M000287828

"Luther has often been made into a hero of modern subjectivity, as if it's all about having faith. Jack Kilcrease corrects the record: it's all about the gracious Word of God, which gives us faith in the heart and every other good gift in Christ. For the Gospel word has the same effect as a sacrament: it gives what it signifies. Kilcrease's book pushes us in the direction of this word-centered path, which is the great gift of Lutheran theology to the larger Christian tradition."

—PHILLIP CARY,
professor of philosophy, Eastern University;
author of *The Meaning of Protestant Theology*

"Most people seem to be impelled to justify themselves in order to convince themselves and others of their acceptability. Even though they may not be religious, they seek to justify themselves in the court of public opinion. They therefore depend on the evaluation, approval, and acceptance of others for their sense of self and their human worth. Given its relevance, it is therefore rather strange that the teaching of justification has recently been downplayed and sidelined in Christian theology and ethics. Commendably, Jack Kilcrease attempts to rectify that deficit in a wide ranging, systematic, ecumenical study from a Lutheran perspective for pastors and teachers to engage with people in their quest for personal validation and acceptance. ... Through God's word the pardon that Christ won for them is delivered to them and received as they put their trust in his word rather than in anything they do or feel or are."

—JOHN W. KLEINIG,
emeritus professor of exegetical theology, Australian Lutheran College;
author of *God's Word: A Guide to Holy Scripture*

"Jack Kilcrease has undertaken a staggering task: a comprehensive summary of what the Bible teaches and what the church in all her manifestations has historically confessed regarding the central article of the Christian faith: justification. Lest you think a weighty tome on a complex topic meticulously researched and copiously documented can be safely ignored, I urge you to think again. The book is a tour de force in that it manages to trace the theme of justification in Scripture from the creation to the eschaton, giving fair consideration to each contrasting (and conflicting) view of justification that has arisen throughout church history. One consistent thread ties the whole magnum opus together: the power and efficacy of the Word of God. The Reformation was not about a doctrinal debate, but a crisis in pastoral care. Kilcrease argues convincingly that Luther's revolutionary teaching on justification was not merely a correction of medieval Catholic excesses, but a rediscovery of the ground of all Christian teaching and ministry: the sacramentality of the Word. Put simply, the Word of God does not merely teach or describe, it creates. If you believe—as I do—that the true care of souls is a ministry of the Word of God and that justification is the ground of consolation and comfort for wounded consciences, this is the book for you. If not, you will still be greatly encouraged by a book so richly drenched in gospel promises."

—HAROLD L. SENKBEIL,
author of *The Care of Souls: Cultivating a Pastor's Heart*

"Too many Christians wring their hands over whether their faith is authentic and thus saving. Instead of looking to Christ alone, as Scripture teaches, they seek instead to assess the genuineness of their feelings or the extent to which their behaviors are changed. Jack Kilcrease tackles this pastoral problem head-on through a sweeping survey of Scripture, early Christian thinkers and medieval theologians, and the thought of Martin Luther along with his disciples and detractors. The upshot: views of justification which fail to honor the truth that God's word not only describes reality but also conveys reality and gives Jesus Christ for faith to grasp, fall short of a scriptural view of the doctrine of justification. Kilcrease's affirmation of the sacramentality of the word is a perspective that contemporary Christians need to hear."

—MARK C. MATTES,
professor of theology and philosophy, Grand View University;
author of *Martin Luther's Theology of Beauty*

Justification
BY THE Word

Justification BY THE Word

RESTORING *SOLA FIDE*

Jack D. Kilcrease

LEXHAM
ACADEMIC

Justification by the Word: Restoring Sola Fide

Copyright 2022 Jack D. Kilcrease

Lexham Academic, an imprint of Lexham Press
1313 Commercial St., Bellingham, WA 98225
LexhamPress.com

Print ISBN 9781683596035
Digital ISBN 9781683596073
Library of Congress Control Number 2022933930

Lexham Editorial: Todd Hains, Caleb Kormann, John Barach, Mandi Newell
Cover Design: Kristen Cork, Brittany Schrock
Typesetting: ProjectLuz.com

Thanksgiving for the Word

IN THE NAME of the Father and of the Son and of the Holy Spirit. Amen.

God gives life to the dead
  and calls into existence the things that do not exist.   *Rom 4:17*
Some sat in darkness and in the shadow of death,
  prisoners in affliction and in irons,
for they had rebelled against the words of God,
  and spurned the counsel of the Most High.   *Ps 107:10–11*
Then they cried to the LORD in their trouble,
  and he delivered them from their distress.
He brought them out of darkness and the shadow of death,
  and burst their bonds apart.   *Ps 107:13–14*
He sent out his word and healed them,
  and delivered them from their destruction.   *Ps 107:20*
Forever, O LORD, your word
  is firmly fixed in the heavens.   *Ps 119:89*
O LORD, I love the habitation of your house
  and the place where your glory dwells.   *Ps 26:8*

Glory be to the Father and to the Son and to the Holy Spirit; as it was in the beginning, is now, and will be forever. Amen.

BLESSED LORD, you sent out your word to heal us and deliver us from destruction. Grant that we might so receive and cherish your word that we might embrace and ever hold fast the blessed hope of everlasting life; through Jesus Christ. Amen.

Contents

Abbreviations

ANF	*Ante-Nicene Fathers*. Edited by Alexander Roberts and James Donaldson. 10 vols. Peabody, MA: Hendrickson, 2004
Ap	Apology to the Augsburg Confession
CA	Unaltered Augsburg Confession
CD	*Church Dogmatics*. Karl Barth. Edited by G. W. Bromiley and T. F. Torrance. Translated by G. T. Thomason et al. 4 vols. Edinburgh: T&T Clark, 1956–1975
FC Ep	Epitome of the Formula of Concord
ICR	*Institutes*. John Calvin. Edited by John T. McNeill. Translated by Ford Lewis Battles. Philadelphia: Westminster, 1960
LC	Large Catechism of Martin Luther
LW	*Luther's Works* [American Edition]. 82 vols. projected. St. Louis: Concordia; Philadelphia: Fortress, 1955–1986, 2009–
NPNF[1]	*Nicene and Post-Nicene Fathers*. First Series. Edited by Philip Schaff. 14 vols. Peabody, MA: Hendrickson, 2004
NPNF[2]	*Nicene and Post-Nicene Fathers*. Second Series. Edited by Philip Schaff and William Wace. 14 vols. Peabody, MA: Hendrickson, 2004
SA	Smalcald Articles of Martin Luther
SC	Small Catechism of Martin Luther
FC SD	Solid Declaration of the Formula of Concord
WA	*D. Martin Luthers Werke: Kritische Gesammtausgabe*. 73 vols. Weimar: Hermann Böhlau and H. Böhlaus Nachfolg, 1883–2009
WABr	*D. Martin Luthers Werke, Kritische Gesamtausgabe: Briefwechsel*. 18 vols. Weimar: Hermann Böhlaus Nachfolger, 1930–1983
WATR	*D. Martin Luthers Werke, Kritische Gesamtausgabe: Tischreden*. 6 vols. Weimar: Hermann Böhlaus Nachfolger, 1912–1921

Introduction

C entral to Christian theology is the question of how a sinner is capable of standing as righteous before a holy God. This is not because, following something like a "Central Dogma Theory,"[1] it is possible to reduce all doctrines to a single soteriological doctrine. Moreover, the centrality of the need for eschatological righteousness before God does not mean that other activities (such as moral formation and works of mercy) are unimportant to the life and identity of the Church. Nevertheless, in that at the end of all things humanity's eternal destiny will be determined by their ability to stand as righteous before a holy God, all other doctrines and works of the Church stand as penultimate to the goal of standing as righteous before the Lord. This status as righteous before God and the eschatological vindication that it brings is what St. Paul called "justification."

Since Christianity, along with Judaism and Islam, agrees that salvation comes about only by way of attaining a status of righteous, then it is necessarily the case that justification is the central doctrine not only of Christianity,[2] but also of the other so-called Abrahamic religions. All religions are defined by the salvation that they offer. As the content of salvation offered by the Abrahamic religions, justification cannot help but be their central doctrine.[3] This being said, contrary to the implication

---

1. For the origins of "Central Dogma" theory see Alexander Schweizer, *Die Protestantischen Centraldogmen in Ihrer Entwicklung inerhalb der Reformirten Kirche*, 2 vols. (Zürich: Orell, Fuessli, 1854–1856). See criticism in Richard Muller, *Post-Reformation Reformed Dogmatics: The Rise and Development of Reformed Orthodoxy, ca. 1520–1720*, 4 vols. (Grand Rapids: Baker Academic, 2003), 1:124–27.

2. Francis Pieper, *Christian Dogmatics* 4 vols. (St. Louis: Concordia, 1951–1953), 2:512–15.

3. Contra R. Michael Allen, *Justification and the Gospel: Understanding the Contexts and Controversies* (Grand Rapids: Baker Academic, 2013), 3–31.

of Lessing's parable of the three rings,[4] Christianity's understanding of justification stands out from the other Abrahamic religions. Whereas Judaism and Islam see no problem with the claim that justification may be wrought through an obedience to the will of the Creator, the project of Christian theology began precisely because the death and resurrection of Jesus called this supposition into question (Gal 2:21). Although broadly speaking, Roman Catholic and Protestant Christians have historically been divided regarding how Jesus's death and resurrection allow humans to stand as righteous before God (i.e., moral transformation vs. imputed righteousness), over against Judaism and Islam they nevertheless agree that it is ultimately through grace that human beings are placed in the status of righteous.

In spite of this historic division between Roman Catholics and Protestants on the question of justification, there has been an unanimity of focus in both groups on the subjective reception of the righteousness of God. That is to say, both Roman Catholics and Protestants have historically tended to center their theologies of justification on what steps individuals must take to appropriate the merit of Christ. Catholics have debated amongst themselves the necessity or lack of necessity of a certain disposition to divine grace as much as Protestants have debated free will and the signs of authentic conversion.[5] Within the Protestant tradition, these debates are rather ironic in light of the Magisterial Reformation's emphasis on the externality and unconditionality of grace.

Particularly with regard to the historic Protestant tradition, this point has been made forcefully by Phillip Cary in his essay "Why Luther is Not Quite Protestant: The Logic of Faith in a Sacramental Promise."[6] When dealing with justification in the theology of Luther and comparing it to subsequent Protestantism, Cary observes that most Protestants have focused on the reality of faith. In this, faith and its authenticity are

---

4. See Gotthold Lessing, *Nathan the Wise, with Related Documents*, trans. Ronald Schechter (Boston: Bedford, 2004).

5. Alister McGrath, *Iustitia Dei: A History of the Christian Doctrine of Justification* (Cambridge: Cambridge University Press, 2020), 227–340.

6. Phillip Cary, "Why Luther is Not Quite Protestant: The Logic of Faith in a Sacramental Promise," *Pro Ecclesia* 14, no. 4 (2005): 447–86. Also see similar argument in Phillip Cary, *The Meaning of Protestant Theology: Luther, Augustine, and the Gospel That Gives Us Christ* (Grand Rapids: Baker Academic, 2019), 258–62.

considered the decisive factor. This gives rise to the soteriological syllogism that Cary outlines thus:

> Major premise: Whoever believes in Christ is saved.
> Minor premise: I believe in Christ.
> Conclusion: I am saved.[7]

Of course, this raises the problem of how one knows that they have authentic faith. Many Protestants have therefore been fixated on discovering secondary signs that confirm the authenticity of faith: a particular kind of conversion experience, good works, wealth, personal holiness or spiritual gifts, and perhaps even snake handling!

When turning to Luther's theology, Cary observes that the focus shifts from the authenticity of faith to the authenticity of God's promise made concrete and tangible in the means of grace. Thus, Cary renders Luther's soteriological syllogism thus:

> Major premise: Christ told me, "I baptize you in the name of the Father, Son and Holy Spirit."
> Minor premise: Christ never lies but only tells the truth.
> Conclusion: I am baptized (i.e., I have new life in Christ).[8]

As Cary correctly observes, although both Luther and the larger Protestant tradition do certainly agree that one receives justification through faith, there is a subtle yet highly significant difference between the two understandings of the righteousness of faith. Whereas most Protestants hold that faith should be reflective regarding its own authenticity, Luther believes in what Cary characterizes as an "unreflective faith"— that is, a faith that does not focus on the question of its own authenticity.[9]

According to Cary, this unreflective faith is possible for Luther because of his belief in the sacramentality of the word.[10] Here Cary echoes the work of the German Luther scholar Oswald Bayer, who claims that it was in fact the sacramentality of the word, and not justification by faith, that

---

7. Cary, "Why Luther is Not Quite Protestant," 450.

8. Cary, "Why Luther is Not Quite Protestant," 451.

9. Cary, "Why Luther is Not Quite Protestant," 450–55.

10. Cary, "Why Luther is Not Quite Protestant," 455–61.

was central to the so-called Reformation breakthrough.[11] The word of justification is objectified in both preaching and the sacraments in such a way as to shift the focus from authentic appropriation of God's grace to the question of the surety of God's promise. Since the risen Jesus is genuinely present in the means of grace, he is capable of mediating a direct assurance of his justifying grace for sinners who look for him there. The tendency of believers to reflect upon and worry about the authenticity of their faith is seen by Luther as a sinful resistance to Jesus's promise that they have already been accepted. Therefore, instead of "justification through faith" it might be appropriate to characterize Luther's position as "justification by the word."

In this book, we will endeavor to show that, although it has been neglected and misunderstood by Protestants and Catholics alike, Luther's "justification by the word" is a better model for understanding salvation in Christ. It will be argued that this is the case not only because it is more faithful to the teachings of the Scriptures, but also because it is the only doctrine of salvation that fully succeeds in de-centering the self and overcoming the self-incurvature of sin (incurvatus in se). As Luther himself observes in his Galatians commentary of 1531: "This is the reason why our theology is certain, it snatches us away from ourselves and places us outside ourselves, so that we do not depend on our own strength, conscience, experience, person, or works but depend on that which is outside ourselves, that is, on the promise and truth of God, which cannot deceive."[12]

11. Oswald Bayer, *Martin Luther's Theology: A Contemporary Interpretation*, trans. Thomas Trapp (Grand Rapids: Eerdmans, 2008), 52–53; Bayer, *Promissio: Geschichte der reformatorischen Wende in Luthers Theologie* (Göttingen: Vandenhoeck & Ruprecht, 1971), 240–41.

12. Lectures on Galatians (1531). WA 40.I: 589; LW 26:387.

CHAPTER 1

Justification and the Word:
Human Experience and Creation

In the opening chapters of his Epistle to the Romans, St. Paul makes the case that all human beings are aware of their creator on either a conscious or unconscious level (Rom 1:20). Humans (with the possible rare exceptions of sociopaths)[1] also possess the law of God written on their hearts and minds (Rom 2:14–15). It is for this reason that something like the Ten Commandments can be found in all societies, albeit with some culturally-based additions or blind spots.[2] According to Paul, this experience of God and his law does not make humans universally capable of becoming "anonymous Christians,"[3] but rather reveals divine wrath at sin and makes human beings accountable to God's justice (Rom 1:18–19).

The fact that humans are universally aware of God and his law makes the question of justification a pressing and central concern of human existence. In that God's law presses down on our species everywhere and at all times, humans find that they need some form of justification. Hence, read from a distinct Reformation perspective, the question of justification can be found not only in the Abrahamic religions, but also

---

1. The best data suggests that sociopaths comprise about 5 percent of the population. See Martha Stout, *The Sociopath Next Door* (New York: Broadway Books, 2005).

2. See C. S. Lewis, *The Abolition of Man* (Oxford: Oxford University Press, 1943).

3. See Paul Imhof and Hubert Biallowons, eds., *Karl Rahner in Dialogue: Conversations and Interviews, 1965–1982*, trans. Harvey D. Egan (New York: Crossroad, 1986), 207.

in a somewhat different form in the Buddhist and Hindu religions teachings regarding karma.[4] Indeed, because of the question of justification's
ubiquity in human experience, it cannot be escaped even in an ostensibly
modern secular life.[5] As Oswald Bayer observes:

> In the other's view of us, and also in our own view, we always find
> ourselves to be the ones who are already being questioned and
> who have to answer. … We are forced to justify ourselves, and as
> we do so, we usually want to be right. … The world of the court
> is not a special world of its own, but just a particular instance—a
> very striking one—of what is being done always and everywhere.
> There is no escaping the questions and evaluation of others. If
> one accepts and welcomes the other or not, if one greets the other
> or not, if one acknowledges the other—either through praise or
> reproach, affirmation or negation—or if one does not acknowledge
> the other and regards the other as worthless, a decision is made
> concerning our being or non-being.[6]

Eberhard Jüngel similarly observes:

The fact that people want to justify their conduct, their behavior,
their past life and their claim to a future life is linked with the fact
that people require recognition. It is essential for people to be recognized. Their personhood depends on it. As human beings we
demand recognition of ourselves. The wish for justification has
its source in this basic human need for *recognition*. The fact that
people *must* justify themselves, that they can be *compelled* to do so,
points to a further basic human requirement: to be human means
the necessity of being accountable. … As beings who are relational
in every aspect, human beings exist *in a state of accountability to*

---

4. See Wendy Doniger, ed. *Karma and Rebirth in Classical Indian Traditions* (Los Angeles University of California Press, 1980).

5. See critique in Oswald Bayer, "With Luther in the Present," *Lutheran Quarterly* 21 (2007): 1–16.

6. Oswald Bayer, *Living by Faith: Justification and Sanctification,* trans. Geoffrey Bromiley (Grand Rapids: Eerdmans, 2003), 1.

others. That is why they can, when the need arises, be *brought to account.* At that time they must *justify* themselves.[7]

As Bayer and Jüngel correctly note, to be a person and have standing before others within the world of the legal and the social requires the act of justification. In this sense personhood as a concept depends on justification. Since humans are relationally constituted, to fail to justify oneself before the bar of legal judgment is to become socially or biologically a non-entity: "For the wages of sin is death" (Rom 6:23).

Moreover, humans cannot escape judgment by refusing to act. Human must make decisions and therefore must be held accountable for them. Taking some inspiration from Kierkegaard in *The Concept of Anxiety,*[8] George Wolfgang Forell observes:

> [M]an's freedom is his bondage. Man may indeed be free to make any number of important decisions about his life. He may have something to say about the choice of his job, his spouse, his friends, or the kind of life he wants to lead. But there is one choice he cannot make: he cannot choose not to choose. He cannot escape his freedom. He is bound to be free. Whether he likes it or not, whether he believes in it or not, he must live a life of constant and unavoidable decisions.[9]

Therefore, merely by making decisions, humans are bound to engage in a constant effort of self-justification. They must give an account for all their decisions, not only before other human beings but before God and his law. This is true whether or not they consciously or unconsciously acknowledge God's ultimate authority.

Hence, the need for justification is a pervasive one in human life and cannot be ignored. The need for self-justification presupposes an awareness (albeit at times vague) of human sin and God's wrath (Rom 1:18;

---

7. Eberhard Jüngel, *Justification: The Heart of the Christian Faith,* trans. Jeffrey Cayzer (Edinburgh: T&T Clark, 2001), 6–7. Emphasis original.

8. Søren Kierkegaard, *The Concept of Anxiety: A Simple Psychologically Orienting Deliberation on the Dogmatic Issue of Hereditary Sin,* trans. Reidar Thomte (Princeton: Princeton University Press, 1980).

9. George Wolfgang Forell, *The Ethics of Decision: An Introduction to Christian Ethics* (Philadelphia: Muhlenberg Press, 1955), 3.

2:15). The social and existential need for justification is an expression of
the universal knowledge of the law and the creator God behind the law.
Werner Elert famously described human existence in the fallen world as
one that was "nomological" insofar as humans stand in a constant confrontation with the law.[10] As the backdrop of all human experience, Elert
terms the experience of the law and divine hiddenness to be the "primal
experience" (*Das Urerlebnis*).[11] The law of God envelops fallen human
existence so that, as Gustaf Wingren observes, all of human life is a "continual foretaste of the Last Judgment."[12]

From this constant experience of divine wrath stems all the great world
religions, with their need either to justify human behavior through ritual
deeds of righteousness, or to abrogate one's status as an accountable being
through the mystical disillusion of personal identity (moksha, nirvana,
etc.). The need for self-justification is also the basis of ancient and modern
rationalism in its various permutations, holding that it can avoid the entire
problem of justification by arguing away the primal human awareness
of guilt before a righteous creator by denying his existence or ultimate
judgment.[13]

Ultimately, we are confronted with our need for justification through
being addressed by another. It is only through language (or at minimum,
an imitation of language) that one can be held accountable. Humans are
hearing and speaking creatures. They are capable of processing the words
addressed to them by their fellow creatures and by their creator. Humans
are capable of responding to these addresses with affirmation or negation.[14]
In this, humans are moral agents precisely because they are linguistic

---

10. Werner Elert, *Law and Gospel*, trans. Edward Shroeder (Philadelphia: Fortress, 1967), 28.
Also see lengthier description of existence under sin and law in Werner Elert, *The Christian Faith:
An Outline of Lutheran Dogmatics*, trans. Martin Bertram and Walter Bouman (Gettysburg, PA:
unpublished manuscript, 1974), 30–67.

11. Werner Elert, *The Structure of Lutheranism*, trans. Walter Hansen, vol. 1 (St. Louis: Concordia,
1962), 17–28.

12. Gustaf Wingren, *Creation and Law*, trans. Ross McKenzie (Philadelphia: Muhlenberg, 1961),
174.

13. Adolf Koberle aptly summarizes human attempts at self-justification as comprising mysticism,
legalism, and rationalism. See Adolf Koberle, *The Quest for Holiness: Biblical, Historical, and Systematic
Investigation*, trans. John Mattes (Eugene, OR: Wipf & Stock, 2004), 1–47. See similar argument in
Forell, *Ethics of Decision*, 47–63.

14. See comments in Werner Elert, *The Christian Ethos: The Foundations of a Christian Way of
Life*, trans. Carl Schindler (Philadelphia: Muhlenberg, 1957), 25–26.

agents. The core of moral agency is to be true to one's words—that is, to be able to enter into covenants. If one is not a linguistic agent, one cannot pledge to fulfill one's promises in the future. Without linguistic agency, neither can one testify to the truth of previous events or be held accountable for one's fulfillment of their past obligations.

This connection between linguistic and moral agency that can be gleaned from an analysis of general human experience correlates well with the Bible's characterization of God's agency as being exercised through his word starting from the very first chapter of Genesis. As we will argue, the fact that human existence is formed, judged, and redeemed by God's address is the very thing that drives the biblical narrative.

JUSTIFICATION IN THE BIBLE:
CREATION BY WORD

Central to the biblical narrative is the creative and redemptive power of the Word of God. God calls both the old and new creation into existence by means of his efficacious Word (*creatio per verbum*). This is why Oswald Bayer, in his exposition of Luther's doctrine of creation, has argued that creation itself is a form of justification.[15] In calling creation into existence, God judicially affirms its status and identity as his good creation. Moreover, just as Christians are justified and sanctified by the work of the Word and the Spirit (John 3:5; Eph 5:26), so too creation comes about by way of God speaking his Word in the power of the Spirit: "By the word of the LORD the heavens were made, and by the breath of his mouth all their host" (Ps 33:6). As Luther observes in his Genesis commentary, this makes creatures created words in analogy to God's eternal created Word: "God, by speaking, created all things and worked through the Word, and ... all His works are some words of God, created by the uncreated Word."[16]

Much like human words, God's Word possesses a number of different dimensions. Scripture speaks of God's will and reality as being revealed by his Word. Indeed, the idea of the Word of God as the "testimony" of God's previous creative and redemptive acts is of central importance in

---

15. Bayer, *Martin Luther's Theology*, 95–101.

16. Lectures on Genesis (1535–1545), LW 1:47. See Bayer's description of Luther's position in "Creation as Speech Act," in Bayer, *Martin Luther's Theology*, 101–5.

the Bible (Pss 71:15–18; 119:46; 2 Tim 1:8; 1 John 1:1–4; Rev 12:11).[17] In John's Gospel, Jesus is consistently described as the true and eternal Word of God because he reveals and represents the Father (John 14:9). Luther in his own writings referred to this dimension of the divine Word as "Call-Words" (*Heissel-Wort*).[18] Call-words are signifiers that signify states of affairs that are already an actuality. Hence call-words include propositional truths about God and his activities, as well as his commandments which he bids humanity to obey. In revealing the truth about himself, God desires his creatures to know who he eternally is and to imitate him (Phil 2:5; Eph 5:1).

Although it is important to not give short shrift to the propositional and legal content of God's Word, there are nevertheless other dimensions to God's revelational speech. The second dimension of God's Word is its efficacious nature. The word functions in such a way so as not merely to testify to states of affairs that already are actualized (testimony), but to call into existence new realities: "He sent out his word and healed them, and delivered them from their destruction" (Ps 107:20) and "God … gives life to the dead and calls into existence the things that do not exist" (Rom 4:17). Luther called this phenomenon "Deed-Words" (*Thettel-Wort*).[19] God calls creation into existence (Gen 1), Jesus heals by his word, and the word of the disciples forgives and binds sins because of Jesus's divine promise and command (John 20). Human language functions analogously when effective statements are made such as: "I pronounce you man and wife" or "I bestow this office upon you." This efficacious quality of language

---

17. Gerhard von Rad described this as the theme of "Recitation." See Gerhard von Rad, *Old Testament Theology: Single Volume Edition*, trans. D. M. G. Stalker, 2 vols. (Peabody, MA: Prince, 2005).

18. David Steinmetz, "Luther and the Two Kingdoms," in *Luther in Context* (Bloomington: University of Indiana Press, 1986), 115.

19. See Confession Concerning the Lord's Supper (1528), LW 37:180–88 for Luther on the different dimensions of the word. On Luther's position, David Steinmetz writes: "Luther draws a distinction between two kinds of words in order to make clear what the Bible means when it speaks of the Word of God. There is, of course the *Heissel-Wort*, the Call-Word, the word which people use when they apply names to things which already exist. The biblical story of Adam in the garden is a fine example of this. He names all the biblical creatures. He does not create them; he only sorts them out and gives them labels. But there is a second kind of word, the *Thettel-Wort* or Deed-Word, which not only names but effects what it signifies. Adam looks around him and says, 'There is a cow and an owl and a horse and a mosquito.' But God looks around him and says, 'Let there be light,' and there is light.' Steinmetz, "Luther and the Two Kingdoms," 115.

encompasses what modern speech-act theory has parsed into the categories of "illocutionary" and "perlocutionary" speech.[20]

When turning to the creation narrative of Genesis 1, several important points should be made regarding God's creative activity through the Word. First, God's speech bestows being on creatures peacefully and out of a purely unilateral grace.[21] Since creatures do not exist from eternity, they cannot merit their creation. Other civilizations of the Ancient Near East saw the creator god's (Marduk, etc.) action in establishing the order of the cosmos as one of violent imposition of order upon chaos (*Chaoskampf*).[22] By contrast, the grace of creation by the divine Word is itself not coercive but is instead a pure gift. This is not because the grace of creation waits upon the decision of willing subjects. After all, no willing subjects yet exist. Rather, the grace of the Word is peaceful and non-coercive because it freely grants creaturely identity and new possibilities out of nothing.

As a gift, the creative divine Word establishes rest and secures peace, rather than calling upon creaturely activity that, if left to itself, would possess an infinite task in establishing its own identity. Due to the evolving nature of time, identity based on activity is always provisional and calls forth the anxious need to be ever vigilant in one's actions. A creature may establish themselves through works as a particular sort of being ("a good father" or "good citizen," for example), only to have it overturned by the works of the next day. This task of creating one's essence through works never ends because one can always invalidate previous works through new works. By contrast, in Genesis 1 the identity and essence of the creature bestowed by the divine Word comes from outside the creature. It firmly establishes creaturely identity by God's decision about who the creature is within the matrix of the divine narration of the primal seven days. This being said, creatures in their freedom may indeed reject their identity as graciously bestowed on them by their creator and fall into the

---

20. See J. L. Austin, *How to Do Things with Words* (Cambridge, MA: Harvard University Press, 1975).

21. I recognize that it is disputed by many whether or not the doctrine of creation *ex nihilo* is taught by Genesis 1. For a defense of creation *ex nihilo* in Genesis 1 see Paul Copan and William Lane Craig, *Creation Out of Nothing: A Biblical, Historical, and Scientific Exploration* (Grand Rapids: Baker Academic, 2004), 30–60.

22. See Debra Scoggins Ballentine, *The Conflict Myth and the Biblical Tradition* (Oxford: Oxford University Press, 2015).

power of nothingness (i.e., sin). Nevertheless, rejection and acceptance do not cause God to bestow his free gift.

Just as God provides identity to creatures through his protological Word of grace, he also bestows a final fulfillment of that identity through inviting them into his own eternal Sabbath rest. Throughout the Genesis creation narrative, the security and peace offered by the bestowal of identity *extra nos* by the divine Word finds its fulfillment at the end of the week in the establishment of the divine rest of the Sabbath. As numerous interpreters have pointed out, unlike the previous six days of creation, the protological Sabbath of the seventh day possesses neither morning nor evening.[23] Rather, this first Sabbath points ahead to the eschatological and eternal Sabbath of creation, wherein creaturely freedom and identity will find eternal security through participating in God's own eternal rest.[24]

This eternal Sabbath is proleptically present to God's creatures in time. It is the ever-present possibility for creaturely repose in a God who has freely given and secured their identity and destiny through the working of the powerful divine Word (Heb 4:9). Creatures find their reality suspended between protology and eschatology. On the one hand creatures find their identity and authenticity in their passive receptivity to the identity bestowed upon them by God's protological word. On the other hand, because creaturely identity necessarily must also anticipate the future, it can repose in the promise of final Sabbath rest rather than an identity anxiously established by works performed throughout time. In time, humans can participate in an eschatological fellowship with God's own eternal rest, already proleptically present to them in time through God's word of grace.

From all this it becomes clear that because creation comes through the word of grace, creatures do not possess their being through a static interior essence or by their external activity. Instead, they find their identity outside of them in the Word of God. Hence for Genesis 1, it might be said that creaturely identity is something "ecstatic," rather than "centered." That is to say, creatures do not possess their being or identity on the basis of something centered within themselves, but on something external to

---

23. For examples see C. F. Keil, *The Pentateuch* (Peabody, MA: Hendrickson, 1996), 43; Gerhard von Rad, *Genesis: A Commentary*, trans. John Marks (Philadelphia: Westminster, 1972), 63.

24. Keil, *The Pentateuch*, 42–43.

themselves. Creatures are "ecstatically" constituted in that they live on the basis of the divine address external to themselves.

The second thing to notice about the Genesis 1 creation narrative is that God's speech possesses a narrative shape. God speaks creation into existence through the narrative of the seven primal days. From this it may be inferred that created beings possess their identity as a result of their being embedded in a story that God narrates.[25] Unlike in the Greek philosophical tradition, created entities do not possess their identity on the basis of a static essence internal to them.[26] Neither do creatures create themselves through their actions (*autopoesis*), as in the modern conception.[27] Rather, in the Bible, creatures gain their essence and status from their place in the narrative that God enacts by his speech.

In this, creaturely identity is shaped by a unity of freedom and determination. By analogy, an author determines the plot and the characters of his novel through his narration. Yet he does not coerce the characters into choices they make. Rather, he shapes them so that their actions spontaneously and organically grow out of who they are as persons. Likewise, God's linguistic agency in the primal and continual creation determines the life and status of his creatures by speaking them into existence through the ongoing story of creation and redemption. God determines his creation, but he does not do so as a superior force overriding inferior forces. Because God shapes secondary causes through his Word, they act spontaneously out of the nature that God has bestowed upon them.[28]

25. See this approach in Hans Urs von Balthasar, *Theo-Drama*, trans. Graham Harrison, 5 vols. (San Francisco: Ignatius, 1983–1998); Oswald Bayer, "Creation as History," in *The Gift of Grace: The Future of Lutheran Theology*, ed. Niels Hendrik Gregersen, et al., (Minneapolis: Augsburg Fortress, 2005), 253; Bayer, "God as Author of My Life History," *Lutheran Quarterly* 2 (1988): 437–56; Bayer, "Poetological Doctrine of the Trinity," *Lutheran Quarterly* 15 (2001): 43–58; Robert Jenson, "Can We Have a Story?" *First Things* 11 (March 2000): 16–17; Jenson, "How the World Lost Its Story," *First Things* 4 (October 1993): 19–24; Jenson, *Story and Promise: A Brief Theology of the Gospel about Jesus* (Philadelphia: Fortress, 1973).

26. See Aristotle, *Metaphysics*, trans. Hugh Lawson-Tancred (New York: Penguin, 1998).

27. See Jean-Paul Sartre, *Existentialism Is Humanism*, trans. Carol Macombe (New Haven: Yale University Press, 2007).

28. William Placher makes a similar analogy using the play *Death of a Salesman*. See William Placher, *The Domestication of Transcendence: How Modern Thinking about God Went Wrong* (Louisville: John Knox, 1996), 148.

THE WORD AND THE
LITURGY OF CREATION

The third point to be made about the nature of creation through the divine Word in Genesis 1 follows from the second. The narrative nature of creation is also liturgical. Contrary to much of Herman Gunkel's theory of Genesis's dependency on the Ancient Near Eastern motif of the *Chaoaskampf*,[29] much of contemporary scholarship has come to recognize a connection between the Genesis 1 creation narrative and the Israelite liturgy and the Tabernacle and Temple.[30]

P. J. Kearney has demonstrated that the creation narrative in Genesis 1 and the description of the erection of the Tabernacle in Exodus 25–32 have many verbal similarities. Not only is this the case, but the pattern of the seven days of creation corresponds directly with God's seven speeches regarding the construction of the Tabernacle.[31] Although Jon Levenson does not find every aspect of Kearney's exegesis persuasive, he argues that it is impossible to completely deny the connection between the Genesis creation account and the construction of the Tabernacle and Temple.[32] Levenson notes that in Exodus 40:2, the erection of the Tabernacle occurs on the day of the vernal New Year. Genesis tells us that Noah likewise emerged from the ark into the post-diluvium world (i.e., the new creation) on the vernal New Year.[33] Along similar lines, 1 Kings 6–7 informs us that Solomon's dedication of the Temple took seven years and occurred on the seventh month during the Feast of Tabernacles. This seven-day feast suggests a connection with the primal week of creation.[34]

G. K. Beale generally agrees with Kearney and has argued that each major section of the Temple and Tabernacle represents a part of the

---

29. See Jo Ann Scurlock and Richard Henry Beal, eds., *Creation and Chaos: A Reconsideration of Hermann Gunkel's Chaoskampf Hypothesis* (University Park, PA: Eisenbrauns, 2013).

30. Much of this material appears in a slightly different form in Jack Kilcrease, "Creation's Praise: A Short Liturgical Reading of Genesis 1–2 and the Book of Revelation," *Pro Ecclesia* 21, no. 3 (2012): 314–25.

31. P. J. Kearney, "Liturgy and Creation: The P Redaction of Exodus 25–40," *Zeitschrift für alttestamentliche Wissenschaft* 89 (1977): 375–87.

32. Jon Levenson, *Creation and the Persistence of Evil: The Jewish Drama of Divine Omnipotence* (San Francisco: Harper and Row, 1988), 83.

33. Levenson, *Creation and the Persistence of Evil*, 78.

34. Levenson, *Creation and the Persistence of Evil*, 78.

created order.[35] In both the original Tabernacle and the First Temple, the basin of water represented the sea, the courtyard represented the land, while the Holy Place and Holy of Holies represented the starry and celestial heavens (or possibly Eden, since it is the locus of divine self-communicating presence in the original creation). This theory is further bolstered by the fact that the curtains covering the Holy Place and the Holy of Holies were woven to resemble the sky (Exod 25), something also mentioned by Josephus concerning Herod's Temple.[36] The seventh speech establishing the Tabernacle concerns the Sabbath (Exod 31:12–18). This directly corresponds to the seventh day of creation and the protological Sabbath. The Tabernacle and Temple are therefore microcosms of the macrocosm of creation. If the Tabernacle and Temple and creation possess the same structure it is safe to assume that they possess the same purpose, namely, the glorification of God.

Regarding the second chapter of Genesis, Gordon Wenham has argued for significant connection between the structure of the garden of Eden (Gen 2–3) and the later Levitical cult. Wenham notes similarities between Eden and the Temple and Tabernacle, such as the opening of both to the east and the function of each as the locus of the divine presence (Gen 2:15).[37] Wenham has also argued that the text's descriptions of Adam's activity in the garden possess verbal similarities with the ministrations of the priesthood elsewhere in the Pentateuch.[38] This means that Genesis describes Adam and Eve's care for creation as a true act of grateful worship, which makes it a liturgical activity. In Wenham's commentary on Genesis, he also notes that Adam's reception of the first commandment in the garden parallels the storage of the book of the law in the Israelite Tabernacle.[39] Adding to all this, Beale has noted the verbal similarities between the arboreal imagery in Genesis 2–3 and in the description of

35. G. K. Beale, *The Temple and the Church's Mission: A Biblical Theology of the Dwelling Place of God* (Downers Grove, IL: InterVarsity Press, 2004), 31–36.

36. See discussion in Beale, *Temple and Church's Mission*, 46. Also see Josephus, *The Jewish War*, 5.5.4 in *The Works of Josephus*, trans. William Whiston (Peabody, MA: Hendrickson, 1995), 707.

37. Gordon Wenham, "Sanctuary Symbolism in the Garden of Eden Story," in *Proceedings of the Ninth World Congress of Jewish Studies*, ed. Moshe Goshen-Gottstein (Jerusalem: World Union of Jewish Studies, 1988), 19–37.

38. Wenham mentions verbal parallels in Num 3:7–8; 8:26; 18:5–6.

39. Gordon Wenham, *Genesis 1–15* (Waco, TX: Word, 1987), 64.

Solomon's Temple in 1 Kings 6–7.[40] Jon Levenson has demonstrated the
verbal parallels between the description of Eden and the Temple mount,
particularly in Ezekiel. Ezekiel 28:14 locates Eden on a cosmic mountain
much like Zion.[41]

With regard to the significance of the number seven for time, Beale
also mentions the importance of the number seven in the liturgical calendar of Israel (specifically the seven-day week and the forty-nine year
cycle of Jubilee) and in the imagery of the Tabernacle.[42] He argues that
the use of the number seven corresponds to the seven planets visible to
the ancient world. In the Tabernacle, the seven planets were represented
by the seven lampstands.

Therefore, as can be observed from this exegesis, creation's existence
subsists on the basis of God's Word as both liturgical time and space. As
liturgical space, the cosmos and the Tabernacle and Temple mirror one
another. Creation is established to reflect God's glory back to him through
the appropriate response of praise. As liturgical time, the primal narrative of creation is the prototype of Israel's week and Sabbath rest (Exod
20:8–11; 31:14–17; Deut 5:12–15), as well as the cycle of Jubilee (Lev 25).

Consequently, in building the Tabernacle and Temple and following its
liturgical calendar, Israel lives out the vocation of the true humanity as a
"kingdom of priests" (Exod 19:6). The fact that it is the human vocation to
be priests who glorify God within the cosmic Temple sheds light on what
it means in Genesis 1 to be made in the image of God (*tzelem Elohim*, Gen
1:26–27). Throughout the Old Testament we are told that God's theoph-
anic presence and image is one of "glory" (*kavod*, Exod 33:14–23; Deut
5:24; Ezek 43:2). In Hebrew, *kavod* has both the connotation of physical light and praise.[43] If God is fundamentally glorious, then his image
reflected in humans must be as well (Rom 3:23). This would suggest that
humans as priests over the cosmic Temple of creation are created in order
to receive and reflect God's glory back to him. As Peter Brunner observes:

---

40. Beale, *Temple and the Church's Mission*, 23–29.

41. Levenson, *Creation and the Persistence of Evil*, 93.

42. Beale, *Temple and the Church's Mission*, 35.

43. Walther Eichrodt, *Theology of the Old Testament*, trans. J. A. Baker, 2 vols. (Philadelphia:
Westminster, 1961–1967), 2:30–32.

As God created man in His image, He created a creature in which His own reality, glory, might, and beauty are reflected within the boundaries implicit in the creatureliness of the foremost creature. The special feature of the mirrored image, by which this creature is distinguished from the reflection of the divine essence in the other earthly creatures, consists in the fact that man became an "I" through God's fatherly address. ... The reality of God, reflected mutely and unconsciously, as it were, in nonhuman earthly creatures, is perceived, recognized, acknowledged, and returned to the Creator with thanks and adoration. ... Man cannot be God's image without the immediate, adoring word of acknowledgement, of gratitude, of glorification addressed to the Creator. Without the prayer and laudation, man would not be the mirror of God's glory, would not be a man.[44]

Nevertheless, this raises the question of how unique the human role in creation actually is—as we have observed already, since the whole of the created order is pictured by Genesis as a cosmic Temple made to glorify God. In this sense, all creation receives this image of divine glory and goodness, thereby reflecting it back to God. As Genesis states: "God *saw all that he had made*, and it was *very good*" (Gen 1:31, emphasis added).

THE WORD AND THE *IMAGO DEI*

Perhaps the key to understanding how human beings are uniquely made in God's image is the fact that not only does God call them into existence through his address, but as linguistic agents humans have the capacity to respond through a trusting reception of that divine address. In Genesis 1 we read that, unlike the rest of God's creation, the first humans are not only spoken into existence, but are then afterwards called upon and addressed directly by their creator through a promise of blessing: *God blessed them*. And God said to them, "Be fruitful and multiply and fill the earth and subdue it and have dominion over the fish of the sea and over the birds of the heavens and over every living thing that moves on

---

44. Peter Brunner, *Worship in the Name of Jesus*, trans. M. H. Bertram (St. Louis: Concordia, 1968), 36.

the earth" (Gen 1:28, emphasis added). It should be highlighted that in
the first section of the verse we are told that the subsequent statement is
to be characterized as an act of "blessing" (*waybārek*).

As a promise of blessing to the first humans, the Word of God calls
forth faith that in turn also gives rise to the action of obedience and grateful praise. In this sense, the blessing functions simultaneously as promise
and imperative. While being given the task of "subduing" the earth, they
are promised that they will possess the freedom of dominion in that they
will be dominated by no other creatures. In telling them to multiply, God
also implicitly promises that he will guarantee their life—that is, their fertility. Hence, the divine-human relationship is anchored in a promise of
life and freedom.

This determination and structure of human personhood around language finds a point of contact with the general existential analysis that we
described at the beginning of the chapter. As Hermann Sasse observes,
that God's Word is directed to humans as linguistic agents is what makes
humans persons:

> The Christian faith understands the nature of the human person
> from this vantage. Man becomes "person" through the call of God.
> "I have called you by name." [Isaiah 43:1] This is how the per-
> sonhood of man is established. God's creative Word has called
> everything into existence: "He bears all things through his pow-
> erful Word." [Hebrews 1:3] In this mystery of the world, this is
> not "nature," or something independent, which exists of itself. It is
> rather "creature," something that God has called into existence out
> of nothing. Therein man has a part in all creation. But this distin-
> guishes him from the rest of the world. He is a creation "according
> to the image of God." God has created man to be person, to be
> an "I" who can hear the word of God. Man is an "I" whom God
> stands over against as a "thou," who can answer to him and is
> answerable to him. This distinguishes man from other creatures.
> So the person of man is conjoined with the person of God. Only
> because God is person and has set himself as a person over against
> man, therefore there is life as personhood. Not as though God and
> man stand over against each other as equals! God is the creator

and man a creature. The boundaries are not blurred. Man does not have life as a person because man is a divine essence. He has such life because the creator created him as a "thou." The divine call alone makes man a person. Because it is so, no philosophy may decipher the mystery of the human person, the mystery of the "I." It cannot be understood from nature, or from a participation in a realm of the intellect. It can be understood only from of the word of the creator: "I have called you by name."[45]

As Werner Elert observes, such an address leads to an active response on the part of humans as conscious subjects in a manner that cannot be said of the rest of the creation:

He [God] becomes the Creator through his word by which the nonexistent is called into existence. That fact alone constitutes the immediate reality of the creation. The image is already given in the act of creation. Obviously the creature cannot be like its maker in creativeness. Man bears God's image in the sense that he is a creature endowed with speech just as God himself speaks. The ability to use language as a means of communication distinguishes man from the lower creatures and establishes a "telling" likeness with his Creator. Speech is more than a technical facility, otherwise human speech would belong in the same category as the bark of a dog or the murmur of a brook. The ability to employ speech means the ability to express oneself as a personality. ... Man can [therefore] achieve what no animal can do—he can address God and express himself before God. This act of expression is a form of response to the God who called man into existence by his word. When God created man, he immediately instituted a form of communication which implies man's response to God's call. ... God's call demands a response, and by responding man becomes a responsible being. Those who bear the image of God are also responsible before him.[46]

45. Hermann Sasse, "What is the State?" (1932), trans. Matthew Harrison (unpublished manuscript, 1932; trans. Matthew Harrison, 2015), 12–13.

46. Elert, *Christian Ethos*, 25–26.

This understanding of the *imago Dei* as connected both with God's linguistic agency and glory fits well with Luther's concept of the righteousness of faith found in Luther's *Freedom of a Christian*. Because the first humans were perfect believers in God's Word, they glorified God by their trust in his Word:

> It is a further function of faith that it honors him whom it trusts with the most reverent and highest regard since it considers him truthful and trustworthy. There is no other honor equal to the estimate of truthfulness and righteousness with which we honor him whom we trust. Could we ascribe to a man anything greater than truthfulness and righteousness and perfect goodness?[47]

Therefore, reception of God's Word by faith establishes the divine image in human beings. Through believing in the truthfulness of the divine Word, humans reflect God's glory back to him. Of course, the flipside of this dialogical relationship based on grace and glorification is the possibility of that relationship breaking down through unbelief. The rest of the narrative of the Genesis speaks to that possibility by describing both the actuality of human sin as well as God's effort in reversing human sin through the election of Israel by the power of his Word.

---

47. Freedom of a Christian (1521), LW 31:350.

CHAPTER 2

Justification and the Old Testament:
Salvation through the Word in the Hebrew Bible

The account of Genesis 2 begins with the creation of human beings (Gen 2:15–5:32) and their subsequent placement in the garden of Eden. Although as it has become clear from our earlier exegesis Eden in many respects prefigures the later Tabernacle and Temple, it also prefigures the land of Palestine itself. We are told in Genesis 13:10 that Canaan is "well-watered everywhere like the garden of the LORD." Indeed, much like Canaan, Eden is a place where humanity works the soil (Gen 2:15) and where the fertility of the earth is guaranteed. Much as YHWH would later dwell in the land with his people in the Temple, so too God is directly present to Adam and Eve.

For Israel, the restoration of God's self-giving presence enjoyed before the fall also occurs. We are told that YHWH's glory (*kavod*) traveled with Israel during the entire period of the exodus under the form of a cloud (Exod 40:36–38). When the Tabernacle's construction was completed, a thick cloud filled the camp and the glory of YHWH descended into the Tabernacle (Exod 40:34–35). The Lord thereby guarantees his favor to the first humans as he would later do with Israel (Gen 3:8).

In the Genesis narrative, humanity sins in the garden by falling into unbelief and disobeying God by listening to the voice of the serpent (Gen 3:10). This leads to the exile of Adam and Eve from the garden, which brings with it their removal from God's gracious presence and the guarantee of the fertility of the soil (Gen 3:17). The first humans are also denied the immortality which they gained by consuming the fruit of the Tree of Life (Gen 3:19, 22).[1] Again, as many interpreters have recognized, such a narrative prefigures Israel's own story. Much as Israel would later by carried off east to Babylon, so too Adam and Eve are driven east of the garden (Gen 3:24).[2]

As Peter Leithart has shown, Genesis structures creation in a manner that parallels the Tabernacle and Temple with its three sections (Courtyard, Holy Place, Holy of Holies):

> When Adam is first created, he is put in the garden of Eden. The Garden is one of several different areas that God makes in the world. ... In Genesis 2, we learn that the middle floor, earth, is divided into three "rooms." The Garden is only one of them. Genesis 2:8 tells us that the Lord God plants a garden "toward the east, in Eden," which means that the Garden is on the east side of the land of Eden. Eden is larger than the Garden, and outside Eden there were other lands, which are named in Genesis 2:11–13. If Adam had taken time on the first day to make a map, he would have drawn a map with several areas: the Garden, the land of Eden, and the larger world.[3]

Although sin begins in the garden, Genesis recounts how sin spreads to the land of Eden and the larger world. In each zone of the created world, sin disrupts the various dimensions of human inter-personal relationships: the divine-human relationship, family relations, and relations among the nations. Adam and Eve sin in the garden, disrupting the divine-human relationship. The disruption of the divine-human relationship spreads to strife within the family, when Cain kills Abel in the land east of the garden and is cast into the land of Nob east of Eden (Gen 4:16). Finally, in this land of Nob (part of the zone of the larger world outside of Eden and the garden), the marriage of the sons of God to the daughters of men

---

1. Lectures on Genesis (1535–1545), LW 1:86, 1:92.

2. Beale, *Temple and the Church's Mission*, 120–21.

3. Peter Leithart, *A House for My Name: A Survey of the Old Testament* (Moscow, ID: Canon, 2000), 52.

results in morally corrupt children and the spread of violence within the peoples of the earth (Gen 6).[4]

God's response to this spread of sin to each sphere of creation is the judgment of the flood. In this, God effectively returns world to its state in Genesis 1:2 and begins the creation process all over again.[5] When Noah and his family leave the Ark, they become new Adams and Eves.[6] The promises given to them in the Noahic covenant directly mirror those made in Genesis 1 to the first humans. Their fertility is blessed, and they are given the ability to kill and eat animals (Gen 9:1-3)— the latter promise suggesting a reassertion of the divinely guaranteed dominion of humanity over creation, including animals.[7] Beyond this, we are told that Noah plants a vineyard, reminiscent of the garden of Eden (Gen 9:20).[8] In a sense, we find humanity back in the position it lost in Genesis 3.

Unfortunately Noah, like Adam, falls into sin in the garden or vineyard. He does so by becoming drunk on wine (fruit of the vine, much like Eden's forbidden fruit) and afterwards removes his clothing so as to become nude like Adam (Gen 9:21).[9] Subsequently, when Ham speaks of his father's nakedness to his brothers, the sin of strife within the family arises in the same manner as Cain and Abel (9:22-23). As a result, Ham's son is cursed like Cain (Gen 9:24-25). Finally, sin spreads among the nations at the Tower of Babel (Gen 11:1-8). The Tower of Babel is in effect an artificial Eden—that is, a humanly constructed cosmic mountain meant to storm heaven and gain God-like power (Gen 9:4). Such an attempt to storm heaven is met with judgment over the diverse peoples of the earth gathered in one place. In all this, sin again spreads from Noah's new Eden to

---

4. Leithart, *House for My Name*, 56.

5. Tremper Longman and Raymond Dillard, *An Introduction to the Old Testament* (Grand Rapids: Zondervan, 2006), 58.

6. Leithart, *House for My Name*, 56-57.

7. Leithart, *House for My Name*, 56-57; Von Rad, *Genesis: A Commentary*, 131.

8. James Jordan, *Through New Eyes: Developing a Biblical View of the World* (Eugene, OR: Wipf & Stock, 1999), 175.

9. Joseph Blenkinsopp, *The Pentateuch: An Introduction to the First Five Books of the Bible* (New York: Doubleday, 1992), 58; Warren Gage, *The Gospel of Genesis: Studies in Protology and Eschatology* (Eugene, OR: Wipf & Stock, 2001), 7-16.

the family, and again, finally, to the nations gathered at Babel. As a result, creation and the fall are recapitulated a second time.[10]

As sin spreads through the various zones of the world, Genesis does not envision God as standing by and idly allowing his creation to sink into destruction. Just as in the beginning God called creation into existence out of nothing, so too in the midst of the nothingness of sin God's Word calls forth new possibilities for creation by its creative power: "Remember not the former things, nor consider the things of old. Behold, I am doing a new thing; now it springs forth, do you not perceive it?" (Isa 43:18–19). Salvation is enacted and mediated through God speaking his Word first as judgment and then grace. God's response to Adam and Eve's sin is judgment, followed by the promise of the seed of the woman that will overcome the seed of the serpent (Gen 3:15).[11] As we have already seen, following the judgment of the flood God speaks virtually the same promises that humanity received in Genesis 1 to Noah and his sons, thereby reaffirming his love and solidarity with humanity.

Hence, in the midst of the judgment wrought by both the fall from Eden and the confusion of Babel, God's solidarity with his creation continues to deepen through the giving of the binding redemptive promise. Analogously, in common human life the one who engages in the speech-act of making a promise binds himself to the one to whom he makes a promise to. The language of covenant or testament (*berith*) in the Bible recognizes this reality, in that covenants or testaments create a bond between the parties involved.[12] Therefore, as humans distance themselves from God with their sin, God binds himself to them all the more closely. In the election and covenant with Abraham enacted by God's saving Word, Genesis sees the beginning of a new humanity that will finally succeed where Adam and Noah failed.

God's election throughout the Old Testament comes by a saving word that calls first the patriarchs and then Israel from nothingness into new life.

---

10. Longman and Dillard, *Introduction to the Old Testament*, 58. Longman and Dillard observe a similar pattern of sin, speech, migration, and punishment.

11. See the thorough defense of the messianic nature of the *protevangelium* in E. W. Hengstenberg, *Christology of the Old Testament*, trans. Theodore Meyer and James Martin, 4 vols. (Grand Rapids: Kregel, 1956), 1:17–30. Also see the discussion in Herbert Leupold, *Exposition of Genesis*, 2 vols. (Grand Rapids: Baker, 1958–1959), 1:163–70.

12. See R.J. Faley, *Bonding with God: A Reflective Study of Biblical Covenant* (New York: Paulist, 1997).

This is evident in several ways. First, the Hebrew Scriptures repeatedly present the reader with pairs of rejected and elect ones: Cain and Abel, Ishmael and Isaac, Esau and Jacob, Saul and David, Israel and Judah.[13] The rejected ones are consistently the ones with seemingly legal claims on election, while the accepted ones are not. Indeed, not infrequently (though not uniformly) these pairs are brothers and therefore subject to the law of primogeniture, also taught in the Old Testament (Deut 21:17).[14] Nevertheless, the youngest, a non-entity as far as legal standing for inheritance, is elected over the older legal heir. As Jesus would later say: "So the last shall be first, and the first last" (Matt 20:16). Much as God calls creation into being from nothingness, so too his election calls forth new possibilities out of the nothingness of legal disinheritance.

This calling of new creation through the redemptive and electing word can also be found in the manner of the giving of the promise. The elect patriarchs receive the promise passively. Like Adam in his deathlike sleep receiving Eve (Gen 2:21–22), Abraham is given the unilateral covenant of blessing while asleep (Gen 15:12). As Gerhard von Rad observes, God performs the entire covenant ceremony over Abraham while the patriarch is utterly passive.[15] Jacob and Joseph are also given the promise of their blessing while in a state of sleep as well (Gen 28:11; 37:5–11). In this, the patriarchs are new Adams receiving again God's good gifts of creation through the word. Likewise, one should not also forget the numerous matriarchs and other holy women in the Bible who are unable to bear children (Sarah, Rebekah, Hannah, Elizabeth) but yet who receive children through the miraculous intervention of God's promising word. God brings life from death and emptiness through his creative word of promise.

Indeed, the imagery of redemptive death and resurrection is present throughout the narrative of Genesis. As Jon Levenson has observed, the book of Genesis is filled with instances of apparently dead sons coming back to life.[16] Abraham forfeits his son's life in Genesis 22, only to have it

---

13. See Karl Barth's fascinating meditation on these texts in CD II/2.306–508.

14. Incidentally, God calls Ephraim "my first-born son" (Jer 31:9), so the principle applies to Israel and Judah as well.

15. Von Rad, *Old Testament Theology*, 2 vols., 1:131.

16. Jon Levenson, *The Death and Resurrection of the Beloved Son: The Transformation of Child Sacrifice in Judaism and Christianity* (New Haven: Yale University Press, 1995), 55–172.

returned, and thereby receives the universal promise of blessing. Jacob
returns to Canaan after the death of his exile (Gen 30–35). Joseph, believed
to be dead by his father, comes back from the living death of slavery in
Egypt to reestablish his relationship with his father.

In light of creational imagery in the Genesis narratives, it should
become clear that the history of the election of the patriarchs suggests
that Israel itself is the beginning of the restoration of the Adamic humanity.
N. T. Wright observes that: "Thus, at major turning-points in the story
[the Pentateuchal narrative] Abraham's call, his circumcision, the offering
of Isaac, the transition from Abraham to Isaac and from Isaac to Jacob,
and the sojourn in Egypt—the narrative quietly insists that Abraham and
his progeny inherit the role of Adam and Eve."[17] YHWH's promise to the
patriarchs that he will multiply their descendants and give them dominion in the land of Canaan (Gen 12:2; 17:2–8; 22:16; 26:3, 24; 28:3; 35:11;
47:27; 48:3) directly parallels the promises that are given to the first man
and woman at the end of Genesis 1.[18]

Indeed, as Leithart shows, Genesis portrays Abraham and his descendants overcoming where humanity, in the first eleven chapters of the same
book, failed. First, Abraham offers up Isaac, showing his faith and obedience to God on the seeming location that the future Temple would be
built (Gen 22:2; 2 Chr 3:1). Since the Tabernacle or Temple and Eden are
typological of one another, it becomes clear that Genesis 22 implicitly
suggests that Abraham has been obedient in the garden where Adam
fell. Similarly, we read in the story of Esau and Jacob of brothers in
strife because of the election of the younger over the older. Nevertheless,
whereas Cain and Abel's relationship ended in murder, we find Esau and
Jacob reconciled with one another (Gen 33). Lastly, Joseph rules wisely
as Pharaoh's prime minister, thereby bringing harmony and unity among
the nations (i.e., Hebrews and Egyptians) countering the violence before
the flood and the peoples of Babel's unwise rule. Indeed, Joseph serves
as an interesting *inclusio* for the book of Genesis in that he re-creates the
harmonious and wise pre-lapsarian rule of Adam. Also, unlike Adam,

---

17. N. T. Wright, *The New Testament and the People of God*, Christian Origins and the Question of God 1 (Minneapolis: Fortress, 1992), 263.

18. Wright, *The Resurrection of the Son of God*, Christian Origins and the Question of God 3 (Minneapolis: Fortress, 2003), 720. Wright lists the examples of Gen 12:2; 17:2–8; 22:16; 26:3, 24; 28:3; 35:11; 47:27; 48:3.

Joseph flees the temptation of the woman (Potiphar's wife) and runs away in Adamic nudity (Gen 39:12).[19]

In Exodus, as Israel becomes a populous nation, the imagery of redemptive creation and re-creation through the word persists. YHWH condemns Egypt and its gods in, under, and through the words spoken by Moses to Pharaoh (Exod 12:12). In the plagues, the natural phenomenon of the land of Egypt are destroyed or destabilized. In this, the ten plagues correspond well with the ten words God speaks to establish the created order in Genesis 1.[20] Therefore, in the ten plagues, Egypt is attacked with God's systematic de-creation through his condemning word. Divine judgment finds its fulcrum in the waters of the Red Sea, wherein YHWH condemns Pharaoh and his host to return to Genesis 1:2, much like those condemned in the earlier flood. In contrast to all this, by the end of Exodus the new Adams and Eves of Israel have come to God's holy mountain where the Lord re-establishes the garden of Eden through the construction of the Tabernacle (Exod 25-31; 35-40). Whereas at the beginning of Exodus Israel labored as slaves tasked with achieving demonic Pharaoh's building projects, by the end of the book Israel is the free covenant partner of God, working on the divine building project of the new creation spoken forth by God's Word through Moses.[21]

If then Edenic harmony and its restoration in the election of Israel means the renewal of creation and a return of the Lord's presence, then sin and its consequence of exile mean the very opposite of these blessings.[22] Therefore, at Sinai God establishes a second covenant with Israel (Exod 20; 24), standing in direct contrast with God's redemptive promise in Eden (Gen 3:15) renewed with Abraham with the promise of universal blessing through the same "seed" (Gen 12; 15; 17; 22).[23] In the covenant of

---

19. Leithart, *House for My Name*, 64–65.

20. See the similar, but not identical argument in John Currid, *Egypt and the Old Testament* (Grand Rapids: Baker, 1997), 113–17; Meredith Kline, *Images of the Spirit* (Grand Rapids: Baker, 1980), 13–42. We acknowledge a debt of gratitude to Prof. Richard Simon Hanson of Luther College for originally giving us this insight.

21. Victor Hamilton, *Exodus: An Exegetical Commentary* (Grand Rapids: Baker Academic, 2011), 9.

22. Much of my exegesis in this section appears in a similar yet modified form in Jack Kilcrease, *The Self-Donation of God: A Contemporary Lutheran Approach to Christ and His Benefits* (Eugene, OR: Wipf & Stock, 2013), 8–13.

23. Hengstenberg, *Christology of the Old Testament*, 1:53–56; Walter Kaiser, *Recovering the Unity of the Bible: One Continuous Story, Plan, and Purpose* (Grand Rapids: Zondervan, 2009), 144.

Sinai, God places conditions on his favor and establishes a law to judge Israel's faithfulness or unfaithfulness to its creator and redeemer.

The contrast between the Abrahamic and Sinai covenants can be observed from the mode of their reception. As we already noted above, in the unilateral Abrahamic covenant of grace, the patriarch lies passive as YHWH performs the covenantal ceremony (Gen 15). Indeed, just as in the Ancient Near East a vassal would pledge to be split in two like the columns of animal carcasses he walked through in the covenant ritual,[24] YHWH moves between the animal parts himself and pledges his own death if he fails to bless Abraham.[25] Nevertheless, unlike the first covenant which called for the passive reception of God's self-surrender to Israel, the Sinaitic covenant calls Israel to fulfill the covenant through an active obedience to YHWH as sovereign. Exodus describes the Israelites standing before Sinai and pledging their submission to the Lord and his covenant of law: "Moses came and told the people all the words of the LORD and all the rules. And all the people answered with one voice and said, "All the words that the LORD has spoken we will do" (Exod 24:3).

The Sinaitic covenant not only contains the Ten Commandments, but the whole law as a condition of God's continuing favor on Israel. Failure to obey the voice of God will result in the curse of death and exile, much as it had been for Adam and Eve. YHWH repeatedly warns the Israelites through Moses and tells them that "if you spurn my statutes, and if your soul abhors my rules, so that you will not do all my commandments, but break my covenant, then I will do this to you: I will visit you with panic, with wasting disease and fever that consume the eyes and make the heart ache. And you shall sow your seed in vain, for your enemies shall eat it" (Lev 26:15–16). Indeed, "I will discipline you again sevenfold for your sins." In the exile "I will break the pride of your power, and I will make your heavens like iron and your earth like bronze" (Lev 26:18–19). Leviticus also suggests that there will be a loss of Israel's restored dominion in the

---

24. Robert Davidson, *Genesis 12–50* (Cambridge: Cambridge University Press, 1979), 45; Victor Hamilton, *The Book of Genesis: Chapters 1–17* (Grand Rapids: Eerdmans, 1990), 429–38; G. F. Hasel, "The Meaning of the Animal Rite in Gen 15," *Journal for the Study of the Old Testament* 19 (1980): 61–78; von Rad, *Genesis*, 181; Claus Westermann, *Genesis 12–36: A Commentary*, trans. John Scullion (Minneapolis: Augsburg, 1995), 228.

25. See argument in Davidson, *Genesis 12–50*, 45; Leupold, *Exposition of Genesis*, 1:488–89.

land: "I will set my face against you, and you shall be struck down before your enemies. Those who hate you shall rule over you, and you shall flee when none pursues you" (Lev 26:17). Later Ezekiel also attests the loss of the divine presence in the restored Eden of the Temple (Ezek 10:18).

Indeed, this second covenant is necessary because of the reality of human sin. Although as we have seen, God remains committed to his creation and binds himself ever deeper to humanity through pure grace, even his post-lapsarian covenants of grace contain within them the basic assumption that the divine-human relationship is in need of repair. The *protoevangelium* of Genesis 3:15 is a promise of grace, but one in response to the reality of human fallenness. The Noahic covenant, although in some measure a restoration of the gracious relationship of Genesis 1, nevertheless also contains the command to impose the death penalty on murderers so that evil and violence never reach their anarchical level prior to the flood (Gen 9:5–6).

The same obtains for the Tabernacle as the restored Eden and microcosm of creation. Although Israel is in a sense restored to the position of Adam and Eve by enjoying the divine *kavod* in her midst, there remains a distance between God and his people. Humanity is sinful and therefore it would be destroyed through a direct contact with the Lord (Exod 33:20), unlike Adam, who in pre-lapsarian righteousness had direct access to the unmediated presence of God. Now the only way that humanity can enter into God's presence in the Most Holy Place is through bloody sacrifice that atones for sin: "For the life of the flesh is in the blood, and I have given it for you on the altar to make atonement for your souls, for it is the blood that makes atonement by the life" (Lev 17:11). Since sin is a rejection of God the creator and the source of life, then sin means forfeiting one's life.[26]

---

26. For a discussion of atoning sacrifice in Leviticus, see the following: Nobuyoshi Kiuchi, *Leviticus* (Downers Grove, IL: InterVarsity Press, 2007), 32–46, 288–326; Martin Noth, *Leviticus: A Commentary*, trans. J. E. Anderson (Philadelphia: Westminster, 1965), 115–32; Mark Rooker, *Leviticus* (Nashville: Broadman & Holman, 2000), 211–37. Note discussion in Jacob Milgrom, *Leviticus 1–16: A New Translation and Commentary* (New York: Doubleday, 1991), 1079–84. Milgrom considers the idea of the "sin offering" to be erroneous and theologically "foreign" (254) to Leviticus. He believes that the offering has nothing to do with personal guilt, but rather has the function of the "ritual detergent" of sacred space. This interpretation has been challenged by Nobuyoshi Kiuchi who has pointed out that the texts of Leviticus are clear that sin offerings are indeed meant to cleanse from personal guilt of sin. See Nobuyoshi Kiuchi *The Purification Offering in the Priestly Literature: Its Meaning and Function* (Sheffield: JSOT, 1987). Also see John Kleinig, *Leviticus* (St. Louis: Concordia, 2003), 117.

The logic of this follows perfectly the *lex talionis* (law of retaliation) one finds in the civil codes of the Bible (Gen 9:5–6; Exod 21:24).[27]

Therefore, just as Adam and Eve were exiled from the garden, Israel cannot enter the Most Holy Place where the divine *kavod* is enthroned between the cherubim (Isa 37:16) except through atoning sacrifice (Lev 16). It may be recalled that God set an angel with a fiery sword before the gate of the garden of Eden in order to block entrance to Adam and Eve (Gen 3:24). As Leithart notes, in the Levitical cult, Israel (through the mediation of the high priest) is allowed to return into the presence of God only through the bloody sacrifice and a burnt offering—that is, in a sense passing through the same "fire and the sword" that blocked the first humans return to Eden.[28] The main implication is that although the Tabernacle and Temple remain a microcosm of the macrocosm of creation, they represent a picture of creation modified by the situation of sin and under the condemnation of the law. That is to say, the Tabernacle and Temple represent a cosmic order where humans are separated from God and can reenter his gracious fellowship only by fulfilling the law (i.e., through bloody atoning sacrifice).

What is striking about God's relationship with Israel is that it reveals a divine-human relationship paradoxically configured under the two seemingly contradictory words of law and grace. Indeed, much like creation, the narrative of the Old Testament is driven along by God speaking forth his word of judgment and redemption. Every time Israel sins in its history, God in his grace makes a provision for a renewal. God has pledged himself to Israel and will fulfill his promises to it in spite of every obstacle. Simultaneously, the covenant of Sinai is equally valid and demands on the part of Israel a real heartfelt obedience to God's commandments. Both words from God are valid and binding. As a result, the unconditional nature of covenant of grace continuously came into conflict with the conditional nature of the covenant of law throughout the history of Israel.

Indeed, this situation gives rise to the bridal metaphor used through the Bible. For example, in Hosea the prophet enacts the sign of Israel's

---

27. See Jonathan Burnside, *God, Justice, and Society: Aspects of Law and Legality in the Bible* (Oxford: Oxford University Press, 2011), 275–82.

28. Peter Leithart, *Delivered from the Elements of the World: Atonement, Justification, Mission* (Downers Grove, IL: InterVarsity Press, 2016), 106–7.

paradoxical situation under law and grace by marrying the prostitute Gomer (Hos 1, 3). As a sign of Israel's state of affairs, Hosea's marriage presupposes the validity of the covenant of the law, as well as God's unilateral and unconditional faithfulness to Israel. Israel is rightly charged with sin for having broken the law by prostituting itself to the nations and to their false gods. Nevertheless, YHWH must remain true to his promise and remains "married" to Israel in spite of her apostasy.

Part of God's solution to the tension posed by the simultaneous existence of Israel under law and promise is the election of mediators between God and his people.[29] As the relationship with God and Israel developed throughout the Old Testament period, in his grace YHWH elected mediators to serve in the place of and overcome the unfaithfulness of Israel. Much like Israel was elected in Genesis in order to overcome the failures of Adam and Eve, so too, mediators of the covenant were elected by God in order to overcome when corporate Israel failed in its vocation.

In that these mediators were intended to facilitate the proper functioning of the covenants, they embody the unity of God and his people bound together through God's self-donating grace.[30] As a sign that these mediators embodied Israel's corporate destiny as an elect people set apart, they were frequently anointed with oil to signify their special status as ones set apart (Exod 28:41; 1 Sam 16:13).[31] In this, the mediators of the covenant represented God and his faithfulness before his people and before God himself. Likewise, they also represented before Israel the covenant faithfulness that they themselves should embody, while simultaneously serving as intercessors before God on behalf of Israel (Exod 32:30–33; Lev 16:1–34; Num 14:13–16; 2 Sam 24:17–25).

As noted above, mediation developed in the Old Testament through failure of the people of Israel to fulfill their Adamic vocation. As a receiver of God's Word, Adam was a prophet; as a chief worshipper in the cosmic Temple, he was a priest; and as a possessor of dominion in creation, he was a king. Likewise, we see in Exodus 20 God speaking the Ten Commandments directly to Israel and thereby attempting to make them

---

29. See similar, yet modified discussion in Kilcrease, *Self-Donation of God*, 13–15.

30. See similar observations in Hans Urs von Balthasar, *A Theology of History* (New York: Sheed & Ward, 1963), 42–43.

31. Walter Kaiser, *The Messiah in the Old Testament* (Grand Rapids: Zondervan, 1995), 16–17.

collectively into prophets. In light of their terror at hearing the voice of God and therefore their inability to receive the Word of God, Moses was elected to receive the law in their place. Similarly, Israel's failure not only to hear the Word of God, but to practice it as a "kingdom of priests" (Exod 19:6) resulted in the election of Levites to serve as substitute priests within the Tabernacle and Temple after the false worship of the golden calf (i.e., failure at priestly vocation, Exod 32). Finally, Israel's priests' inability to rule and communicate the Word of God properly throughout the book of Judges (culminating in the failed leadership of Eli and his sons at the beginning of 1 Samuel) resulted in the establishment of the monarchy. Since all these forms of mediation failed due both to the sin of Israel and its mediators (Ezek 34), the exile of the new Adamic humanity east of the new Eden (Canaan) in Babylon was only logical.

This salvation-historical process of failure, judgment, and election reveals the internal logic of justification in the Old Testament. Election and justification come by the creative Word of God. By fiat, the creative Word of God raises up a substitute in the place of those who have failed. We have already observed this reality in the concept of sacrifice and atonement, wherein because of God's command and promise the death of the animal occurs in the stead of the individual Israelite. Although there certainly are exegetical problems with Augustine's use of the Old Latin version of Romans 5:12,[32] and the later Reformed concept of Adam's "Federal Headship,"[33] it still cannot be denied that Genesis describes Adam as the representative of humanity before God and that his actions possess permanent consequences for his descendants. Indeed, although the name "Adam" very clearly refers to a historical person in the Bible who is the father of the human race (Gen 5:3–5; 1 Chron 1:1–4), the name also simply means "humanity."[34] This suggests that Adam is a representative of humanity as a whole and what happens in his person is imputed to the rest of humanity.

This is true of the later elect mediators of Israel as well. On the Day of Atonement, the high priest bears the sins of Israel. On behalf of Israel,

---

32. See Gerald Bonner, "Augustine on Romans 5:12," *Studia Evangelica* 2 (1968): 242–47.

33. McGrath, *Iustitia Dei*, 246–49.

34. Bruce Waltke and Charles Yu, *An Old Testament Theology: An Exegetical, Canonical, and Thematic Approach* (Grand Rapids: Zondervan Academic, 2007), 254.

he sacrifices the goat for YHWH and places its blood on the mercy seat (Lev 16:15–19). He also confesses the sins of Israel over the scapegoat as if they were his own (Lev 16:20–22). In this, the high priest stands in Israel's place as a representational person. His behavior is imputed to the people he represents, just as their behavior (i.e., sin) is imputed to him. In a similar manner, 2 Kings 23:26–27 states that God allowed the people of Judah to be condemned for the misdeeds of their representative king, Manasseh. Implicitly, this is the reason that Josiah, although righteous, is killed at Meggido. We can also observe a similar situation earlier in 2 Samuel 24, when Israel suffers because of David's sin of counting his fighting men. Ultimately, the imputed sin and righteousness of Israel and the mediators are a two-way street. The sin of the mediator can be imputed to those whom he represents, just as the righteousness of the mediator can also be imputed to those whom he represents.[35]

The fact of the election of mediators and their representational character reveals the ability of God's gracious saving Word to transcend the law. Israel in no sense merits the election of mediators; God does so purely out of grace. This grace is the extension of his covenant of salvation with Adam and Eve (Gen 3:15), which was renewed with Abraham (Gen 15; 17; 22). God's continuing solidarity with Israel and humanity through his Word is what drives all divine electing and saving activity in the Old Testament, not human legal obedience.

God's activity in electing Israelite mediators paradoxically unites two seemingly disparate realities. First, God's salvation does not ignore the covenant of the law and its need to be fulfilled. This is evident not only from the sacrificial system of the Tabernacle and Temple, but in God's election of mediators to be what others fail to be. Nonetheless, at the same time, God's will mysteriously transcends the law. As we have already seen, God does not elect on the basis of the law. By fiat, he can also transfer guilt and righteousness between persons. The notion that one person can represent another, or even more radically, have his deeds or misdeeds imputed to another is at very minimum in some tension with the law of the Old Testament. According to the law, each person must bear responsibility for their own actions (Deut 24:16; Ezek 18:20). The fact that the

---

35. See similar argument in Leithart, *Delivered from the Elements of the World*, 163–64.

Lord elects mediators and salvifically transfers righteousness and sin from
one person to another, suggests that although God's will is revealed in
the law, the divine creative and redemptive Word nevertheless possesses
possibilities beyond the mere constraints of the law.

ESCHATOLOGICAL WORD OF REDEMPTION

Ultimately, the story of the Old Testament is one of Israel failing just as
Adam and Noah did before them. Deuteronomy 28–32 prophesies of
Israel's coming exile even before it enters into the land. As the prophets
make clear, Israel and humanity are bent by the power of sin, and therefore cannot establish or maintain their relationship with YHWH by obeying the covenant of the law. The Psalmist speaks of himself (and implicitly
of humanity) as inherently sinful from the moment of his conception
when he states: "Behold, I was brought forth in iniquity, and in sin did
my mother conceive me" (Ps 51:5). This situation of total human fallenness is recognized early on, just before God sends the flood in Genesis:
"The LORD saw that the wickedness of man was great in the earth, and
that every intention of the thoughts of his heart was only evil continu-
ally" (Gen 6:5). According to Jeremiah, this inborn sinful nature makes it
impossible for Israel to be faithful to YHWH: "Can the Ethiopian change
his skin or the leopard his spots? Then also you can do good who are
accustomed to do evil" (Jer 13:23). Humans are incapacitated in their
relationship with God and in their moral duties to other humans because
of their "uncircumcised hearts and ears" (Jer 6:10; 9:26) and "hearts of
stone" (Ezek 11:19; 36:26).[36]

In light of human moral incapacity due to sin, the giving of the law
at Sinai takes on a character that some might find surprising. Again, it
should be noted that even before Israel enters the land of Canaan God
predicts their failure to keep the covenant because of their inherent wickedness (Deut 31:15–22). Oddly, YHWH seems to do nothing to prevent
this foreseen disaster. He simply gives Israel the law, and then ushers them
into Canaan on their doomed mission to maintain covenant faithfulness.

---

36. See a discussion of original sin in the Bible in James Hamilton, "Original Sin in Biblical
Theology," in *Adam, the Fall, and Original Sin: Theological, Biblical, and Scientific Perspectives*, ed.
Michael Reeves and Hans Madueme (Grand Rapids: Baker Academic, 2014), 189–208.

Similarly, in calling Isaiah in the Temple, God instructs the prophet to preach God's law not because it will result in better behavior, but because it will harden Israel in their sin so that death, destruction, and exile will be certain to ensue (Isa 6:9–13).

In light of these statements, YHWH's purposes in giving the law cannot be seen as serving the purpose of eliciting obedience. Rather, the law served an alternative purpose of humbling the elect people so that they might be receptive to his grace, as Deuteronomy 31:1–10 suggests. Similarly, Leviticus also states that the purpose of exile will be humbling: "I will break the pride of your power" (Lev 26:18). Indeed, God later tells the prophet Ezekiel that he gave Israel a law that would never lead to righteousness: *"I gave them statutes that were not good and rules by which they could not have life, and I defiled them* through their very gifts in their offering up all their firstborn, *that I might devastate them. I did it that they might know that I am the* LORD" (Ezek 20:25–26, emphasis added). Being humbled, Israel would come to justify God in his words and acknowledge him to be the true God (Ps 51:4).

Although God's course of action may seem strange or even counterproductive to many, it fits well into the biblical pattern of salvation and election. As we have already seen, God exalts the humble, and humbles the exalted (Ps 138:6; Prov 3:34; 29:23). All the legally disinherited younger brothers among the patriarchs became the elect inheritors. Moreover, before the elect ones were exalted, they had to be humbled: Abraham was driven from his own land to the unknown Canaan, Jacob was separated and driven from his family under the threat of murder from his brother, Joseph was given over the slavery in Egypt by his own siblings, Israel had to suffer as slaves in Egypt before inheriting the land of Canaan. Therefore, for one to be among the elect, saved, and exalted, one must first be moved into the category of judged and rejected. The corporate history of the people of God is no different.

Ultimately, the Word of YHWH's promise of salvation to Israel and humanity remains truthful in spite of the exile. The Lord and his Word would ultimately be triumphant in the face of human sin. Therefore, Deuteronomy 28–32 not only speak of Israel's sin and impending exile, but also of the second exodus and renewal of the divine-human relationship.

Isaiah 40–66 goes further and envisions a universal end to the exile that began in Eden. This salvation will be worked by God's Word, which is both unchanging in its purpose in the face of every challenge and at the same time capable of calling into being new salvific realities: "The grass withers, the flower fades when the breath of the LORD blows on it; surely the people are grass. The grass withers, the flower fades, but the word of our God will stand forever" (Isa 40:7–8).

Because God's promise of salvation remains good, the new Eden with God's attending presence will be restored and find its final eschatological fulfillment. Although God had previously withdrawn his personal presence from his people by abandoning the Temple (Ezek 10), he is said to be returning through a miraculous desert highway (Isa 40:3–6). He will do this because he will forgive Israel's sin (Isa 40:2) in accordance with his promise of grace. Not only will Israel return to Zion, the city of YHWH's presence (Isa 44–45), but the gentiles who also suffer the universal exile from God's presence will stream from the whole expanse of creation to worship the true God (Isa 45:23) in the eschatological Temple. All this will occur because of the faithfulness of God to his Word (Isa 40:7–8).

Jeremiah also envisions God's faithfulness to his Word as the means by which Israel and humanity will be saved. The Sinaitic covenant of the law was inadequate to secure the divine-human relationship, therefore by his grace God will establish a new covenant with Israel:

Behold, the days are coming, declares the LORD, when I will make a new covenant with the house of Israel and the house of Judah, not like the covenant that I made with their fathers on the day when I took them by the hand to bring them out of the land of Egypt, my covenant that they broke, though I was their husband, declares the LORD. For this is the covenant that I will make with the house of Israel after those days, declares the LORD: I will put my law within them, and I will write it on their hearts. And I will be their God, and they shall be my people. And no longer shall each one teach his neighbor and each his brother, saying, 'Know the LORD,' for they shall all know me, from the least of them to the greatest, declares the LORD. For I will forgive their iniquity, and I will remember their sin no more. (Jer 31:31–4)

As should be noticed, the content of the new covenant will encompass both what the later Christian theological tradition will term "justification" (i.e., forgiveness) and "sanctification" (making holy). It should also be noticed that the Spirit who forgives and sanctifies sinners works through the promulgation of the covenant itself (which is, by definition, words of promise)—that is, the giving of a new divine word of grace.

Ezekiel also speaks of the Spirit's redemption through a new eschatological word of redemption. The prophet writes of God's eschatological "covenant of peace" (Ezek 34:25) and an "everlasting covenant" (Ezek 37:26). Then later, in a manner similar to Jeremiah, Ezekiel describes the coming justification and sanctification of the people through a new covenant:

> I will sprinkle clean water on you, and you shall be clean from all your uncleannesses, and from all your idols I will cleanse you. And I will give you a new heart, and a new spirit I will put within you. And I will remove the heart of stone from your flesh and give you a heart of flesh. And I will put my Spirit within you, and cause you to walk in my statutes and be careful to obey my rules. (Ezek 36:25–27)

Although they use somewhat different terminology, it would appear that Jeremiah and Ezekiel echo Deuteronomy's claim that God would himself circumcise the hearts of his people (Deut 29:4; 30:6). Here again, God's Word is able to work salvation apart from the law, while at the same time ensuring the fulfillment of the law.

Although Isaiah 26 and other Old Testament texts also witness to the same reality (Job 19:26, etc.), Daniel and the later Jewish apocalyptic tradition emphasize that God's promise of continued faithfulness finds its logical conclusion in the resurrection of the dead: "And many of those who sleep in the dust of the earth shall awake, some to everlasting life, and some to shame and everlasting contempt." (Dan 12:2). [37] Here we may observe that Daniel posits a final restoration for some—an eternal return from exile and reversal of the effects of the fall of Genesis 3. God's

---

37. R. K. Harrison, *Introduction to the Old Testament* (Peabody, MA: Hendrickson Publishers, 2004), 1127–32.

covenantal faithfulness is viewed as being so great that it extends even beyond the grave. God resurrects the dead so that he might have persons to whom he can fulfill his promises of restoration. In this sense, the promise of God to Israel of life and freedom are fulfilled and expanded.

This restoration does not merely extend to new and eternal bodily life. The presence of God will not merely return (as in Isaiah), but the resurrected redeemed will share the glory (*kavod*) of the Lord: "And those who are wise shall shine like the brightness of the sky above; and those who turn many to righteousness, like the stars forever and ever" (Dan 12:3). Eichrodt observes: "The Daniel passage is unique in laying stress on the share in the divine light-glory, an image which is in any case entirely in keeping with the conception of God's new world as a revelation of the divine *kavod* [glory]."[38]

Daniel 2 and 7 also envision the restoration of Edenic harmony and the return from cosmic exile in the form of the destruction of the pagan demonic kingdoms (envisioned as unclean monsters), and their replacement by God's own kingdom. Much like in the account of Genesis 1, where the humans made in God's image are given dominion on the earth, a mysterious messianic figure described as "one like a son of man" (Dan 7:13) is given "dominion and glory and a kingdom" (Dan 7:14). Moreover, Daniel 2, the vision of the growing mountain which fills the entire creation is suggestive of the universalization of the Temple mount and therefore the donation of divine presence to the whole creation.[39] Eden, the protological Temple, is restored and expanded to the whole of the cosmos. Heaven and earth are filled with the divine presence which will guarantee the divine favor.

THE ESCHATOLOGICAL FULFILLMENT OF COVENANTAL MEDIATION[40]

As the later prophetic works of the Old Testament make clear, God's faithful Word and the eschatological redemption of creation comes about through the final fulfillment of mediation—that is, the coming of

---

38. Eichrodt, *Theology of the Old Testament*, 2:515.

39. Beale, *Temple and the Church's Mission*, 144–53.

40. See similar, but modified discussion in Kilcrease, *Self-Donation of God*, 15–50.

the Messiah. As the "anointed one" (the literal meaning of Messiah)[41] the Messiah was the supreme embodiment of election, in that as we saw earlier, the anointing of the mediators was a way of designating their chosen status.[42] Just as the earlier mediators of Israel were elect representational persons, the Messiah as he is described by the Old Testament fulfills the destiny of both Israel and humanity. At the same time, the Messiah is the final and definitive manifestation of God's glory and covenant faithfulness.

As we have already seen, this eschatological fulfillment of mediation is suggested by Daniel's description of a kingly figure known as "one like the Son of Man."[43] The Son of Man is a second Adam, in that he takes up Adam's position of universal dominion in the new creation. This parallels the eschatological promise of universal dominion to the Davidic king (Ps 2:8–9) found elsewhere in the Old Testament. Indeed, the form that the eschatological fulfillment of mediation takes in much of the prophetic literature is talk of the renewal of the Davidic covenant (Amos 9:11, Isa 7:14–16; 9:1–7; 11:1–16; 55:3; Jer 23:5; 30:8; 33:14–26; Ezek 34:20–24; 37:24–25; Hos 3:5; Zech 6:12–13; 12:10), since God promised to secure David's throne eternally (2 Sam 7:14–5). In that the universal reign of the Davidic king also happens at the eschaton like that of Danielic Son of Man, there is a strong suggestion that the two figures are identical.

Just as the mediators of the Old Testament embodied God's own faithfulness to the covenant of grace, so too, the future Davidic Messiah is increasingly spoken of throughout the Old Testament as taking on divine qualities. In Isaiah, he is described as "Immanuel" (Isa 7:14) that is, "God with us."[44] In chapter 9 of the same book, the future Davidic savior is described as giving those in darkness a "great light" (v. 2); that is, his presence is reminiscent of the divine *kavod*. Later, in the same chapter he

---

41. Kaiser, *Messiah in the Old Testament*, 16.

42. Kaiser, *Messiah in the Old Testament*, 16–17.

43. See discussion in Delbert Burkett, *The Son of Man: A History and Evaluation* (Cambridge: Cambridge University Press 1999); Joseph Fitzmeyer, "The New Testament Title 'Son of Man,'" in *A Wandering Aramean: Collected Aramaic Essays* (Missoula: Scholars, 1999), 143–60; Charles Gieschen, "The Name of the Son of Man in 1 Enoch," in *Enoch and the Messiah Son of Man: Revisiting the Book of Parables*, ed. Gabriele Boccaccini (Grand Rapids: Eerdmans, 2007), 238–49; Douglas Hare, *The Son of Man Tradition* (Minneapolis: Fortress, 1990); Sigmund Mowinkel, *He That Cometh*, trans. G.W. Anderson (Nashville: Abingdon, 1959), 346–451.

44. Franz Delitzsch, *Biblical Commentary on the Prophecies of Isaiah*, 2 vols. (Grand Rapids: Eerdmans, 1954), 1:220–23.

is described as "Wonderful Counselor, Mighty God, Everlasting Father, Prince of Peace" (v. 6). The adjectives "Mighty" and "Everlasting" are consistently associated with God elsewhere in the Old Testament.[45]

This divine identity of the Davidic Messiah is witnessed to elsewhere in the later prophets. Ezekiel states that at the coming restoration of creation, "My servant David shall be king over them, and they *shall all have one shepherd*" (Ezek 37:24, emphasis added). In chapter 34, God earlier states that he alone will shepherd Israel: "I myself will be the shepherd of my sheep" (Ezek 34:15). Although the text does not explicitly teach a divine Messiah, it is strongly implied that God and the Davidic Messiah are a single subject in that there will be one shepherd of the people of God.[46] God's solidarity with Israel through his promise of grace is therefore envisioned as becoming so deep and totalizing that he literally makes himself into an individual Israelite.

Beyond the image of the mighty savior king,[47] other images of the eschatological fulfillment of mediation are also present in the Old Testament. Isaiah describes redemption as coming through the work of the "Servant of the Lord."[48] The Servant functions primarily as the fulfillment of prophetic and priestly mediation. Nevertheless, although it is never stated directly as such, there is much to suggest that the Servant spoken of in the chapters of Isaiah is paradoxically the same as the promised Davidic king. Earlier, the Davidic Messiah is spoken of as "a shoot from the stump of Jesse, and a branch from his roots shall bear fruit" (Isa 11:1) and "root of Jesse who shall stand as a signal for the peoples—of him shall the nations inquire" (Isa 11:10). Similarly, the Servant is spoken of as a "shoot" coming "out of dry ground" (Isa 53:2) and a "light to the nations" (Isa 49:6). Moreover, the Davidic Messiah and the Servant are both described as redeemers and servants of YHWH.[49]

45. Hengstenberg, *Christology of the Old Testament*, 1:89–90. Also see Leupold, *Isaiah*, 1:185–86.

46. Horace Hummel, *Ezekiel*, 2 vols. (St. Louis: Concordia, 2007), 2:1003–7; Gerard Van Groningen, *Messianic Revelation in the Old Testament* (Grand Rapids: Baker, 1990), 771–78.

47. See discussion in Mowinkel, *He that Cometh*, 155–86.

48. Van Groningen, *Messianic Revelation in the Old Testament*, 62–42; Mowinkel, *He that Cometh*, 187–260.

49. Van Groningen, *Messianic Revelation in the Old Testament*, 646–47.

Indeed, like the Davidic Messiah, the Servant takes on divine qualities as well. As we observed earlier, Isaiah informs us that YHWH himself will return to Zion (Isa 40). This returning presence appears to be
identical with the Servant of the Lord. As previously noted, the Servant
is God's luminous glory in that he is a "light to the nations" (49:6). This
description clearly parallels the manifestation of the *kavod* in Isaiah 40:5.
Furthermore, he is described as the "arm of the Lord"(Isa 53:1; 63:12). He
is also the divine "angel of the presence" sent to save (Isa 63:9).[50]

Because the Servant embodies the destiny of God and his people
united together, the same title of "Servant" is given to the redeemed people
of God (Isa 41:8). Nevertheless, as the most famous description of the
Servant makes clear, this anointed one is an individual person who is distinct from Israel and the rest of humanity.[51] In Isaiah 53, the Servant of
the Lord is described as a righteous individual who has been set apart by
God to atone for sin. Whereas all of humanity has gone astray and fallen
into sin, the righteous Servant has not sinned (Isa 53:9) but has served
as a sacrifice for sin for all (Isa 53:10). In this, the Servant is a representational elect person whose righteousness is imputed to others: "Out of the
anguish of his soul he shall see and be satisfied; by his knowledge shall
the righteous one, my servant, *make many to be accounted righteous* [or "be
justified"], and he *shall bear their iniquities*" (Isa 53:11, emphasis added).[52]

As a result, the Servant is a new Passover Lamb for Isaiah's new exodus:
"[he was] like a lamb that is led to the slaughter" (Isa 53:7). In spite of his
suffering he will be vindicated and be exalted by YHWH (Isa 53:12). His
sacrifice and exaltation parallel that of the "one like the Son of Man" who
ascends to the heavenly throne room (i.e., the heavenly counterpart of
the Holy of Holies) on a cloud (Dan 7:13). The ascension of the Son of
Man parallels the high priest's entry into the Holy of Holies on a cloud
of incense on the Day of Atonement when he brings his blood offering
into the presence of the Lord (Lev 16:12–13). This suggests that the Son

50. Note that this is one reading. The LXX version states "not an ambassador, nor an angel, but
he himself [God] saved them." See discussion in Gieschen, *Angelomorphic Christology: Antecedents
and Early Evidence* (Leiden: Brill, 1998), 116–19. Also see Michel Rene Barnes, "Veni Creator Spiritus,"
4. Barnes notes that the rabbinical interpreters treated the two readings as if they were identical.

51. Van Groningen, *Messianic Revelation in the Old Testament*, 629.

52. Van Groningen, *Messianic Revelation in the Old Testament*, 630–32.

of Man not only is a high priestly figure, but is the same person as the Servant who also offers up an eschatological sacrifice. The Son of Man appears to have made some sort of high priestly sacrifice (much like the Servant) and will offer it before the Ancient of Days in the heavenly court in order to make intercession for sinners.[53]

Likewise, as the great eschatological prophet of the new exodus, the Servant is also a new Moses. We are told: "He [will] sprinkle many nations" (Isa 52:15). Moses sprinkled the Israelites with the blood when inaugurating the Sinaitic covenant (Exod 24), which suggests that the Servant inaugurates a new covenant. Nevertheless, instead of a covenant of law, this new covenant that the Servant mediates appears to be the same as that spoken of by Ezekiel and Jeremiah. We are told by Isaiah that Servant and his work of removing sin are themselves the content of this covenant: "Thus says the LORD: "In a time of favor I have answered you; in a day of salvation I have helped you; I will keep you and *give you as a covenant to the people*" (Isa 49:8, emphasis added). Therefore, we are told that the Servant will proclaim a universal Jubilee (Isa 61:2), based on his own person and work.[54] As should be observed, there is another parallel with the prophesies of Daniel. At the time of eschatological judgment and redemption, we read that an "anointed one" (Messiah) will be "cut off" and will confirm a "covenant with many" (Dan 9:26–27).[55]

CONCLUSION

In our survey of the Old Testament, we have come to observe a number of important themes. First, all reality is dependent on God's creative Word. God's Word does not merely augment already existing realities and impose its stamp on them (as in Ancient Near Eastern creation myths) but calls into existence new possibilities by its creative power. Second, although

---

53. Crispin H. T. Fletcher-Louis, "The High Priest as Divine Mediator in the Hebrew Bible: Daniel 7:13 as a Test Case," *Society of Biblical Literature Seminar Papers* (1997): 169–74.

54. Hengstenberg, *Christology in the Old Testament*, 3:351–53. Leupold agrees that this is a reference to Jubilee. See Leupold, *Isaiah*, 2:321.

55. Van Groningen, *Messianic Revelation in the Old Testament*, 836–38; C. F. Keil, *Biblical Commentary on Daniel* (Grand Rapids: Eerdmans, 1955), 360–62; Andrew E. Steinmann, *Daniel* (St. Louis: Concordia, 2008), 474–76. Also see Brant Pitre, *Jesus, the Tribulation, and the End of Exile* (Grand Rapids: Baker Academic, 2005), 51–62.

God's Word opens up new possibilities to his creatures, he is nevertheless faithful to his original creation purpose.

Because God was faithful to his creation, subsequent to the fall God's Word took the form of covenants that promise judgment and grace. Because God's commitment to the promises embodied in these covenants is total and complete, in order to ensure their fulfillment he elected representational persons to fulfill these covenants in the face of sinful human failure and opposition. Nevertheless, since Israel and its elect mediators proved faithless, God promised the later prophets that he would in a final and definitive way fulfill his promise of salvation in the person of the Messiah. It is to this definitive fulfillment in the era of the New Testament that we now turn.

CHAPTER 3

Justification and Christ:

Salvation Through the Word in the Ministry of Jesus

H aving examined the power of the saving divine Word in the Old Testament, we will now describe the culmination of the redemptive process of history in the person of Christ. Christ is the very Word of God himself (John 1), who comes to fulfill God's gracious promises to Israel and humanity by speaking forth a new creation. As will become evident, Christ does this by the creative power of his word of forgiveness. Christ does this not with human cooperation, but against the final and most terrible resistance of all of humanity (both Jews and gentiles) in the crucifixion. Nevertheless, in spite of human and satanic resistance, Christ succeeds in overcoming sin, death, the devil, and the law, in order to elect and justify the ungodly through his atoning death and resurrection.

Below we will describe the collective witness of the Gospels to Christ's work of justification. Throughout the Gospel tradition, Jesus portrayed himself as the coming Son of Man, both a priest-king figure and a cosmic judge. As the Son of Man, Jesus claimed to be the theanthropic cosmic judge come ahead of the eschaton to share his proleptic verdict in the present. As a result of his death and resurrection, and the coming of the Spirit, Jesus's disciples were empowered to make the same proleptic judgment of election and justification through the apostolic ministry.

THE REDEMPTIVE ADVENT OF THE DIVINE
WORD IN THE BIRTH OF THE MESSIAH[1]

Although both the Markan and Johannine witnesses commence with the revelation of Christ's identity through John the Baptizer's ministry, both Matthew and Luke inform us of the virginal conception and birth of the Messiah. These narratives are significant in themselves because they highlight that the birth of the Messiah is a fulfillment of God's saving and re-creative activity through the Word in the Old Testament.

In discussing the virgin conception of Jesus in the first Gospel, it should be observed that Matthew structures his Gospel around an *inclusio* of the divine Name and presence.[2] Matthew identifies Jesus in his conception and ministry with this divine Name and Word. At the beginning of the first Gospel, Jesus's earthly father Joseph is informed that "you are to give him the name Jesus, because *he will save his people from their sins*" (Matt 1:21). Although many have imputed to Matthew a low and ascending Christology,[3] Jesus's divine identity is revealed in the fact that the name "Jesus" means "God is our salvation."[4] Matthew also reports the angel's explanation of the name: "for he will save his people from their sins" (Matt 1:21). In this, Matthew clearly identifies Jesus as the agent of salvation and therefore as the returning divine presence (Isa 40). The Evangelist then cites Isaiah's prophecy that a virgin will give birth to Immanuel, "God with us" (Matt 1:23).

This explanation of Jesus as the divine Name and presence coincides with the events at the end of the Gospel. Here again we see the divine Name repeated: "make disciples of all nations, baptizing them in the *name of the Father and of the Son and of the Holy Spirit*" (Matt 28:19,

---

1. In this section, see similar arguments in a modified form in Kilcrease, *Self-Donation of God*, 57–62.

2. David Scaer, *Discourses in Matthew: Jesus Teaches the Church* (St. Louis: Concordia, 2004), 172.

3. James D. G. Dunn, *Christology in the Making: An Inquiry into the New Testament Origins of the Doctrine of the Incarnation* (Grand Rapids: Eerdmans, 1989), 202.

4. Daniel Harrington, *The Gospel of Matthew* (Collegeville, MN: Liturgical, 1991) 35; John P. Meier, *Roots of the Problem and the Person*, vol. 1 of *A Marginal Jew: Rethinking the Historical Jesus* (New York: Doubleday, 1991), 207.

emphasis added).[5] Again, the Name coincides with the divine presence: "And behold, *I am with you always*, to the end of the age." (Matt 28:20).[6] In both instances, salvation comes by God's continuing solidarity with his people manifest in his Name and presence given in the incarnation, and, as we will later see, the word and sacrament ministry of the apostles. As the background of Matthew's theology of the incarnation, we are reminded that God's Name and presence are identical in the Old Testament.[7] God's Name is the means by which he is present to his people and identifies with them through his promise. Through his Name, God is also identified with his previous saving act in salvation history: "I am the God of ... " etc. The Temple, wherein God is graciously present to his people is called "a house for my name" (2 Sam 7:13). Eschatologically, it should also be remembered that God told Ezekiel that because he had identified his Name with Israel he must redeem them in order to vindicate his Name (Ezek 36:23). As we have earlier noted, this eschatological vindication of the divine Name coincides with the return of the divine presence, as well as the justification and sanctification of the people of God by the word of the new and everlasting covenant.

It is also important to recognize that throughout the Old Testament the divine Name is identified with the Word of God itself. As Johann Michael Reu observes: "So His [God's] name is much like His Word—in fact, it is the shortest form of His Word; and whatever we do to God's Word we are also doing to His name."[8] Much like with the divine Word, Israel identified God's Name with his powerful and saving presence. God's Name was not a mere label.

When God gives Moses his Name in Exodus 3:14, it is often translated as "I am what I am." Nevertheless, many have suggested that it would be more appropriate to translate it as "I will be who I will be" or even "I am the one who brings into being" (*'ehyeh asher 'ehyeh*, condensed into

---

5. Charles Gieschen, "The Divine Name in Ante-Nicene Christianity," *Vigiliae Christianae* 57 (2003): 124–25.

6. Scaer, *Discourses in Matthew*, 202.

7. See brief discussion in Sandra L. Richter, *The Deuteronomistic History and the Name Theology: Lešakkēn Šemô Šām in the Bible and the Ancient Near East* (New York: De Gruyter, 2002), 11–12.

8. Johann Michael Reu, *An Explanation of Dr. Martin Luther's Small Catechism* (Minneapolis: Augsburg, 1964), 138.

the divine Name YHWH).[9] This seems to form a connection between the divine Name in Exodus 3 and the Word of God's speech in Genesis 1. The Lord first creates with the words: "Let there be" (Gen 1:3). Charles Gieschen has demonstrated that a significant number of early Jewish interpreters drew a connection between the divine speech in Genesis 1 and the divine Name in Exodus 3. In their interpretation, the Word of God and the divine Name were identical because they both contained the verb "to be."[10] In a word, God's Name and presence were identical with his Word through which he established the original creation, as well as the means by which he might call into existence a new creation through his covenantal promises.

Luke's infancy narratives echo the many stories of the Old Testament matriarchs who longed to conceive and yet remained childless.[11] Luke does not begin his account with Mary's virginal conception of Jesus, but rather with Zechariah and Elizabeth, Mary's cousin and her husband. Luke highlights the redemptive power of the Word of God in bringing about the conception of both John and Jesus. Nevertheless, at the same time it should not go unnoticed that Luke constructs his narrative in order to highlight the fact that Zechariah and Elizabeth are people of the time of preparation and law. By contrast, Mary is described as a Spirit-filled person of the new dispensation of grace.[12]

Luke begins his narrative by telling us that Zechariah and his wife are old and are unable to conceive (Luke 1:5–7). Already, we hear an echo of the childless matriarchs of the Old Testament (particularly the elderly Abraham and Sarah) and God's ability to bring forth the promised seed. Zechariah is a Levite serving his appointed time in the Temple, the center of the people of God's relationship with Israel in the old dispensation. In this, Luke identifies John's parents as people of the old covenant, in that

---

9. See the debate about the meaning of the Tetragrammaton in G. H. Parke-Taylor, *Yahweh: The Divine Name in the Bible* (Waterloo, ON: Wilfrid Laurier University Press, 1975), 46–62.

10. Gieschen, *Angelomorphic Christology*, 74, 103–107; Charles Gieschen, "The Real Presence of the Son Before Christ: Revisiting an Old Approach to Old Testament Christology," *Concordia Theological Quarterly* 68 (2004): 105–26.

11. Kenneth Litwak, *Echoes of Scripture in Luke-Acts: Telling the History of God's People Intertextually* (New York: Bloomsbury, 2005), 72–80.

12. See similar observations in John Carroll, *Luke: A Commentary* (Louisville: Westminster John Knox, 2012), 43–44.

they embody Israel's relationship with God during the Old Testament
through their infertility and crucial role in the Levitical cult. Later in the
Lukan narrative, Jesus tells us that John was the last of the prophets and
therefore the end of the older and inferior dispensation: "The Law and
the Prophets were until John" (Luke 16:16).

While serving in the Temple, Zechariah encounters the angel Gabriel
who informs him that although his wife is elderly and infertile, she will
miraculously give birth to the new Elijah who will prepare the way for
the Messiah (Luke 1:8–17). Zechariah doubts the Word of God spoken
by the angel and is therefore silenced as punishment until the fulfillment
of the promised son. Zechariah's resistance to the Word of God seems
similar to that of ancient Israel, whom Luke characterizes as "resisting"
(Acts 7:51) the work of the Spirit through the word. Moreover, the silence
of Zechariah seems similar to the silence of the prophets in the intertestamental period. In this, Luke treats the story of Zechariah typologically.
That is, his story is foreshadowed by other events in the Old Testament.
The Evangelist describes Zechariah as one who fulfills and takes over
the roles of Israel in exile and indeed all the rejected older brothers in
the stories in the Hebrew Bible. Both Israel and the older brothers of the
Old Testament failed to find divine favor because of their resistance to
the Word of God. In a word, in spite of his high position in the Levitical
cult, he is brought low by Gabriel's condemning word of law.[13]

When Luke recounts the Annunciation later in the same chapter, there
is a significant shift. Gabriel announces that Mary is the object of God's
electing grace: "Greetings, O favored one, the Lord is with you!" (Luke
1:28). Therefore, Mary will become the mother of Christ purely by grace
and not by any works that she has done. Her secondary placement in the
narrative seems to put her in the role of the younger elect brothers of the
Old Testament. This sets up a series of contrasts between Zechariah and
Elizabeth on the one hand and Mary on the other. Although Zechariah
and Elizabeth are also elected by grace, it is interesting that Luke mentions
their righteousness before the law (Luke 1:6), whereas he does no such
thing with Mary. Likewise, Zechariah encounters Gabriel while performing the works of the law in the Temple. In contrast to this, Mary becomes

---

13. Carroll, *Luke*, 44.

the new living Temple by grace alone. She will conceive Jesus by being "overshadowed" by the Holy Spirit just as the Tabernacle was when the divine *kavod* descended into it according to the LXX version of Exodus 40 (Luke 1:35, LXX Exod 40:34).[14]

Mary's status as one who will be the mother of the Messiah by the grace of the word is deepened by the fact that she will conceive although she is a virgin. By God's unilateral grace and without human cooperation, Mary will conceive the Messiah by the divine Word and Spirit. In contrast to this, Zechariah and Elizabeth still live in the era of the Old Testament and therefore bear a son through carnal generation (albeit a miraculous one).[15] In a word, whereas Zechariah and Elizabeth are asked to perform a work (i.e., sexual intercourse), Mary conceives through the faith created by the Word of God proclaimed to her (*conception per aurem—*conception through hearing): "Behold, I am the servant of the Lord; *let it be to me according to your word*" (Luke 1:38, emphasis added).[16]

At the end of the chapter, the Magnificat and the Song of Zechariah are both lyrical soliloquies to God's redemptive power exercised through his Word. Mary speaks of God as the exclusive agent of salvation (Luke 1:47). God's agency in salvation consists in his electing and saving Word exalting the lowly and humble exalted ones (Luke 1:48–54). We are told that God has mercy on those who fear him (Luke 1:50), but those who fall into this category do so because God has humbled them (i.e., Zechariah). God has performed his alien and saving work and done this in accordance with his promises to Abraham, which he has now fulfilled in his election of Mary to be the mother of the Messiah (Luke 1:55). In this, God's Word of grace saves, re-creates, and breaks through every barrier to fulfill its ultimate purpose.

This theme of the judging and redemptive work of the word is deepened in the Song of Zechariah as well. Once John is born, Zechariah, who has been supernaturally silenced by God, communicates via writing his insistence that his son be named John in accordance with the word of

14. Arthur Just, *Luke*, 2 vols. (St. Louis: Concordia, 1996–1997), 1:69.

15. Carroll, *Luke*, 44.

16. See Luther's position in That the words of Christ "This is My Body" shall stand firm against the fanatics, (1527), WA 23:185. Also see Martin Chemnitz, Polycarp Leyser, and Johann Gerhard, *The Harmony of the Evangelists*, trans. Richard Dinda, vol 1. (Malone, TX: Repristination, 2009), 120.

the angel Gabriel. As a result of the faith he displays in the Word of God, his tongue is loosened (Luke 1:60–64). Having been humbled in order to be exalted through faith, Zechariah sings a song of praise emphasizing the all-powerful working of God's promise of grace in the Abrahamic and Davidic covenants (Luke 1:69, 73). In this, the rejected elder son of the old dispensation of law has become a justified and elect one of the new era of grace. All this is possible because of the humbling and recreative power of God's Word.

THE COMING OF THE SON OF MAN[17]

As Ernst Käsemann once correctly observed, Jewish apocalypticism is the mother of all Christian theology.[18] Apocalyptic theology and writing deal with the revelation and enactment of God's final eschatological plan for creation. The Gospels frame the ministry of Jesus as an apocalyptic event.[19] It begins the description of Christ's career with John the Baptizer's ministry announcing the Day of the Lord and ends with the proleptic eschaton of Jesus's resurrection from the dead. In a word, the apocalypse that John announces Jesus finally enacts in his resurrection.[20]

As the Gospels present him, John the Baptizer appears to operate with a typical first-century Jewish way of conceiving the coming day of redemption.[21] For John, God was in a process of redeeming and judging

---

17. My presupposition in dealing with the Gospels is that they are accurate histories, albeit condensed and stylized in accordance with the genre of history practiced in the ancient world. I believe this controversial claim can be justified by references to the following studies: Richard Bauckham, *Jesus and the Eyewitnesses: The Gospels as Eyewitness Testimony* (Grand Rapids: Eerdmans, 2006); Craig Blomberg, *The Historical Reliability of the Gospels* (Downers Grove, IL: InterVarsity Press, 2007); Craig Blomberg, *The Historical Reliability of John's Gospel: Issues and Commentary* (Downers Grove, IL: InterVarsity Press, 2011); Peter Williams, *Can We Trust the Gospels* (Wheaton, IL: Crossway, 2018); N. T. Wright, *Jesus and the Victory of God, Christian Origins and the Question of God* 2 (Minneapolis: Fortress, 1997); Martin Hengel, *The Four Gospels and the One Gospel of Jesus Christ: An Investigation of the Collection and Origin of the Canonical Gospels,* trans. John Bowden (Harrisburg, PA: Trinity International, 2000).

18. Ernest Käsemann, "The Beginnings of Christian Theology," in *New Testament Questions of Today,* trans. W.J. Montague (Philadelphia: Fortress, 1969), 102.

19. See Frederick Murphy, *Apocalypticism in the Bible and Its World: A Comprehensive Introduction* (Grand Rapids: Baker Academic, 2012), 281–306.

20. Wolfhart Pannenberg, *Jesus: God and Man,* trans. Lewis Wilkins and Duane Priebe (Philadelphia: Westminster, 1977), 58, 60, 391, 397.

21. See summary and major themes in John Collins, *The Apocalyptic Imagination: An Introduction to Jewish Apocalyptic Literature* (Grand Rapids: Eerdmans, 1998); N. T. Wright, *New Testament and the People of God,* 280-338.

his people.[22] When the Lord's kingdom breaks into the world, it will result in a cosmic judgment that will divide humanity between the redeemed and the condemned (Matt 3:1–11; Mark 1:1–8, Luke 3:1–20). As we saw in the previous chapter, Daniel and the apocalyptic tradition of the later prophets teach that the relationship between God and Israel will find the final fulfillment at a great and terrible "Day of the Lord" (*Yom YHWH*).[23] Whereas earlier prophets speak of the temporal exile and return of Israel (which mirrors the universal exile of humanity from the garden), Daniel speaks of a final and definitive end of exile and return in the form of the resurrection of the dead. Some will be raised to eternal life and others to eternal shame (Dan 12). Although Daniel presents a clearer picture of judgment, resurrection, and an eternal universal kingdom, the basic concept of the Day of the Lord is already present as early as the prophet Amos (Amos 5:18–24).[24]

The concept of the eschaton as involving the resurrection of the dead and the coming of cosmic judgment is in many respects the logical and final outworking of Old Testament covenant theology. As the threats and promises of Leviticus and Deuteronomy prophesy, and the Deuteronomic history witnesses, covenantal theology allows for cycles of judgment and redemption over time as the relationship of God and Israel evolves.[25] This evolution of the relationship between God and humans may be seen as having its ups and downs, much as all interpersonal relationships. Ups and downs in personal relations are only meaningful insofar as they are interpreted within the framework of an anticipated whole. The anticipated whole presupposes a

22. See summary in Wright, *Jesus and the Victory of God*, 2:160–62.

23. See Yair Hoffmann, "The Day of the Lord as a Concept and a Term in Prophetic Literature." *Zeitschrift für die alttestamentliche Wissenschaft* 93 (1981): 37–50; James Nogalski, "The Day(s) of the Lord in the Book of the Twelve," in *Thematic Threads in the Book of the Twelve*, ed. Paul L. Redditt, Aaron Schart (New York: Walter De Guyter, 2003), 192–213. Gerhard von Rad, "The Origin of the Concept of the Day of Yahweh," *Journal of Semitic Studies* 4 (1959): 97–108.

24. C. van Leeuwen, "The Prophecy of the YOM YHWH in Amos V 18–20," *Old Testament Studies* 19 (1974): 113–34.

25. See the discussion in C. Marvin Pate, et al., *The Story of Israel: A Biblical Theology* (Downers Grove, IL: InterVarsity Press, 2004), 50–70.

final completion of the relationship that will contextualize individual events within it.[26]

This analogy in part makes sense of why the Old Testament insists that there must be a final and definitive fulfillment of God's relationship with humanity. The divine-human relationship, as well as the revelation of the character of God himself, will inevitably be infinitely deferred without a final and definitive event of their completion. Such a fulfillment must involve judgment and redemption (or law and grace), because such are the contents of the two great covenants (Abrahamic and Sinaitic) of the Old Testament. The completion of the divine-human relationship must involve the resurrection of the dead because God's faithfulness runs so deep it transcends the grave. God's grace will not break faith with the elect even in the face of death.[27] Similarly, the wicked will not escape judgment even after their temporal death. Therefore, this definitive fulfillment also reveals God's character as God. It is the supreme and definitive self-revelation of God: "And the glory of the LORD shall be revealed, and all flesh shall see it together, for the mouth of the LORD has spoken" (Isa 40:5).[28]

After the Maccabean crisis of the second century BC, a new concept of the Day of the Lord began to develop. Such a conception finds its expression scattered through the Pseudepigraphal apocalyptic literature of the period, as well as to a lesser extent the Rabbinical literature of the post-Second Temple period.[29] Specifically, the martyrdom of many Jews during the Maccabean crisis placed the concept of the resurrection of the dead into new prominence.[30] Although the martyrs of the Maccabean period could not expect God to reward them in this life (i.e., unlike the promises of temporal blessing in Leviticus and Deuteronomy), the Lord

---

26. See the similar argument in Wolfhart Pannenberg, "Dogmatic Theses on the Doctrine of Revelation," in *Revelation as History,* ed. Wolfhart Pannenberg, et al., trans. David Granskou (New York: Macmillan, 1968), 131–55.

27. Wright, *The Resurrection of the Son of God,* Christian Origins and the Question of God 3 (Minneapolis: Fortress, 2003), 102-3.

28. See Wolfhart Pannenberg, *Systematic Theology,* trans. Geoffrey W. Bromiley, 3 vols. (Grand Rapids: Eerdmans, 1991–1993), 1:169. "There thus arises the question of a future definitive self-demonstration of the deity of God, a question which arose in Israel especially in exilic prophecy and was later taken up by apocalyptic into expectation of end-time events."

29. See discussions of Second Temple and Rabbinic personal eschatology in Casey Deryl Elledge, *Resurrection of the Dead in Early Judaism, 200 BCE–CE 200* (Oxford: Oxford University Press, 2017).

30. Shaye J. D. Cohen, *From the Maccabees to the Mishnah* (Louisville: Westminster John Knox, 1987), 92.

would vindicate them against their unrighteous enemies (gentiles and apostate Jews) at the general resurrection.[31]

As is clear from reading much of the literature of the period, universal human history came to be seen in terms of trial and vindication. The current age is evil in that it is ruled by demonic forces (sin, death, Satan, pagans, apostate Jews, etc.) that pressure faithful Jews to give in to their evil intentions.[32] After this trial of the present, at the end of time faithful Jews will be vindicated in their righteousness (that is, "justified") because they had adhered to the Sinaitic covenant.[33] As should be evident, the Maccabean crisis served as a microcosm of this historical macrocosm for Second Temple Jews. Jewish fulfillment of the works of the law was quite specifically challenged by Antiochus Epiphanes's Hellenizing policies.[34] If one anticipated being vindicated by God in refusing to give in to gentiles or apostate Jews when challenged to give up obedience to Torah (quite specifically circumcision, food laws, etc.), then it was only logical to assume that one gained the status of justified or vindicated at the end of time at least in part by being obedient to the works of the law. Indeed, this teaching appears to have fulfilled the theodicy needs of the Second Temple Jews, who worried that they were not being rewarded for obeying the covenant of law.[35] Incidentally, although there were a number of sources of disunity among post-Maccabean Jews, one major dividing point among the differing post-Maccabean parties was which interpretation of the law one needed to follow in order to be eschatologically vindicated. The Essenes appear to have seen the "Teacher of Righteousness" as the

---

31. Geza Vermes, *The Resurrection: History and Myth* (New York: Doubleday, 2008), 29–39.

32. Richard Bauckham, *The Jewish World Around the New Testament* (Grand Rapids: Baker Academic, 2010), 57–63.

33. Wright, *The New Testament and the People of God*, 1:334–38. Wright outlines this scenario, but at the same time unconvincingly says that this vindication on the basis of works "demonstrates" covenant faithfulness but does not "earn" salvation. Gathercole shows this is an inaccurate interpretation: Simon J. Gathercole, *Where is Boasting? Early Jewish Soteriology and Paul's Response in Romans 1–5* (Grand Rapids: Eerdmans), 37–196. Bauckham's discussion also seems to show the importance of works in the final judgment. See Bauckham, *The Jewish World Around the New Testament*, 269–324.

34. Wright, *The New Testament and the People of God*, 1:157–59.

35. J. R. Daniel Kirk, *Unlocking Romans: Resurrection and the Justification of God* (Grand Rapids: Eerdmans, 2008), 14–32; Lidija Novakovic, *Resurrection: A Guide for the Perplexed* (New York: Bloomsbury, 2016), 5–48.

definitive interpreter of Torah, whereas the Pharisees appealed to the "Tradition of the Elders."[36]

As E. P. Sanders correctly pointed out a generation ago, the distinction between grace and works was not an issue for the Jews of the time of Christ.[37] With few exceptions, for most of Second Temple Judaism the Sinaitic covenant was in actuality one with the Abrahamic covenant.[38] As Sanders famously argued, one "got in" to the covenant through the grace of Abraham's election and "stayed in" and was vindicated at the end of time through works of the Sinaitic covenant.[39] Sanders calls this view of soteriology "covenant nomism."[40] As a result, contrary to some negative Christian stereotypes, it would be fairer to describe the general outlook of Second Temple Judaism as being a system of belief that mixed grace and works, rather than being blatantly legalistic.[41] As we will later see, this does not invalidate the "Lutheran" interpretation of Paul (or Jesus), since the mixing of grace and works in fact forms a significant point of contact between Second Temple Judaism and the late medieval Church.[42]

Nevertheless, although the so-called "New Perspective on Paul" is right to call attention to elements of grace in the Second Temple Jewish theology of salvation, ultimately the Jews of the time of Christ very clearly did believe that their works were the determining factor in their final salvation.[43] No matter which way one got into the covenant, or however many times God mercifully overlooked Israel's disobedience, or how one gained forgiveness from the sacrificial system, ultimately, at the end of time

---

36. Wright, *The New Testament and the People of God*, 1:335. Wright makes this point, although again he insists that the works of the law are "badges" of covenant membership. Again, as Gathercole and others show, this is false. Obedience is a genuine criterion for salvation.

37. E. P. Sanders, *Paul and Palestinian Judaism: A Comparison of Patterns of Religion* (Philadelphia: Fortress, 1977), 4, 100, 297.

38. Sanders, *Paul and Palestinian Judaism*, 75, 236.

39. Sanders, *Paul and Palestinian Judaism*, 422, 427.

40. Sanders, *Paul and Palestinian Judaism*, 236. See Timo Laato, *Paul and Judaism: An Anthropological Approach* (Atlanta: Scholar's, 1995), 147–68.

41. Sanders, *Paul and Palestinian Judaism*, 297; Stephen Westerholm, *Justification Reconsidered: Rethinking a Pauline Theme* (Grand Rapids: Eerdmans, 2013), 29–34.

42. See similar, but not identical, observation in Thomas Schreiner, *The Law and Its Fulfillment: A Pauline Theology of Law* (Grand Rapids: Baker, 1998), 115–19.

43. Westerholm, *Justification Reconsidered*, 31–32.

(as Sanders himself unwittingly documents)[44] those who had genuinely tried to be faithful to the law would be judged righteous.[45] Indeed, Peter Stuhlmacher has pointed to the definitive role of works in the eschatological judgment in the Dead Sea Scrolls and other apocalyptic texts (Bar 14:12–13; 51:7–14; 1 En 61:1–5).[46] Conversely, it is undeniable that first century Jews held that apostate Jews, Jews who did not even try to obey the law ("sinners"),[47] and the pagan gentile oppressors of Israel would be destroyed and condemned to eternal shame.[48]

When considering these eschatological themes, John's baptism is evocative for a number of reasons. Water was part of the purification rituals promulgated in the Old Testament (Lev 15:11, 13–14), and for this reason it was part of the ritual practice of a number of Jewish groups in the first century.[49] The most notable example of this is the Essenes.[50] Ezekiel speaks of an eschatological purification with water: "I will sprinkle clean water on you, and you shall be clean from all your uncleannesses, and from all your idols I will cleanse you" (Ezek 36:25).

Another interesting aspect of John's baptism is that it occurred in the Jordan river. Israel had to cross the Jordan when it had entered the promise land (Josh 3). In a sense, those who were baptized re-entered the land and became a renewed Israel coming out of universal exile.[51] Finally, a

---

44. Sanders, *Paul and Palestinian Judaism*, 128–47.

45. Laato, *Paul and Judaism*, 156–57.

46. Peter Stuhlmacher, *Revisiting Paul's Doctrine of Justification: A Challenge to the New Perspective* (Downers Grove, IL: InterVarsity Press, 2001), 41.

47. E. P. Sanders, *Jesus and Judaism* (Philadelphia: Fortress, 1985), 177–79; Wright, *Jesus and the Victory of God*, 2:264–68.

48. Bauckham, *The Jewish World*, 269–324; Gathercole, *Where is Boasting*, 37–196. Also see Peter T. O'Brien, "Was Paul a Covenantal Nomist?" in *Justification and Variegated Nomism*, ed. D. A. Carson, Peter T. O'Brien, and Mark Seifrid, 2 vols. (Grand Rapids: Baker Academic, 2000–2004), 2:268. Quoting Gathercole, O'Brien notes that there is overwhelming evidence that final judgment in first century Judaism is based at least in part on works.

49. Antje Labahn, "Aus Dem Wasser Kommt Leben: aschungen und Reinigungsriten in frühjüdischen Texten," in *Ablution, Initiation, and Baptism: Late Antiquity, Early Judaism, and Early Christian*, ed. David Hellholm, et al. (Berlin: De Gruyter, 2011) 157–220; Sean Feyne "Jewish Immersion and Christian Baptism," in Hellholm, *Ablution, Initiation, and Baptism: Late Antiquity, Early Judaism, and Early Christian*, 221–54.

50. Jodi Magness, *The Archaeology of Qumran and the Dead Sea Scrolls* (Grand Rapids: Eerdmans, 2002), 134–57.

51. N. T. Wright, *The Challenge of Jesus: Rediscovering Who Jesus Was and Is* (Downers Grove, IL: InterVarsity Press, 1999), 39.

number of scholars have noted that there is some evidence that baptismal rituals were used by first-century Jews when inducting gentile converts into Judaism.[52] The implication would appear to be that Israel cannot rely on its status as God's people, but are on the same par with gentiles: "And do not presume to say to yourselves, 'We have Abraham as our father,' for I tell you, God is able from these stones to raise up children for Abraham" (Matt 3:9). Ultimately, because of sin Israel must re-enter fellowship with God through baptism if it seeks vindication on the Day of the Lord.[53]

This leads us to the recognition of a number of significant distinctions between John and his contemporaries. It is important to notice about John that unlike in the typical Second Temple eschatological scenario, Torah obedience is not the thing that places one in the category of the justified. Rather, for John the key distinction between the elect and saved (i.e., the eschatological Israel) and the rest of humanity is repentance and the forgiveness of sins through the ritual of baptism.[54] Of course, John does speak of good works (Luke 3:10–14), but as the fruits of repentance and forgiveness: "Bear fruit in keeping with repentance" (Matt 3:8).

Beyond this, in continuity with his contemporaries John also proclaims a coming eschatological agent of judgment: "he who is coming after me is mightier than I, whose sandals I am not worthy to carry. ... His winnowing fork is in his hand, and he will clear his threshing floor and gather his wheat into the barn, but the chaff he will burn with unquenchable fire" (Matt 3:11–12). Nevertheless, this coming figure (who possesses both messianic and divine attributes) is not simply an agent of judgment, but a worker of salvation.[55] Much as in the Old Testament, salvation never comes without judgment. John's coming eschatological agent will purify Israel from their sins with fire and give them the sanctifying power of the Holy Spirit: "He will baptize you with the Holy Spirit and fire" (Matt 3:11). As we may recall from the last chapter, the giving of the Holy Spirit

52. T. M. Taylor, "The Beginnings of Jewish Proselyte Baptism," *New Testament Studies* 2, no. 1 (1956): 193–97; H. H. Rowley, "Jewish Proselyte Baptism and the Baptism of John," *Hebrew Union College Annual* 15 (1940): 313–34.

53. See a similar observation in Günther Bornkamm, *Jesus of Nazareth*, trans. Irene and Fraser McLuskey (New York: Harper & Row, 1960), 47.

54. Wright, *Jesus and the Victory of God*, 2:323.

55. Gerd Theissen and Annette Merz, *The Historical Jesus: A Comprehensive Guide*, trans. John Bowden (Minneapolis: Fortress, 1996), 200–203.

was associated in the prophets of the Old Testament with the mediation of the new covenant of grace (Jer 31:31–34).

The Gospels inform us that the one that John speaks of is the Messiah Jesus. Christ's identity as God's Son and the Messiah is revealed in a vision reminiscent of the larger tradition of Jewish apocalyptic vision.[56] The New Testament tells us that Jesus is not only the Davidic Messiah, but also God himself returned to Zion (Isa 40 as applied to Jesus in Matt 3; Mark 1; Luke 3). Nevertheless, the title that Jesus most often uses to describe himself is the "Son of Man" (*bar Adam*). The title "Son of Man" can simply mean a human being. Nevertheless, at least in some Second Temple Jewish circles, the Son of Man was understood to be a heavenly cosmic judge who would come at the end of time to mete out judgment and salvation (for example in 1 En 61–2; 64; 4 Ezra 11–13; 2 Bar 39).[57] It should be noted that the Son of Man is identified as a cosmic judge in the non-canonical literature of the intertestamental period and the Gospels, but not directly in the book of Daniel.

As we have already seen in the previous chapter, in Daniel the Son of Man is a heavenly priestly and kingly figure (a parallel with Ps 110 the most frequently cited Psalm in the New Testament)[58] who is exalted and vindicated at the end of time. His status as priest very well may be the reason that both intertestamental literature and the Gospels interpret this figure in Daniel as being a cosmic judge. After all, within the Levitical cult it was the role of the priest to serve as a judge: "You must distinguish between the holy and the common, between the unclean and the clean" (Lev 10:10; 11:47). This discernment and separation of the pure

---

56. Jonathan Knight, *Christian Origins* (Edinburgh: T&T Clark, 2008), 93.

57. For discussion of the meaning of the title see Frederick Borsch, *The Christian and Gnostic Son of Man* (Naperville, IL: Alec R. Allenson, Inc. 1970); Frederick Borsch, *The Son of Man in Myth and History* (Philadelphia: Westminster, 1967); Burkett, *The Son of Man*; Fitzmeyer, "New Testament Title 'Son of Man,'" 143–60; Gieschen, "The Name of the Son of Man in 1 Enoch," 238–49; Hare, *The Son of Man Tradition*; Morna Hooker, *The Son of Man in Mark: A Study of the Background of the Term "Son of Man" and Its Use in St. Mark's Gospel* (London: SPCK, 1967); H. E. Tödt, *The Son of Man in the Synoptic Tradition*, trans. Dorothea Barton (Philadelphia: Westminster, 1965).

58. David Hay, *Glory at the Right Hand: Psalm 110 in Early Christianity* (Nashville: Abingdon, 1973).

and impure would seem to prefigure the cosmic judgment made at the end of time by the Son of Man.

Jesus's contemporaries might be forgiven if they found something amiss in his claim to be the coming Son of Man. The Son of Man was supposed to arrive at the end of time with the eternal kingdom of God, but not ahead of it. Paradoxically, Jesus affirms throughout the Gospels that the kingdom of God is in some sense already here, yet also coming (Mark 1:15 in contrast to Luke 17:21). In the same manner, Jesus as the Son of Man is the theanthropic cosmic judge come ahead of time to enact the eschaton in the present. He does so by his rendering of his proleptic verdict of forgiveness in the present: "the Son of Man has authority on earth to forgive sins" (Mark 2:10).

Such a ministry of reconciliation represents a fulfillment of many of the images of future redemption found in the Old Testament. The words of forgiveness that Jesus announces as the Son of Man are part of universal Jubilee of Isaiah's Servant (note Jesus's self-application of Isa 61:1 in Luke 4:18–21). Implicitly Jesus's ministry is also the culmination of Daniel's seventy-sevens (see Dan 9:20–27 and the parallel language in Matt 18:22).[59] Daniel's eschatological seventy-sevens combines forgiveness and new creation. It is the number of Jubilee (Lev 25:1–4, 8–10) times ten, the number of creation (i.e., the ten words that establish creation in Genesis 1). As a result, Jesus's divine word of absolution also enacts the Sabbath rest that much of Second Temple Judaism held would come with the messianic age[60] (see 1 En 93:2; Ezra 7:4; 12:34; 2 Bar 24:1–4; 30:1–5; 39:3–8; 40:1–4; Jub 1:4–29; 23:14–31): "Come to me, all you who are weary and burdened, and I will give you rest. Take my yoke upon you and learn from me, for I am gentle and humble in heart, and you will find rest for your souls" (Matt 11:28–29).

Because he is the cosmic judge, Jesus's words also condemn when they are resisted: "The one who rejects me and does not receive my words has a judge; the word that I have spoken will judge him on the last day" (John 12:48). Ultimately, this is because all power of judgment has been

<hr>

59. N. T. Wright, *How God Became King: The Forgotten Story of the Gospels* (San Francisco: HarperOne, 2016), 69–71.

60. Herold Weiss, *A Day of Gladness: The Sabbath Among Jews and Christians in Antiquity* (Columbia: University of South Carolina Press, 2003), 25–31.

given to Christ: "The Father judges no one, but has given all judgment to the Son. ... And he has given him authority to execute judgment, because *he is the Son of Man*" (John 5:22, 27, emphasis added). Since he himself is the one who will mete out grace and judgment at the end, his verdict in the present is identical with that of his final judgment. Therefore, people who believe in Jesus's word can be confident of God's final judgment in the end of time in the present: "Truly, truly, I say to you, whoever hears my word and believes him who sent me has eternal life. He does not come into judgment, but has passed from death to life" (John 5:24).

FORGIVENESS AND THE KINGDOM

Jesus communicated his eschatological verdict to his hearers in various ways. In most cases we find Jesus combining his word of absolution with a physical sign such as a common meal or healing. The Synoptic Gospels emphasize the scandals of the common meals with "sinners," that is, those Jews who had ceased to even make an effort to obey Torah.[61] As Sanders has correctly observed, such disapproval from the Pharisees and others should not be equated with self-righteousness or an unwillingness to forgive outcasts as in the typical portrayal of Pharisees in popular Christian preaching. Rather, by eating with sinners and forgiving their sins, Jesus signals that sinners can be reincorporated into Israel through his word of absolution. As a result, these same sinners will share in the future kingdom of the redeemed which the common meals anticipate (Luke 13:29).[62] What appears to have actually offended the Pharisees is the fact that Jesus did all this without asking "sinners" to go through the normal channels of the rites of purification and sacrifice in the Temple.[63]

As N. T. Wright has correctly shown, this suggests that Jesus saw himself as creating a new eschatological Israel defined by their relationship to him and his word, rather than by obedience to Torah.[64] Jesus was also placing himself in the stead of the Temple as the presence of God with his people and as the exclusive channel of grace and forgiveness. Both

---

61. Sanders, *Jesus and Judaism*, 177–79
62. Sanders, *Jesus and Judaism*, 200–211.
63. Wright, *Jesus and the Victory of God*, 2:272–74.
64. Wright, *Jesus and the Victory of God*, 2:405–38.

Temple and Torah were seen in first-century Judaism as being modes of the presence of God with his people, and an appropriate participation in both designated one as member of the elect community.[65] Hence, the implication of all this is that Jesus's own presence and word are identical with God's own presence and word. Likewise, membership in the people of God who would be vindicated at the eschaton meant faith in Jesus and solidarity with his new Israel. Gerhard Barth observes how this theology is present in Matthew's Gospel: "The presence of Jesus in [Matthew's] congregation is here described as analogous to the presence of the Shekinah [i.e., the divine presence with Israel] ... the place of Torah is taken by ... Jesus; the place of the Shekinah by Jesus himself."[66] Jesus's human word mediates the presence of the divine Word and verdict. This is because he is God in the flesh, returned to Zion in order to save and judge his people.[67]

Jesus himself passed on this same redemptive word to his disciples. In both Matthew and Luke, Jesus gives his word to the apostles and commissions them to preach eschatological salvation and judgment in the midst of his own ministry (Matt 10; Luke 10), a mission that they would continue after the resurrection. As Jesus commissions them, he speaks as one who will be supernaturally present through their word: "Whoever receives you receives me, and whoever receives me receives him who sent me" (Matt 10:40). And again: "one who hears you hears me" (Luke 10:16). Just as acceptance of Jesus's word means a redemptive acceptance of Christ himself, so too those who reject the word stand under divine judgment: "And if anyone will not receive you or listen to your words, shake off the dust from your feet when you leave that house or town. Truly, I say to you, it will be more bearable on the Day of Judgment for the land of Sodom and Gomorrah than for that town" (Matt 10:14–15).

That resistance to Jesus's selecting word of justification leads to condemnation is evident throughout the Gospels. As the Parable of the Prodigal Son tells us, God is a loving father who is ever ready to forgive

---

65. Wright, *The New Testament and the People of God*, 1:224–26, 236–37.

66. Gerhard Barth, "Matthew's Understanding of the Law," in *Tradition and Interpretation in Matthew*, ed. Günther Bornkamm, Gerhard Barth, and Heinz Joachim Held, trans. Percy Scott, (Philadelphia: Westminster, 1963), 135.

67. See similar argument in Kilcrease, *Self-Donation of God*, 58.

and invite the sinful humanity to the eschatological feast (Luke 15:20–24). Nevertheless, the son will remain cut off in misery as long as he remains unrepentant in a far-off land.[68] In the Parable of the Royal Wedding Feast (Matt 22:1–14; Luke 14:7–14), the king invites the elites of his kingdom to his son's marriage, an allegory for the eschatological feast that Jesus speaks of as emblematic of the kingdom of God (Matt 8:11). Rejecting the king's invitation and harming his servants leads to bloody reprisals. Alternatively, the king elects the weak and poor as his guest, following the biblical pattern of humbling the strong and exalting the outcasts. Finally, after accepting the wedding invitation a guest is cast out for not wearing his wedding garment, something which some interpreters claim was provided by the host in the first century context (although this is disputed).[69] Read in the wider context of the New Testament, the wedding garment is evocative of all the other instances in which divine justifying and sanctifying grace is spoken of as a garment (Rom 13:14; Rev 7:14; 22:14).[70] Hence, resistance to the word of grace leads to judgment. Therefore, the difference between the damned and the elect comes down to acceptance of the grace given by the word of Jesus.

One objection to this interpretation of Jesus's message might be the Parable of the Sheep and the Goats of Matthew 25.[71] Many see this parable as affirming that Jesus (or at least the author of Matthew) held to salvation by works, since on the surface it at least appears as if the Son of Man's judgment is prompted by the good works of the elect done "to one of the least of these" (Matt 25:45). Traditionally, advocates of the Reformation paradigm have seen these works as the fruits of faith, since the Gospels explicitly teach elsewhere that salvation is through faith alone (Luke 18:7–14; John 3:16).[72]

---

68. See discussion in Just, *Luke*, 2:592–609.

69. R. H. Gundry, *Matthew: A Commentary on His Literary and Theological Art* (Grand Rapids: Eerdmans, 1994), 439; John Walvoord, *Matthew: Thy Kingdom Come: A Commentary on the First Gospel* (Grand Rapids: Kregel, 1998), 164.

70. See similar observation in Joachim Jeremias, *The Parables of Jesus*, trans. S. H. Hooke (New York: Charles Scribner's Sons, 1972), 189.

71. Edward Sri and Curtis Mitch, *The Gospel of Matthew* (Grand Rapids: Baker Academic, 2010), 31–38.

72. For example, R. C. H. Lenski, *The Interpretation of St. Matthew's Gospel* (Peabody, MA: Hendrickson Publishers, 1998), 991–93.

Nevertheless, an alternative interpretation of this parable in keeping with the theme of salvation through the word is also possible. For example, it should not go unnoticed that those who are "naked," "thirsty," "hungry," and "in prison," who bear the presence of Jesus (Matt 25:34–40) and whom the elect are said to have dealt with justly directly parallel Jesus's description of his ministers bringing his word of absolution earlier in the same Gospel. When Jesus sends the disciples out, they are to bring no food or extra clothes, but are to be fed and clothed by those to whom they preach the word (Matt 10:9). This suggests that they are hungry and need to be clothed (i.e., naked at least in a sense). Moreover, Jesus warns that they will be arrested. The implication of this is that they will be thrown in prison (Matt 10:19). Finally, we find that much as the outcasts spoken of in the final judgment manifest Christ ("Truly, I say to you, as you did it to one of the least of these my brothers, you did it to me" Matt 25:40), Jesus's disciples mediate the same presence through their proclamation of the Word of God: "Anyone who welcomes you welcomes me, and anyone who welcomes me welcomes the one who sent me" (Matt 10:40). Read this way, the parable again reaffirms that salvation rests on receiving the word of Jesus and those who proclaim it. This is true, even if reception of the promise of salvation expresses itself in good works, especially in mercy to the downtrodden.

Jesus's word and presence mete out not only justification and condemnation in the present, but also election. Jesus elects through the preaching of the word. Such a word is genuinely efficacious and is preached indiscriminately, yet it only occasionally bears the fruit of genuine faith. In the Parable of the Sower, the sower throws his seed (the word) out indiscriminately and has varying results, in spite of its being real seed rather than merely dummy seed (Matt 13:1–23; Mark 4:1–20; Luke 8:4–15). The soil as soil cannot make itself either good or bad soil. It is passive and must await the activity of the sower's living seed. Nevertheless, the failure of the seed to grow remains with the soil's quality and is not the fault of the farmer or the seed. Still, it remains a mystery why the farmer does not simply dig up the soil and cultivate it so that the seed (word) can find good soil. Jesus summarizes this situation with the words: "For many are called, but few are chosen" (Matt 22:14).

Although the rationale behind God's election mediated through Jesus's sacramental word remains mysterious, it nevertheless follows the pattern of biblical election. The lowly are exalted and the strong are brought low: "So the last will be first, and the first last" (Matt 20:16). And again, "For everyone who exalts himself will be humbled, and he who humbles himself will be exalted" (Luke 14:11). The righteous in Israel (particularly the Scribes and Pharisees) trust in their own righteousness and therefore are not receptive to Jesus's message of unilateral election and justification through the word. It is moral outcasts ("sinners," tax collectors, and prostitutes) who are receptive to Jesus's message because of their lack of inner moral resources to stand as righteous on the Day of the Lord: "Truly I tell you, the tax collectors and the prostitutes are entering the kingdom of God ahead of you" (Matt 21:31). In the Parable of the Pharisee and the Publican, the Pharisee claims to be righteous in himself, whereas the Publican claims to be nothing but sinful. There is no suggestion that the Pharisee is lying when discussing his good works. Yet it is the Publican who goes home "justified" (Luke 18:9–14).[73] Good works performed without true faith, repentance, and love are meaningless and make a person genuinely morally unclean: "Woe to you, scribes and Pharisees, hypocrites! For you are like whitewashed tombs, which outwardly appear beautiful, but within are full of dead people's bones and all uncleanness" (Matt 23:27).

As should be clear from our earlier and extremely brief discussion of Second Temple Judaism's soteriology and eschatology, Jesus's understanding of the terms of vindication on the Day of the Lord was extremely shocking to many of his contemporaries. The Torah-compliant (whatever form that this may take) were supposed to be the ones who would be justified at the final cosmic judgment. Instead, in Jesus's eschatological scenario they were the ones who had become outsiders to the righteous covenant community due to their self-righteousness. Likewise, apart from any Torah compliance, the humble and repentant who relied on Jesus's proleptic word of absolution could already be identified in the present as those who would be vindicated on the Day of the Lord. Indeed, in the minds of his contemporaries Jesus was, in the words of the much later

---

73. See discussion in Just, *Luke*, 2:677–85.

tradition of the Talmud, "leading Israel astray."[74] He was doing so by telling "sinners" that they did not need to follow the Tradition of the Elders
or go through the normal channels of the Temple ritual to reenter the
covenantal community. Instead, they needed merely to rely on his word
of absolution and enter into the community of Jesus's new eschatological
Israel. In light of the fact that Second Temple Jews regarded the "zeal of
Phinehas" (Num 25) to be something of a moral ideal to be followed in
the present,[75] it is not surprising that the Gospels report to us that Jesus's
opponents sought to arrange his death.

ATONEMENT, RESURRECTION, AND THE
RATIFICATION OF THE NEW COVENANT

According to the Gospels, Jesus's claim to forgive sins was by no means
arbitrary. Rather, throughout his ministry Christ predicted his own death
as a sacrifice for sins that he himself had unilaterally forgiven. As the
Messiah, Jesus was the fulfillment of all the elect, representational figures
of the Old Testament. Much like the prophets, priests, and kings of the old
dispensation, Christ's righteousness and atonement represented others as
their substitute. Although in modern New Testament scholarship a great
deal of skepticism has been heaped on Jesus's predictions of his passion,[76]
there are some extremely good reasons to think that they are authentic
statements and genuinely represent Jesus's mindset.[77]

First, Jesus's predictions of his death and resurrection in the Gospels
are by no means made in a passionless and disinterested manner. The
Evangelists describe genuine pathos in Jesus's belief in his coming death:
"I came to cast fire on the earth, and would that it were already kindled! I
have a baptism to be baptized with, and how great is my distress until it
is accomplished!" (Luke 12:49–50). Before his death while praying in the

---

74. Peter Schäfer, *Jesus in the Talmud* (Princeton: Princeton University Press, 2007), 35, 102–5;
Wright, *Jesus and the Victory of God*, 2:439–42.

75. Martin Hengel, *The Zealots: Investigations into the Jewish Freedom Movement in the Period Until
70 A.D.* (Edinburgh: T&T Clark, 1997), 149–76.

76. John Dominic Crossan, *The Historical Jesus: The Life of a Mediterranean Jewish Peasant* (San
Francisco: HarperOne, 1993), 354–95; Paula Fredriksen, *Jesus of Nazareth, King of the Jews: A Jewish
Life and the Emergence of Christianity* (New York: Alfred A. Knopf, 2000), 241–59; Robert Funk, *Honest
to Jesus: Jesus for a New Millennium*, (San Francisco: HarperSanFrancisco 1997), 219–41.

77. Similar, yet modified arguments appear in Kilcrease, *Self-Donation of God*, 242–44.

Garden of Gethsemane (Matt 26:36–46; Mark 14:32–42; Luke 22:39–46) Jesus asks the Father to withdraw the cup that he must drink, a reference to the "cup of wrath" spoken of in a number of Old Testament passages (Isa 51:17, 22; Jer 25:15).[78]

It must be recognized that the Gospels' portrayal of Jesus is incongruous with the moral ideals of first-century culture. In the first century, brave and stoic martyrdom was highly prized. This can be observed in a number of early Christian martyr stories (notably the account of Polycarp's martyrdom), as well as Josephus's account of the binding of Isaac.[79] In his commentary on the Passion narratives, Raymond Brown made a similar point about the martyrs of 2 Maccabees.[80] Jesus's own fear and anxiety regarding his death stands in stark contrast to these ideal cultural figures. Had the Gospel writers invented Jesus's passion predictions they would have done so in accordance with the cultural ideals of their time and made Jesus seem bravely indifferent to his own death. Since they did not, we must conclude that these sayings of Jesus about his coming death, especially the scene in Gethsemane, are authentic.[81] Likewise, it must also be concluded that the atonement theology the passion predictions teach is genuinely that of Jesus and not merely that of the early Church.

Second, our earliest witness to Christ, Paul, gives indirect evidence of Jesus's view of his own death by quoting the words of institution at the Last Supper (1 Cor 11:23–26). Not only is the tradition regarding the Last Supper that Paul quotes corroborated by the Synoptic Evangelists (Matt 26:17–30; Mark 14:12–26; Luke 22:7–39), but according to the passages in 1 Corinthians 15:1–11, Galatians 1–2, and Acts, Paul clearly knew Jesus's original disciples. Paul therefore does not merely have a tradition that has been handed down to him from the Church but was in direct contact with people who were in Jesus's own presence as he had spoken these words

---

78. W. D. Davies and D. C. Allison, *Matthew*, 3 vols. (Edinburgh: T&T Clark 1988–1997), 3:499.

79. Eusebius, *The Church History* 4.14–16 in *Eusebius: The Church History: A New Translation with Commentary*, trans. Paul Maier (Grand Rapids: Kregel, 1999), 145–52; Josephus, *The Antiquities of the Jews* 1.13 in *The Works of Josephus*, trans. William Whiston, (Peabody, MA: Hendrickson Publishers, 1995), 43–44.

80. Raymond Brown, *The Death of the Messiah, From Gethsemane to the Grave: A Commentary on the Passion Narratives in the Four Gospels*, vol. 1 (New York: Doubleday, 1994), 218.

81. Wright, *Jesus and the Victory of God*, 2:606.

on the night of his betrayal. It seems incredible that Paul or these eyewitnesses simply lied about what they had heard.

By citing the words of institution, Paul clearly attests Jesus's understanding of his death as a sacrifice for sins. Jesus presents his flesh and blood as something sacrificially separated.[82] As the sacrifice texts of the Leviticus make clear, atoning sacrifice for Israel was in fact the act of separating body from blood (Lev 17:11). Since in the words of institution Jesus presented his physical substance as something that is separated into body and blood, he therefore treats it as something sacrificed quite specifically for the forgiveness of sins.

Third, it should be observed that Jesus's belief that it was his vocation to die as a sacrifice for sins was not entirely unprecedented within Second Temple Judaism, even if the idea of a suffering Messiah was a novelty. As Wright has shown, it was the belief of many Second Temple Jews that Israel would have to suffer for its previous sins as a condition for the coming of God's kingdom.[83] For at least some, it was held that this suffering could take on a vicarious and representative character. This belief has been attested among a variety of Jewish apocalyptic texts, including the Dead Sea Scrolls produced by the Essene sect.[84] Both Ben Witherington III and Brant Pitre have argued that Jesus's claim to be the bringer and embodiment of the kingdom was closely tied up with the idea of vicarious and representative suffering.[85] Within certain strands of the Jewish apocalyptic worldview, being the agent of the kingdom would have necessitated Jesus's suffering of what have been typically referred to as "the Messianic woes."[86] Pitre makes this judgment after surveying a large number of Second Temple Jewish eschatological texts that refer

---

82. Joachim Jeremias, *The Eucharistic Words of Jesus* (London: SCM, 1966), 222. Jeremias writes that Jesus "is applying to Himself terms from the language of sacrifice. ... Each of the two nouns ["body" and "blood"] presuppose a slaying that has separated flesh and blood. In other words: Jesus speaks of himself as a sacrifice."

83. Wright, *Jesus and the Victory of God*, 1:277–79.

84. Ben Witherington III, *The Christology of Jesus* (Minneapolis: Fortress, 1990), 252. See Wright, *Jesus and the Victory of God*, 2:581–82.

85. See Brant Pitre, *Jesus, the Tribulation and the End of Exile*.

86. Witherington, *The Christology of Jesus*, 123.

to representative and atoning suffering as a necessary prerequisite to the kingdom.[87]

In the Old Testament sacrifice functioned not only as a means of atoning for sin, but as a means of ratifying covenants (Gen 9, 15; Exod 24).[88] That Jesus understood his death in this manner is evident from the words of institution: "this is the new covenant in my blood" (Matt 26:27; Mark 14:23; Luke 22:20; 1 Cor 11:26). Christ's death as sacrifice for sin and ratification of the new covenant were simply two-sides of a single coin. This is because the very content of Christ's new covenant is the unilateral forgiveness of sins. Indeed, as we observed in the previous chapter, the content of Jeremiah's new covenant was the forgiveness of sins and sanctification (Jer 31:31–4). Likewise, the Servant of Isaiah not only atones for sins as the new Passover Lamb (Isa 53), but also in turn brings about a new exodus (Isa 40). Much like the way the first exodus was tied to the establishment of the Sinaitic covenant, this new exodus also means a new covenant. The Servant will "sprinkle many nations" (Isa 52:15) much like Moses did at Mt Sinai in the ratification of the old covenant (Exod 24). Just as the presence of Jesus's sacrificed person in the Lord's Supper is the very giving of the covenant of grace itself, so too God says of Isaiah's Servant: "I will ... give you as a covenant to the people" (Isa 49:8).[89]

This complex of various texts shows how Christ saw his person and mission. The atonement and new covenant that Jesus brings about would result in not simply a private sense of forgiveness for individual believers, but would open up the eschatological floodgates and actualize the fulfillment of all of God's promises to his people: a new creation, a new exodus, a new covenant, and a new eschatological people of God. Just as God spoke forth the original creation, so too Christ sought to speak forth a new creation by his word of forgiveness. Such a word was only made possible by his sacrificial death.

As Jesus entered into his final week, his teaching became increasingly provocative. Upon his arrival in Jerusalem, he faces opposition from the leaders of the Pharisees and the priestly aristocracy. He immediately

---

87. Pitre, *Jesus, the Tribulation and the End of Exile*, 41–127.

88. See similar observations in D. A. Carson, *Matthew* (Grand Rapids: Zondervan, 1984), 537.

89. See similar argument in Craig Keener, *Matthew* (Downers Grove, IL: InterVarsity Press, 1997), 367.

begins to speak in parables about apocalyptic judgment and election. For example, in the Parable of the Wicked Husbandmen, a righteous landlord demands fruits from his tenants who consistently refuse. They abuse his servants, and ultimately kill his son. The ruler finally expels his tenants and replaces them with those who will give him the fruits he is owed.

The point of the parable is not that a church of gentiles will replace a church of Jews, as it has often been read through the centuries by the shameful tradition of "Christian"[90] anti-Judaism, and later anti-Semitism. Beyond the simple fact that Jesus and his followers were ethnic Jews (as well as most of the members of the nascent church), Matthew explicitly tells us that this parable angers the Pharisees and the Temple aristocrats because they know that Jesus is speaking against them (Matt 21:45; Luke 20:19). The wicked husbandmen are therefore not the Jewish people in general, but the elite in Israel who resist Jesus's messianic mission.

The key is that it is not so much that gentiles will replace Jews, but that Jesus will replace Temple and Torah, the means of grace in the Old Testament. The word and sacrament ministry that Jesus inaugurates will not be bound to a specific location controlled by the Temple aristocracy or the works of the law (controlled through the teaching authority of the Pharisees, Matt 23:2), but will be found among all nations where "two or three are gathered in my name" (Matt 18:20). According to Jesus's interpretation, the Pharisees and Temple aristocrats had systematically interpreted Temple and Torah legalistically and had therefore "shut the kingdom of heaven in people's faces" (Matt 23:13). Much as the moral outcasts in Israel had responded to Jesus's justification by word because they had no illusory righteousness on the basis of the law to cling to, so too, the gentiles, who found themselves in the same situation, would respond to the word and sacrament ministry of the Church in the next generation (Rom 9:30–31). Therefore, the biblical pattern of the great reversal would hold on a world-historical scale. The event of the rejected becoming the

---

90. I put "Christian" in quotation marks, because anti-Judaism and anti-Semitism could never be a truly Christian attitude to have. Therefore, by the use of it I mean nominally Christian. By "anti-Judaism" and "anti-Semitism" I mean hatred of the Jewish people because of their religion or ethnicity. Hatred of any group of people can never be a Christian attitude (Matt 5:44; 1 John 3:15). This of course does not mean that Christians must agree with Jewish theology or affirm that any group of people is saved apart from faith in Christ.

elect that Jesus had enacted in Israel would soon become a reality among the nations. Those not compliant with the law among the gentiles would be added to the justified and elect moral outcasts of Israel

Jesus's second great eschatological prophecy is the "little apocalypse" of the Synoptic Gospels, dealing with the destruction of the Temple (Matt 24; Mark 13; Luke 21). Although there are undoubtedly references in this speech to the final eschaton, N. T. Wright has convincingly shown that the majority of the material of the discourse concerns the events of AD 70 and the destruction of the Second Temple.[91] Much of the language that Jesus uses is borrowed from the Old Testament, and many of the details of the destruction of the Temple are hyperbolic rather than literal. In the wake of the actual events of the First Jewish War, the historical details of the events would have been easy to gain access to and could have been placed in Jesus's mouth after the fact had the church so desired. Since the church clearly did not do this, we must conclude that the Synoptic Evangelists are quoting or paraphrasing actual statements of Jesus.[92]

It is interesting to note that much of the language that Jesus uses that involves cosmic collapse ("earthquakes," "the stars fall from the sky," etc.: Matt 24:8; Mark 13:25) is borrowed from the Old Testament's description of the fall of nations. This imagery is meant to portray the failure of the revolution of AD 70, but more importantly the end of the old Levitical cult.[93] The language of cosmic collapse is particularly pertinent to the destruction of the Temple. As we have already seen, the Temple was designed to be a microcosm of the cosmos. In light of this, the destruction of the Temple meant a manifestation of the destruction of the cosmic order.[94]

Moreover, as we noted in the previous chapter, the Temple was not merely an image of the cosmos, but the cosmos under sin and the condemnation of the law. God was present with his people through the Temple, but they could not approach him except through the fulfillment of the law (i.e., bloody sacrifice), which presupposes the existence of sin. Destruction of the Temple would then be a destruction of the cosmic order ruled by sin

---

91. Wright, *Jesus and the Victory of God*, 2:329–68.

92. Wright, *Jesus and the Victory of God*, 2:340, 348–49.

93. Wright, *Jesus and the Victory of God*, 2:364–65.

94. Beale, *The Temple and the Church's Mission*, 189–90.

and the law. Beyond this, the elimination of the Temple means the elimination of the possibility of justification through the law, in that a rather
large percentage of Mosaic legislation dealt with regulations concerning the Temple and Tabernacle. In this, Jesus's prediction rendered Old
Testament religion effectively non-functional. After AD 70, later Rabbinic
Judaism would have to spiritualize the ritual law in order to convince itself
that obedience to the Torah was still possible.[95]

When Jesus dies on the cross, all of his apocalyptic predictions come
true in a kind of proleptic anticipation of AD 70 and the final eschaton.
Matthew's account in many respects illustrates this fact best. First, as we
have already seen, Jesus's death not only atones for sin, but ratifies the
covenant of grace. The darkness and earthquakes at Jesus's death (Matt
27:45, 51) are reminiscent not only of the end of time, but also of the ratification of the Sinaitic covenant (Exod 19–20, 24). Much as in Exodus 24,
where the blood is sprinkled on the people by Moses as a means of covenantal ratification, the crowds cry out at Jesus's trial before Pilate: "His
blood be on us and on our children!" (Matt 27:25). The meaning of this
text is therefore not the perpetual "blood curse" upon the Jewish people
of anti-Jewish and anti-Semitic exegesis,[96] but a recognition that God has
used Israel's resistance to grace to conclude the covenant of grace with
them in spite of themselves. They (along the rest of humanity represented
by the gentile Pilate) will be brought into the time of the new covenant
and new creation, where the only curse will be upon those who reject
God's unilateral forgiveness (Matt 12:30–32).

Second, Jesus's death inaugurates the apocalyptic events of destruction of the Temple, the conversion of the gentiles, and the resurrection of
the dead.[97] As Jesus dies, the Temple curtain rips (Matt 27:51). Not only
does the cosmos constructed around the separation of God and human
through sin come to end through the veil of God's inner sanctum being

95. David Levine and Dalia Marx, "Ritual Law in Rabbinic Judaism," in *The Oxford Handbook of Biblical Law*, ed. Pamela Barmash (Oxford: Oxford University Press, 2019), 471–85.

96. George Smiga, *Pain and Polemic: Anti-Judaism in the Gospels* (New York: Paulist, 1992), 60.

97. Donald Senior, *Matthew* (Nashville: Abingdon, 1998), 334.

torn away,[98] but the process of the Temple's destruction begins.[99] When this happens, the Centurion by Jesus's side declares him to be "the Son of God" and becomes the first gentile convert (Matt 27:54).[100] Finally, the holy dead are raised and show themselves in Jerusalem (Matt 27:52–53).

This is a mere prelude to the proleptic eschaton of Jesus's own resurrection, wherein a new humanity that has moved past death and the condemnation of the law is actualized. Likewise, because of Christ's vindication in the resurrection, the covenant of grace that he promulgated gains a stamp of approval from the Father in the power of the Holy Spirit. In this, the biblical pattern of the great reversal culminates the elect and rejected Christ. Christ (meaning "anointed," and therefore "elect one") has been rejected. Nevertheless, as with the younger sons of the Old Testament, his rejection places him in the category of one elect: "The stone that the builders rejected has become the cornerstone; this was the Lord's doing, and it is marvelous in our eyes'" (Matt 21:42). In Christ and his word, humanity will find its election by grace (Eph 1:4).

As a result of Jesus's vindication in the resurrection, the ministry of the sacramental word continues in the life of the church.[101] Earlier in Jesus's ministry we are told that the presence of Jesus's Name in the midst of those gathered together is identical with the presence of Jesus himself: "where two or three are gathered in my name, there am I among them" (Matt 18:20). In this, Jesus's Name takes on the role of God's own Name in the Old Testament (the divine presence with Israel), and each liturgical gathering becomes a realization of the eschatological Temple ("house for my name" 2 Sam 7:13). From this, the designation of the church as the body of Christ (1 Cor 12:12–14, 27; Eph 4:12; 5:23; Col 1:18, 24; 2:19) and the new Temple (1 Cor 3:16; Eph 2:19–22; Heb 3:6) throughout the New Testament makes perfect sense because Christ is himself the new Temple and Tabernacle (John 1:14; 2:21).

---

98. Daniel Gurtner, *The Torn Veil: Matthew's Exposition of the Death of Jesus* (Cambridge: Cambridge University Press, 2007), 189.

99. Beale, *The Temple and the Church's Mission*, 189.

100. Thomas Weinandy, *Jesus Becoming Jesus: A Theological Interpretation of the Synoptic Gospels* (Washington, DC: Catholic University of America Press, 2018), 387.

101. See similar argument, in a modified form in Kilcrease, *Self-Donation of God*, 192–94.

In the Great Commission at the end of Matthew, how this divine Name of Jesus will be proclaimed among the "two or three" is clarified. Not only are the disciples given the ability to forgive in the Name of Jesus ("repentance for the forgiveness of sins should be proclaimed in *his name* to all nations" (Luke 24:47, emphasis added; also see John 20:23), but they are given Jesus's Name in the form of the sacraments. In Matthew 28:19, they are commissioned to baptize in the Triune name (which includes that of Jesus). This apostolic proclamation and activity of baptism itself will mediate the presence of Jesus in the same manner that the Temple mediated the presence of YHWH to Israel: "And behold, I am with you always, to the end of the age" (Matt 28:20).

Likewise, before his death, Jesus confirms his new testament of forgiveness, by offering them his own body and blood (to which his Name is also attached!) to consume (Matt 26:26–29). As we observed earlier, Jesus's presence at common meals directly mediated the sacramental word of forgiveness to those who ate with him. This is now fulfilled in Jesus's giving an even greater share in fellowship with him and his word of absolution than was possible in the aforementioned common meals. Jesus promises that those who reject his presence in the word preached by the apostles would be subject to condemnation (Matt 10:14–15). In a similar manner, Paul tells us that those who reject Christ's promise and treat the Lord's Supper as ordinary food will suffer divine judgment (1 Cor 11:27–32). In all this, Jesus's presence remains with his church through the exercise of its word and sacrament ministry. As one present with his church, Jesus continues to exercise his role as the Son of Man, making his eschatological judgment of condemnation or vindication proleptically present to those who encounter him through the means of grace.

CHAPTER 4

Justification in Paul:

The Eschatological Redemption by the Word of God

J esus's ministry and his subsequent empowerment of the apostolic mission bring us finally to the writings of St. Paul. Paul's ministry and theology apply this concept of salvation through a proleptic eschatological judgment to the larger question of the role of the law in salvation history, as well as to the question of what are the ultimate means by which both Jews and gentiles will be able to stand as righteous (i.e., "justified") on the Day of the Lord Jesus Christ (Rom 2:16). Although it has been fashionable since the time of Reimarus to drive a wedge between the theology of Jesus and the early church,[1] there is a clearly a direct continuity between the message of Paul and that of Christ. Just as Jesus believed that his word of forgiveness was a proleptic manifestation of his verdict at the end of time, so too Paul believed that the apostolic preaching of "justification" (that is, God's eschatological verdict of vindication) mediates the judgment of the risen Christ in the present through the work of the Spirit (Rom 10:17; Gal 3:2). Likewise, just as Jesus showed his fellowship with sinners through common meals and was reproached for it, Paul's occasion for conflict with Christians who still adhered to the law of Moses was the issue of common meals with gentiles (Gal 1–2). Lastly, Jesus announced

---

1. Samuel Herman Reimarus, *Reimarus: Fragments*, trans. Ralph Fraser (Philadelphia: Fortress, 1970), 133–53.

forgiveness to those who had been outside the normal boundaries of the covenant community (prostitutes, tax collectors, etc.) and pronounced judgment on those who were within it (Pharisees, etc.). Similarly, Paul saw Jews who rejected Christ as outside the number of the redeemed, whereas non-Torah-compliant gentile believers were among the elect. Below we will argue that Paul's theology of justification is a continuation and application of Christ's teaching of justification by the word in the context of the early gentile mission.

UNDER THE LAW

In examining Paul's theology of justification, we will primarily focus on the Epistles to the Romans and the Galatians, with some help from the Apostle's other writings. To understand Paul's soteriological solution (i.e., justification) it is important to understand what problem he is trying to solve. Many of the debates in Pauline studies over the last two centuries on the nature of justification might arguably be traced back to differing opinions as to what problem the Apostle is solving.

Paul's starting point in the Epistle to the Romans is the recognition that the divine-human relationship is fundamentally broken and stands under the condemnation of God's law: "For the wrath of God is revealed from heaven against all ungodliness and unrighteousness of men, who by their unrighteousness suppress the truth" (Rom 1:18). Because of this, neither Jew nor gentile is at any advantage in their relationship with God in terms of legal righteousness (Rom 3:9, 23). Paul starts with his indictment of the gentiles, whose crimes are those not infrequently highlighted by Hellenistic Jewish apologists (idolatry and sexual immorality; Rom 1:21–27).[2] Probably drawing on both popular Stoic philosophy as well as Hellenistic Jewish apologetic wisdom literature,[3] Paul makes the case that the existence of a creator is self-evident from the beauty and order of creation (Rom 1:20). Such a recognition may be glorious to contemplate for the person of faith (Ps 19), but it is condemning to those in thrall to sin. Instead of recognizing the creator in the creature, gentile elevate the

---

2. Victor Furnish, *The Moral Teaching of Paul: Selected Issues* (Nashville: Abingdon, 1985), 74.

3. James D. G. Dunn, *Romans 1–8* (Nashville: Thomas Nelson Publishers, 1988), 58–59; Peter Stuhlmacher, *Paul's Letter to the Romans: A Commentary*, trans. Scott J. Hafemann (Louisville: Westminster John Knox, 1994), 44.

creature to the status of creator by worshipping idols of animals (reversing the natural order of creation, Gen 1:28), and even mortal man (Rom 1:21–23).

In the second chapter Paul goes on to say that the gentiles are also condemned by the fact that they know the law of God that is written on their hearts (Rom 2:15). Indeed, the knowledge of God and his law from nature and conscience is meaningless due to the power of sin. God's punishment is to permit the gentiles to give into their sexually immoral desires, particularly those of the same-sex variety (Rom 1:26–27). Within this situation, Jews are no better off. Although they have the law of God revealed to them on Mount Sinai, they are hypocritical in their obedience and do not practice what they preach (Rom 2:17–24).

This discussion of the condemnation of humanity under the law illuminates what Paul means when he discusses the "works of the law," as well as the problem that the Apostle's doctrine of justification is meant to solve.[4] Put bluntly, Paul's starting point is that God is angry (Rom 1:18). Paul very clearly thinks that both Jews and gentiles are under God's wrath, manifest in the law (revealed in nature, conscience, and historical revelation at Sinai), and this will have negative eschatological consequences for them. Like other first-century Jewish apocalypticists, Paul believed that at the eschaton ("Day of the Lord Jesus Christ," 1 Cor 1:8, an interesting modification of the Old Testament "Day of the Lord"), God would resurrect and judge the dead. Failure to obey the law would result in a negative judgment for both Jews and gentiles.[5] Within this eschatological scenario, what appears to make Paul different from his Jewish contemporaries is the belief that this plight of human sin was not solvable within the framework of the law.

Here a number of interesting contrasts between Paul and his Jewish contemporaries comes into focus. Although later Rabbinical Judaism (which has its roots in first-century Pharisaic Judaism)[6] recognized the existence of evil will in the human heart (*yetzer hara*), it was believed

---

4. Stuhlmacher, *Revisiting Paul's Doctrine of Justification*, 42.

5. Stuhlmacher, *Revisiting Paul's Doctrine of Justification*, 43.

6. Howard Lupovitch, *Jews and Judaism in World History* (London: Routledge, 2010), 49–50.

that such an evil impulse could be tamed by the law.[7] Beyond this, in the rabbis view God did not expect Israel to perfectly adhere to the law, but simply do their best to master their evil impulses. Partially on the merits of the patriarchs (which Israel could draw on as a reserve of good favor),[8] partially on the basis of divine forbearance, and partially on the basis of their own efforts in obeying the law, humanity could stand as righteous on the Day of the Lord.[9]

Although we cannot be certain how many of the traditions of the rabbis go back to the time of Paul, it is not an unreasonable conjecture that at least some of them do. In light of this, it therefore might be suggested that the Apostle may be polemically inverting a number of rabbinical concepts in his treatment of the law. Hence, instead of a *yetzer hara* that merely makes perfect Torah-adherence more difficult, Paul considers human nature completely incapacitated due to the power of sin: "For we know that the law is spiritual, but I am of the flesh, sold under sin. For I do not understand my own actions. For I do not do what I want, but I do the very thing I hate. ... For I know that nothing good dwells in me, that is, in my flesh" (Rom 7:14–15, 18). Indeed, instead of the law serving the role of helping master the evil impulse, Paul claims that the law only eggs on the evil will of humanity: "For I would not have known what it is to covet if the law had not said, 'You shall not covet.' But sin, seizing an opportunity through the commandment, produced in me all kinds of covetousness. For apart from the law, sin lies dead" (Rom 7:7–8).[10]

Finally, God will not overlook any disobedience to Torah. At the eschaton, God will not leave anyone guiltless who has disobeyed even a single commandment: "For all who rely on works of the law are under a curse; for it is written, "Cursed be everyone who does not abide by all things written in the Book of the Law, and do them" (Gal 3:10). Neither is there

---

7. Philip Alexander, "Torah and Salvation in Tannaitic Literature" in Carson, Seifrid, and O'Brien, *Justification and Variegated Nomism*, 1:282.

8. See W. D. Davies, *Paul and Rabbinic Judaism: Some Rabbinic Elements in Pauline Theology* (London: SPCK, 1970), 269–73; Arthur Marmostein, *The Doctrine of Merits in the Old Rabbinical Literature* (London: Jews' College, 1920), 4.

9. Alexander, "Torah and Salvation in Tannaitic Literature," 1:361–402; Sanders, *Paul and Palestinian Judaism*, 84–238.

10. Thomas Schreiner, *Romans* (Grand Rapids: Baker Academic, 2018), 341–42.

any reserve of good will to be found in the merits of the patriarchs. Indeed, in a seeming inversion of the rabbinic concept of the merits of the patriarchs, Paul posits that all humanity is under the curse of sin and death because of the demerit of a much older patriarch, Adam (Rom 5:12, 17; 1 Cor 15:22).

In contrast to the decidedly "Lutheran" reading of Paul that we have offered above,[11] it has recently been argued by followers of the "New Perspective on Paul"[12] that what the Apostle means by the "works of the law" is the cultural boundary markers that designate Jews as the chosen people.[13] It is therefore asserted that what Paul objects to in Galatia and among the Romans is not the idea that people can earn their salvation, but rather the claim that in the era of the New Testament the same Old Testament covenantal boundary markers (circumcision, keeping kosher, etc.) that designated the people of God still apply.[14] Instead of the ritual law of the Old Testament, Paul opted for faith as a more inclusive badge of membership in God's people.[15] It is further claimed that the idea that the "works of the law" meant earning one's salvation could never be the case because first-century Judaism was a religion of grace.[16] The patriarchs were chosen by grace.[17] God would overlook many of Israel's failings because of his gracious character. Instead of applying the standard of absolute fidelity to the law as a means of salvation and blessing, God was

---

11. It should be born in mind, that the author recognizes that he stands in a particular tradition of interpretation. That being said, what one might call the Lutheran "paradigm" can best account for everything that Paul actually says. See Stephen Westerholm, *Perspectives Old and New on Paul: The "Lutheran" Paul and His Critics* (Grand Rapids: Eerdmans, 2004).

12. See James D. G. Dunn, *The Theology of Paul the Apostle* (Grand Rapids: Eerdmans, 1998); James D. G. Dunn, *The New Perspective on Paul: Collected Essays* (Tübingen: Mohr Siebeck, 2005); E. P. Sanders, *Paul and Palestinian Judaism*; Sanders, *Paul, the Law and the Jewish People* (Philadelphia: Fortress, 1983); Krister Stendahl, *Paul among Jews and Gentiles, and Other Essays* (Philadelphia: Fortress, 1976); N. T. Wright, *Paul and the Faithfulness of God*, 2 vols., Christian Origins and the Question of God 4 (Minneapolis: Fortress, 2013); N. T. Wright, *Paul in Fresh Perspective* (Minneapolis: Fortress, 2009); N. T. Wright, *What St. Paul Really Said: Was Paul of Tarsus the Real Founder of Christianity?* (Oxford: Lion, 1997).

13. Dunn, *Theology of Paul*, 363–65.

14. E. P. Sanders, *Paul* (Oxford: Oxford University Press, 1991), 63; Sanders, *Paul, the Law and the Jewish People*, 18–20; Wright, *What St. Paul Really Said*, 120, 130–33.

15. Wright, *Paul in Fresh Perspective*, 110–22.

16. Sanders, *Paul and Palestinian Judaism*, 297, 422, 543; Dunn, *Theology of Paul*, 340–45; Wright, *What St. Paul Really Said*, 32.

17. Sanders, *Paul and Palestinian Judaism*, 100.

viewed as being lenient in his demands for total fidelity of the law. Israel
might fall away from this grace, but God would be patient and provide
forgiveness through the sacrificial system and overlook the weakness of
those who genuinely tried to obey his commandments.[18]

It is notable that although devotees of the New Perspective claim to
have jumped past centuries of "Lutheran" distortions of Paul and have
therefore retrieved the authentic message of the Apostle, they themselves seemingly also stand in a scholarly tradition that has its beginning with F. C. Baur in the early nineteenth century.[19] Basing himself
on Hegelian philosophical principles of thesis, antithesis, and synthesis,
Baur posited a tension in the early church between the phenomenon of
"Judaism" (thesis) and "Hellenism" (antithesis). There was, according
to Baur, a Jewish-Christian party (which was legalistic, fleshly, and sectarian) and a Hellenist party (which was grace-centered, spirit-oriented,
and cosmopolitan). Peter, James, and the author of Matthew were on
the side of the former party, while Paul was on the side of the latter.
Paul's contrast between "law" and "grace" was then a contrast between
Judaism or Jewish Christianity and the new universal and inclusive gentile Christianity. The Hegelian synthesis of these two groups was "early
Catholicism," which mixed grace and works, as well as discipline and
hierarchy with universalism.[20]

Although we do not have the space to trace the genealogy of influences, it could be argued that the New Perspective (either intentionally,
or unintentionally) has revived Baur's interpretation of Paul and the
early Church. As in Baur's thesis about sectarian legalism vs. grace-ori-
ented cosmopolitanism, the New Perspective's Paul is on the side of an
inclusive badge of covenant membership, whereas his opponents are
not. The main difference is the fact that because the New Perspective
developed after the Holocaust it is more sensitive to negative portrayals

18. Sanders, *Paul and Palestinian Judaism*, 130–40.

19. See Horton Harris, *The Tübingen School: A Historical and Theological Investigation of the School of F.C. Baur* (Oxford: Clarendon, 1975). Much of the argument in this section appears in a slightly different form in Jack Kilcrease, "A Genealogy of the New Perspective on Paul," *Logia: A Journal of Lutheran Theology* 29, no. 2 (2020): 62–63.

20. See F. C. Baur, *The Church History of the First Three Centuries*, trans. Allan Menzies, 2 vols. (London: Williams and Norgate, 1878–1879), 1:44–83; F. C. Baur, *Paul the Apostle of Jesus Christ: His Life and Works, His Epistles and Teachings* (Grand Rapids: Baker Academic, 2010).

of Judaism.[21] Nevertheless, the New Perspective and Baur essentially agree on what problem Paul is trying to solve, namely, the problem of social inclusiveness versus social exclusiveness in the early church.

The major difficulty is of course that, as we have seen, Paul's starting point is not the question of God's desire for an inclusive community, but rather divine anger at sin and the coming eschatological judgment (Rom 1:18; 2:16).[22] In light of this, there is a certain irony to the claim of Krister Stendahl that the "Lutheran" reading of Paul projects our modern problems onto the first century.[23] On the contrary, the Lutheran reading of Paul posits that the apostle, like his contemporaries, was concerned about standing vindicated at the eschaton (i.e., justification). Very few post-Enlightenment people worry about such a prospect. In fact, it is the New Perspective which has projected the modern, post-secular problem of how to create unity in the midst of radical pluralism onto the first-century situation.[24]

In a brief response to the exegetical claims made by the New Perspective several observations can be made. To begin with, although it is certainly correct to note that the ritual boundary markers that separated Jews from gentiles are what prompted the confrontation with the "Judaizers" in Galatia, Paul's larger point is that the law of Moses is in fact a single piece: "I testify again to every man who accepts circumcision that he is *obligated to keep the whole law*" (Gal 5:3, emphasis added).[25] Put bluntly, cutting a flap of skin off of one's genitals is a relatively simple task (albeit an extremely painful one!). Loving God and one's neighbor with one's whole heart, mind, and soul is more problematic, especially in light of Paul's belief in universal guilt (Rom 1–3, 5) and morally incapacitating human depravity (Rom 7). Moreover, placing oneself under the law of Moses (through the acceptance of the ritual law) without the ability to

21. Dunn, *New Perspective on Paul*, 196–67.

22. Stuhlmacher, *Revisiting Paul's Doctrine of Justification*, 42.

23. Stendahl, "Paul and the Introspective Conscience of the West," 78–96.

24. See similar argument in Westerholm, *Justification Reconsidered*, 1–22.

25. Timo Laato, "The New Quest for Paul: A Critique of the New Perspective on Paul," in *The Doctrine on Which the Church Stands or Falls*, ed. Matthew Barrett (Wheaton, IL: Crossway, 2019), 305–6.

obey it would be to invite the covenantal curses of Sinai that have proven so disastrous for biblical Israel (Rom 3:10).[26]

For this reason, it should not go unnoticed that Paul's focus in the early chapters of Romans is not at all on "covenantal boundary markers" (i.e., the so-called "ritual law") but on what later Christian exegesis came to call the "moral law" available not only to Jews, but to gentiles in nature and conscience.[27] Paul's argument is never that the ritual law is a problem because it separates Jews from gentiles, but rather that obedience to the ritual law is irrelevant in attaining a positive verdict at the eschaton if one does not obey the moral law: "For circumcision indeed is of value if you obey the law, but if you break the law, your circumcision becomes uncircumcision" (Rom 2:25).

This leads us into the second major issue, namely, that because the New Perspective follows a similar trajectory to Baur, it ultimately tends to wrongly conflate what Paul means by "the works of the law" with the empirical religion of first-century Judaism. As Stephen Westerholm seems to suggest, if one simply systematically examines every statement that Paul makes about the law and its problems, then the arguments made by the New Perspective do not add-up.[28] Cultural boundary markers do not condemn people or call for the redemptive response of the forgiveness of sins. Hence, those scholars who stand within the tradition of the New Perspective do not typically start with what Paul actually says about the law to discern what the phrase "works of the law" means or what problem he is trying to solve. Rather, they start with a particular conception of first-century Judaism established by their scholarly investigations, because they assume what Paul meant by "the law" is "Judaism." For this reason, they tend to assume that Paul cannot mean what he says, specifically that the works of the law condemn, kill, and cannot lead to vindication at the eschaton, since they assert that first-century Judaism was a religion of grace, or at minimum, a religion that mixed law and grace. Paul's concerns

---

26. See Timo Laato, *Paul and Judaism*; Stephen Westerholm, "Paul's Anthropological 'Pessimism' in Its Jewish Context," in *Divine and Human Agency in Paul and His Cultural Development*, ed. J. M. G. Barclay and Simon Gathercole (London: T&T Clark, 2007), 71–98.

27. For example: Walter Houston, *The Pentateuch* (London: SCM, 2013), 54–55.

28. Westerholm, *Perspectives Old and New on Paul*, 297–340. See discussion in Andrew Das, *Galatians* (St. Louis: Concordia, 2014), 245–49.

regarding the law therefore must be about something else, namely, exclusivity vs. inclusivity of covenantal badges of membership in God's people.

What Paul means by the works of the law is very clearly the Sinaitic covenant, which includes both the moral and ritual law.[29] In Galatians 3, the Apostle speaks of "the law" as a distinct covenant established four hundred and thirty years after the first covenant of grace with Abraham (Gal 3:17). This unmistakably is a reference to the giving of the law to Moses on Mt. Sinai.[30] Since the law is the specific legal covenant of God with Israel, when Paul speaks of it he does not mean to exhaust the content of the Old Testament or the religion of ancient Israel. Nor does he mean to say anything about the empirical practice of Judaism in the first century as a supposedly "legalistic religion" or otherwise.[31] Indeed, as Sanders and others have correctly shown, many Jews in the first century certainly did think that God was "gracious" in the sense that he had chosen Israel by grace and would not require a standard of perfect obedience to the law as the price of salvation. Nevertheless, to Paul this would have been an essentially irrelevant point. For him, the key is not what was common opinion in first-century Judaism, but what the Sinaitic covenant actually said, namely, that all were cursed who did not perfectly obey the law (Gal 3:10).[32]

This leads into yet another point of exegetical concern, namely Paul's conception of two distinct covenants of law and grace. As Michael Horton has observed, one of the major difficulties with the New Perspective is that it assumes that Paul thinks in terms of a single covenant, rather than two distinct covenants of law and grace.[33] Read from this perspective, Paul's plea for faith over works has essentially been characterized by the New Perspective as a new stage of evolution in a single covenant from an Old Testament version that had less inclusive cultural boundary markers

---

29. Of course, Paul considers the law to be one piece and does not make a formal distinction between the moral and ritual law. See Heikki Räisänen, *Paul and the Law* (Eugene, OR: Wipf & Stock), 25–26.

30. Westerholm, *Perspectives Old and New on Paul*, 299.

31. Westerholm, *Justification Reconsidered*, 80.

32. See a similar perspective in Andrew Das, *Paul, the Law, and the Covenant* (Grand Rapids: Baker Academic, 2000).

33. Michael Horton, *Justification*, 2 vols. (Grand Rapids: Zondervan, 2018), 2:94–95.

(circumcision, kosher laws, etc.), to a New Testament version that had more inclusive boundary marker (faith).

Nevertheless, Paul very clearly holds that there are two covenants, not simply one. In Galatians 3, he describes the covenant of Abraham as one based on grace and the one at Sinai as based on works. In Galatians 4 he uses an allegory of Sarah and Hagar to reinforce the contrast between the covenants: "Now this may be interpreted allegorically: these women are two covenants" (Gal 4:24). For Paul, these two covenants could not be more different. One works on the principle of grace, which is a gift that does not require works, and the other on the basis of works that earn wages, not unlike a farm worker: "Now to the one who works, his wages are not counted as a gift but as his due. And to the one who does not work but believes in him who justifies the ungodly, his faith is counted as righteousness" (Rom 4:4–5).

Indeed, this appears to be the key difference between Paul and his opponents. The "Judaizers" taught that fulfillment of the law was necessary because there was a single covenant that combined grace and works. To be in fellowship with the church and an inheritor with Abraham, it appears that Paul's opponents held that one had to both be obedient to the law (albeit imperfectly) and also have faith in Christ. This would not be surprising, since if Sanders's interpretation of covenant nomism is correct, first-century Jews typically interpreted the Sinaitic covenant not as a distinct covenant, but simply as a continuation and fleshing out of the covenant with Abraham. This may also explain why the accounts of salvation that Second Temple Jews offered generally tended to be a mixture of grace and works, since they saw the Abrahamic and Sinaitic covenants as dual aspects of a single covenantal order.

If what might be called our "Lutheran" or "Reformational" reading of Paul is correct, then it should be observed that, contrary to what is sometimes charged, the question of works vs. faith in the writings of the Apostle is still nevertheless tied up with the issue of the relationship of Jews and gentiles in the era of the New Testament. Paul is in effect saying that Galatians are trying to achieve the status of being elect and eschatologically vindicated (i.e., justified) by gaining the status of Jews. In a sense, their position is very similar to Sanders's covenant nomism. In Galatia, Paul's audience seem to have come to believe that they could achieve this goal by simply accepting circumcision, among other aspects of the ritual law.[34]

On this point, Sanders's claim that in Second Temple Judaism "getting in" was by grace and "staying in" was by works[35] would have been irrelevant for the Galatians. Beyond the fact that Sanders himself documents that many Jews believed that the patriarchs had actually merited their election (i.e., election obviously was not by grace),[36] for the Galatians "getting in" would have involved following the ritual law and therefore would have been an achievement. Moreover, Paul warns them that even if they accept the "cultural boundary markers" of Jewish identity, this would not result in their justification (i.e., eschatological vindication, not just "getting in"). This is because true justification by the law would mean keeping the whole law, that is, the moral not just the ritual law (Gal 5:3). This is impossible because humans are incapable of fulfilling the moral law due to their depravity (Rom 7).[37]

Ultimately, Paul's point is that the law's historic purpose was never to secure justification and election, since a survey of Israel's history quickly reveals that it did little more than reveal sin and work divine wrath (Rom 4:15; 7:7). It appears that Paul was prompted into reevaluating the law by the recognition that salvation came by the death of the Messiah: "for if righteousness were through the law, then Christ died for no purpose" (Gal 2:21). If Christ and his death are the source of righteousness and salvation, then the law clearly could not be, and consequently it had to serve some other divine purpose. The New Perspective is in some respects correct to point to Paul's "robust conscience," at least prior to his conversion (Phil 3:6).[38] Paul does not appear to have had Luther's experience

---

34. Again, see a similar perspective in the Andrew Das, *Galatians*, 249; Das, *Paul, the Law, and the Covenant.*

35. Sanders, *Paul and Palestinian Judaism,* 17.

36. Sanders, *Paul and Palestinian Judaism,* 87–101.

37. Robert Jewett, "The Anthropological Implications of the Revelation of Wrath in Romans," in *Reading Paul in Context,* ed. W. S. Campbell (London: T&T Clark, 2010), 24–38; Jason Maston, *Divine and Human Agency in Second Temple Judaism and Paul: A Comparative Study* (Tübingen: Mohr Siebeck, 2010), 170–73; Preston Sprinkle, *Paul and Judaism Revisited: A Study of Divine and Human Agency in Salvation* (Downers Grove, IL: InterVarsity Press, 2013), 125–44.

38. Stendahl, "Paul and the Introspective Conscience of the West," 80.

of anxiety about his obedience to the law.[39] Nevertheless, the validity of
the Lutheran or Reformational view emerges from the objective dynamics of God's Word as law and gospel, and not on the basis of a private
religious experience.

THE RIGHTEOUSNESS OF GOD

Paul's solution to the human plight under the law is the righteousness of
God manifest in the gospel: "For I am not ashamed of the gospel, for it
is the power of God for salvation to everyone who believes, to the Jew
first and also to the Greek. For in it the righteousness of God is revealed
from faith for faith, as it is written, 'The righteous shall live by faith'"
(Rom 1:16–17).

What the "righteousness of God" (*dikaiosynē theou*) is has been disputed not only in recent Pauline studies, but also in the history of Christian
thought.[40] As things stand in the present, scholars have suggested several
options for understanding the phrase. One option would be to follow the
traditional interpretation of the Reformation and see the "righteousness
of God" as referring to an alien righteousness that God grants sinners
through the gospel, which is received by faith as a gift.[41] This seems like
the most logical and exegetically sound option, since Paul himself clarifies what he means by the phrase (used first in Rom 1:16–7) in chapter 3
of the same epistle by stating:

> But now the *righteousness of God has been manifested apart from the
> law*, although the Law and the Prophets bear witness to it—*the
> righteousness of God through faith in Jesus Christ for all who believe*.
> For there is no distinction: for all have sinned and fall short of the
> glory of God, and are justified by his grace as a gift, through the
> redemption that is in Christ Jesus. (Rom 3:21–24, emphasis added)

---

39. Scrupuli in supputatione annorum mundi (1543), WA 54:179–87.

40. See an exhaustive discussion of the various option in contemporary scholarship in Desta
Heliso, *Pistis and the Righteous One* (Tübingen: Mohr Siebeck, 2007).

41. See John Calvin, *Instruction in the Faith* (1537), trans. Paul Fuhrmann (Louisville: Westminster
John Knox, 1992), 41–42; Luther's comments in: Lectures on Galatians (1531), WA 40.1:42–45. Also
see the following modern interpreters who maintain the Reformation trajectory: C. E. B. Cranfield,
Romans: A Shorter Commentary (Grand Rapids: Eerdmans, 1985), 18–24; Douglas Moo, *The Epistle
to the Romans* (Grand Rapids: Eerdmans, 1996), 81–86; Thomas Schreiner, *Romans* (Grand Rapids:
Baker Books, 1998), 65–76.

Here Paul clearly states that the gospel is a righteousness that comes from God through the work of Christ and is communicated to faith. This righteousness is contrasted to the sort of righteousness that one finds in the law, which was obviously a failure due to human depravity and the ensuing guilt that it brought upon Jews and gentiles. In Philippians, Paul makes clear that this righteousness is alien in that it is not something achieved by the sinner (even under the power of grace) but is rather something given as a gift by Jesus Christ and received by faith (Phil 3:7–9).

In contemporary Pauline scholarship, there are two other major alternatives to this standard Reformation interpretation of Paul. The first interpretative paradigm might be described as the "continuity model" of God's redemptive purposes. This model has primarily been taken up by the scholars of the New Perspective, notably N. T. Wright and James D. G. Dunn.[42] According to this interpretation, the "righteousness of God" refers to God's faithfulness to his plan of salvation manifested in his covenant with Israel.[43] God's covenantal purpose was to create a single human family for Abraham out the Jews and gentiles. The gospel is a culmination of that process. Sin blocked God's final goal and therefore the crucifixion served the purpose of removing this obstacle. Hence, "justification" does not so much mean being declared righteous for the sake of Christ, but rather means "covenant membership." That is, one gains the status of righteous by being forgiven and then being incorporated into God's new covenantal community.[44]

The major problem with this second interpretation is that although God's righteousness certainly is expressed in his faithfulness to his covenants, the concept of the "righteousness of God" is not directly equivalent to "covenant faithfulness." The Hebrew and Greek words for righteousness (zedek, dikaiosune), mean simply to act correctly in accordance with

---

42. Dunn, *Theology of Paul the Apostle*, 340–46; Wright, *Paul and the Faithfulness of God*, 4:795–815.

43. A number of writers have traced this view back to Ludwig Diestel and Herman Cremer. See Herman Cremer, *Die paulinische Rechtfertigungslehre im Zusammenhange ihrer geschichtlichen Voraussetzungen* (Gutersloh: Bertelsmann, 1899); Ludwig Diestel, "Die idee der Gerrechtigkeit, vorzü im Alten Testament, bibischtheologisch dargestellt," *Jahrbüchen für deutsche Theologie* 5 (1860): 173–253. See discussion in Charles Lee Irons, *The Righteousness of God: A Lexical Examination of the Covenant Faithfulness Interpretation* (Tübingen: Mohr Siebeck, 2015). Also see discussion in Horton, *Justification*, 2:160–68.

44. Wright, *Paul in Fresh Perspective*, 120–22; Wright, *What St. Paul Really Said*, 119.

a standard.[45] As Stephen Westerholm points out, people are judged righteous before the flood and Abraham asks God to look for the "righteous" in Sodom and Gomorrah in Genesis 18. In both cases, divine and human righteousness are invoked without any covenantal relationship.[46] Similarly, "to justify" (*hasdiq, dikaioun*) does not mean "covenant membership" but rather to be declared just (as in a courtroom).[47] The Hebrew and Greek terms can also have the connotation of vindication or forgiveness in both the Hebrew Old Testament and also in the LXX, the latter being the version of the Old Testament with which Paul was most familiar.[48] All these definitions fit well with Paul's eschatological thinking, where there is an expectation of the coming judgment and vindication.

The second option might be described as a "discontinuity model." It has been promoted by Ernst Käsemann, J. Louis Martyn, and more recently by Douglas Campbell.[49] In this reading, the "righteousness of God" is God's "salvation creating power," which bursts into creation and ruptures the entire sinful legalistic order of fallen humanity.[50] Käsemann in particular insisted on the language of apocalyptic rupture and disliked Krister Stendahl and Oscar Cullmann fitting justification into the orderly and continuous development of salvation history.[51] Likewise, Martyn expressed the model of rupture by making the claim (on the basis of Gal 3:19) that at least in Galatians (though not Romans) Paul holds that the law is not actually the will of God, but the work of evil angels.[52] In *The Deliverance of God*, Campbell has even gone so far as to assert that Paul's talk of God's judgment on the basis of the law in the first three chapters of Romans

---

45. Irons, *Righteousness of God*, 337–43; Westerholm, *Perspectives Old and New on Paul*, 261–96.

46. Westerholm, *Justification Reconsidered*, 62–63.

47. See Das, *Galatians*, 243–45; J.A. Ziesler, *The Meaning of Righteousness in Paul: A Linguistic and Theological Enquiry* (Cambridge: Cambridge University Press, 1972), 48.

48. Alister McGrath, *Iustitia Dei*, 23–24.

49. Douglas Campbell, *The Deliverance of God: An Apocalyptic Re-Reading of Justification in Paul* (Grand Rapids: Eerdmans, 2013); Ernst Käsemann, *Commentary on Romans*, trans. Geoffrey W. Bromily (Grand Rapids: Eerdmans, 1980); J. Louis Martyn, *Galatians: A New Translation with Introduction and Commentary* (New York: Doubleday, 1997); Martyn, *Theological Issues in the Letters of Paul* (Nashville: Abingdon, 1997).

50. Käsemann, *Commentary on Romans*, 21–33.

51. Ernst Käsemann, "Justification and Salvation History in the Epistle to the Romans," in *Perspectives on Paul*, trans. Margaret Kohl (Philadelphia: Fortress, 1971), 60–78.

52. Martyn, *Galatians*, 366–67.

is not to be taken seriously. Rather, the apostle puts on the persona of a false teacher who claims that God punishes and rewards on the basis of obedience to divine commandments.[53]

This second "discontinuity" interpretation is problematic because it does not take Paul's statements about the gospel as a fulfillment of both God's covenants of law and grace seriously enough. If the continuity model's weakness was that it saw the gospel as simply a new stage of a single covenant that mixed law and grace, the discontinuity model's weakness is that it seems bent to sweeping away the law altogether. Nevertheless, in Galatians 3, Paul shows that God had two covenants, one of grace with Abraham and one on the basis of the law established at Sinai. The Lord possesses an absolute fidelity to both of them. The apostle compares God's covenant of grace with Abraham to a last will and testament (*diatheke*) that cannot be annulled once it was ratified (Gal 3:17–18).[54] Much like a will of inheritance, the covenant of grace with Abraham was unilateral gift. God is faithful to his promise of grace, even if the covenant of law was established some centuries later, and because of human sin, the law served as an obstacle that God had to overcome to fulfill his covenant of universal blessing.

In Romans 3:21, Paul is clear that although the gospel offers a different kind of righteousness than the law, it nevertheless is testified to by the Old Testament Scriptures. God is faithful to his promises, even if humans were faithless to God (Rom 3:3–4). Indeed, because human faithlessness stands in such profound contrast with divine faithfulness it makes the latter shine all the more brilliantly (Rom 3:5–8). Paul goes on to show how God was completely faithful to both covenants of grace and law by sending Jesus to die as a substitute for humanity's sin:

> For there is no distinction: for all have sinned and fall short of
> the glory of God, and are justified by his grace as a gift, through
> the redemption that is in Christ Jesus, whom God put forward as

---

53. Campbell, *Deliverance of God*, 519–600. See response to Campbell in Douglas Moo, review of *The Deliverance of God: An Apocalyptic Rereading of Justification in Paul* by Douglas A. Campbell, *Journal of the Evangelical Theology Society* 53 (2010): 143–50.

54. Hans Betz, *Galatians: A Commentary on Paul's Letter to the Churches in Galatia* (Philadelphia: Fortress, 1979), 155; Richard Longenecker, *Galatians* (Dallas: Word, 1990), 128; James D. G. Dunn, *The Epistle to the Galatians* (London: A & C Black, 1993), 180–83; Martyn, *Galatians*, 344–45.

a propitiation by his blood, to be received by faith. This was to show God's righteousness, because in his divine forbearance he had passed over former sins. It was to show his righteousness at the present time, so that he might be *just and the justifier of the one who has faith in Jesus.* (Rom 3:22–26, emphasis added)

In other words, in the crucifixion God's absolute fidelity to his covenant of law collided with his absolute fidelity to his promise to Abraham that there would be a universal blessing to the nations.[55] By entering into the flesh in the person of Jesus, God embodied this complete faithfulness by fulfilling his promises of retribution and grace in transferring the guilt of sinful humanity to himself: "For our sake he made him to be sin who knew no sin, so that in him we might become the righteousness of God" (2 Cor 5:21). The law quite literally cursed Christ, and as a result the covenantal curses of Sinai were exhausted (Gal 3:31). God's redemptive and creative word in Christ broke through every barrier (sin, death, law) and emerged Easter morning victorious: "[Christ] was delivered over to death for our sins and was raised to life for our justification" (Rom 4:25, NIV).[56]

In this sense, God in Christ both fulfilled and validated the law (that is, the law's logic of reward and punishment) and yet transcended it in his surprising act of grace (i.e., transferred the guilt of humanity to himself and suffered its curses): "In Christ God was reconciling the world to himself, not counting their trespasses against them" (2 Cor 5:19; also see Rom 8:3). In this, God in Christ fulfills the same pattern that we observed in the Old Testament. The Lord maintains his faithfulness to the covenant of grace by electing a substitutionary representative in order to fulfill the law.

Because of this, there is an element of truth in both the continuity and discontinuity models of divine righteousness. The New Perspective scholars are correct to see Paul as teaching that the gospel is a fulfillment of God's absolute covenant fidelity. Likewise, the discontinuity scholars are correct to see Paul asserting that in the redemption Christ offers, there

---

55. Martin Franzmann, *Commentary on Romans* (St. Louis: Concordia, 1968), 71–72.

56. Michael Middendorf, *Romans*, 2 vols. (St. Louis: Concordia, 2013–2016), 1:365–68; Stuhlmacher, *Revisiting Paul's Doctrine of Justification*, 57–60.

is a surprising rupture and transcendence of the legal order of the world by the power of unilateral grace.

JUSTIFICATION AS THE
PROLEPTIC ESCHATON

Much as we have seen in the Gospels, Paul identifies Christ's advent, death, and resurrection with the proleptic eschaton. The eschaton has mysteriously manifested itself ahead of time in Christ, although it is still a chronologically future event. In some of the most interesting passages in the Apostle's letters, Paul expounds how the redemptive work of Christ is an apocalyptic event that brings about judgment and re-creation. Christ is described as a new Adam, that is, a new representative of humanity and a progenitor of a new creation.[57]

In Romans 5 and 1 Corinthians 15, Paul contrasts the universality of sin and death brought by Adam to the universal grace brought by Christ (Rom 5:13–19). As we noted in the previous chapter, Paul's exegesis on this point is quite sound. The name "Adam" means "humanity,"[58] but also very clearly refers to a historical person named by the Old Testament as the progenitor of the human race (Gen 5:3–5; 1 Chr 1:1–4). Moreover, Adam is a representational person, much like the other elect representational persons of the Old Testament (i.e., prophets, priest, kings). What happened in Adam causes universal sin, death, and judgment (Rom 5:13, 15, 18–19). Paul also contrasts Adam with Christ as being a man of earth rather than heaven (1 Cor 15:45–48). As such, Adam had a mutable body and, although immortal, was vulnerable to the possibility of becoming subject to the power of sin and death. In the fall, Adam succumbed to the temptation and as a result death has become a defining characteristic of human life ever since.[59] Christ in his resurrection inaugurated a new humanity that was glorified by the power of the Spirit. Humanity's natural corruptibility was transcended by Christ's incorruptible resurrected humanity. All believers will share Christ's glorified humanity at the eschaton and will become

---

57. Herman Ridderbos, *Paul: An Outline of His Theology*, trans. John Richard De Witt (Grand Rapids: Eerdmans, 1975), 45–46.

58. Waltke and Yu, *Old Testament Theology*, 254.

59. See comment in Lectures on Genesis (1535), LW 1:86, 92.

invulnerable to physical or moral corruption in a way that Adam was not
(1 Cor 15:35–54).

Therefore, counteracting the universality of sin and death is the universality of grace and life found in the work of Jesus: "But the free gift is not like the trespass. For if many died through one man's trespass, much more have the grace of God and the free gift by the grace of that one man Jesus Christ abounded for many" (Rom 5:15). Indeed, Paul speaks of justification as a universal event that has happened as a result of Christ's death and resurrection: "Therefore, as one trespass led to condemnation for all men, *so one act of righteousness leads to justification and life for all men [pantas anthropos]*" (Rom 5:18, emphasis added). As a result: "For as in Adam all die, so also *in Christ shall all be made alive*" (1 Cor 15:22, emphasis added).[60]

From these passages two main observation should be made. First, implicitly, to the many pairs of elected and rejected persons in the Old Testament (Cain and Abel, Ishmael and Isaac, Jacob and Esau, Saul and David), Paul adds the figures of Adam and Christ. Paul plays out these dualities of election and rejection through the language of sonship and inheritance. In this, it should be noticed that Christ embodies the destinies of both the elected and rejected ones throughout the history of salvation in his person.[61]

Christ is for Paul both first and second born.[62] Since Christ is "the firstborn over all creation" (Col 1:15, NIV), by right of primogeniture he is the inheritor of all that is the Father's. All things were made by the Father "for him" (Col 1:6). Nevertheless, Christ also voluntarily takes upon himself the fate of all firstborn sons of the Old Testament by suffering the curse of the Father's rejection in the crucifixion (Gal 3:13). True to the biblical pattern, Adam as temporally firstborn is rejected as a sinner in the judgment of the crucifixion, but as secondborn from the perspective of eternity, he and his children (i.e., humanity) are among those elected and redeemed by Christ's acceptance of condemnation.

---

60. Middendorf, *Romans*, 1:431–34.

61. See CD II/2.351–409.

62. Observations made by Peter Leithart in a personal conversation.

Consequently, by being placed in the category of the rejected one in the crucifixion, Christ becomes the elect and accepted one in the resurrection. In this, he embodies the destiny of all the suffering second sons of the Old Testament. Moreover, those who are predestined to salvation are elected in him: "he [God the Father] chose us in him before the foundation of the world, that we should be holy and blameless before him [Christ]. In love he predestined us for adoption to himself as sons through Jesus Christ, according to the purpose of his will" (Eph 1:5–6). Hence, not only are the predestined elected by Christ's call through the word (Rom 8:30), but they participate in his election as the Christ (Christ = anointed one = elect one). Therefore, through union with him believers also become "co-heirs" (Rom 8:17) with Christ, the first-born inheritor of all things.

Second, although at certain points in passages like Romans 5 and 1 Corinthians 15 Paul sounds quite universalistic,[63] the Apostle very clearly does not mean that there will be a universal salvation (*apokatastasis*).[64] After all, Paul gives far too many emphatic warnings about eschatological destruction for such a reading to make sense (2 Thess 2:12; 1 Cor 10:1–13; Phil 3:18–19). Rather, a better way of viewing Romans 5 and 1 Corinthians 15 is to interpret the apostle as seeing the crucifixion and resurrection as the proleptic and all-encompassing eschaton. Christ and his eschatological redemption complete and establish an objective state of affairs that defines what is reality and unreality within the new creation. Those who have faith by the grace of God are able to redemptively participate in this new objective reality. In the crucifixion, all human sin (and therefore all humans!) was judged. Indeed, in effect, it was the great and terrible Day of the Lord when humanity received its recompense. By judging sin, God's wrath against sin (spoken of at the beginning of Romans 1) is propitiated. Paul incidentally calls the crucifixion the "Mercy Seat" (*hilasterion*) where God's wrath was propitiated by blood much like on the Day of Atonement (Rom 3:25).[65]

63. Käsemann, *Commentary on Romans*, 157.

64. See Ilaria Ramelli, *The Christian Doctrine of Apokatastasis: A Critical Assessment from the New Testament to Eriugena* (Leiden: Brill, 2013).

65. Stuhlmacher, *Paul's Letter to the Romans*, 58; Douglas Moo, *The Epistle to the Romans* (Grand Rapids:Eerdmans, 1996), 231–36. Also see the famous debate on "expiation" vs. "propitiation" in: C. H. Dodd, "ΙΛΑΣΚΕΣΘΑΙ, Its Cognates, Derivatives, and Synonyms in the Septuagint," *Journal of Theological Studies* 32 (1931): 352–60. See the masterful counter-argument in Leon Morris, "The

Just as the crucifixion was a universal condemnation of sin, so too the resurrection was a pronouncement of universal justification: "[Christ] was delivered over to death for our sins and *was raised to life for our justification*" (Rom 4:25, emphasis added). Much as humanity found its condemnation in the crucifixion even prior to any human response, so too the omnipotent divine Word of absolution that God spoke forth in the resurrection pronounces forgiveness prior its appropriation by faith. Justification is therefore primarily something the Word of God pronounces objectively, rather than a possibility actualized by faith. For Paul, the new Adam and along with it the new creation, have objectively been established by the Word of God. This new creation is reality, even if human beings wish to cling to unreality by their unbelief and thereby condemn themselves.[66]

Although justification is pronounced objectively in the resurrection (Rom 4:25), it is received subjectively through faith that hears the promise: "For with the heart one believes and is justified, and with the mouth one confesses and is saved. ... [And] faith comes from hearing, and hearing through the word of Christ" (Rom 10:10, 17).[67] No one can have faith apart from the electing and regenerative work of the Spirit (1 Cor 2:14; 12:3; Gal 3:2). Christ makes intercession on behalf of believers in heaven on the basis of his sacrifice on the cross (Rom 8:34). The Holy Spirit, who is the spirit of the Son (Gal 4:6), makes the fruits of Christ's intercession, justification, present in the heart of the believer (Rom 10:6–13) through the hearing of the word (Rom 10:7; Gal 3:2). Much as the elect-representational persons stood in the place of Israel in the Old Testament as mediators, so too Christ and his righteousness stand in for the unrighteousness of sinful humans through an act of imputation

---

Use of *ilaskesthai* etc. in Biblical Greek," *Expository Times* 62 (1951): 227–33. Also see other articles relating to the debate: Roger Nicole, "*Hilaskesthai* Revisited," *Evangelical Quarterly* 49/3 (1977): 173–77; Roger Nicole, "C. H. Dodd and the Doctrine of Propitiation," *Westminster Theological Journal* 17 (1955): 117–57. Morris's position seems to best fit the data, although arguably Paul's view of atonement contains elements of both expiation and propitiation.

66. Leithart, *Delivered from the Elements of the World*, 188; Stuhlmacher, *Revisiting Paul's Doctrine of Justification*, 60–62.

67. We interpret the phrase *pistis tou christou* as "faith in Christ" not "Christ's faith." Against Richard Hays, *The Faith of Jesus Christ: The Narrative Substructure of Galatians 3:1–4:11* (Grand Rapids: Eerdmans, 2002). See the counter-argument in Thomas Schreiner, *Faith Alone: The Doctrine of Justification*, Five Solas Series (Grand Rapids: Zondervan, 2015), 124–32.

(Rom 3:25; 4:9, 22; 8:10; 1 Cor 1:30; 2 Cor 5:21; Gal 3:6; Phil 3:9).[68] The concept of representation that we saw in the Old Testament therefore makes sense of Paul's language of imputation in atonement and justification. In atonement, human sin is imputed to Christ, and in justification Christ's righteousness is imputed to humans (2 Cor 5:21).

It is important to notice that Paul uses the eschatological term "justification" for what happens proleptically to believers in the present.[69] As we observed earlier, for Second Temple Jews, at the end of time God would "justify" (judge righteous and vindicate) those who had adhered to the covenant and usher them into the kingdom. For Paul, Christ is the object of election and justification. He is the one who has adhered to the covenant and been vindicated on the eschatological day of his resurrection.[70] Therefore, in the present believers can proleptically receive through Christ what they will receive at the end of time through faith in the promise (i.e., election and justification). This is because the eschaton has already happened for Christ, and therefore when believers enter into him the eschaton happens to them as well.[71] Outwardly, believers remain in the current age weighed down by sin and death, but in their inner being they already have been ushered into the kingdom of the resurrected: "But if Christ is in you, although the body is dead because of sin, the Spirit is life because of righteousness" (Rom 8:10).

One might say that, chronologically (*chronos*), God's pronouncement of judgment and justification in the advent of Christ (Rom 4:25) and at the end of time through the cosmic judgment of Christ are events distant from the believer (Rom 2:16). Nevertheless, kairologically (*kairos*), that is, according to God's breaking into time whereby he establishes his purposes wholly apart from the normal human chronology, God's eschatological

---

68. Against Gundry. See Robert Gundry, "The Nonimputation of Christ's Righteousness," in *Justification: What's at Stake in the Current Debates*, ed. Daniel Trier and Mark Husbands (Downers Grove, IL: InterVarsity Press, 2004), 17–45. In favor of imputation see D. A. Carson's masterful defense in D. A. Carson, "The Vindication of Imputation: On Fields of Discourse and Semantic Fields," in Trier and Husbands, *Justification*, 46–47. Also see Henri Blocher, "Justification of the Ungodly (Sola Fide): Theological Reflections" in Carson, Seifrid, and O'Brien, *Justification and Variegated Nomism*, 2:465–500.

69. George Eldon Ladd, *A Theology of the New Testament* (Grand Rapids: Eerdmans, 1993), 484; Also see Ridderbos, *Paul: An Outline of His Theology*, 50–53.

70. See similar argument in J. Christian Beker, *The Triumph of God: The Essence of Paul's Thought*, trans. Loren Stuckenbruck (Minneapolis: Fortress, 1990), 25.

71. Pannenberg, *Systematic Theology*, 3:236.

judgment and justification on the sinner become a present reality to the believer through the word and sacrament ministry of the church.[72]

In this regard, Paul stresses Abraham as the model for believers (Rom 4). Abraham believed and was justified by faith in Christ long before either the law or before the chronological advent of Christ. Christ was nevertheless kairologically present to him in the promise of the seed (Gal 3:16). Christ has the ability to transcend time and space, thereby becoming present in his word (Rom 10:6–13). Recognizing Paul's understanding on this point goes a long way to explaining his language of the two dispensations of law and grace. Sometimes the law is spoken of as if it were an era that comes before Christ and is now done away with by the time of grace (Rom 3:22; 5:12–21; Gal 3:22–25; 2 Cor 6:2; Eph 1:9–10; Col 1:26). At other times, Paul speaks of the law as a present existential reality even in the new time of grace (Rom 3:20; 7:8–10; Gal 2:19), much as he speaks of Abraham mysteriously participating in the time of grace long before Christ or even the giving of the Sinaitic covenant (Gal 3:17).[73]

For Paul, God transcends time and can break into it at any point, sovereignly establishing his judgment or grace as he so chooses. Although there is very clearly a history of salvation, God's *kairos* creates an interpenetration of the times. When Paul's reasoning on this point is fully exposed, N. T. Wright's supposition that there are in fact two justifications (seemingly one based on faith in the present and another eschatologically based on faith-wrought works) misses the logic of Paul's proleptic understanding of justification.[74] For Paul, much as for Jesus, the eschatological reckoning of righteousness is made present ahead of time to the believer through the power of the word.

The proleptic eschatological nature of the gospel's justifying power can be seen not only in Paul's belief in the risen Christ and the Spirit's work through the word, but also in his teaching regarding the sacraments. For Paul, God works in baptism through the Spirit in order to transcend time

---

72. For the distinction between *kairos* and *chronos*, see Paul Tillich, *The Interpretation of History* (New York: Charles Scribner's Sons, 1936).

73. Pannenberg, *Systematic Theology*, 3:65. "The example of Abraham showed Paul that righteousness before God may be attained, not only after the coming of the Messiah, but always already by faith, and not by works of the law."

74. Wright, *What St. Paul Really Said*, 126–27.

and space, thereby uniting the Christian with the death and resurrection of Jesus. All sin was judged in the cross. Because sinners are defined by their disobedience to God, their sin constitutes their personhood before God. Consequently, by being baptized into the cleansing death of Jesus, the sinner's old being was removed through the justifying power of the water and the word: "We know that our old self was crucified with him in order that the body of sin might be brought to nothing" (Rom 6:6–7; also see Gal 3:26–27). Likewise, through faith in, and baptism into, Christ the believer shares in the resurrected life in the present. Indeed, he is given the full assurance that, having died and risen with Christ in the spirit through baptism, he will rise in flesh with Christ at the end of time: "For if we have been united with him in a death like his, we shall certainly be united with him in a resurrection like his. ... Now if we have died with Christ, we believe that we will also live with him" (Rom 6:5–6, 8).[75]

We find something similar in Paul's teaching on the Lord's Supper. Although there is a distance in time and space between the crucified and risen Christ and the assembly of believers, due to the real presence there is a genuine fellowship of the heavenly Christ's sacrificed flesh and blood for those who receive the eucharistic elements (1 Cor 10:16).[76] Through the elements of the sacrament, Christ's sacrificed flesh and blood, as well as the forgiveness that they have obtained, are directly received by the believer. This is the very content of the new covenant (1 Cor 11:24–25). This substantial presence of Christ's flesh and blood proclaims his saving death and its fruits in the midst of the assembly of believers until the eschaton (1 Cor 11:26).[77]

CONCLUSION

In examining the two main literary blocks in the New Testament (i.e., the Gospels and the Pauline Epistles), it can be observed that the New Testament documents witness to the saving power of the word of the gospel. The Word of God in the form of the saving gospel of Jesus gives the full assurance of eschatological vindication in the present. It does so

75. Udo Schnelle, *Apostle Paul: His Life and Theology*, trans. M. Eugene Boring (Grand Rapids: Baker Academic, 2005), 326–32, 578–81.

76. Gregory Lockwood, *1 Corinthians* (St. Louis: Concordia, 2000), 393–94.

77. Lockwood, *1 Corinthians*, 387–95.

because of the presence of the risen Jesus in the word and sacrament ministry of the church, proclaiming to sinners of his positive verdict ahead of time in the present.

CHAPTER 5

Justification in the
Early Church and Augustine:
The Bishop of Hippo's Theological Foundations

H aving surveyed the biblical material concerning the justifying power
of the Word of God, we now turn to the post-biblical tradition. It
will be the main contention of this chapter that Augustine's theology is
a watershed for the development of the Western theological tradition's
understanding of justification. Augustine revived much of the biblical
understanding of sin and grace that had been lost in the ante-Nicene
church, while simultaneously establishing certain doctrinal paradigms
that significantly distorted the trajectory of the medieval church.

This tension in his thought leads to what we will call the "Augustinian
dilemma," wherein one must choose between an invisible predestination
disconnected or only marginally connected to the word and sacrament
ministry of the church, or a high view of the sacraments that nevertheless makes them efficacious only if grasped as a possibility by human free
will. In either case, the sacramental and efficacious nature of the divine
Word is marginalized in favor of a view of God's Word as a signifier that
merely signifies and does not create. It will be our argument below that the
Augustinian dilemma is ultimately in Augustine's problematic understanding of language. As a number of authors have shown, Augustine operates
with a fundamentally Platonic worldview and concept of language. In this

97

worldview, language is viewed as a sensible sign that at best can point beyond itself to an intelligible reality. Language is an opaque representation that obscures access to reality, or at best is a token of a greater reality behind it that one must move past to gain real knowledge. For Augustine, language is not a medium whereby we receive and participate in reality. Such a conception marginalizes the concept of the word as a genuinely sacramental medium, wherein God sovereignly and incarnationally acts in order to work salvation. In light of this undermining of the sacramentality of the word, Augustine generated a sacramental theology and doctrine of predestination that were in significant tension with one another.

JUSTIFICATION IN THE
ANTE-NICENE CHURCH

As Alister McGrath notes, the discussion of the doctrine of justification is very sparse in the first centuries of Christianity.[1] Part of the reason for this was that there were other theological challenges faced by the early church (i.e., the Gnostic, Ebionite, Modalist heresies) that more indirectly related to the doctrine of justification.[2] A second reason for such a sparse discussion is that the New Testament writings use a variety of terms and images for salvation in Christ. The use of the term "justification" is specifically Pauline.[3] Hence, many of the ante-Nicene Fathers discuss salvation in Christ and justification using different terms for the same reality, much like the other New Testament authors.[4]

For those Christians committed to the Reformation paradigm's interpretation of Paul, the so-called Apostolic Fathers of the late first and early second century present a doctrine of justification that possesses very few bright spots. Indeed, many of these writings are so crassly legalistic that it is difficult to see any connection with the doctrine of grace present in the New Testament documents whatsoever.[5] Probably

---

1. Alister McGrath, *Iustitia Dei*, 30–32.

2. Alister McGrath, *Iustitia Dei*, 30–32. See summary of these heresies in Harold O. J. Brown, *Heresies: Heresy and Orthodoxy in the History of Church* (Peabody, MA: Hendrickson, 1998).

3. Leonhard Goppelt, *Theology of the New Testament: The Variety and Unity of the Apostolic Witness to Christ*, trans. John Alsup, vol. 2 (Grand Rapids: Eerdmans, 1982), 137.

4. McGrath, *Iustitia Dei*, 1, 32–36.

5. Bengt Hägglund, *History of Theology*, trans. Gene Lund (St. Louis: Concordia, 1968), 16.

the works that most clearly deviate from the Pauline concept of justification are the Epistle of Barnabas (ca. AD 130)[6] and the Shepherd of Hermas (ca. AD 110).[7]

The Epistle of Barnabas argues that the Jews did not actually possess a covenant with God. When Moses came down from Mt. Sinai he broke the tablets of stone, thereby ending the covenantal relationship between God and Israel (Barnabas 14:1–5). Instead, an evil angel deceived Israel into believing that it had a covenantal relationship with God through circumcision (Barnabas 9:3). Moreover, the Jews misinterpreted the law of Moses by taking it literally (notably food laws). This led them into acting in ways that were counterproductive to their achievement of salvation (Barnabas 10). Barnabas now introduces the "Two Ways" doctrine, found in Judaism (most notably at Qumran),[8] as well as in a modified form in the Didache and in the Gospel of Matthew (Matt 7:13–14).[9] There is a way of obedience and a way of disobedience to the law—the former leading to salvation and the later to destruction. If Christians read the law of Moses allegorically and obey the commandments, then they can be saved and share in the coming millennial reign of Christ on earth (Barnabas 15:4–5).

The Shepherd of Hermas is an extremely complex work, comprising many visions seemingly reported by a former slave in Rome named Hermas.[10] The contents of the visions focus on the necessity of members of the church living a life of moral rigorism. Moral perfection after baptism is the only means by which human beings can be saved. Indeed, post-baptismal sins exclude people from final salvation—a position that

---

6. See James Carleton Paget, *The Epistle of Barnabas: Outlook and Background* (Tübingen: Mohr Siebeck 1994); Reidar Hvalvik, *The Struggle for Scripture and Covenant: The Purpose of the Epistle of Barnabas and Jewish-Christian Competition in the Second Century* (Tübingen: Mohr Siebeck 1996); Johannes Quasten, *Patrology*, 4 vols. (Allen, TX: Christian Classics, 1983), 85–89.

7. Carolyn Osiek, "The Second Century through the Eyes of Hermas: Continuity and Change," *Biblical Theology Bulletin* 20 (1990): 116–22; Osiek, "The Shepherd of Hermas in Context," *Acta Patristica et Byzantina* 8 (1997): 115–34; Osiek, *Shepherd of Hermas: A Commentary* (Minneapolis: Fortress, 1999).

8. David Flusser, *Judaism of the Second Temple Period: Sages and Literature*, trans. Azzan Yadin, vol. 2 (Grand Rapids: Eerdmans, 2009), 233–47.

9. Helmut Koester, *Introduction to the New Testament: History and Literature of Early Christianity*, vol. 2 (Berlin: De Gruyter, 1987), 158.

10. Christian Tornau and Paolo Cecconi, ed. and trans., *The Shepherd of Hermas in Latin: Critical Edition of the Oldest Translation Vulgata* (Berlin: De Gruyter, 2014), 1.

would be taken up by many in the early church. Hermas introduces the notion that a penance can serve as a second baptism, although this is considered to be final chance to achieve salvation (Shepherd of Hermas, Mandate 4:3).[11]

Within these early works that marginalize the centrality of grace, 1 Clement (ca. AD 95–97)[12] stands out as maintaining the Pauline trajectory. Clement writes as a representative of the council of presbyters that ruled the church of Rome at the end of the first century. He addresses a sister congregation at Corinth regarding their removal and mistreatment of their ministers for reasons of personal preference rather than moral unfitness.[13] In the midst of his exhortation of respect for the office of ministry, Clement states that salvation comes by grace through faith, not on the basis of the works of the law: "And so we, having been called through his will in Christ Jesus, are not justified of ourselves or through our own wisdom or understanding or piety, or works that we have done in holiness of heart, *but through faith, by which the Almighty God has justified all who have existed from the beginning*; to whom be glory for ever and ever, Amen (1 Clement 32:4, emphasis added).[14]

Moving into the later second and early third centuries, the two theologians who arguably did the most to set the trajectory for the later Greek and Latin theological traditions were Irenaeus and Tertullian. Beginning with the former, Irenaeus largely set the soteriological agenda for the Eastern church, although he spent the majority of his career in the city of Lyons in what is modern France.[15]

Irenaeus wrote his magnum opus *Against the Heresies* sometime in the late second century in order to repel the claims made by the Gnostic heretics, as well as the semi-Gnostic heresiarch Marcion.[16] The key to both

---

11. See discussion in Walter Woods, *Walking with Faith: New Perspectives on the Sources and Shaping of Catholic Moral Life* (Eugene, OR: Wipf & Stock, 1998), 104.

12. Holmes, Michael W., trans. *The Apostolic Fathers: Greek Texts and English Translations*, 3rd ed. (Grand Rapids: Baker Academic, 2007), 36. See commentary on justification in the work in Brian Arnold, *Justification in the Second Century* (Berlin: De Guyter, 2017), 19–35.

13. Alan Bandy, *A Greek Reader's Apostolic Fathers* (Eugene, OR: Cascade, 2018), 234.

14. Holmes, *Apostolic Fathers*, 87.

15. Roger Olson, *The Story of Christian Theology: Twenty Centuries of Tradition and Reform* (Downers Grove, IL: InterVarsity Press, 1999), 68.

16. Robert Grant, *Irenaeus of Lyons* (London: Routledge, 1997), 11.

heretical systems was the idea that the creator god was different from the god of redemption.[17] Gnosticism (at least in its Valentinian form) claimed that the creator was actively evil and had enslaved divine human souls that had fallen into the material world from a higher spiritual world.[18] The higher spiritual god of redemption manifested himself in Jesus not as a means of atoning for sins, but of revealing the knowledge (*gnosis*) of the true identity of humans. By gaining access to the knowledge granted by the Savior, humanity was given the means by which they could climb back through the cosmic hierarchy to their original home in the pure spiritual world.[19] Within this system of thought, human beings were pre-determined to have various capacities to achieve spiritual enlightenment. "Animal" persons (*hylics, somatics*) had no capacity to achieve salvation or spiritual enlightenment. "Soulish" persons had a greater ability to become "psychics" and achieve some spiritual enlightenment. Finally, "spiritual" people (*pneumatics*) had the ability to achieve the status of true "Gnostics" (i.e., those who genuinely knew spiritual truth).[20]

In some contrast to this, Marcion held that the god of creation and law was not evil, but morally inflexible and incompetent in his design of the world. Because of the imperfection of the god of creation, evil and decay had infected creation. The creator god stood juxtaposed to Jesus, who was the manifestation of a higher loving and purely spiritual god. In order to save humanity from the inflexible justice of the creator god, Jesus paid himself as a ransom in order to free humanity from the creator god's angry justice.[21]

Marcion was an avowed Paulinist[22] and seemingly created the first New Testament canon comprised of Paul's letters (minus the Pastoral Epistles) and a version of the Gospel of Luke (minus the references to the Old

17. Gerd Thiessen, *A Theory of Primitive Christian Religion* (London: SCM, 1999), 238.

18. David Brakke, *The Gnostics: Myth, Ritual, and Diversity in Early Christianity* (Cambridge, MA: Harvard University Press, 2010), 97.

19. Kurt Rudolph, *Gnosis: The Nature and History of Gnosticism*, trans. Robert McLauchlin Wilson (Edinburgh: T&T Clark, 1983), 118–22.

20. Kurt Rudolph, *Gnosis*, 186.

21. E. C. Blackman, *Marcion and His Influence* (London: SPCK, 1948), 66–102; Brakke, *The Gnostics*, 97.

22. Blackman, *Marcion and His Influence*, 103–12.

Testament, which Marcion rejected *in toto*).[23] His contrast between the law and the gospel was a contrast between the ethic of inflexible justice (associated with the Old Testament era and the Jews) and the ethic of love associated with the god of Jesus. Therefore, Marcion's law and gospel distinction was not as with Paul (or later the Protestant Reformers) the two words or covenants of the single God, one that demanded and the other that promised grace.[24]

Irenaeus attempted to repel these theological claims by more or less inverting them.[25] First, whereas the Gnostics claimed humanity was by nature divine, Irenaeus claimed that, although created, humans could be deified through participating in the divine nature shared with them through Christ, the second Adam.[26] Christ was the fulfillment of the education (*paideia*) of the human race actualized through the history of salvation. Divine grace had been poured out on humans at their creation.[27] Although exegetically dubious,[28] Irenaeus distinguished between the "image" and "likeness" of God in Genesis 1. The divine image was constituted by the faculties natural to the human person, whereas the likeness refers to the holiness and sanctity of the first humans. In the fall, humanity had retained the image, but lost the likeness.[29]

Irenaeus largely ignored (whether intentionally, or unintentionally) the Pauline doctrine of predestination, likely because of the fear of a possible association with the Gnostic soteriological determinism spoken of earlier. Instead, he posited that the divine image gave humans free will to cooperate with God's program of redemption.[30] He thereby established

23. Blackman, *Marcion and His Influence*, 23–65.

24. Jaroslav Pelikan, *The Christian Tradition: A History of the Development of Doctrine*, 5 vols. (Chicago: University of Chicago Press, 1971–1989), 1:71–81.

25. See excellent summary of Irenaeus's theology in Eric Osborn, *Irenaeus of Lyons* (Cambridge: Cambridge University Press, 2004); Gustaf Wingren, *Man and the Incarnation: A Study in the Biblical Theology of Irenaeus*, trans. Ross McKenzie (Eugene, OR: Wipf & Stock, 2004).

26. Irenaeus, *Against the Heresies*, 5.7–9; ANF, 1:532–36.

27. Irenaeus, *Against the Heresies*, 1.10, 4.37–39; ANF, 1:331, 1:518–23.

28. Ray Sherman Anderson, *On Being Human: Essays in Theological Anthropology* (Grand Rapids: Eerdmans, 1982), 216.

29. Osborn, *Irenaeus of Lyons*, 212; Irenaeus, *Against the Heresies*, 3.18, 5.6,10; ANF, 1:445–46, 531–32, 536–37.

30. Irenaeus, *Against the Heresies*, 4.37; ANF, 1:518–21.

a free will theodicy capable of explaining sin in the world without laying the blame of its defects on the creator god.

Moreover, Irenaeus did not so much think of a dialectic of distinct words (law and gospel) that addressed humanity throughout all salvation history, but rather of two eras of the economy of salvation.[31] Hence the disjunction between the law and the gospel that Paul had spoken of, and that Marcion had distorted into a theory of two gods, was smoothed over by Irenaeus into a typological unity of the activity of the single god of creation or law and redemption.[32]

For Irenaeus, the first dispensation was the time of Adamic humanity, where at each stage humanity failed in its vocation.[33] Later in the era of redemption, the second and more mature Adam overcame where the first Adam had failed. Clearly drawing on Paul in Romans 5 and 1 Corinthians 15,[34] Irenaeus posited a theory of "recapitulation" (*anakephalaiosis, recapitulatio*) wherein Christ reversed Adam's curse by doing over everything that Adam had done, but this time acting correctly in accordance with the will of the creator.[35] Whereas Adam had succumbed to Satan at a tree, Christ overcame Satan on the tree of the cross.[36] Again, because the pattern of the first and second Adam mirror one another, Irenaeus implicitly suggests that the God responsible for the first creation must also be the God of redemption and new creation.

Setting the stage for later Western theology, Tertullian wrote in the tradition of North African moral rigorism similar to what we earlier saw in the Shepherd of Hermas.[37] In a surprisingly similar move to Marcion, Tertullian posits that the distinction between law and gospel is to be

31. Irenaeus, *Against the Heresies*, 4.1–2; ANF, 1:463–64.

32. James Bushar, *Irenaeus of Lyons and the Mosaic of Christ: Preaching Scripture in the Era of Martyrdom* (London: Routledge, 2017), 140.

33. Irenaeus, *Against the Heresies*, 5:22; ANF, 1:551–52.

34. D. E. H. Whiteley, *The Theology of St Paul* (Oxford: Blackwell, 1964), 113.

35. L. W. Grensted, *A Short History of the Doctrine of the Atonement* (Manchester: Manchester University Press, 1920), 57–60; R. Mackintosh, *Historic Theories of the Atonement* (London: Hodder & Stoughton, 1920), 89–90; J. K. Mozley, *The Doctrine of the Atonement* (New York: Charles Scribner's Sons, 1916), 100–101.

36. Hans Boersma, *Violence, Hospitality, and the Cross: Reappropriating the Atonement Tradition* (Grand Rapids: Baker, 2004), 125–26; Bushar, *Irenaeus of Lyons*, 167. See examples in Irenaeus, *Against the Heresies*, 3.21–23, 5:16, 5:21; ANF, 1:451–58, 1:544, 1:549–51.

37. Olson, *Story of Christian Theology*, 98.

understood as the opposition between the inferior old law of the Jews and
a new law of the gospel.[38] The Old Testament law was a revelation of God,
but one for the time of preparation. It is superseded by the new, perfect
law of the dispensation of Christ.[39] Much of the North African theologian's
language at these points indicate a conception of the gospel not as a word
of grace, but as a better commandment and means of meriting divine favor.
Indeed, Tertullian spoke in the most crassly legalistic terms of Christians
"making God a debtor" by their good works (*bonum factum deum habet
debitorem, sicuti et malum: quia iudex omnis remunerator est causae*).[40]

According to Tertullian, Christians not only achieve merit (*meritum*)
by doing good works commanded by the Christ, but also by doing more
than they actually need to (*supererogatio*).[41] By performing activities such
as permanently preserving one's virginity[42] or intentionally becoming
a martyr (i.e., by confessing one's Christianity before Roman authorities),[43] a believer could earn extra merit. For this reason, unlike ordinary
believers who repose in a pleasant, albeit inferior region of the afterlife
(*refrigerium interim*),[44] the martyrs are ushered into the direct presence
of God.[45] Here we have the later Roman Catholic doctrine of the saints
and personal eschatology *in utero*.

This theology of law and merit inevitably leads to Tertullian's theology
of penance.[46] Much of early church held that post-baptismal sins were
a problem, since the New Testament speaks of baptism as the rupture
between the old life of sin and new life of grace (Rom 6).[47] One commonly

38. Tertullian, *Against Marcion* 4.1; ANF 3:346.

39. Tertullian, *Answer to the Jews*, 5.6; ANF, 3:157.

40. Tertullian, *On Repentance* 2; ANF, 3:658.

41. Gustaf Aulén, *Christus Victor: An Historical Study of the Three Main Types of the Idea of the Idea of Atonement*, trans. A.G. Hebert (Eugene, OR: Wipf & Stock, 2003), 81–82.

42. Tertullian, *On Exhortation to Chastity*, 10; ANF 3:55–56.

43. Tertullian, *Ad Martyras*; ANF, 3:693–706.

44. Tertullian, *Against Marcion* 4.34; ANF, 3:404-7.

45. Jacques Le Goff, *The Birth of Purgatory*, trans. Arthur Goldhammer (Chicago: University of Chicago Press, 1986), 46–47. See Tertullian, *A Treatise on the Soul*, 55; ANF 3:231.

46. See summary of Tertullian's position in Cornelia Horn, "Penitence in Early Christianity in Historical and Theological Setting: Trajectories in Eastern and Western Sources," in *Repentance in Christian Theology*, ed. Mark J. Boda and Gordon T. Smith (Collegeville, MN: Liturgical, 2006), 160–64.

47. G. R. Beasley-Murray, *Baptism in the New Testament* (Eugene, OR: Wipf & Stock, 2006), 126–45.

held position in the early church was that post-baptismal sins were unforgiveable.[48] At least according to their opponents, the Montanists,[49] as well as other schismatic groups like the Novatians (albeit at a later stage of their theological development), held such a view.[50] As a result, the delay of baptism until immediately before death was a common and logical procedure in order to avoid post-baptismal sin.[51] Other theologians in the early church held that all post-baptismal sins—with the exceptions of murder, fornication or adultery and idolatry—could be forgiven and should be accompanied by outward signs of repentance in the form of penitential acts.[52] Over time the belief arose that such acts of penance were not merely outward signs of contrition, but genuinely effected one's relationship with God.[53] This was particularly the case in North African Christianity.[54]

Tertullian represents this development of penitential theology most clearly.[55] Early in his career he speaks of penance being performed in order to prepare for baptism. In baptism, all sin was forgiven, and the believer was perfectly sanctified. Tertullian thought of original sin taken away in baptism as a sort of veil that covers over and impedes the originally good nature of humanity. With this veil's removal, the good nature of humanity can function perfectly again.[56] Unfortunately, minor sins (but not the major sins of fornication, murder, and idolatry) committed after baptism incur a debt and must be paid for with a one-time

48. Roman Garrison, *Redemptive Almsgiving in Early Christianity* (London: Bloosbury, 1993), 131; Rob Means, *Penance in Medieval Europe, 600–1200* (Cambridge: Cambridge University Press, 2014), 16.

49. William Tabbernee, *Fake Prophecy and Polluted Sacraments: Ecclesiastical and Imperial Reactions to Montanism* (Leiden: Brill, 2007), 365–66.

50. James Papandrea, *Novatian of Rome and the Culmination of Pre-Nicene Orthodoxy* (Eugene, OR: Pickwick, 2011), 69.

51. Holger Hammerich, *Taufe und Askese: Der Taufaufschub in Vorkonstantinischer Zeit* (PhD diss., University of Hamburg, 1994), 96–102.

52. Williston Walker, *A History of the Christian Church* (New York: Charles Scribner's Sons, 1919), 100.

53. See development in Abigail Firey, ed., *A New History of Penance* (Leiden: Brill, 2008).

54. Stuart Donaldson, *Church Life and Thought in North Africa A.D. 200* (Cambridge: Cambridge University Press, 1909), 88–91.

55. Hägglund, *History of Theology*, 56–57, 108–10.

56. Eric Osborn, *Tertullian: First Theologian of the West* (Cambridge: Cambridge University Press, 2003), 166–67; Tertullian, *A Treatise on the Soul*, 16, 39–41; ANF, 3:194–95, 219–21.

second penance.[57] After his conversion to the Montanist movement and his acceptance of the group's perfectionism, Tertullian came to believe that all post-baptismal sin was unforgivable.[58] The only recourse for post-baptismal sins was to become a martyr through a public admission to the Roman authorities that one was a Christian. This "baptism of blood" was the sole means by which sin might be washed away.[59]

One of the major tensions in the conception of salvation raised the question of whether the merit of Christ was sufficient for salvation. In many of his statements about the work of Christ, Tertullian holds to something like what would later be called the doctrine of substitutionary atonement.[60] Nevertheless, if one can atone for their own sins committed after baptism by penance or martyrdom, the question is raised whether work of the Savior is genuinely sufficient, or even necessary. Later medieval theologians would nuance this approach and create the distinction between "temporal" and "eternal punishment," something that will be touched on in a later chapter.[61] Nonetheless, such conceptions remain an implicit tension in the Latin tradition of theology down to contemporary Roman Catholic theology.

AUGUSTINE ON BEING, DESIRE, AND ORIGINAL SIN

The first major debate in the early church on the doctrine of justification occurred in the early fifth century in the conflict between Pelagius and Augustine over original sin and grace.[62] Some writers suggest that Augustine's distinctive views on the subject emerged only as a result of the conflict. Nevertheless, as Alister McGrath has observed, this is

---

57. Tertullian, *On Repentance*, 7; ANF, 3:662–63.

58. Tertullian, *On Modesty*, 16; ANF 4:91. As Eric Osborn observes, for Tertullian, "We are not baptized so that we may stop sinning, but because we have stopped sinning." Osborn, *Tertullian*, 171.

59. Tabbernee, *Fake Prophecy and Polluted Sacraments*, 247; Tertullian, *On Baptism*, 16; ANF 3:677.

60. See discussion in Peter Ensor, "Tertullian and Penal Substitutionary Atonement," *Evangelical Quarterly* 86, no. 2 (2014):130–42.

61. Isnard Wilhelm Frank, *A History of the Medieval Church* (London: SCM, 1995), 19.

62. See John Ferguson, *Pelagius: A Historical and Theological Study* (Cambridge, UK: W. Heffer, 1956); Stuart Squires, *The Pelagian Controversy: An Introduction to the Enemies of Grace and the Conspiracy of Lost Souls* (Eugene, OR: Pickwick, 2019); Benjamin Warfield, *Augustine and the Pelagian Controversy* (Edinburgh: Crossreach, 2018).

not the case. It is true that during the early period after his conversion Augustine's own views appear not to have differed much from those of his later Pelagian opponents.[63] In his early works, in continuity with the ante-Nicene tradition, Augustine speaks of God's election by grace as being little more than divine prescience regarding who would use their free will appropriately and who would not.[64] Nevertheless, in the mid-390s, Augustine's friend Simplicianus raised the question with him as to why Jacob was elected, while Esau was not.[65] From this point on, Augustine began to develop his radical response to the question of sin and grace in two letters he wrote to his friend (*Ad Simplicianus*) between AD 396 and 397.[66] This development in Augustine's thinking occurred long before the emergence of the Pelagian heresy.

To understand Augustine's mature answer to the question of justification, as well as the closely related issues of original sin and predestination, we must comprehend the converging streams of intellectual tradition that inform his thought. In his now classic (though older) work, *History of Dogma*, Adolf von Harnack suggested that Augustine's thought can be properly seen as the convergence of three distinct intellectual traditions: Neoplatonism, North African Latin theology, and Paulinism.[67] The blending of these three influences explains the structure and some of the incoherencies present in Augustine's doctrine of justification.

In his spiritual autobiography *The Confessions*, Augustine makes clear that as a young man he rejected his mother's somewhat simplistic and superstitious version of North African Christianity first in favor

---

63. McGrath, *Iustitia Dei*, 43.

64. Phillip Cary, *Inner Grace: Augustine in the Traditions of Plato and Paul* (Oxford: Oxford University Press, 2008), 48–50; Jairzinho Lopes Pereira, *Augustine of Hippo and Martin Luther on Original Sin and Justification of the Sinner* (Göttingen: Vandenhoeck & Ruprecht, 2013), 81–93.

65. Cary, *Inner Grace*, 50–52.

66. Pereira, *Augustine of Hippo and Martin Luther*, 98–128.

67. Adolf von Harnack, *History of Dogma*, trans. Neil Buchanan, 7 vols. (New York: Dover, 1961), 5:104. It should be noted that when Harnack speaks about Augustine's ecclesiastical position as an influence, he is speaking of the influence of North African theology. Moreover, Harnack also sees Manichaean elements at work in Augustine, but we do not concur with this judgment as shall be discussed later in the chapter.

of Manichaeism[68] (a form of syncretistic dualism)[69] and then later for
Neoplatonism before his final return to the catholic faith.[70] Whereas the
Manichaeans were a heretical sect that stood in direct opposition to orthodox Christianity,[71] various forms of Platonism had been utilized by both
Jews (such as Philo) and Christians for some time.[72] Because of a number
of points of contact between the biblical revelation and the works of
Plato, Platonism was seen as a means of translating biblical truth to the
wider gentile world. Indeed, Augustine often credited Neoplatonism as the
means by which he finally intellectually reconciled himself to Christianity.[73]

Although certainly Augustine was aware of the existence of the man
Plato, we cannot be certain that he had direct knowledge of his works.
Rather, it appears that Augustine absorbed Platonism primarily through
the filter of Neoplatonic thinkers such as Plotinus.[74] The key to Augustine's
interest in these systems of thought lay in their intellectual rigor and
their answer to the question of evil that plagued him in his youth.[75] The
older Augustine remained interested in the existence of evil and would
come to reflect upon it in an even more systematic manner through his
anti-Pelagian writings and his grand theory of history put forward in *The
City of God*.[76]

Whereas the young Augustine found convincing the Manichaean claim
that evil was the result of the existence of two equally powerful substances
in the universe—a good one composed of spirit or light and an evil one

---

68. Augustine, *Confessions*, 4.1; NPNF[1], 1:68.

69. See Michel Tardieu, *Manichaeism*, trans. M. B. DeBervoise (Chicago: University of Illinois Press, 2008).

70. Augustine, *Confessions*, 7.20–21; NPNF[1], 1:113–15. Also see Brian Dobell, *Augustine's Intellectual Conversion: The Journey from Platonism to Christianity* (Cambridge: Cambridge University Press, 2009).

71. Jason BeDuhn, *Augustine's Manichaean Dilemma: Conversion and Apostasy, 373–388 C.E.*, vol. 1 (Philadelphia: University of Pennsylvania Press, 2010), 28.

72. Everett Ferguson, *Backgrounds of Early Christianity* (Grand Rapids: Eerdmans, 2003), 386–88.

73. Augustine, *Confessions*, 7.20; NPNF[1], 1:113–14. Also see John Peter Kenney, *The Mysticism of Saint Augustine: Re-Reading the Confessions* (London: Routledge, 2005), 15–16.

74. Samuel Angus, "The Sources of the First Ten Books of Augustine's *De Civitate Dei*" (PhD diss., Princeton University, 1906), 240–41; Peter Brown, *Augustine of Hippo: A Biography* (Berkley: University of California Press, 2000), 93–107; Laela Zwollo, *St. Augustine and Plotinus: The Human Mind as Image of the Divine* (Leiden: Brill, 2018).

75. Gerald Bonner, *St Augustine of Hippo: Life and Controversies* (Atlanta: Canterbury, 1986), 194.

76. See a systematic discussion of Augustine's view of evil in G.R. Evans, *Augustine on Evil* (Cambridge: Cambridge University Press, 1990).

composed of matter or darkness[77]—Neoplatonism, which the Bishop of Hippo later adopted, claimed that evil was simply the absence of good, that is, a form of ontological incompleteness (*privatio boni*).[78] For example, a "bad cow" lacks any positive quality of evil, but simply does not give milk. This view was taken over by Christians like Augustine to explain the existence of both evil in the world, as well as God's pronouncement on his creation in Genesis 1 that it was "very good."[79]

For Plotinus and the other Neoplatonists of late antiquity, reality was understood as a cosmic hierarchy moving from being beyond being downward to mere being, and finally down further to nothingness.[80] At the top of the cosmic hierarchy was the "One" (*Monad*), the very ground of being itself. The One is properly speaking not a being, but rather transcends all categories of being. It is a being beyond being, in which all temporal and derivative being participates in order to possess its reality.[81] The One was so filled with a plenitude of reality that it emanated (*aporrhoe*)[82] out from itself "Mind" (*Nous*), a lower and inferior copy of the One.[83] This Mind then emanated the world-soul and the material world.[84] Although trapped in the world of sense experience, humans possessed reason and free will. Humanity was therefore capable of re-orienting itself away from its desires for the fleeting goods of the temporal world to the source of being. Since all temporal being moves out from the eternal ground of being in a kind of fall, the goal of rational beings should be to reorient

---

77. Jeffrey Burton Russell, *Satan: The Early Christian Tradition* (Ithaca: Cornell University Press, 1981), 163–64.

78. Dmitri Nikulin, *Neoplatonism in Late Antiquity* (Oxford: Oxford University Press, 2019), 194–95.

79. Augustine, *Confessions*, 7.11–3; NPNF¹, 1:110–11.

80. See lengthy discussion in Geoffrey Scott Bowe, *Plotinus and the Platonic Metaphysical Hierarchy* (New York: Global Scholarly Publication, 2003).

81. Plotinus, *The Enneads*, 6.9; Plotinus, *The Six Enneads*, trans. Stephen McKenna and B. S. Page (Chicago: Encyclopedia Britannica, 1984), 353–60. See John Rist, "Plotinus and Christian Philosophy," in *The Cambridge Companion to Plotinus*, ed. Lloyd P. Gerson (Cambridge: Cambridge University Press, 1996), 386–414.

82. Plotinus, *The Enneads*, 5.4; Plotinus, *The Six Enneads*, 226–28.

83. Plotinus, *The Enneads*, 5.1.7; Plotinus, *The Six Enneads*, 211–12.

84. Plotinus, *The Enneads*, 3.4.1; Plotinus, *The Six Enneads*, 97–100.

themselves from the inauthenticity of temporality and return (*henosis*) to the supreme reality of the One (*exitus-reditus*).[85]

Augustine took over this scheme and adapted it to Christian theology.[86] Augustine held to what might be referred to as a downward causality. God, who is an intelligible spirit, is at the top of the causal hierarchy, human and angelic souls hold an intermediate position, and finally, at the bottom level is matter. Entities at the bottom of the hierarchy are incapable of acting upon entities higher in the hierarchy.[87] Moreover, entities lower in the cosmic hierarchy must know their position and subordinate themselves to entities higher in the cosmic hierarchy. Ultimately, the true end of all things is God himself, who is the ground and exemplary cause of all being.[88]

For Augustine then, sin is fundamentally thought of under the heading of egoistic pride (*superbia*)[89] and misdirected desire (*concupiscence*).[90] Since evil is privation, the ultimate cause and result of sin is non-being.[91] Similar to Plato in the *Phaedrus*, Augustine thinks of humans are primarily desiring creatures. That is to say, humanity's ethical activities as directed by our desire for being.[92] Plato spoke of this motivating force as a kind of *eros*. In the *Phaedrus*, Socrates posits that the erotic love is really our misdirected desire for the eternal form of the Good, from whose presence we were exiled in a pre-temporal fall of the soul from eternity into time.Erotically desiring beautiful bodies who remind us of the form of the Good (the form of the Beautiful participates in the form of the Good), humans come to desire the shadow in the place of the real thing.[93] Plato then develops (for want of a better term) an "eschatology" wherein human desire may be redirected away from the unsatisfying ephemeral beauty

85. Plotinus, *The Enneads*, 3.8; Plotinus, *The Six Enneads*, 129–36.

86. Chad Tyler Gerber, *The Spirit of Augustine's Early Theology: Contextualizing Augustine's Pneumatology* (London: Routledge, 2012), 13–24.

87. Augustine, *City of God*, 5.9; NPNF1, 2:90–92. See Phillip Cary, *Outward Signs: The Powerlessness of External Things in Augustine's Thought* (Oxford: Oxford University Press, 2008), 6–8.

88. Augustine, *City of God*, 11.16; NPNF1, 2:214.

89. Augustine, *City of God*, 14.12–14; NPNF1, 2:272–74.

90. Augustine, *City of God*, 14.16; NPNF1, 2:275–76.

91. Augustine, *Confessions*, 7.11–13; NPNF1, 1:110–11.

92. Lewis Ayres, "Augustine on Redemption," in *A Companion to Augustine*, ed. Mark Vessey (Oxford: Wiley-Blackwell, 2012), 417.

93. Plato, *Phaedrus* 249d–e; in Plato, *Complete Works*, ed. by John M. Cooper (Indianapolis: Hackett, 1997), 527.

of sexual encounters and back to the eternal.[94] Human faculties are compared to a winged chariot, whose horses are trained to move upward toward the heavenly world of the form of the Good.[95]

Augustine replaced Platonic *eros* with what Anders Nygren famously called the "*Caritas* Synthesis."[96] *Caritas* (love) is according to Nygren a synthesis of elements of the New Testament's disinterested and spontaneous *agape* and Platonic *eros*. Humans are made to enjoy God for his own sake,[97] not because he is the self-centered longing of their hearts as in Plato's conception. Nevertheless, in agreement with Plato, Augustine held that the fundamental problem with humanity is its love of things temporal instead of eternal. In the state of sin, humans order their desires toward things that are not God, especially themselves.[98] It is important to note at this point that unlike Paul (Rom 14:23), and later Luther, Augustine follows Plato in seeing love as the primary basis of the divine-human relationship and not faith.[99]

For Augustine wrong love is inevitably connected with the supreme vice, pride. Pride means making oneself the supreme object of ordered love within the cosmic hierarchy, when such a position properly belongs to God. Such pride prevents humans as finite beings to return to the ground of their being (God) to be fully satisfied with his unchanging and immutable goodness: "The true objects of enjoyment, then, are the Father and the Son and the Holy Spirit, who are at the same time the Trinity, one Being, supreme above all, and common to all who enjoy Him."[100] Hence, human love for temporal beings is fundamentally in competition with their love of the eternal being of God.[101] Since sin is the love of lesser goods instead of the highest good (God) and therefore

---

94. Plato, *Phaedrus* 250a; Plato, *Complete Works,* 527–28.

95. Plato, *Phaedrus* 253d–254e; Plato, *Complete Works,* 530–31.

96. Anders Nygren, *Agape and Eros,* trans. Philip Watson (Philadelphia: Westminster, 1953), 464–558.

97. Augustine, *Confessions,* 1.1; NPNF1, 1:45.

98. Augustine, *City of God,* 12.8; NPNF1, 2:30–31. See Oliver O'Donovan, *The Problem of Self-Love in St. Augustine* (New Haven: Yale University Press, 1980).

99. John Rist, *Augustine Deformed: Love, Sin, and Freedom in the Western Moral Tradition* (Cambridge: Cambridge University Press, 2014), 62–83.

100. Augustine, *On Christian Doctrine,* 1.5; NPNF1, 2:524.

101. Augustine, *On Christian Doctrine,* 1.22; NPNF1, 2:527–28.

is inherently irrational,[102] anything that militates against reason's vision of
and enjoyment of the eternal good in favor of the temporal is necessarily
bad. Humans should therefore use (*uti*) temporal beings for sustenance
and reproduction, and refrain from enjoying them (*frui*) as if they are
ends in themselves: "For to enjoy a thing is to rest with satisfaction in it
for its own sake. To use, on the other hand, is to employ whatever means
are at one's disposal to obtain what one desires, if it is a proper object of
desire; for an unlawful use ought rather to be called an abuse."[103]

As a result, the desire for all earthly things, especially sex, becomes a
problem. Although it is often said that Augustine's negative preoccupa-
tion with sex was the result of his youthful indiscretions, this misses the
larger reality of his Christian-Platonic worldview. Indeed, when examined
closely, Augustine's youthful sexual dalliances and his later relationship
with his unnamed mistress appear trite by modern standards. Augustine
admits that he lived with his mistress for nearly a decade as a common-law
wife to whom he was faithful while raising a son.[104] Moreover, although
celibacy was certainly a prized ideal in the early church, Christian clergy
and bishops regularly married in late antiquity.[105] That all Christians did
not share Augustine's negative attitude to sex is clearly demonstrated by
his late debate with Julian of Eclanum.[106]

Hence, from a strictly Christian moral standpoint (1 Cor 7:38) there
was no particular reason why marriage and lawful sexual activity was not
an option open to Augustine. Nevertheless, Augustine chose celibacy and
insisted on the problematic nature of all sexual desire. In light of this, it
would be more accurate to see Augustine's negative attitude toward sex
as being a result of his desire to be a Christian-Platonic philosopher who
sought the eternal over the distraction of the temporal.[107] In discussing
the matter in his *Soliloquies* (written just before his baptism) Augustine

---

102. Augustine, *On Free Choice of the Will*, 1.16; Augustine, *On Free Choice of the Will*, trans. Thomas
Williams (Indianapolis: Hackett, 1993), 27.

103. Augustine, *On Christian Doctrine*, 1.4; NPNF1, 2:53.

104. Augustine, *Confessions*, 4.2; NPNF1, 1:68–69.

105. William Philipps, *Clerical Celibacy: The Heritage* (London: Continuum, 2004), 81–96.

106. Gerald Bonner, "Pelagianism and Augustine" in *Doctrinal Diversity: Varieties of Early
Christianity: A Collection of Scholarly Essays*, ed. Everett Ferguson (New York: Garland, 1999), 203–4.

107. Gary Wills, *Augustine's Confessions: A Biography* (Princeton: Princeton University Press,
2011), 59–62.

comments that he is committed to giving up sex completely in order to purely pursue the life of the mind.[108]

Hence, within Augustine's Christian-Platonic framework, much as in the cosmic hierarchy the baser and more material is to be hierarchically ordered to the greater and more spiritual, so too the human heart should be ordered to the eternal and spiritual, and not to enjoyment of the temporal.[109] Indeed, in the pre-lapsarian state, the baser desires did not interfere with the exercise of reason. Adam and Eve would not have enjoyed or even desired sex, but instead would have engaged in the sex-act purely for the rational purposes of reproduction.[110] The orderly nature of the cosmos—where the material was subordinate to the spiritual—would have been reproduced in the human heart as a microcosm of the macrocosm. Adam and his bride would have never burned with desire for one another but would have simply called their genitals to attention by an act of will, engaged in reproductive act without pleasure, and deactivated their genitals just as easily.[111]

Augustine saw his own struggle to quiet his sexual desires and live an unadulterated life of reason to be a symptom of the fall. Sinful desire which interferes with reason (*concupiscence*) is a punishment for sin.[112] Just as creation is in revolt against the creator, so too the desires of the fallen person are at war with the rational and spiritual centers of the self: "In short, to say all in a word, what but disobedience was the punishment of disobedience in that sin? For what else is man's misery but his own disobedience to himself, so that in consequence of his not being willing to do what he could do, he now wills to do what he cannot?"[113]

Even without sin, created being is inherently unstable.[114] Creation comes from nothingness and has a tendency of drifting back into

---

108. Augustine, *Soliloquies*, 1.17; NPNF1, 7:543.

109. Steven Schafer, *Marriage, Sex, and Procreation: Contemporary Revisions to Augustine's Theology of Marriage* (Eugene, OR: Pickwick, 2019), 28–29.

110. Augustine, *City of God*, 14.24; NPNF1, 2:280–81.

111. Augustine, *City of God*, 14.24; NPNF1, 2:280–81.

112. Timo Nisula, *Augustine and the Functions of Concupiscence* (Leiden: Brill, 2012), 258–59.

113. Augustine, *City of God*, 14.15; NPNF1, 2:275.

114. Augustine, *City of God*, 12.15; NPNF1, 2:235–36.

nothingness.[115] For this reason, humans and angels are in need of grace to prop them up even in their state of integrity.[116] It is only by receiving a special grace can humans and angels not drift back into nothingness through falling into sin.[117] In Augustine's thought—much as in later Roman Catholicism—although "grace" (*gratia*) certainly comes by God's undeserved favor (i.e., the Pauline *charis*), it is primarily defined as supernatural assistance and self-communication to his rational creatures in order that they might achieve higher and greater degrees of moral regeneration.[118]

Even with God's supernatural assistance, humans in the state of integrity were capable of using their free will to turn away from God and fall into sin. Nevertheless, unlike Origen, who was at least read by some of his critics as envisioning the possibility of a second Fall in heaven,[119] Augustine thought that humans would finally reach a stage of existence whereby through a supreme grace they would achieve the state of confirmation in the good.[120] As a result, they would remain eternally in fellowship with God and would cease to be capable of falling away from the good: "[The redeemed will have] no power to sin, and neither shall have any power to choose death; but the ... [redeemed] shall live truly and happily in eternal life."[121] Augustine divided human existence into four stages: able to sin or not to sin (prelapsarian), incapable of avoiding sin (post-lapsarian), capable to imperfectly do the good (post-conversion), and confirmed in the good (heaven).[122]

Matching the redeemed rational creature's confirmation in the good is the eternal confirmation in evil for the damned.[123] According to Augustine, God's fallen angels had already reached the state of being permanently confirmed in evil, just as the good angels had been permanently confirmed

---

115. Paul Blowers, *Drama of the Divine Economy: Creator and Creation in Early Christian Theology and Piety* (Oxford: Oxford University Press, 2012), 298.

116. Augustine, *Enchiridion on Faith, Hope, and Love*, 106; NPNF1, 3:271.

117. Augustine, *City of God*, 14.2; NPNF1, 2:282.

118. Augustine, *On the Grace of Christ*, 1.15–16; NPNF1, 5:223–24.

119. Brian Daley, *Hope of the Early Church: A Handbook of Patristic Eschatology* (Grand Rapids: Baker Academic, 2002), 237.

120. Augustine, *City of God*, 11:13; NPNF1, 2:212–13.

121. Augustine, *Enchiridion on Faith, Hope, and Love*, 111; NPNF1, 3:273.

122. Augustine, *Enchiridion on Faith, Hope, and Love*, 118; NPNF1, 3:275.

123. Augustine, *Enchiridion on Faith, Hope, and Love*, 111–13; NPNF1, 3:273.

in the good.[124] After the eschaton, unbelieving humans would experience
the same fate.[125] In contrast to humans, the angelic confirmation in the
good or evil was almost immediate.[126] The good angels' adherence to God
was a result of God's gracious gift of perseverance to them. Conversely,
God had denied both Satan and his evil angels the gift of perseverance and
as a result they fell away.[127] In establishing the human race, God sought
to create the humans in order to replenish the number of the angels and
restore the heavenly city's mystic harmony.[128] When speaking of his doctrine of predestination, Augustine argued that the rationale behind God's
choice of the specific number of the elect was conditioned by the need to
replace the number of the lost angels.[129]

In *The City of God*, Augustine speaks of two cities at war in history:
the city of God and the city of man.[130] In keeping with his Platonic claim
that love is the fundamental orienting faculty of the self, the Bishop of
Hippo posits that the distinction between the two cities lies in the fact
that the city of God is centered on the love of God, whereas the city of
man love is centered on pride and self-love.[131] The origins of the city of
man lie with the fall of the angels,[132] whose sin spilled over into the fall
of humanity through the temptation of Satan.[133] Augustine argues that
the existence of the two cities and the strife between good and evil in
human history is in fact part of a larger divine plan to beautify the universe. Speech that plays with the dissonance of differing words is more
beautiful. Hence, God permitted evil and the existence of two cities in

---

124. Russell, *Satan: The Early Christian Tradition*, 207–8.

125. Augustine, *City of God*, 11:13; NPNF1, 2:212–13.

126. Augustine, *City of God*, 11:13–15; NPNF1, 2:212–14.

127. Augustine, *City of God*, 14.27; NPNF1, 2:282; Russell, *Satan: The Early Christian Tradition*, 211–12.

128. Augustine, *Enchiridion on Faith, Hope, and Love*, 29; NPNF1, 3:2247. See discussion in Elizabeth Klein, *Augustine's Theology of Angels* (Cambridge: Cambridge University Press, 2018), 93–94.

129. Roy Wesley Battenhouse, *A Companion to the Study of St. Augustine* (Grand Rapids: Baker, 1979), 349.

130. See Gerard O'Daly, *Augustine's City of God: A Reader's Guide* (Oxford: Clarendon, 1999). See summary and discussion in: Matthew Levering, *The Theology of Augustine: An Introductory Guide to His Most Important Works* (Grand Rapids: Baker Academic, 2013), 113–50.

131. Augustine, *City of God*, 11.1; NPNF1, 2:205.

132. Augustine, *City of God*, 11.11, 13–15; NPNF1, 2:211, 212–14

133. Augustine, *City of God*, 14.11–13; NPNF1, 2:271–74

history because the contrast created by the conflict between good and
evil is beautiful to behold.[134]

As a result of falling into sin, Adam and Eve were derailed in their
movement toward confirmation in the good. Although they did not lose
their individual agency, their ability to choose between good and evil was
destroyed.[135] This incapacity for the good was transmitted to all their progeny, since Augustine claimed that all humans had been present in Adam.
He based this judgment on the Old Latin version of the Bible's (*Vetus
Latina*) rendering of Romans 5:12 as "in whom all sinned [i.e., in Adam]"
(*in quo omnes peccavarunt*) rather than the original Greek "because all
sinned" (*ep' ho pantes hemarton*).[136]

Because of the loss of divine grace, humans ceased to be able not to
sin (*non posse non peccare*). Humans now cannot help but sin, but not
because they are being coerced by an outside force.[137] Rather, as creatures of desire they do what they desire, namely, they engage in sin. Fallen
humans love earthly things to the exclusion of eternal things and therefore cannot help but idolatrously cling to things that are not God.[138] Left
to their own devices, humans constitute a "mass of perdition" (*massa
perditionis*) incapable of accepting divine grace and achieving salvation
by their own works or merits.[139]

Indeed, in this fallen state humans are not merely partially sinful, but
totally and completely. Everything human beings do after the fall is sinful:
"The free will taken captive does not avail for anything except for sin."[140]
Of course, in individual external deeds, people can certainly behave in
ways that make them virtuous in the eyes of others. Nevertheless, from
God's perspective the intention behind any action colors its moral status.
A greedy person who does not rob someone because of his fear of the

134. Augustine, *City of God*, 11.18; NPNF1, 2:214–15.

135. Augustine, *City of God*, 14.15; NPNF1, 2:274–75.

136. Augustine, *Sermons*, 294.15; Augustine, *Sermons 273–305*, trans. Edmund Hill (Hyde Park,
NY: New City, 1994), 190. See Bonner, "Augustine on Romans 5:12," 242–47.

137. Augustine, *On Nature and Grace*, 57–58; NPNF1, 5:140–41.

138. Augustine, *Confessions*, 2.5; NPNF1, 1:57–58.

139. Augustine, *Enchiridion on Faith, Hope, and Love*, 25–27; NPNF1, 3:246–47.

140. Augustine, *A Treatise Against Two Letters of the Pelagians*, 3.24.8; NPNF1, 5:414.

loss of even greater amounts of money cannot be considered virtuous.[141] Likewise, without an inner faith and love of God as the supreme good, every action taken by human beings is sinful since it does not possess the correct motivation of expressing love for God. Only by acting out of the supreme love of God can our works be deemed good and not totally sinful.[142]

---

141. Augustine, *Against Julian*, 4.21; Augustine, *Against Julian*, trans. Matthew Schumacher (Washington, D.C.: Catholic University of America Press, 1957), 186–87.

142. Augustine, *Against Julian*, 4.21–25; Augustine, *Against Julian*, 186–90.

CHAPTER 6

Augustine on Justification:

The Origins of the Augustinian Dilemma

B ecause of Augustine's belief in the morally incapacitating nature of original sin, the Bishop of Hippo invariably ran headlong into a conflict with the more optimistic anthropology promoted by the British ascetic teacher Pelagius. In the late fourth century, Pelagius migrated from Britain to Rome, where he became famous by teaching a brand of moral rigorism reminiscent of the North African Fathers and in harmony with the nascent ascetic movements that had emerged in late antiquity.[1]

Based on our fragmentary sources, it appears that Pelagius asserted that Adam and Eve had actually only harmed themselves by falling into sin. They had spread sin to their children only through providing a bad example, not through transmission by generation. Indeed, Pelagius did not think of Adam and Christ as elect representational persons, but as bad and good examples that humans by their free will could follow or not follow.[2] Adam's children had therefore not inherited any original guilt. Although humans are guilty because of their own individual sin and need Christ's atonement, they remain good by nature and are therefore not morally deformed by the fall. Rather, humans still possess free will and

---

1. Richard Fletcher, *Who's Who in Roman Britain and Anglo-Saxon England* (London: Shepheard-Walwyn, 2002), 11–12.

2. Pelagius, *Commentary on St Paul's Epistle to the Romans*, trans. Theodore de Bruyn (Oxford: Clarendon, 1993), 92–95.

can establish their own relationship with God through obedience to the divine commands.[3]

There are a number of obvious theological concerns lying behind Pelagius's teaching. As noted earlier, early Christian apologists generally sought to exalt the claims of created nature (even after the fall) as a way of counteracting the Gnostic assertion that creation was evil. Beginning with Irenaeus, free will theodicy was a way of pushing back against the idea that there was an evil god behind the damaged creation by shifting blame to humans and angels' misuse of free will. Pelagius appears to have inherited this tradition and drove its logic to its natural conclusion.[4] Conversely, many of Augustine's opponents highlighted his former life in the Manichaean sect (which taught that the material world was evil) as a way of explaining his belief in the moral impotence of humans after the fall.[5] In their minds, Augustine's radical doctrine of original sin was in effect a claim that created nature was evil. Since Augustine taught that evil was a privation of the good and not a substance, as well as that the origin of evil lies in human and angelic free will, this was obviously not a fair interpretation of his position.

Beyond this, some contemporary scholars have stressed that for Pelagius there was a less clear contrast between nature and grace than there was in Augustine.[6] Indeed, one reading of Pelagius might be that since nature (which includes free will and the knowledge of the law) is a gift of God, God's sovereignty in salvation is by no means compromised by a high view of human moral agency.[7] Free will's ability to establish and make progress in the divine-human relationship is a gift of God, albeit one granted by the gift of nature and not a special intervention of divine grace.[8]

---

3. See summary in Pier Franco Beatrice, *The Transmission of Sin: Augustine and the Pre-Augustinian Sources*, trans. Adam Kamesar (Oxford: Oxford University Press, 2013), 15–37. Also see Brinley Rees, *Pelagius: A Reluctant Heretic* (Woodbridge: Boydell, 1988).

4. See similar argument in Ali Bonner, *The Myth of Pelagianism* (Oxford: Oxford University Press, 2018), 29–196.

5. Gerald Bonner, "Pelagianism and Augustine" 203–4.

6. Stephen Duffy, *The Dynamics of Grace: Perspectives in Theological Anthropology* (Eugene, OR: Wipf & Stock, 2007), 84–90.

7. De Bruyn, *Pelagius's Commentary*, 65, 81.

8. Duffy, *Dynamics of Grace*, 84–90.

Against Pelagius's rejection of original sin, Augustine taught that God's grace was the sole cause of salvation.[9] Nevertheless, the Bishop of Hippo also stressed that salvation was a life-long process that did not occur without the grace-induced activation and cooperation of human free will.[10] Whether or not Augustine could actually maintain the doctrine of free will in light of his premises remains a point of debate among contemporary scholars.[11] That being said, Augustine sincerely affirmed that he held that there was a grace-shaped human cooperation in salvation, which he broke down into several stages.

According to the mature Augustine, since humans were radically damaged by the power of sin, God's grace must act on the sinner so that they may be disposed to begin the process of salvation. Augustine called this kind of divine grace "prevenient grace" (*gratia preveniens*).[12] Prevenient grace preceded all conversion and prepared humans for conversion. Beyond this, operative and cooperative grace (*gratia operata, gratia cooperata*) were also necessary.[13] Operative grace was the grace whereby humans are converted by a supernatural act of God. Since God did not destroy human freedom but augmented and elevated it in his act of conversion and regeneration, cooperative grace was also necessary as a means of giving the individual human the desire and ability to cooperate with God in the process of salvation.

This formulation of the nature of grace partially clarifies Augustine's belief that divine monergism did not contradict the reality of human free will (*liberum arbitrium*). The key is that for Augustine doing the good is true freedom, and not being able to spontaneously will either good or evil (*libertas indifferentiae*).[14] Therefore fallen humans had a captive will (*liberum arbitrium captivatum*) and not a truly free will. In a sense, fallen humans therefore have *liberum arbitrium* (willing what they want to will),

---

9. Jeff Nicoll, *Augustine's Problem: Impotence and Grace* (Eugene, OR: Resource Publications, 2016), 64.

10. Pereira, *Augustine of Hippo and Martin Luther*, 258.

11. See Eleonore Stump, "Augustine on Free Will," in *The Cambridge Companion to Augustine*, ed. Eleonore Stump and Norman Kretzmann (Cambridge: Cambridge University Press, 2001), 124–47; N. P. Williams, *The Grace of God* (London: Longmans, 1930), 19–43.

12. Augustine, *A Treatise Against Two Letters of the Pelagians*, 2.21; NPNF1, 5:400–401.

13. McGrath, *Iustia Dei*, 55–56.

14. McGrath, *Iustia Dei*, 42.

but not *libertas* (willing the good).[15] Hence, the Bishop of Hippo held to what is often called a "compatibilist" view of free will,[16] rather than "libertarian free will."[17] Therefore, if God communicated to the human heart the desire to do the good, humans would become more authentically free in doing the good that God had placed within them by his grace. Augustine was therefore able to conceptualize human cooperation with divine grace as simultaneously a free act of the human subject and one wholly determined by God.[18]

Such a conception of human agency and divine grace invariably led Augustine to revive aspects of Paul's doctrine of predestination (Rom 8–9). Irenaeus and many of the rest of the ante-Nicene Fathers simply ignored or creatively reinterpreted Paul on this point. Instead, they preferred to see free will and grace working together, along with predestination as mere divine prescience.[19] Indeed, they very well might have been allergic to this doctrine because, as we saw, the Gnostic tradition taught a form of predestination on the basis of a deterministic conception of differing human capacities to achieve salvation.[20] Nevertheless, it should be stressed that, as we have already seen, the Gnostic form of predestination was one of nature and not of grace. This makes it qualitatively different from the predestinarian teaching of Paul or Augustine.

In light of Augustine's teaching that humans are incapacitated by sin and it is only by the intervention of God's supernatural grace that they are converted and justified,[21] the question naturally arises as to why some come to faith and not others.[22] The difference in human fortunes could not lie in human free will since none had the ability to cooperate with salvation apart from God's grace. The answer for Augustine was

---

15. McGrath, *Iustia Dei*, 41–43.

16. See Phillip Cary, *The Meaning of Protestant Theology: Luther, Augustine, and the Gospel that Gives Us Christ* (Grand Rapids: Baker Academic, 2019), 95.

17. Stump, "Augustine on Free Will," 168. Stump makes this comment on a number of Augustine's writings.

18. See Phillip Cary, "Augustinian Compatibilism and the Doctrine of Election," in *Augustine and Philosophy*, ed. Philip Cary, John Doody, and Kim Paffenroth (Lanham, MD: Lexington, 2010), 79–102.

19. George Park Fisher, *History of Christian Doctrine* (Edinburgh: T&T Clark, 1896), 165.

20. Henry Chadwick, *The Early Church* (New York: Penguin, 1993), 38.

21. Augustine, *On the Predestination of the Saints*, 13; NPNF1, 5:504–5.

22. Augustine, *On the Predestination of the Saints*, 11; NPNF1, 5:503–4.

to be found in the fact that God has predestined some to salvation, but not others.[23] All who are baptized receive the gift of the remission of sins and regeneration (i.e. justification).[24] Nevertheless, much like the fallen angels, not all receive the gift of perseverance (that is, the ability to maintain their faith until the end) and therefore many ultimately fall away.[25] Indeed, believers can never be certain that they possess the gift of perseverance and must perpetually pray for it—indeed, that they must pray for it shows it to be a special divine gift.[26] Ultimately, Christians must labor their whole lives to live a morally upright existence and maintain their faith to find final salvation.[27] It should be noted that Augustine did not explicitly teach a doctrine of double predestination as Calvin did later on. Rather, God elected those whom he wished to save and simply left the rest of humanity to their sin and its logical consequences.[28]

Although to many, Augustine's teaching initially sounds very much like that of Paul and Luther, it would be a mistake to not take into account some significant differences.[29] Notably, when Augustine speaks of justification, he describes it as being "made righteous" rather than being "declared righteous": "For what else does the phrase being justified signify than being made righteous—by Him, of course, who justifies the ungodly man, that he may become a godly one instead?"[30] As noted earlier, from this it also followed that "grace" was not only divine favor, but a divine power that regenerated the sinner.[31] Once God "made" the sinner righteous not only by forgiving their sins, but also by communicating

---

23. Augustine, *On the Gift of Perseverance*, 35; NPNF1, 5:539.

24. Friedrich Loofs, *Leitfaden zum Studium der Dogmengeschichte* (Halle: Niemeyer, 1906), 309–13.

25. Augustine, *On the Gift of Perseverance*, 58; NPNF1, 5:549.

26. Augustine, *On the Gift of Perseverance*, 16; NPNF1, 5:541.

27. Augustine, *City of God*, 11.12; NPNF1, 2:212.

28. Larry Sharp, "The Doctrine of Grace in Calvin and Augustine," *Evangelical Quarterly* 52 (1980): 89.

29. See Alister McGrath, "Forerunners of the Reformation? A Critical Examination of the Evidence for Precursors of the Reformation Doctrines of Justification," *Harvard Theological Review* 75, no. 2 (1982): 220.

30. See Augustine, *On the Spirit and the Letter*, 45; NPNF1, 5:102. See lengthy summary in V. H. Drecoll, *Die Entstehung der Gnadenlehre Augustins* (Tübingen: Mohr Siebeck, 1999); J. Lössl, *Intellectus Gratiae: Die erkenntnistheoretische und hermeneutische Dimension der Gnadenlehre Augustins von Hippo* (Leiden: Brill, 1997); David Wright, "Justification in Augustine," in *Justification in Perspective*, ed. Bruce McCormack (Grand Rapids: Baker Academic, 2006), 55–72.

31. Augustine, *On the Grace of Christ*, 26; NPNF1, 5:227–28. J.B. Mozley, *A Treatise on the Augustinian Doctrine of Predestination* (London: John Murray, 1855), 157–59.

the ability through baptismal regeneration to merit their salvation in a positive sense, Augustine affirmed that: "We are to understand, then, that man's good deserts are themselves the gift of God, so that when these obtain the recompense of eternal life, it is simply grace given for grace."[32] Faith—which was identified as belief in the propositions of the faith—according to Augustine, was a necessary prerequisite for salvation not because it grasped the promise of Christ (i.e., the position of the Protestant Reformers), but because believers had to know who God was before they would be made capable of directing their works of love toward him.[33]

As should be clear, Augustine's understanding of justification is both incongruous with the later Protestant Reformers, as well the reading of the Bible that we offered in the first few chapters.[34] This raises the question as to how the Bishop of Hippo arrived at his distinctive understanding of this central theological issue. Here several reasons may be suggested. One reason lies simply in the fact that Augustine by his own admission was unskilled in Greek[35] and was wholly reliant on the inferior biblical translations of the Old Latin edition (*Vetus Latina*), and late in his career, the Vulgate.[36] In both translations, the Greek word that Paul had used to describe justification *dikaioō* (meaning to "judge righteous")[37] was incorrectly translated as the Latin *justificare* (to "make righteous").[38] As we will see, since the later medieval and post-Tridentine church both relied on the inaccurate Vulgate, a similar error was transmitted to later Roman Catholicism.

Other factors influencing Augustine's view of justification have largely to do with the Bishop's intellectual framework. Returning to Harnack's earlier description of the three intellectual streams that converge in Augustine (Neoplatonic, Pauline, North African), the inheritance of the penitential theology and concept of merit in North African church is a clearly an

32. Augustine, *Enchiridion on Faith, Hope, and Love*, 107; NPNF1, 3:272.
33. John Burnaby, *Amor Dei* (London: Hodder and Stoughton, 1938), 79–81.
34. Hägglund, *History of Theology*, 138–89.
35. Augustine, *Confessions* 1.13–14; NPNF1, 1:51–52.
36. McGrath, *Iustia Dei*, 24–25.
37. Ziesler, *Meaning of Righteousness in Paul*, 48.
38. McGrath, *Iustia Dei*, 12–16, 46–47; Wright, "Justification in Augustine," 72.

influence on the Bishop of Hippo's thinking. Hence, although Augustine very clearly learned from Paul the principle of *sola gratia*, he still operated with the North African theory of merit and penance. Therefore, Augustine's solution to the problem of justification was seemingly to combine the Pauline and North African paradigms together. Humans were wholly dependent on divine grace for salvation. Nevertheless, the form that that grace took was divine assistance in meriting salvation before the divine court of judgment. As we shall see, in later centuries this same line of reasoning became the standard Catholic view of justification, albeit in increasingly complex forms.[39]

On this last point, it is important to pause for a moment and consider the seeming internal incoherence of Augustine's view of justification. This is inevitable in that he sought to combine the incongruous Pauline and North African theological traditions that (according at least to the reading we have offered above) suggest significant different answers to the question of salvation.

Perhaps one interesting way of elucidating these tensions might be to draw upon a model of different theological construals of the doctrine of justification as used by the nineteenth century liberal Protestant theologian Albrecht Ritschl in his monumental three-volume work on the doctrine of justification, *Christliche Lehre von der Rechtfertigung und Versöhnung*.[40] Although Ritschl's model is imperfect, it possesses much heuristic value in categorizing different systematic explications of justification. Utilizing Kantian philosophical terminology, Ritschl argued that one can classify doctrines of justification in the history of Christian thought in two main categories: analytic and synthetic.[41]

---

39. McGrath, *Iustia Dei*, 277–340.

40. See Albrecht Ritschl, *Die christliche Lehre von der Rechtfertigung und Versöhnung*, 3 vols. (Bonn: Adolph Marcus, 1870–1874). See English translation, which will be referenced throughout this chapter and which encompass only the first and third volumes: Albrecht Ritschl, *A Critical History of the Christian Doctrine of Justification and Reconciliation*, trans. John Black (Edinburgh: T&T Clark, 1872); Ritschl, *The Christian Doctrine of Justification and Reconciliation: The Positive Development of the Doctrine*, trans. H. R. Macintosh and A. B. Macauley (Edinburgh: T&T Clark, 1900).

41. Ritschl, *Christian Doctrine of Justification*, 38, 81, 90, 97, 217.

First, there are theologies that make justification into an "analytic judgement."[42] Analytic judgments are judgments where the predicate is contained in the subject: "All bachelors are unmarried." Hence, in theologies of justification that are analytic, God's judgment affirms what the redeemed already are: "All who are obedient to the law are saved." They depend on recognizing that the sinner is already righteous.[43]

Second, there are theological systems that make justification into a "synthetic judgment."[44] Synthetic judgments are ones in which the predicate is not contained in the subject but must be made by applying a definition to a contingent set of circumstances: "Jim is a bachelor." Theologies of justification that are synthetic make righteousness dependent on God's action adding something to the empirical reality of the sinner through his judgment of external reality: "Jim is righteous because God has given him righteousness through his positive judgment." In other words, justification is dependent on God's decision to grant a righteous status to a sinner.[45]

Seen from the perspective of Ritschl's (albeit imperfect) categorization, Augustine's position contains an element of both an analytic and synthetic view of justification. From the North African tradition, the Bishop of Hippo picks up the notion of merit as a necessary condition of salvation. The North African concept of merit is analytic, since it presupposes that God is in some sense prompted to judge the sinner righteous based on analyzing their empirical state. Put simply, the merits or demerits of humanity causes God's positive or negative judgment. From Paul, Augustine absorbed the idea of *sola gratia* and the attending doctrine of predestination. This would presuppose a synthetic theory of justification. If, as Augustine states, one is predestined to salvation, then merit ceases to have a purpose. That is to say, if one is elect, then God has made his decision about the believer apart from merit. As a result, merit is meaningless because it ceases to have the function assigned to it by the North African tradition of prompting God's positive judgment in one's favor.

---

42. Immanuel Kant, *The Critique of Pure Reason, introduction*, 4; Immanuel Kant, *The Critique of Pure Reason, The Critique of Practical Reason, and The Critique of Judgment*, trans. Thomas Kingmill Abbott (Chicago: Encyclopedia Britannica, 1984), 16–17.

43. For example: Ritschl, *Christian Doctrine of Justification*, 90.

44. Kant, *The Critique of Pure Reason, introduction*, 4; Kant, *Critique of Pure Reason*, 16–17.

45. For example: Ritschl, *Christian Doctrine of Justification*, 38, 80–82.

This brings us finally to the potential influence of Neoplatonism on Augustine's view of reconciliation and redemption. Perhaps one way of reading the apparent tension between analytic and synthetic motifs in Augustine's doctrine of justification is that it might be seen as a necessary move within the intellectual framework of Neoplatonic ontology. That is to say, if, as Augustine's Christian Neoplatonism claimed, God is the embodiment of the good (*summum bonum*) and if goodness is identical with ontological completeness, God cannot very well recognize something as being ontologically complete when it is not. From this it follows that God's election or imputation of sinners could never be the sole basis of redemption. In a word, sinners (i.e., the ontologically incomplete) cannot be recognized as righteous (ontologically complete) when they simply are not. Doing so would militate against God's nature as the supremely good one, who desires all things that are ontologically similar to his good nature. Because God embodies goodness and being, he necessarily loves being. He cannot very well love non-being since by definition it cannot be the object of love. In Augustine's conception, grace makes sinners righteous by augmenting their being to make them more ontologically complete and desirable. Hence, it could be argued that it is necessary to predestine the elect to salvation through regeneration and merit, because God could not maintain his faithfulness to his own nature as the supreme good otherwise.[46]

It should be observed that the Neoplatonic matrix within which Augustine conceptualized the problem of justification is probably the most powerful reason he deviated from the biblical understanding of justification. Indeed, from what we have seen already in our study regarding how extensively Augustine utilized Neoplatonic models in his thinking, it would appear that philosophical influences played an even more significant role than Augustine's unfamiliarity with the original languages of the Bible.

Incidentally, the philosophical background of the theologians of the early church (including Augustine) largely explains why much of the early church lost or ignored Paul's teaching. When confronted by the fact that

---

46. See similar argument in J. V. Fesko, *Justification: Understanding the Classic Reformed Doctrine* (Philipsburg, NJ: P&R, 2008), 13–14.

Paul's language for justification is purely forensic, Catholic apologists often object that the Greek Fathers who spoke the language of the original New Testament nevertheless still mostly developed sanative models of salvation. This defense of Catholic teaching does not ultimately deal with the linguistic issue (as we have seen, the evidence is overwhelming that Paul does speak of justification as a forensic act) and fails to take into consideration that certain Greek Fathers like John Chrysostom anticipate Reformation teaching on justification.[47] Nevertheless, more importantly, the aforementioned Catholic defense does not recognize that, much like Augustine, the Greek Fathers overwhelming worked with a Middle Platonic and Neoplatonic framework[48] that for the reasons outlined above made it exceedingly difficult to understand justification in the New Testament's eschatological and forensic terms in spite of their knowledge of koine Greek.

LANGUAGE, SACRAMENTS, AND PREDESTINATION

Augustine's conception of divine grace both correlates to and stands in some tension with his notion of the sacraments. Augustine's thinking on the sacraments and external signs in general was ultimately rooted in the Platonic tradition's ontology and philosophy of language. Sensible signs and sensible realities are in the Augustinian and Platonic tradition inherently inferior to intelligible and invisible realities.[49]

As we have already observed, in Plato and the subsequent Platonic tradition, just as the temporal world is constituted by inferior material copies of eternal forms, so too the descent of the human soul into the realm of matter represents a form of self-alienation and inferior existence. In the *Phaedrus*, Plato states that the human soul can only gradually be weaned off its attachment to material things and brought back to the ground of

---

47. See comments in John Chrysostom, *Commentary on Galatians*, 3:8; NPNF1, 13:26; Chrysostom, *Homilies on Genesis 18–45* (Washington, DC: Catholic University of America Press, 1990), 167; Chrysostom, *Homilies on the Epistle of Paul the Apostle to the Romans*, 8; NPNF1, 11:385–88.

48. John Marenbon, *Early Medieval Philosophy 480–1150: An Introduction* (London: Routledge, 2002), 13–18. Also see Andrew Louth, *The Origins of the Christian Mystical Tradition: From Plato to Denys* (Oxford: Oxford University Press, 2007).

49. Phillip Cary, *Outward Signs*, 3–6, 11–16, 87–121.

all being through an erotic desire for divine wisdom.[50] Plato explains that the human soul that has become a philosopher ascends back to the realm of the forms using the desires of the soul, which are compared to a chariot drawn by winged horses.[51] In such a case, the tragic fall from the pre-mundane world is overcome by a reversion to the origin, that is, a reversal of the tragic movement of degeneration from the original vision of the Good to the temporal and mutable copy.

Seen within this metaphysical framework, the Platonic conception of truth and language comes into clearer focus. Indeed, Plato's philosophical project begins in Socrates's hostility to the abuse of language and rhetoric as something that obscures truth, as had been the case with the Sophists.[52] Embedded in the *Phaedrus* and its discussion of personal eschatology and ethics, there is something of a brief excursus in which Plato recounts the myth of the invention of writing by the god Thoth in Egypt. Thoth tells the Pharaoh that writing is a wonderful gift, insofar as it will supplement memory and facilitate learning. Nevertheless, the ruler rejects this claim and instead insists that writing will allow people to appear wise but will not lead to a pure and authentic internalization of knowledge.[53]

In light of this, Socrates comments in the dialogue that human beings pre-existed in the realm of the forms prior to their earthly existence and has direct vision of the forms, without the admixture of language and sense-experience. Therefore, the external word teaches human beings nothing in regard to the reality of transcendental truth. All written words and the temporal entities they refer to are in fact derivative and inauthentic copies of the supreme truth that they already possess within their own hearts by way of intellectual vision.[54] At best, the philosopher may prompt this recollection (*anamnesis*) of the truth that is already known through the use of dialectic, but such conversation only gives rise to the growth of the seeds of knowledge that are already there.[55]

---

50. Plato, *Phaedrus*, 249d–257b; Plato, *Phaedrus* in Cooper, *Works of Plato*, 527–33.

51. Plato, *Phaedrus*, 246a–254e; Plato, *Phaedrus*, 524–32.

52. See David Corey, *The Sophists in Plato's Dialogues* (Albany: SUNY Press, 2015).

53. Plato, *Phaedrus*, 274b–275b; Plato, *Phaedrus* in Cooper, *Works of Plato*, 519–20.

54. Plato, *Phaedrus*, 275cb; Plato, *Phaedrus*, 520–21.

55. Plato, *Phaedrus*, 276e–277a; Plato, *Phaedrus*, 522.

It should be observed that Plato consistently conceptualizes this recollected knowledge in the form of an intellectual "vision" of the forms and ultimately the supreme reality of the Good.[56] Contrary to the biblical conception (John 10:27; Rom 10:17), hearing is a faculty inferior to seeing. Hence, just as the written word is a degeneration away from the spoken word, so too, the material world is a tragic falling away from the eternal and intelligible realm of the forms. All communication of truth in external language is likewise a falling away from the eternal truths that can only be recovered from the interior spiritual realm of the human mind.[57]

The French Post-Structuralist philosopher Jacques Derrida famously argued that Plato's discussion of writing in the *Phaedrus* showed an aversion to what he refers to as supplementarity.[58] By supplementarity, Derrida meant the signifier that aims at representing a particular reality. For example, the word "chair" signifies an actual entity known as a chair, while not being a chair. The word "chair" is therefore supplemental to actual chairs. The word "chair" is not the presence of the chair or even the exact repetition of the chair. The referent (actual chairs) lies behind the signifier (the word "chair"). According to Derrida, because of the influence of Plato there is a prejudice in Western thought against the supplemental signifier as something less authentic than the referent behind it.

In many respects, this critique works very well when applied to Plato. Plato sees language and text as inauthentically "representing" things, much as he sees the whole of the temporal world as inauthentically "representing" the archetypal realities in the realm of the forms. When we encounter a signifier (a word, or representation of an entity) we do not encounter the thing itself. As an incomplete representation of the original, such representation is "supplemental" to the original. From this, the implications for Plato's project are clear. If the supplementary signifier is merely derivative

---

56. Plato uses the analogy of sight for knowledge and of the sun for the form of the Good. See Plato, *The Republic*, 1127–32.

57. Peter Leithart, *Deep Comedy: Trinity, Tragedy, and Hope in Western Literature* (Moscow, ID: Canon, 2006), 76.

58. See Derrida's discussion of supplementarity in Jacques Derrida, *Of Grammatology*, trans. Gayatri Chakravorty Spivak (Baltimore: John Hopkins University Press, 1976); Derrida, *Writing and Difference*, trans. Alan Bass (London: Routledge, 1978), 97–192; Derrida, *Disseminations*, trans. Barbara Johnson (Chicago: University of Chicago Press, 1981), 63–171. See the excellent critique and the source of many of my developed thoughts here in Leithart, *Deep Comedy*, 73–95.

and inauthentic, it must necessarily obscure the reality that it represents. Much like it is the philosopher's goal to move past the visible temporal world to the invisible eternal world of truth, so too, he must move past language to see the actual reality beyond.

The young post-conversion Augustine followed a Christianized version of the Platonic tradition and held that God taught Christians inwardly.[59] According to Augustine's thinking at this early date, language did not in fact convey any information to believers. In a quintessential work of this period, The Teacher (AD 389), Augustine suggested that at best language can prompt humans to remember what we already possess an intellectual vision of.[60] Being a Christian, Augustine suggests that humans gain an intellectual vision of the truth only by virtue of God's inner illumination. Christ is the true inner teacher, although pedagogues can certainly point their students to take the right steps to come to recognize the truth that Christ offers.[61] Ultimately, the key assertion in the Platonic conception of knowledge that Augustine draws upon is that real knowledge is a form of direct intellectual vision. Language and other signs are signifiers that can at best prompt a memory but that obscures the signified. It is necessary to move past the less authentic signifier to the direct vision of the referent.

As should be clear, Augustine's conception of language and truth at this early stage parallels his conception of sin as attachment to becoming (creation) over being (God). Attachment to signs over reality obscures truth, just as attachment to the sensible over the eternal results in idolatry. Since the quest for knowledge has its summit in the participation in the divine, the young Augustine wrote and planned on continuing to write works on philosophy and liberal arts.[62] In this sense, the knowledge of all truths available to the divinely illuminated human mind would serve as a ladder to ascend to God.[63] Augustine identified Plato's Good with the Christian God.[64] Just as in Plato's thought all forms participate in the

---

59. Cary, Outward Signs, 87–113.

60. Cary, Outward Signs, 91–96. See Augustine, Against the Academics and The Teacher, trans. Peter King (Indianapolis: Hackett, 1995).

61. Cary, Outward Signs, 97–101.

62. Cary, Outward Signs, 116.

63. Cary, Outward Signs, 110–15.

64. Augustine, Soliloquies, 1.9; NPNF1, 7:540.

form of the Good, for Augustine all truth originates as thoughts in the mind of the Christian God.[65]

In the work of the mature Augustine, such a conception of knowledge and language was significantly modified. This appears to be part of what Peter Brown memorably described as Augustine's "lost future" of self-perfection by fully comprehending divine wisdom in the present life.[66] Although true knowledge remains (as in Plato) a matter of intellectual vision, such an unmediated vision (*visio beatifica*) is not fully possible in this life. Rather, in order to humble the pride of sinners like Augustine, God gives authoritative signs (such as the Bible and the sacraments), which point beyond themselves to a higher intelligible reality beyond them. To submit to the sign is to humble oneself to an authority that testifies to something that cannot be directly seen or experienced in this life but will become intellectually visible in eternity. Hence, faith is fundamentally a submission to the authority of the divinely appointed signs.[67]

Augustine's utilization of Plato (indirectly by way of Neoplatonism)[68] results in a sharp separation of the external word or sign and the will and presence of the invisible God behind it. As we will see, this separation of signs and the reality beyond them had a significant influence on later Catholics and Protestants. The clearest and most definitive development of the idea of signs in relation to realities can be found in Augustine's sacramental writing in response to the Donatists.

The Donatists were a schismatic group in North Africa who held the view that sacraments were not valid or efficacious if they were administered by a priest who was morally corrupt.[69] In understanding Augustine's response to this teaching, it must be recognized that the term of "sacrament" (*mysterium, sacramentum*) was much looser in the early church than it would later become in the medieval and Reformation churches. For Augustine, sacraments meant any external sign that pointed beyond

65. Philip Cary, *Augustine's Invention of the Inner Self: The Legacy of a Christian Platonist* (Oxford: Oxford University Press, 2000), 54.

66. Brown, *Augustine of Hippo*, 139–49.

67. Cary, *Outward Signs*, 116–26.

68. See John O'Meara, "The Neoplatonism of St. Augustine," in *Neoplatonism and Christian Thought*, ed. Dominic O'Meara (Albany: SUNY Press, 1982), 34–44.

69. W. H. C. Frend, *The Donatist Church: A Movement of Protest in Roman North Africa* (Oxford: Oxford University Press, 1952).

itself to the invisible grace granted to the individual believer in fellowship with the church.[70] Such signs facilitated the unity of believers with Christ's mystical body, the church (*totus Christus*). It is key to recognize that for Augustine sacraments absolutely guaranteed the presence of divine grace available to those in fellowship with the institutional church.[71] It of course remains a point of debate as to whether Augustine held with the medieval theologians that the sacraments literally contain grace.[72]

Following Plato's understanding of language and cognition,[73] Augustine's sacramentology mirrored Platonism's aversion to the supplementary. For Augustine, language, even the Word of God itself,[74] functions merely to "signify" things. As we have already seen, this stands in significant contradiction to our earlier interpretation of the biblical texts, which uniformly see God's action taking place through the human proclamation of the word. To signify a thing, words point beyond themselves to something else that is a reality (*res*).[75] Hence, as "visible words," sacraments "signify" (*signum*) an invisible, spiritual "reality" (*res*) distinct from visible tangibility.[76] Just as Plato's philosopher raises his mind above the supplementarity of the world of appearances, within Augustine's scheme the believer raises his intelligible mind above the sensible *signum* to the *res* of divine grace beyond it.

By separating the signifier and the signified, Augustine created a further problem: If the signified was spiritual and invisible, how one could be certain it was present when one encounters the signifier? His solution to this difficulty was to synthesize the dual sacramental traditions of the ante-Nicene Latin church.[77] With the Roman tradition, Augustine agreed

70. Cary, *Outward Signs*, 158–64.

71. Cary, *Outward Signs*, 193–97; Pelikan, *Christian Tradition*, 1:305–6.

72. For example, Pelikan, *Christian Tradition*, 1:302–7, which tends to be a more sacramental realist reading. In contrast to this see Cary, *Outward Signs*, 155–92.

73. Emmanuel Cutrone, "Sacraments," in *Augustine through the Ages: An Encyclopedia*, ed. Allan Fitzgerald (Grand Rapids: Eerdmans, 1999), 741–42.

74. John Norris, "Augustine and Sin in the Tractatus in Iohannis Euangelium," in *Augustine: Biblical Exegete*, ed. Frederick van Fleteren and Joseph C. Schnaubelt (New York: Peter Lang, 2004), 216–17.

75. B. Darrell Jackson, "The Theory of Signs in Augustine's De Doctrina Christiana," *Revue des Etudes Augustiniennes* 15 (1969):11–12.

76. Cary, *Outward Signs*, 155–64.

77. See Stuart Hall, *Doctrine and Practice in the Early Church* (Grand Rapids: Eerdmans, 1991), 91–94.

that the *verba* (word) and the element guaranteed the validity of the sacrament. Nevertheless, he qualified this by stating that although the *verba* and the physical element made for a valid sacrament, they did not make for an effective one.[78] For a sacrament to become effective, it must be celebrated in fellowship with the institutional Catholic Church, the true conduit of grace. In the case of a onetime sacrament such as baptism, the sacramental action was valid no matter the circumstances of its performance. Nevertheless, the person only received the benefits of baptism if they stood in proper fellowship with the institutional Catholic Church.[79]

In this teaching, Augustine also accepted a modified version of the North African tradition regarding the sacraments, which held that sacraments gain their validity and efficacy on the basis of the character of the person administering them.[80] Augustine rejected the notion of Cyprian and the Donatists that this character was a charisma of moral purity.[81] Rather, Augustine spoke of an "indelible character" (*character indelebilis*) that made him a conduit of divine grace irrespective of his moral lapses or defects.[82] Ultimately then, the work of the Spirit was not effective and present in, under, and through the power of the external word itself, but through the invisible unity of grace manifest externally through the fellowship of the institutional church.[83]

THE AUGUSTINIAN DILEMMA: PREDESTINATION OR SACRAMENTS?

As Benjamin Warfield once wrote, "The Reformation inwardly considered was the ultimate triumph of Augustine's doctrine of grace over his doctrine of the Church."[84] One could also reverse the statement as well: Modern Catholicism is the triumph of Augustine's view of the church over his view of grace and predestination. As Warfield hints, the difficulty with

---

78. See Geoffrey Willis, *Saint Augustine and the Donatist Controversy* (Eugene, OR: Wipf & Stock, 2005), 154–56.

79. Augustine, *On Baptism, Against the Donatists*; NPNF1, 4:411–514.

80. Chadwick, *The Early Church*, 221–22; Hall, *Doctrine and Practice in the Early Church*, 91–94.

81. Willis, *Saint Augustine and the Donatist Controversy*, 145–51.

82. Augustine, *On Baptism, Against the Donatists* 1.2; NPNF1, 4:412.

83. Cary, *Outward Signs*, 194–97.

84. Benjamin Warfield, *Calvin and Augustine* (Philadelphia: Presbyterian & Reformed, 1956), 322.

Augustine's doctrinal stance on predestination is that it stood in considerable tension with his view of the church and sacraments.

To put this more clearly, Augustine appears to pursue two distinct (and at times, seemingly contradictory) lines of reasoning regarding the sacraments and predestination. On the one hand, Augustine asserts that the church and its sacraments were absolute guarantees of the presence of God's grace. On the other hand, the Bishop of Hippo asserted against Pelagius that the grace of God is absolutely efficacious and irresistible. Taken together this raises the problem: If God's grace is irresistible and guaranteed by the means of grace, then why is not everyone who encounters the means of grace saved? In part, Augustine's answer was to emphasize that the grace of perseverance (gained particularly by prayer) is necessary to stay in a genuine fellowship with the church and its perpetual offer of grace. As a result, the role of the church and its ministry seems then to be relativized by God's hidden plan of election. Hence, the question is raised as to whether in the end the external means of grace are really a definitive guarantee of God's favor and forgiveness.

The tension between what might be called the sacramentalist and predestinarian tendencies in Augustine's thought establishes what we will call the "Augustinian dilemma." As Jaroslav Pelikan observes:

> To interpret Augustine as a partisan of either scholastic or Protestant doctrine about grace and the means of grace would resolve the inconsistencies of his thought and language, but it would also resolve the paradox of grace. The sovereignty of grace, with its inevitable corollary in the doctrine of predestination, could make the means of grace incidental to the achievement of the divine purpose. ... The mediation of grace, with its emphasis on the obligation to attend upon the services and sacraments of the church, could substitute a righteousness based on works of piety for a righteousness based on works of morality. Each of these possibilities was present in the theology of Augustine, and each has manifested itself in the subsequent history of Augustianism.[85]

---

85. Pelikan, *Christian Tradition*, 1:306.

Following a similar line of reasoning to Pelikan's, it is easy to discern two distinctive trajectories in Augustine's thought. In one trajectory, one might argue that if grace is irresistible and the result of God's predestinating act, the external means of grace become understood as only indirectly connected with the operation of God's grace. As a result, the means of grace possess little function other than to point beyond themselves to God's eternal act of predestination and grace's attending invisible enactment among the elect. The means of grace in effect become symbols of what God has already done in eternity. Many who encounter them are not converted because they are not real mediums of grace. As we will see below and in future chapters, as a result of this line of reasoning many Western theologians have rejected sacramental realism in favor of sacramental symbolism and spiritualism.

Following a second possible trajectory, if the sacraments do contain real grace (or, at minimum, guarantee the presence of divine grace), then the fact that not all who encounter them are saved is explained by the argument that although sin has damaged free will, it remains operative to a certain extent. Because human free will remains partially operative, people can decide whether or not to participate in the sacramental life of the church. To use an analogy: Although a patient who is ill cannot make themselves well by simply willing it, they can certainly agree to cooperate with the doctor and take medicine that will make them well. In this perspective, grace is seen not so much as something that unilaterally makes salvation an actuality, but as a possibility to be accepted or rejected by free will. Free will's grasping onto the possibilities offered by the means of grace results in the actualization of salvation.

The problem posed by the Augustinian dilemma was felt in the Western church immediately following the Bishop of Hippo's death. It must be recognized that although the consensus of the Catholic Church was against Pelagius (who was condemned both in local African synods and in the canons of the ecumenical Council of Ephesus),[86] Augustine's solution to the problem of sin and grace elicited considerable resistance. Indeed, many attempted to modify Augustine's position in the centuries following the Pelagian controversy.

---

86. B. R. Rees, ed., *Pelagius: Life and Letters* (Woodbridge, MA: Boydell, 1998), 4.

One notable example may be found in the work of John Cassian, an early promoter of Western monasticism.[87] Cassian held a position that many later authors described in a somewhat anachronistic manner as "Semi-Pelagian."[88] Cassian promoted the view that free will was still strong enough to allow for humans to decide whether or not they wanted to cooperate with grace present in the sacraments, but not strong enough to achieve salvation without the assistance of grace.[89]

Similarly, Prosper of Aquitaine softened Augustine's teaching on grace—which at the very least strongly implied a double predestination to salvation and damnation.[90] Prosper emphasized a sharp distinction between foreknowledge and the active operation of God's grace, as well as God's earnest wish for all nations to be saved.[91] Although God actively worked regeneration in believers, he merely passively foreknew the resistance of the damned.[92] In part, the Second Council of Orange (529) ultimately affirmed a similar modification of Augustine's position.[93]

By the ninth century one can observe the sacramentalist and predestinarian trajectories in Augustine's thought coalescing into distinct and contradictory theologies that began to enter into conflict with one another. This can be seen in the debates between Radbertus and Ratramnus,[94] as well as later debates between Gottschalk of Orbais and Hincmar of Reims.[95] On the one side, Radbertus and Hincmar supported a weak-

---

87. John Cassian, *Conferences*, trans Colm Luibheid (New York: Paulist, 1985); John Cassian, *The Institutes*, trans. Boniface Ramsey, (New York: Newman, 2000); Owen Chadwick, *John Cassian* (Cambridge: Cambridge University Press, 1950).

88. Squires, *The Pelagian Controversy*, 161.

89. Squires, *The Pelagian Controversy*, 262–77.

90. Alexander Hwang, *Intrepid Lover of Perfect Grace: The Life and Thought of Prosper of Aquitaine* (Washington, DC: Catholic University of America Press, 2009).

91. Pelikan, *Christian Tradition*, 1:325–27

92. See summary in Prosper of Aquitaine, *The Call of All Nations*, trans. P. De Letter (New York: Newman, 1952).

93. Heinrich Denzinger, *Enchiridion Symbolorum et Definitionum et declarationum de rebus fidei et morum* (Freiberg: Herder & Herder, 1955), 375–77.

94. Celia Chazelle, "Exegesis in the Ninth-Century Eucharistic Controversy," in *The Study of the Bible in the Carolingian Era*, ed. C. Chazelle and Burton van Name Edwards (Turnhout: Brepols, 2003), 167–87; Willemien Otten, "Between Augustinian Sign and Carolingian Reality: The Presence of Ambrose and Augustine in the Eucharistic Debate between Paschasius Radbertus and Ratramnus of Corbie," *Nederlands archief voor kerkgeschiedenis* 80, no. 2 (2000): 137–56

95. G. R. Evans, "The Grammar of Predestination in the Ninth Century," *Journal of Theological Studies* 33, no. 1 (1982): 134–45; Victor Genke and Francis Gumerlock, *Gottschalk and A Medieval*

ened, but not incapacitated free will after the fall, along with sacramental realism. This sacramentalism finds its particular expression in their
confession of the substantial presence of Christ in the Eucharist. On the
other side, both Ratramnus and Gottschalk taught a consistent doctrine
of absolute predestination along with a rejection of the substantial presence of Christ in the Eucharist.[96]

In these conflicts, we see both sides of the Augustinian dilemma manifest in the clearest possible terms. Indeed, it is easy to perceive the two
main modern manifestations of the Augustinian dilemma (major strains
of post-Tridentine Catholicism and Calvinism) *in utero*. Despite censure
from the institutional church through the Middle Ages, the sacramental
anti-realist position (usually, though not always connect with hard pre-
destinarianism) manifested itself throughout the Middle Ages in everything from the heresy of Berengar of Tours to the theology of the so-called
proto-Reformers (Wycliffe, Hus, etc.).[97]

In giving a theological evaluation, it should be observed that the difficulty with both trajectories within the Augustinian tradition is that they
destroy the biblical emphasis on the divine Word's ability to enact salvation through the sacramental medium of human words. For Augustine,
the word is not a divine deed that contains within it the coming of the
reality of which it speaks. Rather, the word is a mere signifier that signifies things to be truly known more authentically through the experience
of vision beyond them. As a result, according to the first option outlined
above the elect are predestined by invisible grace which merely coincides
with the means of grace but is not literally present in them. Therefore, the
external medium of the word and sacraments does not enact salvation;

Predestination Controversy (Milwaukee: Marquette University Press, 2010); Matthew Bryan Gillis,
Heresy and Dissent in the Carolingian Empire: The Case of Gottschalk of Orbais (Oxford: Oxford
University Press, 2017).

96. See Mark Vaillancourt, "Sacramental Theology from Gottschalk to Lanfranc," in *The Oxford
Handbook of Sacramental Theology*, ed. Hans Boersma and Matthew Levering (Oxford: Oxford
University Press, 2018), 187–92.

97. See Stephen Lahey, "The Sentences Commentary of Jan Hus," *A Companion to Jan Hus*, ed. Ota
Pavlicek and František Šmahel (Leiden: Brill), 147–49; A. J. Macdonald, *Berengar and the Reform of
Sacramental Doctrine* (London: Longmans, Green, 1930); Stephen Penn, "Wycliffe and the Sacraments,"
in *A Companion to John Wyclif, Late Medieval Theologian*, ed. Ian Levy (Leiden: Brill, 2006), 241–93;
John Adam Robson, *Wyclif and the Oxford Schools: The Relation of the "Summa de Ente" to Scholastic
Debates at Oxford in the Later Fourteenth Century* (Cambridge: Cambridge University Press, 1961).

they signify a salvation that God has already enacted in his eternal choice. Conversely, following the second option, if grace is contained in the word and sacraments but not enacted through them, it logically follows that the means of grace come to function as a signifier that signifies the possibility of grace to be actualized by free will. It is not the Word of God that actualizes the redemption of the individual sinner, but free will accepting grace.

Ultimately, the competing sacramentalist and predestinarian trajectories fail to counteract the reality of sin as it is defined within the Augustinian tradition. For Augustine, sin is self-incurvature (*incurvate in se*) and self-orientation.[98] Grace must break this self-orientation and reorient the sinner toward God. Nevertheless, if the means of grace do not actually contain grace and God invisibly elects believers, then it is up to the individual to discern the signs of the presence of God's grace within him or herself. In discerning God's electing grace, they must necessarily return to their own self-focus and trust. Conversely, if the means of grace do contain real grace that one is expected to grasp with their free will, then one will again turn inward to discern whether one has appropriately utilized one's free will to take hold of the offer of grace. In either trajectory, the root of sin is ultimately not defeated, and the Augustinian tradition fails to combat sin based on its own internal criterion.

Indeed, the self-orientation exacerbated by both options invariably leads to a form of legalism. If one looks either to works of cooperation or works that evidence election, one is necessarily caught up in the law and its demand for self-justification. Gerhard Forde makes a similar observation in writing:

> I am promised [moral] progress and improvement "by the power of grace" but what if I actually don't seem to be getting anywhere in particular? Talk about grace becomes just the problem! I keep trying, perhaps, and I go to church to get this thing called "grace," but it just doesn't seem to work. What then? The church assures me that there is nothing wrong with the "delivery system." The "grace" is there, especially in the sacraments. Not even a bad priest— say one who has committed mortal sin—can frustrate the delivery.

---

98. Brian Gregor, *A Philosophical Anthropology of the Cross: The Cruciform Self* (Bloomington: Indiana University Press, 2013), 61.

That being the case, I could come to one of two conclusions, or perhaps a mixture of both. One, and perhaps the most plausible, is that the fault must lie with me. Perhaps I just have not done the proper things or done enough to get this thing the theologians call "grace." Perhaps I just don't know the right "combination." But suppose I do as much as anyone else, or more. Suppose I really do everything prescribed, and even more, and I still don't seem to make any progress. What then? Then I might come to the second possible conclusion, the one much more terrifying: Perhaps the reason lies with God! Perhaps God, the giver of all such grace—at least so I am told—has decided not to give it. Perhaps God has turned thumbs down. ... I am left suspended between a futile quest for self-salvation or the terrors of predestination.[99]

CONCLUSION

Having discussed Augustine's doctrine of justification, we will next move on to Luther and his engagement with the medieval tradition. As we will see, Luther's genius lies in the fact that he was finally able to overcome the Augustinian dilemma through his return to the biblical doctrine of the sacramentality of the word. In this, the Reformer saw the word of absolution as bringing with it the reality that it promised, namely, the crucified and risen Christ. Christ present in the word grants eschatological pardon, thereby killing old sinful being and resurrecting new beings of faith.

---

99. Gerhard Forde, *Justification by Faith: A Matter of Death and Life* (Mifflinton, PA: Sigler, 1990), 26–27.

CHAPTER 7

Justification in the Middle Ages:
Augustinian and Aristotelian Legacies in Latin Theology

I n the previous chapter we discussed Augustine and the early church's
theology of justification. As was observed, although Augustine to a
large extent overcame what might be called the naïve semi-Pelagian of the
ante-Nicene church, his critique of the previous tradition was in many
ways not radical enough. In spite of Augustine's revival of the biblical
principle of *sola gratia*, he left a number of traditions that had grown up in
the North African church (i.e., the theology of merit and penance) largely
untouched. Instead of doing away with the North African theology of
merit and penance, the Bishop of Hippo synthesized it with the Pauline
principle of *sola gratia*. He thereby created a theology of justification that
was not only unbiblical, but in many respects was internally incoherent.

Although it does not explain all the tensions in Augustine's theology
of grace, the notion of the Word of God as a signifier that merely signifies
things that already are played a significant role in generating such a theology. There is no sense in Augustine's thought (as in the Bible) that beyond
signifying things that have already come to be, the Word of God can bring
into existence that which is not (2 Cor 4:6). Hence, Augustine's philosophy
of language significantly contributed to the formation of what we have called
the Augustinian dilemma. In this dilemma, grace is merely signified to the
believer through the means of grace either by their pointing beyond themselves to what god has acomplished in eternity (i.e., the predestinarian

tendency), or by their making grace objectively possible if there is the cooperation of human free will (i.e., the sacramentalist tendency).

Standing on the shoulders of Augustine and his first reformation of the doctrine of grace, Luther sought to bring the church of the sixteenth century back to the biblical doctrine of justification. Central to Luther's Reformation theology was his resolution of the Augustinian dilemma through the concept of the sacramentality of the word. In this regard, our thesis stands contrary to the popular understanding that holds that Luther's czzentral project was the doctrine of justification by faith. Faith is of course of paramount importance to Luther, but faith is only meaningful insofar as it relies on a word from God that sacramentally gives the reality that faith receives. Luther doesn't emphasize the subjective act of belief, but the reality of God's saving righteousness in Christ that creates and bestows the reality of which it speaks through the word and sacrament ministry of the church. Luther's belief in justification by the word transcends the Augustinian conception of the word merely as a form of signification, a concept that drives most Catholic and Protestant theologies of justification down to the present.

PRELUDE TO LUTHER:
JUSTIFICATION IN THE MIDDLE AGES

In order to fully understand Luther's theology of justification, we must first give a brief description of the doctrine of justification in the Middle Ages. As a number of authors have noted, there is a sense in which all medieval theology is Augustinian.[1] As Jaroslav Pelikan observed, the history of the West (and not just Western theology) after the fifth century is a series of footnotes to Augustine.[2] Augustine towers over almost any other theologian writing in Latin prior to the eleventh century, and consequently Augustine became the singular authority in the West during the early Middle Ages.[3] Likewise, even after the revival of academic theology after the twelfth century, the main textbook of theology in the Middle Ages

---

1. McGrath, *Iustitia Dei*, 58.
2. Jaroslav Pelikan, *Christian Tradition*, 1:330.
3. McGrath, *Iustitia Dei*, 60.

was Peter Lombard's *Sentences*, 80 percent of which consists of quotations taken from works attributed to or by Augustine.[4]

That being said, although Augustine's theology established the main intellectual paradigms for dealing with justification (and all other theological topics), this does not mean that theologians reproduced or even sought to reproduce his theology in a one-to-one correspondence. Part of this non-correspondence has to do with barriers faced by medieval theologians regarding a genuine encounter with Augustine's work. Many pseudo-works of Augustine circulated in the Middle Ages attributed positions (particularly on the issues of sin and grace) to the bishop of Hippo that he did not hold.[5] Similarly, with limited access to books, for the most part medieval theologians did not encounter Augustine through direct reading to his works cover-to-cover, but through collections of quotations and aphorisms (*florilegia*).[6]

In terms of the actual definition of justification, the medieval theologians largely maintained Augustine's concept of being made righteous (*justificare*).[7] After all, such a conception was in accordance with the standard Vulgate translation of the term,[8] and although knowledge of Greek was not totally lacking in the medieval church, it was not very common.[9] For early medieval theologians, being "made righteous" encompassed three realities: turning from sin, being forgiven of sin, and being regenerated.[10] Later, this was modified to a fourfold movement: an infusion of grace, a movement from sin, contrition, and the forgiveness of sins.[11] The key debates in the Middle Ages revolved around the role of human agency in achieving these aspects of being made righteous.

---

4. McGrath, *Iustitia Dei*, 60.

5. Alister McGrath, *The Intellectual Origins of the European Reformation* (Malden, MA: Blackwell, 2004), 23.

6. James Ginther, *The Westminster Handbook to Medieval Theology* (Louisville: Westminster John Knox, 2009), 68–69.

7. McGrath, *Iustitia Dei*, 68.

8. Peter Harrison, "Philosophy and the Crisis of Religion," in *The Cambridge Companion to Renaissance Philosophy*, ed. James Hankins (Cambridge: Cambridge University Press, 2007), 244.

9. Frans van Liere, *An Introduction to the Medieval Bible* (Cambridge: Cambridge University Press, 2014), 102–3.

10. McGrath, *Iustitia Dei*, 71–73.

11. McGrath, *Iustitia Dei*, 73–74.

AQUINAS AND THE SIGNIFICANCE
OF ARISTOTLE

One significant development with regard to the question of human agency in the process of salvation was the rediscovery of Aristotle in the twelfth century.[12] Aristotle provided the medieval academy with state-of-the-art biology, physics, political science, and ethics[13]—albeit mediated through Arabic commentary and mostly thirdhand translations (Greek to Arabic to Latin).[14] Beginning in the thirteenth century, Aristotle's works played a significant role in the debates regarding justification in the medieval Latin church.[15]

According to Aristotle, "being" is to be identified with "doing."[16] Formal realities (*eidos*) of various entities are not static archetypes (Plato) but are the inner realities of the various entities in the world that dynamically bring those entities from a state of potentiality to actuality. Unlike Plato, who taught that the formal reality of all entities existed in the far off intelligible "Realm of the Forms,"[17] Aristotle insisted that all forms are embedded in matter.[18] All entities are a unity of form and matter (hylomorphism).[19] For example, a statue of George Washington is made up of bronze (matter) and the intelligible idea of the image of George Washington (form). Adding the formal reality to the matter through the bronze mold moves the entity from a potential statue to an actual statue.[20]

For Aristotle, all things in the universe are moving from potency to act. Within this great cosmic order, all entities have a true end (*telos*) to become fully actualized.[21] Failure to reach their true *telos* makes entities defective and less than fully authentic. Since all things in the cosmos are

---

12. Etienne Gilson, *History of Christian Philosophy in the Middle Ages* (Washington, DC: Catholic University of America Press, 2019), 235.

13. See Richard Rubenstein, *Aristotle's Children: How Christians, Muslims, and Jews Rediscovered Ancient Wisdom and Illuminated the Dark Ages* (New York: Harcourt, 2004).

14. Edward Grant, *The Foundations of Modern Science in the Middle Ages: Their Religious, Institutional, and Intellectual Contexts* (Cambridge: Cambridge University Press, 1998), 29.

15. McGrath, *Iustitia Dei*, 190.

16. See Zev Bechler, *Aristotle's Theory of Actuality* (Albany: SUNY Press, 1995).

17. R. M. Dancy, *Plato's Introduction of Forms* (Cambridge: Cambridge University Press, 2004).

18. Aristotle, *Metaphysics*, trans. W.D. Ross (Oxford: Clarendon, 1963), 1036b.1–5.

19. Aristotle, *Metaphysics*, 1028a.10–1045b.20.

20. Aristotle, *Physics*, trans. R.P. Hardie and R.K. Gaye (Oxford: Clarendon, 1962), 191a.8–12.

21. Aristotle, *Physics*, 198b.32–199a.8

continuously moving, there must be an ultimate source of motion who is supremely actualized. Therefore, a god ("the prime mover" or "unmoved mover") must exist in order to explain the motion of the whole cosmic order from all eternity. Since God is pure actuality (as the Scholastics would later put it, *actus purus*), he is the most real thing.[22]

True to his general metaphysical outlook, Aristotle designated ethics as a practical science that helps humans to achieve their *telos* as fully actualized just persons. Because "doing" is "being," for Aristotle being a righteous person meant engaging in right activity.[23] Nevertheless, the key to being a just agent was not to be found in merely going through the motions of right action. Rather, it was a matter of being trained to spontaneously behave correctly and live up to one's full potential. Becoming a good person then was a matter of actualizing the form of justice in the matter of the human subject.[24]

Aristotle developed this notion of the good life by articulating the classical statement of what has come to be called "virtue ethics."[25] According to his theory, human nature possessed universal potencies for what were later called the "cardinal virtues": prudence, temperance, fortitude, and justice.[26] Such potencies in human nature were referred to as "habits" (*habitus*). Habits were aptitudes. Humans have aptitudes to ethical action, in the same manner that a person may have a greater or lesser aptitude to learn to play a musical instrument or speak a language.[27] In a manner similar to other aptitudes, ethical potencies in human nature need practice to become second nature or what is called a "virtue" (*virtus*). Therefore, much as a person who repeatedly practices the piano can develop their musical aptitude into an actual skill, so too, through repeated action a person with the potential to be a virtuous person could actualize themselves as someone who habitually behaved in the right ways. A child who

22. Aristotle, *Metaphysics*, 1072a.21–36.

23. Aristotle, *Nicomachean Ethics*, trans. W. D. Ross (Oxford: Oxford University Press, 1963), 1134a.1–5.

24. Aristotle, *Nicomachean Ethics*, 1104a.27–1104b.18.

25. See discussion in Howard Curzer, *Aristotle and the Virtues* (Oxford: Oxford University Press, 2012); Alasdair MacIntyre, *After Virtue: A Study in Moral Theory* (Notre Dame, IN: Notre Dame University Press, 1984).

26. Aristotle, *Nicomachean Ethics*, 1115b–1131a.9.

27. Aristotle, *Nicomachean Ethics*, 1103a.14–25.

is taught to save their money in a piggy bank to purchase toys will likely grow into an adult who lives within their financial means.[28]

Working with the Augustinian conception that being justified meant becoming righteous and combining it with the Aristotelian notion of how one became just led the Latin church of the twelfth and thirteenth centuries to develop the doctrine of justification in new directions.[29] The classical articulation of this can be found in the theology of Thomas Aquinas. Like Aristotle, Aquinas posited that being is doing. Human identity is defined by what humans do. In this regard, it can be observed that Aristotelian ethics possessed a point of contact with the Latin tradition's doctrine of penance and merit. Righteousness in the eyes of God was constituted by meritorious behavior. Hence, becoming righteous meant being moved so as to act in a habitually just manner by having the form of justice impressed upon the soul that would result in meritorious behavior.[30] Nevertheless, although Aquinas agreed with Aristotle that there were universal potencies in the human soul to the cardinal virtues (hence, the possibility of virtuous pagans), the cardinal virtues did not constitute righteousness before God.[31]

Rather, human righteousness before God was only possible by the intervention of divine grace to give access to certain supernatural or theological virtues spoken of by Paul (1 Cor 13:13): faith, hope, love.[32] Following Augustine, Aquinas stated that faith was constituted by correct belief as a kind of pre-knowledge of one's final vision of God (*visio beatifica*). Likewise, hope gave humans the ability to humbly anticipate the eschatological reward of their correct behavior. Finally, love drew believers to God as the supreme object of enjoyment and fueled meritorious behavior that would propel them on their journey into the divine life.[33]

---

28. Aristotle, *Nicomachean Ethics*, 1103a.26–1103b.26.

29. See Anthony Celano, *Aristotle's Ethics and Medieval Philosophy: Moral Goodness and Practical Wisdom* (Cambridge: Cambridge University Press, 2015).

30. ST, IaIIae, q. 113, art. 1; Thomas Aquinas, *Summa Theologiae*, trans. Fathers of the Dominican Provence (Notre Dame, IN: Ave Maria, 1981), 1144–45.

31. ST, IaIIae, q. 61, art. 2; Aquinas, *Summa Theologiae*, 846.

32. ST, IaIIae, q. 62, art. 1; Aquinas, *Summa Theologiae*, 851.

33. ST, IaIIae, q. 62, art. 1–4; Aquinas, *Summa Theologiae*, 851–53.

Much as for Aristotle virtue helped one become a fully developed person in the earthly realm, so too for Aquinas the supernatural virtues helped the human person reach their true *telos* lying above mere nature in the spiritual realm.[34] The true goal of all humans was to ascend to the divine life and spiritually see God in his essence (*visio beatifica*).[35] Here Aquinas assumes a distinction between the natural and supernatural developed by Philip the Chancellor.[36] The natural is the givenness of creation and its capacities. Although nature is good, on its own it is unequal to its ultimate task of eternal fellowship with God. In the case of human nature, there is a natural desire and intrinsic recognition that one's true end lies in the ultimate happiness of possessing the beatific vision.[37] Therefore, nature needs supernatural capacities (i.e., the created habits of faith, hope, and love) to reach its true *telos*—although these are not intrinsic to human nature. The communication of these supernatural capacities is dependent on divine initiative and therefore based on grace.[38] Grace does not destroy or supersede nature, but helps nature come to its true and final goal, that is, the eternal happiness of fellowship with God.[39]

Through the sacrament of baptism, humans were endowed with the capacities necessary for achieving the beatific vision lost in the fall.[40] In baptism, all previous sins were washed away,[41] the uncreated grace of the Holy Spirit was given, and the habits of faith, hope, and love were "infused" (*diffusa*, "poured" see Vulgate Romans 5:5) into the heart of the believer.[42] In this, grace becomes a predicate of the human person. Since the mere aptitude toward faith, hope, and love were received in baptism, they need to be developed by repeated right behavior and grace from the other sacraments of the medieval church to develop into virtues.[43] Such

---

34. ST, IaIIae, q. 62, art. 1; Aquinas, *Summa Theologiae*, 851.

35. ST, Ia, q. 12, art. 1; Aquinas, *Summa Theologiae*, 49.

36. Duffy, *Dynamics of Grace*, 151–52.

37. ST, IaIIae, q. 3, art. 8; Aquinas, *Summa Theologiae*, 601–2.

38. ST, IaIIae, q. 109, art. 1–10; Aquinas, *Summa Theologiae*, 1123–31.

39. ST, Ia, q. 1, art. 8; Aquinas, *Summa Theologiae*, 6.

40. ST, IIIa, q. 69, art. 5; Aquinas, *Summa Theologiae*, 2405–6.

41. ST, IIIa, q. 69, art. 1; Aquinas, *Summa Theologiae*, 2402–3.

42. ST, IIIa, q. 69, art. 4; Aquinas, *Summa Theologiae*, 2405.

43. ST, IaIIae, q. 52, art. 1–3; Aquinas, *Summa Theologiae*, 806–10.

virtues could generate behavior that would be meritorious of salvation.[44] It must be emphasized in the strongest possible terms that although Aquinas holds that righteousness is by works, such works are impossible apart from divine grace.[45] Indeed, Aquinas affirms that those who are saved receive salvation because of God's predestinating act and that human merit is merely an efficient cause that God uses to enact salvation.[46]

Following Aristotle, Aquinas posited that matter must be properly disposed before a form can be added to it and applied it to his doctrine of grace.[47] Much as a human soul (which serves as the form of the human body) could not simply be added to any matter (a rock, a ball of mud, etc.) and be actualized a human person, likewise, baptizing random adults with no interest in becoming Christians will not somehow cause them to become Christians. Hence, if justification meant having the form of justice impressed upon the soul by means of the supernatural virtues, it followed that the human subject (who serves as the matter) must be disposed. This Aristotelian principle gave rise to a debate over the issue of the necessary conditions for preparation in the reception of divine grace.[48]

In his commentary on Lombard's *Sentences*, the young Aquinas states that human beings may prepare themselves for salvific grace by acting in such a way so as to imperfectly merit the first grace.[49] Nevertheless, in the *Summa Theologiae*, the elderly Aquinas argues that God in his grace disposes humans to the reception of the supernatural graces received in baptism. Independent of divine grace, humans have no ability to initiate or maintain their relationship with God. Much like for Augustine, for Aquinas the whole process of salvation is based on the principle of *sola gratia*.[50]

44. ST, IIIa, q. 69, art. 5; Aquinas, *Summa Theologiae*, 2405–6.

45. ST, IaIIae, q. 114, art. 2; Aquinas, *Summa Theologiae*, 1154–55.

46. ST, Ia, q. 23, art. 1–8; Aquinas, *Summa Theologiae*, 125–33.

47. Fredrick Christian Bauerschmidt, "Augustine and Aquinas," in *The T&T Clark Companion to Augustine and Modern Theology*, ed. C. C. Pecknold and Tarmo Toom (Edinburgh: T&T Clark, 2013), 114.

48. McGrath, *Iustitia Dei*, 129–45.

49. Heiko Oberman, *Forerunners of the Reformation: The Shape of Late Medieval Thought*, trans. Paul Nyhus (Cambridge: James Clarke & Co., 2002), 130.

50. ST, IaIIae, q. 109, art. 6; Aquinas, 1127–28.

The ability of humans to earn the first grace does not, in the thinking of many medieval theologians, take away divine initiative in the process of salvation.[51] Rather, God by his own initiative has set up a system
wherein humans may act even in their state of sinful privation to merit
(however imperfectly) the first grace. Such merit in the later medieval
system was referred to as "congruous merit" (*meritum de congruo*), since
it was not strictly earned, but given due to God's gracious initiative and
imputation. A child who earns money for cleaning their room is not being
paid strictly on the basis of market prices but gains their money because
of the good pleasure of the parent. Having disposed themselves and then
being given actual grace (*gratia gratis data*), humans could now engage
in genuinely meritorious behavior and earn salvation according to the
strict measure of justice. This merit was referred to as "condign merit"
(*meritum de condigno*).[52]

WILLIAM OF OCKHAM
AND THE VIA MODERNA

Whereas theologians from the Dominican Order largely (though not uniformly) took the position of the elderly Aquinas, the Franciscans followed
a position that followed the trajectory of the young Aquinas which had
also been popular among older theologians of the same order.[53] Among
the late medieval Franciscan theologians, probably the most sophisticated
and internally consistent articulation of the latter theology of grace and
merit can be found in the late thirteenth and early fourteenth century
theologian, William of Ockham (sometimes spelled "Occam").[54]

William of Ockham was part of a movement known as the *via moderna* ("the modern way") in the later Middle Ages. This stood in contrast
to the *via antiqua* ("the old way") of Peter Lombard, Thomas Aquinas

---

51. Von Harnack suggests that this concept of grace destroys the Augustinian synthesis. *History of Dogma*, 6:275–317.

52. McGrath, *Iustitia Dei*, 158–60.

53. See Heiko Oberman, "Via Antiqua and Via Modern: Late Medieval Prolegomena to Early Reformation Thought," in *The Impact of the Reformation* (Grand Rapids: Eerdmans, 1994), 3–23.

54. See Marilyn McCord Adams, *William of Ockham*, 2 vols. (Notre Dame, IN: University of Notre Dame Press, 1989).

and John Duns Scotus.[55] Although the difference between the two theological and philosophical trajectories is still debated, one clear difference between them is that the *via moderna* was nominalist (or sometimes called "Terminist") and the *via antiqua* was realist.[56]

Realism held that universals ("catness," "dogness," "squareness," "circleness," etc.) are real ideas eternally existing in God's mind (much like Plato's forms). Nominalists held that universals are merely names applied to individual objects in the world. For example, there are simply a series of furry animals that hunt mice and love to drink cream. Since these animals look similar, humans apply the name "cat" to them—there is no eternal archetype of "cat" in the mind of God.[57] Although to some readers the issue of universals may seem like an abstract question with no bearing on our subject matter, as we will see below how one answers this question does affect one's doctrine of justification.

According to Ockham, God was supremely sovereign will. Whereas Augustine, Aquinas, and the realist tradition in general at times spoke of God more as the embodiment of certain ideals ("wisdom, "beauty," "goodness," etc.), Ockham saw God primarily as a personal entity that related to his creation by his sovereign decisions.[58] Unlike Augustine and Aquinas, who held that God's activities were shaped by certain transcendental ideals (i.e., the eternal universals present in the divine mind), Ockham held that God established the created order purely on the basis of his unbound will.[59]

Because God's decisions were not shaped by metaphysical ideals internal to his essence, the question was naturally raised as to why and how the Lord had enacted his plan of salvation. As we saw earlier, for Augustine and Aquinas, God was himself the embodiment of transcendental goodness, and because of the structure the plan of salvation that he enacted was

55. Fredrick Copleston, *Medieval Philosophy: An Introduction* (Mineola, NY: Dover, 2001), 118–19; Steven Ozment, *The Age of Reform, 1250–1550: An Intellectual and Religious History of Late Medieval and Reformation Europe* (New Haven: Yale University Press, 1981), 22–72.

56. Anthony Levi, *Renaissance and Reformation: The Intellectual Genesis* (New Haven: Yale University Press, 2002), 57.

57. Joseph Koterski, *An Introduction to Medieval Philosophy: Basic Concepts* (Oxford: Wiley-Blackwell, 2011), 87–110.

58. Adams, *William of Ockham*, 2:1033–1256.

59. Rémi Brague, *The Law of God: The Philosophical History of an Idea* (Chicago: University of Chicago Press, 2007), 236–37.

shaped by this. In light of this, God could be trusted to help his creatures achieve salvation and would be responsive to their grace-inspired meritorious good works because he was himself the embodiment of goodness as a transcendental ideal. Since Ockham's God was a person who made sovereign decisions, logically there was no particular guarantee that he would respond to human merit.

In order to solve this problem, Ockham utilized an earlier medieval distinction between God's "absolute power" (*de potentia absoluta*) and his "ordered power" (*de potentia ordinate*).[60] Before the creation of the world, God could simply create whatever sort of order he so desired (within the limits of the law of non-contradiction) according to his absolute power. Nevertheless, after creating the world and establishing the order of redemption, God was self-constrained to act predictably according to the order that he had sovereignly established. Specifically, this took the form of God establishing covenants with humanity (*pactum*) and fulfilling the promises that he had made within the covenantal order.[61]

Alister McGrath has described this shift in how theologians understood divine agency in relationship to creation as a movement from ontological to "covenantal causality."[62] In other words, God acts in particular ways not because he is the embodiment of some philosophically established transcendental notion of the good (*summum bonum*), but rather because of his covenantal promises.[63] Although Anglican and Roman Catholic authors frequently decry Ockham as another step on the road to nihilism (initiated by Duns Scotus),[64] another way of looking at the *Venerabilis Inceptor* is that he returned Western theology to a much more

60. William Courtenay "Dialectic of Omnipotence in the High and Late Middle Ages," in *Divine Omniscience and Omnipotence in Medieval Philosophy: Islamic, Jewish, and Christian Perspective*, ed. Tamar Rudavsky (Dordrecht: D. Reidel, 1985), 246–69.

61. Adams, *William of Ockham*, 2:1257–98; Heiko Oberman, "The Shape of Late Medieval Thought: The Birthpangs of the Modern Era," in *The Dawn of the Reformation: Essay on the Late Medieval and Early Reformation Thought* (Grand Rapids: Eerdmans, 1992), 26–29.

62. Alister McGrath, *Luther's Theology of the Cross: Martin Luther's Theological Breakthrough* (Oxford: Wiley-Blackwell, 1990), 59.

63. See discussion in Miyon Chung, "Faith, Merit, and Justification: Luther's Exodus from Ockhamism *En Route* to Reformation," *Torch Trinity Journal* 6 (2003):21.

64. Brad Gregory, *The Unintended Reformation: How a Religious Revolution Secularized Society* (Cambridge, MA: Belknap Press, 2012), 25–73; John Milbank, *Theology and Social Theory: Beyond Secular Reason* (Malden, MA: Blackwell Publishers, 2008), 14–15.

biblical concept of God as a person who interacts with humanity through covenantal promises.

This brings us to the final issue, the nature of the covenant of salvation between God and humanity. As a Franciscan, Ockham held that humans were capable of meriting the first grace, albeit in an incomplete and imperfect way (*meritum de congruo*—congruent merit). God made a covenant with humanity that if they did what was within their limited moral capacities (*facere quod in se est*—do what lies within you) he would impute to them as having merited the first grace—although in reality their efforts had not genuinely met the standard of divine justice. After meriting the first grace, humans would be given sufficient grace to actually merit salvation.[65] Again, although to many this would appear to be a form of outright Pelagianism, Ockham and the other *moderni* invariably would argue that since this whole system of salvation was initiated by God's sovereign decision, no one could be saved apart from the grace of God.[66]

---

65. Oberman, "The Shape of Late Medieval Thought, 29. Also see Heiko Oberman, " '*Facientibus Quod in Se Est Deus Non Degenat Gratiam*': Robert, O. P., and the Beginnings of Luther's Theology," *Harvard Theological Review* 75 (1962): 317–42.

66. See Alister McGrath, "The Anti-Pelagian Structure of 'Nominalist' Doctrines of Justification," *Ephemerides Theologicae Lovanienses* 57 (1981), 107–19.

CHAPTER 8

Justification and Young Luther:
The Genesis of *Humilitastheologie*

O ur discussion of Ockham in the previous chapter invariably leads us to the struggles of the young Luther. Luther's undergraduate studies at the University of Erfurt were focused on theologians of the *via moderna*. This included Ockham himself, as well as the German *moderni* theologian Gabriel Biel.[1] As we will see, even after Luther had abandoned the Ockhamist theology of sin and grace, he retained commitments to certain aspects of the *via moderna*, most notably the aforementioned covenantal causality. Indeed, in later life, Luther referred to Ockham as his "master,"[2] and according to Melanchthon, the Reformer could recite long passages from the works of Biel by heart even in old age.[3] Moreover, Graham White famously documented that Luther's late Christological and Trinitarian disputations stand in continuity with the *via moderna* and that Luther remained committed to philosophical nominalism until the end of his

---

1. See discussion of Luther and his relationship to *via moderna* in Bernhard Lohse, *Martin Luther's Theology: Its Historical and Systematic Development* (Minneapolis: Fortress, 1999), 21–22; Alister McGrath, *Reformation Thought: An Introduction* (New York: Wiley-Blackwell, 2012), 67–69; Heiko Oberman, *The Two Reformations: Journey from the Last Days to the New World* (New Haven: Yale University Press, 2003), 21–43; Harry McSorley, *Luther: Right or Wrong?: An Ecumenical Theological Study of Luther's Major Work, The Bondage of the Will* (Minneapolis: Augsburg, 1969), 191–223.

2. The Collection of Konrad Cordatus (1532), WATR 2:516.

3. Heiko Oberman, *Luther: Man Between God and the Devil*, trans. Eileen Walliser-Swarzbart, (New York: Image, 1992), 138.

life.[4] Finally, and most importantly for our study, Ockhamism forms the matrix within which Luther's early spiritual crisis took place.

As is well known, after completing his undergraduate studies at Erfurt, the young Luther was on track to study law in accordance with his father's wishes.[5] On a trip to visit his parents, Luther became stuck in a thunderstorm. Fearing death, Luther made a vow to St. Anne (the patron saint of miners, his family's industry) that he would take monastic vows.[6] Luther chose to join the Augustinian Order in Erfurt.[7] Although possibly recounted with much exaggeration (the Augustinians were not a particularly severe order and allowed the pursuit of Humanistic learning),[8] Luther certainly engaged in much obsessive spiritual practice and self-mortification. This behavior eventually led him to the brink of spiritual despair, something that proved fruitful for his later theological development.[9] A number of things probably fueled Luther's spiritual distress and obsessive devotional practice. These factors would include his distinctive psychological disposition, familial pressure to succeed,[10] and late medieval apocalyptic anxiety brought on by the plague and other social or cultural disruptions.[11]

Beyond these factors, many scholars have determined that Luther's personal disposition for spiritual anxiety was being exacerbated by the Ockhamist theology of sin and grace that he absorbed at Erfurt.[12] Most notably, the afore-discussed principle of *facere quod in se est* appears to

4. Graham White, *Luther as Nominalist: A Study of the Logical Methods Used in Martin Luther's Disputations in the Light of Their Medieval Background* (Helsinki: Luther-Agricola-Society, 1994).

5. Lohse, *Martin Luther's Theology*, 32.

6. Richard Marius, *Martin Luther: The Christian between God and Death* (Cambridge, MA: Belknap, 1999), 44.

7. Martin Brecht, *Martin Luther*, trans. James Schaf, 3 vols. (Philadelphia: Fortress, 1985–1994), 1:55–63.

8. Franz Posset, *The Real Luther: A Friar at Erfurt and Wittenberg* (St. Louis: Concordia, 2011), 54–61.

9. James Kittelson, *Luther the Reformer: The Story of the Man and His Career* (Minneapolis: Fortress, 2016), 30.

10. See Erik Erikson, *Young Man Luther: A Study in Psychoanalysis and History* (New York: W. W. Norton & Co., 1958).

11. See Johan Huizinga, *The Autumn of the Middle Ages*, trans. Rodney J. Payton and Ulrich Mammitzsch (Chicago: University of Chicago Press, 1997); Barbara W. Tuckman, *A Distant Mirror: The Calamitous 14th Century* (New York: Random House, 1987).

12. Rob Sorensen, *Martin Luther and the German Reformation* (London: Anthem, 2016), 16.

play a significant role in forming the young Luther's conscience and religious practice.[13] If taken to its logical conclusion, the principle of grace being given to those who "did their best" would invariably drive people to the most extreme levels of scrupulosity. The principle of "doing one's best" breeds uncertainty as to whether or not one has actually done their best since there is no objective way of measuring one's "best."[14]

As a result, uncertainty of grace opened the late medieval mind to the terrors of eternal torment in hell or at minimum temporal torture in purgatory after the swiftly arriving eschaton.[15] These possibilities were strongly present in the popular mind as can be illustrated by the increasingly frequent depictions of hell in late medieval artwork as a hell mouth swallowing up the damned.[16] Likewise, unlike Dante's largely benign portrait in *Purgatorio*,[17] the late medieval portrayals of purgatory were ones of pure torture at the hands of malevolent angels. The most prominent example of this can be found in the visions of Bridget of Sweden that were regularly utilized by popular preachers.[18]

All these images of the afterlife were enough to send Luther and many others into a state of spiritual panic. Indeed, the situation was further exacerbated by the fact that the consensus of medieval theology explicitly taught that one could never be certain that they were in a state of grace.[19] The shape of the spiritual life of someone under the sway of such a theology necessarily would look something like that of Luther's life in the monastery: a period of hyperactive devotional practice, followed by periods of despair and self-recrimination.

---

13. Lohse, *Martin Luther's Theology*, 33. See Luther's description in 1545 in LW 34:323–338.

14. Robert Kolb, *Martin Luther: Confessor of the Faith* (Oxford: Oxford University Press, 2009), 32–34; Lohse, *Martin Luther's Theology*, 32–34.

15. Bernard McGinn, *Visions of the End: Apocalyptic Traditions in the Middle Ages* (New York: Columbia University Press, 1998), 259–83.

16. Clifford Davidson, *Studies in Late Medieval Wall Paintings, Manuscript Illuminations, and Texts* (London: Palgrave Macmillan, 2017), 27–29.

17. See George Corbett, *Dante's Christian Ethics: Purgatory and its Moral Contexts* (Cambridge: Cambridge University Press, 2020).

18. See Eamon Duffy, *The Stripping of the Altars: Traditional Religion in England 1400–1580* (New Haven: Yale University Press, 2005), 338–43.

19. Berndt Hamm, *The Reformation of Faith in the Context of Late Medieval Theology and Piety: Essay by Berndt Hamm*, ed. Robert Bast (Leiden: Brill, 2004), 186.

Since it has been the scholarly consensus of the previous century that Luther's scrupulosity was largely (though not exclusively) caused by Ockhamism, it has often been a Catholic line of defense that Luther's spiritual troubles were the result of his ignorance of the late Aquinas and his theology of *sola gratia*. In this narrative, Ockhamism is viewed as not being the "real" Catholicism, but a late medieval aberration from the pure Catholicism of Aquinas. Joseph Lortz famously argued that Luther sadly did not know Aquinas's theology and therefore fell victim to the inadequate doctrine of grace found in Ockham and Biel.[20] In this, Lortz was moderating a harsher earlier judgment of Heinrich Denifle that Luther was effectively a theological ignoramus who simply did not understand the Catholic doctrine of grace.[21]

There are several difficulties with this argument. First, characterizing "Thomism" as the "real Catholicism" is anachronistic. Thomism took on special importance within the Catholic Church in the period of the Catholic Reformation or Counter-Reformation,[22] and only finally became the official position of the Catholic Church in the late nineteenth century under the pontificate of Leo XIII.[23] Second, it should also be noted that as Denis Janz has demonstrated, Luther was certainly very familiar with the theology of Thomas Aquinas (albeit indirectly, primarily through quotations in the works of Biel) and found it as wanting as Ockhamism in light of his discovery of the biblical gospel.[24]

Third and most important, it must be emphasized that the *via moderna* is not merely an anomaly in Western Christian thought, but simply the culmination of the failure of the entire Augustinian reformation of

20. See Joseph Lortz, *Die Reformation in Deutschland*, 2 vols. (Voraussetzungen: Herder Verlag, 1949).

21. Heinrich Denifle, *Die abendlandischen Schriftausleger bis Luther über Iustitia Dei (Rom 1:17) und Iustificatio* (Mainz: Kircheim, 1905); Denifle, *Luther und Luthertum in der ersten Entwickelung: quellenmässig dargestellt*, 2 vols. (Mainz, Kircheim, 1904), 392–95, 404–15.

22. Vivian Boland, *St. Thomas Aquinas* (London: Bloomsbury, 2007), 108.

23. See brief discussion of Thomas's status in the Catholic Church in Hans Küng, *Great Christian Thinkers: Paul, Origen, Augustine, Aquinas, Luther, Schleiermacher, Barth* (London: Continuum, 1994), 114. For Thomas's standing in the modern Catholic Church, see Leo XIII, *Aeterni Patris: On the Restoration of Christian Philosophy* (Boston: St. Paul Editions, n.d.).

24. See Denis Janz, *Luther and Late Medieval Thomism: A Study in Theological Anthropology* (Waterloo, ON: Wilfrid Laurier University Press, 2009); *Luther on Thomas Aquinas: The Angelic Doctor in the Thought of the Reformer* (Stuttgart: Franz Steiner Verlag, 1989).

the doctrine of grace. As we saw, the key problem with Augustine's doctrine of grace is that it gave rise to a profound dilemma due to the tension between his doctrine of sin and grace on one hand and the sacraments on the other. In either trajectory, sinners are driven inward to the question of whether they are genuinely elect, or conversely have appropriately used their free will to cooperate with the grace objectified in the sacraments.

Indeed, as we saw in the previous chapters, in his late teaching on predestination Augustine emphasized the uncertainty of the believer's apprehension of grace. Believers have no assurance that they are elect or possess the gift of perseverance. Believers must spend their entire lives humbly praying for perseverance until their temporal death. The sacramentalist trajectory does not do much better in lending certainty to the believer's apprehension of grace. In this, Ockham's theology of sin and grace was simply the culmination of the sacramentalist trajectory of the Augustinian dilemma. God's grace is present in the sacraments as a possibility to be grasped by sinners who do their best. Indeed, if sin is mere privation of the good as Augustine claims, why would there not be an expectation that the will (which still has some capacities left after the fall) would do at least a small thing in preparation for grace? Nevertheless, humans can never genuinely be certain of their moral capacities or what decisions they will make in the future. Therefore, reliance on the mechanism of human freedom to apprehend grace sows as much uncertainty and fear as the secret predestinating will of God. Humans are as hidden from themselves as God is to them apart from revelation.

With this uncertainty of grace came extreme spiritual agony for many individuals in the late Middle Ages, including Luther. The effect of the uncertainty of grace and salvation is not to make sinners humble (as Augustine and the later Catholic tradition believed), but to drive them to back to self-trust, that is, the very root of sin (Rom 14:23). Berndt Hamm has noted that one of the fundamental contradictions of late medieval piety is that it instructed the faithful to speak humble prayers, while insisting that they actually be worthy of God's favor.[25] As we saw in the previous chapter, in a sense Augustine undermines his own project of reorienting

---

25. Berndt Hamm, *The Early Luther: Stages in a Reformation Reorientation*, trans. Martin Lohrmann (Grand Rapids: Eerdmans, 2014), 34–37.

human nature to God by exacerbating the self-focus of the sinner by making grace uncertain. In attempting to discern the certainty of grace, the sinner becomes self-trusting and uses good works not for the glory of God or the love of neighbor, but to build their own certainty of salvation.

Nevertheless, it must be observed that the main reason Augustine's theology of grace does not solve the problem of calming the anguish of the scrupulous is that it was never designed to do so in the first place. The uncertainty of salvation and the fear of hell was a problem that Augustine's theology seems totally unprepared for. As Philip Cary correctly notes, although Augustine certainly believed in eternal damnation, it does not appear to be something that he was particularly worried about or that motivated his conversion to Christianity.[26]

In this, Augustine was certainly not alone in the early church. As we have seen in the previous chapter, the two trajectories which inform early Christian soteriological concerns center on the fear of Gnosticism or Manichaeism and Pelagianism. On the one hand, early Christian authors generally believed that the claims of created nature and therefore free will must be sufficiently exalted to emphasize that the created order (and therefore also the creator god) is good. The desire to bolster the goodness of created nature remained a major motivating factor for theologians throughout the Middle Ages in light of the periodic outbreak of heretical Manichaean movements like the Bogomils and the Cathars.[27] On the other hand, Augustine and the post-Augustinian church wanted to emphasize that created nature must be sufficiently impotent in its ability to achieve salvation so as to need the grace of God and support the divine sovereignty of taking the initiative in salvation. How these two factors are to be balanced off against each other and how they intersect with the Christological and Trinitarian teaching of the early church is aptly illustrated by Schleiermacher's model of the four natural heresies of Christianity (Manichaeism or Docetism vs. Pelagianism or Nazarenism [Ebionism]).[28]

---

26. Phillip Cary, *Meaning of Protestant Theology*, 104.

27. Malcolm Barber, *The Cathars: Dualist Heretics in Languedoc in the High Middle Ages* (London: Routledge, 2004); Dimitri Obolensky, *The Bogomils: A Study in Balkan Neo-Manichaeism* (Cambridge: Cambridge University Press, 1948).

28. Friedrich Schleiermacher, *The Christian Faith*, trans. H. R. Mackintosh and J. S. Stewart (Edinburgh: T&T Clark, 1999), 374–76.

As should be clear, balancing these dual pressures became the driving force of most medieval theologians' doctrine of grace and justification, as it has remained for Roman Catholic theologians up to the present. Providing a form of assurance of divine grace was not the goal of this system. Indeed, such assurance was considered to be spiritually harmful since it might make a sinner feel prideful either for being specially favored by God (the predestinarian trajectory) or for properly using their free will so that they had a reason to boast (the sacramentalist trajectory). Although Augustine's theology was certainly able to coherently explain how one could harmonize the claims of nature and grace, it was very poor at comforting sinners suffering terrors of conscience brought on by the apocalyptic fear of the late medieval "rupture of the times."[29]

LUTHER'S FIRST TURNING:
DICTATA SUPER PSALTERIUM, 1513–1515

Luther's superior in the Augustinian Order, Johannes von Staupitz, attempted to counteract the young Augustinian friar's spiritual fears by pointing to the crucified Jesus.[30] Staupitz reasoned that if God in Christ had out of love suffered for sinners, it was in the crucified Jesus that the scrupulous could find assurance of divine grace.[31] In his own preaching, Staupitz spoke in terms reminiscent of Augustine by positing the morally incapacitating nature of original sin and the radical nature of predestinating grace.[32] Nevertheless, unlike Augustine, Staupitz's writing is considerably more Christologically focused.[33] In predestining the elect, God binds himself to the elect and owes them salvation because of his sovereign choice, not because of their deserts. Staupitz speaks of the mediatorial works of Christ as a way that God pays the "debt" (*ex debito*

---

29. Oswald Bayer, "Martin Luther," in *The Reformation Theologians: Introduction to Theology in the Early Modern Period*, ed. Carter Lindberg (Malden, MA: Blackwell, 2002), 51.

30. David Steinmetz, *Luther and Staupitz: An Essay in the Intellectual Origins of the Protestant Reformation* (Durham: Duke University Press, 1980), 32–33. Also see Franz Posset, *The Front-Runner of the Catholic Reformation: The Life and Works of Johann von Staupitz* (Surrey, UK: Ashgate, 2003).

31. Graham Tomlin, *Luther and His World: An Introduction* (Oxford: Lion Books, 2002), 37.

32. See Johannes von Staupitz, "Eternal Predestination and its Execution in Time," in *Forerunners of the Reformation: Illustrated by Key Documents*, ed. Heiko Oberman (Philadelphia: Fortress, 1981), 175–204.

33. See Julius Köstlin, *The Theology of Luther in Historical Development and Inner Harmony*, trans. Charles Hay, 2 vols. (Philadelphia: Lutheran Publication Society, 1897), 1:65.

gratie) he owes to the elect by atoning for their sins.[34] The key is that God's election and grace were to be comprehended through the encounter with the crucified Jesus, a theme that would continue in the theology of Luther.

Although Staupitz is seen by much of modern scholarship as essentially eclectic in his thinking,[35] many of his views on the doctrine of grace appear to have been influenced by a new form of Augustinianism that had arisen in the early modern church. There was of course a late medieval school of Augustinian thought, begun by Thomas Bradwardine[36] and later systematically expounded by Gregory of Rimini,[37] often referred to as the *Schola Augustiniana Moderna*. The *Schola Augustiniana Moderna* combined an Augustinian doctrine of grace with a nominalist philosophical orientation.[38]

Nevertheless, Staupitz's movement was different from the *Schola Augustiniana Moderna* because it was inspired by the new availability of critical editions of Augustine's works published in Basel in 1506 by Johannes Amerbach.[39] Direct interactions with Augustine's works (rather than reading collected quotations, as was typical of most medieval theology) led to a greater appreciation of Augustine's theology on its own terms throughout the early modern period. It goes without saying that this direct reception of Augustine's theology was an outgrowth of the Renaissance Humanist principle of *ad fontes*.[40]

Augustine had a significant impact on the young Luther.[41] Luther read Augustine's writings in collections as early 1509,[42] and finally gained access

---

34. David Steinmetz, *Misericordia Dei: The Theology of Johannes von Staupitz in Its Late Medieval Setting* (Brill: Leiden, 1968), 55.

35. Lohse, *Martin Luther's Theology*, 24.

36. See Heiko Oberman, *Archbishop Thomas Bradwardine, a Fourteenth Century Augustinian: A Study of His Theology in Its Historical Context* (Utrecht: Kemink, 1957).

37. Gordon Leff, *Gregory of Rimini: Tradition and Innovation in the Fourteenth Century Thought* (Manchester: University of Manchester Press, 1961).

38. McGrath, *Intellectual Origins*, 82–87; Heiko Oberman, *Masters of the Reformation: The Emergence of a New Intellectual Climate in Europe*, trans. Dennis Martin (Cambridge: Cambridge University Press, 1981), 64–112.

39. Pereira, *Augustine of Hippo and Martin Luther*, 300.

40. Lewis Spitz, *The Religious Renaissance of the German Humanists* (Cambridge: Harvard University Press, 1963); Lewis Spitz, "Humanism in the Reformation," in *Renaissance: Studies in Honor of Hans Baron*, ed. Anthony Molho and John Tedeschi (DeKalb, IL: Northern Illinois University Press) 643–62.

41. See the classic study: Adolf Hamel, *Der junge Luther und Augustin: Ihre Beziehungen in der Rechtfertigungslehre mach Luthers erstem Vorlesungen 1509–1518 untersucht*, 2 vols. (Gütersloh: C. Bertelsmann, 1934–1935).

42. Lohse, *Martin Luther's Theology*, 23.

to the aforementioned Amerbach editions in 1515.[43] As David Steinmetz had shown, this interaction with Augustine's theology through Staupitz was likely the thing that inspired his movement toward a new Reformation theology and is the source of Augustinian influence in his thought.[44] This interpretation of the Augustinian influence on Luther's theology appears to be considerably more warranted than Heiko Oberman's claim that the Reformer was influenced by the *Schola Augustiniana Moderna*. Contrary to Oberman's claim, it must be observed that although it is clear that Luther directly read Augustine's works,[45] it is unclear that he read those of other late medieval Augustinian authors. Oberman presents the evidence that such works were available to Luther in the Wittenberg university library, but this does not prove his interaction with them.[46]

The shift of Luther's thinking in an Augustinian direction during this period is significant. In his handwritten notes in his copy of Lombard's *Sentences* in 1509, it may be discerned that Luther was still at that stage very much under the thrall of Ockham's doctrine of sin and grace.[47] As we will see below, by the time he began to write his first commentaries on the Psalms, Luther had clearly adopted an Augustinian doctrine of grace.[48]

Luther had visited Rome in 1510 on a mission for his order and was appalled at what he had seen.[49] When the Reformer returned to Germany that same year, he was assigned by Staupitz (contrary to his wishes) to become a professor of biblical studies at the fledging Wittenberg University.[50] In the wake of earning his doctorate in 1512, Luther began his course of instruction by lecturing on the Psalms to his students

43. Arnoud Visser, *Reading Augustine in the Reformation: The Flexibility of Intellectual Authority in Europe, 1500–1620* (Oxford: Oxford University Press, 2011), 25.

44. Steinmetz, *Luther and Staupitz*, 3–34.

45. Visser, *Reading Augustine in the Reformation*, 25.

46. Heiko Oberman, "*Tuus sum, salvum me fac*: Augustinreveil zwischen Renaissance und Reformation," in *Scientia Augustiniana: Studien über Augustinus, den Augustinismus und den Augustinerorden. Festschrift Adolar Zumkeller zum 60*, ed. C. P. Mayer and W. Eckermann (Würzburg: Augustinus Verlag, 1975), 349–94.

47. Lohse, *Martin Luther's Theology*, 45–50.

48. Lohse, *Martin Luther's Theology*, 23.

49. E. G. Schwiebert, *Luther and His Times: The Reformation from a New Perspective* (St. Louis: Concordia, 1950), 174–92.

50. Schwiebert, *Luther and His Times*, 193–98.

between 1513 and 1515.[51] These lectures represent a series of emerging themes in Luther's early theology.

In expounding the Psalms to his students, Luther made significant use of Augustine's own commentaries on the Psalms.[52] Central to Augustine's exegesis was the idea that the Psalms were Christological, an exegetical decision that Luther also makes.[53] As a result, Luther reads the Psalms as the prayers of Jesus, or David's prophesies of Jesus: "Whatever is said [in the Psalms] of the Lord Jesus Christ in his person must be understood allegorically of the help that is in him, and of the church conformed to him in everything. It must also be understood tropologically of every spiritual and inner person: in opposition to the flesh and outer person."[54]

There is both continuity and discontinuity with the earlier tradition in Luther's approach to the Psalms. Throughout his Psalm commentaries, Luther sees Jesus as a man of sorrows. As Marc Lienhard shows, in this point, Luther broke with Augustine to a certain extent by attributing the Psalms of repentance and degradation to the man Jesus. Augustine had considered it to be impious to attribute the words of repentance to the sinless Christ.[55] Luther nevertheless taught that because Christ had taken upon himself the sins of humanity, it was perfectly reasonable to attribute even the penitential Psalms to him: "Let us, I say, understand our sins and His [Christ's] punishment at the same time, expressed in the same words. ... Therefore, Christ was stuck in our mud, namely, in the lust of our flesh, which leads Him into the deep and abyss."[56] Luther's position on this point is not absolutely unique. For example, Aquinas also attributed the penitential Psalms to Christ, seeing the crucifixion as a confession of human sin.[57] Nevertheless, as we will see, Luther's belief that that sin was imputed to Christ does in large measure anticipate his

---

51. Lohse, *Martin Luther's Theology*, 51–67.

52. Uuras Saarnivaara, *Luther Discovers the Gospel: New Light upon Luther's Way from Medieval Catholicism to Evangelical Faith* (St. Louis: Concordia, 2005), 60.

53. Jared Wicks, *Man Yearning for Grace: Luther's Early Spiritual Teachings* (Washington, D.C.: Corpus, 1968), 42–43.

54. Lectures on the Psalms (1513–1515), WA 55:1. Cited in Lohse, *Martin Luther's Theology*, 52–53.

55. Marc Lienhard, *Luther: Witness to Jesus Christ: Stages and Themes of the Reformer's Christology*, trans. Edwin Robertson (Minneapolis: Augsburg, 1982), 25.

56. Lectures on the Psalms (1513–1515), LW 10:354–55.

57. Christine Helmer, *The Trinity and Martin Luther* (Bellingham, WA: Lexham Press, 2017), 174.

notion of justification as an exchange of realities between Christ and the believer that deviated in some significant ways from how redemption had been conceived in the medieval tradition.

In the early Psalms commentaries, it must be observed that Luther's description of Christ to some extent also shows the influence of a group of thinkers known as the "Rhineland Mystics."[58] Luther encountered these mystics both through Staupitz's counsel and his own personal reading.[59] Rhineland mysticism had originated with Meister Eckhart, a Saxon Dominican of the fourteenth century tried for heresy by the Avignon Papacy.[60] Some of Eckhart's ideas had been spread in a modified and more popular form through the writings of Johannes Tauler,[61] as well as a work known as the *Theologia Germanica* (sometimes circulated under the title of *Theologia Deutsch, Theologia Teutsch,* or simply as *Der Franckforter*), written by an anonymous author.[62]

Eckhart had been heavily influenced by Neoplatonism and held that genuine spiritual experience came through something called "the birth of God in the soul" (*Gottesgeburt*),[63] culminating in a mystical breakthrough into fellowship with God's absolute transcendent being (*Der Durchbruch*).[64] This mystical birth was facilitated by emptying the human soul of the images of all temporal things.[65] Temporal things alienate humans and prevent them from fellowship with the absolutely transcendent Godhead (*Gottheit*), which Eckhart described as a "silent desert" (*stille Wüste*).[66] Therefore, becoming emptied was the prerequisite for being filled with the

58. Steven Ozment, "Eckhart and Luther: German Mysticism and Protestantism," *The Thomist* 42 (1978): 258–80.

59. Michael Mullett, *Martin Luther* (London: Routledge, 2015), 87–88.

60. Jeanne Ancelet-Hustache, *Master Eckhart and the Rhineland Mystics* (London: Longmans, 1957). Bernard McGinn, *The Mystical Thought of Meister Eckhart: The Man from Whom God Hid Nothing* (St. Louis: Herder & Herder, 2003). Also see Meister Eckhart, *The Complete Mystical Works of Meister Eckhart* (St. Louis: Herder & Herder, 2010).

61. Bernard McGinn, *The Harvest of Mysticism in Medieval Germany* (St. Louis: Herder & Herder, 2005), 240–96.

62. Bengt Hoffman, trans., *The Theologia Germanica of Martin Luther* (New York: Paulist). Also see discussion in McGinn, *The Harvest of Mysticism,* 392–404.

63. Robert K. C. Forman, *Meister Eckhart: Mystic as Theologian, An Experiment in Methodology* (Rockport, MA: Element, 1991), 126–66.

64. Forman, *Meister Eckhart,* 167–94.

65. Forman, *Meister Eckhart,* 138–39.

66. Forman, *Meister Eckhart,* 66–67.

divine fullness of spiritual union. As can be inferred, this idea that proper preparation of spiritual fulfillment was emptying could very easily lend itself to a kind of mysticism of the cross, already present in the Western tradition from figures like Bernard of Clairvaux,[67] who also exerted significant influence on Luther.[68] Although Eckhart himself did not take much interest in a mysticism of the cross, his followers certainly did, and therefore became a source of the young Luther's thinking.

Within this mysticism of the cross that we find in the later Rhineland mystics and Bernard of Clairvaux, Christ becomes the model for the self-emptying that is a necessary preparation for the coming of God's grace. According to Tauler, the mystic moves through the stages of purification, illumination, and then union.[69] All creatures are empty when compared to the divine fullness. Hence, recognizing one's own emptiness through utter passivity, humbleness, and self-effacement found in the example the crucified Christ.[70] That is to say, utter passive receptivity (*Gelassenheit*) was the prerequisite for divine grace.[71]

As should be clear from this cursory reading of Luther's early Psalm commentaries, here we see the young Luther taking up the medieval question regarding the necessary preparation for grace and the role of human agency. First, whereas the Franciscan tradition (Scotist and Ockhamist) had said it was possible for creatures to love God above all things (although this in itself did not merit salvation),[72] Luther following Augustine holds that humans are completely morally incapacitated by sin: "For we are still unrighteous and unworthy before God, so that whatever we can do is nothing before him."[73]

67. See Anthony N. S. Lane, *Bernard of Clairvaux: Theologian of the Cross* (Collegeville, MN: Liturgical, 2013).

68. Theo Bell, *Divus Bernhardus: Bernhard von Clairvaux in Martin Luthers Schriften* (Mainz: P. von Zabern, 1993); Franz Posset, *Pater Bernhardus: Martin Luther and Bernard of Clairvaux* (Kalamazoo: Cistercian, 2000).

69. Josef Schmidt, "Introduction," in *Johannes Tauler: Sermons*, trans. Maria Shrady (New York: Paulist, 1985), 15.

70. See Ferdinand Vetter, *Die Preditigen Taulers* (Zürich: Weidmann, 1910), 170–76.

71. Brecht, *Martin Luther*, 1:139–40.

72. Marilyn McCord Adams, "Genuine Agency, Something Shared? The Holy Spirit and Other Gifts," in *Oxford Studies in Medieval Philosophy*, vol. 1, ed. Robert Pasnau (Oxford: Oxford University Press, 2013), 53.

73. Lectures on the Psalms (1513-1515), LW 10:236.

Second, in light of his acceptance of the Augustinian *sola gratia* and the theology of humble self-emptying (*humilitas*) that he received from the Rhineland mystics and Bernard, his answer to the question for the preparation is an almost perfect inversion of the Ockhamist principle of *facere quod in se est* (do what lies within you). Whereas Ockhamism called for moral hyperactivity as the prerequisite for the first grace, Luther now called for hyper-passivity. The humble, suffering, self-effacing Christ served here as the model for the Christian.[74] He had not engaged in hyper-activity in order to curry favor with God, but rather had stood in total solidarity with humanity and passively received God's judgment for it.

Therefore, in commenting on Psalm 51, Luther observes that to be justified, the sinner must justify God in his accusation, much as the humiliated Christ did in taking upon himself the sins of the world: "God is not justified by anyone except the one who accuses and condemns and judges himself."[75] Interestingly enough, although Luther at this stage has abandoned the Ockhamist claim that humans by the powers of nature are capable of meriting the first grace (albeit only according to congruous merit), he has not abandoned the notion that the preparation for grace is made possible by covenantal causality: "Yes, even faith and grace, through which we are today justified, would not of themselves justify us *if God's covenant did not do it*. It is precisely for this reason that we are saved: *He made a testament and covenant with us* that whoever believes and is baptized shall be saved."[76]

LUTHER'S ROMANS COMMENTARY OF 1516

Luther's abandonment of the Ockhamist *facere quod in se est* in favor of a theology of humbleness and self-effacement based on the Augustinian principle of *sola gratia* in the Psalms commentaries became even more pronounced in his commentary on Romans of 1516. In this work, the quest for self-imposed emptying and humbleness in the preparation for grace becomes a quest to cultivate an attitude of self-hatred (*odium sui*) and resignation to damnation (*resignatio ad infernum*). Luther's commentary on

---

74. Gerhard Ebeling, *Lutherstudien*, vol. 1 (Tübingen: Mohr Siebeck, 1971), 1–68.

75. Lectures on the Psalms (1513-1515), LW 10:236.

76. Lectures on the Psalms (1513-1515), LW 10:237. Emphasis added.

Romans also promotes a more clearly defined view of justification. This view of justification remains a transformational model, although there are elements of teachings that would later germinate into the Reformer's mature reformational theology.

As previously noted, Luther begins his commentary on Romans within a similar trajectory that one finds in the Psalms commentary. As an Augustinian theologian influenced by the Rhineland mysticism, Luther asserts that the reception of divine grace is only possible if the believer is hollowed out and brought to nothing first. The truly elect believer will have no basis left within them for carnal security. The truly justified will regard themselves as utterly sinful and without inner resources that can serve as a temptation to self-incurvature (*incurvatus in se*). In the introduction to the commentary, the young Reformer writes:

> The chief purpose of this letter is to break down, to pluck up, and to destroy all wisdom and righteousness of the flesh. This includes all works which in the eyes of people or even in our own eyes may be great works. No matter whether these works are done with a sincere heart and mind, this letter is to affirm and state and magnify sin, no matter how much someone insists that it does not exist, or that it was believed not to exist.[77]

Of course, much of the above statement could be easily agreed to by Augustine and the majority of medieval theologians. After all, Christian theologians have universally agreed throughout the ages that humans should be humble before their creator. Moreover, Catholic along with Protestant theologians have uniformly agreed that human beings should not trust in themselves above God. Nevertheless, Luther's key difference with his predecessors is that in the Romans commentary he asserts for the first time that for the self-incurvature of sin to be truly overcome all self-love and any inner resources that humanity might claim must be removed from the soteriological equation. If a theology asserts that humans have any goodness left in them that grace can build on, then it will inevitably promote self-love rather than the love of God for his own sake.[78]

---

77. Lectures on Romans (1516), LW 25: 135.
78. Cary, *Meaning of Protestant Theology*, 130–35.

As we saw earlier, medieval and later Catholic theologians would resist Luther's total emptying of the sinner as a movement in the direction of Manichaeism. In other words, would it not imply that nature itself was evil if there is no good within human nature that grace can cultivate and augment? Augustine and the medieval theologians consistently taught that although the human will and inner disposition can not merit salvation on their own, God's grace does not negate but rather builds on humanity's natural disposition, desires, and agency in the process of salvation. For both Augustine and Aquinas, even self-love is perfectly natural and good, although it must be subordinated to the supreme love of God as the true source of goodness.[79] As we will see below, Luther completely abandons this line of reasoning and claims that for the Christian love of God to be truly authentic, it must be one of pure self-negation.

Luther's hollowing out of human potential before God is quite specifically worked out in the Romans commentary through the young Reformer's all-out assault on Augustine and the medieval tradition's appropriation of the Greek philosophical tradition's ethical Eudaemonism.[80] As we have seen in previous chapters, for Augustine and the later medieval tradition, justification was fit into an ethical scheme, taken over from Platonism and Aristotelianism, in which human authenticity and moral rectitude may be found in reaching one's true end (telos). For Augustine and the medieval theologians, reaching one's true potential meant receiving the intelligible vision of God in his essence (visio beatifica) and from this the achievement of true happiness and satisfaction (eudaemonia).[81] Within this scheme, one was made righteous (i.e., justified) in order that one might make this heavenly journey and reach one's full fulfillment and satisfaction. Self-love and the desire to be happy are therefore not bad, but essentially misfire in the act of sin by thinking that created goods will serve as a source of ultimate satisfaction rather than the eternal good

79. O'Donovan, The Problem of Self-Love in Augustine, 56; Eberhard Schockenhoff, "The Theological Virtue of Charity," in The Ethics of Aquinas, ed. Stephen Pope (Washington, DC: Georgetown University Press, 2002), 254–55.

80. O'Donovan, The Problem of Self-Love in Augustine, 16; Joseph J. McInerney, The Greatness of Humility: St. Augustine on Moral Excellence (Eugene, OR: Pickwick, 2016), 66.

81. O'Donovan, The Problem of Self-Love in Augustine, 56–59; Rik van Nieuwenhove, An Introduction to Medieval Theology (Cambridge: Cambridge University Press, 2012), 195–200.

(God). Divine grace therefore does not negate the desire to be happy and the wish for good things for oneself but builds on them.[82]

In his commentary on Romans, Luther engages in a radical critique of Eudaemonism. In doing this, the young Reformer turns many of Augustine's assumptions on him without specifically naming him. Having studied Augustine, Luther seems to implicitly perceive a certain level of contradiction between his Eudaemonism and his doctrine of sin.[83] On the one hand, as we observed in a previous chapter, Augustine insists that self-love and self-centeredness is the root of all sin. On the other hand, as we also saw, Augustine consistently argues that fellowship with God is a higher form of fulfillment for desires of the human heart and its need to be happy. Taken to its logical conclusion, Luther reasons that Augustine and medieval theology's Eudaemonism simply made fellowship with God another tool of self-indulgent satisfaction and self-incurvature. In this, the central goal of the Bishop of Hippo's *caritas* theology failed because it covertly made the love of God about personal fulfillment.

Hence, Luther asserts that although human nature is ontologically good because it is God's creation, it is wrongly oriented because of the totalizing effects of original sin. Original sin is defined as the "total lack of uprightness and the power of all the faculties both of body and soul and of the whole inner and outer man. On top of all this, it is a propensity toward evil."[84] The Ockhamist tradition is seriously mistaken to think that humans are still capable of loving God above all things by their natural powers and that somehow the real difficulty is that the "works of the Law [are merely performed] according to the substance of the act, even if not according to the intention of Him who gave the command, because he is not in the state of grace."[85]

Of course, Augustine would have agreed to both these points, since as we have seen the Bishop of Hippo affirms the total corruption of human nature by original sin. Nevertheless, Augustine also claimed that although everything in human nature is damaged by sin, humans remain correctly

82. Jeff Steele, "Happiness," in *The Cambridge Companion to Medieval Ethics*, ed. Thomas Williams (Cambridge: Cambridge University Press, 2019), 127–49.

83. Cary, *Meaning of Protestant Theology*, 133–34.

84. Lectures on Romans (1516), LW 25:299.

85. Lectures on Romans (1516), LW 25:261.

oriented toward the good even if they cannot achieve it. In their corruption, humans wrongly grasp at temporal goods when they should be seeking after the full satisfaction of God's eternal goodness. The key point for Augustine, though, is that humans still desire the good.

By contrast, Luther holds that humans are oriented in precisely the wrong direction and the desire to serve that which is not God is not a confused apprehension of the good; it is a total falling away from God. The Reformer avoids Manichaeism because his concept of the orienting power of sin is relational, rather than ontological. Humanity's main difficulty is not their incapacitating weakness or confusion about what is genuinely satisfying, but their trust in and desire for that which is not good: "If we were to say that in particular cases human nature knows and wills what is good, but in general neither knows nor wills it. The reason is that it knows nothing but its own good, or what is good and honorable and useful for itself, but not what is good for God and other people."[86]

For Luther humans do not will the good at all because willing anything but to love God for his own sake places one relationally outside of fellowship with the divine. There is no scale of goodness as with Augustine and Aquinas, but a zero-sum game between loving God and loving creatures. Therefore, because human nature has been completely reoriented by sin, it takes even the good gifts of God and turns them into means of self-centered enjoyment:

> The reason is that our nature has been so deeply curved in upon itself because of the viciousness of original sin that it not only turns the finest gifts of God in upon itself and enjoys them (as is evident in the case of legalists and hypocrites), indeed, it even uses God Himself [i.e., the true *telos* of human existence] to achieve these aims, but it also seem to be ignorant of this very fact, that in acting so iniquitously, so perversely, and in such a depraved way, it is even seeking God for its own sake.[87]

In other words, if people seek after God because they find him to be the fulfillment of their self-centered desires, then even the religious quest

---

86. Lectures on Romans (1516), LW 25:345.
87. Lectures on Romans (1516), LW 25:291.

becomes yet another expression of human self-incurvature. Therefore, religious striving (Augustine) and attempts to live up to one's full potential (Aristotle and Aquinas) will only exacerbate original sin. Unlike Augustine and the medieval tradition, original sin is not so much a privation of the good (Augustine), or a privation of proper activity (Aquinas), but a total-izing wrong orientation of the self.

In light of Luther's totalizing notion of sin, humans must radically question all their motives and cling to nothing good or upright in their nature. Indeed, they must stand before God as total sinners (*totus pecca-tor*), in that they are completely morally alienated from God. As a result, two major aspects of late medieval justification theology are repudiated by Luther in the Romans commentary: the role of *habitus* in the process of justification and the non-sinful nature of concupiscence in believers. Since both doctrines have at least some basis in Aristotelianism, the Romans commentary marks the beginning of Luther's career long assault on the use of Aristotle in theology.[88]

First, the young Reformer completely rejects any account of justi-fication wherein the created grace of the *habitus* is infused into sinners, thereby allowing them to actualize themselves as just persons by culti-vating good works. The habits of created grace (faith, hope, love) were supposed to impose a form of justice on sinners, but contrary to this Luther writes: "But this word 'formed' (*formatum*) is under a curse, for it forces us to think of the soul as being the same after as before the out-pouring of love and as if the form were merely added to it at the time of the action, although it is necessary that it be wholly put to death and be changed before putting on love and working in love."[89]

In other words, human nature under sin should not merely be thought of as being too weak to achieve its true *telos* to which it is properly ori-ented. If this were the case, then created grace as a means of augmenting the soul's capacities with virtues would be an appropriate solution to the problem of sin. But as we have seen, for Luther the problem of sin is a matter of a totalizing orientation toward evil, not merely weakness in the quest to achieve one's true end. Since the configuration of the self

---

88. See Theodor Dieter, *Der junge Luther und Aristoteles* (Berlin: De Gruyter, 2001).

89. Lectures on Romans (1516), LW 25:325.

under the thrall of original sin is a complete self-incurvature, then the infused habits of created grace would only make the situation worse. If grace actually became a predicate of our being, then the sinful self would simply abuse that grace as a means of self-love and glorification. The gifts would become something to be conceited about. Therefore, Luther holds that unless we find nothing but sin within ourselves, we will inevitably have grounds for self-incurvature. Although he still uses the language of "infusion" of grace throughout the commentary, Luther[90] follows the earlier tradition of Peter Lombard and teaches that the love by which we love God is the Holy Spirit dwelling in our hearts rather than a created *habitus*.[91]

The second implication in Luther's campaign to totally hollow out the sinner is a reevaluation of a common (though not universal) medieval interpretation of Romans 7, as well as an insistence that concupiscence of believers is genuinely sin. In the medieval tradition, concupiscence is not identical with sin.[92] "Concupiscence" is typically defined as the involuntary desire to sin, most frequently associated in Augustine with sexual sin. In particular, some medieval theologians claimed that for believers that concupiscence was merely the "tinder" of sin (*fomes peccati*) that had the potential to flair up into real sin (i.e., an unlawful act that possesses the consent of the will) while not constituting genuine sin in and of itself.[93]

Although this interpretation of concupiscence certainly pre-dates the medieval encounter with Aristotle, the predominance of Aristotelianism in the Western church after the thirteenth century helped solidify the existing consensus. In favor of the non-sinful nature of post-baptismal concupiscence, Aquinas following Aristotle[94] states that that which is involuntary cannot be blameworthy.[95] Hence, concupiscence must not be thought of as sin in and of itself.[96]

---

90. Lectures on Romans (1516), LW 25:147–48.

91. Peter Lombard, *The Sentences*, trans. Giulio Silano, 4 vols. (Toronto: Pontifical Institute of Medieval Studies, 2007–2010), 1:191.

92. Tatha Wiley, *Original Sin: Origins, Developments, Contemporary Meanings* (New York: Paulist, 2002), 95–96.

93. Ozment, *Age of Reform*, 30.

94. Aristotle, *Nicomachean Ethics*, 1139a19-1138a23.

95. ST, IaIIae, q. 21, art. 3; Aquinas, *Summa Theologiae*, 686.

96. ST, IaIIae, q. 77, art. 6; Aquinas, *Summa Theologiae*, 938–39.

This interpretation of the role of concupiscence in the life of the believer also colored the interpretation of Romans 7. Many (though, by no means all) Scholastic theologians of the Middle Ages and early modern period argued that the chapter was about Paul's life before his conversion.[97] It was claimed that Paul could only be speaking about his experience before conversion since he describes his sinful desires as being both involuntary and at the same time blameworthy (Rom 7:15–20).

As implausible as this interpretation of Romans 7 is (grammatically, Paul is very clearly speaking in the present tense),[98] what is important to recognize is that for many theologians if concupiscence was actually sinful their conception of progress in the Christian life would be rendered completely impossible. That is to say, if concupiscence were counted as sin, the implication would be that in spite of one's best efforts or intentions, wrong desires would perpetually taint all believer's meritorious works. For example, if concupiscence were blameworthy, the merit of resisting sexual temptation would be canceled out if the believer felt in any way enticed while resisting said temptation (Matt 5:27–28). As a result, even under the power of grace, humanity would never make any genuine progress in the process of salvation.

Much as he rejected the concept of grace as a *habitus*, so too Luther insists that Paul is speaks of himself in the present after regeneration in Romans 7: "Therefore only the perfectly spiritual man says: 'Wretched man that I am!' " But the carnal man does not desire to be liberated and be set free but shudders terribly at the freedom that death brings, and he cannot recognize his own wretchedness."[99] Likewise, the desire to sin is itself also sin, even without the consent of the will: "Therefore, act of sin (as it is called by the theologians) is more correctly sin in the sense of the work and fruit of sin, but sin itself is the passion, the tinder, and the

---

97. David Steinmetz "Divided by a Common Past: The Reshaping of the Christian Exegetical Tradition in the Sixteenth Century," *Journal of Medieval and Early Modern Studies* 27, no. 2 (1997): 251. Steinmetz notes that many Scholastics held that Romans 7 pertained to Paul after conversion, although the pre-conversions position was quite mainstream. Luther is probably reacting to this latter exegetical tradition.

98. Daniel Wallace, *Greek Grammar Beyond the Basics: An Exegetical Syntax of the New Testament* (Grand Rapids: Zondervan, 1996), 531–32.

99. Lectures on Romans (1516), LW 25:335.

concupiscence, or the inclination, toward evil and the difficulty of doing good, as he says below (Rom 7:7)."[100]

It should again be stressed that although in taking both of these positions Luther was breaking with the medieval consensus, neither were absolutely novel in the history of Christian thought. Augustine considered concupiscence to be sin, as did Peter Lombard.[101] Similarly, in writing The Retractions at the very end of his life, the Bishop of Hippo reversed his earlier position and asserted that Paul had been speaking about himself after conversion in Romans 7—although taking this position would seem to cause some tensions with his view of justification and merit.[102] Nevertheless, taken together along with the radical critique of Eudaimonism, Luther's teachings on these points represent important elements in a new conception of grace and justification.

As should be evident already, Luther's hollowing out of any pretense of the human subject under the thrall of sin correlates to a new conception of grace. Unlike Augustine, at this stage Luther ceased to see grace as something thaat fills in our gaps (privatio boni) and heals the privation of our being. Neither does Luther hold that humans are primarily defined by their activity, and therefore the purpose of grace cannot be to augment their capacity for right performance (Aquinas). Humans are not defined by ontological completeness or correct agency, but by receptivity to divine action. Right action remains important, but it is secondary and derivative of right receptivity. This why Luther claims (in an oft misunderstood statement) that the Christian life is not a movement from vice to virtue (i.e., Thomistic or Aristotelian potency to act), but from "virtues to the grace of Christ"[103] (i.e., from glorying in right performance to a passive receptivity to God's gracious action).

In salvation humans are passive and God is active: "To the first grace, as well as to the glory we always adopt a passive attitude."[104] In a manner reminiscent of the mystical tradition, Luther asserts that in pure passivity

100. Lectures on Romans (1516), LW 25:259.

101. Wiley, Original Sin, 94–96.

102. Augustine, The Retractions 2.27; Augustine, The Retractions, trans. Mary Inez Bogan (Washington, DC: Catholic University of America Press, 1968), 119.

103. Lectures on Romans (1516), LW 25:136.

104. Lectures on Romans (1516), LW 25:368.

the believer should simply receive all that the Lord gives him. God's act of predestination is the sole cause of salvation and it is unknowable. The true believer remains agnostic and resigns himself to whatever God's eternal decree might be. For this reason, the Christian must not rely on works or self-judgment, but also accept God's totalizing judgment on him and indeed resign himself to damnation (*resignatio ad infernum*):

> But those who are truly righteous in that they abound in love achieve this resignation without great sadness. For because of their abounding love for God they make all things possible, even enduring hell. And by reason of this facility they immediately escape the penalty of this kind. Indeed they have no need to fear being damned, for they willingly and happily submit to damnation for the sake of God. Rather it is they who are damned who try to escape damnation.[105]

Indeed, since all within the sinner is negated by God's judgment, the righteous and grace-filled life of the truly elect believer consists in self-negation and self-hatred (*odium sui*):

> [W]e must do this not only with our voice and with a deceitful heart, but with our whole mind we must confess and wish that we might be damned and destroyed. For we must act toward ourselves in the same way that a man does who hates another man. For he does not hate him in imagination, but he sincerely desires to destroy and kill and damn the person whom he hates. Therefore if we so sincerely want to destroy ourselves that we offer ourselves to hell for the sake of God and His righteousness, we have already made true satisfaction to His righteousness, and He will be merciful and free us.[106]

Much like in the Psalms commentaries, it is Christ himself who is the model for the Christian in this resignation to hell: "For even Christ suffered damnation and desertion more than all the saints ... and in His human nature He acted in no way different than a man to be eternally

---

105. Lectures on Romans (1516), LW 25:382.
106. Lectures on Romans (1516), LW 25:384.

damned to hell. ... This all His saints should imitate."[107] As David Yeago observes, for Luther: "He [God] will crucify and torture you as He did Christ, your pattern, and thus leave you no reason to cling to Him except for His own sweet sake."[108]

As should be clear by now, the young Luther's theology of self-hatred and resignation to damnation (*humilitastheologie*, as Ernst Bizer calls it)[109] is a radicalization of the Augustinian theology of the love of God. If God is to be loved exclusively and for his own sake, then any other love is sin. Indeed, Augustine's view that there is an inherent competition between the love of creatures and the Creator is pushed by Luther to the point where hating oneself is the only sensible resolution of the conflict. This is because in order to be fully authentic the love of God must not become a tool of human self-fulfillment. Therefore, God imposes suffering on his saints and gives them an attitude of resignation to hell as a means of removing from them any ulterior motives for the love for him:

> For to love is to hate oneself, to condemn oneself, and to wish the worst. ... But if someone says: "I do not love my life in this world because I am seeking what is good for it in the life to come," I reply: "You are doing this out of love for yourself, which is a worldly love, and therefore you still love your life in this world." He who loves himself in this way truly loves himself. For he loves himself not in himself but in God, that is, in accord with the will of God, who hates, damns, and wills evil to all sinners, that is, to all of us.[110]

In passages like this, we begin to see the emergence not only of Luther's new concept of grace, but of his new concept of righteousness and justification. Luther asserts that the believer is righteous because he accuses himself as a sinner: "For in this way [self-accusation] we conform ourselves to God, who does not regard or consider anything in us as good."[111]

---

107. Lectures on Romans (1516), LW 25:382.

108. David Yeago, "The Catholic Luther," *First Things* (March, 1996), 39.

109. Ernst Bizer, *Fides ex auditu. Eine Untersuchung über die Entdeckung der Gerechtig-keit Gottes durch Martin Luther* (Neukirchen: Neukirchener Verlag, 1966) 22, 51. Also see discussion in Steinmetz, *Luther and Staupitz*, 78–91.

110. Lectures on Romans (1516), LW 25:382.

111. Lectures on Romans (1516), LW 25:383.

To be righteous is to will what God wills. God wills death, hatred, destruction on sinners, and hence the more the sinner wills himself to be the object of God's destructive judgment then paradoxically the more righteous he becomes.[112] The self-negation of the sinner then stands as righteousness before the judgment seat of God. In the end, woundedness and deathlike passivity manifest one's election by grace of God, rather than ontological healing (Augustine) or an increase in right performance (Aquinas).

Nevertheless, it should be observed that Luther's view of justification at this stage is still about being made righteous, albeit in an unusual and paradoxical manner. This fact has confused a number of interpreters, in that Luther does speak at many points in the Romans commentary of justification as a kind of imputed righteousness. Nevertheless, such talk generally has to do with the believer's present humble anticipation of being made righteous in the future (sinner in *re*, righteous in *spe*)[113] and not with the reception of the alien righteousness of Christ through faith:

> It is similar to the case of a sick man who believes the doctor who promises him a sure recovery and in the meantime obeys the doctor's order in the hope of the promised recovery and abstains from those things which have been forbidden him, so that he may in no way hinder the promised return to health or increase his sickness until the doctor can fulfill his promise to him. Now is this sick man well? The fact is that he is both sick and well at the same time. He is sick in fact, but he is well because of the sure promise of the doctor, whom he trusts and who has reckoned him as already cured, because he is sure that he will cure him; for he has already begun to cure him and no longer reckons to a sickness unto death. In the same way Christ, our good Samaritan, has brought His half-dead man into the inn to be cared for, and He has begun to heal him, having promised him the most complete cure unto

112. See similar argument in Gerhard Forde, "Forensic Justification and Law in Lutheran Theology," in *Justification by Faith: Lutherans and Catholics in Dialogue VII*, ed. H. George Anderson, T. Austin Murphy, and Joseph Burgess (Minneapolis: Augsburg, 1985), 281–87.

113. See Karl Holl, "Die Rechtfertigungslehre in Luthers Vorlesung über den Römerbrief mit besonderer Rücksicht auf die Frage der Heilsgewißheit," in *Gesammelte Aufsätze*, 3 vols. (Tübingen: Mohr, 1928), 1:111–54. Holl sees Luther's view of justification at this stage as one of genuine progressive sanctification (*reale Gerechtmachung*).

eternal life, and He does not impute his sins, that is, his wicked desires, unto death, but in the meantime things by which his cure might be impeded and his sin, that is, his concupiscence, might be increased. Now, is he perfectly righteous? No, for he is at the same time both a sinner and a righteous man; a sinner in fact, but a righteous man by the sure imputation and promise of God, that he will redeem him from sin until he heals him totally.[114]

In this passage, much of the language is deceptively similar to Luther's later understanding of justification, but it should be cautioned that there are many significant differences. In the mature Luther (as well as later Protestantism), humans are at the same time saint and sinner (*simul iustus et peccator*). This is due to the fact that justification is imputed righteousness for the sake of Christ. The believer comprehends this on the basis of the promise of God by faith alone.[115]

By contrast, in Luther's early Romans commentary, justification certainly does include an imputation of righteousness, but the nature of this imputation is significantly different. Imputation occurs on the basis of future righteousness when the sinner will be fully healed from the illness of sin. Unlike the Reformer's later theology where the *signum* of the word contains the *res* of Christ's alien righteousness, the Luther of the Romans commentary teaches that justification as a future eschatological righteousness distant from the word that promises it.[116] The promise of the doctor (God) is not an effective and saving word that communicates the alien righteousness of Christ, but a promise that if one continues to mortify the flesh and strive after righteousness sin will eventually be overcome at the eschaton. Therefore, despite some superficial similarities (particularly regarding the idea of promise),[117] this picture of justification in Luther's Romans commentary remains essentially sanative in accordance with Augustine and the medieval tradition.[118] Indeed, the image of

---

114. Lectures on Romans (1516), LW 25:260.

115. Freedom of a Christian (1521), LW 31:344–47.

116. I owe this insight to Charles Lehmann and Naomichi Masaki.

117. Bizer, *Fides ex auditu*, 48.

118. Axel Gyllenkrok, *Rechtfertigung und Heiligung in der frühen evangelischen Theologie Luthers* (Uppsala: Wiesbaden, 1952), 4.

the divine physician appears to be directly taken from Augustine's Psalm commentaries.[119]

Likewise, it also should not go unnoticed that there appears to be a significant tension between Luther's insistence in the passage cited above that Christians should hope in and trust the word of redemption and his other aforementioned remarks in the commentary that believers should despair and resign themselves to damnation. Similarly, the image of healing of a patient that appears in the passage also seems at odds with the young Reformer's earlier talk of grace killing, destroying, and negating sinners.[120]

One way of reading the passage could be that Luther is asserting that healing paradoxically takes place by negation and wounding, just as hope arises paradoxically under the outward form of divine damnation. In support of this reading, in another passage after Luther speaks of the believer's self-condemnation, he states: "Thus our life is hidden under death, love for ourselves under hate for ourselves, glory under ignominy, salvation under damnation, our kingship under exile, heaven under hell, wisdom under foolishness, righteousness under sin, power under weakness."[121] In this passage, we can observe the beginnings of Luther's doctrine of God's action *sub contrario*,[122] which we will explore more fully in a later chapter. In spite of this paradoxical explanation, it is difficult to see how Luther could coherently maintain this theology of self-negation without a genuine theology of the assurance of the grace of God through the word. This development would begin in the next stage of his thought to which we now turn.

---

119. Augustine, *On the Psalms*, 147:7 [Masoretic Text: Psalm 146:7]; NPNF1 8:666. See Hamel, *Der junge Luther und Augustin*, 118–19.

120. Cary, *Meaning of Protestant Theology*, 132.

121. Lectures on Romans (1516), LW 25:382–83.

122. McGrath, *Luther's Theology of the Cross*, 169.

CHAPTER 9

The Reformation Breakthrough:
Luther's Rediscovery of the Sacramentality of the Word

H ans Urs von Balthasar once famously observed that all theologians go through two great conversions. This description, which Balthasar applied to Augustine and Karl Barth, can also easily be applied to Luther. As we have already seen, at some point in the early 1510s, Luther transitioned from being a consistent follower of the *via moderna* (Ockham and Biel) to developing a *humilitastheologie* (Humility theology) drawing on biblical humanism, Augustinianism, and mysticism (Rhineland mystics and Bernard of Clairvaux). In this chapter, we follow the model of Luther's development proposed by Uuras Saarnivaara, Ernst Bizer, and Oswald Bayer in opposition to that of Karl Holl and the Luther Renaissance.

What should have become clear by now in our review of the history of the young Luther's theological development is that the Reformer unlocked the true extent of the destructive nature of the dilemma that Augustine had bequeathed to the medieval church. In effect, Luther took the sacramentalist and predestinarian options in the Augustinian dilemma to their logical extremes. In his Ockhamist phase, Luther attempted to follow the most logically consistent version of the sacramentalist option and gain access to divine grace as a possibility objectified in the sacraments by utilizing the full power of his limited free will (*facere quod in se est*). This attempt resulted in systematic spiritual self-abuse, which very nearly destroyed Luther physically and mentally. After his transition to *humilitastheologie*, the young Reformer attempted to solve his spiritual problems by inverting the Ockamist *facere quod in se est* and thereby adopting an attitude of pure passivity to God's terrifyingly secret predestinating will. This resulted in a bizarre and equally unhealthy theology of self-hatred and resignation to damnation as a sign of true election.

Both options in the Augustinian dilemma ultimately threw Luther back on his own moral efforts, which could give him neither spiritual peace nor certainty about God's will toward him. This was as true of the Ockhamist phase as it was of the later *humilitastheologie*. In spite of Luther's assertion in the Romans commentary of the need to rely on God's electing grace alone in a state of deathlike passivity, the young Reformer's emphasis still lies on the sinner's agency in cultivating such an attitude (albeit by the power of grace). Below, we will argue that it was only the discovery of the sacramentality of the word that allowed Luther to transcend the Augustinian dilemma and develop his mature theology of justification.

THE 95 THESES

In 1517, Luther became involved in a controversy over the late medieval practice of indulgences.[1] As a result of a corrupt financial deal between Albrecht the Archbishop of Mainz and Pope Leo X (the ultimate goal of which was to pay for new St. Peter's Basilica in Rome), the Dominican Friar Johann Tetzel was empowered to sell indulgences just over the border from Saxony, the duchy in which Wittenberg was located. Many of Luther's parishioners purchased these indulgences and asked Luther if they were authentic.[2] Although Luther did not reject indulgences at this point, he nevertheless saw Tetzel as seriously abusing the practice,[3] a sentiment that Pope Leo would also eventually agree with.[4]

An indulgence was the remitting of temporal punishment by the church under the authority of the pope.[5] Medieval Latin penitential theology

---

1. Scott Hendrix, *Luther and the Papacy: Stages in a Reformation Conflict* (Philadelphia: Fortress, 1981), 22–32.

2. Roland H. Bainton, *Here I Stand: A Life of Martin Luther* (Nashville: Abingdon, 1978), 51–60.

3. Hendrix, *Luther and the Papacy*, 30–31.

4. Thomas Schirrmacher, *Indulgences: A History of Theology and Reality of Indulgences and Purgatory: A Protestant Evaluation* (Eugene, OR: Wipf & Stock, 2014), 88.

5. Alan Spence, *Justification: A Guide for the Perplexed* (Edinburgh: T&T Clark, 2012), 61.

distinguished between eternal punishment (remitted by absolution) and temporal punishment (remitted through penitential works, or time in purgatory).[6] Beginning with Clement VI in the bull *Unigenitus Dei Filius* of 1343, the medieval popes claimed to possess access to and control over something referred to as the "Treasury of Merits" (*thesaurus ecclesiae*).[7] Because of the mystical unity of the body of Christ, there was a single reservoir of merit made up of the merit of Christ (which was infinite) and the saints (who had performed more good works than necessary to achieve salvation). Because the pope possessed the office of the keys given originally to Peter in Matthew 16, he could release (in the sacramental system) or withhold (as in the case of papal interdict) these merits any time he wished.[8]

Under normal circumstances, the merits of Christ were released through the sacramental ministry of the church. Because the Catholic Church was in fellowship with the pope, his power of the keys guaranteed the presence of divine grace in the means of grace.[9] Beyond this, the late medieval popes claimed to be able to release merits from the Treasury of Merits in the form of an indulgence so as to abrogate penance or even time in purgatory in exchange for a certain good work.[10] Such good works included the giving of money to the church.[11] Therefore, the theology of the Treasury of Merits stood as the justification for the practice of selling indulgences. In light of the uncertainty that one had performed enough penance and the fear of purgatory as a quasi-hell, the inoculation of an

---

6. Thomas Tentler, *Sin and Confession on the Eve of the Reformation* (Princeton, NJ: Princeton University Press, 1977), 23. Also see: Robert Shaffern, *The Penitents' Treasury: Indulgences in Latin Christendom, 1175–1375* (Scranton, PA: University of Scranton Press, 2007).

7. David Bagchi, "Luther's *Ninety-Five Theses* and the Contemporary Criticism of Indulgences," in *Promissory Notes on the Treasury of Merits: Indulgences in Late Medieval Europe*, ed. Robert Norman Swanson (Leiden: Brill, 2006), 344.

8. Robert Shaffern, "The Medieval Theology of Indulgence," in *Promissory Notes on the Treasury of Merits: Indulgences in Late Medieval Europe*, ed. Robert Norman Swanson (Leiden: Brill, 2006), 31–33.

9. See discussion in W. H. Principe, "The School Theologians' Views of the Papacy," in *The Religious Roles of the Papacy: Ideals and Realities 1150–1300* (Leiden: Brill, 1989), 106–8.

10. Heiko Oberman, *The Harvest of Late Medieval Theology: Gabriel Biel and Late Medieval Theology* (Grand Rapids: Baker Academic, 2000), 405–6.

11. G. R. Evans, *A Short History of Medieval Christianity* (London: I. B. Tauris, 2017), 79.

indulgence to remove any potential remaining temporal punishment was attractive to late medieval Christians.[12]

Contrary to what is popularly believed, the Ninety-Five Theses are not genuine Reformation theology. Luther's protest against the sale of indulgences is essentially in keeping with his *humilitastheologie* that we examined in the last two sections. The key to his objection to how Tetzel was preaching indulgences was that it made it possible to pay a fee in order to forego actually living the Christian life.[13] If the real penance was *humilitas*, then by telling people that they could avoid satisfaction by paying a fee inculcated the idea in them that they could forgo the genuine repentance (which penitential acts merely externally expressed) in exchange for money.

Luther begins the Ninety-Five Theses with the statement: "When our Lord and Master Jesus Christ said, 'Repent' (Matt 4:17), he willed the entire life of believers to be one of repentance."[14] Relying on the humanist principle of *ad fontes*, Luther clarifies in the commentary on the Ninety-Five Theses that this does not refer to the penitential works as the Vulgate version of Jesus's words in Matthew seemed to imply: "Do penance, for the kingdom of heaven is at hand" (*paenitentiam agite adpropinquavit enim regnum caelorum*, Matt 4:17). Rather, in the original Greek Jesus speaks of repentance (*metanoia*), meaning to change one's mind.[15] Indeed, this attitude of repentance is identical with the self-hatred that Luther spoke of in the Romans commentary: "The penalty of sin remains as long as the hatred of self, that is, true inner repentance, until our entrance into the kingdom of heaven."[16] In the commentary on the Ninety-Five Theses Luther identifies this inner-hatred of the self with contrition (genuine sorrow for sin), and not mere attrition (repentance based on the fear of divine wrath).[17]

Luther asserts that because the interior action of humble repentance for one's sins is the real essence of the sacrament of penance, several

---

12. Bernhard Lohse, *Martin Luther: An Introduction to His Life and Work,* trans. Robert Schultz (Philadelphia: Fortress, 1986), 43.

13. Hendrix, *Luther and the Papacy,* 28–29.

14. 95 Theses (1517), LW 31:25.

15. Explanation of 95 Theses (1517), LW 31:84.

16. 95 Theses (1517), LW 31:26.

17. Explanation of 95 Theses (1517), LW 31:99.

consequences follow. One clear implication is that the pope or any priest only has the right to declare that God has forgiven a sin; he does not have the right in and of himself to forgive sins: "The pope cannot remit any guilt, except by declaring and showing that it has been remitted by God."[18] In a sense, it is hard to see how most late medieval theologians would disagree with this assertion. After all, medieval theologians did not claim that God had ceded his sovereignty to the pope, but merely that the actions of the institutional church represented divine decisions. Nevertheless, the deeper point Luther seems to be making is that the priest lacks the judicial ability to release the merits of Christ and apply them to the sinner apart from the sinner's attitude. Rather, it is actually the humble and contrite attitude of the believer that is the genuine instrument whereby God remits guilt. The priest merely recognizes God's absolution manifest in the contrition of the sinner with his judgment of absolution.

On this last point, as Bayer has observed it should be noticed that at this stage of his theological development Luther still labors under the Augustinian conception of linguistic signification.[19] The young Reformer views the act of absolution as a signifier that points to a signified beyond itself, namely, the contrition of the sinner and God's invisible act of forgiveness. The priest's word simply witnesses to the invisible act of grace causing the penitence of the sinner and therefore his justification. Much as in the Romans commentary, the instrument of God's justification and election of sinners is inner *humilitas*.

As the Ninety-Five Theses progress, Luther becomes more provocative. Contrition is the true punishment of sin (not works of penance) and will continue on into purgatory.[20] As Paul Hinlicky insightfully observes, for Luther at this stage the Christian life of contrition for sin means that "purgatory is now."[21] Nevertheless, contrition needs an outward means of expression and penance is that medium: "inner repentance is worthless unless it produces various outward mortifications of the flesh."[22] The

---

18. 95 Theses (1517), LW 31:26.

19. Bayer, *Martin Luther's Theology*, 52.

20. 95 Theses (1517), LW 31:26.

21. Paul Hinlicky, "Purgatory Now!" *Christian Century* 134, no. 14 (July 5, 2017): 30–34.

22. 95 Theses (1517), LW 31:25.

pope and priests may impose outward penance as a means of expressing inward repentance in accordance with canon law. The pope may even remit the punishments that he himself imposes in the form of an indulgence. Nevertheless, the pope cannot remit the need of the Christian to possess contrition, since this was commanded by Jesus.[23] Similarly, the pope cannot remit the necessary purgation that the contrition enacts either in this life or in the next in purgatory. Indeed, the pope has no power over purgatory.[24] If he did control it, then why would the pope not simply release all the souls in purgatory with the stroke of a pen instead of holding them hostage to be ransomed by poor Christian peasants for the sake of being able to build the new St. Peter's Basilica?[25]

The key concept in the Ninety-Five Theses remains the same as it does in the Psalms and Romans commentary, but now weaponized into a critique of the ecclesiastical hierarchy. It is an attitude of *humilitas* that is the actual mechanism that gains access to the merits of Christ and defines the Christian as a true believer. The merits of Christ are not released by the pope and he has no authority over purgatory. Beyond the Vatican's obvious unhappiness with Luther's limitation of the pope's authority, the Ninety-Five Theses also were received poorly because they raised the uncomfortable question: If inner contrition is the actual instrument whereby the forgiveness is accessed, what becomes of the mediatorial role of the church and its hierarchy? It is for this reason and many others that after some wrangling the Vatican eventually dispatched Cardinal Cajetan to question Luther and demand his recantation.[26]

ENCOUNTER WITH CAJETAN AND THE REFORMULATION OF ABSOLUTION

Cardinal Cajetan was sent to Augsburg to question Luther in the summer of 1518.[27] In his meeting with Luther, Cajetan was unhappy with what appeared to be a new element in Luther's thinking about confession and

---

23. 95 Theses (1517), LW 31:25–26.

24. 95 Theses (1517), LW 31:27.

25. 95 Theses (1517), LW 31:33.

26. James Tracy, *Europe's Reformations, 1450–1650: Doctrine, Politics, and Community* (Lanham: Rowman & Littlefield, 2006), 52.

27. Hendrix, *Luther and the Papacy*, 56–66.

absolution.[28] In his writings subsequent to the Ninety-Five Theses and the exchange with Cajetan, instead of speaking about self-hatred and humility Luther began to speak about faith as being the central factor in the sacrament of penance.[29] Much like the sick had gained access to Jesus's healing power by their faith ("your faith has made you well" Lk 17:19), so too sinners acquired absolution from the sacramental word of the priest by believing the words "I absolve you."[30] Luther also explicitly rejected the doctrine of the Treasury of Merits on the grounds that it was never mentioned in Scripture.[31] Luther therefore implied (though did not specifically say) that faith and the existence of the church are constituted by Jesus's historical promise to work through the means of grace. The institutional church is itself not a channel of grace.

Following a typical medieval conception of faith, Cajetan countered Luther that belief in the doctrine of the sacrament of penance was part of the infused faith (*fides infusa*) that God placed in Christians by his grace. That the individual administration of penance had been efficacious was part of acquired faith (*fides acquisita*), that is, a kind of discernment built up by the activity of correct spiritual judgment. In Cajetan's thinking, it was unnecessarily burdensome to make the efficacy of penance dependent on the faith of the penitent. According to his understanding, Luther's claims about faith and efficacy made the validity of God's grace dependent on a subjective factor, that is, the belief or unbelief of the sinner.[32]

Going back to Augustine's distinction between validity and efficacy of a sacrament discussed in a previous chapter, it should be recognized that Cajetan and Luther both agree that the sacrament's validity is dependent on Christ's historic promise. In turning to the question of sacramental efficacy, much like Augustine and subsequent medieval tradition, Cajetan believes that the efficacy depends on the objective reality of the institutional church, in particular, its role as a conduit of grace in the form of the Treasury of Merits. By contrast, the efficacy of the

---

28. Hendrix, *Luther and the Papacy*, 59.

29. Proceedings at Augsburg (1518), LW 31:270.

30. Proceedings at Augsburg (1518), LW 31:270–71.

31. Scott Hendrix, *Martin Luther: Visionary Reformer* (New Haven: Yale University Press, 2015), 74.

32. Tommaso de Vio Cajetan, "Augsburg Treatises 1518," in *Cajetan Responds: A Reader in Reformation Controversy*, ed. Jared Wicks (Eugene, OR: Wipf & Stock, 2011), 49–55.

sacrament for Luther depends on faith. Sinners tap into the merits of Christ by believing God's promises, rather than the pope's will to release them or not release them.

On the surface Luther's belief that faith in the promise is central to the efficacy of the sacrament might appear subjectivistic. It might be argued that this confines the work of God to the human choice to believe. This is a charge that has been frequently made against Luther by Roman Catholic apologists.[33] Nevertheless, such an interpretation would be incorrect. As we will see below, Luther holds that because the risen Jesus himself speaks through the means of grace in the power of the Holy Spirit, the sacrament carries within itself the ability to create and sustain the faith that receives it. For this reason, it would be more proper to say that Jesus's historically objective word and its divine power constitute both the validity and efficacy of the sacrament.[34] As will later be observed, it is Jesus's word of promise that trumps all things, including subjective human psychological states, or the discernment of contrition by a priest.

Although Luther's theology of justification was by no means fully formed at this point, the centrality of faith in the promise emerges during this period. What is key in the Reformer's encounter with Cajetan is that he has begun to see faith not merely as assent to supernaturally revealed doctrine (although this is still an important element of faith), but primarily as trust in the promise of God's grace and forgiveness. Indeed, as Lowell Green has demonstrated, there is a gradual conceptual shift regarding the nature of faith in 1518–1519. In his early period, Luther tends to follow the medieval concept of faith as *credulitas* (belief in supernaturally revealed dogma). After 1518, there is a movement to describing faith as *fiducia*[35] (i.e., trust in the promise, in keeping with the Pauline *pistis*).[36]

Luther's theological shift during this period can probably be accounted for by several factors. First, an event resembling the famous "Tower Experience" (*Turmerlebnis*) probably did occur at this time. In this event,

---

33. See Paul Hacker, *Das Ich im Glauben bei Martin Luther* (Graz: Styria Verlag, 1966).

34. Robert Kolb and Charles Arand, *The Genius of Luther's Theology: A Wittenberg Way of Thinking for the Contemporary Church* (Grand Rapids: Baker Academic, 2008), 135–43.

35. Lowell Green, *How Melanchthon Helped Luther Discover the Gospel: The Doctrine of Justification in the Reformation* (Fallbrook, CA: Verdict, 1980), 143–49.

36. See discussion in Moo, *Epistle to the Romans*, 225–26.

Luther recounted in later life that he had the epiphany that the "righteousness of God" spoken of in Romans 1:17 was actually the righteousness by which God makes believers righteous.[37] The Luther Renaissance of the early twentieth century paid exaggerated attention to this event.[38] Nevertheless, as Robert Kolb has noted, Luther's evolution is discernibly much more gradual than the Luther Renaissance allowed.[39] More importantly, Luther's struggle with the Papacy over confession and absolution forced him to come to terms with the odd and contradictory elements of his somewhat unstable *humilitastheologie*. As we saw before, Luther seems to counsel an attitude of both despair and trust toward the possibility of salvation all at the same time. Such a theology is at least on the surface both unstable and contradictory. Finally, as Green helpfully suggests, although Luther had already studied both Hebrew and Greek, Melanchthon's arrival in August 1518 created conditions wherein the Reformer greatly benefited from the young humanist's theological and philological scholarship.[40] This enhanced knowledge helped the Reformer come to a better understanding of the key biblical concepts of faith, grace, and imputation. Green therefore suggests that it was not a coincidence that Melanchthon's arrival coincides with the advent of Luther's mature theology.[41]

Luther's new theology can be found most clearly in two important writings of the late 1518 and 1519 period. The first significant work is the Heidelberg Disputation of April 1518.[42] Here Luther begins his theses with an assault on Aristotelian theory of virtue,[43] at least as it pertains

---

37. Preface to Latin Writings (1545), LW 34:323–38.

38. James Stayer, *Martin Luther, German Saviour: German Evangelical Theological Factions and the Interpretation of Luther, 1917–1933* (Montreal: McGill-Queen's University Press, 2000), 13–14, 30–33, 102–5.

39. Kolb, *Martin Luther*, 42–43.

40. Green, *How Melanchthon Helped Luther Discover the Gospel*, 117–23.

41. Green, *How Melanchthon Helped Luther Discover the Gospel*, 111–36.

42. See the following books on the subject: Gerhard Forde, *On Being a Theologian of the Cross: Reflections on Luther's Heidelberg Disputation, 1518* (Grand Rapids: Eerdmans, 1997); Walther von Loewenich, *Luthers Theologia Crucis* (München: Kaiser Verlag, 1954); Herman Sasse, "The Theology of the Cross," in *We Confess Anthology*, trans. Norman Nagel (St. Louis: Concordia, 1998), 35–45.

43. Carl Trueman, "*Simul Peccator et Justus*: Martin Luther and Justification," in *Justification: Historical and Contemporary Challenges*, ed. Bruce McCormack (Grand Rapids: Baker Academic, 2006), 32n, 87.

to the divine-human relationship: "The law of God, the most salutary doctrine of life, cannot advance man on his way to righteousness, but rather hinders him. Much less can human works, *which are done over and over again with the aid of natural precepts*, so to speak, lead to that end."[44] Humanity is not self-creating by their actions (*autopoiesis*).[45] Humans are creatures and therefore their actions are derivative of their being as it has been established by sin, or by grace. A good tree bears good fruit (Matt 7:17–18)— fruit does not make the tree:

> For the righteousness of God is not acquired by means of acts frequently repeated, as Aristotle taught, but it is imparted by faith, for "He who through faith is righteous shall live" (Rom 1:17), and "Man believes with his heart and so is justified" (Rom 10:10). Therefore I wish to have the words "without work" understood in the following manner: Not that the righteous person does nothing, but that his works do not make him righteous, rather that his righteousness creates works. For grace and faith are infused without our works. After they have been imparted the works follow. Thus Rom 3:20 states, "No human being will be justified in His sight by works of the law," and, "For we hold that man is justified by faith apart from works of law" (Rom 3:28). In other words, works contribute nothing to justification.[46]

This justification and sanctification are due to the active agape-love of God, not based upon our desirability: "The love of God does not find, but creates, that which is pleasing to it."[47]

It should of course not be overlooked that Luther still uses the language of infusion of grace and sees grace as making sinners righteous. Nevertheless, this "sanctification" (as later Protestantism would call it) is something achieved by the passive receptivity of faith in the promise of grace. Sanctification is the result of faith. Faith decenters the self. Faith

---

44. Heidelberg Disputation (1518), LW 31:39. Emphasis added.

45. Oswald Bayer, "Justification: Basis and Boundary of Theology," in *By Faith Alone: Essays on Justification in Honor of Gerhard O. Forde*, ed. Joseph A. Burgess and Marc Kolden (Grand Rapids: Eerdmans, 2004), 75–76.

46. Heidelberg Disputation (1518), LW 31:55–56.

47. Heidelberg Disputation (1518), LW 31: 57.

lives outside of itself upon the alien righteousness of Christ (*iustia alie-num*) obtained on the cross and therefore ends self-incurvature: "He is not righteous who does much, but he who, without work, believes much in Christ. ... The law says, 'do this,' and it is never done. Grace says, 'believe in this,' and everything is already done."[48] Indeed, "Christ is just and has fulfilled all the commands of God, wherefore we also fulfill everything through him since he was made ours through faith."[49] Hence, although Luther does think the grace of God is effective in making a good tree out of a bad tree (Matt 7:17–18), our righteousness before God is something "already done" in Christ's fulfillment of the law. This stands in profound contrast with the Romans commentary's progressive-proleptic sanative model of justification.

In light of Luther's new concept of the righteousness of Christ communicated to the sinner through the promise passively received by faith, the law now takes on a different function. The law does not generate righteousness, even with the assistance of divine grace. Grace does not give us the capacity to become righteous on the basis of genuinely doing the law (Augustine). Grace is not a seed of virtue that is actualized by doing the law (Aquinas). Rather, the function of the law is to work wrath and cause repentance in order to prepare the sinner for reception of divine grace by the promise: "The 'law brings the wrath' of God (Rom 4:15), kills, reviles, accuses, judges, and condemns everything that is not in Christ."[50] And again: "the Lord humbles and frightens us by means of the law and the sight of our sins so that we seem in the eyes of men, as in our own, as nothing, foolish, and wicked, for we are in truth that."[51]

It should not go unnoticed that there is a profound continuity at this point between Luther's new concept of the law and his earlier *humil-itastheologie*. Humans must be reduced to nothing in order to be prepared for grace: "The Lord kills and brings to life; he brings down to Sheol and raises up"[52] Death is that absolute passivity that the law must reduce believers to in preparation for the gospel's resurrecting power.

---

48. Heidelberg Disputation (1518), LW 31:56.
49. Heidelberg Disputation (1518), LW 31:56.
50. Heidelberg Disputation (1518), LW 31:54.
51. Heidelberg Disputation (1518), LW 31:44.
52. Heidelberg Disputation (1518), LW 31:44.

Nevertheless, there are a number of key differences between Luther's earlier position and the one present in the Heidelberg Disputation.

First, unlike *humilitas*, the Luther of the Heidelberg Disputation sees repentance and faith as worked by God through his creative Word. The law kills and humbles believers in repentance. They do not actively cultivate such an attitude in themselves, even under the influence of invisible divine grace—in a word, the grace of God is always tethered to the word. God is active in his Word of law and promise, whereas humans are fundamentally passive. Second, although when they look within themselves human should despair, they should trustingly look outside themselves to God's promise in Christ. Christ is now no longer the model of humble despair,[53] but a savior. There is no sense in which sinners should cultivate a sense that God wishes to damn them or is perpetually angry with them.

Therefore, the experience of divine wrath through the law is not an end in itself but ordered toward the recognition of God's grace manifest in the promise of the gospel. It could be argued that Luther resolves the odd contradiction in his theology of justification in the Romans commentary where believers should somehow hope and despair before God all at the same time. After 1518, the Reformer is able to resolve the tension between despair and trust in the Christian life through the discovery of the biblical distinction between law and promise.[54] Believers despair by looking at the law and in themselves, whereas they find peace, assurance, and hope by looking outside of themselves to the promise of God in Christ. From this point forward, this fleeing from wrath to grace will become the basic structure of the Christian life for Luther.

Luther's belief in the divine power and sacramentality of the Word of God can be observed all the more clearly in a significant catechetical sermon of 1519. In "The Sacrament of Penance," Luther begins to radically modify his theory of confession and absolution in light of his discovery of the gospel as a pure promise of righteousness and salvation for the sake of Christ. The medieval church had spoken of three parts to penance:

---

53. Bizer, *Fides ex auditu*, 22, 51.

54. Thomas Donough, *Law and Gospel in Luther: A Study of Luther's Confessional Writings* (London: Oxford University Press, 1963).

confession, absolution, satisfaction.[55] By contrast, Luther now speaks of
the three elements as being absolution, grace, and faith.[56]

In the beginning of the sermon, Luther boldly states that absolution is
a unilateral and unconditional divine action: "It follows, then, in the first
place, that the forgiveness of guilt, the heavenly indulgence, is granted to
no one on account of the worthiness of his contrition over his sins, nor
on account of his works of satisfaction, but only on account of his faith in
the promise of God, 'What you loose ... shall be loosed.' "[57] The validity
of the word is established by Jesus's historical promise and its efficacy is
based on receiving it in faith "For as you believe, so it is done for you."[58]
Here we can observe Luther's use of the Ockhamist concept of covenantal
causality, albeit used in a way so as to guarantee the promise of grace
rather than the meritorious character of congruous merit.

Absolution is a divine efficacious word (*Thettel-Wort*) and is not a mere
piece of information (*Heissel-Wort*).[59] The word that the priest speaks is
a sacramental instrument wherein God is present and communicates his
grace: "This is why it [confession and absolution] is called a sacrament,
a holy sign, because in it one hears the words externally that signify spiritual gifts within, gifts by which the heart is comforted and set at peace."[60]
Since the heart is only set at peace by the divine grace present in the
objective word, it follows that the word is itself the divine instrument that
creates faith in the heart. As suggested earlier, the logical implication of
this is that validity of the sacrament and the efficacy are all contained in
the Word of God itself.[61]

As a result of this understanding of absolution, Augustine's concept of
res and *signum* in a sacrament is significantly modified. Although there
is still a distinction between the visible sign and the invisible grace, the
signum (the word of absolution) does not somehow point beyond itself

55. Kenneth Appold, *The Reformation: A Brief History* (Malden, MA: Wiley-Blackwell, 2011),
43–44.

56. The Sacrament of Penance (1519), LW 35:11.

57. The Sacrament of Penance (1519), LW 35:12.

58. The Sacrament of Penance (1519), LW 35:11.

59. Confession Concerning the Lord's Supper (1528), LW 37:180–88. See Steinmetz, "Luther
and the Two Kingdoms," 115.

60. The Sacrament of Penance (1519), LW 35:11.

61. Kolb and Arand, *Genius of Luther's Theology*, 176–88.

to the invisible *res* (the work of the Holy Spirit). Rather, the *res* is present and communicated through the outward *signum* (i.e., word). When faith appropriates the word, it appropriates divine grace and forgiveness itself. As Bayer observes:

> That the *signum* itself is already the *res*, that the linguistic sign is already the matter itself —that was Luther's great hermeneutical discovery, his reformational discovery in the strictest sense. … Since the sign is itself already the thing it declares, this means, with reference to absolution, that the statement "I absolve you of your sins!" is not a judgement, which merely establishes that something is true already. … Instead, in this instance, a speech act actually constitutes a reality.[62]

The faith that appropriates the promise is not an autonomous action of the human person, but rather a product of divine grace. Faith is not an independent factor that transmutes absolution as a possibility into an actuality. Rather, the absolution is an objective and fully actualized reality that faith can receive: "Christ, your God, will not lie to you, nor will he waver; neither will the devil overturn his words for him. If you build upon them with a firm faith, you will be standing on the rock against which the gates and all the powers of hell cannot prevail."[63] In other words, faith does not make the word a reality any more than a house that is built on a rock is secure because of the act of building. The house built on a rock is foundationally secure because of what it is built on (Matt 7:24–27).

Luther's emphasis on the objectivity of the Word of God can be especially seen in how he deals with the reality of unbelief: "By such disbelief [in the word of grace] *you make God to be a liar* when, through his priest, he says to you, 'You are loosed from your sins,' and you retort, 'I don't believe it,' or, 'I doubt it.' "[64] If the absolution became true by believing it, then Luther would not accuse the unbeliever of making God a liar. If the believer makes absolution occur by his faith, then unbelief would prevent the word of absolution from becoming a true word. As a consequence,

---

62. Bayer, *Martin Luther's Theology*, 52–53.
63. The Sacrament of Penance (1519), LW 35:12.
64. The Sacrament of Penance (1519), LW 35:13–14. Emphasis added.

God would not be insulted as a liar, since without faith no absolution would take place. What Luther claims instead is that although unbelief blocks divine grace and forgiveness from being received, faith does not actualize absolution as a reality. To borrow a term from Gerhard Ebeling,[65] the "word-event" (*Wortgeschehen*) of the giving of absolution exists prior to faith and determines its reality. Grace and forgiveness are already actualized in the word-event of absolution; faith merely receives and participates in them.

Indeed, as Luther observes in the Large Catechism of 1529, we pray forgiveness in the Lord's Prayer not to enact it, but to recognize that God has already enacted it: "Therefore there is here again great need to call upon God and to pray: Dear Father, forgive us our trespasses. *Not as though He did not forgive sin without and even before our prayer (for He has given us the Gospel, in which is pure forgiveness before we prayed or ever thought about it)*. But this is to the intent that we may recognize and accept such forgiveness."[66] Therefore, the absolution is reality; unbelief is merely the sinner obstinately clinging to the unreality of his sin.

Absolution present in the word of the minister is a channel for the objective and universal reality of the absolution of the whole world in Christ. Although this notion is not present in "The Sacrament of Penance" (1519), the older Luther drew out the implications of the unconditional nature of absolution and made an argument for the objective and universal validity of absolution in his sermons on the Gospel of John of 1538. Here Luther states that all sin and its consequences have simply been forgiven unilaterally in Christ. The world is only accounted guilty because it obstinately opposes the forgiveness that Christ won and proclaims to all:

> Now the joyful message follows that the judgment is over; this means that the wrath of God, hell, and damnation are no more. For the Son of God came that we might be saved and delivered from death and hell. Then what is still lacking? Faith. People refuse to believe this. ... [Therefore, Christ says] "Whoever believes, does not go to hell; whoever does not believe, already has the sentence of death pronounced on him." Why? Well, because he does not

---

65. Gerhard Ebeling, "Word of God and Hermeneutics," *Word and Faith*, trans. James Leitch (Philadelphia: Fortress, 1963), 325–32.

66. LC, 3.5; CT, 723. Emphasis added.

believe in Christ. This is the judgment: that such an ineffably comforting doctrine of God's grace, procured for the world through
Christ, is proclaimed, but that the world still wants to believe the
devil rather than God and His beloved Son. And this despite the
fact that God assures us: "Sin, hell, judgment, and God's wrath
have all been terminated by the Son." We wretched people might
well bewail the sin into which we fell through Adam, the death
which resulted, and all the attendant misery, also the judgment of
God which we must bear. All this often makes it appear that God
is angry with us, that God is too harsh and stern, like an unfair
judge. But God wants to inform us in this text: "*Good and well.
Through My Son I shall cancel My charge against you so that you
need lament no more. To be sure, you have sinned, and with this sin
you have deserved the judgment of God. But your sin shall be par-
doned, death shall be abolished; I shall no longer remember man's
sin, in which he is born and in which he lived. The accounts are to be
considered settled. God will not again call a single sin to mind. Just
believe in My Son.*" Now what is still lacking? Why the judgment
if all sin has been removed by the Son? The answer is that the
judgment is incurred by man's refusal to accept Christ, the Son
of God. Of course, man's sin, both that inherited from Adam and
that committed by man himself, is deserving of death. *But this
judgment results from man's unwillingness to hear, to tolerate, and
to accept the Savior, who removed sin, bore it on His shoulders, and
locked up the portals of hell.*[67]

Therefore, appropriating the categories and terminology of later Lutheran
theology in our description,[68] it could be said that Luther holds that there
is a universal and objective justification of the whole world in Christ. This
is objective reality that determines God's relationship to all humanity
through Christ—even if outside of Christ his relationship to humanity
remains one of judgment. Through faith, there is a subjective justification

67. Sermons on the Gospel of John (1538), LW 22:382. Emphasis added.

68. For the later Lutheran terminological distinction between objective and subjective justification see Pieper, *Christian Dogmatics*, 2:321, 2:347–48, 2:508–12; Eduard Preuss, *The Justification of the
Sinner before God*, trans. J.A. Friedrich (Ft. Wayne, IN: Lutheran Legacy, 2011), 29–61.

that appropriates this objective fact. Humans are damned only in that they resist the reality of this objective justification and cling to the false subjective reality of their unbelief.

The divine power and sacramentality of the word of justification also raises the issue of predestination. Although we will discuss this question in greater detail on the basis of Luther's answer in *The Bondage of the Will* (1525) in a future chapter, it is important to note at this point how Luther deals with the issue in light of his doctrine of the sacramentality of the gospel.

Although Luther comments on predestination somewhat infrequently, there is a clear doctrine of predestination in Luther derived from his engagement with Paul and Augustine.[69] Nevertheless, unlike Augustine, Luther describes election as something that God executes in and through the preaching of the promise in Christ. In a passage in "A Sermon on Preparing for Dying" (1519), Luther writes:

> Therefore fix your eyes upon the heavenly picture of Christ, who for your sake went to hell and was rejected by God as one damned to the eternal perdition, as He cried on the cross, "Eli, Eli, lama sabachthani? My God, my God, why has thou forsaken me?" Behold, in that picture your hell is overcome and *your election assured*, so that if you but take care and believe that it happened for you, you will certainly be saved in that faith.[70]

Here it should be noted that, much as the word of absolution sacramentally contains within itself the coming of God's justification of the sinner, so too God's eternal judgment of predestination supervenes on the word of the cross. Unlike in Augustine, there is not a gap between God's eternal, hidden, predestinating will, and the word of the preacher. To apprehend in faith the word of promise that God has attached to Christ's death and resurrection is to be assured of God's eternal election of the believer.

---

69. See Fredrik Brosché, *Luther on Predestination: The Antinomy and the Unity Between Love and Wrath in Luther's Concept of God* (Stockholm: Almqvist & Wiksell, 1978).

70. Sermon on Preparing to Die (1519), LW 42:105–6. Emphasis added.

In 1531, Luther offered similar counsel to Barbara Lisskirchen (formerly Weller), a woman who wrote the Reformer due to her deep anxiety about the question of her predestination. Luther writes in a response letter:

> The highest of all God's commands is this, that we ever hold up before our eyes the image of his dear Son, our Lord Jesus Christ. Every day he should be our excellent mirror of how much God loves us and how well, in his infinite goodness, he has cared for us in that he gave his dear son for us. In this way I say, and in no other, does one learn to properly deal with the question of predestination. *It will be manifest to you that you believe in Christ. If you believe then you are called. And if you are called you are most certainly predestinated.* Do not let this mirror and throne of grace be torn away from your eyes. If such thoughts still come and bite like fiery serpents, *pay no attention to the thoughts or serpents. Turn away from these notions and contemplate the brazen serpent, that is, Christ given for us.*[71]

Although many might point out that Luther's emphasis is on connecting recognition of election with faith, such a faith is grounded in the external "call" through the Word of God. The key point to notice in this passage is not only that God's eternal election is embodied in the crucified Christ and received by faith in him, but that the faith that apprehends Christ is what Philip Cary calls "unreflective faith,"[72] that is, a faith that does not worry about its own authenticity. Likewise, as Randall Zachman helpful summarizes: "[For Luther] faith means believing with certainty that God's Word is true even when the whole world, the heart of the believer, and even God himself contradict the truth that is revealed in the word, particularly the word of promise."[73] Faith therefore looks outside of itself (*extra nos*) to Christ himself and his word of promise. Again, to look away from Christ would be to return to self-trust and self-incurvature, the very definition of sin. Throughout the letter, Luther emphasizes that

---

71. Martin Luther, *Luther: Letters of Spiritual Counsel*, trans. Theodore Tappert (Vancouver, BC: Regent College Press, 2003), 116. Emphasis added. See the lengthier argument in Luther's Genesis commentary along the same lines in Lectures on Genesis (1535-1545), LW 5:43-50.

72. Cary, "Why Luther is Not Quite Protestant," 450-55.

73. Randall Zachman, *The Assurance of Faith: Conscience in the Theology of Martin Luther and John Calvin* (Louisville: Westminster John Knox, 2005), 9.

all questionings of one's election and justification are satanic temptations. Faith accepts God's trustworthiness in his word as absolute reality and rejects the unreality of unbelief.

Luther's theology of election in these passages nevertheless raises a series of uncomfortable problems. First, if God's decree of election is executed in and through the means of grace, then why do all not believe who come into contact with them? Is there a difference between a real inner call and a mere outward call? Clearly Luther resists this latter claim since his belief in the sacramentality of the word absolutely identifies God's will for the sinner with the external word. Similarly, one might ask how the universality and objectivity of justification that we see in the sermons on John is coherent with the particular and individual understanding of election in *The Bondage of the Will* and other writings. Having raised these issues, we will postpone our full discussion of them for a future chapter dealing with election and justification.

JUSTIFICATION AS AN EXCHANGE OF REALITIES: *FREEDOM OF A CHRISTIAN* (1521) AND THE GREAT GALATIANS COMMENTARY (1531)[74]

In the previous section we have observed the emerging outlines of Luther's theology of justification by the word and how it overturns much of Augustine's Platonic view of language. In Luther's understanding of the means of grace, Augustine's *res* and *signum* dualism is collapsed in a theology where the *res* is present in and through the *signum*.[75] As we will see in this section, Luther's theology of the sacramental Word of God reflects a larger concept of God's redemption action as an exchange of realities. Moreover, this concept of redemption as an exchange of realities facilitated by the word also shaped Luther's view of the incarnation, the work of Christ, and finally the justification of the sinner.

---

74. Much of this material appears in a somewhat different form in Jack Kilcrease, "The Bridal-Mystical Motif in Bernard of Clairvaux and Martin Luther," *The Journal of Ecclesiastical History* 65, no. 2 (2014): 263–79; Kilcrease, *The Doctrine of Atonement: From Luther to Forde* (Eugene, OR: Wipf & Stock, 2018), 45–50.

75. Bayer, *Martin Luther's Theology*, 52.

Johann Anselm Steiger has helpfully described the *communicatio idiomatum* (that is, the exchange of the divine and human in the incarnate Christ) as the "axel and motor" of Luther's mature theology.[76] In Luther's later theology of the incarnation (developed polemically in relationship to Zwingli's theology of the sacraments)[77] the divine is fully communicated to the human and participates in the life of the man Jesus down to its very depths. So too, as we have already seen, in Luther's theology of absolution there is a *communicatio idiomatum* between the Word of God and the word of the confessor or preacher: "I hear a human voice, but faith says it is the Word of God."[78] Luther also writes: "[God] has lowered the Savior enough and put him in the oral word to present him to the human being who should preach it, and it shall be accepted as if were preached by [God] himself."[79] As a result, Luther states regarding absolution and the justification of the sinner in the Small Catechism, "we receive absolution, or forgiveness, from the confessor, as from God Himself, and in no wise doubt, but firmly believe, that our sins are thereby forgiven before God in heaven."[80]

As Steiger shows, the presence of the divine word in the human word in absolution is grounded in Luther's Christology and helps to explain the Reformer's mature doctrine of atonement and justification. In the incarnation, God fully communicates himself to the human nature of Christ (what later Lutheranism would call the *genus majestaticum*).[81] On the cross, the second person of the Trinity fully accepts having sin imputed to him and receives the penalty of death by way of its unity with the human nature (what later Lutheran theology would call the *genus apotelesmaticum* and *genus idiomaticum*).[82] Because the divine is in the human and the human

---

76. Johann Anselm Steiger, "The *Communicatio Idiomatum* as the Axel and Motor of Luther's Theology," *Lutheran Quarterly* 14, no. 2 (2000): 125–58.

77. See Lohse, *Martin Luther's Theology*, 169–77; Hermann Sasse, *This is My Body: Luther's Contention for the Real Presence in the Sacrament of the Altar* (Eugene, OR: Wipf & Stock, 2001).

78. Afternoon Sermon for the Third Day After Christmas (1527), WA 23:747. Cited from Steiger, "The *Communicatio Idiomatum*," 144.

79. Afternoon Sermon for St. Stephen's Day (1538), WA 46:527. Cited from Steiger, "The *Communicatio Idiomatum*," 145.

80. SC 5; CT, 553.

81. Martin Chemnitz, *The Two Natures in Christ*, trans. J. A. O. Preus (St. Louis: Concordia, 1971), 241–47.

82. Chemnitz, *The Two Natures in Christ*, 157–232.

is in the divine, to borrow a term from Trinitarian theology, it would be appropriate to say that there is a full perichoresis between the divine and human natures. As Steiger observes, this account of the incarnation is the presupposition for Luther's understanding of justification through the sacramental word. Steiger writes:

> Thus, the whole doctrine of justification stands on the foundation of the doctrine of the *communicatio idiomatum* because the justification of the impious and the imputation of alien righteousness happens as a perichoresis and antidosis between God and the human. In return, the Son of God appropriates human corruption and sin, is made sin for us (2 Corinthians 5:21), and more still: through the sin attributed to him Christ becomes the greatest sinner and liar.[83]

Faith grasps Christ through the word. This unity of word and faith is the medium by which the exchange of sin and alien righteousness takes place. Nevertheless, faith is meaningless with the *communicatio idiomatum* of the preached word:

> But the presupposition for the fact that the human can grip that which is offered in faith is preaching, through which the Word of God grips human hearts. Preaching is the real place in which the *communicatio idiomatum* between God and the human is set in motion in the form of a verbal communication. In the oral proclamation of the divine message the liberating forgiveness of sins is given and the righteousness of Christ is attributed to the sinner. In preaching, the Word and the thing coincide, since the sermon, like the Word of the Creator himself, is an active Word that does what it says and says what it does.[84]

Luther's theology of justification as a great exchange between God and humanity through Christ and his authorized preached word can best be observed in two seminal writings of the Reformer on the subject of

---

83. Steiger, "The *Communicatio Idiomatum*," 129–30.
84. Steiger, "The *Communicatio Idiomatum*," 131.

justification: *Freedom of a Christian* of 1521 and the Great Galatians commentary of 1531.

Freedom of a Christian begins by asserting that because Christians are justified through the promise of the gospel, they are paradoxically free and a servant simultaneously: "[The Christian is] perfectly free lord of all, subject to none [and] ... a perfectly dutiful servant of all, subject to all."[85] Luther resolves this seemingly paradoxical statement by first showing that faith makes the inner person a free lord of all by removing the condemnation and subjection of the law. Second, he shows that external person of the believer is the dutiful and free servant of all because he now serves his neighbors purely out of love and not the compulsion to earn his salvation.

Following the same law-gospel pattern found in the Heidelberg Disputation, Luther speaks of the inner person as first being emptied by the preaching of the law and made ready for the reception of Christ's alien righteousness by the proclamation of the gospel-promise: "[through the proclamation of] the commandments [the believer comes] to recognize his helplessness."[86] Recognizing this makes the sinner "truly humble and reduced to nothing."[87]

By faith, the believer receives the fullness of Christ's righteousness through the sacramental Word of God. The word of promise contains within it the coming of the risen Jesus. Therefore, in the promise of the gospel, Christ fully donates himself to the believer. In the word of the gospel Christ communicates all his benefits to the soul: "this absorbing of the Word, [in faith] communicate[s] to the soul all things that belong to the Word."[88]

In describing justification, Luther does not use a courtroom metaphor ubiquitous in later Protestantism. Rather he takes over the image of the exchange of goods when a marriage occurs between bride and groom. The exchange of goods between man and wife is analogous to the exchange of realities between Christ and the believer:

---

85. Freedom of a Christian (1520), LW 31:344.
86. Freedom of a Christian (1520), LW 31:348.
87. Freedom of a Christian (1520), LW 31:348.
88. Freedom of a Christian (1520), LW 31:349.

Accordingly, the believing soul can boast of and glory in whatever Christ has as though it were its own, and whatever the soul
has Christ claims as his own. Let us compare these and we shall
see inestimable benefits. Christ is full of grace, life and salvation.
The soul is full of sins, death, and damnation. Now let faith come
between them and sins, death, and damnation will be Christ's,
while grace, life, and salvation will be the soul's; for if Christ is a
bridegroom, he must take upon himself the things which are the
bride's and bestow upon her the things that are his.[89]

The result of this union with Christ through the sacramental word of the
gospel is a "happy exchange" (*der fröhlicher wechsel, admirabile commercium*) between Christ and the believer. Christ receives sin and death, and
his bride (the believing soul) receives life, righteousness, and freedom.

In utilizing the bridal motif, Luther appears to be borrowing an image
taken not only from Scripture (Eph 5), but also from Rhineland mystics like Tauler[90] as well as Staupitz's work.[91] One also can point to the
bridal-mystical motif in the work of Bernard of Clairvaux, whom Luther
thought of very highly, and who also serves as an interesting contrast to
Reformer's teaching in *Freedom of a Christian*.

St. Bernard wrote a lengthy collection of sermons on the Song of Songs
where he took the book to be an allegory for the relationship between
Christ and the soul.[92] Furthermore, in this same work and in *On Loving
God*, the Saint argues that the bride (who is the believing soul) has a
responsibility to use the power of grace communicated to it in order to
adorn herself with virtues that will make it sufficiently attractive to make
Christ desire her.[93] By contrast Luther sees the soul as being filled with sin

89. Freedom of a Christian (1520), LW 31:351.

90. Paul Chung, *The Spirit of God Transforming Life: The Reformation and Theology of the Holy
Spirit* (New York: Palgrave Macmillan, 2009), 7–8; Dietmar Lage, *Martin Luther's Christology and
Ethics* (Lewiston, NY: Edwin Mellen, 1990), 77–78, 86; Oberman, *Luther: Man Between God and
the Devil*, 184.

91. Steinmetz, *Luther and Staupitz*, 29–30; Steinmetz, *Misericordia Dei*, 90–91.

92. See: Bernard of Clairvaux, *On the Song of Songs: Sermons in Cantica Canticorum*, trans. and
ed. A Religious of C. S. M. V. (London: A. R. Mowbray, 1952).

93. See Bernard of Clairvaux, *On Loving God: An Analytical Commentary with an Analytical
Commentary by Emero Stiegman* (Kalamazoo: Cistercian, 1995).

and death, and therefore it brings nothing attractive to the union. Christ surrenders himself to the sinner as sinner out of pure unilateral *agape*-love.

Luther's belief in the unilateral and unconditional nature of divine love in the union between Christ and believers did not go unnoticed by his contemporaries. The Dominican inquisitor Jakob Hochstraten wrote that Luther had made the divine-human relationship into incoherent nonsense. Hochstraten asked: Could God be enticed to have fellowship with the sinner without any of the attraction of the beauty of holiness?[94] In Hochstraten's response, we clearly see the logic of the platonizing Augustinian theology of *caritas* at work.

It therefore should also not go unnoticed that Luther implicitly rejects the Augustinian concept of God as the supreme object of desire. God in Christ is the supremely trustworthy object of human faith, not the fulfillment of all desire. Indeed, Christ is not beautiful or attractive to the believer (Isa 53:2). God's attractive grace and love are hidden under the ugliness of the cross. Earlier in the Heidelberg Disputation, Luther states that faith "comprehends the visible and manifest things of God seen through suffering and the cross."[95] Later in Luther's Galatians commentary of 1531, he states: *"Thus faith is a sort of knowledge or darkness that nothing can see. Yet the Christ of whom faith takes hold is sitting in this darkness as God sat in the midst of darkness on Sinai and in the temple."*[96] Desire is always provoked and enticed by a vision of its object. For Luther, as we observed going all the way back to the Romans commentary, faith relies on a word attached to something contrary to vision (*sub contrario*). The love of God is hidden under the ugliness of the cross and is only detected by the promise God attaches to the cross.

In light of this view of the righteousness of faith, the old Augustinian conception of the divine-human relationship configured around right-love is rejected and replaced by right-trust. For Luther, faith's recognition of God as supremely trustworthy properly orients the self and results in true obedience to the law. Faith gives glory to God by identifying him as fully faithful to his promises: "Nothing more excellent than this can be ascribed

---

94. See Jacob Hochstraten, "Iacobi Hoochstrati Disputationes contra Lutheranos," in *Bibliotheca Reformatoria Neerlandica*, vol. 3, ed. S. Cramer and F. Pijper ('s-Gravenhage: Martinus Nijhof, 1905), 609–10.

95. Heidelberg Disputation (1518), LW 31:52.

96. Lectures on Galatians (1531), LW 26:129–30. Emphasis added.

to God. The very highest worship of God is this that we ascribe to him truthfulness, righteousness, and whatever else should be ascribed to one who is trusted. When this is done, the soul consents to his will."[97] In this faith is the source of obedience to the whole law. Conversely, unbelief is the source of all sin. Luther would write in his commentary on Genesis of the 1530s and 1540s: "Unbelief is the source of all sins; when Satan brought about this unbelief by driving out or corrupting the Word, the rest was easy for him."[98]

Since the self is properly oriented in its relationship with God by faith as trust, Luther now redirects love to the task of correctly orienting the external person in the earthly sphere. This represents a total inversion of the Augustinian doctrine of love. For the Bishop of Hippo, the love of earthly things functions as a distraction from the love of God. Indeed, in spite of being a biblical theme, at this stage of his development Luther seems uncomfortable about even talking about the love of God. Later in the Catechism, he again returned to the formula of "We should fear and love God, etc.," and lost his aversion to talk of the love of God. Nevertheless, in *Freedom of a Christian*, Luther consistently argues that love's proper orientation is in fact an earthly object, namely the neighbor: "This is truly Christian life. *Here faith is truly active in love* [Gal 5:6], that is, it finds expression in works of freest service, cheerfully done, with which a man willing *serves another* [i.e. the neighbor] without hope of reward ..."[99]

Hence, the creative Word of God brings about a faith that orients believers toward God in Christ, whereas love is primarily directed toward the neighbor: "We conclude, therefore, that a Christian lives not in himself, but in Christ and the neighbor. He lives in Christ *through faith*, and in his *neighbor through love*."[100] Whereas the person under the power of sin and self-justification stood curved in on himself (*incurvatus in se*), now the believer lives a life externalized in the other: first in Christ through faith,

---

97. Freedom of a Christian (1520), LW 31:350. Emphasis added.
98. Lectures on Genesis (1535-1545), LW 1:147.
99. Freedom of a Christian (1520), LW 31:365. Emphasis added.
100. Freedom of a Christian (1520), LW 31:371. Emphasis added.

then to the neighbor in love.[101] In this, the self becomes radically decentered in the form of ecstatic existence (*raptus, exstasis*). In this, Luther borrows yet another theme from the mystical tradition,[102] yet remolds it around the biblical themes of faith in God and the love of the neighbor.

In the Galatians commentary of 1531, Luther expands and deepens the theme of justification through the word as an exchange of realities between God and humanity. Apart from the means of grace, God hidden in his majesty and wrath (what Luther called *Deus absconditus* in his earlier *The Bondage of the Will*, 1525)[103] stands in an absolute conflict with human sin. Through becoming incarnate in Christ, God ruptures this condemning relationship to the world by giving himself over to humanity in order to battle his own judgment: "Thus the curse, which is divine wrath against the whole world, has the same conflict with the blessing, that is, with eternal grace and mercy of God in Christ. Therefore, the curse clashes with the blessing and wants to damn it and annihilate it. But it cannot."[104] This paradoxical conflict takes place because whereas God as active and incarnate in Christ unilaterally gives himself to humanity in love, God operative outside of his gracious relationship to humanity in Christ persists in his wrath and absolute opposition to sin. God's law and judgment are manifested in his wrathful activities through the "masks" of his creatures.[105]

Through the *communicatio idiomatum* of the incarnation, Christ enters into total solidarity with humanity. Christ bears within himself the total burden of human sin and the condemnation of the law.[106] As Erich Seeberg rightly observes, Christ anticipates the fact that the believer is "at the same time saint and sinner" (*simul justus et peccator*) in that he unites in himself

---

101. See a good description of Luther's position here in George Wolfgang Forell, *Faith Active in Love: An Investigation into the Principles Underlying Luther's Social Ethics* (Eugene, OR: Wipf & Stock Publishers, 1999).

102. See Karl-Heinz zur Mühlen, *Nos extra nos: Luthers Theologie zwischen Mystik und Scholastik* (Tübingen: Mohr, 1972).

103. See Hans-Martin Barth, *The Theology of Martin Luther: A Critical Assessment*, trans. Linda Maloney (Minneapolis: Fortress, 2013), 101–34; Robert Kolb, *Bound Choice, Election, and Wittenberg Theological Method: From Martin Luther to the Formula of Concord* (Minneapolis: Fortress, 2017), 31–43; Lohse, *Martin Luther's Theology*, 160–68.

104. Lectures on Galatians (1531), LW 26:281.

105. Lectures on Galatians (1531), LW 26:95. Luther writes, "the whole creation is a face or mask of God."

106. Lienhard, *Luther: Witness to Jesus Christ*, 281.

both blessedness and the curse, sin and death with life and righteousness.[107] Indeed, for Luther in the Galatians commentary Christ truly is *simul justus et peccator*, albeit in the opposite manner of the believer: righteous in himself yet imputed as sinful by the judicial curse of the Father.[108]

As Tuomo Mannermaa correctly notes, in the Galatians commentary Luther asserts that Christ becomes three things through identifying with humanity and its sin: he is the "greatest person," "the greatest sinner," and the "only sinner."[109] As Luther himself writes: "because in the same Person, who is the highest, the greatest, and the only sinner, there is also eternal and invincible righteousness, therefore two converge: the highest, greatest and only sin; and the highest, the greatest, and the only righteousness."[110] Consequently, Mannermaa correctly concludes that according "to Luther ... the *Logos* [the divine Son] did not take upon himself merely human nature, in a 'neutral' form, but precisely the concrete and actual human nature. This means that Christ really has and bears the sins of all human beings in the human nature he has assumed."[111]

This *communicatio idiomatum* of sin and death is an extension of the *communicatio idiomatum* of divine and human in the person of Christ. To redeem humanity, Christ had to take all sin upon himself and suffer the wrath of God. Luther writes: "all the prophets saw this, that Christ was to become the greatest thief, murder, adulterer, robber, desecrator, blasphemer, etc., there has ever been anywhere in the world. ... He is a sinner."[112] But if Christ was sinless in himself, how then could this take place? Luther explains it was possible because of God's forensic imputation:

> Thus a magistrate regards someone as a criminal and punishes him if he catches him among thieves, even though the man has never committed anything evil or worthy of death. Christ was not

---

107. Erich Seeberg, *Luthers Theologie: Christus, Wirklichkeit und Urbild*, vol. 2 (Stuttgart: W. Kohlhammer, 1937), 8.

108. Lienhard, *Luther: Witness to Jesus Christ*, 283–85; Olli-Pekka Vainio, *Justification and Participation in Christ: The Development of the Lutheran Doctrine of Justification from Luther to the Formula of Concord (1580)* (Leiden: Brill, 2008), 22–23.

109. Tuomo Mannermaa, *Christ Present in Faith: Luther's View of Justification*, trans. Kirsi Sjerna (Minneapolis: Fortress, 2005), 13–19; Vainio, *Justification and Participation in Christ*, 22–23.

110. Lectures on Galatians (1531), LW 26:281.

111. Mannermaa, *Christ Present in Faith*, 13.

112. Lectures on Galatians (1531), LW 26:277.

found among sinners; but of His own free will and by the will of the Father He wanted to be an associate of sinners and thieves and those who were immersed in all sorts of sin. Therefore, when the Law found Him among thieves, it condemned and executed Him as a thief.[113]

For God to judge human sin it was necessary that Christ be imputed as a sinner: Luther states that the result is universal and objective atonement of all sin: "He [Jesus] has and bears all sins of all men in His body—not in the sense that He has committed them but in the sense that He took these sins, committed by us, upon His body, in order to make satisfaction for them with His own blood."[114] Christ objectively took the sins of the whole human race upon himself and rendered satisfaction for them: "He [God the Father] sent His Son into the world ... and said to Him ... be the person of all men, the one who committed the sins of all men. And see to it that You pay and make satisfaction for them."[115] By describing Christ as the righteous one imputed with humanity's sin, Luther appears to anticipate the second-generation Lutheran theologian Matthias Flacius's distinction between Christ's "active" and "passive" righteousness.[116]

Through the promise of the gospel, faith receives the total person of the risen Christ.[117] Just as Jesus once gave himself over to the imputation of sin, he now gives himself over to sinners through the imputation of righteousness as mediated by word and sacrament. The sacramental word of the gospel effects the total union of Christ and the believer:

But faith must be taught correctly, namely, that by it you are so cemented to Christ that He and you are as one person, which cannot be separated but remains attached to Him forever and declares "I am as Christ." And Christ in turn says "I am as that

113. Lectures on Galatians (1531), LW 26:277–78.

114. Lectures on Galatians (1531), LW 26:277.

115. Lectures on Galatians (1531), LW 26: 280. Emphasis added.

116. Heinrich Schmid, The Doctrinal Theology of the Evangelical Lutheran Church, trans. Charles A. Hays and Henry E. Jacobs, (Minneapolis: Augsburg, 1961), 342–70; Vainio, Justification and Participation in Christ, 25.

117. Lienhard, Luther: Witness to Jesus Christ, 287–88; Mannermaa, Christ Present in Faith, 39–42; Vainio, Justification and Participation in Christ, 38–42.

sinner who is attached to Me, and I to him." For by faith we are joined together into one flesh and one bone.[118]

Therefore, much as in *Freedom of a Christian*, through faith in the word, the believer receives all that is Christ's: "The one who has faith is a completely divine man, a son of God, the inheritor of the universe. He is victor over the world, sin, death, and the Devil."[119] Luther observes that although the scholastics' claim that the *habitus* of love makes the faith living, but this is incorrect. Love is not the "form" (in the Aristotelian sense) of faith, rather Christ is.[120] Faith holds Christ like a ring holds onto a jewel.[121] In other words, faith lives on and subjectively justifies the sinner because it takes its reality from Christ and his alien righteousness. As Regin Prenter observes: "Faith lives completely and alone by the real presence of Christ. To the same extent that Christ is really present, faith is really present, and only to that extent."[122]

Moreover, to use the terminology of later Protestantism, for Luther the Word of God and the saving faith that it creates do not simply justify persons of faith, but also sanctify them. Here the Reformer mirrors Jeremiah's description of the Holy Spirit working through the proclamation of the New Covenant to write the commandments on the heart of believers (Jer 31:33). Although the Reformer clearly rejects the medieval church's belief that the sanctified Christian is formed by habits implanted in the soul, interestingly he does not totally abandon the language of formation taken from peripatetic philosophy. Nevertheless, instead of using Aristotle's concept of ethical formation through habits (i.e., augmentation of human agency and right performance), Luther uses Aristotelian epistemology's concept of objects of consciousness imposing their form on the knower's intellect.

In Luther's interpretation, through the divine power of the gospel, the form of Christ is impressed upon the heart and mind of the believer.

---

118. Lectures on Galatians (1531), LW 26:168.

119. Lectures on Galatians (1531), LW 26:247.

120. Lectures on Galatians (1531), LW 26:88–89.

121. Lectures on Galatians (1531), LW 26:89, 132, 134.

122. Regin Prenter, *Spiritus Creator: Luther's Concept of the Holy Spirit*, trans. John Jensen (Philadelphia: The Muhlenberg Press, 1953), 43.

Aristotle taught that in beholding an object of sense, the form of the object was impressed upon the "Agent Intellect" (*intellectus agens*). Knowledge of a particular entity forms the human intellect in the same way that a signet ring makes an impression when it is pressed against wax.[123] Because of the divine power present in it, the proclamation of the word impresses itself on the mind of the believer and conforms him to the sanctifying image of Christ:

> Now the form of the Christian mind is faith, the trust of the heart, which takes hold of Christ, clings only to Him and to nothing else besides. ... For the Word proceeds from the mouth of the apostle and reaches the heart of the hearer; there the Holy Spirit is present and impresses that Word on the heart, so that it is heard. In this way every preacher is a parent, who produces and forms the true shape of the Christian mind through the ministry of the Word.[124]

As Robert Jenson correctly observes, the key difference between Luther and Aristotelian or medieval scholasticism on this point is that the Reformer sees this formation as occurring through hearing, rather than through physical or intellectual vision.[125] Because the forensic proclamation of the word impresses upon the Christian the sanctifying image of the risen Christ, forensic justification is effective.[126] Indeed, as Gerhard Forde observes, "The old argument about whether justification is 'only' forensic or also 'effective' is transcended. ... It is, to be sure, 'not only' forensic, but that is the case only because the more forensic it is, the more effective."[127]

123. Aristotle, *De Anima*, trans. J.A. Smith (Oxford: Oxford University Press, 1963), 424a.17.

124. Lectures on Galatians (1531), LW 26:430.

125. Robert Jenson, "Luther's Contemporary Theological Significance," in *The Cambridge Companion to Martin Luther*, ed. Donald McKim (Cambridge: Cambridge University Press, 2003), 282–83. Also see Cary, *Meaning of Protestant Theology*, 186–92.

126. Mark Mattes, "Luther on Justification as Forensic and Effective," in *The Oxford Handbook of Martin Luther's Theology*, ed. Robert Kolb, Irene Dingel, and L'Ubomir Batka (Oxford: Oxford University Press, 2014), 264–74.

127. Forde, *Justification by Faith*, 36.

FORENSIC JUSTIFICATION
OR MYSTICAL UNION?

Due to Luther's strong emphasis on the union of Christ with the believer in *Freedom of a Christian* and the Galatians commentary of 1531, it has in recent decades been argued by the Finnish school of Luther research that the Reformer actually conflates mystical union with justification.[128] In this conception, Christ unites himself with the believer through faith in the word. Subsequently, God recognizes the divine-human person of Christ present in the believer by faith in the word as being the believer's righteousness *coram Deo*.[129] It is then claimed by the Finnish scholars that the emphasis of later Lutheranism on the exclusively forensic nature of justification is a distortion of Philipp Melanchthon and was transmitted to the rest of Lutheranism as a result of the negative reaction to Andreas Osiander's[130] description of justification as the indwelling uncreated righteousness of God.[131]

It should be kept in mind that both more traditional Lutheran readings of Luther (i.e., ones that see Luther teaching a forensic doctrine of justification, that is nevertheless also effective) and the Finnish school agree that justification results in both imputation and in mystical union. The Finnish scholars acknowledge that Luther is extremely explicit that the imputation of righteousness is necessary[132] because believers remain sinners

---

128. See Robert Jenson and Carl Braaten, eds., *Union with Christ: The New Finnish Interpretation of Luther* (Grand Rapids: Eerdmans, 1998); Tuomo Mannermaa, *Christ Present in Faith: Luther's View of Justification*, trans. Kirsi Sjerna (Minneapolis: Fortress, 2005); Mannermaa, *Two Kinds of Love: Martin Luther's Religious World*, trans. Kirsi Sjerna (Minneapolis: Fortress, 2010); Olli-Pekka Vainio, ed., *Engaging Luther: A New Theological Assessment* (Eugene, OR: Cascade Books, 2010); Vainio, *Justification and Participation in Christ*.

129. Mannermaa, *Christ Present in Faith*, 87–88. Also see discussion in Dennis Bielfeldt, "The Ontology of Deification," in *Caritas Dei: Beiträge zum Verständnis Luthers und der gegenwärtigen Ökumene: Festschrift für Tuomo Mannermaa zum 60. Geburtstag*, ed. Oswald Bayer, Robert Jenson, and Simo Knuuttila (Helsinki: Luther-Agricola Society, 1997), 92–95.

130. Henry Hamann, "The Righteousness of Faith before God," in *A Contemporary Look at the Formula of Concord*, ed. Robert Preus and Wilbert Rosin (St. Louis: Concordia, 1978), 137–62; Emanuel Hirsch, *Die Theologie von Andreas Osiander und ihre Geschtlichen Voraussetzugen* (Göttingen: Vanderhoeck und Ruprecht, 1919); Carl Lawrenz, "On Justification: Osiander's Doctrine of the Indwelling of Christ," in *No Other Gospel: Essays in Commemoration of the 400th Anniversary of the Formula of Concord, 1580–1980*, ed. Arnold Koelpin (Milwaukee: Northwestern, 1980), 149–74.

131. Vaino, *Justification and Participation in Christ*, 69–81.

132. Mannermaa, *Christ Present in Faith*, 56–57.

until temporal death: "acceptance or imputation is extremely necessary, first because we are not yet purely righteous, but sin is still clinging to our flesh during this life."[133] Believers, considered in themselves apart from the imputation of Christ's righteousness, remain worthy of judgment. Sin is "so great, so infinite and invincible, that the whole world could not make satisfaction for even one of them."[134] Hence, Luther's mature doctrine of *simul iustus et peccator*[135] is based on the imputed righteousness of Christ: "I am a sinner in and by myself apart from Christ. Apart from myself and in Christ I am not a sinner."[136] Likewise, the Formula of Concord (1577) and later Lutheran Scholasticism affirms that Christians are united with Christ (along with the whole Trinity) by mystical union (*unio mystica*).[137] Indeed, seventeenth century theologians like Johann Gerhard were even comfortable with the language of deification in a manner similar to the Greek Fathers.[138]

The disagreement of the two interpretations actually lies in the question of whether imputation occurs logically prior to or is a consequence of mystical union. Returning to the helpful distinction of Ritschl mentioned in the previous chapter,[139] the point of dispute between orthodox Lutherans and the Finnish school is the question of whether justification is a synthetic judgment or analytic judgment. Orthodox Lutherans view justification as a synthetic judgment. The Formula of Concord makes the claim that the imputation of righteousness comes first and subsequently

133. Lectures on Galatians (1531), LW 26:132–33; WA 40.1:233.

134. Lectures on Galatians (1531), LW 26:33.

135. See discussion in Gerhard Ebeling, *Lutherstudien: Dispuatio de homine. Part 3: Die theologischen Definition des Menschen. Kommentar zu These 20–40*, vol. 2 (Tübingen: Mohr Siebeck, 1989), 536–37.

136. The Private Mass and the Consecration of Priests (1533), LW 38:158.

137. FC SD III.54; *Concordia Triglotta: The Symbolical Books of the Evangelical Lutheran Church, German-Latin-English*, trans. and ed. F. Bente, W. H. T. Dau, and Lutheran Church Missouri Synod (St. Louis: Concordia, 1921), 934–35; Schmid, *Doctrinal Theology of the Evangelical Lutheran Church*, 495–96.

138. Johann Gerhard, *Theological Commonplaces: On Christ*, trans. Richard Dinda (St. Louis: Concordia, 2009), 144. Gerhard cites Irenaeus: "Because of His immense love, the Son of God became what we are, to perfect us to be what He is. He became a partaker of our nature to make us sharers in the divine nature." Also see Johann Gerhard, *Sacred Meditations*, trans. C. W. Heisler (Philadelphia: Lutheran Publication Society, 1896), 76.

139. Ritschl, *Christian Doctrine of Justification and Reconciliation*, 38, 80–82.

causes regeneration and mystical union.[140] Therefore, Christians are not righteous because they are mystically united with Christ but are declared righteous for the sake of Christ through the promise prior to being mystically united with Christ. The Finnish school makes righteousness *coram Deo* an analytic judgment. In faith one is unified with Christ and God imputes the believer as righteous because of their union with Christ and his righteousness.

The Finnish interpretation of Luther does not fit the material that we have examined for three main reasons. First, claiming that Melanchthon and Luther had a completely different conception of justification and did not notice it strains credulity. The two theologians worked in close proximity with one another for two and a half decades. They mutually agreed to,[141] and also corroborated with each other on, a number of confessional documents, notably the Apology to the Augsburg Confession (Melanchthon being the official author, Luther having added material).[142] The judgment that Melanchthon and Luther must have understood each other's views on justification is confirmed by a series of letters sent to the Swabian Lutheran Reformer Johannes Brenz, which Melanchthon and Luther both contributed to. When challenged on the issue of what actually causes believers to be judged righteous *coram Deo*, Luther asserted with absolute clarity in consultation with Melanchthon that justification consists of the imputed alien righteousness of Christ.[143]

Secondly, the Finnish interpretation is inconsistent with the logic of justification by word that we have observed in Luther's writings already. If, as we have already seen, the judgment that God makes about sinners in the proclamation of the gospel is forensically true even before they accept it, then it follows that God's forensic and judicial judgment is prior to mystical union. The Finns are of course correct that Christ is himself present in the word of the gospel and uses it as a medium of the gospel

---

140. FC SD 3.18–19; CT, 921.

141. Trueman, "*Simul peccator et justus*," 90.

142. Charles Arand, Robert Kolb, and James Nestingen, *The Lutheran Confessions: History and Theology of the Book of Concord* (Minneapolis: Fortress, 2012), 107.

143. See Luther's Postscript to Melanchthon's Letter to Johannes Brenz on May 12, 1531, WABr 6:100. See discussion in Trueman, *Simul peccator et justus*," 91; Timothy Wengert, *Defending Faith: Lutheran Responses to Andreas Osiander's Doctrine of Justification, 1551–1559* (Tübingen: Mohr Siebeck, 2012), 68–69.

to unite himself with believers. But Luther repeatedly affirms that the gospel speaks its forensic truth prior any unification between the believer and Christ in faith. In a word, Christ is for believers before he is in them.

Third, the logic of mystical union as justification contradicts Luther's conception of sanctification. Beginning with the Romans commentary of 1516, Luther rejects any description of divine grace that locates the basis of righteousness *coram Deo* inside the sinner. The externalization of grace for the sake of the decentering of the incurved self is ultimately the reason why the Reformer rejects the medieval conception of the *habitus*. If the Finnish school is to be believed, in his later theology Luther effectively replaces the *habitus* as a predicate of the believer with mystical union. Such a conceptual move on Luther's part could only undermine his own soteriological premises and reorient the sinner back to a form of self-incurvature.

Luther's goal in externalizing grace (*extra nos*) is to have the believer live an ecstatic rather than centered existence: outside of themselves in Christ by faith, and outside of themselves in the human community by love. Seen from this perspective, mystical union does not serve the function vacated by the medieval concept of infused grace. Rather, mystical union inculcates in the believer the reality of the promise by giving the being of the very promiser to them. As we have seen, for Luther the union of Christ and believers through justification mirrors marriage, where there are both wedding vows (forensic promise) and a consummation (mystical union). Implicit in Luther's marriage analogy, it could be observed that the vows made at the wedding are subsequently guaranteed and made concrete by the bride and groom's physical mutual self-gift to one another. To give one's very self to another is to give the ultimate pledge of one's loyalty and trustworthiness to the other.

CONCLUSION

Luther speaks about justification using a variety of metaphors and analogies in his mature theology (i.e., bridal and judicial). Nevertheless, the key concept that holds them together is the *communicatio idiomatum* that takes place through Christ and his word. Because of the exchange of humanity and divinity in Christ, Jesus is able to engage in a *communicatio idiomatum* of sin and death with humanity on the cross. Because of

Christ's exchange of realities on the cross and incarnation, a *communicatio idiomatum* between the divine and human word is made possible in the means of grace. Finally, this *communicatio idiomatum* of the sacramental word effects subjective justification in the believer as a "happy exchange" between himself and Christ (*der fröhlicher wechsel, admirabile commercium*). In this, the Augustinian dilemma is overcome by the teaching that God enacts his elected and justifying grace in, under, and through the sacramental word of the gospel. Sadly, as we will see in the next chapter, as compelling as an account of justification as Luther's is, subsequently Protestant theology largely abandoned the Reformer's approach and returned to the parameters of the Augustinian dilemma, albeit in new forms.

CHAPTER 10

Justification and Post-Luther Lutheran Theology:
The Outworking of Luther's Legacy

A s we saw in the previous chapter, Luther's doctrine of justification's strength lay in its reviving the biblical theme of God working salvation through his powerful Word. The Reformer was able to critique and overcome the internal incoherencies Augustine's soteriology had bequeathed to the Western church. This being said, Luther's concept of justification was not fully shared by the other Protestant Reformers of the sixteenth century. Most of the Magisterial Reformers superficially agreed with Luther's teachings on the role of faith and alien righteousness, but ultimately could not break past the standard parameters of the Augustinian tradition.

As will be discussed below, the reason most forms of Protestantism returned to the Augustinian dilemma lies in the fact that most of the Magisterial Reformers never fully assimilated Luther's belief in the sacramentality of the word. The rejection of Luther's sacramental realism by most Protestants also played a significant role, something we will explore more fully in a future chapter. This rejection of sacramental realism invariably led to the return to the basic structural tensions in the Bishop of Hippo's soteriology, albeit in different forms than existed in the Middle Ages. Below we will discuss the role of justification in the Lutheran and non-Lutheran Protestant traditions.

THE EVOLUTION OF LUTHERAN
TEACHING ON JUSTIFICATION:
PHILIPP MELANCHTHON

As we observed in the previous chapter, it would be a mistake to place a wedge between Luther and Melanchthon on the issue of justification. As their joint letters to Johannes Brenz and their mutual approval of a series of confessional documents (Augsburg Confession, Apology to the Augsburg Confession, Smalkald Articles, etc.) demonstrate, the two reformers discussed the doctrine of justification with each other frequently over their careers and shared the same doctrine of faith receiving imputed righteousness.[1]

Robert Kolb has helpfully argued that instead of seeing Luther and Melanchthon as isolated Promethean geniuses (i.e., a Romantic concept of the Reformation), it would be truer to historical reality to see both theologians as being part of a wider "Wittenberg Circle."[2] This Wittenberg Circle was composed of a number of early Lutheran theologians (Luther, Melanchthon, Amsdorf, Bugenhagen, etc) who engaged in mutual critique and cross pollination of one another.[3] This being said, between Luther and his younger co-reformer, there are some differences in points of emphasis. Also, in terms of their teaching on free will and grace, Melanchthon implicitly deviated from the teaching of Luther, though only in his later career.[4] Melanchthon's emphasis on the role of human agency eventually put him at odds with second generation "Gnesio-Lutherans" ("Genuine Lutherans") and the later authors of the Formula of Concord.[5]

Melanchthon dealt with the doctrine of justification in many of his personal writings, as well as confessional writings that he penned on behalf of the nascent Lutheran church. These individual writings included

---

1. Carl Trueman, "*Simul Peccator et Justus*: Martin Luther and Justification," in *Justification: Historical and Contemporary Challenges*, ed. Bruce McCormack (Grand Rapids: Baker Academic, 2006), 88–92.

2. Robert Kolb, *Bound Choice, Election, and Wittenberg Theological Method: From Martin Luther to the Formula of Concord* (Minneapolis: Fortress, 2017), 4.

3. Timothy Wengert, "Melanchthon and Luther/Luther and Melanchthon," *Luther-Jahrbuch 66* (1999): 55–88.

4. Hägglund, *History of Theology*, 248–51.

5. Irene Dingel, "The Culture of Conflict in the Controversies Leading to the Formula of Concord (1548–1580)," in *Lutheran Ecclesiastical Culture, 1550–1675*, ed. Robert Kolb (Leiden: Brill, 2008), 45–50.

biblical commentaries (Romans, etc.) as well as his series of dogmatic textbooks published from 1521 to 1559 referred to as *Loci Communes Theologici* ("Theological Commonplaces" or "Common Theological Topics").[6] Melanchthon's dogmatic textbooks were the first Protestant systematic theologies and became the basis of theological method utilized in both the Lutheran and Reformed traditions until the early eighteenth century.[7] In another sign of theological unity between the two reformers, Luther hyperbolically commented that he was so thoroughly pleased with Melanchthon's dogmatic textbooks that he believed them to be second only to the Bible.[8]

The structure and method of Melanchthon's dogmatic textbooks rested on a Renaissance rhetorical theory originated by the fifteenth century German Humanist Rudolf Agricola and transmitted to Melanchthon through Erasmus.[9] Known as the "Loci-Method,"[10] Melanchthon's theory claimed that there are grammatically clear passages of Scripture that deal with specific articles of the faith called the "seats of doctrine" (*sedes doctrinae*).[11] The theologians should gather these grammatically clear passages together and allow them to mutually interpret one another. From the pattern of scriptural judgments about a particular doctrine, a teaching of the faith would organically emerge from the text of the Bible.[12]

The first edition of *Loci Communes Theologici* (1521) dealt almost exclusively with the questions of sin and grace. Melanchthon opines that the doctrine of the Trinity is itself a far too lofty and speculative article of

6. Timothy Wengert, "Biblical Interpretation in the Works of Philip Melanchthon," in *A History of Biblical Interpretation: The Medieval Though the Reformation Periods*, vol. 2, ed. Alan J. Hauser and Duane F. Watson (Grand Rapids: Eerdmans, 2009), 331–53.

7. See Richard Muller, *Post-Reformation Reformed Dogmatics: The Rise and Development of Reformed Orthodoxy, ca. 1520 to ca. 1725*, 4 vols. (Grand Rapids: Baker Academic, 2003), 1:96–102, 1:177–79.

8. "Table Talk for Winter 1542–1543," LW 54:439–40.

9. Willem van Asselt, *Introduction to Reformed Scholasticism* (Grand Rapids: Reformation Heritage Books, 2011), 87–92; Richard Muller, *The Unaccommodated Calvin: Studies in the Foundation of a Theological Tradition* (Oxford: Oxford University Press, 2000), 109–10.

10. See Robert Kolb, "The Ordering of the Loci Communes Theologici: The Structuring of the Melanchthonian Dogmatic Tradition," *Concordia Journal* 23, no. 4 (1997): 317–37.

11. Muller, *Unaccommodated Calvin*, 109–110.

12. Kolb, "The Ordering of the Loci Communes Theologici," 317–37; Muller, *Post-Reformation Reformed Dogmatics*, 1:96–102, 1:177–79.

the faith to be discussed in his text.[13] Instead, Melanchthon focuses on Pauline-Augustinian themes of the incapacitating sinfulness of humanity and the centrality of *sola gratia* in the divine-human relationship.[14] Although in their external relationships they are free and capable of rationally weighing their decisions regarding what course of action to take,[15] humans are ruled in their inner-person by their "affections."[16] This is not only true for the divine-human relationship, but in life the driving force is the passions. For humans to be driven to some course of action, one passion must overcome another passion.[17] God prepares his creatures for faith by working repentance through the law and giving the Holy Spirit through the gospel. The righteousness of faith is then described as being an appropriation by faith of Christ's alien righteousness:

> Therefore, we are justified when, put to death by the law, we are made alive again by the word of grace promised in Christ; the gospel forgives our sins, and we cling to Christ in faith, not doubting in the least that the righteousness of Christ is our righteousness, that the satisfaction Christ wrought is our expiation, and that the resurrection of Christ is ours. In a word, we do not doubt at all that our sins have been forgiven and that God now favors us and wills our good.[18]

Here Melanchthon uses language almost identical to what we observed in Luther of the same period. In both cases, the emphasis lies on the alien nature of Christ's righteousness, as well as faith's appropriation of it through the promise of the gospel.

Some of Melanchthon's longest and most detailed discussion of the doctrine of justification comes in the confessional writings that he composed. For example, the Preceptor's discussion of the doctrine of justification in

---

13. Philipp Melanchthon, "*Loci Communes Theologici* 1521," in *Melanchthon and Bucer*, ed. Wilhelm Pauck (Philadelphia: Westminster, 1969), 21.

14. Melanchthon, "*Loci Communes Theologici* 1521," 22–49.

15. Melanchthon, "*Loci Communes Theologici* 1521," 26–27.

16. Melanchthon, "*Loci Communes Theologici* 1521," 27.

17. Melanchthon, "*Loci Communes Theologici* 1521," 27–28.

18. Melanchthon, "*Loci Communes Theologici* 1521," 88–89.

the Apology to the Augsburg Confession (1531) lasts roughly two hundred pages in modern editions of the Book of Concord.

Beginning with the Augsburg Confession of 1530, Melanchthon outlines a description of the work of Christ and the justification of sinners in harmony with Luther's writings after 1518. After affirming the moral impotence brought on human nature by original sin in the second article of the Augustana, Melanchthon states regarding the work of Christ: "Christ, [who is] true God and true man, who was born of the Virgin Mary, truly suffered, was crucified, dead, and buried, that He might reconcile the Father unto us, and be a sacrifice, not only for original guilt, but also for all actual sins of men."[19] Regarding justification, Melanchthon writes, "men cannot be justified before God by their own strength, merits, or works, but are freely justified for Christ's sake, through faith, when they believe that they are received into favor, and that their sins are forgiven for Christ's sake, who, by His death, has made satisfaction for our sins. This faith God imputes for righteousness in His sight."[20] As can be seen, Melanchthon's description is completely conceptually consistent with the theology that we have seen in Luther thus far. That being said, Luther's motif of the exchange of realities tends to be muted in favor of more judicial sounding language.[21]

In terms of the actual definition of justification, initially Melanchthon defined justification according to both the biblical forensic and medieval sanative definitions. An example of this can be found in the Apology to the Augsburg Confession (1531), where Melanchthon describes justification in the following manner: " '[T]o be justified' means that out of unjust men just men are made, or born again, it means also that they are pronounced or accounted just. For Scripture speaks in both ways. The term 'to be justified' is used in two ways: to denote, being converted or regenerated; again, being accounted righteous."[22]

---

19. Augsburg Confession, III; *Concordia Triglotta: The Symbolical Books of the Evangelical Lutheran Church, German-Latin-English*, trans. and ed. F. Bente, W. H. T. Dau, and Lutheran Church Missouri Synod (St. Louis: Concordia, 1921), 45.

20. Augsburg Confession, IV; *Concordia Triglotta*, 45.

21. Alister McGrath, *Iustitia Dei: A History of the Christian Doctrine of Justification* (Cambridge: Cambridge University Press, 2020), 209.

22. Apology of the Augsburg Confession, IV; *Concordia Triglotta*, 141.

Let it be noted that Melanchthon's formula in the Apology of 1531 is conceptually identical with Luther's formulation in his commentary on Psalm 51 of 1538.[23] Nevertheless, it should be recognized that although both Luther and Melanchthon at this early stage of the Reformation both allow justification can have a secondary meaning of what later Protestantism would call "sanctification," they still clearly reject that notion that this renewal makes believers righteous before God in a way that contributes to salvation. Christ alone is the believer's righteousness before the court of divine judgment.

As Stephen Strehle notes, in the Romans commentary of 1532 Melanchthon shifts over almost entirely to using the term "justification" to mean being imputed as righteous. This linguistic usage of the term was not only in keeping with the Bible but would become standard for later Protestant theology. Melanchthon writes: "[W]e know for certain that in these disputations of Paul justification signifies the remission of sins and the acceptance to eternal life, as the fourth chapter testifies in a sufficiently clear manner, where it defines justification as the forgiveness of sins."[24] Strehle notes that in the Romans commentary there is a "pronounced emphasis upon the forensic terms "imputation" and "acceptation," along with a clear demarcation between justification and any "newness" or "quality" in the believer"[25] Melanchthon of course emphasizes that regeneration does necessarily follow from being declared righteous, but this is not to be confused with the justification itself.[26]

In developing the conceptual and linguistic framework for his soteriology, Melanchthon therefore preferred to use the term "acquittal" (*acceptilatio*) or "imputation" (*imputatio*) to describe the fundamental reality of

---

23. Commentary on Psalm 51 (1532), LW 12:331: "These are the two parts of justification. The first is grace revealed through Christ, that through Christ we have a gracious God, so that sin can no longer accuse us, but our conscience has found peace through trust in the mercy of God. The second part is the conferring of the Holy Spirit with His gifts, who enlightens us against the defilements of spirit and flesh (2 Cor 7:1). Thus we are defended against the opinions with which the devil seduces the whole world. Thus the true knowledge of God grows daily, together with other gifts, like chastity, obedience, and patience."

24. Philipp Melanchthon, *Commentary on Romans*, trans. Fred Kramer (St. Louis: Concordia, 1992), 25.

25. Stephen Strehle, *The Catholic Roots of the Protestant Gospel: Encounter Between the Middle Ages and the Reformation* (Leiden: Brill, 1995), 66–67.

26. Melanchthon, *Commentary on Romans*, 25.

justification.[27] As we saw, Luther agreed on the importance of the forensic nature of justification and the imputation of Christ's righteousness.
In light of our discussion in an earlier chapter, it may also be observed
that these terms accurately mirror Paul's language of being "justified" and
"reckoned" as righteous (Rom 4:3). Indeed, *acceptilatio* is the word that
Erasmus had used in his Latin re-translation of the New Testament to
render the aforementioned Pauline terms from the original Greek, a move
followed by Melanchthon.[28] The term *acceptilatio* had originally meant the
remitting of a debt in its old Roman usage.[29] Moreover, as we have already
seen, the concept of imputation was not totally unknown to medieval
theology. Specifically, the concept of imputation had been utilized in the
late Middle Ages by the Ockhamist tradition as a way of describing how
God accepted good works that did not meet the full standard of justice
in order to merit the first grace (*meritum de congruo*).[30]

Of course, in utilizing the concept of imputation Melanchthon (like
Luther before him) does not develop the doctrine in terms of an acceptance of human works based on a covenantal promise as in Ockhamism.[31]
Rather, imputation occurs for Melanchthon on the basis of Christ's substitutionary sacrifice.[32] In this context, Christ's work is described in terms
somewhat reminiscent of those of Anselm's *Cur Deus homo*.[33] The main
way Luther and Melanchthon differ from Anselm is that the Wittenberg
reformers saw Christ as imputed with human sin and punished for it,[34]
whereas Anselm saw the death of Christ as a meritorious act of *superero-
gation*.[35] As a result of the connection that Melanchthon affirmed between
the work of Christ and justification, the acceptance of sinners by imputation was not seen as an arbitrary judgment, but something achieved by

27. McGrath, *Iustitia Dei*, 210.

28. McGrath, *Iustitia Dei*, 210.

29. McGrath, *Iustitia Dei*, 209–10.

30. Strehle, *Catholic Roots of the Protestant Gospel*, 69–70.

31. Bengt Hägglund, *The Background of Luther's Doctrine of Justification in Late Medieval Theology* (Philadelphia: Fortress, 1971), 23–24.

32. Melanchthon, *Commentary on Romans*, 100.

33. Strehle, *Catholic Roots of the Protestant Gospel*, 87–90.

34. Lecture on Galatians (1531), LW 26:280; Melanchthon, *Commentary on Romans*, 100.

35. Anselm of Canterbury, *Cur Deus Homo?* 2.18, in *A Scholastic Miscellany: Anselm to Ockham*, trans. and ed. Eugene R. Fairweather (Philadelphia: Westminster, 1966), 179.

acceptance *propter christum per fidem*. Faith in the promise receives the imputation of Christ's real righteousness *coram Deo*.[36]

Although, as we have seen so far, Luther and Melanchthon agreed fundamentally on the doctrine of justification (albeit with different emphases), genuine differences over the question of grace and free will began to emerge between the two theologians shortly after Luther's death. Even before Luther's death, Melanchthon became increasingly worried about the implications of Luther's doctrine of the bondage of the human will. He saw the bondage of the will as giving impetus to various forms of philosophical determinism that had been revived at the time of the Renaissance (notably, Stoicism).[37] Incidentally, Melanchthon's concern about philosophical determinism is somewhat ironic in light his belief in and practice of astrology.[38]

As Jaroslav Pelikan has observed, the mature Melanchthon's concept of faith was developed using the Aristotelian faculty psychology.[39] Following Aristotle's teaching in *De Anima*,[40] Melanchthon speaks of the will and intellect as distinct faculties within the human soul.[41] Pelikan notes that this is different from Luther's approach, which tended to speak of human beings as being defined in totalities based on their relationship to God's Word of condemnation or grace (*ganzer Kerl*).[42] According to Melanchthon's understanding, the intellect comes to learn the truth of the gospel. Based on the knowledge of divine grace in the intellect, the will is then moved to trust in the gospel.[43]

---

36. Melanchthon, *Commentary on Romans*, 103–4.

37. Kolb, *Bound Choice, Election, and the Wittenberg Theological Method*, 90.

38. Sachiko Kusukaw, *The Transformation of Natural Philosophy: The Case of Philip Melanchthon* (Cambridge: Cambridge University Press, 1995), 170–71.

39. Jaroslav Pelikan, *From Luther to Kierkegaard: A Study in the History of Theology* (St. Louis: Concordia, 1963), 26–28.

40. See Aristotle, *De Anima*, trans. Christopher Shields (Oxford: Clarendon, 2016).

41. Pelikan, *From Luther to Kierkegaard*, 27–28.

42. Pelikan, *From Luther to Kierkegaard*, 16–17, 27–28.

43. Antti Raunio, "Divine and Natural Law in Luther and Melanchthon," in *Lutheran Reformation and the Law*, ed. Virpi Mäkinen (Leiden: Brill, 2006), 54–59.

Therefore, for the first time[44] in *Enarratio symboli Niceni* (written sometime between 1547 and 1550)[45] and then later more systematically in *Loci Communes* 1559,[46] Melanchthon posits three causes of conversion (*tres causae*). Basing himself on a modified version of Aristotle's causal paradigm[47] the Preceptor suggests that "good action" within believers is due not only to the Word of God and the Holy Spirit, but also to the assent of the human will.[48] In adding the human will, Melanchthon at the very least seems to imply a form of synergism, although as Lowell Green has demonstrated there is little evidence that he explicitly taught synergism. Indeed, the "conversion" and "good action" that Melanchthon often speaks of does not necessarily mean the initial act of coming to faith, but in the parlance of the sixteenth century could also simply mean the Spirit-wrought believing life of repentance and cooperation with grace.[49] Nevertheless, Melanchthon often does speak of the will's possibility of rejecting of the offer of grace wrought by the word and the Spirit. It is therefore easy to see how to many this implied a form of synergism that became more explicit in the Preceptor's later Philippist followers.[50]

In addition to this, in his earlier *Loci Communes Theologici* 1535, while not explicitly denying the doctrine of predestination, Melanchthon decries any talk of predestination as a "labyrinth." Instead, sinners should look to the general offer of grace in the word of the gospel with trust and ignore speculating about any hidden will of God.[51] This approach is in many

---

44. Lowell Green, "The Three Causes of Conversion in Philipp Melanchthon, Martin Chemnitz, David Chytraeus, and the Formula of Concord," *Lutherjahrbuch* 47 (1980): 91.

45. Philipp Melanchthon, "Enarratio symboli Niceni" in *Corpus Reformatorum*, ed. Karl Gottlieb Bretschneider, 28 vols. (New York: Johnson Reprint Corporation, 1963), 23:193–96.

46. Philipp Melanchthon, *The Chief Theological Topics: Loci Praecipui Theologici 1559*, trans. J. A. O. Preus (St. Louis: Concordia, 2011), 61.

47. Green, "The Three Causes of Conversion in Philipp Melanchthon, Martin Chemnitz, David Chytraeus, and the Formula of Concord," 97.

48. See Timothy Wengert, "Philip Melanchthon and the Origins of the 'Three Causes' (1533–1535): An Examination of the Roots of the Controversy over the Freedom of the Will," in *Philip Melanchthon: Theologian in Classroom, Confession, and Controversy*, ed., Irene Dingel; et al. (Göttigen: Vandenhoeck & Ruprecht, 2012), 183–208.

49. Green, "The Three Causes of Conversion in Philipp Melanchthon, Martin Chemnitz, David Chytraeus, and the Formula of Concord," 93–94.

50. Kolb, *Bound Choice, Election, and the Wittenberg Theological Method*, 93–94.

51. Philipp Melanchthon, *Loci Communes 1535*, trans. Paul Rydecki (Malone, TX: Repristination, 2020), 168–71.

ways not dissimilar to Luther, but as we have seen Luther is quite a bit
more comfortable with suggesting that the faithful can have confidence
that the decree of election supervenes on the sacramental promise of the
gospel. Beyond this, as we will discuss at some length in a later chapter, Luther held that God's omnipotence meant that nothing occurred
contingently and that God's foreknowledge was genuinely causative.[52]
By contrast, Melanchthon held that God could foreknow future events
contingently. God's contingent foreknowledge included the demise of
the damned, thereby absolving him of any responsibility of their fate.[53]
Combined with the Preceptor's accent on the role of the human will, this
view of divine providence suggested that election was nothing but a form
of divine prescience as to who decides to cooperate with divine grace and
who did not. It must nevertheless be strongly stressed that Melanchthon
never directly says this about the nature of predestination, while his later
followers drew out many of these implications in their theology.

Melanchthon's teaching on free will and grace initially elicited little
reaction. The one exception was Nicholas von Amsdorf who privately
complained of Melanchthon's position because it contradicted God's
absolute causal sovereignty.[54] Nevertheless, in the second generation of
Lutheranism, Melanchthon's teaching was increasingly perceived by many
of Luther's followers as promoting a form of synergism.[55] As noted earlier,
Melanchthon's doctrine of grace was refined and expanded by students
into a theology that arguably gave a greater role to the human will than
Luther would likely have been comfortable with. This move toward
a theology of grace that also gave some weight to human choice ultimately resulted in open theological warfare with Luther's most ardent
followers referred to as the "Gnesio-Lutherans" led by Amsdorf and the
Croatian-born Lutheran theologian Matthias Flacius.[56] On the other side,
a school of thought known as "Philippism" grew up around Melanchthon
and fought against the Gnesio-Lutherans in what came to be known as the

52. The Bondage of the Will (1525), LW 33:36–42, 184–92.
53. Melanchthon, Loci Communes 1535, 59–62.
54. Kolb, Bound Choice, Election, and the Wittenberg Theological Method, 95–96.
55. F. Bente, Historical Introduction to the Lutheran Confessions (St. Louis: Concordia, 2005), 300.
56. Arand, Kolb, and Nestingen, The Lutheran Confessions, 183–89.

"Synergistic Controversy,"[57] along with numerous others.[58] The Gnesio-Lutherans agreed with Luther that humanity was dead in sin and was only converted from sin by a monergistic action of the Holy Spirit.

Flacius went so far as to claim, in a heated exchange with one Melanchthon's moderate followers, Victor Strigel, that sin had become the very "substance" (within the substance and accidents Aristotelian ontological scheme) of humanity after the fall. Such a theologically inaccurate formulation suggested that either God was the author of evil in creating the human substance or that in fact Satan was a quasi-god who had created fallen humanity. In actuality, Flacius did not mean by "substance" that humanity had been ontologically transformed into evil, but rather that the damage of sin was so deep and pervasive that it completely defined humanity in relation to God after the fall.[59] Nevertheless, as innocently as Flacius might have meant the statement, his theological formulation regarding original sin led to an accusation of the Manichaean heresy and his exile from the Lutheran community.[60] Ultimately, the controversy was only resolved in the Formula of Concord (1577), which we will discuss at some length below.[61]

In light of this, we can observe that the older Melanchthon took Luther's doctrine of the sacramentality of the word and reinterpreted it along the lines of the typical sacramentalist trajectory of the Augustinian dilemma. The Word of God is genuinely sacramental for Melanchthon in that it contains the coming of the Holy Spirit who works faith. Nevertheless, in Melanchthon's teaching it is at minimum very strongly implied that the Holy Spirit's work is dependent on the human will's consent to cooperate with him. Hence, in Melanchthon's later work, grace can be construed as ultimately a possibility that is actualized by human decision. Such

57. Eugene Klug, "Free Will, or Human Powers," in *A Contemporary Look at the Formula of Concord*, ed. Robert Preus and Wilbert Rosin (St. Louis: Concordia, 1978), 122–36.

58. Robert Kolb, "Historical Background of the Formula of Concord" in Preus and Rosin, *A Contemporary Look at the Formula of Concord*, 12–87.

59. Kolb, *Bound Choice, Election, and the Wittenberg Theological Method: From Martin Luther to the Formula of Concord* (Grand Rapids: Eerdmans, 2005), 118–20; Heinrich Vogel, "On Original Sin, The Flacian Aberration" in *No Other Gospel: Essays in Commemoration of the 400th Anniversary of the Formula of Concord, 1580–1980*, ed. Arnold Koelpin (Milwaukee: Northwestern, 1980), 126–31.

60. Luka Ilić, *Theologian of Sin and Grace: The Process of Radicalization in the Theology of Matthias Flacius Illyricus* (Göttingen: Vandenhoeck & Ruprecht, 2014), 155–62.

61. SD I and Ep I; *Concordia Triglotta*, 779–85, 859–79.

a human decision can be called into question regarding its sincerity, thereby returning the sinner to the authenticity of his works (in this case, not external works, but rather a psychological event of conversion). Therefore, the logical implication of the older Melanchthon's theology of justification is that Luther's unreflective faith is to be denied in favor of an extremely reflective faith. As we will see, psychologizing of faith and the implicit call for self-examination as the sincerity of one's conversion would become a standard feature in many strands of the later Protestant tradition.

THE EVOLUTION OF LUTHERAN TEACHING ON JUSTIFICATION: THE OSIANDERIAN CONTROVERSY

Besides the Synergistic Controversy, the Osianderian Controversy was likely the most significant debate in the second generation of Lutheranism over the nature of justification.[62] By his contemporaries, Osiander was largely remembered as having collapsed justification into sanctification.[63] Nevertheless, the truth regarding Osiander's actual position is far more complicated and directly touches on the question of the sacramentality of the word.

Osiander's early teaching on confession and absolution is often ignored, yet it is extremely illuminating for understanding his later view of justification especially when juxtaposed to that of Luther. Being an early follower of Luther, Osiander eventually became a pastor in southern German city of Nürnberg.[64] In 1533, the Nürnberg city council called for Luther and Melanchthon's opinion regarding a controversy that originated with Osiander and group of pastors that he led.[65] Specifically, Osiander and his group had come to reject the practice of the pastor granting a general

62. Hamann, "The Righteousness of Faith before God," 137–62; Robert Kolb, "Historical Background of the Formula of Concord," in Preus and Rosin, *A Contemporary Look at the Formula of Concord*, 36–41; Carl Lawrenz, "On Justification, Osiander's Doctrine of the Indwelling of Christ," in Koelpin, *No Other Gospel*, 149–74.

63. Wengert, *Defending Faith* (Tübingen: Mohr Siebeck, 2012), 74.

64. Ronald Rittgers, *The Reformation of the Keys: Confession, Conscience, and Authority in Sixteenth Century Germany* (Cambridge: Harvard University Press, 2004), 64.

65. Ronald Rittgers, *The Reformation of the Keys*, 141, 143.

absolution during church services.[66] Instead, he demanded that all con-
gregants engage in private confession and absolution as a prerequisite of
being admitted to the Lord's Supper.[67]

Osiander held a view of confession and absolution that had much in
common with, while at the same time possessing subtle differences from
Luther.[68] As we have already seen, for Luther faith is created and sustained by the proclamation of absolution while at the same time being
the receptive organ of that same absolution. Just as there is no separating Christ's humanity and divinity (the Lutheran teaching on the *genus
apotelesmaticum, genus majestaticum*), so too there is no separating God's
invisible act of absolution and the human word of the pastor. When God
forgives through the minister, his mighty divine deed-word is present in
the human word. There is no danger in publicly pronouncing absolution
to the unbelieving (whose hearts and minds one cannot read anyway)[69]
because the word of the gospel will create the conditions for its acceptance. Moreover, as we have also seen, for Luther God has forgiven the
whole world in Christ, and so the word of absolution is objectively true
for all people even if it is not received. Although Luther does not directly
say it, the implication is that when a minister uses the power of the keys
to bind the sin of sinners, it is not a matter of God's unwillingness to forgive them. Rather, in the act of binding, the minister acknowledges that by
their unrepentant behavior the congregant is signaling their unwillingness
to receive this forgiveness. As Luther writes in his response to Osiander:

> We cannot censure or reject general absolution for this reason: *the
> preaching of the holy gospel itself is a general absolution in which the
> forgiveness of sins is proclaimed* to many people in the congregation
> publicly or to a single person alone, either publicly or privately. For
> this reason, although not all believe the absolution, it is not to be
> rejected. For every absolution, whether it takes place in a commu-
> nal or individual setting must still be understood to demand faith

---

66. Ronald Rittgers, *The Reformation of the Keys*, 140.

67. Ronald Rittgers, *The Reformation of the Keys*, 140.

68. See a helpful contrast between the two positions in Ronald Rittgers, "Luther on Private
Confession," in *The Pastoral Luther: Essays on Martin Luther's Practical Theology*, ed. Timothy Wengert
(Minneapolis: Fortress, 2017), 211–32.

69. Rittgers, *The Reformation of the Keys*, 157–58.

and to help those who accept it ... *the gospel proclaims forgiveness to everyone in the whole world and excepts no one from the universal [proclamation]."*[70]

To use a Christological analogy, in contrast to Luther's view of absolution, which was Neochalcedonian (i.e., the divine and human fully united), Osiander's view was Nestorian (i.e., a separation of the divine and human). We will see below that this "Nestorianism" could also be said to characterize Osiander's view of theology of atonement and justification.[71] As Ronald Rittgers notes, for Osiander, absolution should only be given if the right spiritual disposition is present.[72] Pastors possess a judicial power to objectively forgive sins, irrespective of whether there is any repentance or faith.[73] If a pastor granted forgiveness to a person without genuine repentance, divine wrath would necessarily be incurred for both the pastor and the penitent. God would judge the pastor for abusing his office. The unrepentant person who had been objectively absolved would incur divine wrath by abusing and rejecting the forgiveness he had been granted.[74] As Timothy Wengert comments: "Andreas Osiander objected to [general absolution after the sermon], worrying that hardened sinners would take it as *carte blanche* to continue sinning and neglect private confession."[75] Here lay the problem with giving a general absolution. Namely, if Osiander could not examine the individual spiritual state of those who sought absolution, he could not decide who would spiritually benefit from his pronouncement of absolution.[76] He did not view the divine power of the sacramental word as creating the conditions for its acceptance.

Hence, as should be clear, for Osiander the divine and human were in some ways united and in others disunited in the act of absolution. In the forensic aspect of absolution, the pastor possesses the objective divine power to forgive irrespective of faith. Nevertheless, the absolution wielded

70. Letter to the Honorable and Wise Mayors, and to the Council of the City of Nürnberg (1533), WABr 6:454. Cited in Wengert, *Defending Faith*, 70. Emphasis added.
71. See Wengert, *Defending Faith*, 88–92.
72. Rittgers, *The Reformation of the Keys*, 153.
73. Rittgers, *The Reformation of the Keys*, 153.
74. Rittgers, *The Reformation of the Keys*, 153–54.
75. Wengert, *Defending Faith*, 69.
76. Rittgers, *The Reformation of the Keys*, 153–54.

by the pastor is a merely forensic word and not also an effective one. In other words, the word of absolution is not a deed-word that creates faith; it is merely a judicial pronunciation. The word of the pastor was a mere signifier that accurately signifies the divine decision, not a deed-word that creates faith in those who hear it. Ultimately, Osiander's worries about general absolution were rooted in the fact that he assumed that the divine grace that created faith and repentance was separated from the external word. Osiander was a "Nestorian" in the sense that just as Nestorius separated the divine and human in Christ, Osiander separated divine grace from the external word of the pastor.

After relocating to northern Germany in the midst of the Augsburg and Leipzig Interim, in the early 1550s Osiander became embroiled in a second great controversy that united the Philippists and the Gnesio-Lutherans in their opposition to him.[77] Decades later, the Formula of Concord would condemn and somewhat misrepresent Osiander's theology of atonement and justification (without naming him) by largely drawing on the misunderstanding of Melanchthon and Martin Chemnitz's interpretation of his position.[78]

In developing his own theology of justification, Osiander was critical of Melanchthon's purely forensic understanding of justification. Osiander considered the Preceptor's teaching on the subject to amount to little more than a banal legal process that was as "cold as ice."[79] In his early career Osiander had been heavily influenced by both Neoplatonism and the Jewish tradition of Kabbalah, and, it could be argued, displayed significant mystical tendencies in his writings.[80] Based on these influences, Osiander appears to have come to reject Luther's concept of the incarnation. Instead of Luther's theology of exchange between the human and divine in Christ, Osiander sought to separate the physical and the spiritual in a manner

---

77. Eric W. Gritsch and Robert W. Jenson, *Lutheranism: The Theological Movement and Its Confessional Writings* (Philadelphia: Fortress, 1976), 54.

78. Olli-Pekka Vainio, *Justification and Participation in Christ: The Development of the Lutheran Doctrine of Justification from Luther to the Formula of Concord (1580)* (Leiden: Brill, 2008), 99–103, 209–13.

79. Eduard Böhl, *The Reformed Doctrine of Justification,* trans. C. H. Riedesel (Grand Rapids: Eerdmans, 1946), 38.

80. Robert Kolb, "Confessional Lutheran Theology," in *The Cambridge Companion to Reformation Theology,* ed. David Bagchi and David Steinmetz (Cambridge: Cambridge University Press, 2004), 73.

similar to the mystical traditions that exercised influence on his thinking. Osiander saw the two natures in Christ as playing completely separate roles from one another in achieving atonement and justification.[81]

Osiander agreed with Luther and Melanchthon on the substitutionary nature of atonement.[82] Luther had emphasized the fact that God himself had to die in the man Jesus's death. Atonement through the suffering of the divine Son was necessary for the sake of rendering complete satisfaction to the Father. God himself had to sit on the scale of justice in order to redeem humanity:

> We Christians should know that if God is not in the scale to give it weight, we, on our side, sink to the ground. I mean it this way: if it cannot be said that God died for us, but only a man, we are lost; but if God's death and a dead God lie in the balance, His side goes down and ours goes up like a light and empty scale. Yet He can also readily go up again or leap out of the scale! But He could not sit on the scale unless He became a man like us, so that it could be called God's dying, God's martyrdom, God's blood, and God's death. For God in His own nature cannot die; but now that God and man are united in one person, it is called God's death when the man dies who is one substance or one person with God.[83]

By contrast, Osiander saw the righteousness won by Jesus's obedience and death as being merely an act of his human nature. Therefore, the satisfaction rendered by Jesus's obedience and death was merely "human righteousness" that was capable of canceling the debt of sin but did not make a person positively righteous *coram Deo*.[84] In addition to this cancelation of the debt of sin, the believer had to be rendered positively righteous before the judgment seat of God. Osiander used the simile of the son of a doctor who upon drinking a potion or medicine is poisoned

---

81. Strehle, *The Catholic Roots of the Protestant Gospel*, 75–8; Vainio, *Justification and Participation*, 98–100.

82. Vainio, *Justification and Participation*, 100.

83. On the Councils and the Church (1539), LW 41:103–4. See excellent discussion in Johannes Zachhuber, *Luther's Christological Legacy: Christocentrism and the Chalcedonian Tradition* (Milwaukee: Marquette University Press, 2017), 70–71.

84. Vainio, *Justification and Participation*, 100.

by it.[85] Even if his father forgave him this offense, he would nevertheless suffer the consequences of drinking poison unless an antidote was given. Therefore, even with the forgiveness of sin, there remained a need for humanity to stand positively righteousness before God. The solution was that God's eternal righteousness must be mystically communicated to the sinner and dwell in him. In this regard Osiander writes:

> Since we are in Christ through faith and he is in us, we also became the righteousness of God in him, just as he became sin for us [2 Cor 5:21]. That is, he showered us and filled us with this divine righteousness, as we showered him with our sins, so that God himself and all the angels see only righteousness in us on account of the highest, eternal, and infinite righteousness of Christ, which is His Godhead itself dwelling in us.[86]

In this, Osiander treated divine righteousness not just as God's holy faithfulness to his promises or his moral will, but as a kind of ontological predicate of the divine being that could dwell in the believing human subject through mystical union.[87]

Melanchthon and Chemnitz interpreted Osiander's conflation of positive righteousness *coram Deo* with mystical union to mean that sanctification was identical with justification. After examining Osiander's writings in detail, Olli-Pekka Vainio has suggested that in actuality there is no claim in the Nürenberg pastor's work that one merits salvation by one's sanctification. Although there is some ambiguity in his rhetoric, Osiander does not appear to have considered works meritorious or seen inner renewal as meriting God's favor.[88] Indeed, the indwelling of God's eternal divine righteousness remains an alien righteousness. Vainio writes: "When Osiander speaks about God acting wrongly if he reckons as righteous someone who is not righteous *in re* [in themselves], he does not refer to human properties but to God, who is the justifying righteousness

---

85. Vainio, *Justification and Participation*, 104.

86. Andreas Osiander, "Concerning the Only Mediator (1551)," in *Documents from the History of Early Lutheranism: 1517–1750*, ed. Eric Lund (Minneapolis: Fortress, 2002), 206.

87. Vainio, *Justification and Participation*, 98, 102.

88. Vainio, *Justification and Participation*, 101–2.

through faith."[89] Indeed, it should also be observed that Stephen Strehle has pointed out that even Joachim Mörlin (one of strongest critics of Osiander) thought that Melanchthon's accusations of works righteousness were essentially baseless.[90]

Nevertheless, as we have seen, a more cogent critique of Osiander is that the failure of his view of justification is ultimately rooted in the same line of thinking that caused the problems in his view of confession and absolution. Osiander separated the divine and human in Christ in the same way that he had separated the human and divine words in absolution. As Vainio observes, "What Christ does is therefore separated from who Christ is."[91] Christ's human obedience and death is hermetically sealed off from his divinity and therefore lacks the divine power and efficacy to justify and sanctify the sinner. Rather, the human deeds of Christ are merely human and can only forensically release from sin—much like the judicial power of the human pastor can only forgive but not genuinely create faith.

In his response to Osiander, Flacius came closest to identifying the actual difficulty, which was the problematic division of person of Christ. Though he does not make reference to Osiander's troubling concept of the *communicatio idiomatum,* in developing his distinction between the active and passive righteousness in Christ,[92] Flacius assumed that Christ's divine person worked in and through the human obedience and death of Christ to achieve salvation and to justify sinners:

> The justice of God, as revealed in the Law, demands of us, poor, unrighteous, disobedient men, two items of righteousness. The first is, that we render to God complete satisfaction for the transgression and sin already committed; the second, that we thenceforth be heartily and perfectly obedient to His Law if we wish to enter life. If we do not thus accomplish this, it threatens us with eternal damnation. And therefore the essential justice of God includes us

---

89. Vainio, *Justification and Participation,* 102.

90. Strehle, *The Catholic Roots of the Protestant Gospel,* 74.

91. Strehle, *The Catholic Roots of the Protestant Gospel,* 99.

92. Strehle, *The Catholic Roots of the Protestant Gospel,* 116. See Vainio, *Justification and Participation,* 230n96. Also see Lauri Haikola, *Gesetz und Evangelium bei Matthias Flacius Illyricus: Eine Untersuchung zur Lutherischen Theologies vor der Konkordienformel* (Lund: Gleerup, 1952), 172–76.

under sin and the wrath of God. ... Therefore the righteousness of the obedience of Christ, which He rendered to the Law for us, consists in these two features, viz., in His suffering and in perfect obedience to the commands of God.[93]

Although Luther does not use Flacius's terminology, he held with Flacius that Christ was the "greatest and only sin; and the highest, the greatest, and the only righteousness."[94] That is to say, through his divine person active in and through the activity of the man Jesus, the of the human nature stands in the place of and represents sinful humanity who has not been obedient. Likewise, the divine person's death through the human nature renders infinite satisfaction to the Father in the place of the infinite debt of sin accumulated by humanity's sin. Divine righteousness and human righteousness are not separate from one another in atonement and justification, but divine righteousness is present in and through human righteousness, much like the divine Word is present in the human word of the pastor.

THE EVOLUTION OF LUTHERAN TEACHING ON JUSTIFICATION: THE FORMULA OF CONCORD AND SUBSEQUENT LUTHERAN TEACHING ON JUSTIFICATION

In 1577, a group of Saxon and Swabian Lutheran churchmen led by Jakob Andreä and Martin Chemnitz composed a confession of faith aimed in part at putting to rest the debates that had plagued second-generation Lutheranism.[95] This confession of faith known as the "Formula of Concord" quickly won wide acceptance throughout the main Lutheran principalities of Germany.[96] After this, it was swiftly incorporated in a larger collection of Lutheran symbolic writings known as the "Book of Concord" in 1580.[97] This book of confessions became the standard

---

93. Schmid, *The Doctrinal Theology of the Evangelical Lutheran Church*, 354. Also see Haikola, *Gesetz und Evangelium*, 318–23.

94. Lectures on Galatians (1531), LW 26:281.

95. Arand, Kolb, and Nestingen, *The Lutheran Confessions*, 265–76.

96. Arand, Kolb, and Nestingen, *The Lutheran Confessions*, 277–80.

97. Arand, Kolb, and Nestingen, *The Lutheran Confessions*, 275.

articulation of Lutheran doctrine among "confessional Lutherans" down to the present.

Regarding the doctrine of justification, the Formula of Concord reaffirmed Luther and Melanchthon's belief in the forensic nature of justification.[98] Unlike earlier Lutheran confessions (notably the Apology to the Augsburg Confession), justification is defined in strictly forensic terms and differentiated from regeneration.[99] As noted in a previous chapter, mystical union with the Trinity is affirmed, but only subsequent to justification. Mystical union, though real, does not constitute believer's righteousness *coram Deo*.[100] This tendency of strictly distinguishing justification from sanctification and making each a distinct stage of conversion found fuller expression later in Lutheran Orthodoxy's discussion of the *ordo salutis*.[101]

In regard to the doctrine of original sin, the terminology of the Philippist Viktor Strigel is affirmed.[102] Original sin is an accident of human nature, not the substance of human nature.[103] Nevertheless, this does not minimalize original sin, which has damaged human nature to the point that humans cannot contribute anything to their salvation. Hence, Luther and Flacius's view of original sin is conceptually affirmed simultaneously with Philippist terminology regarding original sin.[104] As Robert Jenson wryly observed, ultimately the Concordists were not Flacians with regard to original sin only because they said they were not.[105]

The manner in which the doctrine of predestination was presented by the Formula of Concord inaugurated a complicated legacy for subsequent Lutheranism. Like Luther and the Gnesio-Lutherans, the Formula of Concord affirmed the doctrine of predestination regarding

---

98. FC SD, III; *Concordia Triglotta*, 917–37; Hamann, "The Righteousness of Faith before God," 137–62.

99. FC SD, III.17; *Concordia Triglotta*, 920–21.

100. FC SD III.54; *Concordia Triglotta*, 934–35.

101. Elert, *The Structure of Lutheranism*, vol. 1, 102; McGrath, *Iustitia Dei*, 244–45.

102. Robert Schultz, "Original Sin: Accident or Substance—the Paradoxical Significance of FC I, 53–62 in Historical Context," in *Discord, Dialogue, and Concord: Studies in the Lutheran Reformation's Formula of Concord*, ed. Lewis Spitz and Wenzel Lohff (Philadelphia: Fortress, 1977), 38–57.

103. FC SD, I.57; *Concordia Triglotta*, 876–79.

104. FC SD, I.5; *Concordia Triglotta*, 860–61.

105. Robert Jenson, *On Thinking the Human: Resolutions of Difficult Notions* (Grand Rapids: Eerdmans, 2003), 64.

those redeemed.[106] Believers are saved because of an eternal decree of God's election made possible by Christ and his atoning work.[107] Unlike Augustine and Calvin, and in agreement with Luther and Melanchthon, the Formula of Concord also simultaneously affirms the universality of God's grace.[108] Indeed, one finds the full assurance of one's election by looking to the universal promise of grace in Christ.[109] This is highly paradoxical and can appear incoherent (as it has to many Calvinists) if not viewed within the conceptual framework provided by Luther's distinction between the hidden and revealed God, something that we will engage in a future chapter. Unfortunately, the Formula does not make mention of Luther's distinction of the hidden and revealed God directly (though, it seems to implicitly assume the distinction), leading to much confusion among subsequent generations of Lutherans.[110]

Unlike Luther and more in line with Melanchthon, the Concordists sharply distinguish between divine foreknowledge and predestination.[111] Whereas true believers are saved by God's eternal active predestination of them in Christ,[112] the unbelievers are damned by God's mere foreknowledge of their resistance to divine grace.[113] The fact that humans are capable of resisting God's grace is not due to the fact that the grace of God is contingent on the active cooperation of the human will as Melanchthon had implied. Rather, because the grace of God is only at work in the means of grace and humans have freedom in earthly things (though not in their relationship with God), they are capable of choosing to engage in the means of grace or not. Ultimately, unwillingness to engage or ignorance of the means of grace can prevent conversion.[114] When the means of grace are

---

106. FC SD, XI.8–9; *Concordia Triglotta*, 1064–65. Also see Robert Preus, "Predestination and Election," 271–77.

107. FC SD, XI.64–66; *Concordia Triglotta*, 1082–84. Also see Arand, Kolb, and Nestingen, *The Lutheran Confessions*, 215.

108. FC SD, XI.68–70; *Concordia Triglotta*, 1084–85.

109. FC SD, XI.40; *Concordia Triglotta*, 1074–77.

110. Joel Beeke, *Debated Issues in Sovereign Predestination: Early Lutheran Predestination, Calvinian Reprobation, and Variations in Genevan Lapsarianism* (Göttingen: Vandenhoeck & Ruprecht, 2017), 50–51; Kolb, *Bound Choice, Election, and the Wittenberg Theological Method*, 268.

111. FC SD, XI.4; *Concordia Triglotta*, 1062–65. Also see Elert, *The Structure of Lutheranism*, 137.

112. FC SD, XI.44; *Concordia Triglotta*, 1077.

113. FC SD, XI.83–85; *Concordia Triglotta*, 1077.

114. FC SD, XI.38–43; *Concordia Triglotta*, 1072–75.

engaged, God's grace works monergistically to create and preserve faith. Humans have no free will to convert or regenerate themselves.[115] Since the Formula of Concord emphasized that God works monergistically purely through the medium of the word and sacrament ministry of the church, it successfully upheld the core of Luther's teaching on the sacramental character of the word.

Although the Formula of Concord affirmed Luther's concept of justification by the word, Lutherans of the late sixteenth and early seventeenth century quickly returned to the problematic paradigm bequeathed to the West by Augustine. In this, Lutheran theology tended to take the sacramentalist trajectory in the Augustinian dilemma.[116] This is probably partially based on the early Lutheran desire to polemically differentiate itself as a confessional tradition from Calvinism. It is also possible that there were lingering Melanchthonian undercurrents regarding how the question of sin and grace was conceptualized. Nevertheless, the largest catalyst for the almost total abandon of the doctrine of election lay in the overreaction to the teaching of a Swiss Lutheran theologian named Samuel Huber.[117]

Samuel Huber began his career in the Reformed communion.[118] Having been censored for some of his views of divine grace, he left the Reformed confessional camp to become a Lutheran and taught at Wittenberg.[119] Huber held that because the grace of God was universal, as the Formula of Concord had taught, then it must logically follow that election was also universal.[120] In teaching this, he was not affirming universalism as many

115. FC SD, XI.29–32; *Concordia Triglotta*, 1072–73.

116. Beeke, *Debated Issues in Sovereign Predestination*, 72.

117. Robert Preus, "The Influence of the Formula of Concord on Later Lutheran Orthodoxy," in Spitz and Lohff, *Discord, Dialogue, and Concord*, 99.

118. Walter Arthur Copinger, *A Treatise on Predestination, Election, and Grace, Historical, Doctrinal, and Practical* (London: James Nisbet, 1889), 59.

119. Christian Moser, "Reformed Orthodoxy in Switzerland," in *A Companion to Reformed Orthodoxy* ed. Herman Selderhuis (Leiden: Brill, 2013), 203.

120. Samuel Huber, *Compendium of Theses by Samuel Huber, On the Universal Redemption of the Human Race, Accomplished by Jesus Christ Against the Calvinists*, trans. Andrew Huss, unpublished manuscript, 2013.

of his contemporaries claimed, but merely conflated election with the gracious invitation of humanity to trust in the gospel.[121]

In response to Huber's claim, Aegidius Hunnius[122] and Leonhard Hütter[123] asserted that election is merely God's passive foreknowledge regarding who would come to faith and preserve it to the end of their lives (*ex praevisa fide*). Although humans cannot initiate their relationship with God,[124] humans can lose their faith as Luther had himself affirmed.[125] From the possibility of apostasy, later Lutheran theologians like Johann Gerhard drew the conclusion that preserving or wrecking faith was a matter of contingent human volition (albeit, supported by the power of the Holy Spirit), and hence not subject to the predestinating will of God.[126] Because God clearly foreknew who would continue to cooperate with him after regeneration and who would fall away, predestination was little more than divine foreknowledge of human faith.[127]

This deviation from Luther and the teaching of the Formula of Concord came to be known as the teaching of *intuitu fidei* ("in view of faith") and was eventually established the standard teaching of Lutheran Scholasticism with surprisingly little resistance.[128] Lutherans generally held to the *intuitu fidei* teaching until the nineteenth century when the Neo-Lutheran movement rediscovered Luther's doctrine of election. In the United States, this rediscovery sparked the "Election Controversy" of

---

121. Gottfried Adam, *Der Streit um die Prädestination im ausgehenden 16. Jahrhundert, eine Untersuchung zu den Entwürfen vom Samuel Huber und Aegidius Hunnius* (Neukirchen: Neukirchener Verlag, 1970).

122. Aegidius Hunnius, *A Clear Explanation of the Controversy Among the Wittenberg Theologians Concerning Regeneration and Election*, trans. Paul Rydecki (Malone, TX: Repristination, 2013); Aegidius Hunnius, *Theses in Opposition to Huberianism: A Defense of the Lutheran Doctrine of Justification*, trans. Paul Rydecki (Bynum, TX: Repristination, 2012).

123. Leonhard Hütter, *Compendium of Lutheran Theology*, trans. H.E. Jacobs and G.F. Spieker (Watseka, IL: Just and Sinner, 2015), 125–36.

124. Johann Gerhard, *On Creation and Providence*, trans. Richard Dinda (St. Louis: Concordia, 2013), 236.

125. SA III.3.42–43; *Concordia Triglotta*, 490.

126. Gerhard, *On Creation and Providence*, 126.

127. Beeke, *Debated Issues in Sovereign Predestination*, 73; Rune Soderlund, *Ex praevisa fide: Zum Verstandnis der Pradestinations-lehre in der lutherischen Orthodoxie* (Hannover: Lutherisches Verlaghaus, 1983).

128. Kolb, *Bound Choice, Election, and the Wittenberg Theological Method*, 266; Schmid, *The Doctrinal Theology of the Evangelical Lutheran Church*, 272–92.

the 1870s and 1880s fought between a series of midwestern German and Norwegian immigrant denominations.[129]

The teaching of *intuitu fidei* had many difficulties, not least among them that it was conceptually incoherent. The premise of the Lutheran Scholastics remained that God actively created and sustained faith in Christians.[130] What the teaching of *intuitu fidei* suggested was that God passively foreknew his own active work of communicating and sustaining the faith in the elect. To say that God passively foreknew his own active work is absurd and incoherent. Pastorally, the teaching proved to be a disaster because it held that believers could never genuinely possess assurance of their election, but only that God had at the present moment justified them if they were not actively resisting his grace. The late Lutheran Scholastic David Hollaz baldly claimed that believers could never have full assurance of their salvation until their deathbed.[131] Thus, *intuitu fidei* placed the accent very heavily on the human subject's initiative in continuing to worthily cooperate with the divine grace offered in the means grace. Indeed, it ultimately assumed that humans did indeed contribute something to their salvation.[132] Inevitably, this teaching led to a return to the anxiety over whether one had appropriately cooperated with divine grace, albeit now following a line of reason anticipated by Melanchthon's psychologization of faith.

In the last decades of the seventeenth century there emerged a tradition within Lutheranism called "Pietism."[133] Pietism is often seen as the antithesis of Scholastic Orthodoxy, with which it fought for theological supremacy well into the eighteenth century.[134] Nevertheless, there is a continuity between the two theological traditions in that they both

129. Eugene Fevold, "Coming of Age: 1875–1900," in *The Lutherans in North America*, ed. E. Clifford Nelson (Philadelphia: Fortress, 1980), 313–25.

130. Schmid, *The Doctrinal Theology of the Evangelical Lutheran Church*, 458–80.

131. Schmid, *The Doctrinal Theology of the Evangelical Lutheran Church*, 292.

132. Kolb, *Bound Choice, Election, and the Wittenberg Theological Method*, 266.

133. See Douglas H. Shantz, *An Introduction to German Pietism: Protestant Renewal at the Dawn of Modern Europe* (Baltimore: Johns Hopkins University Press, 2013); Heinrich Schmid, *The History of Pietism* (Milwaukee: Northwestern, 2007).

134. F. Ernest Stoeffler, *German Pietism During the Eighteenth Century* (Leiden: Brill, 1973), 57–58. See Lutheran Orthodoxy's classic critique of Pietism in Valentin Ernst Loescher, *The Complete Timotheus Verinus*, trans. James Langebartels and Robert Koester (Milwaukee: Northwestern, 2006).

accorded a definitive role to the human subject in cooperating with divine grace. Therefore, it is arguably the case that Pietism inherited Scholastic Orthodoxy's problematic theology of sin and grace and simply drove the disastrous pastoral implications of *intuitu fidei* heresy to its logical conclusion.

Philipp Spener[135] and other early Pietists argued that true faith could only be discerned through holy living and an interior emotional experience of the Spirit.[136] It should be strongly emphasized that Spener and the other Pietists did not reject forensic justification and clearly distinguished it from sanctification.[137] Nevertheless, it cannot be denied that the logical implication of their teaching is that justification can only be definitively known from sanctification. Many of the Pietists emphasized the need to discover if one had an authentic faith. Conversion experiences quickly became an important marker of genuine spirituality.[138]

Because like Orthodoxy the Pietists emphasized the possibility of placing barriers to the proper reception of God's grace, it was important cultivate a right disposition in terms of personal piety. This proper disposition was to be cultivated in believers' conventicles (the direct ancestor of modern "small group" ministries) and Bible studies,[139] as well as personal prayer and individual piety.[140] These practices marked a vanguard within the church who were willing to genuinely live the Christian life and renew God's people as a whole (*ecclesiola in ecclesia*).[141] As helpful as such devotional practices might be,[142] they placed a significant burden on believers of

---

135. Philip Jacob Spener, *Pia Desideria*, trans. Theodore Tappert (Eugene, OR: Wipf & Stock, 2002).

136. Dale Brown, *Understanding Pietism*, (Grand Rapids: Eerdmans, 1978), 109.

137. Roger Olson, "Pietism: Myths and Realities" in *The Pietist Impulse in Christianity*, ed. Christian Collins Winn and Christopher Gehrz (Eugene, OR: Pickwick, 2011), 15.

138. Jonathan Strom, "Pietist Experience and Narratives of Conversion," in *A Companion to German Pietism, 1680–1800*, ed. Douglas Shantz (Leiden: Brill, 2015), 293–318.

139. Peter Goodwin Heltzel, "The Inner Church Is the Hope for the World," in Winn and Gehrz, *The Pietist Impulse in Christianity*, 273.

140. Carter Lindberg, "Introduction" in *The Pietist Theologians*, ed. Carter Lindberg (Malden, MA: Blackwell, 2005), 8.

141. Fred van Lieburg, "The Dutch Factor in German Pietism," in Shantz, *A Companion to German Pietism*, 67.

142. As much as our evaluation of Pietism is negative, the movement must be credited with encouraging lay study of the Bible, Christian mission efforts, and personal devotion.

having to worry if they had properly disposed themselves to the means of grace and were showing the signs of real faith through holy living.

Ultimately, the implication of Pietism was that the Word of God did not guarantee salvation in and of itself, but rather reflection on whether or not a person had actually properly received God's grace. Indeed, in some respects Pietism returned to the theology of the late medieval church (which Luther had rejected) by holding that one could properly dispose oneself toward justification.

CHAPTER 11

Post-Reformation Protestant Theology:
The Return of the Augustinian Dilemma

The Lutheran and Reformed traditions have a great deal in common. Both developed out of similar early modern encounters with the original text of the Bible as facilitated by the methodological tools of humanism and certain currents in late medieval thought. Both the Lutheran and Reformed traditions believe in the centrality of the biblical principles of *sola gratia* and *sola fide*.[1] That being said, there are not insignificant divergences in the two traditions, particularly with regard to their differing receptions of Augustine and evaluations of what had gone wrong in late medieval religion. As we will suggest below, these differences primarily have to do with competing concepts of what constitutes idolatry and how salvation in Christ solves the problem of idolatry.[2]

Arguably, Zwingli and Calvin were more consistent Augustinians than Luther was. We have already observed the profound influence of Augustine on Luther, notably in his early interpretation of Paul. That being said, Luther was not a complete Augustinian. In fact, his doctrine of the word is a wholesale reversal of Augustine's theory of what Philip

---

1. See the unity and differences between the Reformed and Lutheran traditions in Robert Kolb and Carl Trueman, *Between Wittenberg and Geneva: Lutheran and Reformed Theology in Conversation* (Grand Rapids: Baker Academic, 2017).

2. See the observation in Paul Hinlicky, *Luther and the Beloved Community: A Path for Christian Theology After Christendom* (Grand Rapids: Eerdmans, 2010), 98.

Cary has called "the powerlessness of outward things."[3] Luther's theology could be correctly characterized as "a Cyrillian Christ for Augustinian humanity."[4] Just as the Cyrillian or Neo-Chalcedonian tradition of early church Christology emphasized the unity of the divine and the human in Jesus,[5] so Luther argued that the only way to finally break the Augustinian self-incurvature of humanity was make God so tangible in the person of Christ and in the means of grace that he can be "grasped"[6] (to use Luther's favorite term) as an object of unassailable trust.

Luther's concept of how faith and the promise work then inexorably led to a negative evaluation of late medieval religion in light of the fact that it promoted a form of idolatry rooted in trusting in that which was not divine. Ockhamism emphasized human agency in salvation and promoted human self-trust. Popular late medieval religion promoted wrong trust by exalting objects of trust that lacked the sanction and promise of the true God (i.e., the veneration of the saints, Masses for the dead, etc.).[7] Ultimately, the issue with these practices for Luther was not that they were superstitious in that they assumed that God came to humans in physical objects. Rather, it was that late medieval religious practice caused humans to trust in things that did not possess the promise and sanction of God. In reality, humanity only interacts with God through physical objects, namely, the Word of God (which is made of physical sound waves), the sacraments, and the divine "masks" (*larva Dei*) of the created order.[8]

The Reformed tradition operates in a different trajectory. It could be claimed with some justification that despite their not inconsequential differences, Zwingli's and Calvin's theologies represent the most systematically consistent articulation of the Augustinian dilemma's predestinarian

---

3. Cary, *Outward Signs*.

4. Paul Hinlicky, *Beloved Community: A Critical Dogmatics after Christendom* (Grand Rapids: Eerdmans, 2015), 400.

5. John Meyendorff, *Christ in Eastern Christian Thought* (Washington, DC: Corpus Books, 1975).

6. LW 34:110.

7. LC I.1; *Concordia Triglotta*, 580–89.

8. Lectures on Galatians (1531), LW 26:95. See discussion in Gerhard Ebeling, *Luther: An Introduction to His Thought*, trans. R. A. Wilson (Philadelphia: Fortress, 1970), 198; Philip Watson, *Let God Be God: An Interpretation of the Theology of Martin Luther* (Philadelphia: Fortress, 1947), 76–77, 162–63.

trajectory and its attending platonizing concept of language ever to be developed. With few qualifications, both theologians sought to separate the *res* from the *signum*, in contrast to Luther's total identification. Whereas Luther saw the idolatry of late medieval religion primarily as a matter of wrong trust (saints over Jesus, the sinful heart over the sacramental word), Zwingli and Calvin saw the idolatry as being primarily a matter of confusing the glory of the Creator with the finite and fallen creature.[9] Therefore, whereas Luther's trajectory sought to make God all the more tangible by locating the divine presence ever more deeply in the flesh of Christ and the means of grace, the Zwinglian and Calvinist trajectories sought to systematically avoid any possible confusion of creature and creator. This attempt at avoiding any confusion of the divine and the creaturely expressed itself in accounts of Christology that emphasized the duality of the two natures, along with a sacramental theology that was overtly symbolicist or spiritualist.

ZWINGLI'S THEOLOGY OF GRACE

The southern Reformation began slightly later than Luther's and developed differently. Zwingli focused more intensely on the northern Humanist project of reforming public worship and morality in accordance with the Word of God.[10] This is not to suggest that Zwingli lacked interest in justification or Christian freedom. He believed with Luther in *sola fide* and *sola gratia*.[11] Moreover, his final definitive break with the local Roman Catholic bishop occurred when he watched with approval while his parishioners in Christian freedom consumed sausage during Lent in defiance of pre-Vatican II Catholic practice.[12] In summary, Zwingli's views on justification were generally quite similar to those of Luther's, although he did emphasize the transformative aspect of the

9. William A. Dyrness, *Reformed Theology and Visual Culture: The Protestant Imagination from Calvin to Edwards* (Cambridge: Cambridge University Press, 2004), 57–72.

10. McGrath, *Reformation Thought*, 52–54.

11. Ulrich Zwingli, "Short Christian Instruction," in *Huldrych Zwingli: Writings*, vol. 2, trans. and ed. H. Wayne Pipkin (Repr., Eugene, OR: Pickwick Publications, 1984), 55–61.

12. Andrew Atherstone, *The Reformation: Faith and Flames* (Oxford: Lion, 2011), 56.

Christian life in a manner more reminiscent of Augustine's interpretation of *sola gratia*.[13]

From the beginning, Zwingli's interest in morality caused him to focus on God's authority as creator and his glory in ways that differed markedly from Luther's accent on God incarnate.[14] Zwingli took Augustine's concept of God's omni-causality with extreme seriousness, while moving it in directions that the Doctor of Grace would likely not have approved of. Instead of trying to make room for compatibilist free will as Augustine did (whether successfully, or unsuccessfully), Zwingli promoted an absolute determinism of divine power.[15] In his *De Providentia Dei* (1530), Zwingli described God as being the source of all events that occur in the created universe.[16] Without the nuance of distinguishing between differing kinds of necessity as Luther had (necessity of immutability vs. the necessary of compulsion),[17] Zwingli envisions God as almost coercing his creatures in order to fit them within his great cosmic plan.[18] Zwingli's language here appears to be a crude anticipation of the metaphysical univocity and occasionalism that would find its perfection in the thinkers of the later seventeenth century (Suarez, Malebranche, Leibniz, Wolf, Grotius).[19]

According to Zwingli, God can dispense with the universe as his property with the ruthlessness of an early modern merchant.[20] God caused humanity to fall in order to redeem humanity through the incarnation.[21] Just as a woodsman who owns a forest can cut down or save trees that he owns based on his own inclination, so too God can do with his creatures

---

13. McGrath, *Iustitia Dei*, 250–51.

14. Kurt Guggisberg, *Das Zwinglibild des Protestantismus im Wandel der Zeiten* (Leipzig: Verlag von M. Heinsius Nachfolger, 1934), 212–13.

15. W. Peter Stephens, *The Theology of Huldrych Zwingli* (Oxford: Clarendon, 1986), 96.

16. Ulrich Zwingli, "Reproduction from Memory of a Sermon on the Providence of God, Dedicated to His Highness Philip of Hesse," in *On Providence and Other Essays*, trans. and ed. Samuel Macauley Jackson (Durham: Labyrinth, 1983), 220.

17. The Bondage of the Will (1525), LW 33:37–44, 64–70, 151, 192–95, 213.

18. Arthur Cushman McGiffert, *Protestant Thought Before Kant* (New York: Charles Scribner's Sons, 1919), 67–69.

19. William Placher, *The Domestication of Transcendence: How Modern Thinking about God Went Wrong* (Louisville: Westminster John Knox, 1996), 71–87.

20. Zwingli, "Reproduction from Memory of a Sermon on the Providence of God," 223.

21. Zwingli, "Reproduction from Memory of a Sermon on the Providence of God," 221–22.

as he pleases.[22] Therefore, the glory of God lies with his power and his ability to dispense with his creation in accordance with his caprice. The alternative would seem to be the meaninglessness of Epicurean randomness (a live option gaining wide interest in the sixteenth century),[23] or to falsely attribute causality to the creature and rob the Lord of his omnicausal glory.[24]

Zwingli's anxiety about the confusion of the creature and the creator lent itself to the pattern of his church reform. Just as the recognition of divine causality negates any autonomous action on the part of creatures, so too God will not allow any of his glory to be removed from him and attributed to a creaturely medium. Like Luther's onetime colleague and later theological adversary Andreas Karlstadt,[25] Zwingli began his reform with a program of iconoclasm—albeit considerably less violent than that of Karlstadt. According to Zwingli's thinking, all church artwork and aesthetic delights focus the mind of the creature away from the Creator and glorify earthly things.[26] For the highly sense-oriented medieval piety that had preceded him, Zwingli substituted lengthy expository sermons.[27]

This degradation of the visible and the sensual paralleled another belief that Zwingli shared with Karlstadt: a rejection of the substantial presence of Christ in the Lord's Supper in favor of a sacramental symbolicism.[28] Here can be observed the most consistent application of the Augustinian concept of words as a mere signifier that points beyond itself. The sensual has less value than the intelligible and spiritual. At best, the visible can serve as a springboard to the invisible and eternal.

Therefore, according to Zwingli, the words of institution are not powerful divine words that create the reality of which they speak. The words of

22. Zwingli, "Reproduction from Memory of a Sermon on the Providence of God," 222.

23. See Ada Palmer, *Reading Lucretius in the Renaissance* (Cambridge, MA: Harvard University Press, 2014); Catherine Wilson, *Epicureanism at the Origins of Modernity* (Oxford: Clarendon, 2008).

24. Zwingli, "Reproduction from Memory of a Sermon on the Providence of God," 220.

25. Bridget Heal, *A Magnificent Faith: Art and Identity in Lutheran Germany* (Oxford: Oxford University Press, 2017), 18–19.

26. Carlos Eire, *War Against the Idols: The Reformation of Worship from Erasmus to Calvin* (Cambridge: Cambridge University Press, 1986), 73–86.

27. Ruth A. Tucker, *Parade of Faith: A Biographical History of the Christian Church* (Grand Rapids: Zondervan, 2011), 245.

28. Amy Nelson Burnett, *Debating the Sacraments: Print and Authority in the Early Reformation* (Oxford: Oxford University Press, 2019), 77–120.

institution are but signifiers that place a label on the bread and wine of the
Eucharist as a means of symbolic representation.[29] The bread and wine
themselves do not contain the reality of which they speak, but "signify"
(*significat*) the flesh and blood of Christ once sacrificed for Christians and
now present at right hand of God in a semi-local heaven.[30] The mind of
believers is not to look at the bread and wine (the *signum*) but to the invisible *res* (i.e., the flesh and blood of Christ) located above and beyond it.

Likewise, Zwingli also rejected the practice of confession and absolution that Luther held so dear.[31] Again, from the Swiss Reformer's perspective, since the word of the pastor is simply a signifier that signifies things,
it cannot enact divine forgiveness. Zwingli emphasized that genuine certainty does not come from the sacramentality of the external word, but
from the Holy Spirit received and experienced in the hearts and minds
of believers.[32] Indeed, Zwingli was so comfortable with the disassociation
between the work of the Spirit and the external means of grace that he
argued that God had elected many of the righteous pagans who lacked
knowledge of or faith in Christ.[33]

Such an account of the Lord's Supper and confession was rooted in an
account of the person of Christ where the *communicatio idiomatum* was
merely verbal and notional.[34] The sharp division between the spiritual
and physical in the word and sacraments translated into the distancing of
the two natures in Christ even to a point beyond what the later Reformed
tradition would find acceptable. To maintain the distinction of the two
natures in Christ, Zwingli held that there could be no communication of
properties between them.[35] Referring to his segregation of the two natures

29. Ulrich Zwingli, "On the Lord's Supper," in *Zwingli and Bullinger*, trans. G. W. Bromiley (Philadelphia: Westminster, 1953), 222–30.

30. Zwingli, "On the Lord's Supper," 216.

31. Jeffrey Watt, "Reconciliation and the Confession of Sins: The Evidence from the Consistory in Calvin's Geneva," in *Calvin and Luther: The Continuing Relationship*, ed. R. Ward Holder (Göttingen: Vandenhoeck & Ruprecht, 2013), 119.

32. Susan Schreiner *Are You Alone Wise? The Search for Certainty in the Early Modern Era* (Oxford: Oxford University Press, 2011), 62–66.

33. Ulrich Zwingli, "An Exposition of the Faith," in Bromiley, *Zwingli and Bullinger*, 275–76.

34. Christof Gestrich, *Zwingli als Theologe Glaube und Geist beim Zürcher Reformator* (Zürich: Zwingli-Verlag, 1967), 23; Stephens, *The Theology of Ulrich Zwingli*, 113.

35. See the lengthy discussion in Richard Cross, *Communicatio Idiomatum: Reformation Christological Debates* (Oxford: Oxford University Press, 2019), 73–77.

from one another as *alleosis*, Zwingli believed that one could read the New Testament and divide up passages that referred to what Jesus did as God (miracles, etc.) and as man (suffer and die, etc.).[36] Again, the outward reality (Christ's humanity) is separated from the inner reality (Christ's divine nature), just as the external word is separated from the work of the Spirit in justifying sinners.

CALVIN'S THEOLOGY OF GRACE

A more significant theologian for the history of the development of the Reformed tradition can be found in the person of John Calvin.[37] Although technically a contemporary of Luther's, Calvin was twenty-six years the junior of the Wittenberg reformer and can be more properly classified as a second-generation reformer.[38] Not only because of his superior intellect to his contemporaries but also because of his hindsight as a child of the second-generation of Reformation,[39] Calvin was able to refine many of the doctrinal concepts of Zwingli as well as other major figures in the southern Reformation (Bucer, Oecolampadius, etc.).[40] Like Melanchthon, Calvin sought to organize the theology of the southern Reformation in the constantly updated editions of his *Institutes of the Christian Religion* published between 1536 and 1559.[41]

Although Calvin developed his doctrine of election and justification in distinct sections of the *Institutes*,[42] it could be argued that justification tends to be a derivative function of the doctrine of election.[43] This is not to say that Calvin somehow deduces the doctrine of the justification from the doctrine of election in the form of some kind of central-dogma

36. Ulrich Zwingli, "Friendly Exegesis, that is, Exposition of the Matter of the Eucharist to Martin Luther, February 1527," in *Huldrych Zwingli: Writings*, vol. 2, trans. and ed. H. Wayne Pipkin (Repr., Eugene, OR: Pickwick Publications, 1984), 319–22. Also see August Baur, *Zwinglis Theologie: Ihr Werden und Ihr System*, 2 vols. (Zürich: Georg Olms Verlag, 1983–1984), 2:425, 460, 473, 484–510.

37. John Leith, *An Introduction to the Reformed Tradition: A Way of Being the Christian Community* (Louisville, KY: John Knox, 1981), 189.

38. Carter Lindberg, *The European Reformation* (Malden, MA: Wiley-Blackwell, 2010), 235.

39. F. Bruce Gordon, *Calvin* (New Haven: Yale University Press, 2009), 145–46.

40. See Paul Helm, *John Calvin's Ideas* (Oxford: Oxford University Press, 2004).

41. Muller, *Unaccommodated Calvin*, 118–39.

42. Paul Helm, *Calvin: A Guide for the Perplexed* (London: Bloomsbury, 2008), 86

43. See comments in Hans Emil Weber, *Reformation, Orthodoxie, und Rationalismus*, Pt. 1, vol. 1 (Gütersloh: Gerd Mohn, 1937), 244.

scheme.[44] Rather, in Calvin's theology as expressed in the *Institutes*, justification occurs because God must reconcile those whom he has elected by his sovereign unconditional will (*decretum absolutum*).[45] This is the case even if, as many contemporary historians of dogma have pointed out, traditionally there has been an overemphasis on the place of the doctrine of election in Calvin's theology as a result of the subsequent Calvinist and Arminian debates.[46] In Calvin's treatment of the doctrines of election and justification we can observe one of the more significant contrasts with Luther. As we have seen earlier, the Wittenberg Reformer tended to subordinate election to atonement and justification.

Though by no means a crass determinist in the vein of Zwingli, Calvin, much like the Zurich Reformer, primarily defines God on the basis of his otherness and power.[47] Whereas Luther in discussing the nature of idolatry in his treatment of the first commandment in the Large Catechism worries about trusting in things that are not God as a means of self-justification,[48] Calvin mainly shows concern about superstitious worship that will confuse the creator with the creature.[49] Indeed, much like the later Heidelberg Catechism,[50] the Genevan Reformer sees the Decalogue's rejection of graven images as not merely an example of sin against the First Commandment (as Luther does),[51] but as a distinctive commandment in and of itself.[52] The idea that physical objects can contain God (or his grace) is seen by Calvin as being the essence of superstition and idolatry.[53] This is true even though as we will see below, the Genevan Reformer is

---

44. Paul Helm, "John Calvin and the Hiddenness of God," in *Engaging the Doctrine of God Contemporary Protestant Perspectives*, ed. Bruce McCormack (Grand Rapids: Baker Academic, 2008), 67.

45. ICR, 3.21.7; John Calvin, *The Institutes of the Christian Religion*, ed. John T. McNeill, trans. Ford Lewis Battles, 2 vols. (Philadelphia: Westminster, 1967), 2:930–32.

46. Donald Wilcox, *In Search of God and Self: Renaissance and Reformation Thought* (Long Grove, IL: Waveland Press, 1975), 318.

47. Timothy George, *Theology of the Reformers* (Nashville: Broadman & Holman, 2013), 125–30, 197–201.

48. LC I.1; *Concordia Triglotta*, 581–89.

49. ICR, 1.12.1–3; Calvin, *Institutes*, 1:116–20.

50. Zacharias Ursinus, *Commentary on the Heidelberg Catechism* (Columbus: Scott and Bascom, 1852), 517–35.

51. William Marsh, *Martin Luther on Reading the Bible as Christian Scripture: The Messiah in Luther's Biblical Hermeneutic and Theology* (Eugene, OR: Wipf & Stock, 2017), 73.

52. ICR, 2.8.16–19; Calvin, *Institutes*, 1:116–20, 1:383–86.

53. ICR, 1.11.1–3; Calvin, *Institutes*, 1:116–20, 1:99–103.

considerably more comfortable with tying the *res* of divine grace to the *signum* of the external means of grace than Zwingli was.

In keeping with Calvin's emphasis on God's power and otherness, the causal foundation of atonement and justification is election. By his eternal decree, God chooses those whom he wishes to save and elects Christ to be the head of the new humanity whom he has rescued out of the mass of those condemned in Adam. More so than Luther, Calvin emphasizes the idea of Christ as the elected one (the literal meaning of "anointed one" i.e., "Christ") who is the head of redeemed.[54] Although Luther does not address the issue, later Lutheranism in contrast to Calvin saw Christ's atoning work coming logically prior to God's choice of the believers in Christ.[55] As a result, God's choice of the redeemed is conditioned by Christ's universal grace and atoning work (Lutherans), rather than atonement being the result of a prior decision of election (Calvin).

Although Calvin is not as clear as the later Synod of Dordrecht,[56] there is nevertheless at the very least strong implication in the *Institutes* that Christ suffered punishment for the sins of the elect alone.[57] Unlike Anselm and Luther,[58] and more in accordance with Duns Scotus's position[59] (though not identical to it), Calvin held that there was no inherent value to Christ's sacrifice on the cross. Rather, God in his sovereignty merely accepted it (*acceptatio divina*) as being a sufficient payment for the sins of the elect and hence it came to be so.[60]

As a student of Augustine and a deep reader of the scriptural narrative, Calvin shares much in common with Luther on the issue of justification. Most notably, along with Luther, Calvin appropriated the scriptural

---

54. ICR, 3.24.5; Calvin, *Institutes*, 2:970–71.

55. Schmid, *Doctrinal Theology of the Evangelical Lutheran Church*, 270–73.

56. Lee Gatiss, "The Synod of Dort and Definite Atonement," in *From Heaven He Came and Sought Her: Definite Atonement in Historical, Biblical, Theological, and Pastoral Perspective*, ed. David Gibson and Jonathan Gibson (Wheaton, IL: Crossway, 2013), 143–65.

57. Paul Helm, "Calvin, Indefinite Language, and Definite Atonement," in Gibson and Gibson, *From Heaven He Came and Sought Her*, 97–120.

58. See comparison in Burnell Eckhardt, *Anselm and Luther on the Atonement: Was It "Necessary"?* (Lewiston, NY: Edwin Mellen, 1992).

59. Richard Cross, *Duns Scotus* (Oxford: Oxford University Press, 1999), 104. Also see discussion of the acceptance theory of the atonement in Macintosh, *Historic Theories of the Atonement*, 110–11.

60. ICR, 2.17.1; Calvin, *Institutes*, 1:52.

and patristic language of salvation in Christ according to the motifs of exchange and union:

> This is the wonderful exchange which, out of his measureless benevolence, he has made with us; that, becoming Son of man with us, he has made us sons of God with him; that, by his descent to earth, he has prepared an ascent to heaven for us; that, by taking on our mortality, he has conferred his immortality upon us; that, accepting our weakness, he has strengthened us by his power; that, receiving our poverty upon himself, he has transferred his wealth to us; that, taking the weight of our iniquity upon himself (which oppressed us), he has clothed us with his righteousness.[61]

Calvin sees Christ as the elect one, whom the elect enter into union with. In becoming united with Christ, believers find their election and justification.

Calvin's emphasis on the motif of union does not mean that he believes in the importance of forensic justification any less than Luther or subsequent Lutheran Orthodoxy, even if he conceptualizes it somewhat differently. Indeed, Calvin spends a great deal of time in the 1559 *Institutes* arguing against Osiander and his collapse of justification into mystical union.[62] Nevertheless, as Todd Billings has convincingly argued, for Calvin forensic justification was subsumed under the wider reality of the spiritual union between Christ and the elect.[63] Christ was the mystical head of the elect and died for their sins.[64] The effect of Christ's work and his spiritual union with the elect was the "twofold grace" (*duplex gratia*) of justification and sanctification.[65] Calvin writes:

> By partaking of him [Christ], we principally receive a double grace: namely, that being reconciled to God through Christ's blamelessness, we may have in heaven instead of Judge a gracious Father;

61. ICR, 4.17.2; Calvin, *Institutes*, 2:1362.

62. ICR, 3.11.5–12; Calvin, *Institutes*, 1:729–43.

63. J. Todd Billings, *Calvin, Participation, and the Gift: The Activity of Believers in Union with Christ* (Oxford: Oxford University Press, 2007).

64. ICR, 3.24.5; Calvin, *Institutes*, 2:970–71.

65. Mark A. Garcia, *Life in Christ: Union with Christ and Twofold Grace in Calvin's Theology* (Eugene, OR: Wipf & Stock, 2008).

and secondly, that sanctified by Christ's spirit we may cultivate blamelessness and purity of life.[66]

As should be clear from this quote, unlike for Luther and the Formula of Concord, there is no clear indication that justification is logically prior to sanctification and mystical union. It would seem that both justification and sanctification are parallel benefits from union of the elect with Christ through faith.[67]

In spite of these similarities with Luther's model, Calvin did not accept the Wittenberg Reformer's notion of justification by the word. Granted, as noted earlier, Calvin was closer to Luther than he was to Zwingli on the nature of the means of grace. Zwingli saw the sacraments primarily as marks of profession among the Christian community.[68] Calvin by contrast saw the sacraments as not actually containing grace, but nevertheless being genuine signs of the presence of grace.[69] For the Genevan Reformer, the Spirit works alongside the means of grace. For the elect, there is a preestablished harmony between two distinct realities of *res* and *signum*. For those whom God has chosen, when the word is preached, or the sacraments are administered, the Spirt simultaneously does his work on the hearts and minds of believers alongside the outward sign.[70] Unlike Zwingli, Calvin affirmed that God did not elect people apart from the word and sacraments.[71]

Nevertheless, the presence of the means of grace was for Calvin not a direct guarantee of the presence of God's grace.[72] Among those who hear the Word of God preached, it is the elect alone in whom the Holy Spirit is present and active.[73] Calvin's ultimate refusal to definitively tie the work of the Spirit to the word and sacraments appears to be based on his fear

66. ICR, 3.11.1; Calvin, *Institutes*, 1:725.

67. See ICR 3.2.24; ICR, 3.24.5; McNeill and Battles, *Calvin: The Institutes of the Christian Religion*, 1:569–70.

68. Ulrich Zwingli, *Commentary on True and False Religion*, ed. Samuel Macauley Jackson and Clarence Nevin Heller (Durham: Labyrinth, 1981), 179–84, 185–252.

69. ICR, 4.14.1–6; Calvin, *Institutes*, 2:1276–81.

70. ICR, 4.14.7–13; Calvin, *Institutes*, 2:1281–89.

71. ICR, 3.14.1–6; Calvin, *Institutes*, 1:964–73.

72. ICR, 4.14.15; Calvin, *Institutes*, 2:1290–91.

73. ICR, 3.14.1–6; Calvin, *Institutes*, 1:964–73.

that such a theological judgment would result in idolatry and superstition (i.e., confusing creator with the creature). Secondarily, one can infer that Calvin like Augustine before him struggled to find an explanatory model for why not all who come into contact with the means of grace are converted and regenerated. If God is directly tied to the means of grace, the question is raised as to why not all who come into contact with the means of grace believe.

Much like Zwingli, Calvin's interest in distancing creator and creatures is also reflected in his Christology. Although the Genevan Reformer rejected Zwingli's division of the agency of the two natures by affirming that Christ was mediator according to both natures,[74] there is no communication of divine glory to the man Jesus as in the Lutheran *genus majestaticum*.[75] Just as the *signum* does not contain the *res* in Calvin's sacramental theology, so too the humanity of Jesus does not fully participate in his divinity which continues to operate *extra carnum* even after the incarnation (*extra calvinisticum*).[76] For this reason, Calvin argued like Zwingli before him that because Christ's body was finite and in heaven, it could therefore not be substantially present in the Lord's Supper.[77] In contrast to Zwingli, he allowed that it was present spiritually, that is, the Holy Spirit unified the elect with the heavenly Christ's body.[78] At the same time, the reprobate received only the empty external sign of Christ's body.[79] Here Calvin rejected the Lutheran and Roman Catholic *manducatio indignorum*.[80]

Therefore, in spite of his many similarities with Luther, there emerges an inherent conflict between the approaches to justification of the Wittenberg Reformer and Genevan Reformer. The differences between the two Reformers' approaches is due primarily to a peculiar incongruity

---

74. ICR, 2.14.2–3; Calvin, *Institutes*, 1:484–87.

75. ICR, 4.17.29–30; Calvin, *Institutes*, 2:1398–1403.

76. See E. David Willis, *Calvin's Catholic Christology: The Function of the So-Called Extra Calvinisticum in Calvin's Theology* (Leiden: Brill, 1966), 60–100.

77. ICR, 4.17.26–30; Calvin, *Institutes*, 2:1393–1403.

78. ICR, 4.17.31–33; Calvin, *Institutes*, 2:1403–8.

79. ICR, 4.17.34; Calvin, *Institutes*, 2:1408–11.

80. B. A. Gerrish, "Sign and Reality: The Lord's Supper in the Reformed Confessions" in *The Old Protestantism and the New: Essays on the Reformation Heritage* (New York: T&T Clark International, 2004), 129–30.

between Calvin's description of salvation in Christ and his theology of the means of grace.

It should be observed that not only do Luther and Calvin agree in their use of the motifs of union and exchange to describe justification, but when faced with the question of the assurance of one's justification and election the Genevan Reformer like the Wittenberg Reformer before him pointed the believers to Christ.[81] For Calvin, Christ reveals God's fatherly heart and therefore also is the "clearest mirror of [our] free election."[82] This is not only because Christ's humanity was elected and anointed with the Spirit unconditionally much like that of the believer, but since he is the spiritual head of the church believers find their election and justification in him.[83] As we have seen, Luther likewise holds that one should look to Christ crucified in order to find one's election and justification.

Nevertheless, when it comes the question of how one comes to know the loving heart of the Father manifest in Christ, Calvin's doctrine of the means of grace ultimately undermines the assurance of grace through Christ that he wishes to inculcate. For Luther, there is no separation of the means of grace and the risen Jesus who is present in them. For the Wittenberg Reformer, God's unambiguous and unequivocal forgiveness and grace in Christ is as certain as the means by which God's salvific judgment is manifest to the believer.

By contrast, in Calvin, there is a separation between the *res* and *signum* in the means of grace. Not only do the word and the sacraments not genuinely contain grace, but the external sign may or may not be intended for those to whom it is proclaimed. For Calvin, there is a general external call and a particular inner call of the elect.[84] Since the preached word is actually not meant for all, the means of grace therefore constitute ambiguous signs. Because the means of grace are the only access that the believer has to Christ who is the mirror of election, the ambiguity of the outward sign makes Christ a highly opaque mirror. The believer can only be certain that the means of grace were intended for himself by assuming the stance of

---

81. ICR, 3.24.5; Calvin, *Institutes*, 2:970–71.

82. ICR, 3.22.1; Calvin, *Institutes*, 2:933.

83. Richard Muller, *Christ and the Decree: Christology and Predestination in Reformed Theology from Calvin to Perkins* (Grand Rapids: Baker Academic, 2008), 17–38.

84. ICR, 3.14.8; Calvin, *Institutes*, 2:974–75.

a highly reflective faith. Calvin suggests that true faith will have an inner certainty of election and that the elect believer will never fall away.[85] The latter course is extremely unhelpful since no one can be certain that they will not fall away, and when people sin gravely they will invariably come to wonder whether they ever had real faith. Even worse, Calvin at one point argues that it is possible to be deluded into thinking one has real faith when it is in fact not the case: "For though only those predestined to salvation receive the light of faith, and truly feel the power of the gospel, yet experience shows that the reprobate are sometimes affected by almost the same feeling, so that even in their own judgment they do not in any way differ from the elect."[86]

Therefore, without any assurance that the means of grace genuinely contain grace, one must discern the presence of grace by its effect on one's person. It logically follows that focus of the eyes of the believer shift from the promise of Christ to the inner reflection aimed at discerning the Spirit's work: genuine conversion, faith, and sanctification. Contrary to the claims of Wilhelm Niesel,[87] Calvin's theology contains elements of what the later Reformed tradition would call the *syllogismus practicus*.[88] The Genevan Reformer explains that those who were genuinely converted would secondarily show the signs of faith in Christ, good works, and participation in the sacraments.[89]

At the same time, Calvin does still insist that one should not speculate about whether one is truly elect and instead simply look to Christ.[90] Nevertheless, in spite of Calvin's assertion it is difficult to see how this could be the case. One would already have to possess a certainty based on a reflective faith before one could be certain that Christ and the means of grace were intended for him. Merely engaging the sacraments would not give one this assurance, since they may or may not be intended for the

---

85. ICR, 3.14.6–7; Calvin, *Institutes*, 2:971–74.

86. ICR, 3.2.11; Calvin, *Institutes*, 1:551.

87. Wilhelm Niesel, *The Theology of Calvin*, trans Harold Knight (Cambridge: James Clark & Co., 2002), 178–81.

88. R. Michael Allen, *Reformed Theology* (London: Bloomsbury Academic, 2010), 87.

89. ICR, 3.14.18–21, 4.14.4–5, 4.14.7–13; Calvin, *Institutes*, 1:784–88, 2:968–71, 2:1281–89.

90. ICR, 3.24.4–5; Calvin, *Institutes*, 2:968–71.

person who receives them. Moreover, if one already possesses assurance through the interior certainty of faith, then it would also follow that the sacraments are simply superfluous, since they cannot give more certainty than the believer already has.[91]

Whereas Calvin downplayed the significance of these secondary signs of election in favor of finding one's election and justification in Christ,[92] the incongruous relationship between assurance in Christ and the ambiguity of the means of grace in his theology inevitably gave rise to historic Protestantism's hyper-reflective faith and the almost wholesale abandonment of Luther's emphasis on the sacramentality of the word. The rejection of the notion that the means of grace genuinely contain grace propelled the later Reformed tradition to seek the assurance of justification through subjective signs of sanctification (*syllogismus practicus*) rather than the external word and the sacraments.

Particularly in the Anglo-American Calvinist tradition (i.e., Puritanism and the First Great Awakening), the *syllogismus practicus* took on ever increasing significance.[93] One can observe this in everything from the Puritans' spiritual journals that aimed at tracking sanctification (or conversely, discovering the lack thereof)[94] to Jonathan Edwards's theories about authentic conversion and the unusual spiritual experiences that people in his congregation had after he abolished the so-called Halfway-Covenant.[95]

Ultimately though, all the spiritual experiences and signs that later forms of Calvinism generated in order to confirm election had significant problems associated with them. Put succinctly, all such signs possess an exegetically tenuous basis in Scripture and are easily faked. Hence, the

---

91. See the similar argument in Cary, *Meaning of Protestant Theology*, 287–94.

92. Joel Beeke, *The Quest for Full Assurance: The Legacy of Calvin and His Successors* (Edinburgh: Banner of Truth, 1999), 65–66.

93. Joel Beeke, "Personal Assurance of Faith: The Puritans and Chapter 18.2 of the Westminster Confession," *Westminster Theological Journal* 55, no.1 (1993): 1–30; John Howard Smith, *The First Great Awakening: Redefining Religion in British America, 1725–1775* (London: Fairleigh Dickinson University Press, 2015).

94. Kathleen M. Swaim, *Pilgrim's Progress, Puritan Progress: Discourses and Contexts* (Urbana: University of Illinois Press, 1993), 145.

95. Michael J. McClymond and Gerald R. McDermott, *The Theology of Jonathan Edwards* (Oxford: Oxford University Press, 2012), 373–89, 424–50.

syllogismus practicus could never actually give genuine assurance of salvation. Moreover, although theoretically salvation was by grace alone, believers were driven back to finding assurance in their works, albeit this time through psychological reflection and the counting of secondary fruits of the Spirit. In a word, instead of finding assurance in the gospel believers were compelled to find it in the law. Ultimately, the self-incurvature that the medieval synthesis of grace and works exacerbated simply reemerged in a different form.

In the challenge of overcoming the problematic implications of reflective faith Arminianism offered no better solution than Calvinism. Although Arminianism is often characterized as the opposite of Calvinism, as an outgrowth of the Reformed tradition it shares many of the same premises.[96] Indeed, Arminianism's founder, Jacobus Arminius, was a Dutch student of Theodore de Beza, Calvin's successor in Geneva.[97] It is arguably the case that Arminius began his theological program as a polemical response to De Beza's fine tuning of Calvin's system.[98] Moreover, as Roger Olson has helpfully observed, what is not often appreciated is that classical Arminianism is not identical with its more popular Semi-Pelagian form that began in the Anglo-American world with Charles Finney's theology[99] and the Second Great Awakening.[100] Like Calvin and unlike Finney, Arminius affirmed the completely incapacitating nature of original sin.[101] Humanity on its own cannot choose God or utilize its free will.[102] Nevertheless, Arminius believed in the universality of prevenient grace rather than its particularity (i.e., the position of Augustine, Calvin, etc.).[103] Universal prevenient grace granted humanity a will capable of choosing

96. Roger Olson, *Arminian Theology: Myths and Realities* (Downers Grove, IL: InterVarsity Press, 2006), 44–60.

97. Keith D. Stanglin and Thomas H. McCall, *Jacob Arminius: Theologian of Grace* (Oxford: Oxford University Press, 2012), 27.

98. Stanglin and McCall, *Jacob Arminius: Theologian of Grace*, 94–140.

99. Charles Finney, *Finney's Systematic Theology* (Minneapolis: Bethany House, 1994). See Olson, *Arminian Theology: Myths and Realities*, 27.

100. Sydney E. Ahlstrom, *The Religious History of the American People* (New Haven: Yale University Press, 2004), 415–28.

101. Stanglin and McCall, *Jacob Arminius: Theologian of Grace*, 145–48, 194.

102. James Arminius, "Private Disputations," in *The Works of James Arminius*, trans. James Nichols and William Nichols (Grand Rapids: Baker, 1996), 2:400.

103. Olson, *Arminian Theology: Myths and Realities*, 66.

to cooperate or resisting the gospel when confronted with it.[104] Under the influence of the Jesuit Louis de Molina, Arminius made predestination merely God's passive foreknowledge based on his "Middle Knowledge" (*scientia media*) of who would accept salvation in Christ and who would reject it.[105]

Although Arminius did not return to the medieval view of the sacraments as inherent guarantors of divine grace, his view of faith in many respects embodies the same logic as the sacramentalist trajectory of the Augustinian dilemma. For Arminius, salvation was again characterized as a possibility actualized by human choice, albeit it not in the form of grasping the grace as objectified in the sacraments of the medieval church, but through the believer's personal application of the message of the gospel to himself. Yet again, for Arminius the Word of God is a mere signifier that signifies grace, rather than God's mighty Word that calls faith into existence.

Whereas Calvin's rejection of Luther's absolute unity of *res* and *signum* created the problem of the ambiguity of the assurance given by the external word, both classical and popular Arminianism possess the same problem of Calvinism due to the ambiguity of human decision-making. Humans can never be certain of their motives in making a decision. Moreover, once a decision has been reached there is no way to prove that a commitment will last. Because humans are mutable, their psychological motives and desires change over time. Therefore, if the certainty of faith rests on the ambiguity of human decisions, then one must invariably return to a theology that promotes something resembling the Calvinist *syllogismus practicus*. If one must rely on the ambiguous certainty of their decisions, one will necessarily seek to augment this certainty with signs of the Spirit's work in order to demonstrate that one was sincere in their decision to accept divine grace. Signs of real conversion and sincere cooperation with the Holy Spirit will therefore invariably take over the place of the means of grace. Hence, although Arminians may theoretically operate with a significantly different doctrine of grace than historic Calvinism,

---

104. Arminius, "Twenty-Five Public Disputations," in *The Works of James Arminius*, 1:664.

105. Richard Muller, *God, Creation, and Providence in the Thought of Jacob Arminius: Sources and Directions of Scholastic Protestantism in the Era of Early Orthodoxy* (Grand Rapids: Baker, 1991), 21, 55, 161–63.

on a practical level Arminian reflective faith gives rise to the same difficulties and solutions.

Hence because of the ambiguities of human agency, Arminianism's
project of granting psychological assurance to sinners quickly evolved
along similar lines to Calvinism and Lutheran Pietism. Among the many
Arminian traditions, John Wesley's theology represents one of the most
theological sophisticated articulations.[106] It is arguably the case that the
Wesleyan tradition began with John Wesley's quest to find the certainty
of his salvation through a series of attempts at discerning the work of the
Spirit in his heart and mind.[107] In spite of his moral discipline and piety
as a member of the "Holy Club" at Oxford,[108] he could not assure himself
of God's favor and the authenticity of his faith until he found his heart
"strangely warmed" while listening to a public reading of Luther's introduction to the Epistle to the Romans.[109]

In should be noted that although the mature Wesley was an Arminian,
early Methodism had both Arminian and Calvinist branches.[110] In other
words, although Wesley had serious disagreements about the theoretical
nature of grace with some of the members of the early Methodist movement, they possessed a profound agreement that genuine faith was to be
discerned through sanctified behavior and a particular interior experience. Calvinism and Arminianism are both guilty of promoted a highly
reflective faith and turning believers away from Luther's teaching that one
gains certainty through looking at the external word and the sacraments
while looking away from one's own works and inner feelings.

Wesley seemingly was not satisfied with his experience of having
his heart "strangely warmed" but went on to develop the doctrine of
"Entire Sanctification" in his *A Plain Account of Christian Perfection* (1777).[111]

---

106. Henry H. Knight III, *John Wesley: Optimist of Grace* (Eugene, OR: Cascade, 2018), 36.

107. Mark Hutchinson and John Wolffe, *A Short History of Global Evangelicalism* (Cambridge: Cambridge University Press, 2012), 25–26.

108. Stephen Tomkins, *John Wesley: A Biography* (Oxford: Lion, 2003), 30–37.

109. Henry Rack, *Reasonable Enthusiast: John Wesley and the Rise of Methodism* (London: Epworth, 1989), 137–57.

110. David Ceri Jones, Boyd Stanley Schlenther, and Eryn Mant White, *The Elect Methodists: Calvinistic Methodism in England and Wales, 1735–1811* (Cardiff: University of Wales Press, 2012).

111. See John Wesley, *A Plain Account of Christian Perfection* (Peabody, MA: Hendrickson, 2007).

Wesley posited that a genuine Christian would actually cease to sin intentionally. Wesley allowed that people could inadvertently sin or succumb to overwhelming temptations against their will.[112] It should not go unnoticed that the doctrine of entire sanctification was the next logical step in the Arminian version of the *syllogismus practicus*. If sanctification were proof of faith and justification, any intentional sin would logically invalidate, or at best make ambiguous, the assurance of salvation. Only a totalizing holiness would logically provide unequivocal proof of true faith and true sanctification.

Wesley's views on sanctification were softened by the mainstream Methodist tradition,[113] while nevertheless finding a more consistent home in the Holiness movement of the nineteenth century.[114] In the early twentieth century, the sign of total sanctification proved insufficient for certain members of the Holiness movement itself as a proof of authentic faith. As a result, the Pentecostal movement in various degrees insisted that tongues, prophecy, and healings were markers of authentic faith.[115] Still other more extreme and marginal members of the Pentecostal and Holiness movements came to hold (basing themselves on the longer and possibly inauthentic ending of the Gospel of Mark) that the only true sign of Christian conversion was the practice of snake handling.[116] In a word, without any objective grounding of faith in the means of grace, the need to prove the authenticity of faith grew ever more extreme.

---

112. Mark Mann, *Perfecting Grace: Holiness, Human Being, and the Sciences* (New York: T & T Clark, 2006), 23.

113. David Bebbington, *Evangelicalism in Modern Britain: A History from the 1730s to the 1980s* (London: Routledge, 1989), 153.

114. See Melvin E. Dieter, *The Holiness Revival of the Nineteenth Century* (Lanham, MD: Scarecrow, 1996).

115. Vinson Synan, *The Holiness-Pentecostal Tradition: Charismatic Movements in the Twentieth Century* (Grand Rapids: Eerdmans, 1997), 84–106.

116. Donald Swift, *Religion and the American Experience: A Social and Cultural History, 1765–1997* (New York: M. E. Sharpe, 1998), 252.

CONCLUSION

Although historically Protestants have theoretically agreed with Luther's principles of *sola gratia* and *sola fide*, in practice their theology has worked quite differently. Without an anchor in both sacramental realism and the sacramentality of the word, the principle of *sola fide* degenerates very quickly into a form of subjectivism and legalism. Without the objectivity of grace present in the word and sacrament ministry of the church, the believer must invariably prove his faith with more and more elaborate works and spiritual experiences. The gaze of the eyes of faith looks away from Christ to the sanctified works of the believer in a manner similar to that of the medieval church's synthesis of works and grace.

Having given an exposition of Luther's doctrine of justification by the word from its biblical roots to its decay in later Protestantism, we will now examine the doctrinal implications of justification for several other areas of Christian doctrine. In subsequent chapters we will explore justi-fication by the word's implications for the doctrine of predestination, the sacraments, and the Christian life.

CHAPTER 12

Justification and Election:
God's Hiddenness in the Means of Grace

I n our earlier discussion of Luther's doctrine of justification, one significant question that we chose to leave unanswered was the relationship
of the doctrine of justification to the doctrine of election by grace. As we
observed in an earlier chapter, there is a certain level of tension between
the universality of God's grace and the reality of God's predestination
of believers to salvation in Luther's thought as well as the subsequent
Lutheran tradition.

Since it is our goal in this study to recommend and defend Luther's
unique approach to the doctrine of justification, it is necessary to discuss
the issue of election for the sake of demonstrating the coherence of the
Reformer's position. There is a direct connection between election and
justification insofar as they are dual aspects of the doctrine of salvation by
grace. A discussion of election is especially pressing in light of subsequent
Protestant debates on predestination (i.e., the Calvinist and Arminian
debate), as well as the common charge of Calvinists that the Lutheran
position on predestination is irrational and incoherent.[1] In examining the
aforementioned issues, our approach in this chapter will be more

1. For example Joel Beeke, *Debated Issues in Sovereign Predestination: Early Lutheran Predestination, Calvinian Reprobation, and Variations in Genevan Lapsarianism* (Göttingen: Vandenhoeck & Ruprecht, 2017), 221.

systematic and less historical in its content than the previous chapters have been.

The lodestar in discussing the doctrine of election is Luther's concept of the "Hidden God" (*Deus absconditus*).[2] Luther's theology of God's hiddenness is one of the most sophisticated and fascinating accounts of divine transcendence in Western thought and is often profoundly misunderstood. Whereas all Christian theologians have in one way or another posited that God is incomprehensible due to the ontological difference between creator and creature, Luther argues that God intentionally hides from his creation (Isa 45:15).[3] Following B. A. Gerrish, we will suggest that Luther holds that God hides in two distinct ways: in revelation and outside of his revelation.[4] This account of how God hides will form our discussion of the divine-human relationship and therefore how God enacts his decree of election in time.

HIDDENNESS 1: TWO WORDS, TWO TREES

In his treatise *The Bondage of the Will*, Luther speaks of God's election connected with his doctrine of the "Hidden God." The use of the motif of divine hiddenness is not without problems. One significant issue raised by the church historian B. A. Gerrish is that when Luther speaks of divine hiddenness he sometimes speaks of a concealment in revelation (as in *The Heidelberg Disputation*) and sometimes apart from revelation (as in *The Bondage of the Will*). In response to this problem, Gerrish cleverly designated a distinction in Luther's thought between what he describes as "Hiddenness 1" (i.e., hiddenness in revelation) and "Hiddenness 2" (i.e., hiddenness apart from revelation).[5] Although these terms are those of Gerrish and not Luther, they

---

2. The Bondage of the Will (1525), LW 33:138–47. Also see: Gerhard Forde, *The Captivation of the Will: Luther vs. Erasmus on Freedom and Bondage*, ed. Steven Paulson (Grand Rapids: Eerdmans, 2005); Robert Kolb, *Bound Choice, Election, and the Wittenberg Theological Method: From Martin Luther to the Formula of Concord* (Grand Rapids: Eerdmans, 2005), 11– 66; Harry McSorley, *Luther: Right or Wrong?, An Ecumenical-Theological Study of Luther's Major Work, The Bondage of the Will* (New York and Minneapolis: The Newman and Augsburg, 1969), 277–354; Bernhard Lohse, *Martin Luther's Theology: Its Historical and Systematic Development*, trans. and ed. Roy A. Harrisville (Minneapolis: Fortress, 1999),16–18.

3. Steven Paulson, "Luther on the Hidden God," *Word & World* 19, no. 4 (1999): 363.

4. B. A. Gerrish, "To the Unknown God: Luther and Calvin on the Hiddenness of God," *Journal of Religion* 53 (1973: 263–93.

5. Gerrish, "To the Unknown God," 268–89.

helpfully serve as a means of explicating and organizing Luther's disparate statements about the nature of divine hiddenness.

According to Hiddenness 1, God condescends to his creatures in his created masks (*larva Dei*) wherein he manifests himself. God does not encounter his creatures in an unmediated way (*Deus nudus*), but paradoxically conceals himself in created mediums as he unveils himself.[6] This theme of hiddenness in revelation has its roots in the Luther's pre-reformational thinking. As we noted in an earlier chapter, divine hiddenness in Christ and in revelation is a motif which is often present in the Reformer's early humilitastheologie. In the Romans commentary, Luther spoke of a kind of hopeful despair. Faith humbly accepts God's condemnation in his revealed Word, and yet at the same time oddly hopes that under the external word there is a hidden eschatological mercy.[7]

The hiddenness of God in revelation as expressed in the Romans commentary finds a further refinement in Luther's *theologia crucis* (theology of the cross) in *The Heidelberg Disputation* of 1518.[8] Here Luther distinguishes between the "theology of the cross" and the "theology of glory." The theology of glory refers to a theology where the believer uses God's manifestations of power in nature and revelation as analogical ladders to climb into eternity and view God in his unmediated glory. Overwhelmed by the gap between themselves and the transcendental majesty of the Lord, the theologian of glory seeks to bridge the gap by becoming like God through outward works of glory. This may be outwardly impressive moral achievements, or merely power and pomp.[9]

By contrast, the "theologian of the cross" looks to Christ where he may perceive God's glory, wisdom, and power hidden under its opposite (*sub contrario*).[10] The theologian of the cross's mind is humbled by the ugly spectacle of the cross because he cannot see through it into God's hidden wisdom and glory present in it. Nevertheless, God has testified

---

6. Gerrish, "To the Unknown God," 268.

7. Lectures on Romans (1516), LW 25:382–83.

8. See Gerhard Forde, *On Being a Theologian of the Cross: Reflections on Luther's Heidelberg Disputation, 1518* (Grand Rapids: Eerdmans, 1997); Walther Von Loewenich, *Luthers Theologia Crucis* (München: Kaiser Verlag, 1954); Sasse, "The Theology of the Cross," 35–45.

9. Heidelberg Disputation (1518), LW 31:53. See: Forde, *On Being a Theologian of the Cross*, 72–73.

10. Heidelberg Disputation (1518), LW 31:52–53.

in his Word that this is precisely the place where it might be found (1 Cor 1:18, 24). Later in the Genesis commentary Luther writes: "Therefore the prophet (Isa 45:15) calls Him 'God who hides Himself.' For under the curse a blessing lies hidden; under the consciousness of sin, righteousness; under death, life; and under affliction, comfort. But one must look at the word, for those who do not have the word follow their own feeling and remain without comfort in their tears and sorrow."[11] For this reason, they must rely on faith in the external word God has attached to the cross and not visible manifestations of divine power and wisdom.[12]

The epistemic humbling caused by the cross also lends itself to a moral humbling that prepares the sinner for grace. Although outwardly human works seem pleasant and God's seem ugly and ignominious, Christ is the divine source of eternal righteousness and therefore condemns all human righteousness apart from him.[13] The recognition of the righteousness of Christ and the depth of human sin empties the believer who looks upon the crucified Christ of any moral pretentions. By finding God hidden in the cross, the believer comes to know that salvation comes by God's promise of grace alone. Central to Luther's claim is that the theologian of the cross does not look past the external form by which God manifests himself into eternity. Rather, he is content with finding him where he desires to be found in the creaturely medium of the flesh of Christ.[14]

In the Galatians commentary of 1531, Luther extends the principle of God addressing humanity under the form of a created covering or mask (as in the incarnation) to the whole of creation: "the whole creation is a face or mask of God" (*larva Dei*).[15] The supreme example of God coming to creation in the creaturely mask nevertheless remains the incarnation of Christ. We should not seek God above his masks in himself (*Deus ipse*), but cling to God in his outward form in the crucified Christ: "I avoid all speculations about the Divine Majesty and take my stand in the humanity of Christ."[16] Yet, much as in *The Heidelberg Disputation* thirteen years

---

11. Lectures on Genesis (1535-1545), LW 4:7
12. Heidelberg Disputation (1518), LW 31:52–53.
13. Heidelberg Disputation (1518), LW 31:44–45.
14. Heidelberg Disputation (1518), LW 31:50–53.
15. Lectures on Galatians (1531), LW 26:95
16. Lectures on Galatians (1531), LW 26:39.

earlier, Christ conceals God as he discloses him: "Thus faith is a sort of knowledge or darkness that nothing *can see*. Yet the Christ of whom faith takes hold is sitting in the darkness as God sat in the midst of darkness on Sinai or in the temple."[17]

In the Genesis commentary of the 1530s and 1540s, Luther speaks of the creation as forming an address of God to his creatures. In harmony with the *creatio per verbum* of Genesis 1, Luther talks of creatures as God's created words in analogy with his uncreated word: "God, by speaking, created all things and worked through the Word, and ... all His works are some words of God, created by the uncreated Word."[18] God makes himself accessible to his creatures hidden under his creatures. As the later Lutheran philosopher Johann Georg Hamann comments in the spirit of Luther, God addresses the "creature through the creature."[19] In this sense, creatures function in a manner similar to the Augustinian sacramental concept of visible words (*verbum visible*).[20] Creatures communicate in a visible manner what the word communicates in an auditory manner. God is not manifest to his creatures apart from created mediums. Indeed, Luther writes that "[i]t is ... insane to argue about God and the divine nature without the Word or any covering."[21] When God reveals himself, he does so by hiding in a created wrapper or veil:

> When God reveals Himself to us, it is necessary for Him to do so through some such veil or wrapper and say: "Look! Under this wrapper you will be sure to take hold of Me." When we embrace the wrapper, adoring, praying, and sacrificing to God there, we are said to be praying to God and sacrificing to Him properly.[22]

Hence, "those who want to reach God apart from these coverings exert themselves to ascend to heaven without ladders. ... Overwhelmed by His [God's] majesty, which they seek to comprehend without coverings, they

17. Lectures on Galatians (1531), LW 26:129–30. Emphasis added.
18. Lectures of Genesis (1535–1545), LW 1:47.
19. Johann Georg Hamann, *Sämtliche Werke*, ed. Josef Nadler, vol. 2 (Vienna: Thomas-Morus-Presse, Verlag Herder, 1950), 198. Cited in Bayer, *Martin Luther's Theology*, 108.
20. Augustine, *Tractates in the Gospel of John*, 80. 3; NPNF1, 7:344.
21. Lectures of Genesis (1535–1545), LW 1:13.
22. Lectures of Genesis (1535–1545), LW 1:15.

fall to their destruction."[23] Here we see echoes of the earlier distinction between the theologies of glory and the cross. God's presence and Word encountered through created mediums goes all the way back the garden of Eden where "our first parents worshiped God early in the morning, when the sun was rising, *by marveling at the Creator in the creature* or, to express myself more clearly, because they were urged on by the creature."[24]

In that God is concealed by the masks and "wrappers" of his creation, he remains unrecognized "without the Word."[25] In one passage in his Eucharistic writings, Luther posits that God never comes to his creatures in his bare Word, but always reveals himself by attaching his Word to a physical, created medium:

> God ... sets before us no word or commandment without including with it something material and outward, and proffering it to us. To Abraham he gave the word including with it his son Isaac [Gen 15:4ff]. To Saul he gave the word including with it the slaying of the Amalakites [I Sam 15:2f]. And so on. You find no word of God in the entire Scripture in which something material and outward is not contained and presented. If we followed the fanatical spirits, we have to say that all these material, outward things were of no avail and simply nothing.[26]

Therefore, much like the later sacraments of the New Testament, the whole creation comes with a word attached that informs humans that the goods they receive come from the hand of God. Luther observes: "We need the wisdom that distinguishes God from his mask [i.e., creature]. ... When a greedy man, who worships his belly, hears that man does not live by bread alone, but by every word that proceeds from the mouth of God' (Matt. 4:4) he eats the bread but fails to see God in the bread; for he sees, admires, and adores only the mask."[27]

---

23. Lectures of Genesis (1535–1545), LW 1:14.

24. Lectures of Genesis (1535–1545), LW1:15. Emphasis added.

25. Lectures of Genesis (1535–1545), LW 1:13.

26. That These Words of Christ " This Is My Body, Still Stand Firm Against the Fanatics (1527), LW 37:135–36.

27. Lectures on Galatians (1531), LW 26:95.

Idolatry lies not in seeing God's work in the medium of creatures, but in not listening to God's Word and acknowledging him behind the creature. In idolatry, one treats creatures as if they are in themselves the ultimate source of the good and not God and his Word. In the Large Catechism Luther writes: "For even though otherwise we experience much good from men, still whatever we receive by His command or arrangement is all received from God. ... For creatures *are only the hands, channels, and means whereby God gives all things*, as He gives to the mother breasts and milk to offer to her child, and corn and all manner of produce from the earth for nourishment, none of which blessings could be produced by any creature of itself."[28]

Luther's sacramental concept of creation and the word helps us clarify both the nature of sin and the grace of election. Beginning with the Genesis narrative's description of the state of integrity, God sacramentally manifested his goodness and grace by attaching his words to his creatures. In Genesis 1, God attaches the words "very good" (Gen 1) to the whole of his creation, signaling that he has made it as a good for humanity. To Adam in Genesis 2, the Lord makes the promise "you may eat" (Gen 2:16) and attaches it to designate the trees of the garden as mediums of divine goodness. Likewise, God also places his Word of command and promise on the male/female relationship in marriages as a medium of the goodness of companionship and procreation (Gen 1:28; 2:24). Much like the promise of redemption in Christ and the sacraments of the New Testament, so too, in the state of integrity God mediated the good to Adam and Eve by faith in his word of promise attached to creatures. The words of promise that God placed before Adam and Eve were not only infallibly true, they were efficacious words that mediated the good of which they spoke.

It should also not go unnoticed in reading the Genesis narrative, God did not merely attach his words of blessing to creatures but also his words of condemnation. In Genesis 2, there is in the garden of Eden both a tree of life and the tree of the knowledge of good and evil. To the former, God attached the promise of eternal life (Gen 3:22), whereas to the latter

---

28. LC I.1; *Concordia Triglotta*, 587. Emphasis added.

a promise of death (Gen 2:17). These two trees therefore embodied and performed God's two words of law and grace. God attached a word of law to the tree of the knowledge of good and evil, and a promise of grace in the tree of life. By placing two trees and attaching two words before Adam and Eve, God called for a response of faith and obedience. The primal humans were meant to flee from the tree of the knowledge of good and evil and its condemning power to the promise of goodness as manifested in the tree of life and the other trees of the garden.

One could also make the same point about the promise of blessing through marital relationship that God establishes in Genesis 1–2. By his word, God makes marriage a channel of blessing to humanity. Likewise, because of the corruption of sin later in the Old Testament, the Lord makes explicit what was implicit in the promise of marital blessing by condemning deviations from the marital relationship. God attached a word of condemnation to sexual relations with persons who are not one's spouse in the command against adultery in the Ten Commandments. Hence, one should flee the condemnation found in sexual relations with person who are not one's spouse, and cling to their spouse to whom God has attached a word of blessing. For this reason, Luther states in his Catechisms that the life of obedient faith is a matter of "fearing and loving" God.[29] In part (though not exhaustively), Luther means that believers fear God by fleeing the place where he has placed his word of condemnation and love him by finding his grace in the places where he has attached his promise of the good.

Returning to the situation in the Genesis narrative it must be observed that there was no gap between God's will and intention, and the word and wrapping or channel in which he presented himself to Adam and Eve. God would be found as gracious and loving in the tree of life, as well as condemning and wrathful in the tree of the knowledge of good and evil. Therefore, for Luther, faith "is something omnipotent."[30] By fleeing from the place of God's wrath, and clinging to the word of grace, Luther suggests that faith has in a sense the infinite power to re-create God. Luther emphasizes that this is not to say that God is actually re-created in himself. Rather, God is re-created by faith or unbelief in the human perception

---

29. SC 1; *Concordia Triglotta*, 539–43.
30. LW 26:227. Lectures on Galatians (1531) WA 40.1: 360.

of him as he is found in different locations and in different words. A God of wrath in the law is re-created as a God of grace and love when he is found in the promise of grace by faith.[31]

Following the patristic and medieval traditions, Luther deduced from the final heavenly glorification of creation (as taught elsewhere in Scripture) that Adam and Eve had an eschatological destiny even before the fall.[32] Because God's Word does what it says, had Adam and Eve continued to look for and sacramentally receive God in the tree of life, they would have been inexorably carried along by the power of the divine Word into eternal life.[33] In such a glorified state, the veil of creaturely masks and words would be removed, and humans would finally come to see *Deus ipse* "face to face" (1 Cor 13:12). Nonetheless, in the pre-eschatological state, humans must harken to God's Word encountered under the "wrappings" and "channels" of his creatures.

Following this interpretative insight, it can be observed that in the Genesis narrative Adam and Eve did not listen to God's Word of grace and decided to look for him in the place of condemnation (i.e., the tree of the knowledge of good and evil). The word that God had spoken in connection with the tree of the knowledge of good and evil did precisely what it promised, namely, it worked spiritual and physical death. Therefore, the word of the law inexorably carried the first humans to eternal death, just as the word of grace would have infallibly carried them along to eternal life. Adam and Eve were then cast outside the garden where "the wrath of God is revealed from heaven against all ungodliness and unrighteousness of men" (Rom 1:18). God's wrath is revealed to all outside the garden

---

31. Lectures on Galatians (1531), LW 26:227.

32. Lectures on Genesis (1535–1545), LW 1:106. "[L]ater on he would have returned to his working and guarding until a predetermined time had been fulfilled, when he would have been translated to heaven with the utmost pleasure."

33. Lectures on Genesis (1535–1545), LW 1:92: "One of these was the tree of life, created that man, by eating of it, might be preserved in full bodily vigor, free from diseases and free from weariness. Here again man is set apart from the brutes, not only in regard to place but also in regard to the advantage of a longer life and one which always remains in the same condition. The bodies of the remaining living things increase in size and are stronger in their youth, but in their old age they become feeble and die. The situation of man would have been different. He would have eaten; he would have drunk; and the conversion of food in his body would have taken place, but not in such a disgusting manner as now. Moreover, this tree of life would have preserved perpetual youth. ... until finally he would have been translated from the physical life to the spiritual." LW 1:110: "Adam ate, he masticated, he digested; and if he had remained as he was, he would have done the other things physical life demands until at last he would have been translated to the spiritual and eternal life."

Justification by the Word

(that is, outside the sphere of divine grace and promise) through God's creaturely masks, because God's "invisible attributes [i.e., including his holiness and wrath], namely, his eternal power and divine nature, *have been clearly perceived*, ever since the creation of the world, *in the things that have been made*" (Rom 1:20, emphasis added).[34]

Nevertheless, God established a new word of promise in the form of the *protoevangelium* in Genesis 3:15. The grace of the *protoevangelium* took on an even more definite form in the corporate life and history of Israel through the promise he attached to Abraham's "seed" (Gen 22:18). God's effective Word of promise pushed the history of Israel inexorably along to its fulfillment in the person of the Messiah, even in the face of human opposition. Nevertheless, the movement of the divine Word toward its final fulfillment could often appear as a failure even as it succeeded. When Moses pronounced the divine Word "Let my people go," it appeared ineffective to both the Egyptians and Israelites. Indeed, Pharaoh was apparently unmoved by the pronouncement of the divine deed-word and in turn increases Israel's labor (Exod 5). Nevertheless, it is through Pharaoh's very obstinacy that God works his redemption and is finally able to bring a plague so horrific that Egypt expels Israel.[35] God likewise tells Isaiah to speak a word of repentance to Israel that they will ignore, thereby ensuring that their suffering in Babylon (Isa 6:9–13). But Israel's destruction was the occasion for their true repentance, something that would prepare them for the grace of restoration and the coming of the Messiah (Isa 40–66). Finally, God's Word of redemption found ultimate fulfillment in the opposition and murder of Jesus by his opponents. By killing God himself, Jesus's enemies brought about the fulfillment of the Word of God they sought to thwart. As Luther's theology of the cross shows, God works under the form of his opposite. God fulfills his Word under the outward appearance of it having failed.

Likewise, throughout the history of Israel, God's pattern of attaching his dual words of condemnation and grace to created masks continued. By doing so, the Lord bid his covenant people to flee from the word of

---

34. Steven Paulson, *Lutheran Theology* (New York: T&T Clark International, 2011), 70–74.

35. Steven Paulson, *Hiddenness, Evil, and Predestination*, vol. 1 of Luther's Outlaw God, 229–43.

condemnation to that of grace. Although Jacob is attacked by God in the night, he demands the name of the shadowy attacker and thereby harkens back to the promise of blessing that God made to him at Bethel (Gen 32:22–32).[36] Moses is also attacked by God on his return to Egypt but flees to the promise of grace found in the circumcision of his son (Exod 4:24–26).[37] God threatened with death those who came near Mt. Sinai, the mountain where he gave his law (Exod 19:10–13), but promised forgiveness and a share in his personal holiness to those who approached him through the sacramental channels of the Tabernacle and Temple at Mt. Zion.[38]

This pattern of fleeing from condemnation to grace also continues in the life of Christ. In the crucifixion, God designated Jesus and the sacraments of the New Testament that flowed from his side (John 19:34) on the hillock of Golgotha as the new place of grace, and the Temple mount and works connected with it as a place of condemnation (Gal 4:25–26). In his resurrection, Jesus insists that the women flee his tomb (the place of death and condemnation) and instructs them to tell his disciples to meet him in Galilee. In Galilee, Jesus tells the disciples to look for him now not in the tomb but in the word and sacrament ministry of the church (Matt 28:8–10, 16–20).

Ultimately, those who embrace Luther's theology find Calvin's theology of election and justification so problematic because it fails to see that God is present and active in his Word in precisely the manner that he promises to be. For Calvin, human salvation and reprobation are to be envisioned from the perspective of a comprehensive plan in eternity operating above and beyond the external word. The harmony of this plan can be discerned by looking past God's words and coverings, in order to see the whole of God's hidden providence.[39] Since some are saved and others not, God must not mean what he says when he presents himself in the word as willing the salvation of all who encounter him there. As a result, in Calvin's theology the external word may or may not do what it

---

36. Lectures on Genesis (1535–1545), LW 6:122–55.

37. Paulson, *Hiddenness, Evil, and Predestination,* 17–18.

38. See the good description in Kleinig, *Leviticus.*

39. See the outline of this approach in the clearest terms in John Calvin, *Concerning the Eternal Predestination of God,* trans. J. K. S. Reid (Louisville: Westminster John Knox, 1997).

promises. Only those who receive the inner call are truly elect and can see through the external word to God's unified plan of grace for them as an individual.[40]

By contrast, Luther sees God as exercising his rule through his Word manifest in and through his created masks. Contrary to the claim of many Calvinists, Luther and the Lutheran tradition do not ultimately make God's grace ineffective. On the contrary, God's Word always does precisely what it speaks. The key though is that God's exercise of his reign is divided between a realm of law and a realm of grace. Those places where God has promised to work death and condemnation inexorably work death and condemnation. By contrast, those who look for God in in the word and sacraments will infallibly find a grace there that performs what it speaks.

Seen from the perspective of the sacramentality of the word, the question of the perseverance of the saints is solved not on the basis of a special spiritual gift given to the elect—as in Augustine[41] and Calvin[42]— but on the basis on the efficacy of the means of grace external to the believer.[43] God is always faithful to his Word regarding the means of grace. The grace of the word and the sacraments will inexorably move one toward the kingdom of heaven, just as a person who gets on a raft in the Mississippi River in Minnesota will inexorably be moved toward the Gulf of Mexico.[44]

It could of course be objected that since Luther and the subsequent Lutheran tradition believe that apostasy is possible, one can never genuinely be certain that the divine Word will carry one along to their eschatological destiny. In response, Lutherans have historically observed that God's promise of grace is objectively true whether or not one believes in it.[45] As we saw in Luther's pronouncement regarding objective justification in an earlier chapter,[46] God's promise of grace in Christ is more real than

---

40. ICR, 3.24.8; Calvin, *Institutes*, 2 vols., trans. and ed. John T. McNeill and Ford Lewis Battles (Philadelphia: Westminster, 1967), 2:974–75.

41. Augustine, *On the Gift of Perseverance*; NPNF1, 5:521–52.

42. ICR, 3.24.7; Calvin, *Institutes*, 2 vols., trans. and ed. John T. McNeill and Ford Lewis Battles (Philadelphia: Westminster, 1967), 2:973–74.

43. See the Lutheran view and critique of the alternatives in Pieper, *Christian Dogmatics*, 3:89–103.

44. Paulson, *Hiddenness, Evil, and Predestination*, 57–158.

45. Pieper, *Christian Dogmatics*, 2:321, 2:347–48, 2:508–12, 2:543.

46. Sermons on the Gospel of John (1538), LW 22:382.

one's refusal to believe it, and therefore remains a valid promise even if one chooses to actively reject it.[47] Hence, to doubt the word of the gospel is not to invalidate it, but rather to place oneself outside of the realm of grace where the word is operative and effective (i.e., the sphere of the church and its ministry), and into the realm of wrath and law which inexorably leads to eternal death (Rom 3:20). Hence, as long as one looks away from one's present or possible future works and to God's promise present in the sphere of grace, one can always have infallible certainty that the living and active word of the gospel will perform precisely what it speaks.

It is therefore important to understand that the differences between Lutheranism and Calvinism does not lie in competing anthropologies or estimations of the severity of original sin. Both Luther and Calvin agreed that in spiritual things humans are bound,[48] whereas in earthly things they are free.[49] That is to say, both Lutherans and Calvinists affirm that humans are free to make mundane decisions (for example: should I wear a green or red tie?), as well as whether to obey the law in a merely external sense (i.e., so-called civil righteousness).[50]

Nevertheless, in their inner person, humans are not free with regard to spiritual things. Augustine long ago showed that in the inner person the passions reign, especially because of the power of sin.[51] As we observed earlier, the young Melanchthon correctly noted that humans are not the authors of their own desires and they cannot control whether they are

---

47. Tom G. A. Hardt, "Justification and Easter: A Study in Subjective and Objective Justification in Lutheran Theology," in *A Lively Legacy: Essays in Honor of Robert Preus*, ed. Kurt E. Marquart, John R. Stephenson, and Bjarne W. Teigen (Ft. Wayne, IN: Concordia Theological Seminary, 1985), 52–78; Eduard Preuss, *The Justification of the Sinner before God*, trans. J.A. Friedrich (Ft. Wayne, IN: Lutheran Legacy, 2011), 29–61; Robert Preus, "Objective Justification," in *Doctrine Is Life: Essays on Justification and the Lutheran Confessions*, ed. Klemet Preus (St. Louis: Concordia, 2006), 147–55.

48. ICR, 2.2.7–8; Calvin, *Institutes*, 1:264–6; LW 33:64–69.

49. ICR, 2.2.12–13; Calvin, *Institutes*, 1:270–72; LW 33:70.

50. Heinrich Heppe, *Reformed Dogmatics*, trans. G. T. Thomson (Eugene, OR: Wipf & Stock, 2007), 361–63; Heinrich Schmid, *The Doctrinal Theology of the Evangelical Lutheran Church*, trans. Charles A. Hays and Henry E. Jacobs, (Minneapolis: Augsburg, 1961), 244–47, 259–68.

51. Han-luen Kantzer Komline, *Augustine on the Will: A Theological Account* (Oxford: Oxford University Press, 2019), 61.

subject to them.[52] Luther later referred to this in *The Bondage of the Will* as the "necessity of immutability."[53] Luther writes:

> This is what we call the necessity of immutability. It means that the will cannot change itself and turn in a different direction but is rather the more provoked into willing by being resisted; as its resentment shows. This would not happen if it were free or had free choice.[54]

Hence, when it comes to things concerning salvation, there can be no question that the will is unable to cooperate with God in conversion. If the will is sinful and unbelieving, then it will necessarily reject the things of God since there is no neutral, middle ground between sin and faith.

To illustrate Luther's teaching on this point with a mundane example, one can choose whether or not one will eat cake, but one cannot choose whether or not one desires cake. The Bible is consistently clear that real conversion means a willing heart, and not simply external obedience (Ps 51:10; Matt 23:27–28). Similarly, in interpersonal relationships, humans act upon one another and inspire love and trust. Nevertheless, one cannot choose to love and trust another person. That is why it is common to say that people "fall in love." Acting as if one loves another person will never cause one person to love another. Since the divine-human is another interpersonal relationship, the same rule of human relations applies to faith in and love of God.[55]

Many who follow the popular version of Arminian theology would reject this line of reasoning and insist that faith is a decision or commitment which humans are capable of.[56] As we have seen in our discussion of Paul, this is a faulty conception of faith. Faith for Paul and the Magisterial

---

52. Melanchthon, "*Loci Communes Theologici* 1521," 27.

53. See discussion in Forde, *The Captivation of the Will*, 47–60.

54. The Bondage of the Will (1525), LW 33:65.

55. Phillip Cary makes a similar point about the interpersonal nature of the divine-human relationship. See Cary, *Meaning of Protestant Theology*, 335–38. The divine-human relationship is an interpersonal encounter like Martin Buber's "I-Thou" (*Ich-Du*) relationship. See Martin Buber, *I and Thou*, trans. Ronald Gregor Smith (Edinburgh: T&T Clark, 1987).

56. See Finney, *Finney's Systematic Theology*, 353. One also thinks here of the popular American Evangelical periodical "Decision Magazine."

Reformers is fundamentally a form of trust (Rom 4:18–25) that gives rise to loving obedience (Gal 5:6).[57] While popular Ariminians are certainly correct that it is possible to make a decision for or commit oneself to Jesus, this is not the same thing as trusting and loving Jesus.[58] In the same manner, choosing or committing oneself to a spouse or business partner is not the same as trusting or loving them.

Since Lutherans and Calvinists agree on bondage in spiritual things as outlined above, they also agree that conversion necessarily means God working monergistically to establish new desires in the human subject by his grace.[59] That being said, the means by which God works new desires in the human subject differs markedly in the two traditions. For Calvin, grace is irresistible because it operates immediately on the human subject, albeit alongside the means of grace.[60] For Lutherans, grace is resistible because it is mediated through the means of grace. Since the means of grace are auditory or physical objects, engaging or disengaging them falls within the sphere of human freedom in earthly things.[61] Because of human freedom in earthly things, one can engage or disengage the means of grace in spite of being spiritually dead. When humans are exposed to the proclamation of the gospel, they are free to listen to it and consider the grace which is preached.[62] All these things fall within the sphere of freedom in earthly things. Jesus illustrates this point perfectly in the parable of the sower, wherein the generative seed (the word) is simply not received by all soil (humanity).

---

57. See brief summary in Donald McKim, *The Westminster Handbook to Reformed Theology* (Louisville: Westminster John Knox, 2001), 127–28.

58. Gerhard Forde, *Theology is for Proclamation!* (Minneapolis: Fortress, 1990), 45.

59. For Reformed examples, see Louis Berkhof, *Systematic Theology* (Grand Rapids: Eerdmans, 1941), 480–92; ICR,2.3.6–7; McNeill and Battles, *The Institutes of the Christian Religion*, 1:296–301; Heppe, *Reformed Dogmatics*, 510–80. For Lutheran examples, see FC SD, XI.29–32; *Concordia Triglotta*, 1072–73; Adolf Hoenecke, *Evangelical Lutheran Dogmatics*, trans. Joel Fredrich, et al., 4 vols. (Milwaukee: Northwestern, 1999–2009), 3:257–87; Theodore Mueller, *Christian Dogmatics: A Handbook in Doctrinal Theology* (St. Louis: Concordia, 1934), 336–66; Schmid, *The Doctrinal Theology of the Evangelical Lutheran Church*, 458–80.

60. ICR, 2.3.6–14; Calvin, *Institutes*, 1:296–309.

61. Mueller, *Christian Dogmatics*, 336–66; Pieper, *Christian Dogmatics*, 2:464–66; Schmid, *The Doctrinal Theology of the Evangelical Lutheran Church*, 459.

62. FC SD, XI.38–43; *Concordia Triglotta*, 1072–75.

Nevertheless, even though humans can engage or disengage the means of grace, they are not free to create faith, or unbelief in their hearts. To use another interpersonal analogy: one can choose whether or not they go on a date, but one cannot choose whether or not one will fall in love with the person that they are dating. Likewise, to say that humans can choose whether or not they enter into the sphere of grace (word and sacrament ministry of the church) or the sphere of wrath (i.e., all reality outside the means of grace) does not mean that they are autonomous in relationship to God. The means of grace are resistible, but God is not. God's wrath or God's love operates through his two words of law and grace and actively determines, shapes, and drives humans on inexorably to the end of either destruction or redemption that they promise.[63]

---

63. Paulson, *Hiddenness, Evil, and Predestination*, 57–158.

CHAPTER 13

Justification and Election:

God's Hiddenness Outside the Means of Grace

Hiddenness 2, "God not preached or *Deus absconditus*" (as Luther terms him in *The Bondage of the Will*), exists above the masks of God. As we observed in the previous chapter, God manifests himself in distinct and seemingly contradictory ways in his creaturely masks. Specifically, in some masks he manifests himself as law or wrath and in others as gospel or love. In spite of these contradictory manifestations of his divine reality and will, God remains unified in his eternal being above them. For this reason, humans can see God's eternal being in this life only "through a glass darkly." At the eschaton, humans will see God "face to face" without any covering or veil (1 Cor 13:12). Until then, God's contradictory manifestations in creaturely masks defy complete rationalization on the basis of any kind of theodicy.

Although Luther does not describe the source of this concept in his thinking, Albrecht Ritschl suggested that there a connection between Luther's distinctive between *Deus absconditus and Deus revelatus* and the earlier medieval distinction between God's absolute and ordered power (*potentia dei absoluta et ordinate*).[1] As we will see below, there does seem

---

1. Ritschl, *Critical History of the Christian Doctrine of Justification and Reconciliation*, 199–200.

to be some kind of connection between the doctrines, even if Luther does not make one explicit. Much like the doctrine of the two powers in God, Luther does talk about God binding himself to a specific order (as we have seen in our earlier discussion of the means of grace)[2] yet remaining free in himself.

In the version of this doctrine that Luther studied at Erfurt under various Ockhamists, it was asserted that God possesses an absolute power wherein he can do all things that are not inherently contradictory (i.e., make a square circle) before he created the world (absolute power). After God creates the world, he commits himself to a certain world order and will use his power in accordance with the covenantal promises that he has made (ordered power). From this brief account of the Ockhamist version of the aforementioned distinction it becomes clear that for the late medieval theologians the concept of God's absolute power is fundamentally a speculative one. God's absolute power was not a present reality, but rather a description about what might have been possible before he created the world.[3]

By contrast, in reshaping the concept of God's absolute power into the notion of *Deus absconditus* Luther describes the very present reality of God's freedom above his masks. As we have already seen, God binds himself by his Word to his creaturely masks in order to reveal how he will act through them. The concept of God's binding himself through his Word appear to have its basis in the Ockhamist notion of ordered power (i.e., what McGrath calls "covenantal causality").[4] Nevertheless, although God binds himself to be present as wrath or grace in specific masks, he remains utterly free above his masks. As sovereign above them, the hidden God (i.e., the God of absolute power) is free to "shuffle" his masks as he

---

2. Scott Hendrix, *Luther* (Nashville: Abingdon, 2009), 15.

3. William Courtenay "Dialectic of Omnipotence in the High and Late Middle Ages," in *Divine Omniscience and Omnipotence in Medieval Philosophy: Islamic, Jewish, and Christian Perspective*, ed. Tamar Rudavsky (Dordrecht: D. Reidel, 1985), 246–69; Heiko Oberman, "The Shape of Late Medieval Thought: The Birthpangs of the Modern Era," in *The Dawn of the Reformation: Essay on the Late Medieval and Early Reformation Thought* (Grand Rapids: Eerdmans, 1992), 26–29.

4. McGrath, *Luther's Theology of the Cross*, 59.

so chooses.[5] Luther writes: "For there [above his masks] he [God] has not bound himself by his word, *but has kept himself free over all things.*"[6]

In his hidden sovereignty, God becomes present to his creatures as wrath or grace according to a genuine plan, but one that cannot be discerned by finite human rationalizations apart from revelation. The book of Jonah represents an excellent example of the mysterious nature of God's electing presence as either wrath or grace. Jonah is commissioned by God to preach repentance to the Ninevites. Knowing the efficacy of God's Word, Jonah does not wish to do this (Jonah 4:1–3). The subtext appears to be throughout the book that the Prophet knows that in the next generation the descendants of the Ninevites will destroy his own people by overthrowing the northern kingdom of Israel.[7] The implication is that God has elected the Ninevites through the grace of his preaching (i.e., his mask of grace), while allowing the northern kingdom to experience the condemnation of the law (i.e., his mask of wrath). Both groups of people are equally sinful, yet God appears to inexplicably elect the gentile Ninevites over his covenant people. Hence, God is reliable in his external Word to work precisely what that word promises, but why he becomes present in his Word as either wrath or grace to specific groups of sinners is not explicable because of God's hiddenness.

Therefore, when dealing with the issue of why some have faith and not others, free will is of limited explanatory power. Ultimately, although it is possible to explain unbelief in part due to human resistance to the means of grace, historically not all have had access to the means of grace (for example, the pre-Columbian Aztecs). In spite of human incapacity to receive the gift of faith apart from the means of grace, Paul nevertheless insists that those who are ignorant of them are to be held accountable and stand under God's wrath (Rom 1:18–20).

More importantly for Luther in *The Bondage of the Will*, God's omnipotence means that although humans are by no means puppets or robots, they ultimately never exercise independent choice. Here, Luther further distances himself from Augustine, for whom the emphasis lay on the fact

---

5. Forde, *Theology is for Proclamation!*, 17.

6. The Bondage of the Will (1525), LW 33:139. Emphasis added.

7. Leithart, *A House for My Name*, 184–85.

that human bondage is largely a function of original sin and not the logical consequence of human createdness.[8] For Luther, human bondage is
the logical consequence of creatureliness:

> Here then, is something fundamentally necessary and salutary for
> a Christian, to know that God foreknows nothing contingently, but
> that he foresees and purposes and does all things by his immutable,
> eternal, and infallible will. Here is a thunderbolt by which free
> choice is completely prostrated and shattered, so that those who
> want free choice asserted must either deny or explain away this
> thunderbolt or get rid of it by some other means.[9]

Luther's claim that all things happen by divine necessity has often
been misunderstood. Contrary to what is often claimed, Luther's point is
not that God acts like a puppeteer capriciously jerking his creatures back
and forth. That would be what Luther calls "necessity of compulsion."[10]
Throughout The Bondage of the Will, Luther emphatically denies that God
works on human agency by means of compulsion or coercion. Rather, as
we have already seen from both Scripture and Luther's interpretation of it,
God's agency is more like a narrator who speaks forth reality according to
his Word. Much as a novelist's linguistic agency determines his characters
while not coercing them into them, God speaks forth both his old creation
and new creation.[11] He thereby determines his creatures through his creative address, which calls them into existence according to their particular
natures and with particular desires. God determines creatures' natures and
the capacities which they act out of by his creative Word. Hence, when
creatures act, they do so out of their own created capacities and desires by
divine determination, but without divine coercion.

Nevertheless, although God is not a coercive tyrant, he is still ultimately the arbiter of all that occurs within his creation and human
agency is incapable of acting without his ordination and foreknowledge.

---

8. Spence, *Justification*, 71.

9. The Bondage of the Will (1525), LW 33:37.

10. The Bondage of the Will (1525), LW 33:65.

11. See Oswald Bayer, "Creation as History," in *The Gift of Grace: The Future of Lutheran Theology*,
eds. Niels Hendrik Gregersen, Bo Holm, Ted Peters, and Peter Widmann, (Minneapolis: Augsburg
Fortress, 2005), 253; Bayer, "God as Author of My Life History," 437–56; Bayer, "Poetological Doctrine
of the Trinity," 43–58.

Nevertheless, God's determination of his creatures must be interpreted from the perspective of human agency's dual horizons of spiritual matters and earthly matters.

In earthly things, although as we have seen Luther holds that we have freedom, human ability to make free choices is bounded by God's foreknowledge, permission, and limitations. In *The Bondage of the Will*, Luther notes that Scripture teaches that Judas betrayed Jesus according to the "definite plan and foreknowledge of God" (Acts 2:23).[12] Because God created Judas with his particular personality, foreknew how he would act, made his foreknown action to be part of the divine plan, and permitted him to do what he did, his betrayal of Jesus happened necessarily.[13] Because of the "definite plan and foreknowledge of God" Judas's betrayal could not have been otherwise than God ordained. Nevertheless, Luther also emphasizes that God did not coerce Judas into his action (i.e., the necessity of compulsion). Judas did what he did freely out of his own heart without the intervention of external compulsion.[14]

One might also make the same point that Luther makes about Judas with regard to the fall of humanity. Although historically Lutherans have rightly registered discomfort with the language that Calvinists use in asserting that God decreed the fall of humanity,[15] it nevertheless cannot be denied that the fall could only have occurred according to God's foreknowledge and permission. Having foreknowledge of what would happen when Adam and Eve were tempted, God could very well have prevented Satan from tempting them. Indeed, God could have simply prevented the fall by never having put the tree of the knowledge of good and evil in Eden in the first place or could have simply created the primal humans already confirmed in the good. Although God certainly does not approve of sin (1 John 1:5; Jas 1:13), if one begins with the premise of God's omnipotence and omniscience, then it is impossible to deny that permitting the fall must in some mysterious sense have been part of God's plan for creation, as Paul seems to imply at least one point (Rom 11:32). Indeed, this opinion

---

12. See discussion in Paulson, *Hiddenness, Evil, and Predestination*, 141–58.

13. The Bondage of the Will (1525), LW 33:192–95.

14. The Bondage of the Will (1525), LW 33:194–95.

15. Heppe, *Reformed Dogmatics*, 144. It should be observed in fairness to Calvinists that they do not hold that in some sense God forced Adam to sin.

is in perfect agreement with the Lutheran confessional writings, since Luther observes in the Large Catechism: "For He [God] has created us for this very object, that He might redeem and sanctify us."[16]

Seen in this light, what has often been perceived as a tension between the Formula of Concord's sharp distinction between foreknowledge and predestination[17] and Luther's insistence that divine foreknowledge is in some sense causative disappears.[18] God foreknows the free actions of his creatures, but such actions would be impossible without his sovereign permission and ordination of them as part of his plan for creation. Hence, from the perspective of his sovereign ordination and permission, it would be correct to say that God's foreknowledge is causative.[19] Nevertheless, as the Formula of Concord affirms, such foreknowledge does not somehow impose a kind of compulsion on creatures to make particular decisions. God does not coerce human or angelic sin, although he does infallibly foreknow that it will occur and can prevent it when he so desires. As Paul Hinlicky aptly states, God "is the cause of all causes but not the maker of all choices."[20]

Likewise, in spiritual things God is the creator and therefore shapes the desires that humans possess. As the sustainer of creation, he concurs in the propagation of human nature with original sin,[21] just as through the word and sacrament ministry of the church he circumcises the heart (Deut 30:6; Jer 31:33; 32:40; Col 2:11–12). The human subjects are either ruled by the desire to sin or by the Holy Spirit. Luther observes that the human will therefore acts out of necessity in spiritual matters, but again this is not a form of compulsion: "Now by 'necessarily' I do not mean 'compulsorily,' but by the necessity of immutability (as they say) and not of compulsion. That is to say, when a man is without the Spirit of God he does not do evil against his will."[22] As Jesus likewise said: "So, every

---

16. LC II.64; *Concordia Triglotta*, 695.
17. FC SD, XI.4; *Concordia Triglotta*, 1062–65.
18. The Bondage of the Will (1525), LW 33:184–92.
19. The Bondage of the Will (1525), LW 33:189.
20. Hinlicky, *Luther and the Beloved Community*, 344.
21. The Bondage of the Will (1525), LW 33:174–75.
22. The Bondage of the Will (1525), LW 33:64.

healthy tree bears good fruit, but the diseased tree bears bad fruit. A healthy tree cannot bear bad fruit, nor can a diseased tree bear good fruit" (Matt 7:17–18).[23] Therefore, the human will cannot be seen as some neutral capacity, but is configured as either good or evil: "[The] will cannot change itself and turn in a different direction but is rather the more provoked into willing by being resisted; as its resentment shows. This would not happen if it were free or had free choice."[24] Hence, when it comes to things concerning salvation, there can be no question that the will is unable to cooperate with God in conversion. If the will is sinful and unbelieving, then it will necessarily reject the things of God since there is no neutral, middle ground between sin and faith.

Luther's description of *Deus absconditus* relentlessly working all things through his created masks raises the issues of why God hides and what the implications of this hiding are for the doctrine of election. As we have already seen, unlike Calvin (and we could also add Augustine and Barth), Luther speaks primarily of God's justification and election of his creatures as something that occurs in and through his creaturely masks.[25] Of course, God's predestination of the elect is clearly something worked out before time (Rom 8:29; Eph 1:4; 1 Pet 1:20), but following the motif of the theology of glory vs. the theology of the cross, when dealing with election Luther is less willing to climb into eternity and discuss God's decrees in the abstract. Therefore, quite to the contrary of the mainstream of the Augustinian tradition, Luther holds that God in eternity has actively chosen to hide himself and can only be discussed from the standpoint of his external works and word: "God reveals himself in no other way than in his word and works; for a man can comprehend them in some measure. But that other, that which properly belongs

23. Freedom of a Christian (1520), LW 31:361. See discussion in Brett Muhlhan, *Being Shaped by Freedom: An Examination of Luther's Development of Christian Liberty, 1520–1525* (Eugene, OR: Pickwick, 2012), 69.

24. Freedom of a Christian (1520), LW 33:65.

25. See the critique in Gerhard Forde, "Karl Barth on the Consequences of Lutheran Christology," in *The Preached God: Proclamation in Word and Sacrament*, ed. Steven Paulson and Mark Mattes (Minneapolis: Fortress, 2017), 69–88; Steven Paulson, "Analogy and Proclamation: The Struggle over God's Hiddenness in the Theology of Martin Luther and Eberhard Jüngel" (PhD diss., Lutheran School of Theology, 1992), 216–17.

to the Godhead can no man comprehend or understand."[26] Why God hides and yet makes himself available to us in certain means as either wrath or grace is then fundamental to understanding how God elects and justifies the ungodly.

In addressing the question of why God actively hides, Luther gives two answers. Together these answers echo Luther's other concerns for the theology of the cross and the proper distinction between law and promise. First, God hides because it is part of his alien work, wherein he "*kills* in order to *make alive*."[27] God's hiddenness is therefore not an anomaly or contradiction in his theology that militates against the Reformer's belief in God's fundamentally loving nature (Ritschl).[28] Nor is God's hiddenness a pure antithesis to his love that sets up an absolute dualism between what God is like outside and inside the gospel (Theodosius Harnack).[29] Rather, as we observed in an earlier chapter, God's alien work of wrath and hiddenness help the creature recognize their own sinfulness and finitude, which is the only proper preparation for the reception of divine grace: "[For most] assuredly he has promised his grace to the humble, those who lament and despair of themselves."[30] Luther writes of his own contemplation of God's hiddenness outside of Christ: "I myself was offended more than once, and brought to the very depth and abyss of despair, so that I wished I had never been created a man, before I realized how salutary that despair was, and how near I was to grace."[31]

Therefore, God's alien work and his hiddenness functionally represent the work of the law by bringing about humble repentance and receptivity to grace: "Thus when God makes alive he does it by killing, when he

---

26. Cited from Gregory Dexter Walcott, *The Kantian and Lutheran Elements in Ritschl's Conception of God* (Lancaster, PA: New Era,1904), 13. Originally taken from Johann Georg Walch, ed., *Dr. Martin Luthers Sämmtliche Schriften*, 24 vols. (Halle, 1740–1753), 1:15.

27. The Bondage of the Will (1525), LW 33:62.

28. Albrecht Ritschl, *The Christian Doctrine of Justification and Reconciliation: The Positive Development of the Doctrine*, trans. H. R. Macintosh and A. B. Macauley (Edinburgh: T&T Clark. 1900), 263–34.

29. Theodosius Harnack, *Luthers Theologie mit besonderer Beziehung auf seine Versöhnungs- und Erlösungslehre*, 2 vols. (Amsterdam: Rodopi, 1969), 1:84–97.

30. The Bondage of the Will (1525), LW 33: 61. This recognition of the distinction between the "proper" and "alien" work of God is a contribution of Karl Holl to the debate between Ritschl and Harnack. See brief discussion in Karl Holl, "Was verstand Luther unter Religion?" in *Gesammelte Aufsätze*, 3 vols. (Tübingen: Mohr, 1928), 1:75–77.

31. The Bondage of the Will (1525), LW 33:190.

justifies he does it by making men guilty, when he exalts to heaven he does it by bringing down to hell."[32] Later in the *Antinomian Disputations* of the 1530s, Luther often spoke of the alien work of God as taking over the accusing and terrifying function of the law even apart from the law's explicit preaching.[33] Hence, God must hide and become terrible outside the means of grace in order to drive sinners to the gospel.

The second reason that God conceals himself is "the nature of Christian faith itself."[34] As we have already observed with regard to the motif of the theology of the cross, when God becomes present in his grace he hides such redemptive power under the outward appearance of the opposite (*sub contrario*).[35] Since Christian faith is a matter of trust in a promise that possesses a fulfillment not directly accessible to human vision (Rom 4:16–21; Heb 11:1), God must hide from believers in order to make faith possible.[36] As we have seen, this principle applies to Hiddenness 1. Whereas humans who are by nature theologians of glory wish to see into God's eternal purposes (including his secret counsels of election), faith bids sinners to humble trust in God's promises even when they are attached to the baser and weaker things of the world such as the cross. Nevertheless, in *The Bondage of the Will* Luther asserts that the *sub contrario* principle also applies to Hiddenness 2: "Thus God hides his eternal goodness and mercy under eternal wrath, his righteousness under iniquity. This is the highest degree of faith, to believe him merciful when he saves so few and damns so many, and to believe him righteous when by his own will he makes us necessarily damnable."[37]

When humans therefore try to look into God's eternal purposes and peer into God's secret counsels of election through the veil of divine hiddenness, they are invariably terrified and confused. As a result they not infrequently develop legalistic theories to control God's election with

32. The Bondage of the Will (1525), LW 33:62.

33. See Martin Luther, "The First Disputation Against the Antinomians, Thesis 18," in *Only the Decalogue is Eternal: Martin Luther's Complete Antinomian Theses and Disputations*, ed. and trans. Holger Sontag (Minneapolis: Lutheran, 2008), 80.

34. The Bondage of the Will (1525), Theses for the Second Disputation Against the Antinomians (1538), LW 33:62.

35. Bernhard Lohse, *Martin Luther: An Introduction to His Life and Work*, Robert Schultz (Philadelphia: Fortress, 1986), 194–95.

36. Forde, *The Captivation of the Will*, 42–43.

37. The Bondage of the Will (1525), LW 33:62.

their good works. If God's will is unbound and working all things, the logic of much of human religion has been to try to argue that obedience to the law can control him.[38] Of course, the difficulty is that if God's will is exhaustively explained by the law, there is no room for him to fulfill and transcend the law by grace. With this, the biblical and Reformation principle of *sola Christus* and *sola gratia* falls to the wayside.

Therefore, God does not wish humans to idolatrously rationalize him into the straitjacket of the *opinio legis* (the mindset of the law). Rather being terrified by his hidden reality, God wishes humans to flee to the word of the gospel wherein he makes himself available as love and promise. As we have already seen, it is through the word of the gospel that Luther sees God as working his election and not outside of it. Luther writes in his Genesis commentary concerning God's act of predestination manifest in the means of grace:

> God did not come down from heaven to make you uncertain about predestination, to teach you to despise the sacraments, absolution, and the rest of the divine ordinances. Indeed, He instituted them to make you completely certain and to remove the disease of doubt from your heart, in order that you might not only believe with the heart but also see with your physical eyes and touch with your hands. Why, then, do you reject these and complain that you do not know whether you have been predestined? You have the Gospel; you have been baptized; you have absolution; you are a Christian.[39]

Therefore, to come into contract with the means of grace is to come into contact with God's saving and electing will. If we cling to the means of grace, we will find a gracious God and will be assured of our election. There is no gap between God's hidden plan of salvation and the external means whereby he graciously makes himself available to sinners.

Recognizing that God elects through his sacramental word of the gospel does not solve every theological problem. One difficulty that arises in both the study of the Scripture and in Luther's theology is the tension

---

38. Gerhard Forde, "The Work of Christ," in *Christian Dogmatics*, ed. Robert Jenson and Carl Braaten, 2 vols. (Philadelphia: Fortress, 1984), 2:66–68.

39. Lectures on Genesis (1535–1545), LW 5:45–46.

between the universality of divine grace and the particularity of election. Perhaps a good place to examine this issue in the Bible from the perspective of Luther's paradigm of hiddenness and humbling is the *locus classicus* on the doctrine of election in Romans 9–11. It has often been asserted in modern New Testament studies that Paul does not actually intend to propagate a doctrine of predestination and election in Romans 9–11, but rather puzzles over ethnic Israel's apostasy in light of the revelation of Christ.[40] This is partially true, in that Israel's unbelief is the occasion for his discussion of election and predestination. Nevertheless, such a claim is ultimately misleading because Paul uses the question of Israel according to the flesh's corporate apostasy in order to launch a larger discussion of election by grace.

The main question that vexes Paul in Romans 9–11 is the one of the certainty of God's promises and the efficacy of the divine Word in relationship to election.[41] In the case of Israel according to the flesh, Paul's argument is ultimately that the Word of God has not failed to fulfill its purpose even if at the present it may appear to have done so: "But it is not as though the word of God has failed" (Rom 9:6). This appearance of failure is so vexing because the people of Israel are the subjects of so many prophesies of redemption in the Old Testament, and yet have largely rejected Christ, the single source of redemption. In order to explain how this can be true, Paul offers essentially two answers to the seeming rejection of the gospel by ethnic Israel.

First, God elects those whom he has predestined by grace alone. He is under no obligation to save anyone since we are the clay and he is the potter (Rom 9:19–21). Nevertheless, has fulfilled his promises to Israel by electing a remnant through the word, including Paul and implicitly his fellow ethnic Jewish Christians (Rom 11:1). Those whom God elects he does so through the word: "those whom he *predestined he also called, and those whom he called he also justified,* and those whom he justified he also glorified" (Rom 8:30, emphasis added). Therefore "not all are children of Abraham because they are his offspring ... but the children *of the promise*

---

40. See Florian Wilk and J. Ross Wagner, eds., *Between Gospel and Election: Explorations in the Interpretation of Romans 9–11* (Tübingen: Mohr Siebeck, 2010).

41. Thomas Schreiner *Paul, Apostle of God's Glory in Christ: A Pauline Theology* (Downers Grove, IL: InterVarsity Press, 2006), 244.

are counted as offspring" (Rom 9:7–8, emphasis added). Ultimately, those who are elected through the word of promise are elected in Christ (Eph 1:3), the rock set in Zion that is both a stumbling stone and a savior to those who encounter him in the promise (Rom 9:33).

Paul's second answer to the question of election is more complicated and paradoxical. It has often proved confusing to interpreters because it embodies the dynamic tension between Paul's insistence on the universality of grace in certain passages (Rom 5:18–19; 1 Tim 2:4) and the particularity of election in others (Rom 9:11–18). Paul discusses the gentiles who have come to faith and the Jews who have been hardened with reference to motif of the two sons in the Old Testament that we have discussed in an earlier chapter. God's election by grace is so radical in these stories that it contradicts the biblical or natural law of primogeniture: "though they were not yet born and had done nothing either good or bad—in order that God's purpose of election might continue, not because of works but because of him who calls— she was told, 'The older will serve the younger.' As it is written, 'Jacob I loved, but Esau I hated' " (Rom 9:11–13).[42]

In the great reversal of Esau and Jacob (as well as numerous others in the Old Testament: Cain and Abel, Ishmael and Isaac, Saul and David, Israel and Judah), the first-born son who has legal right to election has become rejected and those who have no legal standing have been elected. Paul seems to suggest that the same pattern has come to fruition in the era of the New Testament. Much as Jesus's selection of the unrighteous over the righteous in his ministry repeated the biblical pattern (Matt 20:16), so too the pattern has repeated in Paul's ministry: "What shall we say, then? That gentiles who did not pursue righteousness have attained it, that is, a righteousness that is by faith; but that Israel who pursued a law that would lead to righteousness did not succeed in reaching that law" (Rom 9:30–31). In a word, Israel the older brother who had the right to election by legal descent and Torah compliance has been passed over in favor of the unrighteous and disinherited gentiles.

Therefore, to be elect is to be rejected (ethnic Israel or Pharisees) and to be rejected is to be elect (Jesus or "sinners" or gentiles). In light of this pattern of rejection and acceptance Paul's invocation of the stories of

---

42. Lectures on Genesis (1535–1545), LW 4:386–88.

the patriarchs makes a great deal of sense (Rom 9:6–12). The first-born Ishmael and Esau were ultimately rejected and became gentiles, whereas Isaac and Jacob were elected to become the progenitors of the Jews. But Paul tells us that the great reversal happened yet again in his ministry. The Jews having become the elect ones are now in the position of the first-born son, whereas the rejected gentiles are in the position of the second-born sons. This is not because God has rejected Israel and wishes them to be damned (Rom 11:11). Rather their hardening is a necessary stage in humbling them. It is God's gracious purpose in humbling Israel to provoke their jealousy in seeing the gentiles saved: "So I ask, did they stumble in order that they might fall? By no means! Rather, through their trespass salvation has come to the Gentiles, so as to make Israel jealous" (Rom 11:11). Indeed, to be placed into the category of a rejected one makes one into an object of God's grace. It is part of what Luther would later call God's alien work that humbles to exalt (1 Sam 2:6–7).[43]

Indeed, it might be noted in Paul's contrast between Adam and Christ in Romans 5, there is an implicit suggestion that Jesus became the elect one by being placed into the category of being the rejected one. Paul asserts that the same principle holds for Israel according to the flesh. They must be humbled by God's alien work in order to move into the category of the elect and accepted ones: "Lest you be wise in your own sight, I do not want you to be unaware of this mystery, brothers: a partial hardening has come upon Israel, until the fullness of the Gentiles has come in. And in this way all Israel will be saved. ... So they too have now been disobedient in order that by the mercy shown to you they also may now receive mercy. *For God has consigned all to disobedience, that he may have mercy on all*" (Rom 11:25–26, 31–32 emphasis added). In other words, those who are placed in the rejected category and subjected to God's alien work suffer such work as a means of driving them to God's universal grace manifest in the gospel.

That God has "consigned all to disobedience, that he may have mercy on all" (Rom 11:32) makes sense of Paul's earlier talk of "vessels of mercy" and "vessels of wrath" (Rom 9:22). As we have seen, to be hardened is not to be one predestined to destruction as the Calvinistic theory of double

---

43. Heidelberg Disputation (1518), LW 31:50–51.

predestination claims. Hardening is part of God's alien work aimed at humbling so that he might do his proper work of grace. Paul of course allows that theoretically God would be perfectly fair in consigning some to eternal destruction: "*What if* God, desiring to show his wrath and to make known his power, has endured with much patience vessels of wrath prepared for destruction" (Rom 9:22, emphasis added).[44] Nevertheless, although God is the creator and is well within his right to do as he wishes with his creation, Paul is quite clear that the hardening of Israel and that of humanity in general is ultimately intended to result in their salvation (Rom 11:25–32).

Ultimately, Paul does not resolve the tension between the universality of God's grace and the particularity of God's election, but humbly bows before God's hidden purposes. Although it is God's purpose that all Israel and humanity be saved, Paul is also quite clear that not all will be saved, and that God has elected only a few. Indeed, it could also be noted that Pharaoh (mentioned in the discussion of hardening in 9:17) did not repent and God's hardening resulted in his ultimate destruction. Hence, at the end of his discussion of election, Paul allows the mystery of why some are saved and not others to stand as a mystery. Instead of speculating about God above his Word, he breaks into a doxology regarding the incomprehensibility of the hidden God's judgments: "Oh, the depth of the riches and wisdom and knowledge of God! How unsearchable are his judgments and how inscrutable his ways!" (Rom 11:33).

THREE LIGHTS: A TRINITARIAN
THEODICY OF FAITH

In light of our discussion of the hidden and revealed God, what to many has seemed like an outright contradiction in Luther and the Formula of Concord's assertion of both the reality of predestination and the universality of God's grace may conceptualized more coherently as a description of the *aporia* between God preached (i.e., universal grace) and God not preached (i.e., God's inscrutable eternal election). In that God works all things by his hidden will, all who gain salvation do so only because he

---

44. Arland Hultgren, *Paul's Letter to the Romans: A Commentary* (Grand Rapids: Eerdmans, 2011), 368.

has elected them from eternity (Rom 8:30; Eph 1:4). Nevertheless, God as he has been revealed to us in Christ has opened his heart to the whole world on the cross (John 12:32; 19:31–4), so it must be earnestly believed that God's grace is universal and that he wills the salvation of all (John 3:16; 1 Tim 2:4). To look past the external word of grace and attempt to peer into the intentions of the hidden God in order to resolve the seeming contradiction between these claims is to remove oneself from the sphere of grace and place oneself into the realm of the hidden God of wrath. The strength of Luther and the Lutheran symbolic writings' position on predestination and universal grace is that it takes the fact that the New Testament makes both assertions with the utmost seriousness and does not attempt to rationalize such statement with ad hoc exegetical tricks.

In light of this, from the perspective of the Lutheran paradigm, the seemingly intractable Calvinist and Arminian debates possess essentially three problems. First, Calvinists accept the statements of Scripture that affirm predestination and the bondage of the will, but then ignore or explain away statements about God's universal grace. By contrast, Arminians affirm the passages of the Bible that deal with universal grace, and then ignore or explain away statements about predestination and the bondage of the human will.

Second, both Calvinists and Arminians focus their discussion on God in himself (*Deus ipse*), and not how God has presented himself through his creaturely masks. Calvinists extrapolate from the fact that some are saved and others are not to the conclusion that God has a plan above and beyond his external word to predestine some to salvation and others to damnation. They thereby read God's intention over and above how he presents himself in the means of grace and ignore the sincerity of God's universal grace manifest in the gospel. By contrast, Arminians extrapolate from the fact that the call of the gospel is universal to the conclusion that God must be present as grace to all people and not simply in the means of grace. In light of this, they conclude that the reason some are saved and not others is that some appropriately respond to grace and others do not.

Last, both the Calvinist and Arminian paradigms result in significant pastoral problems. Both groups ultimately drive sinners back to the law through speculations about the hidden God. The Calvinist is driven back to works through speculating about God's predestinating act above his word of grace. Because the external word is not meant for all who hear it but only the elect, the Calvinist can never be certain that the word of the gospel was meant for him. As a result, he cannot help but try to prove his election not by looking to the external word, but by the *syllogismus practicus* and its functional legalism. Likewise, the Arminian must convince himself that he has genuinely received the word. The requirement to sincerely receive the gift of grace thereby becomes a new law with no practical difference from the *syllogismus practicus*.

In contrast to the Calvinist and Arminian alternatives, the sacramentality of the word makes it possible to give sinners the full assurance of grace through the comfort both of election and the universality of grace. Indeed, the assertion of both the universality of grace and the particular grace of election is merely to give a theological account of the phenomenology of divine Word of grace. On the one hand, there is no gap between God's will for sinners and what the word says. God's promise of grace is universal and is meant for all those who hear it. Second, because God's Word does what it speaks forth, the promise of justification and election present in the gospel can be relied upon to fulfill its purpose. The word promises salvation and because God immutably rules all things, it will bring those who look for grace there to the kingdom of heaven.[45]

Although historically orthodox Lutherans have rightly confessed the seeming incongruity between the universality of grace and the particularity of election as a paradox of the faith,[46] they have not always explicated this mystery in a coherent manner. This appears to be part of the reason that the generation after the Formula of Concord so easily fell into the *intuitu fidei* heresy. Perhaps a better approach to conceptualizing the tension within the Lutheran doctrine of grace is to view it from a Trinitarian perspective.

The late Wolfhart Pannenberg made an intriguing suggestion regarding how to conceptualize divine hiddenness and the manner in which it relates to the doctrine of grace in Luther's theology. According to Pannenberg, perhaps one way to think of the paradox of hidden and revealed in

---

45. Paulson, *Hiddenness, Evil, and Predestination*, 57–158; Pieper, *Christian Dogmatics*, 3:89–103.

46. Pieper, *Christian Dogmatics*, 3:473–506; Pieper, *Conversion and Election: A Plea for a United Lutheranism in America* (Watseka, IL: Just and Sinner, 2015).

Luther's thought is to recognize that apart from the final vision of God's unity at the eschaton, there is a certain degree of tension between the temporal works of the persons of the economic Trinity.[47] Pannenberg's suggestion has a great deal of merit. In order to observe how the problem of divine hiddenness can be conceptualized within the framework of the economic Trinity, it would perhaps be helpful to review the last section of *The Bondage of the Will* in which Luther speaks according to the late medieval scheme of the "three lights." These three lights are the light of nature, grace, and glory.[48]

Luther begins with the "light of nature," wherein humanity knows of God's existence and his commandments but is then uncertain as to why evil befalls the righteous.[49] This question is answered by the "light of grace," which reveals the reality of original sin, as well as its solution in the cross and empty tomb. God has redeemed the righteous in Christ and the wicked will be judged in the next life. Therefore, God cannot be judged to be unloving or unjust in his application of the law.[50] Although the light of grace reveals God's love and the full depth of sin, it nevertheless does not solve the problem of election. That is to say, in light of the love of God in Christ and the universality of sin, it appears incongruous that the Spirit works faith in some, but not others. At the eschaton in the "light of glory," the problem of election will be resolved as easily as the problem of human suffering by the "light of grace."[51]

It should not go unnoticed that the three lights correspond to the works of the economic Trinity as outlined by the Apostle's Creed: Father/creation, Son/revelation of grace, Spirit/election to glory. Indeed, following Luther's theology of God's masks, we could even speak of each as a mask (*larva*) of the given person of the Trinity. From the human perspective, the activities of the Father are manifest in his mask of creation. Indeed, Luther says of the Father: "The Father gives *himself to us, with heaven and earth and all the*

---

47. See Pannenberg, *Systematic Theology*, 1:339–41.
48. The Bondage of the Will (1525), LW 33:289–92.
49. The Bondage of the Will (1525), LW 33:291.
50. The Bondage of the Will (1525), LW 33:291–92. Note that Luther does not explicitly mention the work of Christ, but he speaks of the "good and evil." Seen within the wider context of his theology, it is clear that the "good" who receive eternal life are those justified by Christ.
51. The Bondage of the Will (1525), LW 33:292.

creatures, in order that they may serve us and benefit us."[52] In the same way, the acitivities of the Spirit in his mask of the means of grace often seem in tension with the work of the Son, his created mask being his incarnate humanity.[53]

Although Luther speaks of the problems present in the light of nature as being resolved in the light of grace, it should be noticed that certain tensions between the first and second article nevertheless remain. Through the veil of the law and creation, God works the death and destruction of sinners (Rom 1:18; 6:23). From the perspective of fallen humanity, creation appears to be a realm of wrath that crushes creatures in a seemingly haphazard fashion (i.e., Job, Ecclesiastes, psalms of lamentation, etc.).

The unilateral love of the gospel also entails the fulfillment of the law and the purpose of the original creation, thereby unveiling the unity of God as creator and redeemer. Nevertheless, it does not fully resolve how God's unrelenting activity of wrath within the realm of creation and law can exist alongside and in total unity with God's unilateral love in the person of his Son in the incarnation and cross. In other words, it is difficult to fully rationally coordinate how it is that the God who redeems unilaterally in Christ simultaneously also applies the law without mercy in the realm of the created orders. Likewise, with regard to the third article, although the basis of the means of grace is the universal love of the Son, from a human perspective the work of the Spirit through them seems arbitrary and uneven. All are equally sinful, yet only a certain number come to faith by the electing power of grace operating in word and sacrament.

The claim that has often been advanced (most notably by Eberhard Jüngel)[54] that the doctrine of the hidden God means that ultimately another sinister God lurks behind the revelation of Christ. Nevertheless, it should be recognized that Luther holds that the work of the Son is central to revealing who God truly is and what his intention is for humanity. In the Large Catechism, Luther emphasizes that the Son and his universal love

---

52. Confession Concerning the Lord's Supper (1528), LW 37:366. Emphasis added.

53. See Luther's comment about Christ's humanity being the "hindquarters of God" here: Heidelberg Disputation (1518), LW 31:52. "Visiblia et posteriora Dei."

54. Eberhard Jüngel, "The Revelation of the Hiddenness of God," in *Theological Essays II*, trans. Arnold Neufeldt-Fast and John Webster (Edinburgh: T&T Clark, 1989), 120–44. Also see a more recent version of this charge in Carl Trueman, *Grace Alone: Salvation as a Gift of God* (Grand Rapids: Zondervan, 2017), 130–31.

are a true revelation of the inner heart of God: "For ... we could never attain to the knowledge of the grace and favor of the Father except through the Lord Christ, who is a mirror of the paternal heart, outside of whom we see nothing but an angry and terrible Judge. But of Christ we could know nothing either, unless it had been revealed by the Holy Ghost."[55]

Therefore, the Son's universal atonement for sin on the cross and his revelation of the Father's universal declaration of justification in his resurrection (Rom 4:25, 5:18; 1 John 2:2)[56] is the true and definitive unveiling of the character of God. The hiddenness of God entails not a God behind the revelation of the Son, but rather the seeming (but, ultimately unreal) tension between the economic works of the Father and Spirit with those of the Son. Nevertheless, as Luther's statement in the Large Catechism proves, the revelation of God in the Son is the true unveiling of the Father's heart (John 14:9), even if the manner in which God's manifestation of himself outside of revelation appears incongruous with the loving character of God revealed in Christ. Faith clings to God's revelation in Christ and trusts that the activities of the Father and the Spirit are coherent with the universal love of the Son even if they appear at times not to be.

Hence, under the veil of divine hiddenness and the false conjectures of fallen human reason, there is an *aporia* between the activities of the Father and the Spirit and with the universal and unconditional love revealed in the Son. In light of this, human reason inevitably tries to rationalistically harmonize these disparate activities and peer into the hiddenness of God. Nevertheless, all rationalistic theodicies ultimately fail because they try to justify God's actions on the basis of the law. This approach demands that God justify himself, when it is humans that need justification.[57] Moreover, because God's will is not exhausted by the law, God can never be made completely explicable on the basis of the law. The good news ultimately consists in the fact that although the law is God's holy and eternal will,

---

55. LC II.66; *Concordia Triglotta*, 695.

56. "He [God the Father] also condemned it, in that He punished our sins in Christ, which were imposed on Him and imputed to Him as to a bondsman. So also, by the very act of raising Him from the dead, He absolved Him from our sins that were imputed to Him, and consequently also absolves us in Him, so that, in this way, the resurrection of Christ may be both he cause and the pledge and the complement of our justification." Johann Gerhard, *Annotations on the First Six Chapters of the St. Paul's Epistle to the Romans*, trans. Paul Rydecki (Malone, TX: Repristination, 2014), 214.

57. Commentary on Psalm 51 (1532), LW 12:311.

God possesses possibilities that transcend the law and that are manifest in the atoning work of Christ.

Instead of creating a rationalistic or legalistic theodicy,[58] Christians must cling to the gospel-promise and operate on the basis of a theodicy of faith.[59] On the basis of faith in the promise, the believer trusts that the divine love manifest in Christ has revealed the hidden coherence of the triune being in a preliminary sense in the means of grace. Only at the eschaton will the full coherence of the works of the one God be revealed to believers. Faith possesses the full confidence of the sacramental Word of God, in which the Son has revealed the Father's true heart to faith through the power of the Spirit. By holding onto the sacramental word, faith comes into contact with the objectified gracious electing will of God and can be certain of salvation.

CONCLUSION

Having examined the nature of predestination worked out through the sacramental word, we now turn to the doctrine of the sacraments and their relationship to the article of justification. As we will see, historically Protestantism has treated the concept of sacraments as difficult to relate to the article of justification. Nevertheless, sacraments and sacramental realism are central to maintaining the objectivity of the message of the gospel and the justification it brings.

---

58. Gottfried von Leibniz, *Theodicy*, trans. E.M. Huggard (New York: Cosmo Classics, 2010).

59. Hinlicky, *Beloved Community*, 72. Though the general thrust of Hinlicky's idea is correct, we should note that we do not endorse all details.

CHAPTER 14

Justification and the Sacraments:
The General Concept of Sacraments

Having discussed election, we will now address the important role of the sacraments in relationship to the doctrine of justification. Central to Luther's account of justification by the word is the reality of the sacraments. According to Luther, although the word alone is sufficient to work justification and create faith, God in his great mercy has given us a multitude of means of grace to preach the gospel to us. These include both auditory words (such as words of evangelical encouragement among believers, biblically based preaching, and absolution) as well as visible words (such as baptism and the Lord's Supper). Not only are these multiple modes by which God proclaims the grace of Christ to humanity a manifestation of God's generosity, but the visible words of the gospel (sacraments) play an important role in maintaining the objectivity of the promise of salvation.[1]

Throughout the history of Protestant theology, the assurance of the justifying word has not infrequently been undermined by the emphasis on the authenticity of faith. It has often been the line of reasoning in Protestant theology that one cannot merely look to the gospel-promise because the condition of appropriating the gospel-promise is having an

---

1. SA III.3; *Concordia Triglotta*, 491.

authentic faith. Inevitably, this leads to the question of what secondary signs validate the authenticity of one's faith. As we saw in the discussion of the history of the Lutheran theology, even those who accepted Luther's sacramental account of the word can, and invariably do, fall into this trap of worrying about the sincerity of their own faith.

Due to the *simul* of Christian existence (that is, Christians are "at the same time saint and sinner," *simul justus et peccator*),[2] the temptation of returning to the self-incurvature of reflective faith is ever present. That is to say, because even true believers now possess a sinful nature, they are subject to the temptation of trusting in their own works or the quality of their faith over what the external word tells them. Such a temptation connects with not only the root sin of unbelief, but what Luther called "Enthusiasm."[3] Enthusiasm means "God withinism."[4] An enthusiast looks inward to his interior thoughts and feelings so as to discover God's will for him, rather than the external Word of God. This tendency can undermine biblical authority, but it is also the source of human doubt in the promise of the gospel.

Because of fallen humanity's orientation toward unbelief and enthusiasm (*incurvatus in se*), temptation to doubt one's own proper reception of the word will invariably arise. When temptation arises, faith in the word must inevitably seek a secondary support in refocusing the believer on the objectivity of grace rather than the subjectivity of their own disposition. Such a secondary support should inculcate the objectivity of grace to the individual believer in a tangible manner and break the focus of the believer on their own inner reception of the external word. This secondary support for faith can be found in the sacraments of the New Testament.

Disappointingly, most forms of Protestantism have failed to maintain the believer's focus on Christ and the word because of their rejection of sacramental realism. Indeed, most (though not all) Protestants rejected

2. See Wilhelm Christe, *Gerechte Sünder: Eine Untersuchung zu Martin Luthers "Simul iustus et peccator"* (Leipzig: Evangelische Verlagsanstalt, 2014).

3. SA III.8; *Concordia Triglotta*, 497.

4. Steven Paulson, *Hidden in the Cross*, vol. 2 of Luther's Outlaw God (Minneapolis: Fortress, 2019), 350.

sacramental realism in favor of sacramental symbolicism or spiritualism.[5] Since both sacramental symbolicism and spiritualism disconnect the *res* from the *signum* in the sacraments, much of the Protestant tradition has denied believers the tangible secondary assurance of God's grace that sacramental realism provides. Believers who reject sacramental realism therefore have had to seek secondary assurance apart from the sacraments in moral athleticism or spiritual experience, thereby exacerbating the problem of unbelief and self-incurvature. Only if the sacraments objectively contain grace can they function as an antidote to religious subjectivism. They perform this task by shifting the focus away from the interior and spiritual reception of grace to grace's tangible external embodiment in a physical medium.

In light of the Protestant tradition's emphasis on the authenticity of faith and its fruits, Catholics have often charged Protestant spirituality with an inappropriate interiority and subjectivism.[6] This charge has some merit to it when applied to Protestants who endorse sacramental symbolicism or spiritualism. Faith that does not cling to the tangible presence of the risen Jesus in the means of grace must invariably accept the authority of its own subjectivity. Unmoored to the sacraments, justification by faith drifts into a form of subjective certainty of one's own psychological state of belief or unbelief. Sacraments make grace tangible and help maintain the life of faith as something objective, thereby de-centering the self of the believer.

LUTHER ON THE NATURE OF THE SACRAMENTS IN LIGHT OF THE REFORMATION PRINCIPLES

One of the reasons that Protestantism has often undermined the spiritual assurance given by the sacraments is that most Protestant traditions have either consciously or unconsciously seen the sacraments as standing in tension with the gospel of justification through faith. It could be argued that the reason for this lies in how the sacraments were

---

5. See the discussion in James F. White, *The Sacraments in Protestant Practice and Faith* (Nashville: Abingdon, 1999).

6. Louis Bouyer, *The Spirit and Forms of Protestantism*, trans. A. V. Littledale (Princeton: Scepter, 2004), 189–90, 206, 254–55.

practiced and thought about in the late medieval church. As its starting point, Protestantism rejected the medieval doctrine of the sacraments in accordance with *sola fide* and *sola gratia*.

The standard medieval teaching on the sacraments was refined in the twelfth century by figures like Peter Lombard and was made official church teaching by the Fourth Lateran Council (1215)[7] and reaffirmed by the Council of Trent (1545–1563) after the Reformation was underway.[8] Lombard and the medieval theologians after him held that the sacraments were spiritually effective signs that genuinely contained grace.[9] Although there was a disagreement as to whether or not just some or all of the sacraments had been instituted by Christ,[10] the medieval church affirmed that when an ordained priest spoke the words and performed the ritual acts authorized by God in the sacrament, there was a divine power operative in those words that made the rite a vehicle of grace.[11] Therefore, it should be noted that Luther's belief in the efficacious divine power of the word was not entirely novel but stands in continuity with the medieval church teaching on the sacraments.[12]

Moreover, because the sacrament were effective signs, they worked simply by virtue of being performed (*ex opere operato*).[13] As long as a believer who received them was not in a state of mortal sin, the sacraments would communicate grace regardless of whether or not one acknowledged the presence of grace in them.[14] By analogy, one must simply be willing to receive a medicine in order to receive the benefits of wellness derived

---

7. Bernhard Lohse, *A Short History of Christian Doctrine*, trans. F. Ernst Stoeffer (Philadelphia: Fortress, 1966), 150–55,

8. Stephen Tomkins, *A Short History of Christianity* (Oxford: Lion Hudson, 2005), 154.

9. Peter Lombard, *The Sentences*, 4 vols., trans. Giulio Silano (Toronto: Pontifical Institute of Medieval Studies, 2007–2010), 4:4

10. ST, IIIa, q. 64, art. 3; Thomas Aquinas, *Summa Theologiae*, trans. Fathers of the Dominican Provence (Notre Dame, IN: Ave Maria, 1981), 2363; Van Nieuwenhove, *An Introduction to Medieval Theology*, 158.

11. ST, IIIa, q. 64, art. 1; Aquinas, *Summa Theologiae*, 2360–61; Hägglund, 193.

12. See the discussion of continuities in Mickey Mattox, "Sacraments in the Lutheran Reformation," in *Oxford Handbook of Sacramental Theology*, ed. Hans Boersma and Matthew Levering (Oxford: Oxford University Press, 2015), 269–82.

13. Lombard, *The Sentences*, 3:170; Alister McGrath, *Christian Theology: An Introduction* (Malden, MA: Wiley–Blackwell, 2011), 406.

14. ST, IIIa, q. 79, art. 3; Aquinas, *Summa Theologiae*, 2476.

from it. One does not ultimately have to believe that the medicine will be effective in their particular case.[15]

To many this concept of sacramental efficacy may appear to be utterly mechanical. Nevertheless, following Augustine, the medieval church held that the principle of *ex opere operato* (by the work performed) guarded the gracious character of the sacraments. In other words, if faith or other dispositions were required to make the sacraments effective, then one would only receive grace from them on the condition of a human work and not on the basis of God's gracious communication within them.[16]

Most of the Protestant Reformers of the sixteenth century (including Luther) drew the opposite conclusion from the medieval church regarding the gracious character of *ex opere operato*. From the perspective of Reformers, the principle of *ex opere operato* made the performance of the sacraments themselves into a work that gave grace.[17] That is to say, the act of performance was made into a condition to gain grace.[18] Although it very well could be argued that this interpretation is not entirely fair to the intention of the medieval theologians (a question that we do not have the space to engage at length), it cannot be denied that in terms of late medieval popular piety and the abusive practices it gave rise to (i.e., private Masses, Masses for the dead, etc.) there was much truth to the critique.[19]

Luther began to significantly reformulate the doctrine of the sacraments in his treatise *On the Babylonian Captivity of the Church* of 1521.[20] Luther understood that the late medieval conception of the sacraments as spiritual medicine that made one better irrespective of one's belief or unbelief was unsustainable in light of the reformational principles of *sola gratia*, *sola fide*, and *sola scriptura*. On the one hand, following the principle of

15. ST, IIIa, q. 62, art. 1; Aquinas, *Summa Theologiae*, 2346.

16. Alister McGrath, *Christian Theology: The Basics* (Malden, MA: Wiley–Blackwell, 2011), 167–69.

17. The Adoration of the Sacrament (1523), LW 36:288–89.

18. Peter Walter, "Sacraments in the Council of Trent and Sixteenth-Century Catholic Theology," in *Oxford Handbook of Sacramental Theology*, 316. See On the Babylonian Captivity of the Church (1520), LW 36:67.

19. C. Scott Dixon, *Contesting the Reformation* (Malden, MA: Wiley–Blackwell, 2012), 194–95. Also see Derek Rivard, *Blessing the World: Ritual and Lay Piety in Medieval Religion* (Washington, DC: Catholic University of America Press, 2008).

20. See Luther's critique of the medieval sacramental system in Brian Brewer, *Martin Luther and the Seven Sacraments: A Contemporary Protestant Reappraisal* (Grand Rapids: Baker Academic, 2017).

sola scriptura, Luther pointed out[21] that many of the seven sacraments that Peter Lombard and the Fourth Lateran Council had affirmed as means of grace had no basis in the Bible at all (confirmation, extreme unction), or were biblically sanctioned, but not as channels of grace (ordination, matrimony).[22] Sacraments must be divinely mandated and have a promise from God attached to them.[23] Without a command and promise recorded in Scripture, one could not draw the conclusion that a particular sacrament would communicate grace.[24]

For those within the Roman Catholic fold who would object that sacraments like extreme unction and confirmation are biblically mandated (according to traditional Catholic exegesis of James 5 and Acts 8), Luther further clarifies in his later *Against the Thirty-Two Articles of the Louvain Theologists* (1545) that sacraments must have a specific dominical command and promise attached to them. For this reason, confirmation cannot be a sacrament as asserted by the theological faculty at Louvain: "That confirmation is a sacrament is asserted without the authority of the Word. And the statement of the Louvainists that it was instituted by Christ is a lie."[25] By contrast regarding absolution: "We gladly confess penance to be a sacrament ... *for on account of Christ it has the promise and faith of the remission of sins.*"[26] Hence sacraments are established by Christ's command and promise alone. Simply pointing to a text where a practice (for example, anointing people with oil) is commended by the New Testament is inadequate. There must be a specific dominical promise of grace attached to a sacrament in order to make it valid and efficacious.

Moreover, invoking the Augustinian distinction between validity and efficacy, Luther affirmed with the medieval church that the biblically sanctioned sacraments (baptism, the Lord's Supper) were objectively valid when performed.[27] Nevertheless, in light of the principle of *sola fide,* the

---

21. On the Babylonian Captivity of the Church (1520), LW 36:18.

22. The Adoration of the Sacrament (1523), LW 36: 302–3.

23. The Adoration of the Sacrament (1523), LW 36:303. The Babylonian Captivity of the Church (1520), LW 36:91–123.

24. The Babylonian Captivity of the Church (1520), LW 36:65–66.

25. Against the Thirty-Two Articles of the Louvain Theologist (1545), LW 34:356.

26. Against the Thirty-Two Articles of the Louvain Theologist (1545), LW 34:356. Emphasis added.

27. The Private Mass and the Consecration of Priests (1533), LW 38:200–201.

sacraments were not salvific unless the promise of grace connected with them was trusted in.[28] In the same way, while the auditory word of the gospel is objectively true whether believed or not, it is not salvific unless received by faith.[29] This is because the sacraments are a visible sign (i.e., the Augustinian "visible words")[30] that give sinners in a physical and tangible form what they received in an auditory form in confession and absolution and the preaching of the promise of the gospel.[31]

On the other hand, like the early and medieval church, Luther affirmed sacramental realism.[32] The sacraments are not mere symbols or representations of the gospel but give the reality of which they speak and thereby are genuinely capable of creating (baptism) and sustaining (the Lord's Supper) justifying faith and sanctification.[33] Much like his concepts of absolution and preached word that we have already examined, Luther's view of the Word of God connected with his belief in the unity of the divine Word in the human word in the proclamation of the sacraments. Indeed, as we saw in an earlier chapter, Luther's understanding of how human language and physical objects can be a vehicle of the divine is rooted in his fundamentally Cyrillian account of *communicatio idiomatum*.[34] Just as in the Cyrillian tradition of Christology there is a full of the communication divine to the human in the person of Christ (what later Lutheran theology called the *genus majestaticum*), so too, in the word and sacrament ministry of the church the divine Word is present and active in the human word.[35]

Luther implicitly utilizes the Ockhamist concept of "covenantal causality" to explain how God binds himself to act in a certain manner in

28. On the Babylonian Captivity of the Church (1520), LW 36:66–67.

29. Sermons on the Gospel of John (1538), LW 22:382.

30. Augustine, *Tractates in the Gospel of John*, 80.3; NPNF¹, 7:344.

31. Lectures on Habakkuk (1526), LW 19:192–93; The Sacrament of the Body and Blood of Christ-Against the Fanatics (1526), LW 36:348–49.

32. Oswald Bayer, *Martin Luther's Theology: A Contemporary Interpretation*, trans. Thomas Trapp (Grand Rapids: Eerdmans, 2008), 264–72.

33. Bernhard Lohse, *Martin Luther's Theology: Its Historical and Systematic Development* (Minneapolis: Fortress, 1999), 299–313.

34. See Cyril of Alexandria, *On the Unity of Christ*, trans. John Anthony McGuckin (Crestwood, NY: St. Vladimir's Seminary, 1995).

35. See Steiger, "The *Communicatio Idiomatum*," 125–58.

relationship to certain established means (*de potentia ordinate*).[36] God has promised to become present and active with the words that he has given to the church (i.e., "I baptize you in the name of the Father, Son, and Holy Spirit," "This is my body," "This is my blood") in connection with certain elements (water, bread, wine).[37] Because of their efficacious power, the words attached to the sacraments are for Luther both consecratory and promissory. Just as Christ is present and efficacious in the words spoken over the sacramental elements (that is, a *communicatio idiomatum* between the divine and human words), so too he becomes present and active in the physical elements of the sacraments. For the Reformer, there is a kind of *communicatio idiomatum* in the form of sacramental union (*unio sacramentalis*) between the Spirit and water in baptism, and the flesh and blood of the risen Jesus and bread and wine in the Lord's Supper.[38]

In the sacramental elements of water, bread, and wine, Christ makes himself available in all his salvific benefits to faith. It is by faith in the promise attached to the sacraments that the benefits of Christ are received.[39] Luther delighted in citing Jesus's words in the longer ending of Mark: "Whoever believes and is baptized will be saved, but whoever does not believe will be condemned" (Mark 16:16).[40] Likewise, regarding the Lord's Supper, Luther (and the Lutheran tradition after him) cited the words of Paul: "For anyone who eats and drinks without discerning the body [i.e., not believing the words of institution] eats and drinks judgment on himself" (1 Cor 11:29).[41]

Luther's theological modification of the sacraments in light of the principles of *sola fide* raises an interesting question: If the auditory means of grace justify and save, then why are physical ones necessary? As we have already noted, one answer that Luther gives in the Smalkald Articles of

---

36. Alister McGrath, *Luther's Theology of the Cross: Martin Luther's Theological Breakthrough* (Oxford: Wiley Blackwell, 1990), 59.

37. That These Words of Christ, This is My Body, Still Stand Firm Against the Fanatics (1527), LW 37:68–69.

38. Gordon Jensen, "Luther and the Lord's Supper," in Kolb, Dingel, and Batka, *The Oxford Handbook of Martin Luther's Theology*, ed. Robert Kolb, Irene Dingel, and L'Ubomir Batka (Oxford: Oxford University Press, 2014), 328. Also see SC IV, VI; *Concordia Triglotta*, 551, 555.

39. On the Babylonian Captivity of the Church (1520), LW 36:67.

40. SC IV; *Concordia Triglotta*, 551.

41. On the Babylonian Captivity of the Church (1520), LW 36:43.

1537 is that God in his generous love gives a multitude of ways of inculcating his grace and forgiveness to human beings.[42] In *The Sacrament: Against the Fanatics* of 1526, Luther gives a rationale for the Lord's Supper that as a principle could be applied to the sacraments in general:

> When I preach his [Christ's] death, it is in a public sermon in the congregation, in which I am addressing myself to no one individually; who grasp it, grasps it. But when I distribute the sacrament, I designate it for the individual who is receiving it; I give him Christ's body and blood that he may have forgiveness, obtained through his death and preached in the congregation. This is something more than the congregational sermon; for although the same thing is present in the sermon as in the sacrament, here there is the advantage that it is directed at definite individuals. In the sermon one does not point out or portray any particular person, but in the sacrament it is given to you and to me in particular, so that the sermon comes to be our own. For when I say: "This is the body, which is given for you, this is the blood which is poured out for you for the forgiveness of sins," I am therefore commemorating him; I proclaim and announce his death. Only it is not done publicly in the congregation but is directed at you alone.[43]

In other words, for Luther, the Eucharist (and by implication baptism as well), confirms for the individual what the word universally proclaims. The word of the gospel is addressed to everyone in the congregation, and therefore it is possible to worry that this promise may not apply to you as an individual or that you have not genuinely received it by faith. Nevertheless, the Lord's Supper contains within it the same promise and presence of the risen Jesus as the sermon. For Luther, words are sacraments and sacraments are a kind of word. The difference between the sermon and the sacrament is that the latter is applied to the individual who directly receives it. When reflective faith invariably worries about whether one has individually received Jesus and his promise of forgiveness, the believer may rely on the sacraments to give them assurance.

---

42. SA III.3; *Concordia Triglotta*, 491.
43. The Sacrament of the Body and Blood of Christ-Against the Fanatics (1526), LW 36:348–49.

There can be here no doubt that you have personally received the promise in the form of the sacrament since it was you as an individual who heard the promise and consumed the elements. By receiving the eucharistic elements, the promise and presence of Jesus are given to you in a tangible and physical way that draws you out of your subjectivity and enthusiasm (Did I truly believe? Did I truly receive the promise?) to the objectivity of the gospel.

HISTORIC PROTESTANTISM'S
DIFFICULTIES WITH SACRAMENTS

From a certain perspective, many Protestants have upheld the popular medieval conception of sacraments as essentially rituals that humans perform. As we have seen, this is at odds with how Luther viewed the sacraments as visible sermons of the gospel. For the Wittenberg Reformation, the problem was not that sacraments were actually legalistic ritual-works in themselves, but that scholastic speculations and popular medieval piety had made them into works when they were proclamations of grace. By maintaining the popular medieval conception of the sacraments as ritual works, most forms of Protestantism not only unwedded them from justification, but largely made them superfluous.

By maintaining the understanding of the sacraments as ritual-works, many Protestants place their thinking about the sacraments in a trajectory whereby to maintain *sola fide* and *sola gratia* they need to reject the sacraments as genuine means of grace. That is to say, if one's basic assumption remains that the sacraments are "works we perform," they cannot be effective signs or have anything to do with salvation since that would mean that works would produce grace. Hence, according to this line of reasoning, if the sacraments genuinely contain God's grace, they nullify the gospel. Instead of being saved by faith alone, we would gain divine grace by "doing works," i.e. participating in the sacraments. Hence, to harmonize the sacraments with *sola fide* and *sola gratia*, a number of Protestant traditions have argued that the sacraments must be something other than mediums of genuine grace.

A prime example of this impulse can be found in the work of Ulrich Zwingli. Zwingli argued that the sacraments were ritual works that outwardly expressed the interior experience of faith in a public and symbolic form.[44] He made this judgment partially on the basis of the etymology of the Latin word *sacramentum* being "oath" or "pledge."[45] This argument proved theologically and linguistically strained. Although the word *sacramentum* generally (though not always) appears in the Vulgate as a translation of the Greek word *mysterion*[46] (a term the patristic tradition after the third century often applied to the sacraments),[47] neither *sacramentum* or its Greek equivalent are ever applied to baptism and the Lord's Supper in the Bible (whether in the Vulgate or original Greek). Hence, using an extra-biblical term (*sacramentum*) to deduce the meaning of a biblical practice makes little sense. As a result, whereas Luther saw the sacraments as being the mediums whereby the risen Jesus preached the promise of the gospel to sinners, Zwingli insisted that the sacraments were works performed in order to publicly "pledge" before others their identity as Christians.[48] The end result was that Zwingli made the sacraments into a form of ritual law that provided no assurance of salvation.

Ultimately Zwingli's view of the sacraments faces the same difficulty that would plague the subsequent Anabaptist and Baptist traditions regarding the nature of the sacraments. If the sacraments are ritual works that publicly testify to faith, are they not superfluous? First, it is ultimately difficult to explain why one needs to publicly testify to their faith through a ritual. Why should others be interested in whether or not you as an individual personally have faith? Moreover, even if the sacraments are ritual works designed to testify to faith, one runs into the further problem that non-believers can participate in the sacraments and pretend to testify to faith that they in actuality do not have. Therefore, the sacraments as public testimonies become ambiguous signs since it is unclear as to whether or not they actually testify to genuine faith. As a result, one cannot help but

---

44. Amy Nelson Burnett, *Debating the Sacraments: Print and Authority in the Early Reformation* (Oxford: Oxford University Press, 2019), 101.

45. Ulrich Zwingli, *Commentary on True and False Religion*, ed. Samuel Macauley Jackson and Clarence Nevin Heller (Durham, NC: Labyrinth, 1981), 180–84.

46. Leonard J. Vander Zee, *Christ, Baptism and the Lord's Supper: Recovering the Sacraments for Evangelical Worship* (Downers Grove, IL: InterVarsity Press, 2004), 28.

47. John Mueller, *Theological Foundations: Concepts and Methods for Understanding Christian Faith* (Winona, MN: St. Mary's, 2007), 182.

48. Zwingli, *Commentary on True and False Religion*, 184.

draw the conclusion that the ritual or symbolic concept of the sacraments effectively makes them pointless.

The Anabaptist tradition inherited much of Zwingli's thinking on the issue of sacraments. It in turn exerted influence on the much later Baptist tradition, and therefore a number of popular Evangelical traditions in the Anglo-American world.[49] Many (though not all) of the early Anabaptist leaders were Zwingli's followers[50] and drove his logic of the sacraments as being public means of professing faith to their logical conclusion by rejecting infant baptism. If infants could not consciously profess their faith, would not then infant baptism represent an inconsistency in Zwingli's position which held that sacraments were means of publicly professing faith? Would not the belief that infants should be baptized maintain a magical conception of the sacraments as physical vehicles of grace? Anabaptist theology argued an unequivocal yes to both of these questions.[51]

To counter many of these aforementioned Anabaptist objections, Zwingli developed a larger theory regarding the place of sacraments in the history of salvation. In a debate with the Anabaptist theologian Balthasar Hubmaier,[52] Zwingli countered that infant baptism made sense because the sacraments were covenantal signs of the New Testament that fulfilled covenantal signs of the Old Testament. Baptism was a fulfillment of circumcision (as Col 2:11–12 appears to teach), and therefore just as infants in the Old Testaments could be pronounced covenant members through their parents and be circumcised, so too children of Christians in the era of the New Testament could also be pronounced covenant members through a public ceremony.[53] Although the mainstream of the Reformed

---

49. James Leo Garrett, *Baptist Theology: A Fourth-Century Study* (Macon, GA: Mercer University Press, 2009), 8–16.

50. William Estep, *The Anabaptist Story: An Introduction to Sixteenth-Century Anabaptism* (Grand Rapids: Eerdmans, 1996), 11–21.

51. See the summary of Anabaptist views of baptism in Hans-Jurgen Goertz, *The Anabaptists*, trans. Trevor Johnson (London: Taylor & Francis, 2013), 68–84.

52. Torsten Bergsten, *Balthasar Hubmaier: Seine Stellung zu Reformation und Täufertum, 1521–1528* (Kassel: Verlag, 1961); Cristof Windhors, *Tatiferisches Taufverstandnis: Balthasar Hubmaiers Lehre zwischen Traditioneller und Reformatorischer Theologie* (Leiden: Brill, 1976).

53. Samuel Macauley Jackson, *Huldreich Zwingli: The Reformer of German Switzerland* (New York: G. P. Putnam's Sons, 1903), 264. See Ulrich Zwingli, "Of Baptism," in Bromiley, *Zwingli and Bullinger*, 132–75.

tradition rejected Zwingli's symbolic view of the sacraments, the concept of the sacraments as New Testament fulfillments of the covenantal signs of the Old Testament gained much currency.[54]

In discussing the sacraments, Calvin stood somewhere between Zwingli and Luther. As we have already seen in a previous chapter, Calvin disagreed with Zwingli on the idea that the sacraments were purely symbolic. This being said, Calvin did appropriate Zwingli's idea of the sacraments as covenantal signs.[55] Both the Old and New Testaments contain a single covenant of grace; they are simply regulated with different signs.[56] Therefore, unlike Zwingli, for Calvin the sacraments are signs of real grace and are therefore not merely symbolic.[57] Because the sacraments are means by which the Holy Spirit confirms faith by working alongside the external material form, a fair description of Calvin's position might be "sacramental spiritualism."[58] Note that like Zwingli, Calvin sees the visible words of the sacraments as functioning as a signifier that signify a reality that exists already (i.e., the invisible workings of God's grace on the elect), rather than a vehicle for enacting grace. Therefore, like Zwingli Calvin rejected Luther's insistence that the sacraments objectively contained grace and therefore enact justification. For the Genevan reformer, in the sacraments the *res* and the *signum* are not in union with one another and coincide only for the elect.[59] For Calvin, to claim otherwise is to return to a form of superstitious worship that confuses the creator and creature.[60]

Nevertheless, as we have already documented, this creates the major problem for Calvin. While the Genevan Reformer clearly describes that sacraments as promoting and inculcating the assurance of grace, it is extremely difficult to see how this could be the case. Since for Calvin the *res* and the *signum* in the sacraments only coincide occasionally for those

---

54. Paul Nimmo, "Sacraments," in *The Cambridge Companion to Reformed Theology*, eds. Paul Nimmo and David Fergusson (Cambridge: Cambridge University Press, 2016), 85.

55. ICR, 4.14.6; Calvin, *Institutes*, 2:1280–81.

56. ICR, 4.14.20–24; Calvin, *Institutes*, 2:1296–1301.

57. ICR, 4.14.1–6; Calvin, *Institutes*, 2:1276–81.

58. ICR, 4.14.7–13; Calvin, *Institutes*, 2:1281–89.

59. ICR, 4.14.15; Calvin, *Institutes*, 2:1290–91.

60. ICR, 1.11.1–3; Calvin, *Institutes*, 1:99–103.

whom God has secretly elected, the means of grace cannot give a genuine
assurance of election and justification. God's Word in the sacraments is
not identical to his hidden intention behind them. The result of Calvin's
position is that the sacraments cannot give assurance to the weak in faith
who fear that the external sign may not be intended for them. Neither
can they give any more assurance than one already possesses due to the
interior work of the Spirit, since a pre-existent inner assurance of the
authenticity of one's faith is the precondition for knowing that the sacrament is intended for you. As a result, the sacraments serve no purpose
and effectively become superfluous. Hence, although sacramental symbolicism and spiritualism are by no means identical positions (as Lutherans
have frequently unfairly charged), they both have the ultimate result of
making the sacraments superfluous.

Although Calvinists and Arminians have held both symbolicist
and spiritualist views of the sacraments through the centuries, in both
cases a lack of sacramental realism has exacerbated the basic problems
with their conception of justification as discussed in previous chapters.
Without sacraments that in a visible and objective sense contain grace,
one must inevitably look for the evidences of grace elsewhere. In the case
of Calvinism, the believer will inevitably worry that he does not have
genuine faith since the inner call of the Spirit does not always coincide
with the external call of the means of grace. With regard to Arminianism,
the fear will be that one's response to the Holy Spirit's offer of grace was
not sincere.

Without sacramental realism, there is no antidote to this problem without a regression into the enthusiastic quest for an inner assurance. That is
to say, lack of objective secondary support for faith inevitably leads to a
self-focus (*incurvatus in se*) that undermines the Christian life. As we have
already documented, historically many Protestants have sought moral
works or spiritual gifts (Christian perfection, *glossolalia*, snake handling)
as secondary supports of faith. In effect, these gifts take over the place
of the sacraments. The difficulty is that these gifts are located inside the
believing person and not external to them, thereby driving the person back
to their own works. Inevitably, such gifts are subject to deception (including self-deception) and are essentially subjective. By focusing on spiritual experience and moral progress as signs of justification and election,

Protestants have more often than not proved the Roman Catholic charge of spiritual subjectivism.[61]

THE REAL PRESENCE OF THE SON OF MAN

In developing our doctrine of the sacraments in relationship to justification, it is important to refer back to the nature of the ministry of Jesus as we discussed in our earlier chapter on the New Testament. Jesus's ministry is of supreme relevance because following Luther and the consensus of much of the Christian tradition (Aquinas, Calvin, etc.) the sacraments of the New Testament derive their validity from having been established by the dominical promise and command of Jesus in his ministry.[62]

As we saw, Jesus refers to himself as the Son of Man throughout both the Synoptic and Johannine traditions.[63] Since the other major blocks of tradition that we find in the New Testament do not refer to Jesus in this manner (i.e., Pauline letters, etc.), it is clearly not a title that was much used in the early church. Therefore, it cannot be denied that it was a title that Jesus applied to himself in discontinuity with the later church. In both some intertestamental Jewish literature (notably 1 Enoch) and the Gospels, the Son of Man is a cosmic judge who would come at the end of time to vindicate the elect and judge the wicked (Matt 25).[64] Jesus described himself as paradoxically coming before the end of time to enact a proleptic eschaton. He forgave sinners, thereby giving them his eschatological verdict ahead of time. Indeed, for those who receive Jesus's word of grace, the eschaton has already come: "I say to you, whoever hears my word and believes him who sent me *has eternal life*. He does not come into judgment, but *has passed from death to life*" (John 5:24, emphasis

---

61. Luigi Giussani, *Why the Church?*, trans. Viviane Hewitt (Montreal: McGill-Queen's University Press, 2001), 19.

62. ST, IIIa, q. 64, art. 3; Aquinas, *Summa Theologiae*, 2363; ICR, 4.14.3; Calvin, *Institutes*, 2:1278; That These Words of Christ, This is My Body, Still Stand Firm Against the Fanatics (1527), LW 37:68–69.

63. Larry R. Helyer, *The Witness of Jesus, Paul, and John: An Exploration in Biblical Theology* (Downers Grove, IL: InterVarsity Press, 2008), 321.

64. See Delbert Burkett, *The Son of Man: A History and Evaluation* (Cambridge: Cambridge University Press 1999); Joseph Fitzmyer, "The New Testament Title 'Son of Man,'" in *A Wandering Aramean: A Collected Aramaic Essays* (Missoula: Scholars, 1999), 143–60; Charles Gieschen, "The Name of the Son of Man in 1 Enoch," in *Enoch and Messiah Son of Man: Revisiting the Book of Parables*, ed. Gabriele Boccaccini, (Grand Rapids: Eerdmans, 2007), 238–49; Douglas Hare, *The Son of Man Tradition* (Minneapolis: Fortress, 1990).

added). In this, Jesus ushered sinners in the present into a realization of a kingdom that had not yet visibly manifested itself.

As the Son of Man, Jesus's proleptic eschatological verdict on sinners was shared both by word and deed. Jesus absolved sinners and gave his disciples the ability to bind and loose sins in the exercise of their ministry on his behalf (Matt 18:18, John 20:23). Likewise, at minimum, the Fourth Gospel suggests that in a few instances Jesus's disciples continued to baptize in the midst of Jesus's ministry (John 3:22), even after the ministry of John the Baptizer was ended. In the same manner, Jesus ate with sinners in common meals that gave them the assurance of their forgiveness and fellowship with him as part of the new Israel (Matt 2:13–17). In light of these facts, Gerd Theissen has observed that the sacraments of the New Testament had a pre-existence in the practices of fellowship that Jesus established in the midst of his ministry. Nevertheless, these practices were transformed into the sacraments of the New Testament by their connection both with the events of Jesus's death and resurrection (Rom 6; 1 Cor 11),[65] as well as the dominical command and promise of the Messiah (Matt 28; Mark 14; Luke 22; 1 Cor 11).

As we have already observed, the post-resurrection church continued Jesus's ministry of reconciliation. Central to the ability of the church to exercise Jesus's ministry was his continuing presence with the church through his Name attached to word and sacrament (Matt 18:20; 28:20; Luke 24:47). Throughout the Gospels and the other writings of the New Testament, the Name of Jesus takes over the function of the Name of YHWH in the Old Testament.[66] In the Old Testament, God dwelt in the Temple in the midst of Israel through his Name which is identical with his presence (2 Sam 7:13; 1 Kgs 5:5).[67] Whereas "YHWH" is a compression of "I will be who I will be"[68] (i.e., God hidden and unbound by his prom-

65. Gerd Theissen, *The Religion of the Earliest Churches: Creating a Symbolic World*, trans. John Bowden (Minneapolis: Fortress, 1999), 124.

66. Charles Gieschen, "The Divine Name in Ante-Nicene Christianity," *Viliae Christianae* 57 (2003): 130–48. David Scaer, *Discourses in Matthew: Jesus Teaches the Church* (St. Louis: Concordia, 2004), 130–48.

67. See Robert Hayward, *Divine Name and Presence, Memre* (Lanham, MD: Rowman & Littlefield, 1982).

68. G.H. Parke-Taylor, *Yahweh: The Divine Name in the Bible* (Waterloo, On: Wilfried Laurier University Press, 1975), 55–56.

ises), "Jesus" means "God is our salvation."[69] Therefore, in Jesus, God who is utterly free above his self-binding ("I will be who I will be," *Deus absconditus*), binds himself definitively to be a gracious God to humanity ("Jesus" meaning "God is our salvation," Phil 2:11). In turn since Jesus has attached his gracious Name to word and sacrament, he has committed himself to make his gracious electing and justifying presence available to sinners through these physical means.

Therefore, just as God gave access to his gracious presence through the forgiveness of sin wrought by the sacrifices of the Levitical cult, so too in the era of the New Testament God gives access to his saving presence in Jesus through the sacraments. Jesus's presence with his church through his Name makes both the individual believer and the corporate church into the eschatological Temple (1 Cor 6:16, 19; Eph 2:20–21; 1 Pet 2:5), that is, the new locus of God's gracious presence in his creation. In this the church anticipates the eschatological fulfillment of creation, wherein God will fill the whole of creation with his self-communicative presence (Dan 2:35; Rev 21:3).

The divine Name (both the Name of Jesus and the Triune Name, Matt 28:19) given through word and sacrament make the life of faith possible. The giving of the Name means the self-donation of God to the believer in the form of the promise. To give his Name means the giving of God's very self through the means of grace to seal the promise of the gospel. Oswald Bayer writes that in the gospel, "God's being is [a] gift and promise as he gives himself wholly and utterly to us."[70] In the Old Testament, unilateral divine promises were sealed by the pledge of God's own person: "By myself I have sworn, declares the LORD" (Gen 22:16; Isa 45:23; Jer 49:13; Heb 6:13). To make an unconditional promise to another is to give oneself over to and bind oneself to the person to whom it is spoken until the promise is fulfilled. The incarnation (the bodily self-gift of God to his people) is therefore the fitting fulfillment of God's unconditional promises of redemption in the Old Testament. Similarly, marriage (a frequent

---

69. Daniel Harrington, *The Gospel of Matthew* (Collegeville, MN: Liturgical, 1991) 35; John P. Meier, *A Marginal Jew, Rethinking the Historical Jesus: Roots of the Problem and the Person*, vol. 1 (New York: Doubleday, 1991), 207.

70. Oswald Bayer, *Living By Faith: Justification and Sanctification*, trans. Geoffrey Bromiley (Grand Rapids: Eerdmans, 2003), 53.

metaphor for divine-human relationship throughout the Bible; see Hos 2:7; Joel 1:8; Ezek 16:8–14; Eph 5), is likewise sealed by a consummation that involves the couple literally giving their very physical beings to one another in the one-flesh union. Since the divine Name is identical with the divine presence, to receive the Name is to receive God's very self as a "down payment" of God's eschatological fidelity (Eph 1:14).

The giving of the divine Name in the word and sacrament ministry of the church enables the life of faith. Faith is described throughout the Bible as being able to "call upon the name of the Lord" (Joel 2:32; Acts 2:21; Rom 10:12). Jesus's Name is described particularly in the book of Acts as the object of saving faith (Acts 4:12). As background to the Old Testament phrase, it should be remembered that in the Ancient Near East a vassal was given the name of his suzerain so that he could call upon him in a time of trouble.[71] Analogously, the believer who receives Jesus's Name in the means of grace can call upon it in repentance and trust in it through faith.

Jesus's continuing presence with his church through word and sacrament is not merely spiritual. Rather, Christ is present to his church as both true God and true man. It is the man Jesus who states that "All authority in heaven and on earth has been given to me" (Matt 28:18). This divine power manifest in the man Jesus in his state of exaltation allows him to truthfully promise "surely I am with you always, to the very end of the age" (Matt 28:20). Indeed, in his ministry it was Jesus's physical and tangible presence that facilitated his ministry of the forgiveness of sin. Jesus was able to assure sinners of their forgiveness and their incorporation into the kingdom not by a mental or spiritual solidarity with them, but by his physical presence with them in communal meals and his personal word of absolution. Jesus's presence as both God and man is not confined to his church, but fills the whole creation with his theanthropic reign: "He who descended is the one who also ascended far above all the heavens, that he might fill all things" (Eph 4:10).[72]

---

71. Michael Horton, *The Christian Faith: A Systematic Theology for Pilgrims on the Way* (Grand Rapids: Zondervan, 2011), 108–9.

72. *Confession concerning Christ's Supper* (1528), LW 37:218.

Luther and the subsequent Lutheran tradition identified continuing presence as the result of the full communication of divine attributes to the man Jesus (*genus majestaticum*): "For in him the whole fullness of deity dwells bodily" (Col 2:9).[73] Because the man Jesus participates in the fullness of divine glory, he can in some mysterious sense be present with his church through the means of grace even after having ascended to his place of exaltation. Jesus has been exalted to the "right hand of God" (Ps 110:1, Rom 8:34; Col 3:1), which is not a physical location, but God's power and glory (Exod 15:6; Isa 48:13; Ps 44:3) which is everywhere (Isa 6:3).[74] Therefore, because the man Jesus possesses the full exercise of God's power and glory, he can transcend both time and space and become present to his church through the means of grace.[75]

By contrast, the Reformed tradition has insisted that the man Jesus's presence is circumscribed and therefore has often applied the passages about the continuing presence of Jesus to the Holy Spirit.[76] Nevertheless, this is not exegetically warranted. Although Jesus does promise the coming of the Holy Spirit (John 14:16; Luke 24:49) and the Holy Spirit is also the Spirit of the Son (Gal 4:6), the Holy Spirit is nevertheless still "another" (John 14:16), that is, a distinct person of the Trinity. Therefore, passages that speak of the Holy Spirit's presence in the church cannot be conflated with passages that speak of the presence of Jesus with his church in the means of grace. Moreover, Jesus's spiritual presence through the Holy Spirit does not exclude the reality of his mysterious presence according to his humanity. Physical and spiritual presences do not categorically exclude one another.

Jesus is able to transcend the normal limitation of creaturely existence in two ways. First, Jesus's possession of the fullness of divine glory allows

---

73. Adolf Hoenecke, *Evangelical Lutheran Dogmatics*, 4 vols., trans. Joel Fredrich, James L. Langebartels, Paul Prange, and Bill Tackmier (Milwaukee: Northwestern, 1999–2009), 3:89–99; Johann Gerhard, *Theological Commonplaces: Exegesis IV: On Christ*, trans. Richard Dinda (St. Louis: Concordia, 2009), 203–87; Francis Pieper, *Christian Dogmatics*, 3 vols. (St. Louis: Concordia, 1951–1953), 2:152–242.

74. Confession concerning Christ's Supper (1528), LW 37:207.

75. Hoenecke, *Evangelical Lutheran Dogmatics*, 3:90–92; Pieper, *Christian Dogmatics*, 2:173–214 Gerhard, *On Christ*, 227–43.

76. David Steinmetz, "The Theology of John Calvin," in *The Cambridge Companion to Reformation Theology*, ed. David Bagchi and David Steinmetz (Cambridge: Cambridge University Press, 2004), 127.

him to transcend the metaphysical "distance" between heaven and earth. This means that there is no gap between Jesus's word and presence, and the means of grace. The absolution of the pastor is the absolution of Jesus. Jesus is present in the Lord's Supper and through the bread and wine he gives a share in his sacrificed body and blood for the forgiveness of sins.

Second, Jesus also transcends time so that his proleptic eschatological ministry can continue in the present. The pardon Jesus offers in the present through the word and the sacraments is identical with and connects the believer to the Father's eschatological verdict enacted in the cross and empty tomb brought two thousand years ago. Likewise, this verdict of the Father in atonement and justification is the proleptic realization of the verdict Christ will mete out at the end of time: condemnation for all who reject Christ and righteousness and life for all those who in faith are in him. In making his judgment of condemnation and grace present in his church, Jesus is not only the man from heaven, but the man from the eschatological future.[77]

---

77. See similar thoughts in Markus Barth and Verne Fletcher, *Acquittal by Resurrection: Freedom, Law, and Justification in Light of the Resurrection of Jesus* (New York: Holt, Rinehart & Winston, 1964).

CHAPTER 15

Justification and the Sacraments:
Baptism and the Lord's Supper

A s we saw in an earlier chapter, the problem of post-baptismal sin was a significant factor in the early church for the development of the doctrine of penance. In turn, as we also observed, it was the doctrine of penance as it had developed in the late Middle Ages that was the ultimate cause of the Indulgence Controversy and Luther's evolution from his transitional Augustinian *humilitastheologie* to his mature Reformation position.[1] Therefore, understanding baptism and its relationship to the Christian life is central to understanding the nature of justification.[2]

As noted earlier, that the concept of post-baptismal sin was considered a problem in the early church was by no means unsurprising in that the New Testament speaks of baptism as the definitive rupture between the old life of sin and death and the new life of faith.[3] Jesus describes baptism as being a matter of being "born again" of "water and the Spirit" (John 3:3, 5). Contrary to what has often been believed in popular Anglo-American

---

1. Ernst Bizer, *Fides ex auditu. Eine Untersuchung über die Entdeckung der Gerechtig-keit Gottes durch Martin Luther* (Neukirchen: Neukirchener Verlag, 1966) 22, 51.

2. See Jonathan Trigg, *Baptism in the Theology of Martin Luther* (Leiden: Brill, 2001).

3. G. R. Beasley-Murray, *Baptism in the New Testament* (Eugene, OR: Wipf & Stock, 2006), 126–45.

Evangelicalism,[4] there is no indication in the text that Jesus speaks of a spiritual experience, or a kind of miraculous moral improvement that is then publicly expressed by the testimony of water baptism. Rather, Christ speaks of the operation of the Holy Spirit through water baptism to bring about a new creation. Note that in the original Greek there is no definite article before "Spirit," although "the" is frequently inserted in English translations ("water and the Spirit").[5] The lack of a definite article suggests that "water and Spirit" are being spoken in tandem as a sacramental unity, rather than as separate events of "water baptism" and "Spirit baptism," as the Pentecostal tradition has sometimes claimed.[6]

In John 3, the imagery that Jesus employs connects baptism with the waters of the original creation. The image of water implies both judgment and redemptive re-creation. Like those who died in the flood and the Egyptians at the Red Sea, individuals who are baptized are having their old nature drowned.[7] This drowning returns them to the primal waters of chaos (Gen 1) in preparation for being re-created in the promise of the gospel. The biblical pattern is that humbling comes before glory, condemning law before redeeming gospel.[8] Therefore, baptism is a condemnation of the old nature and a re-creation of the new person by the Spirit (John 3:6). Water is the media of new creation by the Spirit, much like the Spirit of God hovered over the primal water and brought about the original creation (Gen 1:2).[9] Faith and justification are obviously the byproduct of this work of the Spirit through baptism. Indeed, in the same passage Jesus ties baptism to salvation and eternal life, which he in turn also identifies directly with faith in himself (John 3:3, 5, 16).

Paul also associates baptism to justification and new creation by teaching that baptism is the incorporation of sinners into Jesus's death and resurrection: "We were buried therefore with him by baptism into death,

---

4. See Sean McGever, *Born Again: The Evangelical Theology of Conversion in John Wesley and George Whitefield* (Bellingham, WA: Lexham Press, 2020).

5. Ben Witherington III, *John's Wisdom: A Commentary on the Fourth Gospel* (Louisville: Westminster John Knox, 1995), 97.

6. See Harold Hunter, *Spirit Baptism: A Pentecostal Alternative* (Eugene, OR: Wipf & Stock, 2009).

7. Ronald P. Byars, *The Sacraments in Biblical Perspective* (Louisville: Westminster John Knox, 2011), 23.

8. Arthur Just, *Luke*, 2 vols. (St. Louis: Concordia, 1996–1997), 2:1021–36.

9. David Scaer, "The Sacraments as an Affirmation of Creation," *Concordia Theological Quarterly* 57, no. 4 (1993): 248.

in order that, just as Christ was raised from the dead by the glory of the Father, we too might walk in newness of life" (Rom 6:4).[10] Indeed, baptism condemns and destroys our old nature and raises up a new righteous creature: "We know that our old self was crucified with him in order that the body of sin might be brought to nothing, so that we would no longer be enslaved to sin" (Rom 6:6). If baptism kills sin, it necessarily either reinforces or creates faith because the essence of sin is unbelief: "For whatever does not proceed from faith is sin" (Rom 14:23). This opens up the eschatological dimension of faith. Baptism contains a redemptive promise that can be continuously drawn upon. If one has died with Christ in baptism, then one will also enjoy his eschatological fate: "For if we have been united with him in a death like his, we shall certainly be united with him in a resurrection like his" (Rom 6:5).[11]

Moreover, there is no contradiction in Paul between dying with Christ and Christ dying for one. In chapter 7 of Romans, Paul uses the analogy of a woman who was once married but who is now widowed. When her husband dies, she is free from him and can marry another without committing the sin of adultery. The woman was relationally defined by her husband but is no longer because of his death. Similarly, Christ having died for sinners releases them from the law. The law hardens sinners in their relationship with God by pushing back against the desires of their sinful nature. But once sin has been atoned for and the sinner has been justified *coram Deo*, the sinner is free from the law and the oppositional relationship of sin which it promotes (Rom 7:8). Atonement and justification remove the old person relationally constituted by unbelief and the legal relationship ("nomological existence")[12] by replacing that old relationship with a new one of grace and faith. This new relationship of grace reorients the inner person toward trust in God and the trustworthiness of his eschatological promises in the present and the future (Rom 6:5; 8:29–30). Therefore, by Christ dying for and forensically justifying

---

10. Beasley-Murray, *Baptism in the New Testament*, 127–46.

11. Joseph Plevnik, *Paul and the Parousia: An Exegetical and Theological Investigation* (Peabody, MA: Hendrickson, 1997), 289.

12. Elert, *Law and Gospel*, 28.

believers, they die also, and are raised up as new creatures of faith through the preaching of the word and baptism.[13]

Luther closely followed these biblical descriptions of the reality of baptism in his treatment of the subject in his Catechisms. Baptism is death and resurrection through the work of the Holy Spirit.[14] It destroys the power of sin and creates faith: "What does Baptism give or profit? Answer. It works forgiveness of sins, delivers from death and the devil, and gives eternal salvation to all who believe this, as the words and promises of God declare."[15] This is not due to a view of the sacrament of baptism as a kind of magical bath. Rather, Luther emphasizes that the key to the efficacy of baptism is the power of the word, which is both consecratory and promissory. As we have already seen, the divine word performs what it speaks. It makes a sacrament valid, but it also makes it efficacious by creating a faith that is salvific because it receives the promises that it makes:

How can water [in baptism] do such great things? Answer: It is not the water indeed that does them, but the word of God which is in and with the water, and faith, which trusts such word of God in the water. For without the word of God the water is simple water and no baptism. But with the word of God it is a baptism, that is, a gracious water of life and a washing of regeneration in the Holy Ghost.[16]

Luther emphasizes throughout his writing on baptism that the sacrament grants a divine promise that remains good throughout the whole of one's life.[17] Indeed, it is of secondary importance whether or not one believed the promise of one's baptism at the time one was baptized.[18]

13. See similar argument in: Werner Elert, *The Christian Ethos: The Foundation of the Christian Way of Life*, trans. Carl Schindler (Philadelphia: Muhlenberg, 1957), 182–94. Also see: Wolfhart Pannenberg, *Systematic Theology*, trans. Geoffrey W. Bromiley, 3 vols. (Grand Rapids: Eerdmans, 1991–1993), 2:427: "those whom Jesus represents have the possibility in their death, by reason of its linking to the death of Jesus, of attaining to the hope of participation in the new resurrection life that has already become manifest in Jesus (Rom 6.5)."

14. Trigg, *Baptism in the Theology of Martin Luther*, 92–98.

15. SC IV; *Concordia Triglotta*, 551.

16. SC IV; *Concordia Triglotta*, 551.

17. LC IV.44; *Concordia Triglotta*, 743.

18. LC IV.52; *Concordia Triglotta*, 745.

First, since baptism is a visible word of the gospel, it can create faith.[19] As we saw, Paul says that baptism kills sin and brings forth new life (Rom 6:3–14). Sin is fundamentally unbelief (Rom 14:23) and faith is new life (Gal 2:20).[20] Second, just as the promise of the gospel is objectively true whether or not one has believed it, likewise the promise of one's baptism remains good and can be drawn upon later in life even if one did not believe before or at the time of one's baptism.[21]

Unlike other forms of Protestantism,[22] Luther does not envision justification as a onetime event, but as something that occurs day after day as the Christian repents and returns to the promise of the gospel made in baptism.[23] Therefore, the Christian life means a perpetual participation in the death and resurrection of Christ (Luke 9:23):

What does such baptizing with water signify? Answer. *It signifies that the old Adam in us should, by daily contrition and repentance, be drowned and die with all sins and evil lusts, and, again, a new man daily come forth and arise;* who shall live before God in righteousness and purity forever.[24]

Luther's belief on the continuing efficacy of the sacrament of baptism throughout the Christian's life has a significant effect on how he understands confession and absolution. Although as we saw earlier, Luther considered the word of absolution to be sacramental, in *On the Babylonian Captivity of the Church*, he rejected confession and absolution as being a distinct sacrament.[25] This is partially because Luther insists that sacraments must have a material sign, which confession and absolution lacks.[26] More importantly though, baptism is effective one's entire life: "Baptism ... *now saves you,* not as a removal of dirt from the body *but as an appeal to God for a good conscience,* through the resurrection of Jesus Christ

19. Trigg, *Baptism in the Theology of Martin Luther*, 75–80, 154–65.
20. Lectures on Hebrews (1518), LW 29:182.
21. SC IV; *Concordia Triglotta*, 551.
22. Phillip Cary, *Meaning of Protestant Theology*, 113.
23. LC IV.72–3; *Concordia Triglotta*, 750–51; Trigg, *Baptism in the Theology of Martin Luther*, 151–73.
24. SC IV; *Concordia Triglotta*, 551, emphasis added.
25. On the Babylonian Captivity of the Church (1520), LW 36:124.
26. On the Babylonian Captivity of the Church (1520), LW 36:124.

(1 Pet 3:21, emphasis added). When one believes the words of absolution given by the pastor, one simply returns to the same gospel promise given in baptism: "Whoever believes and is baptized will be saved, but whoever does not believe will be condemned" (Mark 16:16). "For if we have been united with him in a death like his, we shall certainly be united with him in a resurrection like his (Rom 6:5).[27]

Through the perpetual return to baptism the Christian is able to enter the reality of Jesus's death and resurrection, although this event is historically distant. Thus, a key implication of Luther and the historic Lutheran tradition's teaching on the *communicatio idiomatum* is that Christ's humanity is not confined by time and therefore he can make himself available through the promise of the gospel in any era. Herein we again encounter in Luther implicit appropriation of Scripture's distinction between chronological time and kairological time.[28] Even though Scripture does describe the history of salvation as an orderly development, there is a *perichoresis* of the ages. God's kairological time has manifested itself at specific point in chronological history. Nevertheless, the Lord is not bound to the chronological order of history in manifesting his kairological salvation. Hence, the risen Jesus, who transcends time makes the eschaton present to the believer at the appointed time of their redemption in baptism in order to actualize God's electing and justifying purposes. Christ thereby makes it possible to incorporate the believer into the eschatological redemption in the present through a return to the kairological event of their baptism, just as baptism is a return to the kairological event of his death and resurrection. As Oswald Bayer observes:

> Luther's apocalyptic understanding of creation and history opposes modern concepts of progress. For Luther, the only progress is return to one's baptism, the biographical point of rupture between the old and new worlds. Creation, Fall, redemption, and

---

27. Albrecht Peters, *Commentary on Luther's Catechisms: Confession and Christian Life* (St. Louis: Concordia, 2013), 74.

28. Elert, *The Christian Ethos*, 286–89; Paul Tillich, *The Interpretation of History* (New York: Charles Scribner's Sons, 1936).

completion of the world are not sequential advance, one after the other, but perceived in an intertwining of the times.[29]

In emphasizing the possibility of returning to one's baptism, Luther responds to the issues that gave rise to the problem of post-baptism sin, and then in turn generated the Latin doctrines of penance, purgatory, and indulgences that he combated in his early Reformation theology. Like the New Testament and the ante-Nicene church,[30] Luther saw baptism as the apocalyptic rupture between the old person and new person in Christ.[31] Nevertheless, at this point Luther and the early church begin to diverge. Unlike Luther, the early church treated baptism as a onetime purification that could genuinely be lost through either serious sin or any sin at all.[32] Subsequently, the concept of penance was developed as a means of repeating (albeit in a less effective manner) the original purification of baptism. Purgatory likewise followed penance as a means of continuing into the afterlife the incomplete process of repairing the purity lost in post-baptismal sin.[33] The supplementary sacrament of penance (as well as purgatory) was necessary because the barrier of time made it impossible to return to the supreme purification of the original act of baptism.[34]

As a result, in most post-Nicene Christian traditions baptism increasingly ceased to be the final and complete purification from sin and began to be seen more as an act of initiation into the Christian life.[35] Although Catholicism retained the view of baptism as a total purification, it was assumed that for most believers this purification would be almost immediately lost. As a result, the sacrament degenerated into the starting point

29. Oswald Bayer, "Martin Luther," in *The Reformation Theologians: An Introduction to Theology in the Early Modern Period*, ed. Carter Lindberg (Malden, MA: Blackwell, 2004), 51–52.

30. See Everett Ferguson, *Baptism in the Early Church: History, Theology, and Liturgy in the First Five Centuries* (Grand Rapids: Eerdmans, 2009).

31. Trigg, *Baptism in the Theology of Martin Luther*, 92–98.

32. Roman Garrison, *Redemptive Almsgiving in Early Christianity* (London: Bloomsbury, 1993), 131; Rob Means, *Penance in Medieval Europe, 600–1200* (Cambridg: Cambridge University Press, 2014), 16.

33. Jacques Le Goff, *The Birth of Purgatory*, trans. Arthur Goldhammer (Chicago: University of Chicago Press, 1986), 209–89.

34. See development in Abigail Firey, ed., *A New History of Penance* (Leiden: Brill, 2008).

35. See Peter Cramer, *Baptism and Change in the Early Middle Ages, c.200–c.1150* (Cambridge: Cambridge University Press, 2003), 87–266.

of a life of good works and penance for sin.[36] For most Protestants baptism
has similarly been seen as an act of initiation, albeit along significantly different lines. For some baptism has been characterized as a covenant sign
that shows incorporation into the people of God (Reformed).[37] For others,
it has been viewed as a means of publicly displaying one's commitment to
live the Christian life by entering into the life of the church and its discipline (Anabaptists, Baptist).[38] In all cases (both Catholic and mainstream
Protestant), baptism loses its New Testament eschatological finality.

For Luther baptism is not a onetime purification that can be lost, or
merely the ritual inauguration of the Christian life. It is the final and total
incorporation of the believer into Christ's proleptic eschaton of his death
and resurrection.[39] Because baptism is itself the proleptic presence of the
eschaton, Lutherans do not generally talk about the gift of perseverance in
the manner of Augustine and Calvin.[40] The concept of perseverance presupposes that the eschaton and salvation are something in the future that
one moves toward by maintaining their faith. By contrast, for Luther the
eschaton has already occurred in baptism when one enters into Christ's
death and resurrection. The Christian life as death and resurrection is
structured around continuously moving backward in time to one's baptism, not forward to the final triumphant preservation of faith at death.[41]

The eschatological event of baptism justifies and sanctifies the individual completely (Rom 6:2–4), thereby pulling the believer away from his
self-incurvature to a new identity external to themselves in Christ. One's
true identity is not to be found in the empirical person who may fall into
sin, or even apostatize, but in the new being who lives outside themselves
(*extra nos*) in Christ (Gal 2:20, Col 3:3). As a result of baptism, one's true
reality as a person is to be found in an ecstatic existence in Christ, even

---

36. See a contemporary Catholic summary in Kenan Osborne, *The Christian Sacraments of Initiation: Baptism, Confirmation, Eucharist* (New York: Paulist, 1987).

37. John Wheelan Rigg, *Baptism in the Reformed Tradition: A Historical and Practical Theology* (Louisville: Westminster John Knox, 2002), 73–90.

38. Thomas N. Finger, *A Contemporary Anabaptist Theology: Biblical, Historical, Constructive* (Downers Grove, IL: InterVarsity Academic, 2015), 16–83; Harold Rawlings, *Basic Baptist Beliefs: An Exposition of Key Biblical Doctrines* (Springfield, MO: 21st Century, 2014), 243–54.

39. Kolb and Arand, *The Genius of Luther's Theology,* 98.

40. Augustine, *Gift of Perseverance*; NPNF[1], 5:521–52; ICR, 3.14.7; Calvin, *Institutes,* 2:973–74.

41. Bayer, *Martin Luther's Theology,* 270.

if one becomes alienated from that new existence: "We conclude, there-fore, that a Christian lives not in himself, but in Christ and the neighbor. He lives in Christ *through faith*, and in his *neighbor through love*."[42] That is to say, even if one rejects the faith, one can always return to and connect with the eschatological promise in baptism that is constitutive of their true identity, rather than the shadowy false identity of sin (Rom 6:2–3). Although many who fall away from their baptismal promise will finally be lost, it is because they have clung to unreality, not because sin is their genuine reality.

The fact that the empirical person will continue to sin until temporal death is not a failure of the power of baptism, but it is rather a necessary manifestation of the "already" and "not yet" of New Testament eschatol-ogy.[43] Believers are simultaneously sinful and righteous (*simul justus et peccator*) because the New Testament tells us that the righteous kingdom of God is already here (Luke 17:21), although the old evil age persists (Gal 1:4). Sanctification is progressive in the sense that what was already established whole and complete in baptism manifests itself in greater and greater degrees until our death. As Oswald Bayer observes, "Ethical progress is only possible by returning to baptism."[44] At the death of the believer, there is a full manifestation of what already occurred at the time of the believer's baptism. The body of sin is completely condemned in physical death, while simultaneously the believer is completely actualized as a righteous citizen of the kingdom of heaven.[45]

JUSTIFICATION AND THE LORD'S SUPPER

In *On the Babylonian Captivity of the Church*, Luther finds biblical basis for a second sacrament of the New Testament, namely the Lord's Supper.[46] In this particular treatise, Luther's object of critique is the medieval Roman Catholic understanding of the Mass.[47] Later in his career Luther would

---

42. Freedom of a Christian (1520), LW 31:371. Emphasis added.
43. Jeffrey Silcock, "A Lutheran Approach to Eschatology," *Lutheran Quarterly* 31, no. 4 (2017): 375.
44. Bayer, *Living by Faith*, 66.
45. First Sermon Delivered at Elector Johannes's Funeral (1533), LW 51:237–38.
46. On the Babylonian Captivity of the Church (1520), LW 36:18.
47. On the Babylonian Captivity of the Church (1520), LW 36:35.

have an even more contentious debate over the nature of the Eucharist with the Ulrich Zwingli and some of the other southern German reformers.[48]

In light of his commitment to the notion of justification as a unilateral promise, Luther engaged in a sustained critique of the idea that the Mass is a sacrifice throughout his career.[49] Catholics rightly observe that Protestants have frequently misrepresented the idea of the Mass as a sacrifice as teaching that the work of the cross is somehow repeated by the priestly celebrant.[50] This being said, the actual Catholic doctrine of the Eucharist still does not satisfy the Protestant objections against the sacrificial character of the Mass in light of the principle of *sola fide*.

According to the standard late medieval understanding ratified at the Council of Trent, Christ's sacrifice is "re-presented" in the Mass by the priest offering up in an unbloody manner what Christ once offered to the Father in a bloody manner on the cross. The eucharistic sacrifice does not repeat the sacrifice of the cross but rather is in some mysterious sense identical with it. From this re-presented sacrificial offering, the merits of Christ are applied to the assembled congregation who receive the host. The offering of the Mass may even be applied to the dead in purgatory as a means of shortening their sufferings.[51]

Luther's main difficulty with this doctrine of the Mass as a sacrifice is twofold. First, the idea of the sacrificial character of the Mass is unbiblical. When we looking to Christ's word as recorded in the Bible there is no justification for saying that the Mass is a sacrifice, however envisioned.[52] Expanding on Luther's point, it is important to recognize that Scripture simply does not call the Lord's Supper a sacrifice, describe its function as sacrificial, set up a priesthood whose purpose is to offer said sacrifices *in persona Christi*, or speak of the possibility of the Mass being applied to the dead in the equally unbiblical realm of purgatory.

---

48. Lohse, *Martin Luther's Theology*, 169–77.

49. See Robert Croken, *Luther's First Front: The Eucharist as Sacrifice* (Ottawa: University of Ottawa Press, 1990).

50. Christian Smith, *How to Go from Being a Good Evangelical to a Committed Catholic in Ninety-Five Difficult Steps* (Eugene, OR: Cascade, 2011), 117.

51. See B. J. Kidd, *The Later Medieval Doctrine of Eucharistic Sacrifice* (London: SPCK, 1958); "Thirteenth Session" in *Canons and Decrees of the Council of Trent*, trans. H. J. Schroeder (St. Louis: Herder, 1960), 72–87.

52. On the Babylonian Captivity of the Church (1520), LW 36:36.

Second, the sacrifice of the Mass is not evangelical. The Lord's Supper is a visible form of the gospel. As Hermann Sasse writes, "It is really true that *the sacrament is the Gospel, and the Gospel is the Sacrament.*"[53] Hence, the sacrificial concept of the Mass makes the promise of grace on the basis of Jesus's historic death into a priestly offering. What Christ instituted as unilateral grace becomes another grace-enabled meritorious work.[54] As we have already seen, Luther and the other Magisterial Reformers rejected the idea that human works are meritorious, even ones performed by the power of divine grace. Hence, the nature of the gospel itself categorically rules out the possibility that the Mass could be a meritorious sacrifice.[55]

Although Luther does not address the issue in *On the Babylonian Captivity of the Church*, the memorial view of the Lord's Supper promoted by Zwingli and so popular in Anglo-American Evangelicalism, fares just as poorly when judged on the basis of Luther's dual biblical and evangelical criteria. According to this view, the Lord's Supper is a symbolic eating of Christ's body and blood that reminds believers of his death for them. As a memorial, it is inherently symbolic in that symbols remind individuals of realities chronologically and physically distant from them.[56]

First, the reading of the words of institution "do this in memory of me" by the sacramental symbolicist tradition misapprehends what the Bible means when it speaks of memory. In Scripture, knowledge (*yada*) and memory (*zikaron*) are participatory and hence presuppose the real presence of the contemplated reality.[57] To "remember" is to have the reality that one recalls placed before one's eyes as a real presence, not something far off. God "remembering" his covenantal promises means to have them placed before his eyes and as a result acts to fulfill them in the present

53. Hermann Sasse, *This is My Body: Luther's Contention for the Real Presence in the Sacrament of the Altar* (Eugene, OR: Wipf & Stock, 2001), 406.

54. On the Babylonian Captivity of the Church (1520), LW 36:52–56.

55. See summary in Croken, *Luther's First Front*, 26–27.

56. See a contemporary defense in Thomas Schreiner, ed., *The Lord's Supper: Remembering and Proclaiming Christ Until He Comes* (Nashville: Broadman & Holman, 2011).

57. Bruce Birch, et al., *A Theological Introduction to the Old Testament* (Nashville: Abingdon, 2005), 106.

(Gen 8:1; 9:15–6; Exod 2:24; 6:5; Lev 26:42; Deut 4:31).[58] Likewise, the thief on the cross's plea to "remember me when you come into your kingdom" (Luke 23:42) was not a request for Jesus to merely think of the thief when he was enthroned in glory, but to make him present with him in heaven. Hence, "do this in memory of me" does not have the connotation of a symbolic representation of something distant, but rather of making present the fulfillment of God's covenant promises ("this is the new testament in my blood") objectified in Jesus's sacrificed body and blood.

The second point of critique is that the memorial conception of the Lord's Supper makes the Eucharist no less a work than the sacrificial notion of the Mass—albeit not a meritorious work. The accent of the symbolicist view of the Lord's Supper falls entirely upon believers' action of remembering the death of Christ and not the presence of the risen Jesus speaking the promise of the gospel ("this is my body given for you ... this is my blood shed for you") to the individual believer. As a result, the sacrament ceases to be about the promise of grace and is turned into another ritual work.

As an alternative to the sacrificial and memorialist paradigms, the central interpretive lens through which Luther's reads the Lord's Supper is the notion of the sacrament as a "testament" (*diatheke*).[59] The Reformer notes that Jesus says in the words of the institution that the sacrament is a "new testament [*diatheke*] in my blood" (1 Cor 11:25).[60] *Diatheke* often translated as "covenant," largely because it was the word used by the translators of the LXX to render the Hebrew *berith* (chain, ring, or covenant).[61] Nevertheless, the literal meaning of the term *diatheke* in Greek is a last will and testament.[62] In keeping with this it should not go unnoticed that a number of the New Testament authors exploit the testamental meaning

58. Walther Zimmerli, *The Fiery Throne: The Prophets and Old Testament Theology*, ed. K.C. Hanson (Minneapolis: Fortress, 2003), 125.

59. On the Babylonian Captivity of the Church (1520), LW 36:37–38; Croken, *Luther's First Front*, 73–86.

60. On the Babylonian Captivity of the Church (1520), LW 36:37.

61. J. Benton White and Walter Wilson, *From Adam to Armageddon: A Survey of the Bible* (Belmont, CA: Thomason Watson, 2012), 1.

62. J. Behm, "Diatheke," in *Theological Dictionary of the New Testament: Abridged in One Volume*, ed. Gerhard Kittel and Gerhard Friedrich, trans. Geoffrey Bromiley (Grand Rapids: Eerdmans, 1985), 160.

of *diatheke* by describing the promise of the gospel as being like a will (Gal 3:15; Heb 9:16).[63] One of the more interesting examples can be found in the book of Revelation, where the Lamb's book with the seven seals (a symbol of the gospel) possesses this connotation. In the first century last wills and testaments generally were bound with seven seals.[64] Even outside the New Testament in other early Christian literature the testamental concept of the gospel can be found. In the later apocryphal Gospel of Peter, Jesus's tomb is described as being sealed with seven seals (Gos. Pet 8:33), thereby suggesting that the gospel of Jesus's resurrection is a kind of will of inheritance.[65]

All the biblical data (and even some extra biblical data) suggesting an analogy between the gospel and a last will and testament certainly does not exclude the covenantal understanding of the term *diatheke*. After all, as we have seen in our discussion of the Old Testament, covenants of grace are unilateral in the manner of a will. Nevertheless, the analogy that the New Testament authors draw between the covenant of the gospel and wills of inheritance does offer an interesting twist on the manner in which the Lord's Supper gives the gospel to believers.

The gospel is a unilateral divine self-donation, in that an unconditional promise means a gift of the promiser himself in order to fulfill the terms of the promise. Therefore, Christians who receive the unilateral promise of the gospel are heirs to Christ's very sacrificed person as a guarantee that he is at their disposal to fulfill his promise. This means that through the promise of the gospel we inherit Christ and everything that he possesses. Indeed, as Paul states that all true believers in union with Christ are "fellow heirs with Christ" (Rom 8:17). This reality is manifest in the Lord's Supper wherein Christ wills his very physical being (body and blood) wherein he brought about their salvation to believers. Therefore, to paraphrase Luther, in dying Jesus gives the inheritance of his body and

---

63. Hans Betz, *Galatians: A Commentary on Paul's Letter to the Churches in Galatia* (Hermeneia; Fortress, 1979), 155; Scott Murray, "The Concept of *diathēkē* in the Letter to the Hebrews," *Concordia Theological Quarterly* 66 (2002): 59; Frank Thielman, *Theology of the New Testament: A Canonical and Synthetic Approach* (Grand Rapids: Zondervan, 2011), 600.

64. Louis Brighton, *Revelation* (St. Louis: Concordia, 1999), 107.

65. R. Joseph Hoffmann, *Jesus Outside the Gospels* (Buffalo, NY: Prometheus, 1987), 101.

blood to believers in order that they might receive the forgiveness of sins and eternal life through his promise attached to them.[66]

Returning to *On the Babylonian Captivity of the Church*, Luther's second major difficulty with the medieval conception of the Eucharist is the doctrine of transubstantiation.[67] The doctrine of transubstantiation teaches that the bread and the wine in the Lord's Supper are transformed by the words of institution into the body and blood of Christ, although the outward appearance and qualities of bread and wine (Aristotelian "accidents") remain intact.[68] Although Luther affirmed the substantial presence of Christ's body and blood in the Eucharist, he disliked the doctrine of transubstantiation because it contradicts 1 Corinthians 10:16, which states that the bread and wine remain in the Lord's Supper as the medium by which one receives Christ's substantial body and blood.[69] Luther considers the entire idea of transubstantiation an Aristotelian rationalization of the mystery of how the body and blood of Christ can become present through the bread and the wine.[70]

In spite of this criticism of transubstantiation, it is interesting to note that Luther does not consider belief in the doctrine to be tremendously problematic and allows that people could still affirm transubstantiation as a theologoumenon.[71] What is most important to the Reformer is that one affirms the substantial presence of Christ's flesh and blood in the Lord's Supper. Although how one conceptually achieves this mysteriously physical presence is not unimportant, the main point for Luther is that one knows that Christ is substantially present in his body and blood "for you" (*pro me*).[72]

It is for this reason that Luther was considerably less tolerant when it comes to the sacramental symbolism of a figure like Zwingli.[73] From

66. On the Babylonian Captivity of the Church (1520), LW 36:38.

67. On the Babylonian Captivity of the Church (1520), LW 36:28–35.

68. See Brett Salkeld, *Transubstantiation: Theology, History, and Christian Unity* (Grand Rapids: Baker Academic, 2019), 57–138.

69. On the Babylonian Captivity of the Church (1520), LW 36:33–34.

70. On the Babylonian Captivity of the Church (1520), LW 36:34–35.

71. On the Babylonian Captivity of the Church (1520), LW 36:35.

72. Paul Althaus, *The Theology of Martin Luther*, trans. Robert Schultz (Philadelphia: Fortress, 1966), 379.

73. Lohse, *Martin Luther's Theology*, 169–77; Sasse, *This Is My Body*, 134–294.

Luther's perspective, Zwingli ignores the divine promise that Christ's flesh and blood will be present on an rationalistic ground, namely, that bodies cannot be at more than one location at once. As we have seen Luther rejects this logic and affirms that although Jesus's body remains a real body, it participates in God's glory and can transcend the normal boundaries of physicality.[74] After all, in the resurrection Jesus was able to walk through walls and appear and disappear at will. Jesus's body nevertheless remained a real body. Christ could still invite Thomas to place his fingers in the nail holes of his very real hands and eat fish with the apostles. Likewise, the mysterious supernatural quality of Christ's body in the Lord's Supper does not negate its real physicality or his genuine humanity.

As we noted earlier, these difference between Luther and Zwingli on the sacrament are due in part to competing concepts of the *communicatio idiomatum*.[75] Nevertheless, these differences also have implications regarding the nature of how the Word of God functions. For Zwingli, the words of institution are signifiers that merely signify.[76] For Zwingli, how the signifiers "body and blood" can be validly applied to the signified "bread and wine" (which they do not match) is a puzzle that can only be resolved by sacramental symbolicism.[77] For Luther, divine words are not mere signifiers, but promises that effect what they speak.[78] This is the same principle that we have seen earlier in his views of confession and absolution. Hence the words "this is my body ... this is my blood" possess divine power to bring about the presence of Christ's flesh and blood.[79] Faith must simply trusts that God's words perform what they promise. To believe otherwise would be to trust in human reason over God's clearly stated promises.[80]

---

74. Thomas Davis, *This Is My Body: The Presence of Christ in Reformation Thought* (Grand Rapids: Baker Academic, 2008), 41–64; Sasse, *This is My Body*, 148–60.

75. Sasse, *This is My Body*, 148–54.

76. See discussion in Aaron Moldenhauer, "Analyzing the *Verba Christi*: Martin Luther, Ulrich Zwingli, and Gabriel Biel on the Power of Words," in *The Medieval Luther*, ed. Christine Helmer (Tübingen: Mohr Siebeck, 2020), 53–56.

77. Ulrich Zwingli, "On the Lord's Supper," 175–238.

78. Moldenhauer, "Analyzing the *Verba Christi*," 57–61.

79. Confession Concerning the Lord's Supper (1528), LW 37:180–88.

80. That These Words of Christ "This is My Body" Still Stand Firm Against the Fanatics (1527), LW 37:131.

Taking his inspiration primarily from Martin Bucer,[81] Calvin sympathized with the concerns of both the Zwinglian and Lutheran Reformations and attempted to establish a *via media* between the two theological paradigms.[82] Hence, for the Genevan Reformer the Lord's Supper is not merely symbolic, since it does mediate a mode of Christ's presence with his church.[83] Nevertheless, this mode of Christ's presence is not objective for all who are present at the celebration of the Lord's Supper in that it is not received by unbelievers, but only by the elect.[84] Moreover, for Calvin the presence of Christ's flesh and blood is not genuinely substantial. Jesus is not orally received according to his mysterious physicality, as in Roman Catholic and Lutheran doctrine. Rather, Jesus is spiritually present by way of the mediatorial presence of the Holy Spirit.[85] The Holy Spirit connects true believers to Christ in heaven and allows them to feed on him spiritually by faith.[86]

From the perspective of the Lutheran paradigm there are number of difficulties with Calvin's view. First, it is unfounded exegetically. The words of institution promise Christ's substantial flesh and blood and not the presence of the Holy Spirit. Indeed, Calvin's entire position is extremely difficult to justify on the basis of any of the *sedes doctrinae* in the New Testament dealing with the Lord's Supper. There are simply no biblical texts that state that Christ is present in the Supper through the Holy Spirit. In the end, Calvin's doctrine of the Eucharist is an attempt to establish a form of the real presence while simultaneously accepting most (though not all) of the premises of Zwingli's Christology.[87]

Second, the objective bodily presence of Jesus is a necessary corollary of the full assurance that the gospel brings. As we have already seen, in

---

81. Martin Greschat, *Martin Bucer: A Reformer and His Times*, trans. Stephen Buckwalter (Louisville: Westminster John Knox, 2004), 76–77.

82. See B. A. Gerrish, *Grace and Gratitude: The Eucharistic Theology of John Calvin* (Eugene, OR: Wipf & Stock, 2002).

83. ICR, 4.17.33–34; Calvin, *Institutes*, 2:1405–11.

84. ICR, 4.17.33; Calvin, *Institutes*, 2:1407.

85. ICR, 4.17.33; Calvin, *Institutes*, 2:1405–8.

86. ICR, 4.17.32; Calvin, *Institutes*, 2:1403–5.

87. See the summary of Calvin's Christology in Stephen Edmondson, *Calvin's Christology* (Cambridge: Cambridge University Press, 2004); E. David Willis, *Calvin's Catholic Christology: The Function of the So-called Extra Calvinisticum in Calvin's Theology* (Leiden: Brill, 1966).

his earthly ministry Jesus assured sinners of his positive eschatological verdict in their favor by being physically present with them and having fellowship with them through common meals. Our physical bodies are our availability to one another.[88] To pledge one's self to another is to put one's self physically at the disposal of that other. In the giving of the gospel-promise God puts himself at the disposal of his creatures as a servant in order to fulfill the terms of the promise (Phil 2:7). God put himself at the disposal of his creatures first in the Tabernacle and Temple and its sacrifices in the Old Testament. Next the Lord became a human person with a body in the incarnation and continues this act of self-giving by making his bodily presence available through the Lord's Supper.

A God who remains intangible and therefore unavailable to his creatures in a graspable form would invariably remain a terrifyingly numinous presence that could not give the assurance of salvation.[89] We have already seen this reality in our discussion of the hidden God. To use an analogy: Although the concept of ghosts is merely a common human superstition, the reason humans find the very idea of ghosts to be frightening (1 Sam 28:12) is because a spirit without a body would be intangible and available to no one as an objectified presence. In that humans with bodies are objectified and tangible presences, they are at the disposal of others who can grasp their reality. Because of this, if ghosts were real, they would not be objectified, but could act on humans with bodies who are tangible and objectified. In this they would possess a terrifying power of being able to act and not be acted upon.

In keeping with the terrifying reality of unobjectified presences, when Jesus's disciples believed that he was a ghost, they were frightened. Jesus only became a comforting presence to the disciples when he said "See my hands and my feet, that it is I myself. Touch me and see. For a spirit does not have flesh and bones as you see that I have" (Luke 24:39–40). Therefore, whereas people not infrequently find ghosts disturbing, they find the idea of the tangible touch and physical presence of their relatives or friends to be a positive comfort.

---

88. Although we do not endorse all his conclusions, see a series of interesting and provocative arguments in regard to bodily presence and grace in Robert Jenson, "You Wonder Where the Body Went," in *Essays in the Theology of Culture* (Grand Rapids: Eerdmans, 1995), 216–24.

89. See Steven Paulson, "Graspable God," *Word & World* 32, no. 1 (2012): 51–62.

Because our bodily presence and trustworthiness are inexorably tied together in human experience, physicality represents a key manner in which humans inculcate fidelity. Physical intimacy within marriage best exemplifies this truth and is especially relevant to our study in light of the biblical motif of YHWH and Christ as the bridegroom to the people of God (Jer 31:32; Isa 54:5; Hos 2:7; Eph 5). Christians have always rejected premarital sex and adultery not only because of the destructive consequences of disease and unwanted pregnancies, but because giving one's self physically over to one's spouse is the ultimate pledge of one's loyalty and fidelity. To give one's body to another is to give one's very being. If one gives their very physical being away haphazardly, either for the sake of a pleasant weekend or in an affair, how can ultimate fidelity ever be established?[90] If one gives away their very enfleshed selves to anyone who strikes their fancy, nothing will be left over to give to one's spouse as an ultimate pledge. This is why the explanation that an act of infidelity was "just sex" is never convincing to the wronged partner.

Therefore, bodily self-gift is a necessary means of giving assurance of fidelity to the absolute promise of Christ the bridegroom of the church. It is not sufficient to treat the sacraments as small, symbolic tokens of love in the manner of a husband who occasionally gives trinkets to his wife.[91] Any relationship may be poorer without gestures like these small gifts, but a marriage is not a marriage in a biblical sense without fleshly consummation and unity (Gen 2:24; Eph 5:31). Through fleshly self-giving one "knows" (yada) one's spouse, that is, they gain a real participatory knowledge of their very physical being. In the same manner, we can be no more certain of our justification and eternal life than by physically receiving the very flesh and blood that was sacrificed for humanity on the cross (1 Cor 11:26) and raised in anticipation of the general resurrection (John 6:54). There is no ambiguity as to whether or not one is justified by the work of Christ when Christ himself is present and gives believers that same body and blood that was sacrificed for them on the cross. Just as baptism is a proleptic realization of the last judgment, so too paschal

---

90. Robert Jenson, *Systematic Theology*, 2 vols. (New York: Oxford University Press, 1997–1999), 2:91–92.

91. Carl Trueman's analogy for the sacraments. See Trueman, *Grace Alone*, 213–14.

feast of the Lord's Supper is the proleptic realization of the final bridal feast of the Lamb at the end of time (Rev 19:6–9).

CONCLUSION

The work of Christ through the Holy Spirit in the means of grace brings about both justification and sanctification. God's declaration of righteousness becomes a reality in the sanctified life of the Christian through the efficacy of the word. Therefore, in the final chapter we will examine how justification through the word refocuses the life of the believer in living out Christian freedom in receptivity to God's goodness and service to the neighbor in sanctification.

CHAPTER 16

Justification and the Christian Life:
The Sacramental Word in Action

T he word and sacrament ministry of the church mediates the real presence of the risen Jesus. Just as Jesus is the eternal Word who spoke forth the original creation (Gen 1; John 1), so too he speaks forth the new creation by means of the church's proclamation of his re-creative death and resurrection. Although through Christ God has pronounced sinners righteous in an unconditional forensic manner, this same forensic word is also an effective word that contains within itself transformative divine power. Therefore, as Luther puts it in the *Antinomian Disputations* of the 1530s, the law is fulfilled in the believer both by the imputation of Christ's atoning death for sin and by the Spirit working sanctification in the hearts and minds of believers.[1]

Because God works in, under, and through the means of grace, we will examine how Christ's real presence in his effective word establishes and governs Christian existence in anticipation of the final eschaton. From the original creation to the present, believers have always lived suspended between the times and under the authority of the two divine words of the law and the gospel. The original creation possessed an eschatological destiny typologically represented by the Sabbath rest on the seventh day of creation. God's goal of bringing his whole creation into the eternal

---

1. First Antinomian Disputation (1537), LW 73:74.

Sabbath rest did not change with the advent of sin. Nevertheless, after the entry of sin, the fallenness of creation complicated God's effort to bring his creation to fulfill its original goal. Jesus brings about this Sabbath rest by removing sin and bringing the eschaton into the present. Nevertheless, in the interim until the full incorporation of creation into God's eternal rest, Christians must continue to deal with the power of sin and strive to live a God-pleasing life in correspondence to their temporal vocations. Such an existence is lived under and governed by God's two effective words: the law and the gospel. In this chapter will examine how Christian existence in the current age lives out this paradoxical existence suspended between the old and new creation.

WORK AND REST IN THE OLD CREATION

Throughout the Bible, God reveals his character through his works.[2] This is no less true of the events of salvation history as it is in regard to the establishment of the original creation in Genesis 1. In speaking-forth the original creation, God's creative activity is not instantaneous, or continuous, but rather follows cycles of work and rest. The days in Genesis 1 begin at sundown ("there was evening, and there was morning") and end at the next sundown. Taken this way, God rests his powers before he works. Of course, the converse is also true. The six days of God's works lead to the fulfillment of creation in the Sabbath rest. The Sabbath rest is not only for God, but is something he invites his creation to participate in. Seen this way, rest not only makes work possible (as in the individual days of creation) but is also the ultimate byproduct of work. The work of creation actualizes God's cosmic order and allows God to rest his powers. The cosmos must exist in its fullness if it is to participate in God's rest.

Since as we have seen, God is revealed in his works and because we are told at the end of the first chapter of Genesis that humans are made after God's image (Gen 1:26–27), the pattern of work and rest becomes normative for human behavior and destiny. In Exodus, we are told that the cycle of work and rest of the original creation is normative for the

---

2. See discussion in Wolfhart Pannenberg, *Systematic Theology*, 3 vols. trans. Geoffrey W. Bromily (Grand Rapids: Eerdmans, 1991–1993), 1:169.

Israelite institution of the Sabbath rest (Exod 20:8–11).[3] God tells Israel to work for the first six days and rest on the seventh because this is precisely what he did at the beginning of creation. The implication is that because humans are made in God's image, they should also live according to the pattern of God's protological and eschatological works.[4]

The narrative of Genesis 1 is typological of the overall structure of history of creation as it is described in the biblical narrative. As we are told in the Epistle to the Hebrews (Heb 4:9–11), the Sabbath was never merely a day designated for religiously sanctioned rest, but an image of the eternal divine rest that God has sought to bring his creation to fulfillment in.[5] God's rest is identical with his presence. As Moshe Weinfeld has observed, there is a strong parallel between God's rest (sabat) on the seventh day of creation and his resting (sakan) in the Tabernacle in Exodus 40.[6] This fact becomes all the more significant when one realizes that the Tabernacle or Temple is an image of creation, as we saw in an earlier chapter.[7]

In Genesis 1, the coalescing of the image of God in humanity established as the pinnacle of creation on the sixth day and the divine rest/ presence on the seventh day parallel the fulfillment of the history of salvation in the incarnation as the ultimate gift of divine presence and rest. The incarnation prefigures the destiny of the whole creation. At the end of Revelation, we are told that the whole creation has become a Tabernacle of the divine presence (Rev 21:3, 21:22). This correlates well with Daniel's promise that the Temple mount (i.e., the locus of the presence of the divine kavod) would permeate the whole of creation (Dan 2:35).[8]

3. Daniel Timmer, *Creation, Tabernacle, and Sabbath: The Sabbath Frame of Exodus 31:12–17; 35:1–3 in Exegetical and Theological Perspective* (Göttingen: Vandenhoeck & Ruprecht, 2009), 56–57.

4. J. Gerald Janzen, *Exodus* (Louisville: Westminster John Knox, 1997), 269–70.

5. John Dunnill, *Covenant and Sacrifice in the Letter to the Hebrews* (Cambridge: Cambridge University Press, 2005), 137.

6. Moshe Weinfeld, "Sabbath, Temple and the Enthronement of the Lord — the Problem of the Sitz im Leben of Genesis 1:1—2:3," in *Mélanges bibliques et orientaux en l'honneur de M Henri Cazelles*, ed. A. Caquot and M. Delcor (Kevelaer: Butzer & Bercker, 1981), 501–12.

7. G. K. Beale, "Garden-Temple," *Kerux* 18, no. 2 (2003): 3–50; Beale, *Temple and the Church's Mission*, 31–36; P. J. Kearney, "Liturgy and Creation: The P Redaction of Exodus 25–40," *Zeitschrift fur Alttestamentliche Zeitschrift* 89 (1977): 375–87.

8. Beale, *Temple and the Church's Mission*, 144–53.

The promise of God's communicative presence and divine rest are inexorably tied up with the promise of grace found in the gospel. The gospel is a unilateral gift and as such it is an act of self-donation. To make an unconditional promise is to surrender one's being to the other and to cease to place any condition upon them (i.e., the works of the law). As we have already seen, this is also the covenantal imagery of marriage and its consummation (established in Gen 1), which is why the Bible uses the image of the nuptial feast for the eschaton (Luke 14:7–14; Rev 19:6–9).

God's works (and human works in response to God's works) in the protological week culminating in the Sabbath find their typological fulfillment in the eschatological promise of the divine presence and rest from all works.[9] In God's eschatological rest and presence at the end of time, the law of creation is fulfilled and there is no more need to work (i.e., the performance of the law). The fact that law proceeds the gospel in salvation history and in the life of the Christian mirrors the fact that God's works in the first six days preceded the divine rest. In Genesis 1, the week of works fulfilled in rest also prefigures Christ's actualization of the new creation through his works of active and passive obedience culminating in his Sabbath rest in the tomb.[10]

Nevertheless, as we have also seen, in the midst of the protological week, rest also precedes work. Since days are measured from evening to evening God rests before he works, and he establishes a cosmic order in which his creatures do the same. Just as the movement from works to rest (i.e., law to promise) parallels the redemptive movement of humans *coram Deo* through the work of Christ, humans as God's image bearers also imitate the movement of rest to work *coram mundo*.

Grace is fundamentally the promise of rest from need to engage in self-justifying works (Eph 2:8–9). Contrary what is often urged by the Reformed tradition, Genesis 1 and 2 does not envision a kind of covenant of works.[11] Nevertheless, in both the primal and redeemed state, freedom

---

9. Meredith Kline, *God, Heaven and Har Magedon: A Covenantal Tale of Cosmos and Telos* (Eugene, OR: Wipf & Stock, 2006), 195.

10. N. T. Wright, *The Resurrection of the Son of God*, Christian Origins and the Question of God 3 (Minneapolis: Fortress, 2003), 440.

11. Heinrich Heppe, *Reformed Dogmatics*, trans. G.T. Thomson (Eugene, OR: Wipf & Stock, 2007), 281–300; Michael McGiffert, "From Moses to Adam: The Making of the Covenant of Works," *Sixteenth Century Journal* 19 (1988): 131–55.

from the need to engage in justifying works enables active works of obedience in the human vocation of governing creation.[12] Being placed in
their vocation in the original creation, the first man and the first woman
are given the promise of dominion and also fertility, that is, the promise
of freedom and life (Gen 1:26–28). In the era of the new testament this
promise of freedom and life simply exists in different form in Christ's
promise of freedom from the law and eternal life. Enjoying the Sabbath
rest of their conscience *coram Deo*, Adam and Eve may engage in the task
of wisely governing creation and cultivating the garden *coram mundo*. The
same pattern of rest before work also obtains in the era of the new testament. The resurrection (which grants eschatological rest to the conscience
of sinners) occurred on the first day of the week so as enable the obedience
of the faithful in their vocation the subsequent days of the week.[13]

In the prelapsarian state, the primal humans enjoyed both God's rest
from works in their inner person and his presence in the protological
Temple of Eden. When they dwelt in the protological temple, the garden of
Eden, that is, the locus of divine presence in creation, the works of Adam
and Eve in cultivating the garden are described using similar Hebrew
words to those used to denote the activities of the Levitical priests later
in Numbers 3:7–8; 8:26; 18:5–6.[14] The clear implication is that their vocational works in the garden are to be understood in terms of priestly activities. By performing their tasks Adam and Eve are described as engaging
not in meritorious works, but in liturgical responses of praise for the gifts
of grace: dominion, life, freedom.

Moreover, Genesis implies that the Temple and Garden sphere of
grace was intended to be ever expanding. As John Walton has suggested,
as Adam and Eve bore children and humanity increased its numbers,
this would invariably extend the boundaries of the Garden until it filled
the whole creation.[15] Since the divine presence was coterminous with
the garden, the extension of the boundaries of the garden to the whole of

---

12. See Gustaf Wingren, *Luther on Vocation*, trans. Carl Rasmussen (Eugene, OR: Wipf & Stock, 2004).

13. Many thanks to Rev. David Fleming for this insight.

14. See the full discussion of priestly role in John Walton, *The Lost World of Adam and Eve: Genesis 2–3 and the Human Origins Debate* (Downers Grove, IL: InterVarsity Press, 2015), 104–15.

15. John Walton, *Genesis* (Grand Rapids: Zondervan, 2001), 186–87.

creation would then logically mean that the communicative presence of God would fill the whole earth as in Daniel 2 and Revelation 21.[16]

SIN AND THE PROBLEM OF THE LAW

Having discussed the role of humans in the prelapsarian order and its relationship to God's command and promise, it is necessary to examine how sin and its relationship to God's Word complicates and changes the divine and human relationship. The change brought to creation by sin is central to understanding how the new relationship between God and humans that justification inaugurates relates to sanctification and Christian ethics.

Central to the concerns of the Wittenberg Reformation was the proper distinction between law and promise.[17] As we observed in earlier chapters, the fundamental issue between Luther and Rome did not only pertain to the possibilities of human agency in the post-lapsarian state, as in the earlier conflict between Pelagius and Augustine.[18] Rather, Luther held that the divine-human relationship was at its heart structured around God's promise of unilateral favor, and only derivatively around obedience to God's commandments.[19] Therefore, to structure the divine-human relationship around the law (even empowered by grace) is necessarily to distort it. It of course must be urged in the strongest possible terms that both Scripture and all the Reformers of the sixteenth century (Luther included) held that the law is good since it is God's eternal and holy will.[20] This being said, when the law is made the fundamental matrix of the divine-human relationship it will invariably be twisted into an ethos of self-trust.

Because of the distorting effect of making the law the central framework of the divine-human relationship (*opinio legis*), it becomes clear

16. See G. K. Beale, *The Book of Revelation* (Grand Rapids: Eerdmans, 1999), 1111.

17. Jeffrey Silcock, "Luther on the Holy Spirit and His Use of God's Word," in Kolb, Dingel, and Batka, *The Oxford Handbook of Martin Luther's Theology* (Oxford: Oxford University Press, 2014), 300.

18. See Stuart Squires, *The Pelagian Controversy: An Introduction to the Enemies of Grace and the Conspiracy of Lost Souls* (Eugene, OR: Pickwick Publications, 2019).

19. Robert Kolb and Charles Arand, *The Genius of Luther's Theology: A Wittenberg Way of Thinking for the Contemporary Church* (Grand Rapids: Baker Academic, 2008), 104.

20. See discussion in John Witte, "Faith in Law: The Legal and Political Legacy of the Protestant Reformation," in *The Protestant Reformation of the Church and the World*, ed. John Witte and Amy Wheeler (Louisville: Westminster John Knox, 2018), 105–38.

why the historic Roman Catholic insistence that they too believed that salvation was contingent on divine assistance (i.e., grace) could not solve the problem that Luther raised.[21] If one believes that their relationship with God is fundamentally rooted in their performative righteousness, one cannot help but fall into prideful self-trust in the holiness of their works.[22] Conversely, one cannot help but despair if one does not believe that they have met God's standards by not correctly appropriating divine grace. Both stances rule out a total and complete trust in God's promises, which is the condition *sine qua non* of genuinely obeying the law of God. Even if it is acknowledged that a person can only fulfill the law if they are empowered by grace, such a theology will still orient the believer to focus on their own actions to secure their future and not God's promise to bring them to salvation. In the same manner, those who despair in their lack of the fulfillment of the law cannot trust in divine salvation.

Hence, from the standpoint of Luther, the Roman Catholic response that works merit salvation only by the power of grace ultimately fails. As Pelagius correctly observed, nature is also a gift of God,[23] and if humans empowered only by their natural capacities can glory in themselves by believing that they have gained salvation by obeying the law, then a graced human subject could just as easily abuse God's supernatural gifts and trust in himself. Any theology of grace that directs the human's hope of salvation to a quality or action internal to them directs the locus of trust inwardly and not outside the human subject to the divine promissory word of the gospel. The divine-human relationship can only be put right if it is established on the basis of God's "categorical gift"[24] through the word of promise external to the human subject (*extra nos*). This is true in both

---

21. See this excellent summary of the "Catholic Incomprehension" (the title of the third chapter) of the Lutheran critique of their doctrine of grace in: Daphne Hampson, *Christian Contradictions: The Structures of Lutheran and Catholic Thought* (Cambridge: Cambridge University Press, 2001), 97–142.

22. Willard Dow Allbeck, *Studies in the Lutheran Confessions* (Philadelphia: Fortress, 1968), 278.

23. James Bowling Mozley, *A Treatise on the Augustinian Doctrine of Predestination* (London: John Murray, 1883), 49.

24. Oswald Bayer, *Freedom in Response: Lutheran Ethics: Sources and Controversies* (Oxford: Oxford University Press, 2007), 13–20.

creation and redemption, since as we have already seen God establishes both unilaterally by his word of grace.[25]

If the law is not the foundation of the divine-human relationship, a number of other questions are raised. Most importantly among these questions is: How is one to define the law, and in what manner does it relate to Christian existence in the spheres of creation and redemption? Turning to the New Testament data on the subject, it should be observed that one criticism that scholars falling in the trajectory of the New Perspective on Paul make is that Luther was insufficiently cognizant of the differences between his historical situation and that of the Apostle.[26] As we have seen, this is in part because the New Perspective on Paul assumes that the Apostle is almost exclusively concerned with the ritual law whereas Luther is almost exclusively concerned with the moral law.

In responding to these charges, it should first be observed, as we have already shown in an earlier chapter, that the New Perspective on Paul distorts the Apostle's position by not taking into account that one of his key arguments was the inseparability of the ritual and moral law. Beyond this, as Stephen Westerholm has pointed out,[27] Luther was certainly aware of the difference between Paul's situation and his own. In the Great Galatians commentary, Luther explicitly affirms that Paul means the whole content of Sinaitic covenant (moral and ritual law), whereas his application of the term "law" primarily refers to the moral law and the late medieval expansions on it. What Luther recognized is that the principle that Paul established held good across differing historical situations: If the law of Moses (which was commanded directly by God) did not justify, then the ritual works of the medieval church (invented by humans) would not justify either.[28]

Paul's assertion was that Jewish rituals could not be separated out from the need to perfectly perform the moral law. Because of the power of sin,

25. Jaroslav Pelikan, *Luther the Expositor: Introduction to the Reformer's Exegetical Writings* (St. Louis: Concordia, 1959), 50–51.

26. James D. G. Dunn, *The Parting of the Ways: Between Christianity and Judaism and Their Significance for the Character of Christianity* (London: SCM, 2011), 14.

27. Stephen Westerholm, *Justification Reconsidered: Rethinking a Pauline Theme* (Grand Rapids: Eerdmans, 2013), 76.

28. Lectures on Galatians (1531), LW 26:139–41, 407.

it was impossible to be obedient to the moral law. Hence the Judaizers' insistence on the need for Christians to obey Jewish ritual law was meaningless when one realized that they would still be damned by their failure to obey every moral commandment (Rom 2:25). Luther's situation in the sixteenth century was of course quite different, but Paul's principle that right performance could not lead to divine favor or eschatological vindication also be applied to late medieval rituals and theories of merit. Indeed, Paul seems to anticipate this at least in Ephesians by replacing the formula of "the works of the law" with simply "works" in contrast to the "gift" of salvation (Eph 2:8–9).[29]

Since the reality of the law as a principle of legal relationship (morally charged human activity resulting in merit or demerit) as opposed to a principle of grace and promise relationship (i.e., *protoevangelium*, new covenant) applies across cultural and historical situations (Pharisees or Judaizers vs. Ockhamism), Luther gave other more expansive definitions of the law throughout his career rooted in the principles he discovered in his biblical exegesis. Much like many in the early and medieval church, Luther held that God's commandments given to Israel and the church expressed his just and holy eternal divine nature. It logically follows that if God is eternal (as Scripture affirms) then his will (which includes the law) must also be eternal. In his *Antinomian Disputations* of the 1530s, Luther affirmed that "the Decalogue is eternal."[30] Elsewhere Luther states the same doctrine. Since the law is "His [God's] will and counsel,"[31] it "serves to indicate the will of God,"[32] "commands eternally and firmly,"[33] and is "the eternal and immutable judgment of God."[34] Later Lutheran Scholasticism[35] would follow Luther and express the truth that the law is

29. J.V. Fesko, *Justification: Understanding the Classic Reformed Doctrine* (Philipsburg, NJ: P&R, 2008), 184.

30. First Antinomian Disputation (1537), LW 73:112.

31. Lectures on Deuteronomy (1524), LW 9:51.

32. Commentary on Psalm 19 (1531), LW 22:143.

33. WA 5:560, *inaeternum et stabiliter*. Translation my own.

34. Lectures on Genesis (1535-1545), LW 7:275.

35. See Gerhard Forde, *The Law-Gospel Debate: An Interpretation of Its Historical Development* (Minneapolis: Augsburg, 1969), 3–11.

rooted in God's eternal nature through the utilization of the Stoic concept of *lex aeterna* (eternal law).[36]

Beyond affirming that the law was God's eternal and immutable will for his creation, in the *Antinomian Disputation* of the 1530s Luther also spoke of the law as anything in creation that expresses the condemnation of sin. Part of this formulation was aimed at responding to the work of the early Lutheran heretic Johann Agricola. Agricola believed that only a heartfelt love of God could inspire true repentance. Because it was the gospel and not the law that inspires fallen humanity's love for God, it then also followed that preaching the promise of the gospel to the exclusion of the law should occur. The law was good, but only for the use of the civil authority.[37]

Luther countered Agricola's claims by noting that because God's wrath against humanity based on its violation of the law was at work in the whole of creation, then simply excluding certain biblical texts or the word "law" from preaching would do no good. Death, destruction, illness, and all the vicissitudes of the fallen creation preached the law (i.e., the consequences of not following the law) to fallen humans without any explicit word of law from the preacher: "Anything that exposes sin, wrath, or death exercises the office of the law."[38] Hence by the preacher excluding the preaching of the law, they achieved nothing. Indeed, since God mandates the preaching of both the law and the promise, the preacher would be guilty of dereliction of duty by not preaching the law.[39]

It should be noted that the later Formula of Concord agrees with Luther that the law is eternal in defining the law as: "the eternal and immutable righteousness of God."[40] Although later Lutheranism frequently ignored this second way of talking about the law as any manifestation of

---

36. Gunnar Skirbekk and Nils Gilje, *A History of Western Thought: From Ancient Greece to the Twentieth Century* (London: Routledge, 2001), 94.

37. See discussion of Agricola's early position in Timothy Wengert, *Law and Gospel: Philip Melanchthon's Debate with John Agricola of Eisleben over Poenitentia* (Grand Rapids: Baker, 1997), 84–89. Also see description in F. Bente, *Historical Introduction to the Book of Concord* (St. Louis: Concordia, 1965), 161–69.

38. Theses for the Second Disputation Against the Antinomians (1538), LW 73:54.

39. Against the Antinomians (1539), LW 47:111.

40. FC SD III.57; *Concordia Triglotta: The Symbolical Books of the Evangelical Lutheran Church, German-Latin-English*, trans. and ed. F. Bente, W. H. T. Dau, and Lutheran Church Missouri Synod (St. Louis: Concordia, 1921), 935.

wrath in creation, the Formula of Concord approvingly cites passages in which Luther speaks to this effect: "Anything that preaches concerning our sins and God's wrath, let it be done how or when it will, that is all a preaching of the law."[41]

Luther's two different ways of speaking about the law may initially seem contradictory to some readers, but in reality they are easily reconcilable. Because sin is a violation of God's will and commandment, God works his wrath through the death, decay, disease, and many disasters of the old creation (Rom 8:20). God's activities of wrath through his creaturely masks in time are an expression of the fact that his creatures have violated his eternal will (Rom 1:18–19). God's eternal will would be the same if there was no sin, but the law becomes a destructive menace because of sin (Rom 7:10). The law is good in itself and only becomes a problem as a result of sin (Rom 7:11–12).

The late nineteenth century Luther scholar Theodosius Harnack conceptualizes these different ways of speaking about the law in Luther's thought according to his distinction between the "essence" (wesen) and "office" (amt) of the law. According to its essence, the law was for Luther the eternal statutory will of God, while according to its office in a fallen creation, it was God's will to condemn his creatures for standing out of harmony with that eternal law.[42] Although many (though not all) of the texts that Harnack cited in favor of this position were shown to be spurious later interpolations by editors of the Weimar Ausgabe,[43] Harnack's conceptual scheme still possesses much heuristic value in light of the texts that we have cited above.

The connection between the condemning effect of the law and sin also raises the issue of the relationship between the law and the life of the believer. As St. Paul writes, "Now we know that the law is good, if one uses it lawfully, understanding this, that the *law is not laid down for the just but for the lawless and disobedient, for the ungodly and sinners*" (1 Tim 1:8–9, emphasis added). Following Paul's claim that law is only set down

---

41. FC SD V.12; *Concordia Triglotta*, 955.

42. Theodosius Harnack, *Luthers Theologie besonderer Beziehung auf seine Versöhnung und Erlösunglehre*, 2 vols. (Amsterdam: Rodopi, 1969), 1:368–401.

43. See Robert Schultz, *Gesetz und Evangelium in der Lutherischen Theologie des 19. Jahrhunderts* (Berlin: Lutherisches Verlagshaus, 1958), 142.

for sinners, in the *Antinomian Disputations* Luther gives an eschatological account of the law's authority in the life of the believer. The law is of course always normative for the believer since it is eternally the will of God for his creatures. That being said, to the extent that the human subject stands in compliance with the will of God, that eternal will may have a different function in relationship to the believer in time: "the Decalogue is eternal—in its substance, of course, not as Law—for in the life to come, it will simply be what it used to demand here."[44]

Therefore, Luther asserts that insofar as the sin ceases, law also ceases. By this, the Reformer does not mean that God ceases to will the Ten Commandments, but rather that the divine commandments cease to be condemning or function as positive external commandments to the extent that one is justified and sanctified: "[W]e are free even from this Law in a double way, and it ceases through Christ, for He is the one who fulfills that emptiness, (by Himself, outside of me, for He fulfills the Law for us,) and I do so in Him."[45] To use an analogy: although it is always the will of a parent that a child to keep their room clean, they will not ask them to clean their room if it is already clean. If the child began to habitually clean their room, then most parents would never bother to ask their children to clean again. Hence, law is genuinely abrogated by the gospel, but only on the basis of its fulfillment. The preaching of the effective sacramental word justifies and sanctifies believers. A person is forgiven by justification, while being made positively righteous by sanctification. To the extent that sanctification is at work in their hearts and minds, a believer does the law spontaneously as a result of their renewed nature and therefore does not need an external commandment.

The truth that the law functions as a positive command only under sin can also been seen in the example of the prelapsarian state. In the Genesis narrative, Adam and Eve never received the Ten Commandments since the biblical narrative implies that it would never have even occurred to them in the state of integrity to lie, murder, or commit adultery. While in the present age humans are never perfectly sanctified and therefore always subject to the law as a positive demand, at the eschaton the law

44. First Antinomian Disputation (1537), LW 73:112.
45. Second Antinomian Disputation (1538), LW 73:127.

will continue to exist as God's will but will not function as a positive demand in the life of the glorified. The eternal divine law will become a *lex vacua* ("empty law")[46] that cannot command anything to persons who are already in compliance with it: "Where sin ceases, the Law ceases. And to the extent that sin has ceased, to that same extent the Law has ceased, even as in the life to come the Law must cease completely because then it will have been fulfilled, for no trace of sins will survive there nor any in that could be accused by the Law."[47]

Of course, it could be objected that the claim that the law as an external command is coterminous with sin is contradicted by the existence of the commandment not to eat from the tree of the knowledge of good and evil in the state of integrity. Luther acknowledges that some claim that in the state of integrity that there was no law but rejects it by saying that this claim is "full of wickedness and blasphemy."[48] Indeed, if there were no commandments then how could the primal humanity revolt against God by disobeying them (1 John 3:4)? The Formula of Concord agrees that humans were given commandments before the fall into sin: "For the Law of God has been written in their heart, and also to the first man immediately after his creation a law was given according to which he was to conduct himself."[49]

In order to harmonize these statements with Luther's teaching in the *Antinomian Disputations* about law ceasing with sin, a number of things should be kept in mind. First, it is important to recognize that the absence of the law as a positive command does not mean that the law does not exist. It remains God's will, whether humans simply obey it as a matter of course (as in the state of integrity or heaven) or need to be asked to comply with it (as in the state of sin). Second, the prelapsarian state was a unique situation where sin was a possibility, but not yet an actuality. Such a state stands in contrast with the rest of human history under sin or the final glorified state of divine rest from all works. Luther states in the *Antinominian Disputations* that when he says that law ceases with sin,

---

46. Second Antinomian Disputation (1538), LW 73:126.
47. Second Antinomian Disputation (1538), LW 73:125.
48. Lectures on Genesis (1535-1545), LW 1:108.
49. FC SD VI.5; *Concordia Triglotta*, 963.

he is not speaking of the primal state (as in the Genesis commentary), but of the final glorified state. After the eschaton, believers will receive what Augustine called "confirmation in the good"[50] and therefore sin will cease to even be a possibility, unlike in the primal state of integrity. In the glorified state, there will be no need for negative (do not!), or positive commands (do this and live!), since there is will be no sin and no possibility of sin.

Seen in this light, it should be observed that obedience to the commandment not to eat from the tree of the knowledge of good and evil was not a positive commandment (which as we have seen, presupposes sin), but a negative one (which presupposes the possibility of sin). The key point is that Adam and Eve as Genesis describes them were created in compliance with the commandment not to eat from the tree of the knowledge of good and evil. Obedience to the commandment was something that they had already positively achieved in accord with how they were created. Indeed, the primal humans did not need to justify themselves because they were created righteous and dwelling in the sphere of God's grace and presence.[51]

Rather, the command given in Eden not to eat was a boundary that they should not cross. As a negative commandment (you will not!) the commandment not to eat from the tree of the knowledge of good and evil indicated the place where the possibility of sin was open to the primal humans. The command not to eat was a divine word attached to the tree of the knowledge of good and evil, thereby promising that the tree would serve as a medium of condemning law, divine hiddenness, and wrath. As we observed in an earlier chapter, after the primal humans were cast out of the garden (the sphere of grace), they and the rest of humanity could only return to the sphere of grace and fellowship with God by a positive fulfillment of the law. In the Tabernacle or Temple (the reconstituted Eden), this was only achieved by bloody sacrifice and burnt offering on

---

50. Augustine, *Enchiridion on Faith, Hope, and Love*, 118; NPNF[1], 3:275.

51. David Scaer, "Law and Gospel in Lutheran Theology," *Logia* 3, no. 1 (Epiphany, 1994): 30. Scaer writes, "The law as a positive affirmation was understood by man only during his brief stay in paradise. He knew God as his Creator, accepted his responsibility for creation and procreated. He was prohibited from stepping out of this positive relationship with God. But this prohibition is not arbitrarily superimposed on man to test him, but was simply the explanation or description of what would happen to man if he stepped outside of the relationship with God in which he was created."

the Day of Atonement (Lev 16).[52] This prefigured the fact that Christ would remove the barrier to sin by atonement and justification (bloody sacrifice) and sanctification (the fire of Pentecost).[53]

Faith is the essence of righteousness, just as we have already seen that unbelief is the essence of sin (Rom 14:23).[54] Faith gives birth to genuine obedience, because it trusts that God wishes us the best, and his commandments are for our good. Hence, obedience consists in harkening to God's promises wherein he indicates where one may receive the good that he communicates through the mediums of his creatures. As we have likewise seen, the other trees in the garden (including the tree of life) possessed a promise to mediate earthly life and heavenly immortality.[55] In chapters 1–2 of Genesis, God also attaches a word of promise to the fertility of humanity and the male-female relationship of marriage. One complies with the law by finding and passively receiving the good that God wishes to communicate in the trees of the garden (other than the tree of the knowledge of good and evil) and the man and the woman in each other's bodies.

After the entry of sin into the world, the law ceases to be merely a negative command, but also a positive one.[56] Because of original sin, fallen humanity is born already clinging to those things to which God has attached a word of condemnation. In the case of the sixth commandment, he bids humanity to flee the bodies of those to whom they are not married and cling to that of their spouse. The reality of inborn lust makes such a command something positive that humans must work to achieve, that is, loving and desiring one's spouse to the exclusion of others. The very fact that such a commandment is spoken presupposes that it is already being violated and that humans upon hearing it stand condemned (Gal 2:18). God would not need to condemn adultery if humans did not already desire it.

---

52. Peter Leithart, *Delivered from the Elements of the World: Atonement, Justification, Mission* (Downers Grove, IL: InterVarsity Press, 2016), 106–7.

53. Leithart, *Delivered from the Elements of the World*, 169–70.

54. See Lectures on Genesis (1535–1545), LW 1:147, Freedom of a Christian (1520), LW 31:361; Johann Gerhard, *On Sin and Free Choice*, trans. Richard Dinda (St. Louis: Concordia, 2014), 15.

55. Lectures on Genesis (1535–1545), LW 1:92.

56. Contrary to the claims of Elert. See Werner Elert, *Law and Gospel*, trans. Edward Shroeder (Philadelphia: Fortress, 1967), 31–43.

Beyond the sixth command, one could also examine all the commandments and observe how God bids humanity to flee the place where he has attached his word of condemnation and flee to the place where he has promised to communicate the good. For example: God bids humans to find the good in his Lordship (first commandment) and flee from idols, to find the good in the authority of our parents and civil authorities (fourth commandment) and flee our inner desire for rebellion, and to find the divinely communicated good in our own property and not another's (nineth and tenth commandment), etc.

Hence Luther states in the Catechisms that to obey each commandment we must "fear and love God."[57] Humans properly "fear God" when they flee from the place of his wrath. Humans properly "love" God when they find him where he has attached his word of promise and receive the good that he communicates there. Luther states that this is the reason why the first commandment is the sum of all commandments.[58] The first commandment can function either as a command (trust God!) or as a promise that God is infinitely more trustworthy than any idol—that is, the sum of the gospel.[59]

From this it should be clear that the biblical religion categorically rejects the notion that humans can generate the good by their obedience. Rather, the commandments when read within the overarching framework of the promise of the first commandment assert that God freely gives the good in creation and then redemption, and humans passively receive it. God creates the creature-creator relationship, the male-female relationship in marriage, other human beings, and property. Law does not create these goods, but merely protects them and directs humans toward them. Obedience is not a means of actualizing a kind of potency of the good into an actuality, as in the Aristotelian or Thomistic theory of virtue ethics.[60] Neither are humans through their obedience "created co-creators" of the good.[61] Instead, in faith humans trustingly find God's categorical

---

57. SC I; *Concordia Triglotta*, 539–43.

58. LC I.47; *Concordia Triglotta*, 47.

59. LC I.39; *Concordia Triglotta*, 591.

60. See Jörn Müller, Matthias Perkams, Tobias Hoffmann, eds., *Aquinas and the Nicomachean Ethics* (Cambridge: Cambridge University Press, 2013).

61. See Philip Hefner, *The Human Factor: Evolution, Culture, Religion* (Philadelphia: Fortress, 1993).

gift where he has promised to communicate it and flee from where God has promised condemnation. The law protects and directs humans to the good that God creates by his Word, but it does not create it.

THE THREEFOLD USE OF THE LAW

As we observed in the previous section, through the power of sin (Rom 7:14) the law becomes condemning when it once was not (Rom 7:10). It might be objected that the law also possessed a role of condemnation prior to the fall in that it promised judgment to those who would eat of the tree of the knowledge of good and evil. While this is correct in the sense that the law promised a potential condemnation of humans if they disobeyed the command not to eat, it was not an actualized condemnation. By contrast, in the postlapsarian state humans experience relentless condemnation from the law, even when they possess some civil righteousness (Rom 1:18).

Prelapsarian humans did not experienced the commandment not to eat as a form of condemnation or terrifying threat, since they were created in compliance with it and therefore could never feel accused by it as a positive demand that they needed to achieve. Indeed, as Luther states God established the command not to eat not as a means of condemnation or even self-justification (as in the later Reformed doctrine of the "covenant of works"),[62] but as a means of worship.[63] Humans would delight in the command not to eat as a way of showing their gratitude for all that God had given humanity in the form of the promise of freedom and life.[64]

After the entry of sin, the law becomes a threat and condemnation, and therefore also a positive command about how righteousness is to be achieved. Apart from the revelation of the Mosaic law (Exod 19–20), humans possess a knowledge of this threat and condemnation of the law from both their conscience (Rom 2:15) and the natural order of the universe (Rom 1:20). Because of this universal (though somewhat fragmentary) knowledge of the law,[65] humans are ever placed in the position of

---

62. Heppe, *Reformed Dogmatics*, 281–300.
63. Lectures on Genesis (1535–1545), LW 1:103–4.
64. Lecture on Genesis (1535–1545), LW 1:103.
65. See Lewis, *The Abolition of Man*.

being self-justifiers.[66] In this, justification before others and ultimately before God himself becomes the central problem of human existence. It is the quest to justify one's self before God and other humans that has generated all the world religions and secular philosophies of redemption (Marxism, etc.).[67]

Although the law has the office (*amt*) of threat and condemnation after the entry of sin, it exercises such coercive force in a different manner on humans based on whether they are regenerate. In light of the realities of both sin and redemption, the Lutheran tradition (as well as the Reformed) came to speak of the law having several uses (*usus legis*).[68] Although Luther certainly speaks of multiple functions of the law,[69] the concept of *usus legis* originated with Melanchthon and was developed as a result of his debate with Johann Agricola over the place of the law in the Christian's life.[70] Calvin also adopted the notion of the law having various uses, although he numbered them somewhat differently than Lutheran dogmaticians.[71] Both Lutheran and Reformed theologians of the era of Scholastic Orthodoxy and the major confessional documents of both communions affirm the three uses of the law (*triplex usus legis*).[72] This being said, there has been considerable debate in the Lutheran tradition over the third use of the law in the twentieth century.[73]

---

66. Eberhard Jüngel, *Justification: The Heart of the Christian Faith*, trans. Jeffrey Cayzer (Edinburgh: T&T Clark, 2001), 6–7.

67. See George Wolfgang Forell, *The Ethics of Decision: An Introduction to Christian Ethics* (Philadelphia: The Muhlenberg, 1955), 47–63; Adolf Koberle, *The Quest for Holiness: Biblical, Historical, and Systematic Investigation*, trans. John Mattes (Eugene, OR: Wipf & Stock, 2004), 1–47.

68. See Reformed and Lutheran views in Robert Kolb and Carl Trueman, *Between Wittenberg and Geneva: Lutheran and Reformed Theology in Conversation* (Grand Rapids: Baker Academic, 2017), 39–43; Jonathan Linebaugh, ed., *God's Two Words: Law and Gospel in Lutheran and Reformed Traditions* (Grand Rapids: Eerdmans, 2018).

69. See Thomas McDonough, *The Law and the Gospel in Luther: A Study of Martin Luther's Confessional Writings* (Oxford: Oxford University Press, 1963).

70. Wengert, *Law and Gospel*, 195–57.

71. ICR, 2.7.6–12; *Calvin, Institutes*, 1:354–61

72. L'ubomir Batka and Anna Marie Johnson, "Law and Gospel," in *T&T Clark Companion to Reformation Theology*, ed. David Whitford (New York: T&T Clark, 2012), 83.

73. See the controversial essay Gerhard Ebeling, "On the Doctrine of the *Triplex Usus Legis* in the Theology of the Reformation," in *Word and Faith*, trans. James Leitch (Philadelphia: Fortress, 1963), 62–78. See the summary of the conflict in Scott Murray, *Law, Life and the Living God: The Third Use of the Law in Modern American Lutheranism* (St. Louis: Concordia, 2001).

Within the Lutheran schematization, the first use of the law is the civil use of the law (*usus politicus sive civilis*). The Lutheran Formula of Concord describes this use thus: "[T]he Law of God is useful ... to the end that external discipline and decency are maintained by it against wild, disobedient men."[74] The first use of the law describes the use of the law by the state and other social institutions to discipline the unregenerate. The goal of the first use of the law is maintain order, so it involves a watered-down version of the moral law. If everything that is immoral becomes illegal, the law becomes unenforceable and scofflaws are produced. This explains in part why the law of Moses allows breaches of the moral and natural law (divorce on any grounds, slavery, polygamy, etc.), as Jesus himself explains (Matt 19:8).[75]

The nature of the first use of law possesses certain anthropological premises. As we observed in an earlier chapter, human beings are creatures of desire. Humans are not the authors of their own desires, neither can they voluntarily remove their desires.[76] Under the power of sin, they are enslaved to unbelief and hatred of God precisely because it is what they desire to do (John 8:34; Rom 8:7; 1 Cor 2:14; Eph 2:3–5). Nevertheless, in regard to external decision making, humans are capable of restraining their desires and making better or worse moral decisions.[77] This is especially the case if they are given an incentive structure. Therefore, a thief may desire to steal a diamond, but might not do so if he is presented with the possibility that he will go to jail. For this reason, the Formula of Concord assumes that the first use of the law only applies to the unregenerate, since those enslaved to sin only do good in an external and earthly sense (*coram mundo*) as a means of preserving self-interest and status (i.e., self-justification). From God's perspective, every action performed apart from faith is sinful (Rom 14:23), so that although humans can do some good external works from a relative and human perspective

---

74. FC SD VI.1; *Concordia Triglotta*, 963.

75. See the argument in this regard in William Webb, *Slaves, Women & Homosexuals: Exploring the Hermeneutics of Cultural Analysis* (Downers Grove, IL: InterVarsity Press, 2001).

76. The Bondage of the Will (1525), LW 33:65; Gerhard Forde, *The Captivation of the Will: Luther vs. Erasmus on Freedom and Bondage*, ed. Steven Paulson (Grand Rapids: Eerdmans, 2005), 47–60.

77. The Bondage of the Will (1525), LW 33:70.

(Rom 2:14–15), they are incapable of doing anything righteous from God's perspective (Rom 7:18).[78]

The second use of the law (*usus elenchticus sive paedagogicus*) is the law whereby, in the church's proclamation, sinners are convicted of their sins and brought to repentance: "[T]he Law of God is useful ... likewise, that through it men are brought to a knowledge of their sins."[79] Within the Lutheran tradition this is the chief function of the law: "the law always accuses."[80] Indeed, Paul spoke primarily of the law as a revealer of sin: "[I]f it had not been for the law, I would not have known sin. For I would not have known what it is to covet if the law had not said, 'You shall not covet' (Rom 7:7). The law likewise reveals God's wrath at sin: "For the law brings wrath'" (Rom 4:15). For this reason, that Paul asserts that the law is an active worker of death: "For the letter [i.e., the law] kills, but the Spirit gives life" (2 Cor 3:6). Hence as an efficacious divine word of judgment, the law executes the divine judgment on the sinner in order to bring new life.

Again, as we have seen, humans are desiring creatures who under original sin possess desires that are configured against God in unbelief. It is possible that moral exhortation may be able to convince humans to change their external behavior to a certain degree, but it cannot make them change their inner sinful desires. God is concerned with the state of the heart and secondarily with the actual deeds done (1 Sam 16:7; Matt 23:27). Hence, even the unregenerate's good works before God are sinful (Gen 6:5; Isa 64:4; Phil 3:8).

Therefore, human sinful desires must be pacified and killed by the law (Gal 5:24). As a result of the preaching of the law, the sinner must die and be brought to the point of total passivity before the judgment seat of God (Rom 3:19). All self-justification must be ended, so that the sinner can become receptive to God's act of new creation through the preaching of the gospel (2 Cor 5:17). As Gerhard Forde observes, the law-gospel "hermeneutic itself is shaped by death-life language. It takes the shape of the

---

78. See Luther's argument in *Against Latomus* (1521), LW 32:133–260. Also see Anna Vind, *Latomus and Luther: The Debate: Is Every Good Deed a Sin?* (Göttingen: Vandenhoeck & Ruprecht, 2019), 169–311.

79. FC SD VI.1; *Concordia Triglotta*, 963.

80. Ap III.45; *Concordia Triglotta*, 168.

cross: the letter kills the old, and through it, when one at last meets the end of one's sinful ways, the spirit, the life-giving word is given."[81]

By reducing humanity to the state of death, through the preaching of the law the Holy Spirit prepares hearers of the word for the passive receptivity of faith (*vita passiva*).[82] To be passive before God is the proper stance of the creature before God's address. To be a creature is to passively receive one's being and all that is good from God's continuous narration of creation into existence by his Word and his Spirit (Gen 1:1–3; Ps 33:6). Sin makes humans active before God's address of law. This active stance before the Lord takes the form of either revolting against the word that is spoken to one through antinomianism or justifying one's self against the annihilating judgment of the law through legalism. The Holy Spirit working through the preaching of the law ends the creature's rejection of the law accusation and places the creature and the Creator in their proper relationship.

Within the history of mainstream Lutheran and Reformed theology, the first two uses of the law have been relatively non-controversial. Nevertheless, in the twentieth century the third use of the law (*usus didacticus sive normativus*) has been a point of contention among some Lutherans.[83] Part of the reason for this is that Luther generally only speaks of two uses of the law (ordering and condemning)[84] and the third use of the law was first explicated by Melanchthon in his struggle with Johann Agricola.[85] Nevertheless, the majority of the second generation of the Wittenberg Reformation affirmed the third use of the law (a large number of Gnesio-Lutherans and all Philippists),[86] and it therefore was established as normative teaching for the Lutheran church in the Formula of

---

81. Gerhard Forde, *Justification by Faith: A Matter of Death and Life* (Milifinton, PA: Sigler, 1999), 15.

82. Oswald Bayer, *Theology the Lutheran Way*, trans. Jeffrey Silcock and Mark Mattes (Grand Rapids: Eerdmans, 2007), 21–27.

83. See Gerhard Forde, *The Law-Gospel Debate: An Interpretation of Its Historical Development* (Minneapolis: Augsburg, 1969); Scott Murray, *Law, Life and the Living God: Third Use of the Law in Modern American Lutheranism* (St. Louis: Concordia, 2001).

84. See Lectures on the First Epistle to Timothy (1528), LW 28:233–34; Lectures on Galatians (1531), LW 26:308–13. See comment in Oswald Bayer, *Martin Luther's Theology: A Contemporary Interpretation*, trans. Thomas Trapp (Grand Rapids: Eerdmans, 2008), 61; H. H. Kramm, *The Theology of Martin Luther* (Eugene, OR: Wipf & Stock, 2009), 60; Bernhard Lohse, *Martin Luther's Theology: Its Historical and Systematic Development* (Minneapolis: Fortress, 1999), 270–73.

85. Wengert, *Law and Gospel*, 196.

86. See discussion in Eugene Klug, "The Third Use of the Law," in *A Contemporary Look at the Formula of Concord*, ed. Robert Preus and Wilbert Rosin (St. Louis: Concordia, 1978), 187–204.

Concord.[87] This establishment of the third use of the law as part of the official position of the Lutheran church was done in a belief that such a teaching was faithful both the Holy Scripture and essence of Luther's thought.[88]

The Formula of Concord defines the need for the third use of the law thus: "[The] elect, and regenerate children of God need in this life not only the daily instruction and admonition, warning, and threatening of the Law, but also frequently punishments, that they may be roused [the old man driven out of them] and follow the Spirit of God."[89] The key thing to recognize is that for the Formula of Concord the third use of the law is necessary because of the *simul* of Christian existence. This is in harmony with Luther's teaching in the *Antinomian Disputations*, which affirms that the external teaching of law is necessary because of sin.[90] As we have seen, law as an external command presupposes at minimum the possibility of sin (negative commands) or the state of sin (positive commands). The Formula of Concord affirms that if Christians were sinless, they would need no preaching of the law whatsoever: "[I]f the believing and elect children of God were completely renewed in this life by the indwelling Spirit, so that in their nature and all its powers they were entirely free from sin, they would need no law."[91]

The law must be preached to Christians as a moral exhortation (Rom 6:13) because although believers are sanctified in their inner person due to the work of the Spirit, their external person is still subject to the corruption of sin (Rom 7:22–23; 8:10). Believers continue to desire those things to which God has attached his word of condemnation to even as they simultaneously seek engage in behavior consistent with trust in and love of God. The preaching of the law cannot create inner freedom from sin or write the law upon the heart (Deut 30:6). Only the proclamation of the new covenant can do this (Jer 31:33; Ezek 11:19; 2 Cor 3:6). The Formula of Concord expresses this biblical teaching in stating: "For the Law says indeed that it is God's will and command that we should walk

87. FC SD VI; *Concordia Triglotta*, 963–71.
88. The Concordists explicitly affirm their desire to stand in continuity with Luther' thought. See FC SD, Comprehensive Summary, 9; *Concordia Triglotta*, 853.
89. FC SD VI.9; *Concordia Triglotta*, 965.
90. Second Antinomian Disputation (1538), LW 73:125.
91. FC SD VI.6; *Concordia Triglotta*, 963, 965.

in a new life, but it does not give the power and ability to begin and do it; but the Holy Ghost, who is given and received, not through the Law, but through the preaching of the Gospel, Gal 3:14, renews the heart."[92] Therefore although the law cannot circumcise the heart or write the divine commandments upon it, it can instruct the external person, who can consent to making right or wrong moral choices.

The believer's situation of continuing sanctification while still dealing with the power of sin gives the third use of the law both a negative and positive dimension. The state of sin presupposes the existence of potentially sinful behaviors that one should avoid. Because of their remaining sinful desires, the believer is impeded from automatically performing the good. Nevertheless, since the inner person has been renewed, it is capable of listening to the law and restraining the sinful desire that drives the human person toward sinful actions (1 Cor 9:24–27).

The fact that believers not only need to avoid potential sin, but also need to positively perform the good in their actions is why although the Ten Commandment are technically stated as purely negative commands ("you shall not"), Luther suggests in his Catechisms that a negative command necessarily implies a positive command. To avoid any act of murder or harm of our neighbor implies that we conversely find the good in the divine mask (larva Dei) of our neighbor and therefore work for their betterment. Because we are sinful by nature, we need not only to flee from that which is evil, but also to flee toward what is good. Without the knowledge of what good to flee to, we might very well flee from one evil to another.

Hence, it is impossible to subsume the third use of the law under the first use of the law as many twentieth century Lutheran theologians have sought to do.[93] Although Luther seems to have defined the first use of the law expansively according to an ordering function that applies to both believers and non-believers, the Formula of Concord refined Luther's insight in light of the various antinomian controversies that occurred

---

92. FC SD VI.11; Concordia Triglotta, 965.

93. See Werner Elert, Law and Gospel, trans. Edward Shroeder (Philadelphia: Fortress, 1967); Gerhard Forde, "Luther's 'Ethics,'" in A More Radical Gospel: Essays on Eschatology, Authority, Atonement, and Ecumenism, ed. Mark. Mattes and Steven Paulson (Grand Rapids: Eerdmans, 2004), 137–58; Wingren, Creation and Law.

in Lutheranism before and after the Reformer's death.[94] Following the Concordists' schematization, the first use of the law is the minimum of the moral law necessary to keep order in society among non-believers. It is used not by the church (which lacks police powers), but by the state and other coercive institutions in society. The third use of the law is the whole moral law, preached by the church as a form of exhortation, not enforced by police power. It is applied to believers insofar as their empirical behavior remains out of accord with the justification and sanctification that they received in baptism.

It has similarly been charged by some twentieth century Lutheran theologians that there can be no third use of the law because the gospel is eschatological and it must therefore be the final Word of God to the believer.[95] After all Paul writes, "For Christ is the end [telos= end, goal, fulfillment] of the law for righteousness to everyone who believes" (Rom 10:4). The gospel enacts the Sabbath rest of the believer, where they repose in Christ and their works cease: "Come to me, all who labor and are heavy laden, and I will give you rest" (Matt 11:28). As Luther states in the *Antinomian Disputations*, it is correct to say that the preaching of the gospel is the final word that eschatologically abrogates the law because it causes the law to be completely fulfilled through imputation (justification) and renewal of the inner person (sanctification).[96] In that through faith in the word believers receive justification, the law is completely removed.

Nevertheless, in terms of the external person and the earthly life, the law remains a guide and spur to good behavior until the eschaton and temporal death. As we saw, in the first week of creation, works do not merely lead to rest (week of work followed by Sabbath), but rest proceeds work (night of rest before day of work). In the same way, the rest of the believer's conscience from all works simultaneously allows their external person to live out their works of sanctification propelled by both the joy of Christian freedom as well as the threat of negative consequences.

94. Charles Arand, Robert Kolb, and James Nestingen, *The Lutheran Confessions: History and Theology of the Book of Concord* (Minneapolis: Fortress, 2012), 191–200.

95. Gerhard Forde, "The Apocalyptic No and the Eschatological Yes: Reflections, Suspicions, Fears, and Hopes," in Mattes and Paulson, *A More Radical Gospel*, 17–32.

96. Second Antinomian Disputation (1538), LW 73:126–27.

Perhaps one helpful way of conceptualizing how the law can be fulfilled and abrogated *coram Deo*, while remaining a rule of life *coram mundo*
is through Luther's distinction between two (active and passive),[97] or in
some cases three (civil, imputed, sanctified),[98] kinds of righteousness.[99]
Coram Deo, one is righteous or unrighteous not by what they do, but what
they receive. We passively receive our sinful nature from our parents,
which in turn colors everything we do or leave undone. Likewise, faith
is created by a monergistic act of the Holy Spirit, and we receive the gift
of imputed righteousness and a renewed heart passively. This passive
gift of righteousness completely abrogates the law *coram Deo*. From the
perspective of this relational horizon, the law as condemnation moves to
the gospel as freedom from condemnation. Once the gospel has arrived,
the law no longer holds sway since it is completely fulfilled.

In terms of our external person *coram mundo*, humans are good or
bad based on what they do (i.e., active righteousness). Under the first
use of the law, the unregenerate can make better or worse decisions and
likewise be judged as just or unjust by what they do. A person is defined
as a good spouse, parent, or citizen based on the extent to which they
behave well in these roles. Indeed, as far as active and civil righteousness
is concerned, Aristotle and Thomas Aquinas are essentially correct. One
can indeed even train themselves to act in a habitually correct way within
their roles in society. Likewise, under the gospel and the third use of the
law the regenerate can cooperate with the Holy Spirit and can listen to
and obey the commandments of God through specific external actions.
The faithful do this both as an act of gratitude for the gifts of creation
and redemption that they have received, as well as to restrain the wicked
impulses which remain present in them this side of the eschaton.

It should be noticed that fallen humans tend to reverse these two kinds
of righteousness. Rather than being judged by who they are before God
(children of Adam, or redeemed sinners in Christ), humans desire to be

---

97. Lectures on Galatians (1531), LW 26:7–8; Two Kinds of Righteousness (1519), LW 31:297–306.

98. Sermon on Three Kinds of Righteousness (1518), WA 2:43–47.

99. See Charles Arand, "Two Kinds of Righteousness as a Framework for Law and Gospel in
the Apology," *Lutheran Quarterly* 15, no. 4 (2001): 417–39; Robert Kolb, "Luther on the Two Kinds
of Righteousness: Reflections on His Two-Dimensional Definition of Humanity at the Heart of His
Theology," *Lutheran Quarterly* 13, no. 2 (1999): 449–66.

righteous by their works. As a result, humans have created the various world religions (which work on the basis of the *opinio legis*),[100] as well as rationalistic or moralistic schemes of theodicy.[101] *Coram mundo*, humans desire not to be judged righteous and worthy of status on the basis of what they do, but on the basis of who they are. In human history, this has given rise to the sins of racism, sexism, and classism.

SANCTIFICATION AND THE ETHOS
OF CHRISTIAN FREEDOM[102]

Since the time when the Reformation revived the biblical teaching regarding justification, numerous controversies have arisen regarding how justification has been applied to the Christian life. One significant problem is that the necessary distinction between justification and sanctification has hardened to the point that on a popular level many people have come to functionally separate the two.[103] As we saw in an earlier chapter, this was in part necessary conceptually due to the challenge of Osiander's teaching to the unconditional and forensic nature of justification.[104] This being said, in retrospect, the conceptual separation of sanctification from justification caused many to see the proclamation of justification being simply a matter of acquittal, and not a powerful divine word that simultaneously forgives and renews the heart. As we will argue below, as a result of this lack of full appreciation of the efficacy of the gospel, many Protestants have drifted into a form of either an antinomian or pronomian stance. In

100. Chris Marantika, "Justification by Faith: Its Relevance in Islamic Context," *Right with God: Justification in the Bible and the World*, ed. D. A. Carson (Eugene, OR: Wipf & Stock, 2002), 228–42; Sunand Simithra, "Justification by Faith: Its Relevance in Hindu Context," in *Right with God*, 216–27; Masao Uenuma, "Justification by Faith: Its Relevance in Buddhist Context," in *Right with God*, 243–55.

101. Gregory Boyd, *God at War: The Bible and Spiritual Conflict* (Downers Grove, IL: InterVarsity Press, 1997); Boyd, *Satan and the Problem of Evil: Constructing a Trinitarian Warfare Theodicy* (Downers Grove, IL: InterVarsity Press, 2001); Leibniz, *Theodicy*.

102. This section contains material (in an altered form) from the following short essay: Jack Kilcrease, "Sanctification and Concepts of the Self," *Logia: A Journal of Lutheran Theology* 27, no. 4 (2018): 61–62.

103. See one example of this in K. L. Gentry, "Lordship Controversy: Faith Alone/Faith and Submission", in *The Westminster Handbook to Evangelical Theology*, ed. Roger Olson (Louisville: Westminster John Knox, 2004), 317–19.

104. See Wengert, *Defending Faith: Lutheran Responses to Andreas Osiander's Doctrine of Justification, 1551–1559* (Tübingen: Mohr Siebeck, 2012).

our discussion, we will use these terms to broadly designate these two historic tendencies within Protestantism for the sake of convenience without any pejorative intent. These differing factions have become visible in many and various ways throughout the history of Protestantism in conflicts as diverse as the "Marrow Controversy"[105] and the debates among Lutherans in the twentieth century over the validity of the third use of the law.

Speaking in very general terms, in the history of Protestantism those who stand on the "antinomian" side of the debate over sanctification tend to emphasize the totalizing nature of human sin and the purely forensic nature of justification. One can see this tendency in some of persons involved in the second and third antinomian controversies in Lutheranism,[106] as well as some Neo-Lutherans of the twentieth century. Within this theological trajectory, the continued fallenness of the believer is emphasized over any affirmation of regeneration. For the antinomian faction, this is often seen as the proper way of understanding the *simul* of Christian existence. As a result, the Christian is to focus on the imputation of righteousness singularly and find nothing but sin within themselves. The third use of the law is either subsumed under the first use of the law,[107] or simply relabeled as a new, gospel-ethic.[108]

Another faction might be described as the pronomian group. This tendency can be found in Lutheran Pietism,[109] or in Anglo-American

105. See Sinclair Ferguson, *The Whole Christ: Legalism, Antinomianism, and Gospel Assurance—Why the Marrow Controversy Still Matters* (Wheaton, IL: Crossway, 2016).

106. Arand, Kolb, and Nestingen, *The Lutheran Confessions*, 191–200.

107. See Werner Elert, *Law and Gospel*, trans. Edward Shroeder (Philadelphia: Fortress, 1967); Gerhard Forde, "Luther's 'Ethics,'" in *A More Radical Gospel: Essays on Eschatology, Authority, Atonement, and Ecumenism*, ed. Mark. Mattes and Steven Paulson (Grand Rapids: Eerdmans, 2004), 137–58; Wingren, *Creation and Law*.

108. See Paul Althaus, *Gebot und Gesetz: Zum Thema Gesetz und Evangelium* (Gütersloh: Bertelsmann, 1952); Johannes von Hofmann, *Theologische Ethik* (Nördlingen, C. H. Beck, 1878); Nygren, *Agape and Eros*.

109. See Douglas H. Shantz, *An Introduction to German Pietism: Protestant Renewal at the Dawn of Modern Europe* (Baltimore: Johns Hopkins University Press, 2013); Heinrich Schmid, *The History of Pietism* (Milwaukee: Northwestern, 2007).

Puritanism[110] and the Dutch *Nadere Reformatie.*[111] For the pronomian, the antinomian faction's emphasis on the totality of sin kills the possibility of good works or renewal. After all, if humans even in a state of grace are completely and irredeemably sinful, how does one conceptualize sanctification or good works? Is it also then not logical that sanctification and the third use of the law must necessarily be rejected, if not in word, certainly in practice?

For this reason, this pronomian faction in the debate has emphasized the numerous statements of the Bible and the great confessions of the Reformation era regarding the transformation of believers by the power of the Spirit. Genuine faith cannot lie dormant, but necessarily gives rise to a renewal of the inner person and subsequently good works by the external person. Theoretically the pronomian group would continue to affirm the *totus peccator* of believers,[112] while at the same time speaking of sanctification as a gradual removal of sinfulness. As a result, pronomians tend to functionally operate with a sense of believers as only partial (*partim*) sinners.[113]

From the perspective of the antinomian faction, the implicit *partim* of the pronomians is indicative of a return to the Catholic doctrine of infused grace, wherein righteousness is an ontic quality that becomes a predicate of our being. Likewise, the antinomian faction often makes the objection that the pronomian view of progressive sanctification suggests that as sin is gradually removed the believer needs Christ less and less. As a result, it is often argued, the fundamental nature of the Christian life as total reliance on Christ is removed. Hence the pronomian position would theoretically affirm *sola gratia*, but in practice drives sinners to their works as a means of validating the authenticity of their faith.

Broadly speaking, both alternatives regarding sanctification are problematic because they fail to capture the original intention of Scripture

110. Michael Winship, *Hot Protestants: A History of Puritanism in England and America* (New Haven: Yale University Press, 2019).

111. Herman Selderhuis, "The Further Reformation," in *Handbook of Dutch Church History*, ed. Herman Selderhuis (Bristol, CT: Vandenhoeck & Ruprecht, 2014), 338–41.

112. Anne Eusterschulte, *Anthropological Reformations—Anthropology in the Era of Reformation* (Göttingen: Vandenhoeck & Ruprecht, 2015), 215.

113. Commentary on Romans (1516), WA 56:272.

regarding the relationship of sanctification to justification. The antinomian option describes believers as remaining sinners, and therefore max-
imally dependent on Christ. Nevertheless, this seems to imply that there
is no room for sanctification and instruction in the law, something clearly
important to both biblical and Reformation teaching. Conversely, the
second pronomian option would be to describe Christians as sanctified
and experiencing a continuous increase in good works. Sin is removed
from the sinner much like paint can be stripped from a wall. As a result,
sanctification seems to gradually remove the need for justification. This
would again contradict the centrality and sufficiency of Christ's righteousness in both biblical and Reformation teaching.

One angle for approaching the issues raised by both sides of the sanctification debate is by examining the common concept of the human self that
both factions labor under. Specifically, what both sides seem to presuppose
is that human beings are in an ultimate sense defined by qualities internal
to them. On the one side, it could be argued that the antinomian faction
holds that when humans look into their own hearts they find nothing but
sin and death. Therefore, it seems to logically follow that there can be no
change in believers due to sanctification, or perhaps only minimally so. If
there was, the sufficiency of Christ would be undermined. Conversely, it
seems to be the premise of the pronomian faction that if sanctification is
real change, then we find less sin in our hearts over time. If this is not the
case, how could sanctification be a reality? It could also be observed that
the medieval church held a similarly centered concept of the self which
drove on the belief in infused grace. For Augustine and Aquinas, if the self
is defined by qualities internal to it, then it must logically follow that the
grace of Christ cannot become ours in a proper sense without becoming
a predicate of our being.[114]

Perhaps another way to tackle the problem is to recognize that the
presupposition of the biblical worldview is that humans do not find the
center of their identity within themselves, but outside of themselves in
God's address to them. Genesis 1 teaches that creatures have their reality because the Word of God speaks them into existence. For this reason,

---

114. Alister McGrath, *Iustitia Dei: A History of the Christian Doctrine of Justification* (Cambridge:
Cambridge University Press, 2020), 42–58, 67–81, 103–45.

creation's existence is not centered within itself, but is ecstatic (that is, in the sense of existence outside of oneself) in that it is grounded in the external Word of God. Creatures are creatures specifically because they continuously receive their reality from outside themselves by God's sustaining address.[115]

What is true of the old creation is also true of the new creation. In the new creation brought about by Christ's death and resurrection, believers gain their reality and identity not by something within themselves, but by God's external address present in the means of grace. In denying the fact that they are grounded in the Word of God external to them, sinful humans contradict their very status as creatures and seek to find their identity in what is within themselves (*incurvatus in se*). In this, they assert the superiority of their own inner truth and self-judgment (enthusiasm). Therefore, God's address of law empties sinners of the validity of any of their inner judgments through its totalizing judgment of the proclamation of the law. Likewise, the sacramental word of the gospel draws sinners out of themselves so that through faith they can live outside of themselves in Christ, the proper object of their trust and the true source of their identity: "For you have died, and your life is hidden with Christ in God" (Col 3:3).

If humans find their true selves in the word external to them, then there is room to reconceptualize sanctification to overcome the problematic conclusions of both the antinomian and pronomian factions. First, the totalizing judgment of the law means that we cannot find anything within ourselves other than sin and death. Although the Holy Spirit dwells in the hearts of believers, he is a person with whom we have union, and not a quality infused in us. In recognizing their inner sinfulness, believers are drawn out of themselves to live in Christ by faith. This new life in Christ is not idle. As Scripture and all the Protestant Reformers emphasize, such faith gives rise to both a love of God, and a love for one's neighbor.[116] Nevertheless, it should be observed that in light of the ecstatic nature of

115. See Oswald Bayer, "Creation as History," in *The Gift of Grace: The Future of Lutheran Theology,* eds. Niels Hendrik Gregersen, Bo Holm, Ted Peters, and Peter Widmann, (Minneapolis: Augsburg Fortress, 2005), 253; Bayer, "God as Author of My Life History," *Lutheran Quarterly* 2 (1988): 437–56; Bayer, *Martin Luther's Theology,* 101–5; Bayer, "Poetological Doctrine of the Trinity," *Lutheran Quarterly* 15 (2001): 43–58.

116. George Wolfgang Forell, *Faith Active in Love: An Investigation into the Principles Underlying Luther's Social Ethics* (Eugene, OR: Wipf & Stock Publishers, 1999).

the life of faith, this love cannot be thought of as a kind of infused quality that augments our inner moral capacities. Rather, like faith, this sanctifying love draws us into a new ecstatic existence, lived outside of ourselves by the power of the divine Word. The renewed self lives ecstatically both through faith in the promise and in loving service to the neighbor (i.e., the word of the gospel and the third use of the law). Therefore, Luther remarks that the "Christian *lives not in himself*, but in Christ and the neighbor. He lives in Christ *through faith*, and in his *neighbor through love*."[117]

Sanctification is then not the building up of righteous qualities inside of believers, but believers learning to live outside of themselves as a result of their justification. Such an existence lived outside of ourselves neither destroys the *simul* of Christian existence, nor the full and robust reality of sanctification. The more the Christian meditates on the divine Word, the more he or she cannot help but feel the reality of his or her inner sinfulness. This recognition will undoubtedly be augmented by the fact that we sin every day and therefore the older we become the more we have to regret. Nevertheless, such a recognition of our innate sinfulness draws us ever more out of ourselves into Christ through faith. In turn, the love that faith in Christ gives rise to ever increases and overflows into our service to our neighbors.

Of course, Christian love is always imperfect. Hence, there is a genuine insight in Luther's early theology where he describes the believer as *partim peccator*,[118] and *peccatores in re, iusti autem in spe*.[119] In our present life, there is a real distinction between which actions of ours are the fruits of the Spirit and which are sins, as the Pauline delineation of the fruits of the flesh and Spirit demonstrates (Gal 5:19–25). Hence, from the perspective of the paradigm of "active" and "passive" righteousness, believers are *partim peccator* according to the former category. At the same time, any sin within us makes us *totus peccator* before God. One either sins, or does not, and this fact grants us a status of total sinfulness or righteousness before God. Even the good works of believers are imperfect, and therefore judged by the absolute standard of the divine law are in themselves sinful

---

117. LW 31:371. Emphasis added.

118. Commentary on Romans (1516), WA 56:272.

119. Commentary on Romans (1516), WA 56:269.

(Isa 64:6). Hence, we are not *partim peccator* before the eyes of God according to passive righteousness. In the present age, we are always total sinners *coram Deo* and therefore beggars before the divine throne of judgment and mercy.

The believer's sense of their sinfulness drives on their sanctification. If believers honestly contemplate their own actions, they cannot help but feel that their sinfulness outweighs their progress in good works. Indeed, the progress of sanctification cannot be quantified, and at times, we cannot detect any moral progress in our lives at all. Such reflections should inevitably lead us to repentance and ever-deeper faith in Christ. This divinely wrought faith in turn leads to our overflowing love for God and our neighbor. Thus, the Christian life can be seen as a perpetual cycle of believers suffering the work of the Word of God as law and gospel, until they are definitively transformed by their temporal death and resurrection.

CONCLUSION: RETURN TO THE GARDEN, ANTICIPATION OF THE KINGDOM

As we have already observed, the ethos of Christian freedom brought about by the sacramental word of justification returns us to the tasks of creation forfeited by expulsion from the garden: the shepherding of creation and the love of the neighbor. To have faith is not only to gain the certainty of salvation in Christ, but also to return to the garden and be placed in the position of Adam and Eve.[120] Like the primal humanity, believers possess dominion in creation and are free to offer up their vocational works as a doxology of thanksgiving.

As Luther shows in the *Freedom of a Christian*, believers are unified with Christ by faith and therefore possess the same dominion that Christ has achieved by his resurrection and ascension: "[God the Father] raised us up with him and seated us with him in the heavenly places in Christ Jesus" (Eph 2:6). Much as Christ was able to give all because he possessed all (Phil 2:6–8), Christians are now free to be priests because they are kings (1 Pet 2:9; Rev 5:10). To be a priest means to offer up sacrifice (Lev 21:6). As priests, Christians can offer their lives and their vocations to God as a "living sacrifice" (Rom 12:1). Christian can also offer themselves

---

120. Freedom of a Christian (1520), LW 31:360.

as a sacrifice to their fellow human beings, thereby imitating the self-giving nature of Christ in his reconciling work (John 13:14; Phil 2:5). Just as Christ's sacrifice was simultaneously wholly given to God the Father as atonement and wholly given to humans as justification,[121] so too the obedience of believers to God is at the same time wholly given to our neighbor as a work of love.

It therefore follows that although Christian ethical behavior is motivated by the reality of justification, it finds its fulfillment firmly within the sphere of creation. Believers live out this sacrificial ministry within what Luther called "the Three Estates" (*status, ordines, regimina, stände*),[122] or what later Lutherans called "the Orders of Creation" (*schöpfungsordnung*): the family, the church, and the state.[123] These three institutions define God's design for human vocation and therefore shape how believers order their lives and vocations prior to the eschaton.

Therefore, contrary to what many have urged, there is no special "gospel" ethic. The gospel is not a new law. Rather, the gospel is the promise of the forgiveness of sins and eternal life that ushers the believer into the eschatological rest from all works (Heb 4:3). The works of the law praise God and serve the neighbor in the present age prior to the eschaton. The law is a channel whereby we live out our vocation in the sphere of the old creation, and not a means for actualizing the eternal Sabbath rest. Even the Sermon on the Mount, which is often described as a kind of new ethic of the coming kingdom, is in reality Jesus's purification of centuries of misinterpretation of moral law.[124]

Even though there is no special eschatological ethic, the eternal Sabbath nevertheless does find expression in the works performed by believers. As we observed in the earlier section, the implicit mandate that Adam and his offspring had was to extend the liturgical space of the Temple-Garden to the whole of creation, thereby incorporating it into the eschatological rest of God's presence. Through its ministry, the church

121. Charles Porterfield Krauth, *The Conservative Reformation and Its Theology* (St. Louis: Concordia, 2007), 591.

122. See Lectures on Genesis (1535–1545), LW 1:103–6.

123. Adolf von Harless, *A System of Christian Ethics*, trans. A. W. Morrison (Brighton, IA: Just & Sinner, 2014), 416–99; Johann Michael Reu, *Christian Ethics* (Columbus: Wartburg, 1935), 256–354.

124. Dan Lioy, *The Decalogue in the Sermon on the Mount* (New York: Peter Lang, 2004), 138.

bring God's eschatological rest through the proclamation of the forgiveness of sins and the presence of the risen Jesus in the means of grace.

Likewise, having proleptically been given Christ's eschatological rest
in their inner person, through their self-donating vocational works in
the service of others Christians can give a foretaste of God's eternal rest.
As we have already seen, God gives rest to the saints by giving his very
person over to them and thereby ending all conditions of works. By serving the neighbor through their vocations, believers donate their person to
the service of others and give them rest for their works.[125] The vocational
works of believers are all performed in gratitude to God, much like Adam
and Eve performed liturgical works in the garden in gratitude for the gift
of the created order. Through the sharing of the gospel and the love of
the neighbor, Christians offer up a new doxology, which expresses gratitude to God for the gifts not only of creation but also of the new creation
brought about by the redemption of Jesus Christ (Rev 5).

---

125. See similar argument in Peter Leithart, *The Four: A Survey of the Gospels* (Moscow, ID:
Canon, 2010), 68–69.

CHAPTER 17

Six Theses on Justification:
Its Place in Christian Faith and Life

Justification is central to the biblical message about redemption in Christ as well as one of the major driving forces behind the Protestant Reformation. This centrality has in recent years been downplayed and pushed to the side in response to what are often perceived as more pressing challenges faced by the church in the early twenty-first century. Many modern theologians have focused on the Trinity, ecclesiology, or various forms of cultural and political engagement as central tasks of the church in the present era. It is nevertheless our goal in this work to reassert the centrality of justification for a new generation of Christians. The theses discussed below both encapsulate the basic systematic theological themes of this work, as well as give a brief and programmatic statement regarding what we believe the importance of justification is to Christian theology and ethics.

1. Justification is the center of Christian theology. The central task of the church is to proclaim justification through Christ.

2. Justification is a universal and objective event that has already occurred in Christ's resurrection.

3. Justification as an objective reality is made present to and is appropriated by believers through the presence of the risen Jesus in the Word and sacrament ministry of the church.

4. Justification is purely forensic but is efficacious in its proclamation. The proclamation of justification is efficacious precisely because it is purely forensic.

5. For this reason, justification reorients believers outside of
   themselves to what Christ has graciously done and promised,
   and away from all inner securities.

6. The work of the Spirit through the proclamation of justification pulls believers out of their own inner subjectivity to
   live outside themselves through faith in Christ and service
   to their neighbors.

SIX THESES EXPLAINED

1. Justification is the center of Christian theology.

Justification is the center of Christian theology because the salvation of
sinners is the goal of God's revelation in the Bible (*scopus Scripturae*) and
the ministry of the church. In saying this, we do not mean to suggest that
justification exhausts the content of the Christian faith. Obviously without
doctrines such as the Trinity, the divine essence and attributes, and creation,
and so forth, justification would be incoherent and meaningless. Neither
are we claiming that all other doctrines are deduced from the single doctrine of justification, as in so-called Central-Dogma theory. Rather, what
we mean in stating that justification is the central doctrine of Christianity
is that the ultimate goal of all of God's revelation is to clarify and promote
the proclamation of the doctrine of justification in the midst of the church.

2. The central task of the church is to proclaim justification through Christ.

Justification means being unconditionally forgiven and judged positively
righteous for the sake of Christ. Before his ascension, Jesus tasked his
church with the proclamation of repentance and the forgiveness of sins
in his name (Luke 24:47–48). Hence Jesus made the proclamation of justification central to the mission and identity of the church. This does not
exclude other tasks from the church's vocation. The community of believers engages in catechesis and moral formation of its members. It engages
in works of mercy to the marginalized and the suffering. Nevertheless,

these activities are penultimate to the ultimate identity defining task of the proclamation of the gospel of justification. Moreover, the good works performed by the church are ultimately merely a response to God's supreme mercy toward humanity in Christ.

3. Justification is a universal and objective event that has already occurred in Christ's resurrection.

Paul states in his Epistle to the Romans that Jesus was "delivered up for our trespasses and raised for our justification" (Rom 4:25). Paul here distinguishes between atonement, which occurs in the crucifixion, and justification, which occurs in the resurrection. In the crucifixion, Christ paid the Father for the sins of humanity. Having received the Son's payment for sin, on Easter morning the Father raised the Son and pronounced a universal and objective verdict of forgiveness on humanity. Hence: "in Christ God was reconciling the world to himself, not counting their trespasses against them" (2 Cor 5:19). Therefore "as one trespass led to condemnation for all men, *so one act of righteousness leads to justification and life for all men*" (Rom 5:18). The universal reconciliation of humanity with God through Christ is reality, and all resistance to it is unreality.

4. Justification as an objective reality is made present to and is appropriated by believers through the presence of the risen Jesus in the Word and sacrament ministry of the church.

Since the late eighteenth century, Lutheran theology has distinguished between objective and subjective justification. In objective justification, God has pronounced all humans forgiven in Christ's resurrection. Nevertheless, the objective reality of Christ's redemption must be appropriated and received, just as the objective reality of Adam's universal sin is individually appropriated and received by the particular act of human generation (Rom 5:12). The risen Jesus continues to be present in the ministry of the church, thereby communicating his reconciliation through Word and sacrament (Matt 18:20; 28:20; Luke 10:16). The same Jesus who is present in Word and sacrament will also serve as the judge of humanity at the end of time. We can be confident that his judgment of forgiveness and grace in the present will be the same as in the end. For this reason, an encounter with the means of grace is a proleptic realization of the eschaton in the present. Therefore, in subjective justification, faith appropriates this objective reality of justification present in the means of grace. Faith is necessary as a receptive organ to take hold of the redemption in Christ, and all those who reject faith in Christ will not be saved. Nevertheless, faith is not the cause of justification, but merely receives what is already fully realized in objective justification. Entering into fellowship with Christ through the means of grace, faith finds God already reconciled with humanity through the death and resurrection of Jesus (2 Cor 5:19).

5. *Justification is purely forensic but is efficacious in its proclamation. The proclamation of justification is efficacious precisely because it is purely forensic. For this reason, justification reorients believers outside of themselves to what Christ has graciously done and promised, and away from all inner securities.*

The Apostle Paul speaks of justification as an eschatological acquittal by God made for the sake of Christ (Rom 5:1). The metaphor used by Paul throughout his epistles is that of a courtroom. The judicial metaphor is particularly apt in light of the cosmic judgment of humanity by Christ that Paul sees coming at the end of time (Rom 2:16). Justification is God's favorable eschatological judgment of sinners on the basis of the work of Jesus received by faith. It is not dependent on any quality or disposition internal to the believer. This being said, the proclamation of justification as forensic fundamentally reorients sinners to the Word of God outside of themselves. Because justification is purely forensic, through proclamation of justification the Holy Spirit "raptures" (Luther) sinners out of their own subjectivity into the objective reality of salvation in Christ (2 Cor 3:6). Since sin is fundamentally to be curved in on one's self, forensic justification becomes an effective reality in the renewal of the sinner precisely because it is forensic. A forensic judgment is completely external to the sinner and takes away any possibility of looking for salvation or its assurance in anything within themselves. The reality of forensic justification refocuses the believer on the promise outside of themselves and thereby transforms the sinner's total existence.

6. The work of the Spirit through the proclamation of justification pulls believ-
ers out of their own inner subjectivity to live outside themselves through faith
in Christ and service to their neighbors.

Since justification is an objective reality in Christ and its manifestation in the means of grace, believers must continuously look away from anything within themselves to the promise of grace external to them. The promise of salvation gives full assurance because it is not only true, but also efficacious. The divine power of the promise of the gospel will carry the believer along to salvation at the eschaton. If the promise of salvation were untrue or ineffective, then God would be a liar. Because Christians can have confidence in the unconditional nature of salvation, they are freed for good works and desire to do them. Only by God taking away the law as a condition of his salvation is it possible to do good works. Good works are good only to the extent that they are motivated by the genuine love of God and neighbor. Since the legal relationship of fallen humanity to God makes good works the basis of the divine-human relationship, the sinner in this state must necessarily be driven on to do good works in order to curry favor with God. All works motivated by self-justification are tainted, no matter how externally pure and impressive in themselves (Matt 23:27–28). With the law fulfilled and removed as a basis of the divine-human relationship in Christ, the performance of the law for the right motivation is now possible for believers. Sanctification is therefore the process of getting used to living the new existence that justification has enacted. Over time, believers grow in holiness by acclimating themselves to living outside of themselves through faith in Christ and the loving service of their neighbor.

Bibliography

Adam, Gottfried. *Der Streit um die Prädestination im ausgehenden 16. Jahrhundert, eine Untersuchung zu den Entwürfen vom Samuel Huber und Aegidius Hunnius*. Neukirchen: Neukirchener Verlag, 1970.

Adams, Marilyn McCord. "Genuine Agency, Something Shared? The Holy Spirit and Other Gifts." Pages 23–60 in vol. 1 of *Oxford Studies in Medieval Philosophy*. Edited by Robert Pasnau. Oxford: Oxford University Press, 2013.

———. *William of Ockham*. 2 vols. Notre Dame, IN: University of Notre Dame Press, 1989.

Ahlstrom, Sydney E. *The Religious History of the American People*. New Haven: Yale University Press, 2004.

Alexander, Philip. "Torah and Salvation in Tannaitic Literature." Pages 361–402 in vol. 1 of *Justification and Variegated Nomism*. Edited by D. A. Carson, Peter T. O'Brien, and Mark Seifrid. Grand Rapids: Baker Academic, 2000.

Allbeck, Willard Dow. *Studies in the Lutheran Confessions*. Philadelphia: Fortress, 1968.

Allen, R. Michael. *Justification and the Gospel: Understanding the Contexts and Controversies*. Grand Rapids: Baker Academic, 2013.

———. *Reformed Theology*. London: Bloomsbury Academic, 2010.

Althaus, Paul. *Gebot und Gesetz: Zum Thema Gesetz und Evangelium*. Gütersloh: Bertelsmann, 1952.

———. *The Theology of Martin Luther*. Translated by Robert Schultz. Philadelphia: Fortress, 1966.

Ancelet-Hustache, Jeanne. *Master Eckhart and the Rhineland Mystics*. London: Longmans, 1957.

Anderson, Ray Sherman. *On Being Human: Essays in Theological Anthropology*. Grand Rapids: Eerdmans, 1982.

Angus, Samuel. "The Sources of the First Ten Books of Augustine's *De Civitate Dei*." PhD dis., Princeton University, 1906.

Anselm of Canterbury. *Cur Deus Homo?* Pages 100–183 in *A Scholastic Miscellany: Anselm to Ockham*. Translated and edited by Eugene R. Fairweather. Philadelphia: Westminster, 1966.

Appold, Kenneth. *The Reformation: A Brief History*. Malden, MA: Wiley-Blackwell, 2011.

Aquinas, Thomas. *Summa Theologiae*. Translated by Fathers of the Dominican Province. Notre Dame, IN: Ave Maria, 1981.

Arand, Charles. "Two Kinds of Righteousness as a Framework for Law and Gospel in the Apology," *Lutheran Quarterly* 15, no. 4 (2001): 417–39.

Arand, Charles, Robert Kolb, and James Nestingen. *The Lutheran Confessions: History and Theology of the Book of Concord*. Minneapolis: Fortress, 2012.

Aristotle. *De Anima*. Translated by J. A. Smith. Oxford: Oxford University Press, 1963.

———. *De Anima*. Translated by Christopher Shields. Oxford: Clarendon, 2016.

———. *Metaphysics*. Translated by Hugh Lawson-Tancred. New York: Penguin, 1998.

———. *Metaphysics*. Translated by W. D. Ross. Oxford: Clarendon, 1963.

———. *Nicomachean Ethics*. Translated by W. D. Ross. Oxford: Oxford University Press, 1963.

———. *Physics*. Translated by R. P. Hardie and R. K. Gaye. Oxford: Clarendon, 1962.

Arminius, James. "Private Disputations." Pages 9–452 in vol. 2 of *The Works of James Arminius*. Translated by James Nichols and William Nichols. Grand Rapids: Baker, 1996.

———. "Twenty-Five Public Disputations." Pages 390–669 in vol. 1 of *The Works of James Arminius*. Translated by James Nichols and William Nichols. Grand Rapids: Baker, 1996.

Arnold, Brian. *Justification in the Second Century*. Berlin: De Gruyter, 2017.

Atherstone, Andrew. *The Reformation: Faith and Flames*. Oxford: Lion, 2011.

Augustine. *Against Julian*. Translated by Matthew Schumacher. Washington, DC: Catholic University of America Press, 1957.

———. *Against the Academics and The Teacher*. Translated by Peter King. Indianapolis: Hackett, 1995.

————. *City of God.* Pages 1–511 in vol. 2 of *Nicene and Post-Nicene Fathers.* Edited by Philip Schaff. Peabody, MA: Hendrickson, 2004.

————. *Confessions.* Pages 45–208 in vol. 1 of *Nicene and Post-Nicene Fathers.* Edited by Philip Schaff. Peabody, MA: Hendrickson, 2004.

————. *Enchiridion on Faith, Hope, and Love.* Pages 237–76 in vol. 3 of *Nicene and Post-Nicene Fathers.* Edited by Philip Schaff. Peabody, MA: Hendrickson, 2004.

————. *On Baptism, Against the Donatists.* Pages 11–514 in vol. 4 of *Nicene and Post-Nicene Fathers.* Edited by Philip Schaff. Peabody, MA: Hendrickson, 2004.

————. *On Christian Doctrine.* Pages 515–97 in vol. 2 of *Nicene and Post-Nicene Fathers.* Edited by Philip Schaff. Peabody, MA: Hendrickson, 2004.

————. *On Free Choice of the Will.* Translated by Thomas Williams. Indianapolis: Hackett, 1993.

————. *On the Gift of Perseverance.* Pages 521–52 in vol. 5 of *Nicene and Post-Nicene Fathers.* Edited by Philip Schaff. Peabody, MA: Hendrickson, 2004.

————. *On the Grace of Christ.* Pages 214–257 in vol. 5 of *Nicene and Post-Nicene Fathers.* Edited by Philip Schaff. Peabody, MA: Hendrickson Publishers, 2004.

————. *On Nature and Grace.* Pages 116–54 in vol. 5 of *Nicene and Post-Nicene Fathers.* Edited by Philip Schaff. Peabody, MA: Hendrickson, 2004.

————. *On the Predestination of the Saints.* Pages 493–520 in vol. 5 of *Nicene and Post-Nicene Fathers.* Edited by Philip Schaff. Peabody, MA: Hendrickson, 2004.

————. *On the Spirit and the Letter.* Pages 80–115 in vol. 5 of *Nicene and Post-Nicene Fathers.* Edited by Philip Schaff. Peabody, MA: Hendrickson, 2004.

————. *The Retractions.* Translated by Mary Inez Bogan. Washington, DC: Catholic University of America Press, 1968.

————. *Sermons 273–305.* Translated by Edmund Hill. Hyde Park, NY: New City, 1994.

————. *Soliloquies.* Pages 537–60 in vol. 7 of *Nicene and Post-Nicene Fathers.* Edited by Philip Schaff. Peabody, Mass: Hendrickson, 2004.

————. *Tractates in the Gospel of John.* Pages 7–452 in vol. 7 of *Nicene and Post-Nicene Fathers.* Edited by Philip Schaff. Peabody, MA: Hendrickson, 2004.

————. *A Treatise Against Two Letters of the Pelagians.* Pages 374–415 in vol. 5 of *Nicene and Post-Nicene Fathers.* Edited by Philip Schaff. Peabody, MA: Hendrickson, 2004.

Aulén, Gustaf. *Christus Victor: An Historical Study of the Three Main Types of the Idea of the Atonement*. Translated by A. G. Hebert. New York: Macmillan, 1951. Repr., Eugene, OR: Wipf & Stock, 2003.

Austin, J. L. *How to Do Things with Words*. Cambridge, MA: Harvard University Press, 1975.

Ayres, Lewis. "Augustine on Redemption." Pages 416–27 in *A Companion to Augustine*. Edited by Mark Vessey. Oxford: Wiley-Blackwell, 2012.

Bagchi, David. "Luther's *Ninety-Five Theses* and the Contemporary Criticism of Indulgences." Pages 331–55 in *Promissory Notes on the Treasury of Merits: Indulgences in Late Medieval Europe*. Edited by Robert Norman Swanson. Leiden: Brill, 2006.

Bainton, Roland. *Here I Stand: A Life of Martin Luther*. Nashville: Abingdon, 1978.

Ballentine, Debra Scoggins. *The Conflict Myth and the Biblical Tradition*. Oxford: Oxford University Press, 2015.

Bandy, Alan. *A Greek Reader's Apostolic Fathers*. Eugene, OR: Cascade, 2018.

Barber, Malcolm. *The Cathars: Dualist Heretics in Languedoc in the High Middle Ages*. London: Routledge, 2004.

Barnes, Michel Rene. "Veni Creator Spiritus." https://www.marquette.edu/maqom/spiritus.pdf.

Barth, Gerhard. "Matthew's Understanding of the Law." Pages 58–164 in *Tradition and Interpretation in Matthew*. Edited by Günther Bornkamm, Gerhard Barth, and Heinz Joachim Held. Translated by Percy Scott. Philadelphia: Westminster, 1963.

Barth, Hans-Martin. *The Theology of Martin Luther: A Critical Assessment*. Translated by Linda Maloney. Minneapolis: Fortress, 2013.

Barth, Karl. *Church Dogmatics*. Edited by G. W. Bromiley and T. F. Torrance. 4 vols. Edinburgh: T&T Clark, 1956–1975.

Barth, Markus, and Verne Fletcher. *Acquittal by Resurrection: Freedom, Law, and Justification in Light of the Resurrection of Jesus*. New York: Holt, Rinehart & Winston, 1964.

Batka, Ľubomir, and Anna Marie Johnson. "Law and Gospel." Pages 72–85 in *T&T Clark Companion to Reformation Theology*. Edited by David Whitford. New York: T&T Clark, 2012.

Battenhouse, Roy Wesley. *A Companion to the Study of St. Augustine*. Grand Rapids: Baker, 1979.

Bauckham, Richard. *Jesus and the Eyewitnesses: The Gospels as Eyewitness Testimony.* Grand Rapids: Eerdmans, 2006.

———. *The Jewish World Around the New Testament.* Grand Rapids: Baker Academic, 2010.

Bauerschmidt, Fredrick Christian. "Augustine and Aquinas." Pages 113–30 in *The T&T Clark Companion to Augustine and Modern Theology.* Edited by C. C. Pecknold and Tarmo Toom. Edinburgh: T&T Clark, 2013.

Baur, August. *Zwinglis Theologie: Ihr Werden und Ihr System.* 2 vols. Zürich: Georg Olms Verlag, 1983–1984.

Baur, F. C. *The Church History of the First Three Centuries.* Translated by Allan Menzies. 2 vols. London: Williams and Norgate, 1878–1879.

———. *Paul the Apostle of Jesus Christ: His Life and Works, His Epistles and Teachings.* Grand Rapids: Baker Academic, 2010.

Bayer, Oswald. "Creation as History." Pages 253–63 in *The Gift of Grace: The Future of Lutheran Theology.* Edited by Niels Hendrik Gregersen, Bo Holm, Ted Peters, and Peter Widmann. Minneapolis: Augsburg Fortress, 2005.

———. *Freedom in Response: Lutheran Ethics: Sources and Controversies.* Oxford: Oxford University Press, 2007.

———. "God as Author of My Life-History." *Lutheran Quarterly* 2 (1988): 437–56.

———. "Justification: Basis and Boundary of Theology." Pages 67–85 in *By Faith Alone: Essays on Justification in Honor of Gerhard O. Forde.* Edited by Joseph A. Burgess and Marc Kolden. Grand Rapids: Eerdmans, 2004.

———. *Living by Faith: Justification and Sanctification.* Translated by Geoffrey Bromiley. Grand Rapids: Eerdmans, 2003.

———. "Martin Luther." Pages 51–66 in *The Reformation Theologians: Introduction to Theology in the Early Modern Period.* Edited by Carter Lindberg. Malden, MA: Blackwell, 2002.

———. *Martin Luther's Theology: A Contemporary Interpretation.* Translated by Thomas Trapp. Grand Rapids: Eerdmans, 2008.

———. "Poetological Doctrine of the Trinity." *Lutheran Quarterly* 15 (2001): 43–58.

———. *Promissio: Geschichte der reformatorischen Wende in Luthers Theologie.* Göttingen: Vandenhoeck & Ruprecht, 1971.

———. *Theology the Lutheran Way.* Translated by Jeffrey Silcock and Mark Mattes. Grand Rapids: Eerdmans, 2007.

———. "With Luther in the Present." *Lutheran Quarterly* 21 (2007): 1–16.

Beale, G. K. *The Book of Revelation*. Grand Rapids: Eerdmans, 1999.

———. "Garden-Temple," *Kerux* 18, no. 2 (2003): 3–50.

———. *The Temple and the Church's Mission: A Biblical Theology of the Dwelling Place of God*. Downers Grove, IL: InterVarsity Press, 2004.

Beasley-Murray, G. R. *Baptism in the New Testament*. Eugene, OR: Wipf & Stock, 2006.

Beatrice, Pier Franco. *The Transmission of Sin: Augustine and the Pre-Augustinian Sources*. Translated by Adam Kamesar. Oxford: Oxford University Press, 2013.

Bebbington, David. *Evangelicalism in Modern Britain: A History from the 1730s to the 1980s*. London: Routledge, 1989.

Bechler, Zev. *Aristotle's Theory of Actuality*. Albany, NY: SUNY Press, 1995.

BeDuhn, Jason. *Augustine's Manichaean Dilemma: Conversion and Apostasy, 373–388 C.E.* Vol. 1. Philadelphia: University of Pennsylvania Press, 2010.

Beeke, Joel. *Debated Issues in Sovereign Predestination: Early Lutheran Predestination, Calvinian Reprobation, and Variations in Genevan Lapsarianism*. Göttingen: Vandenhoeck & Ruprecht, 2017.

———. "Personal Assurance of Faith: The Puritans and Chapter 18.2 of the Westminster Confession," *Westminster Theological Journal* 55, no.1 (1993): 1–30.

———. *The Quest for Full Assurance: The Legacy of Calvin and His Successors*. Edinburgh: Banner of Truth, 1999.

Behm, J. "Diatheke." Page 160 in *Theological Dictionary of the New Testament: Abridged in One Volume*. Edited by Gerhard Kittel and Gerhard Friedrich. Translated by Geoffrey Bromiley. Grand Rapids: Eerdmans, 1985.

Beker, J. Christian. *The Triumph of God: The Essence of Paul's Thought*. Translated by Loren Stuckenbruck. Minneapolis: Fortress, 1990.

Bell, Theo. *Divus Bernhardus: Bernhard von Clairvaux in Martin Luthers Schriften*. Mainz: P. von Zabern, 1993.

Bente, F. *Historical Introduction to the Lutheran Confessions*. St. Louis: Concordia, 2005.

Bergsten, Torsten. *Balthasar Hubmaier: Seine Stellung zu Reformation und Täufertum, 1521–1528*. Kassel: J. G. Oncken Verlag, 1961.

Berkhof, Louis. *Systematic Theology*. Grand Rapids: Eerdmans, 1941.

Bernard of Clairvaux. *On Loving God: An Analytical Commentary by Emero Stiegman*. Kalamazoo: Cistercian, 1995.

———. *On the Song of Songs: Sermons in Cantica Canticorum*. Translated and edited by a Religious of C. S. M. V. London: A. R. Mowbray, 1952.

Betz, Hans. *Galatians: A Commentary on Paul's Letter to the Churches in Galatia*. Philadelphia: Fortress, 1979.

Bielfeldt, Dennis. "The Ontology of Deification." Pages 90–113 in *Caritas Dei: Beiträge zum Verständnis Luthers und der gegenwärtigen Ökumene: Festschrift für Tuomo Mannermaa zum 60. Geburtstag*. Edited by Oswald Bayer, Robert Jenson, and Simo Knuuttila. Helsinki: Luther-Agricola Society, 1997.

Billings, J. Todd. *Calvin, Participation, and the Gift: The Activity of Believers in Union with Christ*. Oxford: Oxford University Press, 2007.

Birch, Bruce, Walter Brueggemann, Terence Fretheim, and David Petersen. *A Theological Introduction to the Old Testament*. Nashville: Abingdon, 2005.

Bizer, Ernst. *Fides ex auditu: Eine Untersuchung über die Entdeckung der Gerechtigkeit Gottes durch Martin Luther*. Neukirchen: Neukirchener Verlag, 1966.

Blackman, E. C. *Marcion and His Influence*. London: SPCK, 1948.

Blenkinsopp, Joseph. *The Pentateuch: An Introduction to the First Five Books of the Bible*. New York: Doubleday, 1992.

Blocher, Henri. "Justification of the Ungodly (Sola Fide): Theological Reflections." Pages 465–500 in vol. 2 of *Justification and Variegated Nomism*. Edited by D. A. Carson, Peter T. O'Brien, and Mark Seifrid. Grand Rapids: Baker Academic, 2000–2004.

Blomberg, Craig. *The Historical Reliability of John's Gospel: Issues & Commentary*. Downers Grove, IL: InterVarsity Press, 2011.

———. *The Historical Reliability of the Gospels*. Downers Grove, IL: InterVarsity Press, 2007.

Blowers, Paul. *Drama of the Divine Economy: Creator and Creation in Early Christian Theology and Piety*. Oxford: Oxford University Press, 2012.

Boersma, Hans. *Violence, Hospitality, and the Cross: Reappropriating the Atonement Tradition*. Grand Rapids: Baker, 2004.

Böhl, Eduard. *The Reformed Doctrine of Justification*. Translated by C. H. Riedesel. Grand Rapids: Eerdmans, 1946.

Boland, Vivian. *St. Thomas Aquinas*. London: Bloomsbury, 2007.

Bonner, Ali. *The Myth of Pelagianism*. Oxford: Oxford University Press, 2018.

Bonner, Gerald. "Augustine on Romans 5:12," *Studia Evangelica* 2 (1968): 242–47.

———. "Pelagianism and Augustine." Pages 211–42 in *Doctrinal Diversity: Varieties of Early Christianity: A Collection of Scholarly Essays*. Edited by Everett Ferguson. New York: Garland, 1999.

———. *St. Augustine of Hippo: Life and Controversies*. Atlanta: Canterbury, 1986.

Bornkamm, Günther. *Jesus of Nazareth*. Translated by Irene and Fraser McLuskey. New York: Harper & Row, 1960.

Borsch, Frederick. *The Christian and Gnostic Son of Man*. Naperville, IL: Alec R. Allenson, 1970.

———. *The Son of Man in Myth and History*. Philadelphia: Westminster, 1967.

Bouyer, Louis. *The Spirit and Forms of Protestantism*. Translated by A. V. Littledale. Princeton: Scepter, 2004.

Bowe, Geoffrey Scott. *Plotinus and the Platonic Metaphysical Hierarchy*. New York: Global Scholarly Publication, 2003.

Boyd, Gregory. *God at War: The Bible and Spiritual Conflict*. Downers Grove, IL: InterVarsity Press, 1997.

———. *Satan and the Problem of Evil: Constructing a Trinitarian Warfare Theodicy*. Downers Grove, IL: InterVarsity Press, 2001.

Brague, Rémi. *The Law of God: The Philosophical History of an Idea*. Chicago: University of Chicago Press, 2007.

Brakke, David. *The Gnostics: Myth, Ritual, and Diversity in Early Christianity*. Cambridge, MA: Harvard University Press, 2010.

Brecht, Martin. *Martin Luther*. Translated by James Schaf. 3 vols. Philadelphia: Fortress, 1985–1994.

Brewer, Brian. *Martin Luther and the Seven Sacraments: A Contemporary Protestant Reappraisal*. Grand Rapids: Baker Academic, 2017.

Brighton, Louis. *Revelation*. St. Louis: Concordia, 1999.

Brosché, Fredrik. *Luther on Predestination: The Antinomy and the Unity Between Love and Wrath in Luther's Concept of God*. Stockholm: Almqvist & Wiksell, 1978.

Brown, Dale. *Understanding Pietism*. Grand Rapids: Eerdmans, 1978.

Brown, Harold O. J. *Heresies: Heresy and Orthodoxy in the History of Church*. Peabody, MA: Hendrickson, 1998.

Brown, Peter. *Augustine of Hippo: A Biography*. Berkley: University of California Press, 2000.

Brown, Raymond. *The Death of the Messiah, From Gethsemane to the Grave: A Commentary on the Passion Narratives in the Four Gospels*. Vol. 1. New York: Doubleday, 1994.

Brunner, Peter. *Worship in the Name of Jesus*. Translated by M. H. Bertram. St. Louis: Concordia, 1968.

Buber, Martin. *I and Thou*. Translated by Ronald Gregor Smith. Edinburgh: T&T Clark, 1987.

Burkett, Delbert. *The Son of Man: A History and Evaluation*. Cambridge: Cambridge University Press 1999.

Burnaby, John. *Amor Dei*. London: Hodder and Stoughton, 1938.

Burnett, Amy Nelson. *Debating the Sacraments: Print and Authority in the Early Reformation*. Oxford: Oxford University Press, 2019.

Burnside, Jonathan. *God, Justice, and Society: Aspects of Law and Legality in the Bible*. Oxford: Oxford University Press, 2011.

Bushar, James. *Irenaeus of Lyons and the Mosaic of Christ: Preaching Scripture in the Era of Martyrdom*. London: Routledge, 2017.

Byars, Ronald P. *The Sacraments in Biblical Perspective*. Louisville: Westminster John Knox, 2011.

Cajetan, Tommaso de Vio. "Augsburg Treatises 1518." Pages 49–55 in *Cajetan Responds: A Reader in Reformation Controversy*. Edited by Jared Wicks. Eugene, OR: Wipf & Stock, 2011.

Calvin, John. *Concerning the Eternal Predestination of God*. Translated by J. K. S. Reid. Louisville: Westminster John Knox, 1997.

———. *The Institutes of the Christian Religion*. Edited by John T. McNeill. Translated by Ford Lewis Battles. 2 vols. Philadelphia: Westminster, 1967.

———. *Instruction in the Faith (1537)*. Translated by Paul Fuhrmann. Louisville: Westminster John Knox, 1992.

Campbell, Douglas. *The Deliverance of God: An Apocalyptic Re-Reading of Justification in Paul*. Grand Rapids: Eerdmans, 2013.=

Carroll, John. *Luke: A Commentary*. Louisville: Westminster John Knox, 2012.

Carson, D. A. *Matthew*. Grand Rapids: Zondervan, 1984.

———. "The Vindication of Imputation: On Fields of Discourse and Semantic Fields." Pages 46–78 in *Justification: What's at Stake in the Current Debates*. Edited by Daniel Trier and Mark Husbands. Downers Grove, IL: InterVarsity Press, 2004.

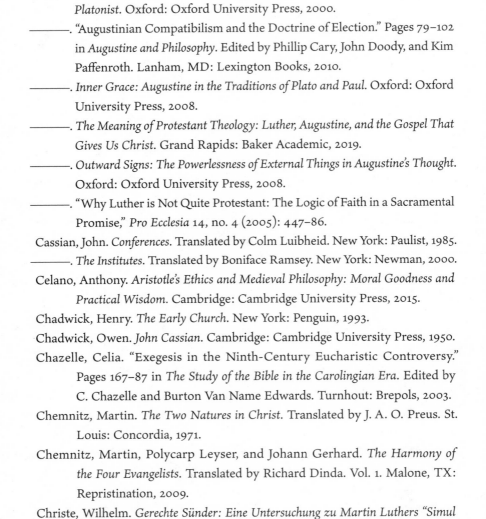

Cary, Phillip. *Augustine's Invention of the Inner Self: The Legacy of a Christian Platonist*. Oxford: Oxford University Press, 2000.

———. "Augustinian Compatibilism and the Doctrine of Election." Pages 79–102 in *Augustine and Philosophy*. Edited by Phillip Cary, John Doody, and Kim Paffenroth. Lanham, MD: Lexington Books, 2010.

———. *Inner Grace: Augustine in the Traditions of Plato and Paul*. Oxford: Oxford University Press, 2008.

———. *The Meaning of Protestant Theology: Luther, Augustine, and the Gospel That Gives Us Christ*. Grand Rapids: Baker Academic, 2019.

———. *Outward Signs: The Powerlessness of External Things in Augustine's Thought*. Oxford: Oxford University Press, 2008.

———. "Why Luther is Not Quite Protestant: The Logic of Faith in a Sacramental Promise," *Pro Ecclesia* 14, no. 4 (2005): 447–86.

Cassian, John. *Conferences*. Translated by Colm Luibheid. New York: Paulist, 1985.

———. *The Institutes*. Translated by Boniface Ramsey. New York: Newman, 2000.

Celano, Anthony. *Aristotle's Ethics and Medieval Philosophy: Moral Goodness and Practical Wisdom*. Cambridge: Cambridge University Press, 2015.

Chadwick, Henry. *The Early Church*. New York: Penguin, 1993.

Chadwick, Owen. *John Cassian*. Cambridge: Cambridge University Press, 1950.

Chazelle, Celia. "Exegesis in the Ninth-Century Eucharistic Controversy." Pages 167–87 in *The Study of the Bible in the Carolingian Era*. Edited by C. Chazelle and Burton Van Name Edwards. Turnhout: Brepols, 2003.

Chemnitz, Martin. *The Two Natures in Christ*. Translated by J. A. O. Preus. St. Louis: Concordia, 1971.

Chemnitz, Martin, Polycarp Leyser, and Johann Gerhard. *The Harmony of the Four Evangelists*. Translated by Richard Dinda. Vol. 1. Malone, TX: Repristination, 2009.

Christe, Wilhelm. *Gerechte Sünder: Eine Untersuchung zu Martin Luthers "Simul iustus et peccator."* Leipzig: Evangelische Verlagsanstalt 2014.

Chrysostom, John. *Commentary on Galatians*. Pages 1–172 in vol. 13 *of Nicene and Post-Nicene Fathers*. Edited by Philip Schaff. Peabody, MA: Hendrickson, 2004.

———. *Homilies on Genesis 18–45*. Translated by Robert Hill. Washington, DC: Catholic University of America Press, 1990.

————. *Homilies on the Epistle of Paul the Apostle to the Romans.* Pages 335–566 in vol. 11 of *Nicene and Post-Nicene Fathers.* Edited by Philip Schaff. Peabody, MA: Hendrickson, 2004.

Chung, Miyon. "Faith, Merit, and Justification: Luther's Exodus from Ockhamism En Route to Reformation." *Torch Trinity Journal* 6 (2003): 210–40.

Chung, Paul. *The Spirit of God Transforming Life: The Reformation and Theology of the Holy Spirit.* New York: Palgrave Macmillan, 2009.

Cohen, Shaye J. D. *From the Maccabees to the Mishnah.* Louisville: Westminster John Knox, 1987.

Collins, John. *The Apocalyptic Imagination: An Introduction to Jewish Apocalyptic Literature.* Grand Rapids: Eerdmans, 1998.

Concordia Triglotta: The Symbolical Books of the Evangelical Lutheran Church, German-Latin-English. Translated and edited by F. Bente, W. H. T. Dau, and Lutheran Church–Missouri Synod. St. Louis: Concordia, 1921.

Copan, Paul, and William Lane Craig. *Creation Out of Nothing: A Biblical, Philosophical, and Scientific Exploration.* Grand Rapids: Baker Academic, 2004.

Copinger, Walter Arthur. *A Treatise on Predestination, Election, and Grace, Historical, Doctrinal, and Practical.* London: James Nisbet, 1889.

Copleston, Fredrick. *Medieval Philosophy: An Introduction.* Mineola, NY: Dover, 2001.

Corbett, George. *Dante's Christian Ethics: Purgatory and Its Moral Contexts.* Cambridge: Cambridge University Press, 2020.

Corey, David. *The Sophists in Plato's Dialogues.* Albany: SUNY Press, 2015.

Courtenay, William. "Dialectic of Omnipotence in the High and Late Middle Ages." Pages 24–269 in *Divine Omniscience and Omnipotence in Medieval Philosophy: Islamic, Jewish, and Christian Perspective.* Edited by Tamar Rudavsky. Dordrecht: D. Reidel, 1985.

Cramer, Peter. *Baptism and Change in the Early Middle Ages, c.200–c.1150.* Cambridge: Cambridge University Press, 2003.

Cranfield, C. E. B. *Romans: A Shorter Commentary.* Grand Rapids: Eerdmans, 1985.

Cremer, Herman. *Die paulinische Rechtfertigungslehre im Zusammenhange ihrer geschichtlichen Voraussetzungen.* Gutersloh: Bertelsmann, 1899.

Croken, Robert. *Luther's First Front: The Eucharist as Sacrifice.* Ottawa: University of Ottawa Press, 1990.

Cross, Richard. *Communicatio Idiomatum: Reformation Christological Debates.* Oxford: Oxford University Press, 2019.

———. *Duns Scotus.* Oxford: Oxford University Press, 1999.

Crossan, John Dominic. *The Historical Jesus: The Life of a Mediterranean Jewish Peasant.* San Francisco: HarperOne, 1993.

Currid, John. *Egypt and the Old Testament.* Grand Rapids: Baker, 1997.

Curzer, Howard. *Aristotle and the Virtues.* Oxford: Oxford University Press, 2012.

Cutrone, Emmanuel. "Sacraments." Pages 741–42 in *Augustine through the Ages: An Encyclopedia.* Edited by Allan Fitzgerald. Grand Rapids: Eerdmans, 1999.

Cyril of Alexandria. *On the Unity of Christ.* Translated by John Anthony McGuckin. Crestwood, NY: St. Vladimir's Seminary Press, 1995.

Daley, Brian. *Hope of the Early Church: A Handbook of Patristic Eschatology.* Grand Rapids: Baker Academic, 2002.

Dancy, R. M. *Plato's Introduction of Forms.* Cambridge: Cambridge University Press, 2004.

Das, Andrew. *Galatians.* St. Louis: Concordia, 2014.

———. *Paul, the Law, and the Covenant.* Grand Rapids: Baker Academic, 2000.

Davidson, Clifford. *Studies in Late Medieval Wall Paintings, Manuscript Illuminations, and Texts.* London: Palgrave Macmillan, 2017.

Davidson, Robert. *Genesis 12–50.* Cambridge: Cambridge University Press, 1979.

Davies, W. D. *Paul and Rabbinic Judaism: Some Rabbinic Elements in Pauline Theology.* London: SPCK, 1970.

Davies, W. D., and D. C. Allison. *Matthew.* 3 vols. Edinburgh: T&T Clark, 1988–1997.

Davis, Thomas. *This Is My Body: The Presence of Christ in Reformation Thought.* Grand Rapids: Baker Academic, 2008.

Delitzsch, Franz. *Biblical Commentary on the Prophecies of Isaiah.* 2 vols. Grand Rapids: Eerdmans, 1954.

Denifle, Heinrich. *Die abendlandischen Schriftausleger bis Luther über Iustitia Dei (Rom 1:17) und Iustificatio.* Mainz: Kirchheim, 1905.

———. *Luther und Luthertum in der ersten Entwickelung, quellenmässig dargestellt.* 2 vols. Mainz: Kirchheim, 1904.

Denzinger, Heinrich. *Enchiridion Symbolorum et Definitionum et declarationum de rebus fidei et morum.* Freiberg: Herder & Herder, 1955.

Derrida, Jacque. *Disseminations.* Translated by Barbara Johnson. Chicago: University of Chicago Press, 1981.

————. *Of Grammatology*. Translated by Gayatri Chakravorty Spivak. Baltimore: John Hopkins University Press, 1976.

————. *Writing and Difference*. Translated by Alan Bass. London: Routledge, 1978.

Diestel, Ludwig. "Die idee der Gerrechtigkeit, vorzü im Alten Testament, biblischtheologisch dargestellt." *Jahrbüchen für deutsche Theologie* 5 (1860): 173–253.

Dieter, Melvin E. *The Holiness Revival of the Nineteenth Century*. Lanham, MD: Scarecrow, 1996.

Dieter, Theodor. *Der junge Luther und Aristoteles*. Berlin: De Gruyter, 2001.

Dingel, Irene. "The Culture of Conflict in the Controversies Leading to the Formula of Concord (1548–1580)." Pages 15–64 in *Lutheran Ecclesiastical Culture, 1550–1675*. Edited by Robert Kolb. Leiden: Brill, 2008.

Dixon, C. Scott. *Contesting the Reformation*. Malden, MA: Wiley-Blackwell, 2012.

Dobell, Brian. *Augustine's Intellectual Conversion: The Journey from Platonism to Christianity*. Cambridge: Cambridge University Press, 2009.

Dodd, C. H. "ΙΛΑΣΚΕΣΘΑΙ: Its Cognates, Derivatives, and Synonyms in the Septuagint." *Journal of Theological Studies* 32 (1931): 352–60.

Donaldson, Stuart. *Church Life and Thought in North Africa A.D. 200*. Cambridge: Cambridge University Press, 1909.

Doniger, Wendy, ed. *Karma and Rebirth in Classical Indian Traditions*. Los Angeles: University of California Press, 1980.

Donough, Thomas. *Law and Gospel in Luther: A Study of Luther's Confessional Writings*. Oxford: Oxford University Press, 1963.

Drecoll, V. H. *Die Entstehung der Gnadenlehre Augustins*. Tübingen: Mohr Siebeck, 1999.

Duffy, Eamon. *The Stripping of the Altars: Traditional Religion in England, 1400–1580*. New Haven: Yale University Press, 2005.

Duffy, Stephen. *The Dynamics of Grace: Perspectives in Theological Anthropology*. Eugene, OR: Wipf & Stock, 2007.

Dunn, James D. G. *Christology in the Making: An Inquiry into the New Testament Origins of the Doctrine of the Incarnation*. Grand Rapids: Eerdmans, 1989.

————. *The Epistle to the Galatians*. London: A & C Black, 1993.

————. *The New Perspective on Paul: Collected Essays*. Tübingen: Mohr Siebeck, 2005.

————. *The Parting of the Ways: Between Christianity and Judaism and Their Significance for the Character of Christianity*. London: SCM, 2011.

———. *Romans 1–8*. Nashville: Thomas Nelson Publishers, 1988.

———. *The Theology of Paul the Apostle*. Grand Rapids: Eerdmans, 1998.

Dunnill, John. *Covenant and Sacrifice in the Letter to the Hebrews*. Cambridge: Cambridge University Press, 2005.

Dyrness, William A. *Reformed Theology and Visual Culture: The Protestant Imagination from Calvin to Edwards*. Cambridge: Cambridge University Press, 2004.

Ebeling, Gerhard. *Luther: An Introduction to His Thought*. Translated by R. A. Wilson. Philadelphia: Fortress, 1970.

———. *Lutherstudien*. Vol. 1. Tübingen: Mohr Siebeck, 1971.

———. *Lutherstudien: Dispuatio de homine. Part 3: Die theologischen Definition des Menschen. Kommentar zu These 20–40*. Vol. 2. Tübingen: Mohr Siebeck, 1989.

———. "On the Doctrine of the Triplex Usus Legis in the Theology of the Reformation." Pages 62–78 in *Word and Faith*. Translated by James Leitch. Philadelphia: Fortress, 1963.

———. *Word and Faith*. Translated by James Leitch. Philadelphia: Fortress, 1963.

Eckhart, Burnell. *Anselm and Luther on the Atonement: Was It "Necessary"?* Lewiston, NY: Edwin Mellen, 1992.

Eckhardt, Meister. *The Complete Mystical Works of Meister Eckhart*. Translated by M. O'C. Walshe. St. Louis: Herder & Herder, 2010.

Edmondson, Stephen. *Calvin's Christology*. Cambridge: Cambridge University Press, 2004.

Eichrodt, Walther. *Theology of the Old Testament*. Translated by J. A. Baker. 2 vols. Philadelphia: Westminster, 1961–1967.

Eire, Carlos. *War Against the Idols: The Reformation of Worship from Erasmus to Calvin*. Cambridge: Cambridge University Press, 1986.

Elert, Werner. *The Christian Ethos: The Foundations of a Christian Way of Life*. Translated by Carl Schindler. Philadelphia: Muhlenberg, 1957.

———. *The Christian Faith: An Outline of Lutheran Dogmatics*. Translated by Martin Bertram and Walter Bouman. Gettysburg, PA: Unpublished Manuscript, 1974.

———. *Law and Gospel*. Translated by Edward Shroeder. Philadelphia: Fortress, 1967.

———. *The Structure of Lutheranism*. Vol. 1. Translated by Walter Hansen. St. Louis: Concordia, 1962.

Elledge, Casey Deryl. *Resurrection of the Dead in Early Judaism, 200 BCE–CE 200*. Oxford: Oxford University Press, 2017.

Ensor, Peter. "Tertullian and Penal Substitutionary Atonement." *Evangelical Quarterly* 86, no. 2 (2014): 130–42.

Erikson, Erik. *Young Man Luther: A Study in Psychoanalysis and History*. New York: W. W. Norton, 1958.

Estep, William. *The Anabaptist Story: An Introduction to Sixteenth-Century Anabaptism*. Grand Rapids: Eerdmans, 1996.

Eusebius. *The Church History: A New Translation with Commentary*. Translated and edited by Paul Maier. Grand Rapids: Kregel, 1999.

Eusterschulte, Anne. *Anthropological Reformations: Anthropology in the Era of Reformation*. Göttingen: Vandenhoeck & Ruprecht, 2015.

Evans, G. R. *Augustine on Evil*. Cambridge: Cambridge University Press, 1990.

———. "The Grammar of Predestination in the Ninth Century." *Journal of Theological Studies* 33, no. 1 (1982): 134–145.

———. *A Short History of Medieval Christianity*. London: I. B. Tauris, 2017.

Faley, R.J. *Bonding with God: A Reflective Study of Biblical Covenant*. New York: Paulist, 1997.

Ferguson, Everett. *Backgrounds of Early Christianity*. Grand Rapids: Eerdmans, 2003.

———. *Baptism in the Early Church: History, Theology, and Liturgy in the First Five Centuries*. Grand Rapids: Eerdmans, 2009.

Ferguson, John. *Pelagius: A Historical and Theological Study*. Cambridge: W. Heffer, 1956.

Ferguson, Sinclair. *The Whole Christ: Legalism, Antinomianism, and Gospel Assurance—Why the Marrow Controversy Still Matters*. Wheaton, IL: Crossway, 2016.

Fesko, J. V. *Justification: Understanding the Classic Reformed Doctrine*. Philipsburg, NJ: P&R, 2008.

Feyne, Sean. "Jewish Immersion and Christian Baptism." Pages 221–54 in *Ablution, Initiation, and Baptism: Late Antiquity, Early Judaism, and Early Christian*. Edited by David Hellholm, Tor Vegge, Øyvind Norderval, Christer Hellholm. Berlin: De Gruyter, 2011.

Fevold, Eugene. "Coming of Age: 1875–1900." Pages 255–358 in *The Lutherans in North America*. Edited by E. Clifford Nelson. Philadelphia: Fortress, 1980.

Finger, Thomas N. *A Contemporary Anabaptist Theology: Biblical, Historical, Constructive*. Downers Grove, IL: InterVarsity Academic, 2015.

Finney, Charles. *Finney's Systematic Theology*. Minneapolis: Bethany House, 1994.

Firey, Abigail, ed. *A New History of Penance*. Leiden: Brill, 2008.

Fisher, George Park. *History of Christian Doctrine*. Edinburgh: T&T Clark, 1896.

Fitzmyer, Joseph. "The New Testament Title 'Son of Man.'" Pages 143–60 in *A Wandering Aramean: Collected Aramaic Essays*. Missoula: Scholars, 1999.

Fletcher, Richard. *Who's Who in Roman Britain and Anglo-Saxon England*. London: Shepheard-Walwyn, 2002.

Fletcher-Louis, Crispin H. T. "The High Priest as Divine Mediator in the Hebrew Bible: Daniel 7:13 as a Test Case." *Society of Biblical Literature Seminar Papers* (1997): 169–74.

Flusser, David. *Judaism of the Second Temple Period: Sages and Literature*. Translated by Azzan Yadin. Vol. 2. Grand Rapids: Eerdmans, 2009.

Forde, Gerhard. "The Apocalyptic No and the Eschatological Yes: Reflections, Suspicions, Fears, and Hopes." Pages 17–32 in *A More Radical Gospel: Essays on Eschatology, Authority, Atonement, and Ecumenism*. Edited by Mark Mattes and Steven Paulson. Grand Rapids: Eerdmans, 2004.

———. *The Captivation of the Will: Luther vs. Erasmus on Freedom and Bondage*. Edited by Steven Paulson. Grand Rapids: Eerdmans, 2005.

———. "Forensic Justification and Law in Lutheran Theology." Pages 281–87 in *Justification by Faith: Lutherans and Catholics in Dialogue VII*. Edited by H. George Anderson, T. Austin Murphy, and Joseph Burgess. Minneapolis: Augsburg, 1985.

———. *Justification by Faith: A Matter of Death and Life*. Mifflinton, PA: Sigler, 1990.

———. "Karl Barth on the Consequences of Lutheran Christology." Pages 69–88 in *The Preached God: Proclamation in Word and Sacrament*. Edited by Steven Paulson and Mark Mattes. Minneapolis: Fortress, 2017.

———. *The Law-Gospel Debate: An Interpretation of Its Historical Development*. Minneapolis: Augsburg, 1969.

———. "Luther's 'Ethics.'" Pages 137–58 in *A More Radical Gospel: Essays on Eschatology, Authority, Atonement, and Ecumenism*. Edited by Mark Mattes and Steven Paulson. Grand Rapids: Eerdmans, 2004.

———. *On Being a Theologian of the Cross: Reflections on Luther's Heidelberg Disputation, 1518*. Grand Rapids: Eerdmans, 1997.

———. *Theology Is for Proclamation!* Minneapolis: Fortress, 1990.

———. "The Work of Christ." Pages 5–99 in vol. 2 of *Christian Dogmatics*. Edited by Robert Jenson and Carl Braaten. Philadelphia: Fortress, 1984.

Forell, George Wolfgang. *The Ethics of Decision: An Introduction to Christian Ethics*. Philadelphia: Muhlenberg, 1955.

———. *Faith Active in Love: An Investigation into the Principles Underlying Luther's Social Ethics*. Eugene, OR: Wipf & Stock, 1999.

Forman, Robert K. C. *Meister Eckhart: Mystic as Theologian: An Experiment in Methodology*. Rockport, MA: Element, 1991.

Frank, Isnard Wilhelm. *A History of the Medieval Church*. London: SCM, 1995.

Franzmann, Martin. *Commentary on Romans*. St. Louis: Concordia, 1968.

Fredriksen, Paula. *Jesus of Nazareth, King of the Jews: A Jewish Life and the Emergence of Christianity*. New York: Alfred A. Knopf, 2000.

Frend, W. H. C. *The Donatist Church: A Movement of Protest in Roman North Africa*. Oxford: Oxford University Press, 1952.

Funk, Robert. *Honest to Jesus: Jesus for a New Millennium*. San Francisco: Harper, 1997.

Furnish, Victor. *The Moral Teaching of Paul: Selected Issues*. Nashville: Abingdon, 1985.

Gage, Warren. *The Gospel of Genesis: Studies in Protology and Eschatology*. Eugene, OR: Wipf & Stock, 2001.

Garcia, Mark A. *Life in Christ: Union with Christ and Twofold Grace in Calvin's Theology*. Eugene, OR: Wipf & Stock, 2008.

Garrett, James Leo. *Baptist Theology: A Four-Century Study*. Macon, GA: Mercer University Press, 2009.

Garrison, Roman. *Redemptive Almsgiving in Early Christianity*. London: Bloomsbury, 1993.

Gathercole, Simon J. *Where is Boasting? Early Jewish Soteriology and Paul's Response in Romans 1–5*. Grand Rapids: Eerdmans, 2002.

Gatiss, Lee. "The Synod of Dort and Definite Atonement." Pages 143–65 in *From Heaven He Came and Sought Her: Definite Atonement in Historical, Biblical, Theological, and Pastoral Perspective*. Edited by David Gibson and Jonathan Gibson. Wheaton, IL: Crossway, 2013.

Genke, Victor, and Francis Gumerlock. *Gottschalk and A Medieval Predestination Controversy*. Milwaukee, WI: Marquette University Press, 2010.

Gentry, K. L. "Lordship Controversy: Faith Alone/Faith and Submission." Pages 317–19 in *The Westminster Handbook to Evangelical Theology*. Edited by Roger Olson. Louisville: Westminster John Knox, 2004.

George, Timothy. *Theology of the Reformers*. Nashville: Broadman & Holman, 2013.

Gerber, Chad Tyler. *The Spirit of Augustine's Early Theology: Contextualizing Augustine's Pneumatology*. London: Routledge, 2012.

Gerhard, Johann. *Annotations on the First Six Chapters of St. Paul's Epistle to the Romans*. Translated by Paul Rydecki. Malone, TX: Repristination, 2014.

————. *On Creation and Providence*. Translated by Richard Dinda. St. Louis: Concordia, 2013.

————. *On Sin and Free Choice*. Translated by Richard Dinda. St. Louis: Concordia, 2014.

————. *Sacred Meditations*. Translated by C. W. Heisler. Philadelphia: Lutheran Publication Society, 1896.

————. *Theological Commonplaces: On Christ*. Translated by Richard Dinda. St. Louis: Concordia, 2009.

Gerrish, B. A. *Grace and Gratitude: The Eucharistic Theology of John Calvin*. Eugene, OR: Wipf & Stock, 2002.

————. "Sign and Reality: The Lord's Supper in the Reformed Confessions." Pages 118–30 in *The Old Protestantism and the New: Essays on the Reformation Heritage*. New York: T&T Clark, 2004.

————. "To the Unknown God: Luther and Calvin on the Hiddenness of God." *Journal of Religion* 53 (1973): 263–93.

Gestrich, Christof. *Zwingli als Theologe Glaube und Geist beim Zürcher Reformator*. Zürich: Zwingli-Verlag, 1967.

Gieschen, Charles. *Angelomorphic Christology: Antecedents and Early Evidence*. Leiden: Brill, 1998.

————. "The Divine Name in Ante-Nicene Christianity." *Vigiliae Christianae* 57 (2003): 115–58.

————. "The Name of the Son of Man in 1 Enoch." Pages 238–49 in *Enoch and the Messiah Son of Man: Revisiting the Book of Parables*. Edited by Gabriele Boccaccini. Grand Rapids: Eerdmans, 2007.

————. "The Real Presence of the Son Before Christ: Revisiting an Old Approach to Old Testament Christology." *Concordia Theological Quarterly* 68 (2004): 105–26.

Gillis, Matthew Bryan. *Heresy and Dissent in the Carolingian Empire: The Case of Gottschalk of Orbais.* Oxford: Oxford University Press, 2017.

Gilson, Etienne. *History of Christian Philosophy in the Middle Ages.* Washington, DC: Catholic University of America Press, 2019.

Ginther, James. *The Westminster Handbook to Medieval Theology.* Louisville: Westminster John Knox, 2009.

Giussani, Luigi. *Why the Church?* Translated by Viviane Hewitt. Montreal: McGill-Queen's University Press, 2001.

Goertz, Hans-Jurgen. *The Anabaptists.* Translated by Trevor Johnson. London: Taylor & Francis, 2013.

Goppelt, Leonhard. *Theology of the New Testament: The Variety and Unity of the Apostolic Witness to Christ.* Translated by John Alsup. Vol. 2. Grand Rapids: Eerdmans, 1982.

Gordon, F. Bruce. *Calvin.* New Haven: Yale University Press, 2009.

Grant, Edward. *The Foundations of Modern Science in the Middle Ages: Their Religious, Institutional, and Intellectual Contexts.* Cambridge: Cambridge University Press, 1998.

Grant, Robert. *Irenaeus of Lyons.* London: Routledge, 1997.

Green, Lowell. *How Melanchthon Helped Luther Discover the Gospel: The Doctrine of Justification in the Reformation.* Fallbrook, CA: Verdict, 1980.

———. "The Three Causes of Conversion in Philipp Melanchthon, Martin Chemnitz, David Chytraeus, and the Formula of Concord." *Lutherjahrbuch* 47 (1980): 89–114.

Gregor, Brian. *A Philosophical Anthropology of the Cross: The Cruciform Self.* Indianapolis: Indiana University Press, 2013.

Gregory, Brad. *The Unintended Reformation: How a Religious Revolution Secularized Society.* Cambridge, MA: Belknap, 2012.

Grensted, L. W. *A Short History of the Doctrine of the Atonement.* Manchester: Manchester University Press, 1920.

Greschat, Martin. *Martin Bucer: A Reformer and His Times.* Translated by Stephen Buckwalter. Louisville: Westminster John Knox, 2004.

Gritsch, Eric W. and Robert Jenson. *Lutheranism: The Theological Movement and Its Confessional Writings.* Philadelphia: Fortress, 1976.

Guggisberg, Kurt. *Das Zwinglibild des Protestantismus im Wandel der Zeiten.* Leipzig: Verlag von M. Heinsius Nachfolger, 1934.

Gundry, Robert. *Matthew: A Commentary on His Literary and Theological Art.* Grand Rapids: Eerdmans, 1994.

———. "The Nonimputation of Christ's Righteousness." Pages 17–45 in *Justification: What's at Stake in the Current Debates.* Edited by Daniel Trier and Mark Husbands. Downers Grove, IL: InterVarsity Press, 2004.

Gurtner, Daniel. *The Torn Veil: Matthew's Exposition of the Death of Jesus.* Cambridge, UK: Cambridge University Press, 2007.

Gyllenkrok, Axel. *Rechtfertigung und Heiligung in der frühen evangelischen Theologie Luthers.* Uppsala: Wiesbaden, 1952.

Hacker, Paul. *Das Ich im Glauben bei Martin Luther.* Graz: Styria Verlag, 1966.

Hägglund, Bengt. *The Background of Luther's Doctrine of Justification in Late Medieval Theology.* Philadelphia: Fortress, 1971.

———. *History of Theology.* Translated by Gene Lund. St. Louis: Concordia, 1968.

Haikola, Lauri. *Gesetz und Evangelium bei Matthias Flacius Illyricus: Eine Untersuchung zur Lutherischen Theologies vor der Konkordienformel.* Lund: Gleerup, 1952.

Hall, Stuart. *Doctrine and Practice in the Early Church.* Grand Rapids: Eerdmans, 1991.

Hamann, Henry. "The Righteousness of Faith before God." Pages 137–62 in *A Contemporary Look at the Formula of Concord.* Edited by Robert Preus and Wilbert Rosin. St. Louis: Concordia, 1978.

Hamann, Johann Georg. *Sämtliche Werke.* Edited by Josef Nadler. Vol. 2. Vienna: Thomas-Morus-Presse, Verlag Herder, 1950.

Hamel, Adolf. *Der junge Luther und Augustin: Ihre Beziehungen in der Rechtfertigungslehre mach Luthers erstem Vorlesungen 1509–1518 untersucht.* 2 vols. Gütersloh: C. Bertelsmann, 1934–1935.

Hamilton, James. "Original Sin in Biblical Theology." Pages 189–208 in *Adam, the Fall, and Original Sin: Theological, Biblical, and Scientific Perspectives.* Edited by Hans Madueme and Michael Reeves. Grand Rapids: Baker Academic, 2014.

Hamilton, Victor. *The Book of Genesis: Chapters 1–17.* Grand Rapids: Eerdmans, 1990.

———. *Exodus: An Exegetical Commentary.* Grand Rapids: Baker Academic, 2011.

Hamm, Berndt. *The Early Luther: Stages in a Reformation Reorientation.* Translated by Martin Lohrmann. Grand Rapids: Eerdmans, 2014.

———. *The Reformation of Faith in the Context of Late Medieval Theology and Piety: Essays by Berndt Hamm.* Edited by Robert Bast. Leiden: Brill, 2004.

Hammerich, Holger. *Taufe und Askese: Der Taufaufschub in Vorkonstantinischer Zeit.* PhD diss., University of Hamburg, 1994.

Hampson, Daphne. *Christian Contradictions: The Structures of Lutheran and Catholic Thought.* Cambridge: Cambridge University Press, 2001.

Hardt, Tom G. A. "Justification and Easter: A Study in Subjective and Objective Justification in Lutheran Theology." Pages 52-78 in *A Lively Legacy: Essays in Honor of Robert Preus.* Edited by Kurt E. Marquart, John R. Stephenson, and Bjarne W. Teigen. Ft. Wayne, IN: Concordia Theological Seminary, 1985.

Hare, Douglas. *The Son of Man Tradition.* Minneapolis: Fortress, 1990.

Harnack, Theodosius. *Luthers Theologie mit besonderer Beziehung auf seine Versöhnungs- und Erlösungslehre.* 2 vols. Amsterdam: Rodopi, 1969.

Harrington, Daniel. *The Gospel of Matthew.* Collegeville, MN: Liturgical, 1991.

Harris, Horton. *The Tübingen School: A Historical and Theological Investigation of the School of F. C. Baur.* Oxford: Clarendon, 1975.

Harrison, Peter. "Philosophy and the Crisis of Religion." Pages 234–49 in *The Cambridge Companion to Renaissance Philosophy.* Edited by James Hankins. Cambridge: Cambridge University Press, 2007.

Harrison, R. K. *Introduction to the Old Testament.* Peabody, MA: Hendrickson, 2004.

Hasel, G. F. "The Meaning of the Animal Rite in Gen 15." *Journal for the Study of the Old Testament* 19 (1980): 61–78.

Hay, David. *Glory at the Right Hand: Psalm 110 in Early Christianity.* Nashville: Abingdon, 1973.

Hays, Richard. *The Faith of Jesus Christ: The Narrative Substructure of Galatians 3:1–4:11.* Grand Rapids: Eerdmans, 2002.

Hayward, Robert. *Divine Name and Presence, Memre.* Lanham, MD: Rowman & Littlefield, 1982.

Heal, Bridget. *A Magnificent Faith: Art and Identity in Lutheran Germany.* Oxford: Oxford University Press, 2017.

Hefner, Philip. *The Human Factor: Evolution, Culture, Religion.* Philadelphia: Fortress, 1993.

Heliso, Desta. *Pistis and the Righteous One.* Tübingen: Mohr Siebeck, 2007.

Helm, Paul. *Calvin: A Guide for the Perplexed*. London: Bloomsbury, 2008.

———. "Calvin, Indefinite Language, and Definite Atonement." Pages 97–120 in *From Heaven He Came and Sought Her: Definite Atonement in Historical, Biblical, Theological, and Pastoral Perspective*. Edited by David Gibson and Jonathan Gibson. Wheaton, IL: Crossway, 2013.

———. "John Calvin and the Hiddenness of God." Pages 67–82 in *Engaging the Doctrine of God Contemporary Protestant Perspectives*. Edited by Bruce McCormack. Grand Rapids: Baker Academic, 2008.

———. *John Calvin's Ideas*. Oxford: Oxford University Press, 2004.

Helmer, Christine. *The Trinity and Martin Luther*. Bellingham, WA: Lexham Press, 2017.

Heltzel, Peter Goodwin. "The Inner Church is the Hope for the World." Pages 269–84 in *The Pietist Impulse in Christianity*. Edited by Christian Collins Winn and Christopher Gehrz. Eugene, OR: Pickwick, 2011.

Helyer, Larry R. *The Witness of Jesus, Paul, and John: An Exploration in Biblical Theology*. Downers Grove, IL: InterVarsity Press, 2008.

Hendrix, Scott. *Luther*. Nashville: Abingdon, 2009.

———. *Luther and the Papacy: Stages in a Reformation Conflict*. Philadelphia: Fortress, 1981.

———. *Martin Luther: Visionary Reformer*. New Haven: Yale University Press, 2015.

Hengel, Martin. *The Four Gospels and the One Gospel of Jesus Christ: An Investigation of the Collection and Origin of the Canonical Gospels*. Translated by John Bowden. Harrisburg, PA: Trinity International, 2000.

———. *The Zealots: Investigations into the Jewish Freedom Movement in the Period Until 70 A.D.* Edinburgh: T&T Clark, 1997.

Hengstenberg, E. W. *Christology of the Old Testament*. Translated by Theodore Meyer and James Martin. 4 vols. Grand Rapids: Kregel, 1956.

Heppe, Heinrich. *Reformed Dogmatics*. Translated by G. T. Thomson. Eugene, OR: Wipf & Stock, 2007.

Hinlicky, Paul. *Beloved Community: A Critical Dogmatics after Christendom*. Grand Rapids: Eerdmans, 2015.

———. *Luther and the Beloved Community: A Path for Christian Theology After Christendom*. Grand Rapids: Eerdmans, 2010.

———. "Purgatory Now!" *Christian Century* 134, no. 14 (July 5, 2017): 30–34.

Hirsch, Emmanuel. *Die Theologie von Andreas Osiander und ihre Geschtlichen Voraussetzugen*. Göttingen: Vanderhoeck und Ruprecht, 1919.

Hochstraten, Jacob. "Iacobi Hoochstrati Disputationes contra Lutheranos." Pages 545–620 in vol. 3 of *Bibliotheca reformatoria Neerlandica*. Edited by S. Cramer and F. Pijper. s-Gravenhage: Martinus Nijhof, 1905.

Hoenecke, Adolf. *Evangelical Lutheran Dogmatics*. Translated by Joel Fredrich, James L. Langebartels, Paul Prange, and Bill Tackmier. 4 vols. Milwaukee: Northwestern, 1999–2009.

Hoffman, Bengt, trans. *The Theologia Germanica of Martin Luther*. New York: Paulist, 1980.

Hoffmann, R. Joseph. *Jesus Outside the Gospels*. Buffalo, NY: Prometheus, 1987.

Hoffmann, Yair. "The Day of the Lord as a Concept and a Term in Prophetic Literature." *Zeitschrift für die alttestamentliche Wissenschaft* 93 (1981): 37–50.

Holl, Karl. "Die Rechtfertigungslehre in Luthers Vorlesung über den Römerbrief mit besonderer Rücksicht auf die Frage der Heilsgewißheit." Pages 11–54 in vol. 1 of *Gesammelte Aufsätze*. Tübingen: Mohr Siebeck, 1928.

———. "Was verstand Luther unter Religion?" Pages 75–77 in *Gesammelte Aufsatze*, 3 vols. (Tubingen: Mohr, 1928).

Holmes, Michael W., trans. *The Apostolic Fathers: Greek Texts and English Translations*. 3rd ed. Grand Rapids: Baker Academic, 2007.

Hooker, Morna. *The Son of Man in Mark: A Study of the Background of the Term "Son of Man" and Its Use in St. Mark's Gospel*. London: SPCK, 1967.

Horn, Cornelia. "Penitence in Early Christianity in Historical and Theological Setting: Trajectories in Eastern and Western Sources." Pages 153–87 in *Repentance in Christian Theology*. Edited by Mark J. Boda and Gordon T. Smith. Collegeville, MN: Liturgical, 2006.

Horton, Michael. *The Christian Faith: A Systematic Theology for Pilgrims on the Way*. Grand Rapids: Zondervan, 2011.

———. *Justification*. 2 vols. Grand Rapids: Zondervan, 2018.

Houston, Walter. *The Pentateuch*. London: SCM, 2013.

Huber, Samuel. *Compendium of Theses by Samuel Huber, On the Universal Redemption of the Human Race, Accomplished by Jesus Christ Against the Calvinists*. Translated by Andrew Huss. Unpublished Manuscript, 2013.

Huizinga, Johan. *The Autumn of the Middle Ages*. Translated by Rodney J. Payton and Ulrich Mammitzsch. Chicago: University of Chicago Press, 1997.

Hultgren, Arland. *Paul's Letter to the Romans: A Commentary*. Grand Rapids: Eerdmans, 2011.

Hummel, Horace. *Ezekiel*. 2 vols. St. Louis: Concordia, 2005–2007.

Hunnius, Aegidius. *A Clear Explanation of the Controversy Among the Wittenberg Theologians Concerning Regeneration and Election.* Translated by Paul Rydecki. Malone, TX: Repristination, 2013.

———. *Theses in Opposition to Huberianism: A Defense of the Lutheran Doctrine of Justification.* Translated by Paul Rydecki. Bynum, TX: Repristination, 2012.

Hunter, Harold. *Spirit Baptism: A Pentecostal Alternative.* Eugene, OR: Wipf & Stock, 2009.

Hutchinson, Mark and John Wolffe. *A Short History of Global Evangelicalism.* Cambridge: Cambridge University Press, 2012.

Hütter, Leonhard. *Compendium of Lutheran Theology.* Translated by H. E. Jacobs and G. F. Spieker. Watseka, IL: Just & Sinner, 2015.

Hvalvik, Reidar. *The Struggle for Scripture and Covenant: The Purpose of the Epistle of Barnabas and Jewish-Christian Competition in the Second Century.* Tübingen: Mohr Siebeck 1996.

Hwang, Alexander. *Intrepid Lover of Perfect Grace: The Life and Thought of Prosper of Aquitaine.* Washington, DC: Catholic University of America Press, 2009.

Ilić, Luka. *Theologian of Sin and Grace: The Process of Radicalization in the Theology of Matthias Flacius Illyricus.* Göttingen: Vandenhoeck & Ruprecht, 2014.

Imhof, Paul, and Hubert Biallowons. eds. *Karl Rahner in Dialogue: Conversations and Interviews, 1965–1982.* Translated by Harvey D. Egan. New York: Crossroad, 1986.

Irenaeus. *Against the Heresies.* In *Ante-Nicene Fathers*, edited by Alexander Roberts and James Donaldson, 10 vols., 1:309–567. Peabody, MA: Hendrickson, 2004.

Irons, Charles Lee. *The Righteousness of God: A Lexical Examination of the Covenant Faithfulness Interpretation.* Tübingen: Mohr Sieback, 2015.

Jackson, B. Darrell. "The Theory of Signs in Augustine's *De Doctrina Christiana.*" *Revue des Etudes Augustiniennes* 15 (1969): 9–49.

Jackson, Samuel Macauley. *Huldreich Zwingli: The Reformer of German Switzerland.* New York: G. P. Putnam, 1903.

Janz, Denis. *Luther and Late Medieval Thomism: A Study in Theological Anthropology.* Waterloo, ON: Wilfrid Laurier University Press, 2009.

———. *Luther on Thomas Aquinas: The Angelic Doctor in the Thought of the Reformer.* Stuttgart: Franz Steiner Verlag, 1989.

Janzen, J. Gerald. *Exodus.* Louisville: Westminster John Knox, 1997.

Jensen, Gordon. "Luther and the Lord's Supper." Pages 323–33 in *The Oxford Handbook of Martin Luther's Theology*. Edited by Robert Kolb, Irene Dingel, and L'Ubomir Batka. Oxford: Oxford University Press, 2014.

Jenson, Robert. "Can We Have a Story?" *First Things* 11 (March 2000): 16–17.

———. "How the World Lost Its Story," *First Things* 4 (October 1993): 19–24.

———. "Luther's Contemporary Theological Significance." Pages 272–88 in *The Cambridge Companion to Martin Luther*. Edited by Donald McKim. Cambridge: Cambridge University Press, 2003.

———. *On Thinking the Human: Resolutions of Difficult Notions*. Grand Rapids: Eerdmans, 2003.

———. *Story and Promise: A Brief Theology of the Gospel about Jesus*. Philadelphia: Fortress, 1973.

———. *Systematic Theology*. 2 vols. New York: Oxford University Press, 1997–1999.

———. "You Wonder Where the Body Went." Pages 216–24 in *Essays in the Theology of Culture*. Grand Rapids: Eerdmans, 1995.

Jenson, Robert and Carl Braaten, eds. *Union with Christ: The New Finnish Interpretation of Luther*. Grand Rapids: Eerdmans, 1998.

Jeremias, Joachim. *The Eucharistic Words of Jesus*. Translated by Norman Perrin. London: SCM, 1963.

———. *The Parables of Jesus*. Translated by S. H. Hooke. New York: Charles Scribner's Sons, 1972.

Jewett, Robert. "The Anthropological Implications of the Revelation of Wrath in Romans." Pages 24–38 in *Reading Paul in Context*. Edited by W. S. Campbell. London: T&T Clark, 2010.

Jones, David Ceri, Boyd Stanley Schlenther, and Eryn Mant White. *The Elect Methodists: Calvinistic Methodism in England and Wales, 1735–1811*. Cardiff: University of Wales Press, 2012.

Jordan, James. *Through New Eyes: Developing a Biblical View of the World*. Eugene, OR: Wipf & Stock, 1999.

Josephus, Flavius. *The Works of Josephus*. Translated by William Whiston. Peabody, MA: Hendrickson, 1995.

Just, Arthur. *Luke*. 2 vols. St. Louis: Concordia, 1996–1997.

Jüngel, Eberhard. *Justification: The Heart of the Christian Faith*. Translated by Jeffrey Cayzer. Edinburgh: T&T Clark, 2001.

————. "The Revelation of the Hiddenness of God." Pages 120–44 in *Theological Essays II*. Translated by Arnold Neufeldt-Fast and John Webster. Edinburgh: T&T Clark, 1989.

Kant, Immanuel. *The Critique of Pure Reason, The Critique of Practical Reason, and The Critique of Judgment*. Translated by Thomas Kingmill Abbott. Chicago: Encyclopedia Britannica, 1984.

Käsemann, Ernst. "The Beginnings of Christian Theology." Pages 82–107 in *New Testament Questions of Today*. Translated by W. J. Montague. Philadelphia: Fortress, 1969.

————. *Commentary on Romans*. Translated by Geoffrey W. Bromily. Grand Rapids: Eerdmans, 1980.

————. "Justification and Salvation History in the Epistle to the Romans." Pages 60–78 in *Perspectives on Paul*. Translated by Margaret Kohl. Philadelphia: Fortress, 1971.

Kaiser, Walter. *The Messiah in the Old Testament*. Grand Rapids: Zondervan, 1995.

————. *Recovering the Unity of the Bible: One Continuous Story, Plan, and Purpose*. Grand Rapids: Zondervan, 2009.

Kearney, P. J. "Liturgy and Creation: The P Redaction of Exodus 25–40." *Zeitschrift für alttestamentliche Wissenschaft* 89 (1977): 375–87.

Keener, Craig. *Matthew*. Downers Grove: InterVarsity Press, 1997.

Keil, C. F. *Biblical Commentary on Daniel*. Grand Rapids: Eerdmans, 1955.

————. *The Pentateuch*. Peabody, MA: Hendrickson, 1996.

Kenney, John Peter. *The Mysticism of Saint Augustine: Re-Reading the Confessions*. London: Routledge, 2005.

Kidd, B. J. *The Later Medieval Doctrine of Eucharistic Sacrifice*. London: S.P.C.K., 1958.

Kierkegaard, Søren. *The Concept of Anxiety: A Simple Psychologically Orienting Deliberation on the Dogmatic Issue of Hereditary Sin*. Translated by Reidar Thomte. Princeton: Princeton University Press, 1980.

Kilcrease, Jack. "The Bridal-Mystical Motif in Bernard of Clairvaux and Martin Luther." *The Journal of Ecclesiastical History* 65, no. 2 (2014): 263–79.

————. "Creation's Praise: A Short Liturgical Reading of Genesis 1–2 and the Book of Revelation," *Pro Ecclesia* 21, no. 3 (2012): 314–25.

————. *The Doctrine of Atonement: From Luther to Forde*. Eugene, OR: Wipf & Stock, 2018.

———. "A Genealogy of the New Perspective on Paul." *Logia: A Journal of Lutheran Theology* 29, no. 2 (2020): 62–63.

———. "Sanctification and Concepts of the Self," *Logia: A Journal of Lutheran Theology* 27, no. 4 (2018): 61–62.

———.

———. *The Self-Donation of God: A Contemporary Lutheran Approach to Christ and His Benefits.* Eugene, OR: Wipf & Stock, 2013.

Kirk, J. R. Daniel. *Unlocking Romans: Resurrection and the Justification of God.* Grand Rapids: Eerdmans, 2008.

Kittelson, James. *Luther the Reformer: The Story of the Man and His Career.* Minneapolis: Fortress, 2016.

Kiuchi, Nobuyoshi. *Leviticus.* Downers Grove, IL: InterVarsity Press, 2007.

———. *The Purification Offering in the Priestly Literature: Its Meaning and Function* Sheffield: JSOT, 1987.

Klein, Elizabeth. *Augustine's Theology of Angels.* Cambridge: Cambridge University Press, 2018.

Kleinig, John. *Leviticus.* St. Louis: Concordia, 2003.

Kline, Meredith. *God, Heaven and Har Magedon: A Covenantal Tale of Cosmos and Telos.* Eugene, OR: Wipf & Stock, 2006.

———. *Images of the Spirit.* Grand Rapids: Baker, 1980.

Klug, Eugene. "Free Will, or Human Powers." Pages 122–36 in *A Contemporary Look at the Formula of Concord.* Edited by Robert Preus and Wilbert Rosin. St. Louis: Concordia, 1978.

———. "The Third Use of the Law." Pages 187–204 in *A Contemporary Look at the Formula of Concord.* Edited by Robert Preus and Wilbert Rosin. St. Louis: Concordia, 1978.

Knight, Henry H. III. *John Wesley: Optimist of Grace.* Eugene, OR: Cascade, 2018.

Knight, Jonathan. *Christian Origins.* Edinburgh: T&T Clark, 2008.

Koberle, Adolf. *The Quest for Holiness: Biblical, Historical, and Systematic Investigation.* Translated by John Mattes. Eugene, OR: Wipf & Stock, 2004.

Koester, Helmut. *Introduction to the New Testament: History and Literature of Early Christianity.* Vol. 2. Berlin: De Gruyter, 1987.

Kolb, Robert. *Bound Choice, Election, and Wittenberg Theological Method: From Martin Luther to the Formula of Concord.* Minneapolis: Fortress, 2017.

————. "Confessional Lutheran Theology." Pages 68–79 in *The Cambridge Companion to Reformation Theology*. Edited by David Bagchi and David Steinmetz. Cambridge: Cambridge University Press, 2004.

————. "Historical Background of the Formula of Concord." Pages 12–87 in *A Contemporary Look at the Formula of Concord*. Edited by Robert Preus and Wilbert Rosin. St. Louis: Concordia, 1978.

————. "Luther on the Two Kinds of Righteousness: Reflections on His Two-Dimensional Definition of Humanity at the Heart of His Theology," *Lutheran Quarterly* 13, no. 2 (1999): 449–66.

————. *Martin Luther: Confessor of the Faith*. Oxford: Oxford University Press, 2009.

————. "The Ordering of the Loci Communes Theologici: The Structuring of the Melanchthonian Dogmatic Tradition." *Concordia Journal* 23, no. 4 (1997): 317–37.

Kolb, Robert, and Charles Arand. *The Genius of Luther's Theology: A Wittenberg Way of Thinking for the Contemporary Church*. Grand Rapids: Baker Academic, 2008.

Kolb, Robert, and Carl Trueman. *Between Wittenberg and Geneva: Lutheran and Reformed Theology in Conversation*. Grand Rapids: Baker Academic, 2017.

Komline, Han-luen Kantzer. *Augustine on the Will: A Theological Account*. Oxford: Oxford University Press, 2019.

Köstlin, Julius. *The Theology of Luther in Historical Development and Inner Harmony*. Translated by Charles Hay. 2 vols. Philadelphia: Lutheran Publication Society, 1897.

Koterski, Joseph. *An Introduction to Medieval Philosophy: Basic Concepts*. Oxford: Wiley-Blackwell, 2011.

Kramm, H. H. *The Theology of Martin Luther*. Eugene, OR: Wipf & Stock, 2009.

Krauth, Charles Porterfield. *The Conservative Reformation and Its Theology*. St. Louis: Concordia, 2007.

Küng, Hans. *Great Christian Thinkers: Paul, Origen, Augustine, Aquinas, Luther, Schleiermacher, Barth*. London: Continuum, 1994.

Kusukaw, Sachiko. *The Transformation of Natural Philosophy: The Case of Philip Melanchthon*. Cambridge: Cambridge University Press, 1995.

Laato, Timo. "The New Quest for Paul: A Critique of the New Perspective on Paul." Pages 295–326 in *The Doctrine on Which the Church Stands or Falls*. Edited by Matthew Barrett. Wheaton, IL: Crossway, 2019.

———. *Paul and Judaism: An Anthropological Approach*. Atlanta: Scholar's, 1995.

Labahn, Antje. "Aus Dem Wasser Kommt Leben: Aschungen und Reinigungsriten in frühjüdischen Texten." Pages 157–220 in *Ablution, Initiation, and Baptism: Late Antiquity, Early Judaism, and Early Christian*. Edited by David Hellholm, Tor Vegge, Øyvind Norderval, Christer Hellholm. Berlin: De Gruyter, 2011.

Ladd, George Eldon. *A Theology of the New Testament*. Grand Rapids: Eerdmans, 1993.

Lage, Dietmar. *Martin Luther's Christology and Ethics*. Lewiston, NY: Edwin Mellen, 1990.

Lahey, Stephen. "The Sentences Commentary of Jan Hus." Pages 130–69 in *A Companion to Jan Hus*. Edited by Ota Pavlicek and František Šmahel. Leiden: Brill, 2015.

Lane, Anthony N. S. *Bernard of Clairvaux: Theologian of the Cross*. Collegeville, MN: Liturgical, 2013.

Lawrenz, Carl. "On Justification: Osiander's Doctrine of the Indwelling of Christ." Pages 149–74 in *No Other Gospel: Essays in Commemoration of the 400th Anniversary of the Formula of Concord, 1580–1980*. Edited by Arnold Koelpin. Milwaukee: Northwestern, 1980.

Leff, Gordon. *Gregory of Rimini: Tradition and Innovation in the Fourteenth Century Thought*. Manchester: University of Manchester Press, 1961.

Le Goff, Jacques. *The Birth of Purgatory*. Translated by Arthur Goldhammer. Chicago: University of Chicago Press, 1986.

Leith, John. *An Introduction to the Reformed Tradition: A Way of Being the Christian Community*. Louisville, KY: John Knox, 1981.

Leithart, Peter. *The Four: A Survey of the Gospels*. Moscow, ID: Canon, 2010.

———. *Deep Comedy: Trinity, Tragedy, and Hope in Western Literature*. Moscow, ID: Canon, 2006.

———. *Delivered from the Elements of the World: Atonement, Justification, Mission*. Downers Grove, IL: InterVarsity Press, 2016.

———. *A House for My Name: A Survey of the Old Testament*. Moscow, ID: Canon, 2000.

Lenski, R. C. H. *The Interpretation of St. Matthew's Gospel*. Peabody, MA: Hendrickson, 1998.

Leo XIII, *Aeterni Patris: On the Restoration of Christian Philosophy*. Boston: St. Paul Editions, n.d.

Lessing, Gotthold. *Nathan the Wise, with Related Documents*. Translated by Ronald Schechter. Boston: Bedford, 2004.

Leupold, Herbert. *Exposition of Genesis*. 2 vols. Grand Rapids: Baker, 1958–1959.

Levenson, Jon. *Creation and the Persistence of Evil: The Jewish Drama of Divine Omnipotence*. San Francisco: Harper and Row, 1988.

———. *The Death and Resurrection of the Beloved Son: The Transformation of Child Sacrifice in Judaism and Christianity*. New Haven: Yale University Press, 1995.

Levering, Matthew. *The Theology of Augustine: An Introductory Guide to His Most Important Works*. Grand Rapids: Baker Academic, 2013.

Levi, Anthony. *Renaissance and Reformation: The Intellectual Genesis*. New Haven: Yale University Press, 2002.

Levine, David, and Dalia Marx. "Ritual Law in Rabbinic Judaism." Pages 471–85 in *The Oxford Handbook of Biblical Law*. Edited by Pamela Barmash. Oxford: Oxford University Press, 2019.

Lewis, C. S. *The Abolition of Man*. Oxford: Oxford University Press, 1943.

Lienhard, Marc. *Luther: Witness to Jesus Christ: Stages and Themes of the Reformer's Christology*. Translated by Edwin Robertson. Minneapolis: Augsburg, 1982.

Linebaugh, Jonathan, ed. *God's Two Words: Law and Gospel in Lutheran and Reformed Traditions*. Grand Rapids: Eerdmans, 2018.

Lindberg, Carter. *The European Reformation*. Malden, Mass: Wiley-Blackwell, 2010.

———. "Introduction." Pages 1–20 in *The Pietist Theologians*. Edited by Carter Lindberg. Malden, MA: Blackwell, 2005.

Lioy, Dan. *The Decalogue in the Sermon on the Mount*. New York: Peter Lang, 2004.

Litwak, Kenneth. *Echoes of Scripture in Luke-Acts: Telling the History of God's People Intertextually*. New York: Bloomsbury, 2005.

Lockwood, Gregory. *1 Corinthians*. St. Louis: Concordia, 2000.

Loescher, Valentin Ernst. *The Complete Timotheus Verinus*. Translated by James Langebartels and Robert Koester. Milwaukee: Northwestern, 2006.

Lohse, Bernhard. *Martin Luther: An Introduction to His Life and Work*. Translated by Robert Schultz. Philadelphia: Fortress, 1986.

———. *A Short History of Christian Doctrine*. Translated by F. Ernst Stoeffer. Philadelphia: Fortress, 1966.

————. *Martin Luther's Theology: Its Historical and Systematic Development.* Translated by Roy A. Harrisville. Minneapolis: Fortress, 1999.

Lombard, Peter. *The Sentences.* Translated by Giulio Silano. 4 vols. Toronto: Pontifical Institute of Medieval Studies, 2007–2010.

Longenecker, Richard. *Galatians.* Dallas: Word, 1990.

Longman, Tremper, and Raymond Dillard. *An Introduction to the Old Testament.* Grand Rapids: Zondervan, 2006.

Loofs, Friedrich. *Leitfaden zum Studium der Dogmengeschichte.* Halle: Niemeyer, 1906.

Lortz, Joseph. *Die Reformation in Deutschland.* 2 vols. Voraussetzungen: Herder Verlag, 1949.

Lössl, J. *Intellectus Gratiae: Die erkenntnistheoretische und hermeneutische Dimension der Gnadenlehre Augustins von Hippo.* Leiden: Brill, 1997.

Louth, Andrew. *The Origins of the Christian Mystical Tradition: From Plato to Denys.* Oxford: Oxford University Press, 2007.

Lupovitch, Howard. *Jews and Judaism in World History.* London: Routledge, 2010.

Luther, Martin. *Dr. Martin Luthers Sämmtliche Schriften.* Edited by Johann Georg Walch. 24 vols. Halle: 1740–1753.

————. *D. Martin Luthers Werke. Deutsche Bibel.* 12 vols. Weimar: Hermann Böhlaus Nachfolger, 1906–1961.

————. *Luther: Letters of Spiritual Counsel.* Translated by Theodore Tappert. Vancouver, BC: Regent College, 2003.

————. *D. Martin Luthers Werke. Kritische Gesamtausgabe.* 120 vols. Weimar: Hermann Böhlau and H. Böhlaus Nachfolger, 1883–2009.

————. *D. Martin Luthers Werke. Tischreden.* 6 vols. Weimar: Hermann Böhlaus Nachfolger, 1912–1921.

————. *Luther's Works.* American Edition. Edited by Jaroslav Jan Pelikan, Hilton C. Oswald, Helmut T. Lehmann, and Christopher Boyd Brown. 82 vols. St. Louis: Concordia, 1955–.

————. *Only the Decalogue Is Eternal: Martin Luther's Complete Antinomian Theses and Disputations.* Translated and edited by Holger Sonntag. Minneapolis: Lutheran, 2008.

Macdonald, A. J. *Berengar and the Reform of Sacramental Doctrine.* London: Longmans, Green, 1930.

Macintyre, Alasdair. *After Virtue: A Study in Moral Theory.* Notre Dame, IN: University of Notre Dame Press, 1984.

Mackintosh, R. *Historic Theories of the Atonement.* London: Hodder & Stoughton, 1920.

Magness, Jodi. *The Archaeology of Qumran and the Dead Sea Scrolls.* Grand Rapids: Eerdmans, 2002.

Mann, Mark. *Perfecting Grace: Holiness, Human Being, and the Sciences.* New York: T&T Clark, 2006.

Mannermaa, Tuomo. *Christ Present in Faith: Luther's View of Justification.* Translated by Kirsi Sjerna. Minneapolis: Fortress, 2005.

———. *Two Kinds of Love: Martin Luther's Religious World.* Translated by Kirsi Sjerna. Minneapolis: Fortress, 2010.

Marantika, Chris. "Justification by Faith: Its Relevance in Islamic Context." Pages 228–42 in *Right with God: Justification in the Bible and the World.* Edited by D. A. Carson. Eugene, OR: Wipf & Stock, 2002.

Marenbon, John. *Early Medieval Philosophy 480–1150: An Introduction.* London: Routledge, 2002.

Marius, Richard. *Martin Luther: The Christian between God and Death.* Cambridge, MA: Belknap, 1999.

Marmostein, Arthur. *The Doctrine of Merits in the Old Rabbinical Literature.* London: Jews' College, 1920.

Marsh, William. *Martin Luther on Reading the Bible as Christian Scripture: The Messiah in Luther's Biblical Hermeneutic and Theology.* Eugene, OR: Wipf & Stock, 2017.

Martyn, J. Louis. *Galatians: A New Translation with Introduction and Commentary.* New York: Doubleday, 1997.

———. *Theological Issues in the Letters of Paul.* Nashville: Abingdon, 1997.

Maston, Jason. *Divine and Human Agency in Second Temple Judaism and Paul: A Comparative Study.* Tübingen: Mohr Siebeck, 2010.

Mattes, Mark. "Luther on Justification as Forensic and Effective." Pages 264–74 in *The Oxford Handbook of Martin Luther's Theology.* Edited by Robert Kolb, Irene Dingel, and L'Ubomir Batka. Oxford: Oxford University Press, 2014.

Mattox, Mickey. "Sacraments in the Lutheran Reformation." Pages 269–82 in *Oxford Handbook of Sacramental Theology.* Edited by Hans Boersma and Matthew Levering. Oxford: Oxford University Press, 2015.

McClymond, Michael J., and Gerald R. McDermott. *The Theology of Jonathan Edwards.* Oxford: Oxford University Press, 2012.

McGever, Sean. *Born Again: The Evangelical Theology of Conversion in John Wesley and George Whitefield*. Bellingham, WA: Lexham Press, 2020.

McGiffert, Arthur Cushman. *Protestant Thought Before Kant*. New York: Charles Scribner's Sons, 1919.

McGiffert, Michael. "From Moses to Adam: The Making of the Covenant of Works." *Sixteenth Century Journal* 19 (1988): 131–55.

McGinn, Bernard. *The Harvest of Mysticism in Medieval Germany*. St. Louis: Herder & Herder, 2005.

———. *The Mystical Thought of Meister Eckhart: The Man from Whom God Hid Nothing*. St. Louis: Herder & Herder, 2003.

———. *Visions of the End: Apocalyptic Traditions in the Middle Ages*. New York: Columbia University Press, 1998.

McGrath, Alister. "The Anti-Pelagian Structure of 'Nominalist' Doctrines of Justification." *Ephemerides Theologicae Lovanienses* 57 (1981), 107–19.

———. *Christian Theology: An Introduction*. Malden, MA: Wiley-Blackwell, 2011.

———. *Christian Theology: The Basics*. Malden, MA: Wiley-Blackwell, 2011.

———. "Forerunners of the Reformation? A Critical Examination of the Evidence for Precursors of the Reformation Doctrines of Justification." *Harvard Theological Review* 75, no. 2 (1982): 219–42.

———. *The Intellectual Origins of the European Reformation*. Malden, MA: Blackwell, 2004.

———. *Iustitia Dei: A History of the Christian Doctrine of Justification*. Cambridge, UK: Cambridge University Press, 2020.

———. *Luther's Theology of the Cross: Martin Luther's Theological Breakthrough*. Oxford: Wiley-Blackwell, 1990.

———. *Reformation Thought: An Introduction*. New York: Wiley-Blackwell, 2012.

McInerney, Joseph J. *The Greatness of Humility: St. Augustine on Moral Excellence*. Eugene, OR: Pickwick, 2016.

McKim, Donald. *The Westminster Handbook to Reformed Theology*. Louisville: Westminster John Knox, 2001.

McSorley, Harry. *Luther: Right or Wrong? An Ecumenical Theological Study of Luther's Major Work, The Bondage of the Will*. Minneapolis: Augsburg, 1969.

Means, Rob. *Penance in Medieval Europe, 600–1200*. Cambridge: Cambridge University Press, 2014.

Meier, John P. *Roots of the Problem and the Person*. Vol. 1 of *A Marginal Jew: Rethinking the Historical Jesus*. New York: Doubleday, 1991.

Melanchthon, Philipp. *The Chief Theological Topics: Loci Praecipui Theologici 1559*. Translated by J. A. O. Preus. St. Louis: Concordia, 2011.

———. *Commentary on Romans*. Translated by Fred Kramer. St. Louis: Concordia, 1992.

———. "Enarratio symboli Niceni." Pages 193–346 in vol. 23 of *Corpus Reformatorum*. Edited by Karl Gottlieb Bretschneider. New York: Johnson Reprint Corporation, 1963.

———. *Loci Communes 1535*. Translated by Paul Rydecki. Malone, TX: Repristination, 2020.

———. "*Loci Communes Theologici 1521*." Pages 3–150 in *Melanchthon and Bucer*. Edited by Wilhelm Pauck. Philadelphia: Westminster, 1969.

Meyendorff, John. *Christ in Eastern Christian Thought*. Washington, DC: Corpus Books, 1975.

Middendorf, Michael. *Romans*. 2 vols. St. Louis: Concordia, 2013–2016.

Milbank, John. *Theology and Social Theory: Beyond Secular Reason*. Malden, MA: Blackwell, 2008.

Milgrom, Jacob. *Leviticus 1–16: A New Translation and Commentary*. New York: Doubleday, 1991.

Moldenhauer, Aaron. "Analyzing the *Verba Christi*: Martin Luther, Ulrich Zwingli, and Gabriel Biel on the Power of Words." Pages 47–63 in *The Medieval Luther*. Edited by Christine Helmer. Tübingen: Mohr Siebeck, 2020.

Moo, Douglas. *The Epistle to the Romans*. Grand Rapids: Eerdmans, 1996.

———. Review of *The Deliverance of God: An Apocalyptic Rereading of Justification in Paul* by Douglas A. Campbell. *Journal of the Evangelical Theology Society* 53 (2010): 143–50.

Morris, Leon. "The Use of ilaskesthai etc. in Biblical Greek." *Expository Times* 62 (1951): 227–33.

Moser, Christian. "Reformed Orthodoxy in Switzerland." Pages 195–226 in *A Companion to Reformed Orthodoxy*. Edited by Herman Selderhuis. Leiden: Brill, 2013.

Mowinkel, Sigmund. *He That Cometh*. Translated by G. W. Anderson. Nashville: Abingdon, 1959.

Mozley, J. B. *A Treatise on the Augustinian Doctrine of Predestination*. London: John Murray, 1855.

Mozley, J. K. *The Doctrine of the Atonement*. New York: Charles Scribner's Sons, 1916.

Mühlen, Karl-Heinz zur. *Nos extra nos: Luthers Theologie zwischen Mystik und Scholastik*. Tübingen: Mohr Siebeck, 1972.

Mueller, John. *Theological Foundations: Concepts and Methods for Understanding Christian Faith*. Winona, MN: St. Mary's, 2007.

Mueller, Theodore. *Christian Dogmatics: A Handbook in Doctrinal Theology*. St. Louis: Concordia, 1934.

Muhlhan, Brett. *Being Shaped by Freedom: An Examination of Luther's Development of Christian Liberty, 1520–1525*. Eugene, OR: Pickwick, 2012.

Müller, Jörn, Matthias Perkams, and Tobias Hoffmann, eds. *Aquinas and the Nicomachean Ethics*. Cambridge: Cambridge University Press, 2013.

Muller, Richard. *Christ and the Decree: Christology and Predestination in Reformed Theology from Calvin to Perkins*. Grand Rapids: Baker Academic, 2008.

——. *God, Creation, and Providence in the Thought of Jacob Arminius: Sources and Directions of Scholastic Protestantism in the Era of Early Orthodoxy*. Grand Rapids: Baker, 1991.

——. *Post-Reformation Reformed Dogmatics: The Rise and Development of Reformed Orthodoxy, ca. 1520–1720*. 4 vols. Grand Rapids: Baker Academic, 2003.

——. *The Unaccommodated Calvin: Studies in the Foundation of a Theological Tradition*. Oxford: Oxford University Press, 2000.

Mullett, Michael. *Martin Luther*. London: Routledge, 2015.

Murphy, Frederick. *Apocalypticism in the Bible and Its World: A Comprehensive Introduction*. Grand Rapids: Baker Academic, 2012.

"The Concept of diathēkē in the Letter to the Hebrews." *Concordia Theological Quarterly* 66 (2002): 41–60.

Murray, Scott. *Law, Life and the Living God: The Third Use of the Law in Modern American Lutheranism*. St. Louis: Concordia, 2001.

Nicole, Roger. "C. H. Dodd and the Doctrine of Propitiation." *Westminster Theological Journal* 17 (1955): 117–57.

——. "*Hilaskesthai* Revisited," *Evangelical Quarterly* 49, no. 3 (1977): 173–77.

Nicoll, Jeff. *Augustine's Problem: Impotence and Grace*. Eugene, OR: Resource, 2016.

Niesel, Wilhelm. *The Theology of Calvin*. Translated by Harold Knight. Cambridge: James Clark & Co., 2002.

Nikulin, Dmitri. *Neoplatonism in Late Antiquity*. Oxford: Oxford University Press, 2019.

Nimmo, Paul. "Sacraments." Pages 79–95 in *The Cambridge Companion to Reformed Theology*. Edited by Paul Nimmo and David Fergusson. Cambridge: Cambridge University Press, 2016.

Nisula, Timo. *Augustine and the Functions of Concupiscence*. Leiden: Brill, 2012.

Nogalski, James. "The Day(s) of the Lord in the Book of the Twelve." Pages 192–213 in *Thematic Threads in the Book of the Twelve*. Edited by Paul L. Redditt and Aaron Schart. New York: De Gruyter, 2003.

Norris, John. "Augustine and Sign in the Tractatus in Iohannis Euangelium." Pages 215–32 in *Augustine: Biblical Exegete*. Edited by Frederick van Fleteren and Joseph C. Schnaubelt. New York: Peter Lang, 2004.

Noth, Martin. *Leviticus: A Commentary*. Translated by J. E. Anderson. Philadelphia: Westminster, 1965.

Novakovic, Lidija. *Resurrection: A Guide for the Perplexed*. New York: Bloomsbury, 2016.

Nygren, Anders. *Agape and Eros*. Translated by Philip Watson. Philadelphia: Westminster, 1953.

Obolensky, Dimitri. *The Bogomils: A Study in Balkan Neo-Manichaeism*. Cambridge: Cambridge University Press, 1948.

Oberman, Heiko. *Archbishop Thomas Bradwardine: a Fourteenth Century Augustinian: A Study of His Theology in Its Historical Context*. Utrecht: Kemink, 1957.

———. "'Facientibus Quod in Se Est Deus Non Degenat Gratiam:' Robert Holcot, O. P., and the Beginnings of Luther's Theology," *Harvard Theological Review* 75 (1962): 317–42.

———. *Forerunners of the Reformation: The Shape of Late Medieval Thought*. Translated by Paul Nyhus. Cambridge: James Clarke & Co., 2002.

———. *The Harvest of Late Medieval Theology: Gabriel Biel and Late Medieval Theology*. Grand Rapids: Baker Academic, 2000.

———. *Luther: Man Between God and the Devil*. Translated by Eileen Walliser-Swarzbart. New York: Image, 1992.

———. *Masters of the Reformation: The Emergence of a New Intellectual Climate in Europe*. Translated by Dennis Martin. Cambridge: Cambridge University Press, 1981.

———. "The Shape of Late Medieval Thought: The Birthpangs of the Modern Era." Pages 18–38 in *The Dawn of the Reformation: Essay on the Late Medieval and Early Reformation Thought*. Grand Rapids: Eerdmans, 1992.

———."Tuus sum, salvum me fac: Augustinreveil zwischen Renaissance und Reformation." Pages 349–94 in *Scientia Augustiniana: Studien über Augustinus, den Augustinismus und den Augustinerorden. Festschrift Adolar Zumkeller zum 60*. Edited by C. P. Mayer and W. Eckermann. Würzburg: Augustinus Verlag, 1975.

———. *The Two Reformations: Journey from the Last Days to the New World*. New Haven: Yale University Press, 2003.

———. "Via Antiqua and Via Modern: Late Medieval Prolegomena to Early Reformation Thought." Pages 3–23 in *The Impact of the Reformation*. Grand Rapids: Eerdmans, 1994.

O'Brien, Peter T. "Was Paul a Covenantal Nomist?" Pages 249–96 in vol. 2 of *Justification and Variegated Nomism*. Edited by D. A. Carson, Peter T. O'Brien, and Mark Seifrid. Grand Rapids: Baker Academic, 2000–2004.

O' Daly, Gerard. *Augustine's City of God: A Reader's Guide*. Oxford: Clarendon, 1999.

O'Donovan, Oliver. *The Problem of Self-Love in St. Augustine*. New Haven: Yale University Press, 1980.

O'Meara, John. "The Neoplatonism of St. Augustine." Pages 34–44 in *Neoplatonism and Christian Thought*. Edited by Dominic O'Meara. Albany: SUNY Press, 1982.

Olson, Roger. *Arminian Theology: Myths and Realities*. Downers Grove, IL: InterVarsity Press, 2006.

———. "Pietism: Myths and Realities." Pages 3–16 in *The Pietist Impulse in Christianity*. Edited by Christian Collins Winn and Christopher Gehrz. Eugene, OR: Pickwick, 2011.

———. *The Story of Christian Theology: Twenty Centuries of Tradition and Reform*. Downers Grove, IL: InterVarsity Press, 1999.

Osborn, Eric. *Irenaeus of Lyons*. Cambridge: Cambridge University Press, 2004.

———. *Tertullian: First Theologian of the West*. Cambridge: Cambridge University Press, 2003.

Osborne, Kenan. *The Christian Sacraments of Initiation: Baptism, Confirmation, Eucharist*. New York: Paulist, 1987.

Osiander, Andreas. "Concerning the Only Mediator (1551)." Pages 206–7 in *Documents from the History of Early Lutheranism: 1517–1750*. Edited by Eric Lund. Minneapolis: Fortress, 2002.

Osiek, Carolyn. "The Second Century through the Eyes of Hermas: Continuity and Change." *Biblical Theology Bulletin* 20 (1990): 116–22.

————. *Shepherd of Hermas: A Commentary*. Minneapolis: Fortress, 1999.

————. "The Shepherd of Hermas in Context." *Acta Patristica et Byzantina*, 8 (1997): 115–34.

Otten, Willemien. "Between Augustinian sign and Carolingian reality: the presence of Ambrose and Augustine in the Eucharistic debate between Paschasius Radbertus and Ratramnus of Corbie." *Nederlands archief voor kerkgeschiedenis* 80, no. 2 (2000): 137–56

Ozment, Steven. *The Age of Reform, 12501–1550: An Intellectual and Religious History of Late Medieval and Reformation Europe*. New Haven: Yale University Press, 1981.

————. "Eckhart and Luther: German Mysticism and Protestantism." *The Thomist* 42 (1978) 258–80.

Paget, James Carleton. *The Epistle of Barnabas: Outlook and Background*. Tübingen: Mohr Siebeck, 1994.

Palmer, Ada. *Reading Lucretius in the Renaissance*. Cambridge, MA: Harvard University Press, 2014.

Pannenberg, Wolfhart. "Dogmatic Theses on the Doctrine of Revelation." Pages 131–55 in *Revelation as History*. Edited by Wolfhart Pannenberg, Rolf Rendtorff, Trutz Rendtorff, and Ulrich Wilkens. Translated by David Granskou. New York: MacMillan, 1968.

————. *Jesus: God and Man*. Translated by Lewis Wilkins and Duane Priebe. Philadelphia: Westminster, 1977.

————. *Systematic Theology*. Translated by Geoffrey Bromiley. 3 vols. Grand Rapids: Eerdmans, 1991–1998.

Papandrea, James. *Novatian of Rome and the Culmination of Pre-Nicene Orthodoxy*. Eugene, OR: Pickwick, 2011.

Parke-Taylor, G. H. *Yahweh: The Divine Name in the Bible*. Waterloo, ON: Wilfrid Laurier University Press, 1975.

Pate, C. Marvin, J. Scott Duvall, J. Daniel Hays, E. Randolph Richards, Preben Vang, and W. Dennis Tucker Jr., *The Story of Israel: A Biblical Theology*. Downers Grove, IL: InterVarsity Press, 2004.

Paulson, Steven. "Analogy and Proclamation: The Struggle over God's Hiddenness in the Theology of Martin Luther and Eberhard Jüngel." Dissertation, Lutheran School of Theology, 1992.

————. "Graspable God." *Word & World* 32, no. 1 (2012): 51–62.

———. *Hidden in the Cross*. Vol. 2 of Luther's Outlaw God. Minneapolis: Fortress, 2019.

———. *Hiddenness, Evil, and Predestination*. Vol. 1 of Luther's Outlaw God. Minneapolis: Fortress, 2018.

———. "Luther on the Hidden God." *Word & World* 19, no. 4 (1999): 363–71.

———. *Lutheran Theology*. New York: T&T Clark International, 2011.

Pelagius. *Commentary on St Paul's Epistle to the Romans*. Translated by Theodore De Bruyn. Oxford: Clarendon, 1993.

Penn, Stephen. "Wycliffe and the Sacraments." Pages 241–93 in *A Companion to John Wyclif, Late Medieval Theologian*. Edited by Ian Levy. Leiden: Brill, 2006.

Pelikan, Jaroslav. *The Christian Tradition: A History of the Development of Doctrine*. 5 vols. Chicago: University of Chicago Press, 1971–1989.

———. *From Luther to Kierkegaard: A Study in the History of Theology*. St. Louis: Concordia, 1963.

———. *Luther the Expositor: Introduction to the Reformer's Exegetical Writings*. St. Louis: Concordia, 1959.

Pereira, Jairzinho Lopes. *Augustine of Hippo and Martin Luther on Original Sin and Justification of the Sinner*. Göttingen: Vandenhoeck & Ruprecht, 2013.

Peters, Albrecht. *Commentary on Luther's Catechisms: Confession and Christian Life*. St. Louis: Concordia, 2013.

Philipps, William. *Clerical Celibacy: The Heritage*. London: Continuum, 2004.

Pieper, Francis. *Christian Dogmatics*. 4 vols. St. Louis: Concordia, 1951–1953.

———. *Conversion and Election: A Plea for a United Lutheranism in America*. Watseka, IL: Just and Sinner, 2015.>

Pitre, Brant. *Jesus, the Tribulation, and the End of Exile*. Grand Rapids: Baker Academic, 2005.

Placher, William. *The Domestication of Transcendence: How Modern Thinking about God Went Wrong*. Louisville, KY: Westminster John Knox, 1996.

Plato. *The Complete Works*. Edited by John Cooper. Indianapolis: Hackett, 1997.

Plevnik, Joseph. *Paul and the Parousia: An Exegetical and Theological Investigation*. Peabody, MA: Hendrickson, 1997.

Plotinus, *The Six Enneads*. Translated by Stephen McKenna and B. S. Page. Chicago: Encyclopedia Britannica, 1984.

Posset, Franz. *The Front-Runner of the Catholic Reformation: The Life and Works of Johann von Staupitz*. Surrey, UK: Ashgate, 2003.

————. *Pater Bernhardus: Martin Luther and Bernard of Clairvaux*. Kalamazoo: Cistercian, 2000.

————. *The Real Luther: A Friar at Erfurt and Wittenberg*. St. Louis: Concordia, 2011.

Prenter, Regin. *Spiritus Creator: Luther's Concept of the Holy Spirit*. Translated by John Jensen. Philadelphia: Muhlenberg, 1953.

Preus, Robert. "The Influence of the Formula of Concord on Later Lutheran Orthodoxy." Pages 86–101 in *Discord, Dialogue, and Concord: Studies in the Lutheran Reformation's Formula of Concord*. Edited by Lewis Spitz and Wenzel Lohff. Philadelphia: Fortress, 1977.

————. "Objective Justification." Pages 147–55 in *Doctrine Is Life: Essays on Justification and the Lutheran Confessions*. Edited by Klemet Preus. St. Louis: Concordia, 2006.

Preuss, Eduard. *The Justification of the Sinner before God*. Translated by J. A. Friedrich. Ft. Wayne, IN: Lutheran Legacy, 2011.

Principe, W. H. "The School Theologians' Views of the Papacy." Pages 45–116 in *The Religious Roles of the Papacy: Ideals and Realities 1150–1300*. Edited by C. Ryan. Toronto: Pontifical Institute of Medieval Studies, 1989.

Prosper of Aquitaine. *The Call of All Nations*. Translated by P. De Letter. New York: Newman, 1952.

Quasten, Johannes. *Patrology*, 4 vols. Allen, TX: Christian Classics, 1983.

Rack, Henry. *Reasonable Enthusiast: John Wesley and the Rise of Methodism*. London: Epworth, 1989.

Räisänen, Heikki. *Paul and the Law*. Eugene, OR: Wipf & Stock, 2010.

Ramelli, Ilaria. *The Christian Doctrine of Apokatastasis: A Critical Assessment from the New Testament to Eriugena*. Leiden: Brill, 2013.

Raunio, Antti. "Divine and Natural Law in Luther and Melanchthon." Pages 21–61 in *Lutheran Reformation and the Law*. Edited by Virpi Mäkinen. Leiden: Brill, 2006.

Rawlings, Harold. *Basic Baptist Beliefs: An Exposition of Key Biblical Doctrines*. Springfield, MO: 21st Century, 2014.

Rees, B. R. *Pelagius: A Reluctant Heretic*. Woodbridge: Boydell, 1988.

————, ed. *Pelagius: Life and Letters*. Woodbridge, MA: Boydell, 1998.

Reimarus, Samuel Herman. *Reimarus: Fragments*. Translated by Ralph Fraser. Philadelphia: Fortress, 1970.

Reu, Johann Michael. *Christian Ethics*. Columbus: The Wartburg, 1935.

———. *An Explanation of Dr. Martin Luther's Small Catechism*. Minneapolis: Augsburg, 1964.

Richter, Sandra L. *The Deuteronomistic History and the Name Theology: Lešakkēn Šemô Šām in the Bible and the Ancient Near East*. New York: De Gruyter, 2002.

Ridderbos, Herman. *Paul: An Outline of His Theology*. Translated by John Richard De Witt. Grand Rapids: Eerdmans, 1975.

Rigg, John Wheelan. *Baptism in the Reformed Tradition: A Historical and Practical Theology*. Louisville: Westminster John Knox, 2002.

Rist, John. *Augustine Deformed: Love, Sin, and Freedom in the Western Moral Tradition*. Cambridge: Cambridge University Press, 2014.

———. "Plotinus and Christian Philosophy." Pages 386–413 in *The Cambridge Companion to Plotinus*. Edited by Lloyd P. Gerson. Cambridge: Cambridge University Press, 1996.

Ritschl, Albrecht. *Die christliche Lehre von der Rechtfertigung und Versöhnung*. 3 vols. Bonn: Adolph Marcus, 1870–1874.

———. *The Christian Doctrine of Justification and Reconciliation: The Positive Development of the Doctrine*. Translated by H. R. Macintosh and A. B. Macauley. Edinburgh: T&T Clark. 1900.

———. *A Critical History of the Christian Doctrine of Justification and Reconciliation*. Translated by John Black. Edinburgh: T&T Clark, 1872.

Rittgers, Ronald. "Luther on Private Confession." Pages 211–32 in *The Pastoral Luther: Essays on Martin Luther's Practical Theology*. Edited by Timothy Wengert. Minneapolis: Fortress, 2017.

———. *The Reformation of the Keys: Confession, Conscience, and Authority in Sixteenth Century Germany*. Cambridge, MA: Harvard University Press, 2004.

Rivard, Derek. *Blessing the World: Ritual and Lay Piety in Medieval Religion*. Washington, DC: Catholic University of America Press, 2008.

Roberts, Alexander, and James Donaldson, eds. *Ante-Nicene Fathers*. 10 vols. Peabody, MA: Hendrickson, 2004.

Robson, John Adam. *Wyclif and the Oxford Schools: The Relation of the "Summa de Ente" to Scholastic Debates at Oxford in the Later Fourteenth Century*. Cambridge: Cambridge University Press, 1961.

Rooker, Mark. *Leviticus*. Nashville: Broadman & Holman, 2000.

Rowley, H. H. "Jewish Proselyte Baptism and the Baptism of John." *Hebrew Union College Annual* 15 (1940): 313–34.

Rubenstein, Richard. *Aristotle's Children: How Christians, Muslims, and Jews Rediscovered Ancient Wisdom and Illuminated the Dark Ages*. New York: Harcourt, 2004.

Rudolph, Kurt. *Gnosis: The Nature and History of Gnosticism*. Translated by Robert McLauchlin Wilson. Edinburgh: T&T Clark, 1983.

Russell, Jeffrey Burton. *Satan: The Early Christian Tradition*. Ithaca: Cornell University Press, 1981.

Salkeld, Brett. *Transubstantiation: Theology, History, and Christian Unity*. Grand Rapids: Baker Academic, 2019.

Saarnivaara, Uuras. *Luther Discovers the Gospel: New Light upon Luther's Way from Medieval Catholicism to Evangelical Faith*. St. Louis: Concordia, 2005

Sanders, E. P. *Jesus and Judaism*. Philadelphia: Fortress, 1985.

———. *Paul*. Oxford: Oxford University Press, 1991.

———. *Paul and Palestinian Judaism: A Comparison of Patterns of Religion*. Philadelphia: Fortress, 1977.

———. *Paul, the Law and the Jewish People*. Philadelphia: Fortress, 1983.

Sartre, Jean-Paul. *Existentialism Is Humanism*. Translated by Carol Macombe. New Haven: Yale University Press, 2007.

Sasse, Herman. "The Theology of the Cross." Pages 35–45 in *We Confess Anthology*. Translated by Norman Nagel. St. Louis: Concordia, 1998.

———. *This is My Body: Luther's Contention for the Real Presence in the Sacrament of the Altar*. Eugene, OR: Wipf & Stock, 2001.

———. "What is the State?" (1932). Translated by Matthew Harrison. Unpublished MS, 2015.

Scaer, David. *Discourses in Matthew: Jesus Teaches the Church*. St. Louis: Concordia, 2004.

———. "Law and Gospel in Lutheran Theology." *Logia* 3, no. 1 (Epiphany, 1994): 27–34.

———. "The Sacraments as an Affirmation of Creation," *Concordia Theological Quarterly* 57, no. 4 (1993): 241–63.

Schaff, Philip, ed. *Nicene and Post-Nicene Fathers*. 14 vols. First Series. Peabody, MA: Hendrickson, 2004.

Schaff, Philip, and William Wace, eds. *Nicene and Post-Nicene Fathers*. 14 vols. Second Series. Peabody, MA: Hendrickson, 2004.

Schäfer, Peter. *Jesus in the Talmud*. Princeton: Princeton University Press, 2007.

Schafer, Steven. *Marriage, Sex, and Procreation: Contemporary Revisions to Augustine's Theology of Marriage*. Eugene, OR: Pickwick, 2019.

Schirrmacher, Thomas. *Indulgences: A History of Theology and Reality of Indulgences and Purgatory: A Protestant Evaluation*. Eugene, OR: Wipf & Stock, 2014.

Schleiermacher, Friedrich. *The Christian Faith*. Translated by H. R. Mackintosh and J. S. Stewart. Edinburgh: T&T Clark, 1999.

Schmid, Heinrich. *The Doctrinal Theology of the Evangelical Lutheran Church*. Translated by Charles A. Hays and Henry E. Jacobs. Minneapolis: Augsburg, 1961.

———. *The History of Pietism*. Milwaukee: Northwestern, 2007.

Schmidt, Josef. "Introduction." Pages 1–34 in *Johannes Tauler: Sermons*. Translated by Maria Shrady. New York: Paulist, 1985.

Schnelle, Udo. *Apostle Paul: His Life and Theology*. Translated by M. Eugene Boring. Grand Rapids: Baker Academic, 2005.

Schockenhoff, Eberhard. "The Theological Virtue of Charity." Pages 244–58 in *The Ethics of Aquinas*. Edited by Stephen Pope. Washington, DC: Georgetown University Press, 2002.

Schreiner, Susan. *Are You Alone Wise? The Search for Certainty in the Early Modern Era*. Oxford: Oxford University Press, 2011.

Schreiner, Thomas. *Faith Alone: The Doctrine of Justification*. 5 Solas Series. Grand Rapids: Zondervan, 2015.

———. *The Law and Its Fulfillment: A Pauline Theology of Law*. Grand Rapids: Baker Books, 1998.

———. ed., *The Lord's Supper: Remembering and Proclaiming Christ Until He Comes*. Nashville: Broadman & Holman, 2011.

———. *Paul, Apostle of God's Glory in Christ: A Pauline Theology*. Downers Grove, IL: InterVarsity Press, 2006.

———. *Romans*. Grand Rapids: Baker Books, 1998.

———. *Romans*. Grand Rapids: Baker Academic, 2018.

Schroeder, H. J., trans. "Thirteenth Session." Pages 72–87 in *Canons and Decrees of the Council of Trent*. St. Louis: B. Herder, 1960.

Schultz, Robert. Gesetz und Evangelium in der Lutherischen Theologie des 19. Jahrhunderts. Berlin: Lutherisches Verlagshaus, 1958.

———. "Original Sin: Accident or Substance—the Paradoxical Significance of FC I, 53–62 in Historical Context." Pages 38–57 in *Discord, Dialogue, and*

Concord: Studies in the Lutheran Reformation's Formula of Concord. Edited by Lewis Spitz and Wenzel Lohff. Philadelphia: Fortress, 1977.

Schweizer, Alexander. *Die Protestantischen Centraldogmen in Ihrer Entwicklung inerhalb der Reformirten Kirche*. 2 vols. Zürich: Orell, Fuessli, 1854–1856.

Schwiebert, E. G. *Luther and His Times: The Reformation from a New Perspective*. St. Louis: Concordia, 1950.

Scurlock, Jo Ann and Richard Henry Beal, eds. *Creation and Chaos: A Reconsideration of Hermann Gunkel's Chaoskampf Hypothesis*. University Park, PA: Eisenbrauns, 2013.

Seeberg, Erich. *Luthers Theologie: Christus, Wirklichkeit und Urbild*. Vol. 2. Stuttgart: W. Kohlhammer, 1937.

Selderhuis, Herman. "The Further Reformation." Pages 338–41 in *Handbook of Dutch Church History*. Edited by Herman Selderhuis. Bristol, CT: Vandenhoeck & Ruprecht, 2014.

Senior, Donald. *Matthew*. Nashville: Abingdon, 1998.

Shaffern, Robert. "The Medieval Theology of Indulgence." Pages 11–37 in *Promissory Notes on the Treasury of Merits: Indulgences in Late Medieval Europe*. Edited by Robert Norman Swanson. Leiden: Brill, 2006.

———. *The Penitents' Treasury: Indulgences in Latin Christendom, 1175–1375*. Scranton, PA: University of Scranton Press, 2007.

Shantz, Douglas H. *An Introduction to German Pietism: Protestant Renewal at the Dawn of Modern Europe*. Baltimore: Johns Hopkins University Press, 2013.

Sharp, Larry. "The Doctrine of Grace in Calvin and Augustine." *Evangelical Quarterly* 52 (1980): 84–96.

Silcock, Jeffrey. "Luther on the Holy Spirit and His Use of God's Word." Pages 294–309 in *The Oxford Handbook of Martin Luther's Theology*. Edited by Robert Kolb, Irene Dingel, and L'Ubomir Batka. Oxford: Oxford University Press, 2014.

———. "A Lutheran Approach to Eschatology." *Lutheran Quarterly* 31, no. 4 (2017): 373–95.

Simithra, Sunand. "Justification by Faith: Its Relevance in Hindu Context." Pages 216–217 in *Right with God: Justification in the Bible and the World*. Edited by D. A. Carson. Eugene, OR: Wipf & Stock, 2002.

Skirbekk, Gunnar, and Nils Gilje. *A History of Western Thought: From Ancient Greece to the Twentieth Century*. London: Routledge, 2001.

Smiga, George. *Pain and Polemic: Anti-Judaism in the Gospels*. New York: Paulist, 1992.

Smith, Christian. *How to Go from Being a Good Evangelical to a Committed Catholic in Ninety-Five Difficult Steps*. Eugene, OR: Cascade, 2011.

Smith, John Howard. *The First Great Awakening: Redefining Religion in British America, 1725–1775*. London: Fairleigh Dickinson University Press, 2015.

Soderlund, Rune. *Ex praevisa fide: Zum Verständnis der Prädestinationslehre in der lutherischen Orthodoxie*. Hannover: Lutherisches Verlaghaus, 1983.

Sorensen, Rob. *Martin Luther and the German Reformation*. London: Anthem, 2016.

Spence, Alan. *Justification: A Guide for the Perplexed*. Edinburgh: T&T Clark, 2012.

Spener, Philip Jacob. *Pia Desideria*. Translated by Theodore Tappert. Eugene, OR: Wipf & Stock, 2002.

Spitz, Lewis. "Humanism in the Reformation." Pages 643–62 in *Renaissance Studies in Honor of Hans Baron*. Edited by Anthony Molho and John Tedeschi. DeKalb, IL: Northern Illinois University Press, 1971.

———. *The Religious Renaissance of the German Humanists*. Cambridge: Harvard University Press, 1963.

Sprinkle, Preston. *Paul and Judaism Revisited: A Study of Divine and Human Agency in Salvation*. Downers Grove, IL: InterVarsity Press, 2013.

Squires, Stuart. *The Pelagian Controversy: An Introduction to the Enemies of Grace and the Conspiracy of Lost Souls*. Eugene, OR: Pickwick, 2019.

Sri, Edward, and Curtis Mitch. *The Gospel of Matthew*. Grand Rapids: Baker Academic, 2010.

Stanglin, Keith D. and Thomas H. McCall. *Jacob Arminius: Theologian of Grace*. Oxford: Oxford University Press, 2012.

Stayer, James. *Martin Luther, German Saviour: German Evangelical Theological Factions and the Interpretation of Luther, 1917–1933*. Montreal: McGill-Queen's University Press, 2000.

Steele, Jeff. "Happiness." Pages 127–49 in *The Cambridge Companion to Medieval Ethics*. Edited by Thomas Williams. Cambridge: Cambridge University Press, 2019.

Steiger, Johann Anselm. "The *Communicatio Idiomatum* as the Axel and Motor of Luther's Theology." *Lutheran Quarterly* 14, no. 2 (2000): 125–58.

Steinmann, Andrew E. *Daniel*. St. Louis: Concordia, 2008.

Steinmetz, David. "Divided by a Common Past: The Reshaping of the Christian Exegetical Tradition in the Sixteenth Century." *Journal of Medieval and Early Modern Studies* 27, no. 2 (1997): 245–564.

———. "Luther and the Two Kingdoms." Pages 112–25 in *Luther in Context*. Bloomington: University of Indiana Press, 1986.

———. *Luther and Staupitz: An Essay in the Intellectual Origins of the Protestant Reformation*. Durham: Duke University Press, 1980.

———. *Misericordia Dei: The Theology of Johannes von Staupitz in Its Late Medieval Setting*. Brill: Leiden, 1968.

———. "The Theology of John Calvin." Pages 113–29 in *The Cambridge Companion to Reformation Theology*. Edited by David Bagchi and David Steinmetz. Cambridge: Cambridge University Press, 2004.

Stendahl, Krister. "Paul and the Introspective Conscience of the West." Pages 78–96 in *Paul among Jews and Gentiles, and Other Essays*. Philadelphia: Fortress, 1976.

Stephens, W. Peter. *The Theology of Huldrych Zwingli*. Oxford: Clarendon, 1986.

Stoeffler, F. Ernest. *German Pietism During the Eighteenth Century*. Leiden: Brill, 1973.

Stout, Martha. *The Sociopath Next Door*. New York: Broadway Books, 2005.

Strehle, Stephen. *The Catholic Roots of the Protestant Gospel: Encounter Between the Middle Ages and the Reformation*. Leiden: Brill, 1995.

Strom, Jonathan. "Pietist Experience and Narratives of Conversion." Pages 293–318 in *A Companion to German Pietism, 1680–1800*. Edited by Douglas Shantz. Leiden: Brill, 2015.

Stuhlmacher, Peter. *Paul's Letter to the Romans: A Commentary*. Translated by Scott J. Hafemann. Louisville: Westminster John Knox, 1994.

———. *Revisiting Paul's Doctrine of Justification: A Challenge to the New Perspective*. Downers Grove, IL: InterVarsity Press, 2001.

Stump, Eleonore. "Augustine on Free Will." Pages 124–47 in *The Cambridge Companion to Augustine*. Edited by Eleonore Stump and Norman Kretzmann. Cambridge: Cambridge University Press, 2001.

Swaim, Kathleen M. *Pilgrim's Progress, Puritan Progress: Discourses and Contexts*. Urbana: University of Illinois Press, 1993.

Swift, Donald. *Religion and the American Experience: A Social and Cultural History, 1765–1997*. New York: M. E. Sharpe, 1998.

Synan, Vinson. *The Holiness-Pentecostal Tradition: Charismatic Movements in the Twentieth Century*. Grand Rapids: Eerdmans, 1997.

Tabbernee, William. *Fake Prophecy and Polluted Sacraments: Ecclesiastical and Imperial Reactions to Montanism*. Leiden: Brill, 2007.

Tardieu, Michel. *Manichaeism*. Translated by M. B. DeBervoise. Chicago: University of Illinois Press, 2008.

Taylor, T. M. "The Beginnings of Jewish Proselyte Baptism." *New Testament Studies* 2, no. 1 (1956): 193–97.

Tentler, Thomas. *Sin and Confession on the Eve of the Reformation*. Princeton: Princeton University Press, 1977.

Tertullian. *Ad Martyras*. Pages 693–696 in vol. 3 in *Ante-Nicene Fathers*. Edited by Alexander Roberts and James Donaldson. Peabody, MA: Hendrickson, 2004.

———. *Against Marcion*. Pages 269–476 in vol. 3 in *Ante-Nicene Fathers*. Edited by Alexander Roberts and James Donaldson. Peabody, MA: Hendrickson, 2004.

———. *Answer to the Jews*. Pages 151–74 in vol. 3 in *Ante-Nicene Fathers*. Edited by Alexander Roberts and James Donaldson. Peabody, MA: Hendrickson, 2004.

———. *A Treatise on the Soul*. Pages 181–242 in vol. 3 of *Ante-Nicene Fathers*. Edited by Alexander Roberts and James Donaldson. Peabody, MA: Hendrickson, 2004.

———. *On Baptism*. Pages 669–80 in vol. 3 of *Ante-Nicene Fathers*. Edited by Alexander Roberts and James Donaldson. Peabody, MA: Hendrickson, 2004.

———. *On Exhortation to Chastity*. Pages 50–58 in vol. 3 of *Ante-Nicene Fathers*. Edited by Alexander Roberts and James Donaldson. Peabody, MA: Hendrickson, 2004.

———. *On Modesty*. Pages 74–101 in vol. 4 of *Ante-Nicene Fathers*. Edited by Alexander Roberts and James Donaldson. Peabody, MA: Hendrickson, 2004.

———. *On Repentance*. Pages 657–68 in vol. 3 of *Ante-Nicene Fathers*. Edited by Alexander Roberts and James Donaldson. Peabody, MA: Hendrickson, 2004.

Theissen, Gerd. *A Theory of Primitive Christian Religion*. London: SCM, 1999.

———. *The Religion of the Earliest Churches: Creating a Symbolic World*. Translated by John Bowden. Minneapolis: Fortress, 1999.

Theissen, Gerd, and Annette Merz. *The Historical Jesus: A Comprehensive Guide*. Translated by John Bowden. Minneapolis: Fortress, 1996.

Thielman, Frank. *Theology of the New Testament: A Canonical and Synthetic Approach*. Grand Rapids: Zondervan, 2011.

Tillich, Paul. *The Interpretation of History*. New York: Charles Scribner's Sons, 1936.

Timmer, Daniel. *Creation, Tabernacle, and Sabbath: The Sabbath Frame of Exodus 1:12–16; 35:1–3 in Exegetical and Theological Perspective*. Göttingen: Vandenhoeck & Ruprecht, 2009.

Tödt, H. E. *The Son of Man in the Synoptic Tradition*. Translated by Dorothea Barton. Philadelphia: Westminster, 1965.

Tomkins, Stephen. *John Wesley: A Biography*. Oxford: Lion, 2003.

———. *A Short History of Christianity*. Oxford: Lion Hudson, 2005.

Tomlin, Graham. *Luther and His World: An Introduction*. Oxford: Lion Books, 2002.

Tornau, Christian, and Paolo Cecconi, ed. and trans. *The Shepherd of Hermas in Latin: Critical Edition of the Oldest Translation Vulgata*. Berlin: De Gruyter, 2014.

Tracy, James. *Europe's Reformations, 1450–1650: Doctrine, Politics, and Community*. Lanham: Rowman & Littlefield, 2006.

Trigg, Jonathan. *Baptism in the Theology of Martin Luther*. Leiden: Brill, 2001.

Trueman, Carl. *Grace Alone: Salvation as a Gift of God*. Grand Rapids: Zondervan, 2017.

———. "*Simul Peccator et Justus*: Martin Luther and Justification." Pages 73–97 in *Justification: Historical and Contemporary Challenges*. Edited by Bruce McCormack. Grand Rapids: Baker Academic, 2006.

Tucker, Ruth A. *Parade of Faith: A Biographical History of the Christian Church*. Grand Rapids: Zondervan, 2011.

Tuckman, Barbara W. *A Distant Mirror: The Calamitous 14th Century*. New York: Random House, 1987.

Uenuma, Masao. "Justification by Faith: Its Relevance in Buddhist Context." Pages 243–55 in *Right with God: Justification in the Bible and the World*. Edited by D. A. Carson. Eugene, OR: Wipf & Stock, 2002.

Ursinus, Zacharias. *Commentary on the Heidelberg Catechism*. Columbus: Scott and Bascom, 1852.

Vaillancourt, Mark. "Sacramental Theology from Gottschalk to Lanfranc." Pages 187–201 in *The Oxford Handbook of Sacramental Theology*. Edited by Hans Boersma and Matthew Levering. Oxford: Oxford University Press, 2018.

Vainio, Olli-Pekka, ed., *Engaging Luther: A New Theological Assessment*. Eugene, OR: Cascade, 2010.

———. *Justification and Participation in Christ: The Development of the Lutheran Doctrine of Justification from Luther to the Formula of Concord (1580)*. Leiden: Brill, 2008.

Van Asselt, Willem. *Introduction to Reformed Scholasticism*. Grand Rapids: Reformation Heritage Books, 2011.

Van Groningen, Gerard. *Messianic Revelation in the Old Testament*. Grand Rapids: Baker Books, 1990.

Van Leeuwen, C. "The Prophecy of the YOM YHWH in Amos V 18–20." *Old Testament Studies* 19 (1974): 113–34.

Van Lieburg, Fred. "The Dutch Factor in German Pietism." Pages 50–80 in *A Companion to German Pietism, 1680–1800*. Edited by Douglas Shantz. Leiden: Brill, 2015.

Van Liere, Frans. *An Introduction to the Medieval Bible*. Cambridge: Cambridge University Press, 2014.

Van Nieuwenhove, Rik. *An Introduction to Medieval Theology*. Cambridge: Cambridge University Press, 2012.

Vander Zee, Leonard J. *Christ, Baptism and the Lord's Supper: Recovering the Sacraments for Evangelical Worship*. Downers Grove, IL: InterVarsity Press, 2004.

Vermes, Geza. *The Resurrection: History and Myth*. New York: Doubleday, 2008.

Vetter, Ferdinand. *Die Preditigen Taulers*. Zürich: Weidmann, 1910.

Vind, Anna. *Latomus and Luther: The Debate: Is Every Good Deed a Sin?* Göttingen: Vandenhoeck & Ruprecht, 2019.

Visser, Arnoud. *Reading Augustine in the Reformation: The Flexibility of Intellectual Authority in Europe, 1500–1620*. Oxford: Oxford University Press, 2011.

Vogel, Heinrich. "On Original Sin, The Flacian Aberration." Pages 123–48 in *No Other Gospel: Essays in Commemoration of the 400th Anniversary of the Formula of Concord, 1580–1980*. Edited by Arnold Koelpin. Milwaukee: Northwestern, 1980.

Von Balthasar, Hans Urs. *Theo-Drama*. Translated by Graham Harrison. 5 vols. San Francisco: Ignatius, 1983–1998.

———. *A Theology of History*. New York: Sheed & Ward, 1963.

———. *The Theology of Karl Barth*. Translated by Edward Oakes. San Francisco: Ignatius, 1992.

Von Harless, Adolf. *A System of Christian Ethics*. Translated by A. W. Morrison. Brighton, IA: Just & Sinner, 2014.

Von Harnack, Adolf. *History of Dogma*. Translated by Neil Buchanan. 7 vols. New York: Dover Publications, 1961.

Von Hofmann, Johannes. *Theologische Ethik*. Nördlingen, C. H. Beck, 1878.

Von Leibniz, Gottfried. *Theodicy*. Translated by E. M. Huggard. New York: Cosmo Classics, 2010.

Von Loewenich, Walther. *Luthers Theologia Crucis*. München: Kaiser Verlag, 1954.

Von Rad, Gerhard. *Genesis: A Commentary*. Translated by John Marks. Philadelphia: Westminster, 1972.

———. *Old Testament Theology: Single Volume Edition*, Translated by D. M. G. Stalker. 2 vols. Peabody, MA: Prince, 2005.

———. "The Origin of the Concept of the Day of Yahweh," *Journal of Semitic Studies* 4 (1959): 97–108.

Von Staupitz, Johannes. "Eternal Predestination and its Execution in Time." Pages 175–204 in *Forerunners of the Reformation: The Shape of Late Medieval Thought*. Edited by Heiko Oberman. Philadelphia: Fortress, 1981.

Walcott, Gregory Dexter. *The Kantian and Lutheran Elements in Ritschl's Conception of God*. Lancaster, PA: New Era, 1904.

Walker, Williston. *A History of the Christian Church*. New York: Charles Scribner's Sons, 1919.

Wallace, Daniel. *Greek Grammar Beyond the Basics: An Exegetical Syntax of the New Testament*. Grand Rapids: Zondervan, 1996.

Walter, Peter. "Sacraments in the Council of Trent and Sixteenth-Century Catholic Theology." Pages 313–28 in *The Oxford Handbook of Sacramental Theology*. Edited by Hans Boersma and Matthew Levering. Oxford: Oxford University Press, 2018.

Waltke, Bruce, and Charles Yu. *An Old Testament Theology: An Exegetical, Canonical, and Thematic Approach*. Grand Rapids: Zondervan Academic, 2007.

Walton, John. *Genesis*. Grand Rapids: Zondervan, 2001.

———. *The Lost World of Adam and Eve Genesis 2–3 and the Human Origins Debate*. Downers Grove, IL: InterVarsity Press, 2015.

Walvoord, John. *Matthew: Thy Kingdom Come: A Commentary on the First Gospel*. Grand Rapids: Kregel, 1998.

Warfield, Benjamin. *Augustine and the Pelagian Controversy*. Edinburgh: Crossreach, 2018.

———. *Calvin and Augustine*. Philadelphia: Presbyterian & Reformed Publishing, 1956.

Watson, Philip. *Let God be God: An Interpretation of the Theology of Martin Luther.* Philadelphia: Fortress, 1947.

Watt, Jeffrey. "Reconciliation and the Confession of Sins: The Evidence from the Consistory in Calvin's Geneva." Pages 105–20 in *Calvin and Luther: The Continuing Relationship.* Edited by R. Ward Holder. Göttingen: Vandenhoeck & Ruprecht, 2013.

Webb, William. *Slaves, Women & Homosexuals: Exploring the Hermeneutics of Cultural Analysis.* Downers Grove, IL: InterVarsity Press, 2001.

Weber, Hans Emil. *Reformation, Orthodoxie, und Rationalismus.* Vol. 1. Güterloh: Gerd Mohn, 1937.

Weinandy, Thomas. *Jesus Becoming Jesus: A Theological Interpretation of the Synoptic Gospels.* Washington, DC: Catholic University of America Press, 2018.

Weinfeld, Moshe. "Sabbath, Temple and the Enthronement of the Lord — the Problem of the *Sitz im Leben* of Genesis 1:1–2:3." Pages 501–12 in *Mélanges bibliques et orientaux en l'honneur de M Henri Cazelles.* Edited by A. Caquot and M. Delcor. Kevelaer: Butzer & Bercker, 1981.

Weiss, Herold. *A Day of Gladness: The Sabbath Among Jews and Christians in Antiquity.* Columbia: University of South Carolina Press, 2003.

Wengert, Timothy. "Biblical Interpretation in the Works of Philip Melanchthon." Pages 331–53 in vol. 2 of *A History of Biblical Interpretation: The Medieval Though the Reformation Periods.* Edited by Alan J. Hauser and Duane F. Watson. Grand Rapids: Eerdmans, 2009.

———. *Defending Faith: Lutheran Responses to Andreas Osiander's Doctrine of Justification, 1551–1559.* Tübingen: Mohr Siebeck, 2012.

———. *Law and Gospel: Philip Melanchthon's Debate with John Agricola of Eisleben over Poenitentia.* Grand Rapids: Baker, 1997.

———. "Melanchthon and Luther/Luther and Melanchthon," *Luther-Jahrbuch* 66 (1999): 55–88.

———. "Philip Melanchthon and the Origins of the 'Three Causes' (1533–1535): An Examination of the Roots of the Controversy over the Freedom of the Will." Pages 183–208 in *Philip Melanchthon: Theologian in Classroom, Confession, and Controversy.* Edited by Irene Dingel; Robert Kolb, Nicole Kuropka, and Timothy Wengert. Göttigen: Vandenhoeck & Ruprecht, 2012.

Wenham, Gordon. *Genesis 1–15.* Waco, TX: Word Book Publisher, 1987.

———. "Sanctuary Symbolism in the Garden of Eden Story." Pages 19–37 in *Proceedings of the Ninth World Congress of Jewish Studies*. Edited by Moshe Goshen-Gottstein. Jerusalem: World Union of Jewish Studies, 1988.

Wesley, John. *A Plain Account of Christian Perfection*. Peabody, MA: Hendrickson, 2007.

Westerholm, Stephen. *Justification Reconsidered: Rethinking a Pauline Theme*. Grand Rapids: Eerdmans, 2013.

———. "Paul's Anthropological 'Pessimism' in Its Jewish Context." Pages 71–98 in *Divine and Human Agency in Paul and His Cultural Development*. Edited by J. M. G. Barclay and Simon Gathercole. London: T&T Clark, 2007.

———. *Perspectives Old and New on Paul: The "Lutheran" Paul and His Critics*. Grand Rapids: Eerdmans, 2004.

Westermann, Claus. *Genesis 12–36: A Commentary*. Translated by John Scullion. Minneapolis: Augsburg, 1995.

White, Graham. *Luther as Nominalist: A Study of the Logical Methods Used in Martin Luther's Disputations in the Light of Their Medieval Background*. Helsinki: Luther-Agricola-Society, 1994.

White, J. Benton and Walter Wilson. *From Adam to Armageddon: A Survey of the Bible*. Belmont, CA: Thomason Watson, 2012.

White, James F. *The Sacraments in Protestant Practice and Faith*. Nashville: Abingdon, 1999.

Whiteley, D. E. H. *The Theology of St Paul*. Oxford: Blackwell, 1964.

Wicks, Jared. *Man Yearning for Grace: Luther's Early Spiritual Teachings*. Washington, DC: Corpus, 1968.

Wilcox, Donald. *In Search of God and Self: Renaissance and Reformation Thought*. Long Grove, IL: Waveland, 1975.

Wiley, Tatha. *Original Sin: Origins, Developments, Contemporary Meanings*. New York: Paulist, 2002.

Wilk, Florian and J. Ross Wagner, eds. *Between Gospel and Election: Explorations in the Interpretation of Romans 9–11*. Tübingen: Mohr Siebeck, 2010.

Williams, N. P. *The Grace of God*. London: Longmans, 1930.

Williams, Peter. *Can We Trust the Gospels?* Wheaton, IL: Crossway, 2018.

Willis, E. David. *Calvin's Catholic Christology: The Function of the So-called Extra Calvinisticum in Calvin's Theology*. Leiden: Brill, 1966.

Willis, Geoffrey. *Saint Augustine and the Donatist Controversy*. Eugene, OR: Wipf & Stock, 2005.

Wills, Gary. *Augustine's Confessions: A Biography.* Princeton: Princeton University Press, 2011.

Wilson, Catherine. *Epicureanism at the Origins of Modernity.* Oxford: Clarendon, 2008.

Windhors, Cristof. *Tatiferisches Taufverstandnis: Balthasar Hubmaiers Lehre zwischen Traditioneller und Reformatorischer Theologie.* Leiden: E. J. Brill, 1976.

Wingren, Gustaf. *Creation and Law.* Translated by Ross McKenzie. Philadelphia: Muhlenberg, 1961.

———. *Luther on Vocation.* Translated by Carl Rasmussen. Eugene, OR: Wipf & Stock, 2004.

———. *Man and the Incarnation: A Study in the Biblical Theology of Irenaeus.* Translated by Ross McKenzie. Eugene, OR: Wipf & Stock, 2004.

Winship, Michael. *Hot Protestants: A History of Puritanism in England and America.* New Haven: Yale University Press, 2019.

Witherington, Ben III. *The Christology of Jesus.* Minneapolis: Fortress, 1990.

———. *John's Wisdom: A Commentary on the Fourth Gospel.* Louisville: Westminster John Knox, 1995.

Witte, John. "Faith in Law: The Legal and Political Legacy of the Protestant Reformation." Pages 105–38 in *The Protestant Reformation of the Church and the World.* Edited by John Witte and Amy Wheeler. Louisville: Westminster John Knox, 2018.

Woods, Walter. *Walking with Faith: New Perspectives on the Sources and Shaping of Catholic Moral Life.* Eugene, OR: Wipf & Stock, 1998.

Wright, David. "Justification in Augustine." Pages 55–72 in *Justification in Perspective.* Edited by Bruce McCormack. Grand Rapids: Baker Academic, 2006.

Wright, N. T. *The Challenge of Jesus: Rediscovering Who Jesus Was and Is.* Downers Grove, IL: InterVarsity Press, 1999.

———. *Jesus and the Victory of God.* Christian Origins and the Question of God 2. Minneapolis: Fortress, 1997.

———. *The New Testament and the People of God.* Christian Origins and the Question of God 1. Minneapolis: Fortress, 1992.

———. *Paul and the Faithfulness of God.* 2 vols. Christian Origins and the Question of God. 4. Minneapolis: Fortress, 2013.

———. *How God Became King: The Forgotten Story of the Gospels.* San Francisco: HarperOne, 2016.

———. *Paul in Fresh Perspective*. Minneapolis: Fortress, 2009.

———. *The Resurrection of the Son of God*. Christian Origins and the Question of God 3. Minneapolis: Fortress, 2003

———. *What St. Paul Really Said: Was Paul of Tarsus the Real Founder of Christianity?* Oxford: Lion Books, 1997.

Yeago, David. "The Catholic Luther." *First Things* (March 1996): 37–41.

Zachhuber, Johannes. *Luther's Christological Legacy: Christocentrism and the Chalcedonian Tradition*. Milwaukee: Marquette University Press, 2017.

Zachman, Randall. *The Assurance of Faith: Conscience in the Theology of Martin Luther and John Calvin*. Louisville: Westminster John Knox, 2005.

Ziesler, J. A. *The Meaning of Righteousness in Paul: A Linguistic and Theological Enquiry*. Cambridge: Cambridge University Press, 1972.

Zimmerli, Walther. *The Fiery Throne: The Prophets and Old Testament Theology*. Edited by K. C. Hanson. Minneapolis: Fortress, 2003.

Zwingli, Ulrich. *Commentary on True and False Religion*. Translated and edited by Samuel Macauley Jackson and Clarence Nevin Heller. Durham: Labyrinth, 1981.

———. "An Exposition of the Faith." Pages 249–79 in *Zwingli and Bullinger*. Translated by G. W. Bromiley. Philadelphia: Westminster, 1953.

———. "Friendly Exegesis, that is, Exposition of the Matter of the Eucharist to Martin Luther, February 1527." Pages 238–369 in vol. 2 of *Huldrych Zwingli: Writings*. Vol. 2. Translated and edited by H. Wayne Pipkin. Repr., Eugene, OR: Pickwick, 1984.

———. "Of Baptism." Pages 132–75 in *Zwingli and Bullinger*. Translated and edited by G. W. Bromiley. Philadelphia: Westminster, 1953.

———. "On the Lord's Supper." Pages 176–238 in *Zwingli and Bullinger*. Translated and edited by G. W. Bromiley. Philadelphia: Westminster, 1953.

———. "Reproduction from Memory of a Sermon on the Providence of God, Dedicated to His Highness Philip of Hesse." Pages 128–235 in *On Providence: and Other Essays*. Translated and edited by Samuel Macauley Jackson. Durham: Labyrinth, 1983.

———. "Short Christian Instruction." Pages 43–73 in vol. 2 of of *Huldrych Zwingli: Writings*. Vol. 2. Translated and edited by H. Wayne Pipkin. Repr., Eugene, OR: Pickwick, 1984.

Zwollo, Laela. *St. Augustine and Plotinus: The Human Mind as Image of the Divine*. Leiden: Brill, 2018.

Subject and Name Index

Zwingli, 305
Baptist, 305, 322
Baptizer, John the, 50, 310
Barnabas, Epistle of, 99
Barth, Gerhard, 60
Barth, Karl, 178,
Baur, F.C., 78–79
Bayer, Oswald, 178, 182, 191, 311, 320, 323
Beale, G.K., 14, 15, 16,
Beza, Theodore de, 254
Biel, Gabriel, 155, 178
Billings, Todd, 248
Bizer, Ernst, 178
Bogomils, 157
Book of Concord, 217, 231
Bradwardine, Thomas, 159
Brown, Peter, 131
Brown, Raymond, 65
Buddhism, 6

C

Cain and Abel, 23, 25, 90, 286
Cajetan, Thomas Cardinal, 183–85
Calvin, John, 233, 239–41, 245, 254, 255, 271, 322
  atonement, 247
  christology, 250
  election/Predestination, 122, 269–70, 281
  God, 246–47
  justification, 247–49, 269
  law, 351
  sacraments, 249–52, 273, 307–8, 309, 330
  syllogismus practicus, 252–53
Calvinism, 137, 234, 253, 254, 255, 256, 271, 308
Calvinist/Arminian Debate, 289–90
Campbell, Douglas, 86
Canterbury, Anselm of, 219, 247
Cary, Philip, 2, 3, 157, 195, 240
Cassian, John, 136
Cathars, 157

Christian Theology, 1, 2, 50, 110, 369, 370
central dogma theory, 1
Chaoskampf, 11, 14
Chemnitz, Martin, 229, 231
Church 1, 54, 65, 71, 78, 79, 94, 97, 100, 132, 133, 135, 141, 143, 157, 159, 178, 180, 213, 214, 298, 309, 330, 332, 369, 370, 371
covenant, 24, 27, 30, 31, 33, 51, 53n33, 54n36, 63, 64, 74, 77, 78, 82, 85, 88, 93, 99, 151, 164, 268, 277, 306, 322, 326, 327
  Abrahamic, 25, 28, 54, 82
  Davidic, 39
  new, 36–38, 42, 46, 57, 64, 67, 70, 71, 81, 87, 88, 95, 206, 307, 342, 355
  Noahic, 23, 29
  of Works, 337, 350
  Sinaitic, 28, 29, 30, 31, 33, 34–35, 42, 47, 53, 54, 67, 70, 81, 82, 87, 88, 94, 341
covenantal causality, 150, 152, 164, 190, 276, 301
creation, 5, 9–17, 19, 21, 22, 23, 24, 25, 26, 27, 29, 30, 31, 36, 37, 39, 40, 42, 43, 44
  by word, 9–11, 24, 67, 334
  ex nihilo, 11–12, 11n21
  liturgical, 14–16
  new creation, 9, 14, 25, 27, 39, 44, 47, 58, 67, 70, 89, 91, 92, 103, 278, 316, 334, 335, 337, 353, 363, 367
  six days of, 12, 14–16
Creator, 2, 5, 8, 11, 17, 18–19, 28, 29, 74–75, 101, 103, 113, 157, 165, 174, 198, 241, 242
Cullmann, Oscar, 86
Cyrillian Christology, 240, 301

D

Daniel, book of, 37–39, 42, 51, 57, 58, 336, 339

Semi-Pelagian, 136, 140, 254
Sentences of Peter Lombard, 142, 147,
    160
simul iustus et peccator, 176, 203–4,
    209, 296, 323, 355, 356, 360,
    364
snake handling, 15, 257, 308
speech-act theory, 11, 24
Spener, Philipp, 237
Staupitz, Johannes von, 158–60
Steinmetz, David, 10n19, 160, 171n97
Stendahl, Krister, 79, 86
Stuhlmacher, Peter, 55
Suarez, Francisco, 242
supplementarity, 129
syllogismus practicus, 252–55, 257, 290

T

Tabernacle, 14–16, 21, 22, 26, 27, 29,
    30, 32, 33, 49, 70, 71, 269, 331,
    336, 347
Tauler, Johannes, 162, 163, 200
tax collectors, 63, 74
telos, 144, 146, 166, 168, 169, 357,
Temple, 14–17, 21, 22, 26, 29, 30, 31,
    32, 33, 35, 36, 38, 46, 47, 48,
    49, 59–60, 64, 68, 69–70, 71,
    72, 201, 263, 269, 311, 331, 336,
    338, 347, 366
Ten Commandments, 5, 28, 31, 266,
    345
testament/*diatheke,* 87, 326–27
Tertullian, 100, 103–4, 105–6
Gerd Theissen, 310
Thomism, 155
tower experience, 186
Treasury of Merits, 180, 184
transubstantiation, 328
Trent, Council of, 298, 324

two ways doctrine, 99

V

Vainio, Olli-Pekka, 229
Vatican II, 241
virtue, 144, 146, 172, 186, 188, 349
virtue ethics, 144–47, 349
visio beatifica, 131, 145, 146, 166
vita passiva, 354
Vulgate, 123, 142, 146, 181, 305

W

Walton, John, 338
Wengert, Timothy, 226
Wesley, John, 256–57
Westerholm, Stephen, 80, 86, 341,
Wittenberg Reformation, 339, 354,
    304
Wolf, Christian, 242
Word of God, 9–10, 10n19, 12, 18, 32,
    44, 46, 47, 48, 49, 50, 62, 92,
    95, 97, 132, 138, 140, 189, 190,
    191, 196, 197, 198, 199, 202,
    206, 221, 223, 238, 240, 241,
    249, 255, 264, 268, 285, 294,
    296, 301, 318, 329, 357, 362–63,
    365, 372
Wright, N.T., 26, 53n33, 54n36, 59, 66,
    69, 85

Y

Yeago, David, 174
yetzer hara, 75, 76

Z

Zwingli, Ulrich, 197, 239, 240, 241–45,
    246, 247, 249, 250, 304-7, 324,
    325, 328-29, 330

Scripture Index

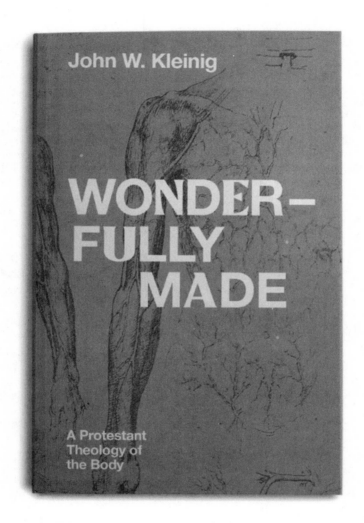